THE LETTERS AND PRIVATE PAPERS OF
WILLIAM MAKEPEACE THACKERAY

VOLUME IV

LONDON : GEOFFREY CUMBERLEGE

OXFORD UNIVERSITY PRESS

THACKERAY IN 1863
From a photograph

THE LETTERS AND PRIVATE PAPERS OF

William Makepeace

THACKERAY

Collected and edited by

Gordon N. Ray

In four volumes

Volume IV: 1857–1863

HARVARD UNIVERSITY PRESS
Cambridge, Massachusetts
1946

PRINTED AT THE HARVARD UNIVERSITY PRINTING OFFICE

CAMBRIDGE, MASSACHUSETTS, U.S.A.

PREFACE TO VOLUME FOUR

The final volumes of this edition appear four years after I turned my manuscript over to Howard Mumford Jones on being ordered to active duty in the United States Navy. Such prolonged delay in publication, made inevitable by war-time conditions, has at any rate enabled me to relieve Professor Jones of the heavy burden of reading proof half way through Volume Three. I take this opportunity of thanking him once more for his generous services, without which no part of the edition would yet have achieved printed form.

Other obligations, contracted during my absence, must also be mentioned. Mr. Roger Scaife, who succeeded Dr. Malone as Director of the Harvard University Press in 1943, has been indefatigable in overcoming the many difficulties attendant on the publication of the *Letters*. Miss Eleanor Dobson of the Harvard University Press has supervised the printing of the edition with a constant vigilance that went far beyond the usual function of a publisher's editor. Phoebe deKay Donald has compiled the elaborate index which concludes this volume, thereby putting all students of Thackeray, and not least the present writer, in her debt. To turn to an obligation of another kind, belated but grateful acknowledgment is made to Macmillan & Company of London for permission to include FitzGerald's letters to Thackeray in this edition.

As was to be expected, a number of minor errors remain to be corrected.[1] One more serious question has been raised. Both Mrs.

---

[1] In Volume One: p.xc, *for* Adam's *read* Adams's; p. 3, note 1, *for* see below, No. 880, *read* see below, No. 882; p. 16, note 4, *for* (1819–1929) *read* (1819 1809); p. 398, *for* Cocher *read* Cocker. (*The mathematical and calligraphic manuals of Edward Cocker (1631–1675) had so great a vogue that the phrase "according to Cocker" became proverbial.*) P. 447, note 71, *for* novel *read* survey.

In Volume Two: p. 3, note 1, *for* Jeanne *read* Jean; p. 57, note 38, *for* No. 224 *read* No. 223; p. 160, note 64, *for* (pp. 274–190) *read* (pp. 274–290); p. 223, *for* respects to Mr. Pryme *read* respects to Mrs. Pryme; p. 240, *for* Mr. Bakewell's *read* Mrs. Bakewell's; p. 291, *for* Hampstead Court *read*

Fuller and Mr. Ritchie are convinced, from recollections of their grandmother as she appeared in old age, that the drawing reproduced in Volume One, opposite page 350, cannot be of Mrs. Thackeray. In the Huntington Library album where the original is to be found, this portrait is identified as being of "Mrs. W. M. Thackeray" in a letter of January 23, 1902, from J. M. Shawe, Warfield, Hampton on Thames, who also states that the drawings in this album can be vouched for "by my cousins Mrs. [later Lady] Ritchie & Mrs. Browne." It is possible, as Mrs. Fuller suggests, that the drawing in question may actually be of Mary Graham, though no final conclusion can be reached on the evidence at hand.

I write this preface from London, where a grant from the Guggenheim Foundation is enabling me to spend the summer in bringing together Thackeray's unpublished letters in English collections and in assembling other materials for his biography. A hasty preliminary survey, which is all that I have as yet had time to make, promises well for an interesting supplementary volume of Thackeray's correspondence drawn from holdings in Great Britain.

GORDON N. RAY

June, 1946.

Hampton Court and cancel note 53; p. 374, note 95, *for* fifth Earl, *read* second Earl; p. 469, note 260, *for* Charles Elton *read* Probably Arthur Elton; p. 530, *for* hausel, *read* hansel; p. 705, text and note 157, *for* St. Britins *read* St. Britius; p. 740, *for* D[obbins] *read* D[obson]; p. 826, note 164, *for* December, 1851 *read* January, 1852.

In Volume Three: p. 68, note 95, *for* Henry Thurstan *read* Henry Thurstan Holland; p. 360, *the correct date for Letter 1040 is* 26 March 1855.

CONTENTS OF VOLUME IV

LETTERS, 1857–1863 3

LETTERS OF UNCERTAIN DATE 305

APPENDIX XVIII. THACKERAY IN NORWICH, MAY, 1857 377

APPENDIX XIX. THE OXFORD ELECTION, 1857 . . . 381

APPENDIX XX. DIARY 3 JANUARY–23 SEPTEMBER 1858 . 390

APPENDIX XXI. DIARY FOR 1861 395

APPENDIX XXII. DIARY FOR 1862 399

APPENDIX XXIII. NUMBER 2, PALACE GREEN, KENSINGTON 405

APPENDIX XXIV. DIARY FOR 1863 408

APPENDIX XXV. THACKERAY AND THE NATIONAL SHAKE-
SPEARE COMMITTEE 416

APPENDIX XXVI. EXCERPTS FROM THACKERAY'S UNPUB-
LISHED LETTERS TO MRS. BROOKFIELD, MRS. ELLIOT,
AND MISS PERRY 418

APPENDIX XXVII. FORGED THACKERAY LETTERS . . . 451

APPENDIX XXVIII. THE MEDICAL HISTORY OF WILLIAM
MAKEPEACE THACKERAY — BY CHESTER M. JONES,
M.D. 453

A THACKERAY GENEALOGY 461

INDEX OF CORRESPONDENTS IN VOLUME IV 471

GENERAL INDEX 477

INDEX OF THACKERAY'S WRITINGS 577

ILLUSTRATIONS IN VOLUME IV

*(The name of the owner of each illustration taken from the original
is noted in parenthesis.)*

Thackeray in 1863 . . . . *Frontispiece*
From a photograph (*Mrs. Fuller*)

"FILBY FECIT. Dr. Goldsmith's New Coat" 70
From a sketch by Thackeray (*Mr. Carlebach*)

Dr. Johnson and Dr. Goldsmith 71
From a sketch by Thackeray, reproduced in *Letters of Dr. John
Brown*, p. 328

Edmund Yates's article on Thackeray 90
From *Town Talk*, June 13, 1858

"The smiler with the knife" (Yates and Thackeray in the
Garrick Club) 102
From a drawing by Thackeray (*Mr. Wylie*)

Edmund Yates in 1865 103
From a photograph, reproduced as the frontispiece to Volume II
of his *Recollections and Experiences*

Drawing in Thackeray's letter to Adelaide Procter . . . 182
From a reproduction in *The Memories of Dean Hole*

"The Belle of the West" 214
From the Currier lithograph (*Mr. Peters*)

Anne Thackeray 230
From a painting by G. F. Watts (*Mrs. Fuller*)

Harriet Thackeray 231
From a painting by G. F. Watts (*Mrs. Fuller*)

Thackeray's letter of 21 October 1861 . . . . 250, 251
(*Berg Collection of the New York Public Library*)

Mrs. Procter in Old Age 274
From a photograph (*Mrs. Fuller*)

Thackeray in 1863 275
From photographs

Thackeray's letter of 20 July 1863 to Sir William and Lady
    Knighton 288, 289
    (*Berg Collection of the New York Public Library*)

A cast of Thackeray's hand, made after death 296
    (*Mrs. Fuller*)

Lucy Baxter 306
    From a photograph (*Miss Frank*)

An undated letter from Thackeray to the Rev. Richard Harris
    Barham 307
    (*Berg Collection of the New York Public Library*)

An undated letter from Thackeray to Mrs. Elliot . . . 324
    From a facsimile in *A Collection of Letters of Thackeray*, opposite
    p. 94

An undated letter from Thackeray to Lady Morley . . 344
    (*Gimbel Brothers*)

An undated letter from Thackeray to Clarkson Stanfield . 358
    From a facsimile in *The Dickensian*, XXII, 204

"Mr. Thackeray's Sentiments on the Sabbath Question" . 382
    From a broadside (*Mr. Parrish*)

"The Sabbath Question. To the Electors of the City of
    Oxford." 383
    From a broadside (*Bodleian Library*)

Thackeray and the National Shakespeare Committee . 416, 417
    From clippings found among Thackeray's papers (*Mrs. Fuller*)

A forged Thackeray letter 452
    (*Berg Collection of the New York Public Library*)

LETTERS, 1857–1863

1281. TO MAJOR AND MRS. CARMICHAEL-SMYTH
1 JANUARY 1857

Hitherto unpublished.

January 1. 1857.

I was busy writing letters till after Paris-post hour last night, and so let us begin the first pen and ink work of the year with a word for my dearest old Granny & G P — not much more than a word — In this business on w^h I am engaged I dont seem to do or think anything or see friends or places or observe or remember — It is like a man playing at roulette, and winning, the whole world and his acquaintance and the newspaper &c being indifferent to him, as he eyes the ball turning round and time after time rakes up his winnings — Mine are growing bigger & bigger — We shall repeat the lectures in London 4 times before 10 February & get very nearly 250 £ for each set of lectures. In the spring they will doubtless bear other repetitions — Well, well, it is an unwholesome life, and when we have made a little more money there must be an end of the game. The game is so much in my favor, that yesterday I had all but treated the young ladies to a Brougham and a pretty little pair of horses w^h were to be had [at] altogether a fair bargain: but I thought I would have Higgins's advice first who is most learned in horse-flesh; and he would not hear of a purchase — one horse in London is as useful as 2, and I can hire one horse carriage coachman for 90 £ for six months, and the end was that my friend & the Brougham & horses drove away again. The Lords & Ladies I am told are very wroth that I should hold the Queens Uncle up to ridicule and I am to be out of favor henceforth — I'm rather glad having had enough of fine parties and not caring to drag about to balls as my daughters' chaperon. Mr Hayter,[1] the Whig Whipper in sent me a message about a borough (not Liskeard) that he thought would suit me — but I sent him back my compliments, and said a man with independent means, who has 15000 subscribers to his books and can bring scores of thousands

[1] William Goodenough Hayter (1792–1878), later (1858) first Baronet, M. P. for Wells, 1837–1865.

of people with half crowns in their hands to hear his lectures —
needn't go into Parliament as a Whig nominee — so if we do
we'll go in independent — & try and see what that new life may be
good for. It mustn't be for a year though or before we have made
those 20000£ we talked of. These are visions all *en l'air* however. I think the idea of turning painter was knocked on the head
at Glasgow where I was so confounded by Mʳˢ Blackburne's prodigious genius and saw that she had a talent so infinitely superior
to my little one — that I thought I had best blow that poor little
farthing candle out, and think of it no more.

And now we have all been & had a jolly breakfast (& didnt I
have a jolly sleep from 8 to 8 last night?) and the last words
of conversation I heard were 'Minny what would you like for
dinner? Minny says gravely 'I should like a vol-au-vent.' Have
a vol au vent you dear little women — I should like to hear, that
our dear old folks had a comfortable New Years dinner and that
my dearest mothers fever was relaxing its grip upon her. Quinine
took away mine in the U. States and I liked it and drank it eagerly.
But the girls tell me you are gone back to your globules, and what
can I think or say but that beliefs are beyond compulsion, and that
you must no doubt follow yours. If the girls come to you from 10
February till about Lady Day whilst I am in the north lecturing
— you'll hardly take that charming companion — If you could
find a cheerful brisk Mʳˢ Gloynish kind of attendant she would
do better perhaps than a genteel faded dame de compagnie — but
here again you'll choose for yourselves — & none else can manage
for you. The best way will be that Chéri should have both those
shares in the canal — that will be paying back his great Grandmothers 450 £ wʰ his parents gave over to me in better days when
poor Mary's heart was more charitable. A man I dont like & dont
know much but clever & learned & in distress got 100£ out of
me yesterday — I know it was wrong but couldn't help helping
him thinking of my own distress & how many a kind hand was ready
to help me — and so the papers full & theres only room for a God
bless my dear old Mother & G P from

W M T.

1282.   TO MRS. CARMICHAEL-SMYTH
6–8 JANUARY 1857

Hitherto unpublished.

January 6–8. 1857.

My dearest Granny will have a long letter from her young ones to day, and mine will be only a scrap to be sent off when the sheet is full. So you have had a little return — well, may they grow littler & littler until they dwindle off into infinitesimality — But pray pray dont send away Martha. Remember how admirably attentive patient and good humoured she has been during your illness how she gave way to Eliza and wasn't jealous of that superior favorite how natural it is for a woman who has to pass night after night alone in that glum kitchen by that one candle to want companionship and amusement from time to time. *We* are no companions to servants, speak condescendingly to them for what we want, can't amuse or talk with them — Let them have their chance of friendship and freedom. their share of light & holyday out of doors. How good my 3 servants have been to us! If I am ill what care they take of me! What a little we pay them back! That word 'master' ought to be abolished I think, and have ideas of a small fund to be placed annually to their secret account and given to them when they leave or are sick or I die.

We have not been to see Mary yet — and it is a matter of very great difficulty. I will not go into a house where George Wood goes — drunk or sober, sane or mad, I wont meet the man who put his hand on my dear old G P's shoulder and uttered those monstrous calumnies about you — And I dont want him to lose the kind friends whom he has got in Charles & Mary or to be the means of thrusting the poor fellow from no doubt the only comfortable home and respectable fireside to w^h he is admitted. Nor do I choose that my daughters should be cast off and their acquaintance resumed at the will of any he or she in Christendom — this sort of humiliation is more than I can swallow, or submit to their suffering — though my dear old Nanny wants to go, and my own heart melts as I think of the kind old Charles.

Thursday   Just before setting out for Bath. Wasn't it odd that on the very day of writing this the Wood difficulty should be solved? Mr George comes drunk for the 10th time to Hyndford Castle — Charles begs him to go and George slaps him on the face! having on other occasions pinioned him got him down on the sofa and at dinner seized him by the throat and playfully put a knife to it! So Charles sends for me and I go and give Mary a kiss — and see as well as possible that we can't get on together. But at least there shall be peace if there cant (and oughtn't) to be love — we shall meet from time to time and be very decent good friends.

Applications for lectures keep pouring in. I dont know what the deuce it all means — but I must reap the corn stands and pocket these hundreds for the children's sake and hope for better days for my dearest old Mother.

Will you do me a favor? Will you see Olliffe (Hotel Talleyrand. R. St Florentin) and ask him to bring the very best French Ladys Physician in consultation? The idea of these sleepless nights and dragging fever, gives me many a bad night too. Hicks says most likely the Irish railway is wound up — the mortgage plan won't do because — never mind the because

Come Charles! pack the bag put in the 2 lectures let us be off with the girls in the brougham (only a hired one) to the Great Western Railway — and come back & lecture again on Saturday, and so work and work until it is time for rest. I have had serious thoughts of shutting up the house and coming off to you and working at my novel at Paris — but it's a pity, it's a pity. Dont you see G P and Granny that there's a great career before me if I will but run it? — and that for it I must be on the ground? — and yet it w^d be sweet wouldn't it to retire and be a twopenny painter and say Get thee behind me Ambition — However no more about this for now   God bless my dearest old mother & G P says

                    W M T.

1283.   TO MRS. CARMICHAEL-SMYTH
9–12 JANUARY 1857

Published in part, *Biographical Introductions*, X, xxix-xxx.

This is begun in the beautiful city [2] where Miss Ann Becher first danced with Captain G P. It is only 4 hours from London now by the slow train, as I came yesterday I thought of the supper at Marlborough and the York House coach. It was dark when I arrived I had to go to dinner and directly afterwards to my lecture-room — The room was crammed with 400 genteel folks and 350 of the wulgar The genteel could not understand what I was talking about I looked into their genteel blank faces and saw they were dullards The vulgar took the jokes understood the points laughed & cheered at the right places. Among the polite were many parsons. They rule here and tyrannize as all parsonic bodies do — A man who has been with me about more lectures this morning told me for taking a walk of a Sunday evening after Church where his clergyman had seen him, he was rebuked by his Reverence who said 'You had better have remained at home.' Between our side & their's ought there not to be war?

To day I get invitations from Ireland declined with thanks, from Devonshire, from Bath again and Bristol, from Yorkshire for the summer, where is this going to stop? What I said about 'a great career' is not swagger but a fair look at Chances in the face. Just when the novel-writing faculty is pretty well used up here is independence a place in Parliament and who knows what afterwards? Upon my word I dont seem much to care, and fate carries me along in a stream somehow — Shall I float with it or jump on shore? I shant be happy in politics and they'll interfere with my digestion — but with the game there, it seems faint-hearted not to play it. 'Retire and paint pooty little pictures' says Ease, perhaps Conscience: 'Retire and work at literature at history — But that game is very tempting. I wonder will it come off or whether this is mere idle vaporing & dreaming? Did I tell you

[2] Bath. See above, No. 794.

about the Whigs whipper in sending to me about a seat in parliament? Sir says I with 15000 subscribers to my books, and hundreds of thousands of hearers all over England I'm not going to be a Whig under strapper? — (All this is entre nous) I think I did tell you — One of the obstacles to getting on perhaps is this dreadful want of memory. What is the use of forming plans & castles in the air? A hundred things may happen to knock down this one. Well, I shan't care.

Bob [3] has just been here in pretty good spirits and I am to go and see his Baby between 3 & 5, poor fellow. And then to Mrs Forrest's and then to Impeys and then to dine again with the Thackeray cousins who won't hear of my eating at my own hour and send me choking into lecture.

I hear sad accounts of the Morning Herald [4] — What a comfort it is to be a popular performer at such moments! — I know where there always are 50£ for honest Paddy.

Monday — My dear old womans comfortable letter has just come in — the pleasantest I have seen for many a long day — & I send off my scrap with good news about all of us — I went to see Bob & his baby and the child is a perfect wonder — the finest child ever seen finer than Mrs Story's [5] — the most jolly handsome broad chested fair-skinned little hero with a look of G P in the Hessian boot picture — and I saw Mrs Forrest & Emmy, and came away very much pleased with kind handsome Bath — where the Miss Thackerays have a house twice as big & handsome as mine w^h costs 700£.

It rains money — This morning I have arranged for 2 sets of lectures at Willis's & Brighton — the 8 hours will bring me four hundred pounds! — I have engaged for the month of April for twenty four lectures for w^h I am to be paid 1200 guineas! — perhaps we may have 2 or 3 months of this sort of money-making. Great Powers! it's prodigious — Meanwhile I don't think I've

[3] Robert Forrest.
[4] Of which Thackeray's friend John Frazer Corkran was Paris correspondent.
[5] Waldo Story, whom Thackeray called "Henry the Eighth" (James, *William Wetmore Story*, I, 367).

above 100£ at Lubbocks or I would send Granny some — Mum about the price of the lectures. It seems a fable. If they come off I have promised Amy 100£. Have anything you like Dont stint God bless you my dear old Granny & G P. What a comfort to see your hand not shaking!

W M T.

1284.   TO WILLIAM HARRISON AINSWORTH
11 JANUARY 1857

Extract published in Ellis's *Ainsworth*, II, 194.

36 Onslow Sq^r January 11.

My dear Ainsworth

One more word to tell you again how extremely pained and annoyed I am that an old friend should have had to suffer such an inconvenience and such a seeming slight.

What has become of my letter saying that the whole party was put off? At Chapman's they remember receiving & forwarding it. The Saturday party fell to the ground on account of a series of 4 Saturdays being taken for a course of lectures — the only days available — and writing from the Club I think, without book I thought I was engaged on Wednesdays & Thursdays to lecture at Bath whereas I found it was on Thursdays & Fridays — rooms taken — word passed — impossible for me to do any thing but give up my dinner-party and apologize all round.

As soon as I heard you had been here I dashed into town in search of you — you cant imagine with what extreme sorrow for the contretemps. Like a kind fellow you must forgive me. The thing annoys me more than it can you — for how can I be other than pained at annoying an old friend whose early kindness & hospitality I always gratefully remember?

Now *do* do me a favor — Come up on Saturday 24th and hear the George III lecture it wont offend your loyalty — We'll dine at 5 and have a good bottle of Claret before we go — and I'll ask one or two cozy friends for Sunday 25th and my daughters will

make you welcome and I have a snug comfortable bed at your
service — If you do this I shall know you have forgiven

Yours always.

W M Thackeray.

1285.   TO ?
13 JANUARY 1857

Hitherto unpublished.

36 Onslow Sq^e Jan 13.

Dear Madam

I kill George III at Reading on Monday 19 or I should have
had much pleasure in coming to you.

Very faithfully yours
W M Thackeray

1286.   TO WILLIAM HARRISON AINSWORTH
13 JANUARY 1857

Extract published in Ellis's *Ainsworth*, II, 194; the whole letter in facsimile
in Joline's *Rambles in Autograph Land*, pp. 193–194, from which my text is
taken.

36 Onslow ☐ . Jany 13. 1857.

My dear Ainsworth

You'll think this correspondence is never a going to stop —
and laugh when I tell you that here's *another* put off! — only
from 5 to 6.30 however and I'll tell you why. Yesterday after
my letter to you was dispatched Mr Beale [6] comes to me for 4

---

[6] Thomas Willert Beale (1828–1894), impresario and music publisher.
The Brighton lectures must have proved remunerative, for Beale writes in
The Light of Other Days (London, 1890), p. 254: "Not satisfied with having
the German Reeds, Jullien and his band, Grisi and Mario, and nearly all the
leading singers and instrumentalists of the day under engagement to me, early
in 1857 I arranged with Thackeray for a second series of his lectures on 'The
Four Georges,' the terms being fifty guineas a lecture for fifty lectures. The
arrangement commenced in May, 1857, at Cheltenham, and continued at
intervals during the summer." It is presumably the negotiations for this

lectures at Brighton to be paid at the extremely moderate figure of 50 guineas per lecture — (this is between ourselves) The only days we could give them are Wednesday Thursday Friday Saturday 24th at 3 o clock — and I shall have to speak again in the evening here.

Now this is the plan of campaign. We start from Brighton [7] by the 5 o'clock train — My servant is in waiting at the station to take our luggage. My (jobbed) Brougham whisks us off to Painters Ship & Turtle [8] Leadenhall Street where a neat dinner awaits us a bottle of East India particular and one of Claret. at 7.30 the Brougham takes us to Edwards St.[9] and at 9.25 whither we like first, and then home to the house where we all insist you must stop & sleep.

And so for the present farewell old friend. Who knows there may [be] ANOTHER letter yet? The Brighton Room may be engaged &c &c. About these matters due notice shall be given but on Saturday & Sunday 24.25. please the Lord you dine with

Yours always

W M Thackeray.

I find I write upright with the steel pens slanting with the quill.[10]

---

second series that Hodder describes in *Memories of my Time*, pp. 268–272. Thackeray continued to lecture on his own account until his contract with Beale began.

[7] Ainsworth lived at 5 Arundel Terrace, Kemp Town, Brighton, from 1853 to 1867 (Ellis, *Ainsworth*, II, 192–193).

[8] George Painter, Ship and Turtle, 129–130 Leadenhall St., City (*London Directory*, 1855).

[9] The Marylebone Literary and Scientific Institution, 17 Edwards St., Portman Square (*London Directory*, 1855).

[10] The bulk of the letter is written in Thackeray's upright hand, the last four words in his slanting hand.

1287.   TO ?
              17 JANUARY 1857

Hitherto unpublished.

                          36 Onslow Sq: W S.
                          January 17, 1857.
Sir

I thank you for your note and grieve to hear the melancholy end of poor Mr Jeffries [11] — I don't touch on his affair in my lecture nor on many another point to the discredit of that unhappy George IV.: though I may have to speak on the subject when I publish the lectures in an enlarged form.   Believe me
                  Yours very much obliged
                  W M Thackeray.

1288.   TO MRS. CARMICHAEL-SMYTH
              23 JANUARY 1857

Published in part, *Biographical Introductions*, X, xxviii–xxix.

                                   Jan. 23.
Before bowling off to Brighton I think I ought to write a scrap to my dearest old Mammy — with the usual announcement, that there's nothing to say immense quantities of the same to do — endless letters constant running from place to place — not particklar good health but it cant be helped; and the illness over

[11] When George IV was Prince of Wales, he bought his jewelry (on credit, as was his custom) from a certain Nathaniel Jeffrys. After waiting some years for payment, Jeffrys brought suit and recovered a large sum for the jewels he had supplied. He shortly afterward went bankrupt, notwithstanding his legal success, and appealed for help to his former patron. His pleas proving futile, he wrote a series of pamphlets attacking the Prince. One of these, *A Review of the Conduct of his Royal Highness the Prince of Wales*, attained great notoriety because it gave renewed currency to an old topic of scandal, the relations between the Prince and Mrs. Fitzherbert. In his note above Thackeray perhaps refers obliquely to this delicate subject, to which he devotes only one sentence in his lecture on George IV, rather than to the troubles of Jeffry, who was very small game.

the best way is to shake it over and think no more about it until the next time I am down. Tomorrow I lecture in Brighton at 2, in London at 8 — I have had a couple of days rest and solitary dining at Club, w^h has done me good. The town is at present placarded with my name in enormous type announcing my lectures at the Surrey Zoological.[12] The bigwigs and great folks are furious. The halls of splendor are to be shut to me — and having had pretty nearly enough of the halls of splendour I shall be quite resigned to a quiet life outside them. I hope my dearest old Mothers improvement goes on a-bettering. How about the girls if they come in February? Where can they be stowed? — I think I ought to send Gray over with them this time. The poor woman has had months of lonely watching in the house here, & deserves an outing. Or perhaps I can get Eyre to come and stay with his sister here — hire a second maid for the time, and keep the house inhabited. The money bag is quite full again though to be sure there are awful pulls on it Mrs Bakewell has just had one. The poor thing's house was robbed of linen forks money coats boots brandy wine — and I have had to pay her rent and her income tax and keep her out of utter bewilderment and ruination O thank God for the full money-bag! And there is plenty more coming in 500£ more in the next 3 weeks at least so that my dear old folks may spend t'other side of the page with comfort and a knowledge that there's lots more when this little supply is used up.

Sunday we are to have dinner for Ainsworth my old friend between whom & me there has been a sort of a coolness since I have got on in the world & he has got off — and that I think is all

---

[12] "MR. THACKERAY will deliver his series of LECTURES on the FOUR GEORGES, in the Music-hall, at the Royal Surrey Gardens, on Wednesday, the 28th inst., Friday, the 30th inst., and Monday and Tuesday, the 2d and 3d February, commencing at 8 o'clock in the evening precisely. Admission to area and upper galleries, 1s.; reserved seats, 2s. 6d.; orchestra chairs, 5s., or 15s. for the four lectures. Tickets may be obtained at the Royal Surrey Gardens; at Jullien and Co.'s, 214 Regent-street; and at Keith, Prowse, and Co.'s, 48 Cheapside. The reserved seats being limited in number, early application will be necessary to secure them." (*Times*, January 26)

my news for my dear old Mother & G. P. I thought Georgy
Forrest very nice ladylike and grown quite good looking — It
was queer to see the old Montague Place furniture and the sideboard where I stole the olive when I was a boy [13] — Mrs Forrest
very cheerful & in wonderful good case — Bob and his baby I
think I told you must be put into a book. Shall I ever write one
again? — Some day please God when these astonishing Georges
have put a few thousands more into my pocket. And now, Come
Charles! Pack up the bag & lets be off to London Super Mare,
after a kiss to the girls and a God bless you to their dear Granny
& G. P.

1289.   TO ?
                   30 JANUARY 1857

Hitherto unpublished.

                              36 Onslow Sq^r S. W.
                              January 30. 1857.

Dear Sir

My rule has been never to solicit a favorable notice from a critic,
and never to thank him, w^h is as it were a request for future favors.
But of course I am glad when I hear that young men like my
books, and read them aright — knowing very well the common
cry against me that I am misanthropical bitter & so forth, whereas,
please God, my heart is full of anything but unkindness towards
the people who believe me such a cynic. No human brain is big
enough to grasp the whole truth — and mine can take in no doubt
but a very infinitesimal portion of it but such truth as I know that
I must tell, and go on telling whilst my pen & lungs last, and the
public and the author are not weary of each other. I am pleased,
you may be sure, if you or any other educated man likes my books,
and can never be indifferent to the expression of honest good will.

I hope the monotony of the Speaker the other night was greater
than usual. I didn't know what the circumstances were, was greatly
annoyed by people coming in 1/2 hour after the time — and besides

[13] Presumably at the home of Dr. Turner.

was just getting ready for a fever and ague fit w^h I had an hour after the lecture.

Believe me your very faithful Servt
W M Thackeray.

1290.   TO THE REV. WHITWELL ELWIN
8 FEBRUARY 1857

Hitherto unpublished.

36 Onslow Sq. S. W. Feb 8.

My dear Elwin. A hurried line to pay a debt and to beg a favor. A Mr Gale, a Winchester & Oxford man wrote me an interesting letter regarding himself and his desire to work as a man of letters, and he sent 2 pleasant books on Cricket & School life [14] w^h amused me, and w^h I almost remember though I read & burned them 2 years ago. Then he tried, me adjuvante, to write for Parker & couldn't get a place in his magazine.[15] Now he has tried yet again, and his subject is novel practical & interesting. 'The Progress of a Railway Bill' I should say promises a good article from a man who knows about it — Mr Gale it appears is Manager in a great Railway Solicitor's house — quite a gentleman in manners — might do for you. Will you, whose mission is to do kindnesses, read his paper & see if he can serve the Q. R.? — And so let us pass over Mr Gale, and get on to that other case. Well sir here it is [*sketch of hand pointing*]

I mean the cheque on the opposite page for young Abeckett. Wasn't it artful of me to bring the page up to this very point, and relieve your mind?

On Tuesday I go off again on a 2 months Northern Tour, in April have sold myself to Mr Beale for an immense bribe some 1500£ per month — and if I can last on till the end of June at this kind of work, shall have filled a wonderful money-bag.[16] My

[14] See above, No. 717, note 129.
[15] *Fraser's Magazine.* "The Progress of a Railway Bill" did not appear in *The Quarterly Review.*
[16] "Thackeray is flourishing," Albert Smith writes to John Blackwood about

girls remain here — We are all very glum at the idea of going away and talk common-places to each other as if we were cheerful and didn't mind it. My dear old friend H. Davison goes to Madras as Puisne-Judge tomorrow and saying good bye to him is rather an awful thing, when one thinks how he is 50 and in bad health, and I not very young nor very well. I've no news I think. I havent even read Lord Raglan in the last Quarterly [17] and only little bits of the cuts in the Sunday papers. Good bye, dear Elwin, and believe me always yours

W M Thackeray.

Mind there's more money whenever you want it.

1291.   TO FREDERICK COZZENS
        8 FEBRUARY–5 APRIL 1857

Published in part, *Thackeray in the United States*, I, 336–338.

36 Onslow Sq: London.

Feb 8 — (It's a Sunday evening) and Im waiting for dinner & thats how you come by an answer

My dear Cozzens. Thank you for a sight of your hand writing, and the kindly reminiscences of those jolly Centurions [18] whose hospitality and affectionateness this ♡ never intends to forget. What pleased me most in your ♡ letter is to have it under your own hand & seal that you are well — I should like to see those pretty little chicks again — that snug cottage — those rosy-tinted palisades that dining-room cupboard up w^h victuals came

---

this time. "Forbes is very funny about him. He told him the other night at the Garrick that as he was making such a pot of money with his four Georges, he had better go on with the eight Henrys, and then the Sixteen Gregories; by which time the public would be so exhausted that he had better wind up with the *One John* — and that (as Jerrold said) a *cheap* one!" Everyone is pleased, Smith goes on to say, with George Eliot's "The sad fortunes of the Rev. Amos Barton," which appeared in *Blackwood's Magazine* in January and February, 1857. "Thack.'s eyes sparkled through his spectacles as he spoke of it yesterday." (Mrs. Porter, *John Blackwood*, p. 43)

[17] January, 1857, pp. 168–202.

[18] See above, No. 999, note 208.

with clangor — that snug bed-room where the celebrated Thacker left the razor strap and could hear for hours Judge Daly talking talking into the midnight. My dear old Judge — I havent forgot what I owe him — I dont like to send it until I hear whether he is married or not;[19] — there was a hitch men told me — the course of true love didnt run smooth — Enlighten me some of you about this and let me pay my debts to my kind host & friend. Where Bayard may be now the Loramussy only knows We liked his pretty sisters, we had brief glimpses of a jolly time together[20] — We hope to meet in April or May when I bragged about taking him into the fashionable world. But I hear that I am in disgrace with the fashionable world for speaking disrespectfully of the Georgyporgies — and am not to be invited myself, much more to be allowed to take others into polight Society. I writhe at the exclusion. The Georges are so astoundingly popular here that I go on month after month hauling in fresh bags of sovereigns, wondering that the people are not tired & that the lecturer is not found out — Tomorrow I am away for 2 months to the North — have found a Barnum who pays me an awful sum for April & May and let us hope June — shall make 10000 £ by my beloved monarchs one way or the other — and then and then & then — well I don't know what is going to happen — If I had not to write 20 letters a day on business I would have written to George Curtis, and given him an old man's blessing on his marriage — But I cant write — no, only for business or for money can this pen bite this paper — As I am talking nonsense to you — all the fellows are present in my mind, I hear their laughter & talk, and taste that 44 Chateau Margaux — and that Champagne do you remember? — And I say again I would like to see those pretty little chicks. So the Athenæum assaults you[21] — to

[19] Judge Daly married Maria Lydig of New York in 1856.

[20] On August 4, 1856, Taylor noted in his diary: "Thackeray was in London, and I found him as jovial and as tender-hearted as ever. His daughters came to see the girls, took them out driving a whole afternoon, and we all dined together in the evening." (Marie Hansen-Taylor and H. E. Scudder, *Bayard Taylor*, I, 321)

[21] A brief and contemptuous notice of Cozzens's *Sparrowgrass Papers* ap-

you now! I never heard of the circumstance — the shot is fired,
the report is over, the man not killed — the critic popgunning
away at some other mark by this time — and you I hope you are
writing some more of those papers. Your book & Bayard Taylors
helped me over the voyage — How curious it is writing! I feel
as if I was back again in New York and shaking hands with 100
of you — the heart becomes warm — God bless all good fellows
say I. Shall I ever see you all again? Providebit Dominus.

I forgot whether you know Bancroft Davis — The folks here
are hospitable to him. He has a pleasant time. Yesterday we
elected him into the Garrick — and on the mantelpiece in my
dining room is a bottle of Madeira w^h he gave it me and w^h I
am going to hand out to some worthies who are coming to dine —
They have never tasted anything like it — thats the fact — As I
go on twaddling I feel I MUST come back & see you all. I praise
Mr Washington five times more here than I did in the States —
Our people cheer — the fine folks look a little glum but the celebrated Thacker does not care for their natural ill-temper. Only 2
newspapers here have abused me, & I have been quite on their side.

April 5. To think this was written on Feb 8 and left in my
portfolio! I went out of town the next day only returned April 3
— have been killing & eating the Georges ever since. I do not
know what this letter is about — I am not going to read so much
M. S. if I can help it — but I remember, when I wrote it, how
I had a great desire to commune with my old chums at New York
and hereby renew the kindest greetings to them. Tell me, Judge
Daly, are you married & happy? If so I will send you them
books I owe you. Poor Kane! [22] I grieved to think of that hero
carried so soon out of our world. There — I can no more —
Goodbye my dear Cozzens — I salute you my excellent Century —
G Curtis & Young & Daly I am

Yours always
Will. Thackeray

---

peared in *The Athenaeum*, September 20, 1856, pp. 1164–1165. The book
of Taylor's to which Thackeray refers below was probably *Poems of Home and
Travel*, published in November, 1855.

[22] Elisha Kane died on February 16, 1857.

1292.   TO ANNE AND HARRIET THACKERAY
13 FEBRUARY 1857 [23]

My text is taken from *Unpublished Letters by W. M. Thackeray*, ed. Clement Shorter, pp. 19–20; the drawing is reproduced from *Thackeray and his Daughter*, p. 108.

White Swan
Halifax
Friday.

My beloved

Although I am still at Halifax instead of going to Sheffield, yet I am greatly better have just eaten 2 wings of a fowl for dinner and wished the pore burd had 4, and have no doubt after the prodigious discipline I have undergone that I shall be able to get through the rest of the campaign without trouble. Min's letter arrived from Leeds this morning — so that was as good as another letter from home. I have been reading Mahon [24] with great comfort — am quite brisk and gay in my spirits, though a trifle weak, and though for reasons w^h my blushes forbid me to mention I am not quite good for a public lecture tonight. Never mind. Tomorrow will begin again. We won't lose heart for a little check or two. I think the D^r I have had here is about the best of them all. His name is Garlick and I like him both in cookery and as a medical man.

God bless my women. Write a famous account of me to Granny, and so good night says Papa.

[23] Written the Friday before Tuesday, February 17, 1857.
[24] See No. 1293, note 26.

1293.   TO ANNE AND HARRIET THACKERAY
17 FEBRUARY 1857

My text is taken from *Thackeray and his Daughters*, pp. 107, 109–111, where the first page is reproduced in facsimile.

Royal Hotel Sheffield
Chewsday. 17 Feb.

This comes rather late for Valentines day — It is copied from 6 mugs in my sitting room at the horrible inn at Halifax. This is a byootiful Inn. I have the gayest parlour looking over three smoky cheerful streets — a clean snug bed room — a snug sleep — a pleasant book to read — Colonel and Mrs. Forrest came to tea last night after the lecture that's why I didn't write to the girls. I liked them both, she pretty and blonde, he very gentlemanlike. The people for the most part didn't understand a word of the lecture. Old Fogy President of Institution introduced me and insisted upon toddling into the room with me on his arm. What, is Mr. Thackeray infirm? asks Mrs. F. of her husband. It was Old Fogy who was infirm. I had a very pleasant calm day at Fryston, and yesterday for dinner here ate a pheasant, one of a brace which old Mr. Milnes insisted on sending to my daughters, though I told him I wasn't going home. The last time I was at F. in the year 41,[25] Mrs. Milnes gave me a ribbon and a little étui, a something for my children — they were little trots of small size then — and she has been in Kingdom Come these 10 years I believe.

I wish those horrible newspapers would leave my health out. Some day the wolf will really come and no one will be frightened. Keep off Wolf for a few months! I want to put my lambs in comfortable shelter.

I am in the 4 vol. of Mahon.[26] It amuses me. I have read Cockburn's *Memorials*,[27] very pleasant too. It is delightful weather and the skeei is blyew through the smoke. Poor old Brookfield was born here my ♡ feels very soft towards him. Do you smell anything in ♡ this ink? It was thick, and I filled the bottle with brandy and soda-water. I have nothing to tell my dawlings but that I am very well busy and cheerful. I go to Leeds lecture, and come back tonight to York. I like the quarters I am in. So you may go on directing to this Royal Hotel till Saturday. I mean you may send by Friday night's post. I am glad you liked the drive to Q, never mind thc 2/6.

Write to Granny and tell her how cheerfully your dear father writes and God bless my women says Papa.

---

[25] See above, No. 203. Milnes's mother died on May 1, 1847.
[26] *History of England from the Peace of Utrecht to the Peace of Versailles. 1713–1783.* Volume IV covers the years 1749 to 1763.
[27] *Memorials of his Time* (1856) by Henry Cockburn (1779–1854), Judge of the Court of Session from 1834 till his death.

1294.   TO ANNE AND HARRIET THACKERAY
22 FEBRUARY 1857

Hitherto unpublished.

Sunday. Feb 22

C. E. Ellison [28] Es 3 George St East. Newcastle

My dearest women.   I hope you'll be able to go to Lady Molesworth & Lady Lyttleton [29] if there's any shaperoon.   I write to
Chesham Place to see if the lady from there is going to Lady M.
You must send me that Atlantic Telegraph letter it's — no, stop!
send it with the accompanying note addressed to Sir John Lubbock Bart & Co.

11 Mansion House S^t
City.

And in a day or 2 a receipt will come back from Lubbocks w^h you
will put on the files in my study.   I arrived quite comfortable last
evening gave me lecture w^h is getting so stale now that I'm not
even disgusted any more and forget all about it — and am staying in a very comfortable house with a nice pretty little married
couple.   He is Police Magistrate here — He & Tom Taylor used
to live in the Temple together, and had my name on the door.
He is at church with his pretty wife now over the way, whilst
your Pa is sitting & writing in the dining-room.   But though I'm
not at Church I think I say my prayers & thank God too — for
good children — for loving them — for the penny post that en-
ables us to talk to each other day by day — for the railroad that
whisks me about to get this money for them — You see without
railroads I couldn't have made this little fortune w^h is dropping
into us, Sheffield, York to Newcastle w^d have been 40 hours
journey instead of 5 1/2 without any fatigue.   Thanks be to God

[28] Cuthbert Edward Ellison (1818?–1883), whom Thackeray had known
as a barrister of the Inner Temple.   He was police magistrate successively
at Newcastle (1854), Manchester (1860), and London (1864).

[29] The former Mary Glynne (1813–1857), who had married Brookfield's
friend of the fourth Baron Lyttleton in 1839.

for his kindness to us on Quinquagesima Sunday and all other days in the year. I am glad you have seen poor old Charles. I am pained not at his wife's wit, but that she should have a cold heart. If she had had a good one, she never would have turned away relatives whom she had injured and slighted and who called to shake hands & be friends with her. She might have had her drive 5 minutes later and seen us although it was only 12/30 o'clock.

— Here lunch came in and stopped the sermon, & after lunch it is decreed that we are to go by railway to Tynemouth 10 miles off, walk by the stormy sea-shore and get an appetite for dinner. So I must shut my packet up, and send a balessing to my daughters from their dear Pa.

1295.   TO ANNE AND HARRIET THACKERAY
FEBRUARY 1857

Hitherto unpublished.

Only a line to day to tell you how I am come back from Carlisle and how it is the prettiest 3 hours possible of drive — I wonder whether we shall ever come & see it? — Think we shall. I am very sorry about my dear old Granny.— anxiety was 1/2 the cause of her bad nights — If I were to have 3 or 4 of them I should be more nervous than she — But Law how I do sleep! I am going to the Blackwoods for next Sunday from Carlisle, and to the Queens Hotel Glasgow afterwards — and the fine weather has broken up, and I am very well to day, and Mrs Ellison is doing everything to coax cuddle comfort me, and it will very soon be the end of March though to be sure it seems a year since I left home. Never mind, there's a good time coming — Good bye my pooty ooty little dears. Give my best regards to Lady Elizabeth — Drive about — make yourselves ahappy and think with respect of your

Pepar.

4 letters about lectures again to day. It isnt near over.

1296.   TO A. EDMONSTON [30]
                26 FEBRUARY 1857

Hitherto unpublished.

Newcastle on Tyne. Feb 26.

Dear M[r] Edmonston.

I am very sorry indeed to hear of your calamity. Eighteen years ago I endured such a one myself: [31] suffer from it even now sometimes, and can fully & heartily sympathize with those who are visited with so severe an affliction.

I propose to come to my friend M[r] Blackwood in Randolph Crescent for Sunday 1, & a part of Monday m[g] until it shall be time to set forth for Glasgow. Perhaps you will make it convenient to call upon me on Monday m[g] about 11? I look at the new programme as settled by M[r] Wood with some alarm — It involves a great deal more travelling than your first proposed plan, and by any study of Bradshaw I can't land myself at Kirkcaldy — perhaps you will be able to make this clear for me when we meet.

I have already refused the hospitality of M[r] Crichton of Cupar, but if your friend lives in the place must do honour to your acceptance and his hospitality. I hope though I hardly expect I shall be able to carry through the months campaign without some such check as I met at Halifax — We must do the best & hope for it meanwhile —

Believe me very faithfully yours
W M Thackeray.

[30] An Edinburgh bookseller.
[31] The death of his second daughter, Jane Thackeray, on March 14, 1839.

1297. **TO JOHN EVERETT MILLAIS**
26 FEBRUARY 1857

Hitherto unpublished.

Newcastle on Tyne. Feb. 26.

My dear Millais.

I thank you very much for your proffered hospitality. I wonder can I accept it and how I am to get from Kirkcaldy where I lecture on the 10th to Perth where I am set down for lecturing the next day — On the 12th I am to be at Dundee: and about that horrible Kirkcaldy can make out nothing after the most desperate study of Bradshaw. You at Perth will be best able to judge what will be the best plan for me — whether, by the nature of things, I shan't arrive late — whether I shan't have to set off early the next morning to keep my Dundee engagement, and whether under these circumstances I had not best go to an Inn where beds are always ready porters and cabs are always in attendance &c — Likewise I am obliged to travel with a servant owing to obstinate attacks of Roman (bilious) fever w^h has had hold of me these 4 years past, and seizes and prostrates me every month or so. If, considering these things, you think a Hotel the best place for me, perhaps you will decide *against* my coming to you. But the offer of hospitality is equally kind on your part and Mrs Millais' & I am very much obliged to you for proposing to have me as your guest.

Always sincerely yours
W M Thackeray.

1298.   TO JOHN EVERETT MILLAIS
                      3 MARCH 1857

My text is taken from John G. Millais's *Life and Letters of Sir John Everett Millais* (London, 1899), I, 277.

Queen's Hotel, Glasgow,
March 3rd.

My dear Millais, — I got the sad news at Edinburgh yesterday — that there is to be no lecture at Perth, my manager not having been able to make arrangements there. So I shall lose the pleasure I had promised myself of seeing you and Mrs. Millais, and the pictures on the easel, and the little miniature Millais [32] by Millais, which I hope and am sure is a charming little work by that painter. I am off in a minute to Edinburgh for Kirkaldy, and have only time to say that I am

Very truly yours always,
W. M. Thackeray.

1299.   TO ANNE AND HARRIET THACKERAY
                      3 MARCH 1857

Extract published, *Biographical Introductions*, X, xxvi.

Queens Hotel Glasgow Tuesday 3

I thought I should ave ad a letter from the Demoiselles Dickory this morning. I had a capital Sunday at Edinburgh, found a wonderful large audience here considering, had a famous long sleep after w.ʰ I woke up strong & hearty, and in a few minutes am off through Edinburgh again to Kirkcaldy where the Provost writes me word that he will be in waiting to carry me off to his Mansion. Several days 3 or 4 have been knocked out of the lecturing I am to have Saturday & Sunday 7th & 8th in Edinburgh likewise Saturday & Sunday 14 & 15 — where those kind hospitable Blackwoods receive me. All the week beginning 16th I am to be at Aberdeen, and perhaps shall knock off the last week of Inverness

32 Everett Millais (1856–1897), later (1896) second Baronet.

& so forth. w^h may bring me home by the 24th or so — and give me a clear week before we begin with Beale. That will be a comfort, won't it?

The Blackwoods were most eager that you should come but theres no use in spending 25 £ on railways in this bad weather — and besides I dont think you would hit it well with her. The clever little kind woman is spoilt by her husband & brother in law and carried off her little legs with prosperity. We are the best of friends but. but &c &c &c. Quite right about the Douglas T fight & I dont think the fib was a harmful one. I had to sit & be called the Greatest Satirist of the Age before 1200 people last night and then went to Mrs Thomson & her nice little sisters and was adored during the evening — Thomson [33] adoring too who is one of the greatest philosophers now alive. What does all this mean dont I know I am a miserable sinner? — Yes but my dear women's affte Father always

W M T.

By Thursdays post address here. By Fridays & Saturdays to Blackwood at Edinburgh.

1300.   TO MRS. FANSHAWE
                        MARCH 1857 [34]

Hitherto unpublished.

My dear f.

Will you kindly take a walk some day to dear Mrs Cappur and pay her what is owing by my darlings? I thought I might have had a line from you. I have been working away at Glasgow & here, and have not been wery well thank you but needs must and I work my best. I send you my best Cupid and to all travellers & ⟨ . . . ⟩ [35]

a penny stamp must be on this cheque.

[33] William Thomson. See above, No. 1262, note 156.
[34] This note appears to have been written from Edinburgh early in March.
[35] The final words of this note have not been preserved.

1301.   TO ANNE AND HARRIET THACKERAY
8 MARCH 1857

Hitherto unpublished.

Sunday.   March 8.

My loaves   It was very comfortable yesterday having nothing to do; and a good dinner and a good sleep also refreshed your dear Papa. The Scotch expedition is a failure as regards money, but pleasant enough otherwise — and this confounded Election [36] too will deprive me of ever so much more. Never mind: We shall only be a little longer getting the 20.000. At Dundee I found and read Pendennis & thought it dreadfully stupid — Here I found and read 2 numbers of Newcomes and thought them — o for shame you conceited creature! — well — I cant help it. If I think its bad I say so with just as much candour — and the desire of pease came over my mind — pease, repoge, and honest labour not this quackery w^h I'm about now. Let us NOT go into parliament: let us retire and take that atelier and work and write honestly and humbly — The frontispiece of Pendennis is verily always going on my mind.

Here is yours of yesterday just come in. I don't think that there would be any good in going over just now to my dear old Mother — the coming away gives her more pain than the meeting gives her pleasure. You see what you do when you marry.— what slaves you become — well? and what immense happiness you enjoy I daresay with the right man. These folks' pleasure has no doubt been very greatly increased during 40 years by their living together — the bottom of the cup is rather bitter. So may other dregs be.

That last was getting to be a very stupid sentence — Cause why? There is somebody sitting in the room   It is Professor Ferrier [37] father of the pretty girl I wrote you about and whom I dont like quite so much on 2^d thoughts — but those good people at Glasgow

[36] See below, No. 1324 and Appendix XIX.
[37] James Frederick Ferrier (1808–1864), Professor of Moral Philosophy and Political Economy at St. Andrews University from 1845 till his death.

are quite as nice and kind. I had a quiet evening on Friday with them after a delightful ride through lovely country from Dundee, by Perth, Sterling, to Glasgow. And tomorrow it is Glasgow again, & Glasgow on Friday, and Dundee Wednesday — care of Mr Chalmers Bookseller — but I dont care about your writing unless there is something pertickular to say as I shall be 3 miles from Dundee at the house of Sir J. Ogilvy [38] wherever that may be.

And so with a benediction on my gals their Papa puts a cigar into his mouth and goes out to take a little walk in Church time. Mind and go to Chesham Place tomorrow night & say I got a letter from there on Saturday only — and give my best love to all there including poor J. O. B.

P. S. A Special Edict. You understand that I distinctly prohibit a visit to Hyndford House — The sending of that poor little innocent olive-branch is all mighty well — But the frequenting of the house can produce nothing but mischief.

[For fragments of a letter to Mrs. Elliot and Kate Perry 8 March, 1857, see Letter 52, Appendix XXVI.]

1302.   TO LADY LOUISA DE ROTHSCHILD
                    17 MARCH 1857

Published in part by Lucy Cohen, *Lady de Rothschild*, p. 37. My text is taken from a transcript supplied by Mrs. Fuller.

Aberdeen, March 17, 1857.

Dear Lady Rothschild — I hope you know that I am murdering the 4 Georges in Scotland and never heard of your beautiful party till the flowers were all dead, the dancers all in bed, the candles all out, the supper all eaten, the ices all melted, and the plate all locked up.

How long this business of George-killing is to last I don't know, but I have months yet of the House of Brunswick before me. Heaven bless them! I never thought my late gracious Sovereign

[38] Sir John Ogilvy (1803–1890), ninth Baronet, of Baldovan House, near Dundee, M. P. for Dundee from 1857 to 1874.

would put so many 100£ in the pockets of --- Yours always
to command.

W. M. Thackeray.

What a fine wedding you have had in your family! [39] What a
parasol! What a pretty bride! — we met them all at Aix-la-Cha-
pelle last autumn, and I think we all liked each other. I know
I did.

1303.   TO ANNE THACKERAY
               17 MARCH 1857

Hitherto unpublished.

Aberdeen March 17. 1857.
Douglas's Hotel.

As usual this is only going to be a scrap of a letter — And am
I not writing it before eight o'clock — because I went to bed before
11, because I am going away to Dundee at 10.45. because I have
ever so many business letters to write besides. Well, the voice of
nature told me of the illness of my eldest daughter, though I felt
confident she would recover and so she has — the same cry of
nature told me she would want money and hadn't the paternal
instinct already forwarded it?

Also I had it in my mind to tell you about the Brougham Horse,
your various infantile letters pointing out to me clearly that you
were awfully working that poor animal — He must have a rest
at times. He musn't be taken out too many times a day — He
is not intended to carry 4 every journey he takes poor horse!
Spare him now & then Tis thoughtlessness I know not cruelty wh
has urged ye.

This is the most awfully hospitable of all the places. Fellows were
in waiting for me at the railway station walked me up and down
the town whether I would or no never left ⟨ . . . ⟩ [40]

---

[39] Baron Alphonse de Rothschild and his cousin Leonora, daughter of Baron
Lionel and Lady Charlotte de Rothschild, were married on March 4, 1857.
[40] Only the first page of this letter has been preserved.

1304. TO LADY JAMES HAY [41]
18 MARCH 1857

Hitherto unpublished.

Douglas's. Wednesday

Dear Lady James. How Can you suppose that I forget? I have this day engaged with a gentleman who keeps a carriage, M[r] Todd, to take me to pay a visit to your Ladyship tomorrow at 3. On Saturday I am engaged to the Provost. On Monday I have to go to Banff, but on Sunday morning, quite early, disguised, & in the grey, may I not come over in a cab to Seaton House and stay that day & tell you & Lord James that I am always

Most faithfully yours
W M Thackeray.

1305. TO ? 20 MARCH 1857

Hitherto unpublished.

Aberdeen. March 20. 1857.

My dear Sir.

I don't see how, with my views, I could be acceptable to any Scottish constituency. As long as the State pays any Church establishment at all (and I desire to see no separation) I think Maynooth [42] must be supported, & the educators of the Irish people educated. I do not care about disturbing the Forbes Mackenzie Act, of w[h] some of the consequences have been good, though the principle I believe is wrong. I would certainly open the Crystal Palace & similar Institutions on Sundays, holding that such a freedom would tend to the happiness and harmless pleasure of the people, and hence to the *majorem Dei gloriam.*

[41] The former Elizabeth Forbes (d. 1861), who had married Lord James Hay (1788–1862), second son of the seventh Marquess of Tweeddale, in 1813. Lord James was a General in the army.
[42] The college for the Catholic clergy at Maynooth, whose support by the government was long a debated parliamentry issue.

The duration of Parliaments I think is of small importance the character of the representation of the very highest, and I would be for the extension of the franchise and heartily vote for the ballot. As any government whatever it shall be must pursue the China War to an issue, there is no need of talking on that point, nor does Lord Palmerstons ministry want the least pressing upon it. But, on questions concerning us at home I think he wants a great deal of pressing, and that reforms of law, representation administration, are most urgent & needful.

> Very faithfully yours
> W M Thackeray.

1306.   TO ANNE AND HARRIET THACKERAY
24 MARCH 1857

Published in part, *Biographical Introductions*, X, xxvi–xxvii.

Inverness. Tuesday. March 24.

This is such a remote and ancient city that I suspect my letter will scarcely reach ye before Thursday noon — and after that let it be hoped there wont be many more letters written by your poor dear Papa to his absent family. It is a jolly little city. I was pained for the honest squires and country gentlemen with noble old fashioned notions about Church & King who thronged to the pretty little lecture room last night and had to listen to a sceptical Londoner sneering at loyalty courts and king-worship. I wonder if sneering is of the Deevil and laughter is not wicked? At a delightful industrial School at Aberdeen (where the children's faces and voices choked me and covered my spectacles with salt water) the founder of the School Sheriff Watson pulled my ballads out of his pocket and bade one of the little ones read out 'A hundred years ago and more a city built by burghers stout and fenced with ramparts round about' [43] &c w^h the little man did in an innocent voice and a strong Scotch accent of course — but the

----

[43] The opening lines of "The Legend of St. Sophia of Kioff" (*Works*, XIII, 80–97).

tone of levity in the ballad pained me coming from guileless lips — and I turned away ashamed and said to myself 'Pray God, I may be able some day to write something good for children' That will be better than glory & parliament. We must try & do it: mustn't we? As soon as we have made a competence for the 2 young ones, we must see if we can do anything for the pleasure of young ones in general. That truth suggested itself to me in the Industrial Schools in Aberdeen.

I was very sulky and disgusted at the prospects of yesterday's journey and a fierce storm of snow & sleet coming on as we were about 10 miles on the railroad from Aberdeen I had serious thoughts of turning back and not trying the coach-ride from Keith to Nairn — but I am very glad I did my duty. Honest folks came in many miles with cloaks furs gig-lamps and smoking post-horses to hear that dreary scepticism about George I. I should have caused many disappointments and sent trusting people angry home — and the coach journey though a little cold turned out very pleasant. To hear the horn sing as we rattled into the little towns and see the horses walk away towards their stables with quivering tails as their fresh successors took their places to see a bluff jolly guard and coachman once more was like being young again — you young folks never saw a bluff jolly guard & coachman; — and already Anny is deploring the departure of her youth. Her gentle sighs breathed on the artless paper, made me wonder whether TOMKINS had not made his appearance; — I shall be very glad to see him — Dont give him the Liverpool Port if you ask him to dinner — that is too good for young fellows — the Balfour wine is excellent, and the Kensington claret mind not the 40 or 60 — the young beggar does not know about wine yet — The coach journey was very pretty quaint & pleasant a sort of pathetic country we drove through little low villages great broad rushing streams hills covered with firs as poor folks put coarse mittens and woollen wrappers round their children whilst the rich have sables silk waddings and warm douillettes (— the Scotch hills are the poor, you see, the firs the cheap worsteds, oaks elms &c I take to be the adornments of wealthy lands and rich soils) —

an immense deal of ploughing going on & neat thrifty agriculture
— all pleasant to see from the coach windows and of w^h one sees
nothing on a railway-journey — All the same I am sulky still at
the notion of having to go 9 hours tomorrow to Banff where I'm
told there are not 4000 people. Never mind tomorrow is soon
over & then Thursday at Aberdeen, & by Friday's post you may send
me any letters care of Edmonston & Douglas Prince's St Edinburgh.
I do believe I might be returned for Edinburgh — a strong party
offered to put me up, and have pressed me, & written & rewritten:
but it w^d be impossible to be at one with these Scotchmen on the
Sabbath question and I wrote them my opinions so that there sh^d
be no possible mistake on that subject. And now I'm at my paper's
end — and to my dearest daughters send this news of their papa
& friends — w^h they will please to Granny lend — My dear old
Granny would like this place w^h seems to be entirely inhabited
by Frasers. Several were at my lecture last night in actual kilts.
W M T.

1307.   TO J. D. MILNE
                        26 MARCH 1857

Address: J. D. Milne Esq^e J^r Hitherto unpublished.

                                              26 March. 1857 —
My dear Sir

   I had not the least idea of the guarantees private convenings &c
by w^h my last lectures in Scotland have been managed. I stipulated
for a certain sum 25 guineas per lecture & half the profits over &
above — Had I not made the arrangement, I could have had
double the price in England during this month.

   But unless, a man has his own employés Secretaries &c, some
one must help him & make a profit out of him — it was thus the
Glasgow Athenæum engaging me to lecture for 100 guineas as
I thought in a hall w^h w^d have held 600 persons — took a hall
for 3000 — pocketed 5 or 600 by the transaction — and thanked
me at the Conclusion of the performances. I have heard of bargains

concluded & broken off at Inverness & Elgin about w.^h I knew no sort of particulars, and am forced to leave these details (annoyed by some of them & regretting them very sincerely) to the hands of Mr Wood.

faithfully yours

W M Thackeray.

1308.   TO ANNE AND HARRIET THACKERAY
26 MARCH 1857

Hitherto unpublished.

Banff Thursday 26.

Your letter just come in. Granny had best have my room and if G. P comes Amy will take a little lodgement like a little darlent, where Miss Shakspeare 44 was or somewhere a bed for Martha in Grannys room — the next for GP in case he wants it — I'll be just as happy upstairs next to you. See about the bells in all the bed rooms. Have the bell hanger over from Mr Freakes 45 immediately — Such a long dreary journey yesterday all in pochaises — poor old Brodie at the lecture to be sure. I gave her 10£. It's 7 o'clock in the bordig. Its raining. I am going in the coach and so God bless all at 36 all sick women all young children all old G Ps and your Pa.

Granny will be off to Aunt Marys at once but not you if you please young ladies.

[For a fragment of a letter to Kate Perry 24 March, 1857, see letter 53, Appendix XXVI.]

---

44 Selina Shakespear.
45 Charles Freak of 55 Onslow Square (*Watkins's London Directory*, 1855).

1309.   TO ROBERT CARRUTHERS [46]
        30 MARCH 1857

Published in part, *Thackeray in the United States*, II, 118–119.

36 Onslow Sq^e Brompton London S. W.
Edinburgh March 30.

My dear Mr Carruthers

Think of the state of mind of the landlord of this hotel and 50 or 60 gentlemen who were to have given me a dinner on Saturday at finding that though I had arrived over night I was ill and couldn't dine on that day! Dinner put off till Tuesday — side dishes all spoiled (let us hope so for it will be the deuce if they are served again) — very kind of them to insist upon having the dinner in spite of the contretemps.

I think the Mackayan letter not bad a trifle grand and solemn as young folks write [47]— and know Wm Jerrold is a clever fellow — My man was quite of a different sort — a man of the world and society w^h these men are not — not so good as either of them very likely in some respects — but we will keep our talk about him mum to ourselves and dont mention him to S. Brooks [48] — I have reason to fancy they dont like each other.

The 2 members for Edinburgh [49] are coming to my dinner on

[46] Carruthers (1799–1878) was editor of *The Inverness Courier* from 1828 till his death.

[47] Mackay, who was perhaps a son of Charles Mackay of *The Morning Chronicle*, had applied for a vacant post on the *Courier*. Among the other applicants were William Blanchard Jerrold (1826–1884), a son of Douglas Jerrold, and Thackeray's candidate, George Augustus Sala.

[48] Charles William Shirley Brooks (1816–1874), a close friend of Thackeray's later life and one of his principal champions among the journalists of the day. As a young man Brooks had been articled to a solicitor, but he soon gave up the law for journalism. After a decade as parliamentary reporter for *The Morning Chronicle*, magazine writer, and playwright, Brooks in 1851 joined the staff of *Punch*. He remained with this magazine until his death, serving as editor after 1870.

[49] Charles Cowan and Adam Black (d. 1874), an Edinburgh publisher who was elected liberal M. P. for the city in 1856.

Tuesday & Sterling of Keir and I hope we shall have a jolly party — I write from Youngs New Royal Hotel. Princes S![^t] and send my London address where I shall be very glad indeed to see you when you visit our village. By the way tell me about that Claret — It is really very good and I want some. How much? a word to

Yours very truly
W M Thackeray.

So my friend the Emperor of China has come round to our side about the Yeh question. His Majesty has a kind heart: I thought he had when he sent me that chest of tea.

1310.   TO LADY JANE OGILVY [^50]
30 MARCH 1857

My text is taken from a facsimile in *Biographical Introductions*, IX, lxi–lxiii.

Edinburgh. Monday 30 March

Dear Madam

Allow me to fling up my hat and cry hurray for the member for Dundee. He is so busy with the lawyers agents baillies & the like that he wont care for a shout more or less — but his wife? They you know are always pleased when good fortune happens to their husbands, and when other folks are pleased at it.

Since I saw you I have had an escape of being M P myself & for this place where two parties, I dont exactly know for what reason, wanted to put out one of the sitting members M![^r] Cowan: [^51] but I manfully said I was for opening the Crystal Palace on Sunday (*ad majorem Dei gloriam* as I thought) and for the grant to Maynooth, & that I didn't think any Scottish constituency would take a stranger with those opinions. I had a delightful tourkin

---

[^50] The former Lady Jane Elizabeth Howard (d. 1861), daughter of the sixteenth Earl of Suffolk and ninth Earl of Berkshire, who had married Sir John Ogilvy in 1836.

[^51] Charles Cowan (b. 1801), who had been liberal M. P. for Edinburgh since 1847.

in the North, was charmed with Inverness, and fell in love with old Aberdeen, an elderly decayed mouldering old beauty who lives quietly on the sea shore near her grand new granite sister of a city — I found old friends of mine, Lord & Lady James Hay there, with a house as hospitable as Baldovan — kindness everywhere — baillies & provosts at every station and dinners in every town. But the pace and incessant travelling and lecture-spouting and dining were too much for me. I broke down on Friday night on my arrival at Edinburgh leaving 50 gentlemen & the landlord of this hotel aghast who were to give me a dinner on Saturday. The dinner is put off till Tuesday I shall avoid the entrées (of w^h I shall have my suspicions) and eat the simple roast, and go back home on Wednesday, let us trust.

Wont you come to London for a little time in the season? I hope very much you may, and think with very great pleasure of the pleasant, restful days you gave me at Baldovan. With best regards to Sir John I am always most faithfully yours

W M Thackeray.

1311.   TO WILLIAM WEBB FOLLETT SYNGE
30 MARCH 1857

Hitherto unpublished.

Youngs New Royal Hotel.   Princess S^t
Edinburgh.   March 30.

So Kinglake has bowled your Uncle out [52] — Think that I might almost have been in for Edinburgh but by way of conciliating them I said I was for opening the Crystal Palace on Sunday & was for Maynooth and even then a strong party pressed me & w^d have

[52] The poll in the parliamentary election at Bridgewater in March, 1857, was as follows:

Lieut.-Col. C. J. K. Tynte 330
Alexander William Kinglake 301
B. Spencer Follett 203

(F. H. McCalmont, *The Parliamentary Poll Book*, London, 1880, p. 30).

had me try. But this is not the pint I hope you & Madam will kyindly dine on Sunday with us at 6.30 and ask Morgan John will you. His cheerful prattle emuses my good old mother. I have just got up after a crack of spasms w^h befel on the first & last day of this campaign — It has been glorious but not hoverendebuv remewnerative

I shant pocket above 700 out of the 7 weeks very different to the terms propoged by the noble Beale and w^h the Election has caused us to postpone very likely to throw over — Well never mind — Its only a little longer getting rich. As soon as I do I shall lapse into hidjous indolence — but meanwhile am

With the highest consideration

Sir

&cccc

[For a fragment of a letter to Mrs. Elliot and Kate Perry, March, 1857, see Letter 54, Appendix XXVI.]

1312.   TO LADY MURRAY
                        2 APRIL 1857

Hitherto unpublished.

Young's New Royal Hotel. Thursday
April 2. 1857 —

Dear Lady Murray — I must go to London tomorrow where my mother has been waiting to spend a week with me, 5 days of w^h will have been consumed when at last we meet tomorrow night. Otherwise I should have waited for your party, and have had very great pleasure in again shaking hands with Lord Murray and you.

Believe me
Most faithfully yours
W M Thackeray.

1313.   TO ANNE AND HARRIET THACKERAY
2 APRIL 1857

Hitherto unpublished.

Edinburgh. April 2.

My dearest women. I hope tomorrow m^g at 9.50 to be in the train going South, and tomorrow ev^g at 9.30 to be at the Great Northern Station at King's Cross, where if it doesn't rain my gals may come for me in the Brougham — or if it's fine they may want a drive during the day — a cab for Charles & the luggage must be had anyway, & I shall only rush into their arms at 10.15 instead of 9.30.

Oof! I wish this dinner [53] & the 2 speeches were over w^h I have to make — they have been throttling me like nightmares all the week, & though I have done 'em I know I shant remember 'em. Never mind It will all be over tomorrow, & then for all Saturday & all Sunday I shall be quiet with my dearest women & mother

W M T.

[53] The dinner given to Thackeray at the Royal Hotel in Edinburgh on April 2 is described in *The Times* of April 4, his two speeches being reported verbatim. Lord Neaves was in the chair, and the other speakers included Stirling of Keir, Professor Blackie, Robert Chambers, James Russell, and Charles Cowan. "Wasn't that beautiful of Lord Neaves," Dr. Brown writes to Mary Crum on April 8, "*Satire* and *Sympathy* rising in his deepest and highest nature, and rising together, though they took each their several ways. I saw [Thackeray] was so surprised and grateful at being so spoken of and understood. If you had seen his pathetic, dumb face, like a great child going to cry, when he stood up to return thanks for his Two Muses, his Daughters, you would have had a good honest cry, you and Jessie, as I very nearly had; only men's tears are seldom honest, and if honest, are Dearly bought. He thought he had made an immense fool of himself in his speech till he saw it next morning." (*Dr. Brown*, p. 111)

1314.   TO THORNTON HUNT
                       7 APRIL 1857

Hitherto unpublished.

                              Onslow Sqʳ   Brompton.
                                    April 7.

Dear Hunt.

Mʳ Bray wrote offering his hospitalities to me; but I am unwell,
and when in that condition like to be at an inn best — so I thank-
fully declined Mʳ Bray's offer. I am full of business at the present
writing, and have only leisure to say that I think that author is
very wrong whose opinion you quote that everybody abuses everybody behind the latter's back.

                          Always yrs
                          W M Thackeray.

1315.   TO LADY JAMES HAY
                      7 APRIL 1857

Hitherto unpublished.

                          36 Onslow Sqʳ   April 7.

My dear Lady James. I didnt send you a Scotsman because
I came away quite early on Friday mᵍ from Edinburgh, and on
Saturday your humble servants speeches were in the Times [54] —
They were very ill delivered for the Speaker is a nervous & sometimes even modest youth. He is going to begin a new book very
soon he hopes — very likely he will come into the North & work
on it, and then wont he be glad to see Seaton House once again &
the kind Lord & Lady there! He is yours (squeezed up at the
bottom of the page) faithfully ever W. M. T.

    [54] See above, No. 1313.

1316.   TO GEORGE FREDERICK PARDON [55]
                    14 APRIL 1857

Hitherto unpublished.

                                    36 Onslow Sq.   April 4
Dear Sir

I have this moment returned home from a 2 months absence in the North, and find your little volume [56] and 2ᵈ note. The first was forwarded to me at Glasgow: but I thought I would look at the book ere I wrote to thank the giver.

Naturally, I have not had time to do that as yet: but answer your second note without delay and with thanks for the little present you have made me.

                        Your very faithful Servᵗ
                        W M Thackeray.

There is no number to your date, but I hope my letter will find you in Beaumont Sq:

1317.   JAMES REYNOLDS YOUNG
                      2 MAY 1857

My text is taken from an Anderson Galleries catalogue, May 15–17, 1916, lot 143.

                                            Saturday Eve.
My dear Young.

I only got your note yesterday just as I was starting for Clifton where I had to lecture.[57] Endless Visitors prevented me from

[55] Pardon (1824–1884) wrote more than twenty volumes on sports and pastimes under the pseudonym "Captain Crawley".

[56] *Billiards*, "by Captain Crawley," the preface of which is dated Christmas, 1856.

[57] Thackeray had now begun the fifty lectures for which his contract with Beale provided. His itinerary included Exeter, Plymouth, Clifton, Birmingham, Oxford, Leamington, and Norwich. Hodder, who accompanied him as manager and secretary, describes the trip in *Memories of my Time* (pp. 272–

writing answers to my heaps of Correspondents, and now lo Monday must come before I can speak to you. I must go back to town on Saturday after lecturing at Leamington — have to dine with a Cousin of mine [58] at Oxford on Friday who is just made fellow of Lincoln so its in vain for me to try and hope to pay you my visit now. I begin at Norwich again on Monday and for a fortnight or 3 weeks more there is no rest for me. It is a bore, but I wish all men could be as well paid for their sermons as yours always my dear Young.

W. M. Thackeray.

Poor old Stoddart!

274, 282–292, and 301–305). Thackeray was by no means as successful as he had been earlier in the year. "After the first five lectures had been delivered," writes Beale (*The Light of Other Days*, p. 262), "I called in Onslow Square with a cheque for £250.

" 'What is this, W. B.?' said Thackeray, reading the cheque. 'Pounds? Our agreement says guineas, and guineas it must be.'

" 'You are well aware the lectures so far have involved a very heavy loss,' I replied by way of apology.

" 'That's not my affair,' he rejoined. 'I am not to know what occult means you have to protect yourself from loss. Guineas, W. B.! Guineas it must be, and nothing less! I must have the shillings.' "

[58] Francis St. John Thackeray, who was a Fellow of Lincoln College from 1857 to 1861. While in Oxford Thackeray met the Rev. Charles Lutwidge Dodgson (1832–1898), later famous as Lewis Carroll, mathematical lecturer in the University from 1855 to 1881. "I breakfasted this morning with Fowler of Lincoln," Dodgson noted in his journal on May 9, "to meet Thackeray (the author), who delivered his lecture on George III. in Oxford last night. I was much pleased with what I saw of him; his manner is simple and unaffected; he shows no anxiety to shine in conversation, though full of fun and anecdote when drawn out. He seemed delighted with the reception he had met with last night: the undergraduates seem to have behaved with most unusual moderation." (Stuart Dodgson Collingwood, *Life and Letters of Lewis Carroll*, New York, 1899, pp. 72–73) Among those present at the large breakfast party given by Thomas Fowler (1832–1904), Tutor at Lincoln College from 1855 to 1881 and President of Corpus Christi College from the latter year until his death, in the Lincoln common room were Mark Pattison and John Morley (Irvine, *Nineteenth Century*, XXXIV, 592).

1318.   TO WILLIAM BRADFORD REED
                    14 MAY 1857

Hitherto unpublished.

                                Norwich.   May 14.   1857.
My dear Reed.

Thank you for that kind little note announcing Your Excellency's speedy departure for China [59]— for without it, I should not have answered the last letter I had from you — our papers all announcing your speedy arrival here to commune with Lord Clarendon and Walewski upon the measures to be pursued at Canton. And I made sure that we would have you for the Literary Fund dinner next week, and that I should get a chance of making a neat speech in your honor & of asking you to dinner at home and having a party of big wigs to meet you — &c &c. Sed Deis aliter visum [60]— I don't at all like the Chinese appointment unless it will lead to an English one afterwards — where I should like of all things to see a scholar and a gentleman out of your country, and a man who could hold his own with our folks in literary talk.

This is written at a very uncomfortable table in an Old Hotel at Norwich [61]— a city w^h would do your heart good to see, with an ancient market place peaked with a hundred gables and surmounted by a huge castle built by the Normans and as grim and as clean it has just been scraped for the first time, as when William Conquerors knights kept ward there. I had a magnificent old Hall to lecture in with honest stupid county families driving in in their carriages — it was a Church once and I approached it through the Cloisters of an old Convent. That lecturing business is very nearly come to an end. I have made as much more by it as I made in America, And am straightway going to a book w^h in consequence of the popularity of these lectures is paid to me twice as much as

[59] Reed was appointed Ambassador to China shortly after President Buchanan took office in March, 1857.
[60] *Aeneid*, II, 428.
[61] See Appendix XVIII.

any former production. That is all my personal news — you see by it that I am flourishing pretty well — in disgrace with the Whigs who have left me off; but much better known to the country and liked by it let us trust. It was good to hear the boys at Oxford cheering the other night. The last time I was there there were not 100 of them. this time there were 500 — so it is that vires acquire riches It will be good for your boys to see the world, to smell powder mayhap; but what an anxious time for you and Mrs Reed! What a wrench at the heart that parting with the little ones — what a meal that last breakfast where you'll all try and look cheerful Amen! Days and griefs pass; and we struggle on in our career, and amass or dissipate or climb upwards to reputation or slip down and flounder, and undergo our Fate. I suppose it will please you (it would me, I'm pretty sure) to hear the frigates salute you as you go into the Canton river → Every man would like to make a mark as a Citizen in his country — and you having that chance may it be a prosperous one to you, may you go back to happy wife and children, my dear Reed. And may we see you in London in a coach emblazoned with the eagle and the stripes and stars. I suppose the pretty daughter will have a husband to console her for Papa's absence. None such has yet appeared about my premises and I hope not to see one for some time to come. How I wish I had you here that I might keep out of blunders in THE VIRGINIANS! w^h is to be D. V. the name of the New Story. I daresay you guess who they are & that Hester Reed's Diary [62] will be very serviceable to me. Salve et Vale my dear Reed says

Yours very sincerely always

W M Thackeray.

And a many kind messages to Mrs Reed though I havent the heart to say them now to her

[62] See above, No. 1079.

1319.   TO GEORGE FREDERICK PARDON
21 MAY 1857

Hitherto unpublished.

May 21.   Onslow Sq.ʳ

Dear Sir

I have been travelling from home, & your note has again been delayed in reaching me. I was not hurt that you should have put Captain Crawleys name to your little book on billiards — and if you remember wrote to you instantly on my arrival from a previous journey to acknowledge your 2 notes & the volume wʰ you sent me.[63] Since then I have been painting my study & the book has disappeared so that I have not had an opportunity of judging of the quality of the text of the book you were so kind as to inscribe to

Your very faithful Servant
W M Thackeray.

1320.   TO BAYARD TAYLOR
29 MAY 1857

Extract published by Mrs. Hansen-Taylor and Scudder, *Bayard Taylor*, I, 333. My text is taken from *Thackeray in the United States*, I, 339–340.

36 Onslow Square, 29 May

My dear Bayard, — I have written a letter to Tennyson [64] containing comments upon your character, which I could n't safely trust to your own hand — and so, you'll go to Freshwater in the Isle of Wight and he'll be prepared to receive you. The girls are sorry not to see the sisters who must have had a famous time and we here shall be delighted to shake hands with you — A month sooner we would not have let you camp out elsewhere, but I have just pulled part of my house down and have only one bed-chamber

[63] See above, No. 1316.
[64] I have not traced this letter.

where there were to be two. But live as close as you can to us and eat, drink, smoke, come in and out as you please, and you'll be sure to please

W. M. T.

1321. TO WILLIAM ALEXANDER MACKINNON [65]
31 MAY 1857

Hitherto unpublished.

Private   May 31.
My dear Mr Mackinnon

I am told that the second seat for Lymington may be had by the person who is secure of your good will. Will you give it to
Yours very faithfully
W M Thackeray.

May I come to talk to you on the subject?

1322.   TO BAYARD TAYLOR
JUNE 1857

Facsimile published in *Thackeray in the United States*, I, 340. *Endorsed*: June, 1857, B. T.

My dear B. T. I was so busy yesterday that I couldn't keep my agreeable appointment with Thompson: & am glad I didn't fetch you to Greenwich Here's a note wh concerns you,[66] & I am ever yours

[65] Mackinnon (1789–1870), author of a *History of Civilization* (1846), had represented Lymington in parliament from 1831 to 1833 and from 1835 to 1852. He was currently liberal M. P. for Rye. His son, William Alexander Mackinnon Jr. (b. 1813), was elected to the second seat for Lymington later in 1857.

[66] The note, which is to Thackeray from Tennyson at Farringford, reads: "Your American friend & poet-traveller has never arrived. he has I suppose

1323.   TO DR. JOHN BROWN
                           22 JUNE 1857

My text is taken from *Letters of Dr. John Brown*, pp. 331–332.

Monday, 22 June.

My Dear Doctor — I am very sorry to hear the bad news about
Madam, whom I don't like to fancy in illness and pain. Nature
gives them a much greater share of it than to us who grumble
and groan so much more; and the hypocrites bear it so well! I
know one, two, three at this minute, all suffering, all cheerful,
when the husband or company arrives, all aches are trifles com-
pared to theirs, and I'm determined to bear my share fortitudi-
nously. . . . Tom Taylor wrote the verses in *Punch*; when I strike
the lyre I think it's to a more original tune than that; it's not the
best music, but it's my own. Jerrold never was Editor of *Punch*.
I wrote to Douglas on that important matter on Saturday. I'm
getting up a new sermon in his behalf,[67] and have done little more
this month past but racket and go to my Doctor, and to parties
with my daughters, and ponder over the new book. The lines
are out of the introduction to Faust, about the prettiest of Goethe's,
and utter sweetly and naturally a selfish, honest feeling of grief.[68]

---

changed his mind. I am sure I should have been very glad to see him for my
'castle' was never yet 'barricaded & entrenched' against good fellows. I
write now this line to say that after the 30th I shall not be here.
    "My best remembrances to your daughters whom I have twice seen once as
little girls & again a year or so back." Taylor visited Tennyson later in June.
    [67] Douglas Jerrold had died on June 8, 1857. Thackeray was a pall-bearer
at his funeral on June 15, and later in the year he read his old lecture on
"Charity and Humour" (otherwise called "Weekday Preachers") for the
benefit of Jerrold's family.
    [68] In the preface (dated April 10, 1857) to volume IV of his *Miscellanies*,
Thackeray writes of *A Shabby Genteel Story*: "The tale was interrupted at
a sad period of the writer's own life. The colours are long since dry; the artist's
hand is changed. It is best to leave the sketch, as it was when first designed
seventeen years ago. The memory of the past is renewed as he looks at it —

die Bilder froher Tage
Und manche liebe Schatten steigen auf."

(*Works*, XI, vii)

I don't think I've any news. I know that I've ever and ever so many letters to write, and that I'm yours always and your wife's and your young ones', my dear Brown.

1324.   TO ANNE AND HARRIET THACKERAY
11 JULY 1857

My text is taken from *Biographical Introductions*, X, xxxi.

Oxford, July 11, 1857.

My dearest little women, as far as I can see,
The independent Woters is all along with me,[69]
But nevertheless I own it, with not a little funk,
The more respectable classes they go with Wiscount Monck;
But a fight without a tussle it is not worth a pin,
And so St. George for England, and may the best man win.

1325.   TO LADY MOLESWORTH
JULY 1857

Hitherto unpublished.

My dear Lady Molesworth,

In such a moment all I ask
Is, thou'lt remember me.[70]

What can I say better than the beautiful words of the poet and leave the rest to hope and your good nature?

Haste, Haste to the poll! Bring up your independent electors! and rally round Titmarsh! Such is the earnest and patriotic appeal of

Your ladyship's most faithful humble Serv!
W M Thackeray

[69] See Appendix XIX.

[70] From Thaddeus's aria in the first scene of the third act of *The Bohemian Girl* (1844) by Michael Balfe:

When hollow hearts shall wear a mask,
'Twill break your own to see —
In such a moment, I but ask
That you'll remember me.

1326.   TO WILLIAM HEPWORTH DIXON [71]
16 JULY 1857

Hitherto unpublished.

Mitre.   July 16.

My dear Mr Dixon

I am not ready with the new lecture Im sorry to say — It is more than 1/2 done, but this election has stopped me and occupies every hour of my time till Tuesday when my fate will be decided. I had thought Saturday w^d be the day, when I sh^d have had plenty of time to finish Week Day Preachers.

Always yours
W M Thackeray.

Our side says we are safe to win — so do the others.
Speirs is on the other side I fear, or at best will not vote.

1327.   TO LADY HOLLAND
23 JULY 1857

Hitherto unpublished.

July 23.   36 Onslow Sq^r

Dear Lady Holland

I have only just returned beaten from Oxford, and found your kind invitation. I wish I had been here to accept it, and hope to pay my best respects to you & Lord Holland on a very early day.

very faithfully yours always
W M Thackeray.

[71] Dixon (1821–1879), editor of *The Athenæum* from 1853 to 1869, was a persistent enemy of Thackeray after the Garrick Club Affair. See Appendix XXV.

1328.   TO THOMAS BUCHANAN READ [72]
                    3 AUGUST 1857

Address: T. Buchanan Read Esq. | at Thornton's Esq^e | Whalley Range | Manchester. *Postmark:* AU 4 57. Published in *Thackeray in the United States,* I, 341.

36 Onslow Sq^r   August 3.

My dear Read

Thank you for your volume [73] — I did not know Where to send you to acknowledge — wont say that I have had time to read it yet — have been away out of town on a business w^h occupied every hour of my time, electioneering — have been ill since my return and So busy that the muse has had to sit in the antechamber, all this while. Tomorrow we go to Brighton and I shall see your Icebergs from the sea-shore there. Thank Mr Thornton [74] for his offer of hospitality: but I am promised if I go to Manchester to my friend Drane, and when I go it will be in force with my daughters in company. I shall be delighted to have a bit of the Ancestral printing: and hope that we may have some more meetings in our country or in your's

Always yours
W M Thackeray.

[72] Read (1822–1872) was a minor American poet and painter who had lived for years in England. Thackeray appears to have met him through Bayard Taylor.

[73] *The Famous History of the Life of the Renowned Prince Palmerin of England,* a copy of which inscribed to him by Read was in Thackeray's library when he died (*Howe Proofs,* p. 512). Read sent Thackeray this Spanish romance of doubtful authorship, which shares with *Amadis of Gaul* the distinction of being one of the two tales of chivalry which the curate and the barber in *Don Quixote* (Book I, chap. VI) spare from the flames, because the title page reads: "London, printed for William Thackeray, in Duck-Lane and Thomas Passinger on London-Bridge. MDCLXXXV."

[74] William Thornton, of Challey Range, Manchester, with whom Read was living.

1329.   TO COLONEL SYKES [75]
                         16 AUGUST 1857

Hitherto unpublished. *Endorsed*: | 57.

> Brighton. 126 Marine Parade.
>   August 16.

My dear Sir

I trouble you once more in behalf of my friend M[r] Crowe the Artist, thank you for entertaining his application so kindly — I am sure if you employ him he will do justice to your Commission, and send you a note from him w[h] has been lying awaiting me here.

Thanking you most sincerely for your willingness to serve my friend believe me dear Colonel Sykes
>   Your obliged faithful Serv[t]
>   W M Thackeray.

1330.   TO MRS. SYNGE
                         SEPTEMBER ? 1857

Address: M[rs] Synge. Hitherto unpublished.

My dear M[rs] Synge

At last it is arranged that we go to Hombourg and herewith Charles Pearman receives orders to join his employer.

My old Stepfather is very shaky and I think I must spend a great part of the winter at Paris, so that the good Grey the Cook must seek for a place elsewhere. I have written her a line to say that I am sure you will be kind enough to answer for me that I have found her 'honest willing intelligent economical & a good cook' And so Eliza will be at your Ladyships service; and the house for some months to come at least. I must come to London to get the first number of my book out;[76] and then further matters

---

[75] Colonel William Henry Sykes (1790–1872), Chairman of the Board of Directors of the East India Company in 1856 and liberal M. P. for Aberdeen from 1857 to 1872.

[76] Chapters 1 to 4 of *The Virginians*, published for November, 1857.

may be arranged. If a young couple who are talking of fitting & furnishing a house don't find themselves too far off at Kensington — why — but we will talk of this when I come.

Meanwhile I send my very best regards to Mrs Synge, and am Mr Synges

Very sincerely
W M Thackeray.

1331.   TO WILLIAM MACREADY
                13 SEPTEMBER 1857

Hitherto unpublished.

36 Onslow Sq.
Sep. 13.

My dear Macready

I am only just home from Hombourg, have no lectures to give but the one I owe you and will pay it on any day that shall be fixed by you & your Institution 77 — There —

I dont write any more. O Lord — if you could see the heap of letters to answer you w^d pity

Yours ever
W M Thackeray.

Please Announce either Week Day Preachers 78 or George III.

1332.   TO JOSEPH PARKES
                25 SEPTEMBER 1857

Hitherto unpublished.

36 Onslow Square.   Brompton
Friday ev^t Sepr 25.

To remind

Mr Thackeray requests the pleasure of Mr Joseph Parkes's company at dinner on Wednesday the 7 October at *6. o'clock precisely*

---

77 Thackeray did not lecture at Sherborne until March, 1858.
78 That is, "Charity and Humour".

1333.   TO LADY OLLIFFE
                        26 OCTOBER 1857?

Hitherto unpublished.

                                        36 Onslow Sq: S. W.
                                            October 26.

My dear Lady O   Those stupid reporters at the Reform Club
have only given me your note of the 19ᵗʰ just now. I am too busy
and alas! too unwell to be able to leave town just now else
you know how glad I should be to see you. Mʳ W Russell the
Times Correspondent is talking so cheerfully at my back that I
cant make grammatical sentences, but I can briefly and with real
sincerity aver that I am yours

                            Most respectfully
                            J. B. O'Meagher.

1334.   TO A. I. HOPKINS
                        31 OCTOBER 1857

Address: A. I. Hopkins Esqᵉ | 38 Great Pulteney Sᵗ | Golden Square. Hitherto
unpublished.

                            Athenæum.   October 31. 1857
Sir

I found your note on my return to town yesterday. The paper [79]
about wʰ you enquire has just been republished in (I am not certain wʰ volume of) my miscellanies — I am very glad it pleased
you & your children.   'Sedan Court' of wʰ I forget the real name,
is close by Great Pulteney Sᵗ and I assure you the scene was
accurately described.

                        Your very faithful Servt
                        W M Thackeray

[79] "The Curate's Walk".

1335.   TO THE BAXTERS
31 OCTOBER–27 NOVEMBER 1857

Address: Mʳˢ Baxter | Second Avenue | New York. | U. S. A. | via Liverpool.
Postmark: LONDON NO 27 57. Published in part, *American Family*, pp.
155–160.

36 Onslow Square.
November 1.
but begun yesterday at the
Athenæum where I found
your letter.

These are pretty reproaches indeed Ladies! — I should like
to know who wrote last to both of you? I flatter myself its I who
am the injured party — though that it may be months ago since
I wrote I confess. And I have been thinking of you all the time
of this panic [80] and actually was too frightened to write. Last
Monday I came home to the girls and announced that the carriage
and one must be sold (we keep a carriage and one a very pretty
open carriage and a brougham if you please.) that Jeames must
certainly go, if not chawls too (Mr. Chawls is such a great man
now that he cant do without a young man in livery to help him)
that all the American savings were gone to smash, including the
500£ from Harper Brothers for the Virginians — It is astonishing
how well we took our ruin. Next day however things began to
brighten again: and it appears we are not done for, as yet at least.
What shall I tell I have just come back from Oxford after that
little electioneering freak. I should have won but for the Sabbath
question, and on that point I wont truckle or change to get any
possible promotion or glory — and am quite as well out of Parliament as in. Tell Sally my fits of blue devils continue — that I
have fallen in love with nobody else and intend to dont — that
nobody is come after my homely girl who is the delight of her

[80] The transatlantic mails brought news early in October of the failure of
many American banks. In the ensuing panic several English firms had to close
their doors, the largest being the Western Bank of Scotland, which had
liabilities of £8,911,000. (*Annual Register,* 1857)

father when he sees her. I have had the parents with me for the last 3 months: or with the girls rather my visits being only occasional. I dont think the Virginians is good yet though it has taken me an immense deal of trouble but I know it will be good at the end. I tremble for the poor publishers who give me 300£ a number — I dont think they can afford it and shall have the melancholy duty of disgorging. Sure I think this is all my news; but I think about America a many & many times and in so friendly a manner that I am perfectly certain I shall be walking Broadway again ere long. Do write and tell me that you are not severely hurt in the panic. I took a share in the Transatlantic Telegraph (deeming it a sort of duty) but the Oxford Election cost me so much that I was obliged to sell the Transatlantic-share, so that that money was so much saved — Only 2 people of all those I canvassed had ever heard of my name. It wouldn't be so in America, would it? It was a good lesson to my vanity.

My summer trip was confined to a house at Brighton and a little excursion to Hombourg & Paris. The girls rode hack horses and bathed and were happy. My mother who has been ailing for more than a year has improved very much during her 3 months visit to us. I am rather better in health I think but becoming more silent & selfish every day. Women know how to dissemble when they are bored, and appear cheerful though they are yawning in spirit. I wish I could be a little more of a hypocrite sometimes. Your daughter S. H. writes glumly that she is a wreck: a wreck with a pooty ittle boy floating on it is always an interesting object — Let us carry the young ones safe to shore. Ha! There is a large tear w^h my pen has shed. It is one of a box of pens w^h I bought in Washington D. C. What about the boys? Is Wyllie working hard and as good as ever Has George begun to grow a moustache? Is that tiresome fever and ague out of the house? I have not had a touch since the 4 of July when I was sitting quite happy and unprepared, after a good dinner, listening to Lord Brougham & Lord Lyndhurst telling wicked old stories, and lo! I felt the enemy creeping down my back. Mysterious chill & fever! — Prattling w^h nonsense my paper has come to an end. Was it a grand marriage of Miss Libbie? Mind, I consider it is my privilege to send each of those young ladies a tea-pot. The girls and I will go into town today to look for one: & when Madame Jandon uses it she will please remember her & your

Here it is the 28 November [81] and the letter begun on the 1st still lying in my box. Do you know why it was not sent? First we went out to look for a T. pot, then we couldnt find a pretty little oné such as befits a young bride who wishes to console herself with Bohea in the absence of her hearts darling. Then when in about a week I had got scent of a pretty little old tea pot it is a fact I had NO MONEY — that is to spare — That is times are so bad and every man so hard pressed that 1, 2, 3, 4 up to 14 people have been to me for gold and silver in the course of the month, and I couldnt refuse them in their distress and didn't dare to buy even a two penny halfpenny present whilst all these unfortunates were calling out for help. As I came in just now Charles says Mr C's servant just called with a note wh he was to leave in case you were at home' Do you suppose I dont know what that means? Mr C. will call himself tomorrow morning before 11 (the wretch!) and say My dear fellow the times are so bad that if you can lend me &c and how on airth with all this can I go and get that teapot? Never mind. Wait a while, Libbie, It must and SHALL be bought, meanwhile take the benediction of your affectionate Uncle — wh is I think my relationship to you. What has happened since the 1st? Nothing particular. My good old parents are gonc away after a good long visit — The old Major grows to be more and morc like Colonel Newcome every day. My mothers health has greatly improved She enjoyed her visit here. We are very smart. You should see our new Brougham if you please, &c &c &c. God bless you all — a very merry Xmas to you, to brides to bridegrooms to spinsters piccaninnies Grandmothers Grandfathers grand and common uncles, and to S S H from yours evcr

[81] A mistake for November 27, as the postmark shows.

1336.   TO BRADBURY AND EVANS
               3 DECEMBER 1857

Hitherto unpublished.

Brighton. Decr 3 . 1857.

Dear Sirs

I hear that Messrs Harper of New York have forwarded funds
to meet their engagements in this country, and shall be glad to
have payment for my 2 numbers of the Virginians. Will you or
Mr Joyce call on M^{ess}^{rs} Low and receive the monthly money on
behalf of

                         Yours very faithfully
                         W M Thackeray.

Messrs Bradbury & Evans.

1337.   FROM CHARLES DICKENS
               4 DECEMBER 1857

Published by Dr. Rosenbach, *Widener Catalogue*, II, 51.

                         Tavistock House
                    Friday December Fourth. 1857.

My Dear Thackeray

Your second note stopped me from coming to you, to talk over
the subject of your first [82]— which reached me within an hour
before the receipt of a similar proposal from Forster.

In the intervale which has followed through your absence from
town, I have communicated with Marguerite Power, and have
asked her plainly, whether such a subscription would be acceptable
and accepted? She replies, most gratefully and without hesitation,
"Yes". It seems to me that the best thing we can do, is, to take
out 20 names of old visitors at Gore House and make a subscription
of £10 each. This will give us a purse of £200 to present to her.

---

[82] I have not traced these letters.

I will come to you at Brompton, or meet you anywhere, any day you can name, between 10 and 5. Let us do it as soon as we can, and get it done.

Ever Faithfully
Charles Dickens.

W. M. Thackeray. Esquire

1338. TO CHARLES DICKENS
7 DECEMBER 1857

Published by Dr. Rosenbach, *Widener Catalogue*, II, 51.

36 O. □. Decr 7.

My dear Dickens

I cant ask, but you may, a gentleman by the name of Alb-rt Sm-th, (who has made a good deal of money by ascending a place called M-nt Bl-nc) for 10£ towards that purse, and I think he will give it.

A man assaulted him in a public club the other day for his stinginess to an old friend, and the man as it appears was egregiously wrong, and Sm-th's conduct has been quite right and generous towards his unfortunate friend R-b-ns.[83]

Of course I am good for 10£. for the Subscription

Yours ever
W M T.

[83] Serjeant Ballantine (*Some Experiences of a Barrister's Life*, I, 136) explains that "Albert Smith . . . and a poor fellow now dead, Joe Robbins, had been associates and friends; the latter, who originally had been in a lucrative business, quitted it for the stage and got into a very sad plight. I know that Albert Smith had been most considerate and kind to him, but had on one occasion refused to join in some subscription that had been set on foot in his behalf. Thackeray circulated throughout the club a caricature, in which the likenesses were unmistakable. Robbins was represented wounded by thieves and being assisted by some good Samaritan, also portrayed, whilst Albert Smith, the Pharisee of the parable, was passing scornfully upon the other side."

In *The Roundabout Papers* Thackeray tells of the apology that he made to Arthur Smith (1825–1861) for his injustice to Albert. "Years ago," he

1339.   TO S. LOW AND SONS
                 11 DECEMBER 1857

Published in part, *Biographical Introductions*, X, xxxvii.

36 Onslow Sq^re London
December 11. 1857

Dear Sirs

I am sorry to hear from you that the N Y. Tribune is reprinting
The Virginians, and no doubt hurting the Messrs Harpers' Issue
of the story, who pay me 100$ per month for early impressions.
But I do not see what good any remonstrances of mine can effect.
If American houses choose to reprint our books we can't prevent
them, and the Tribune will doubtless take it's own course, in spite
of any objections of mine or Messrs Harper. Could English writers
have remonstrated with any effect we should have done so
years ago: but I am sure an outcry at present would neither be
useful nor dignified; and can only express my regret that I dont
see how, in the present instance, I can be of any service to a House
w^h shows itself inclined to act in a kind and friendly manner to
English literary men.

Faithfully yours
W M Thackeray.

Messrs S. Low & Son.

----

writes (*Works*, XII, 373–374), "I had a quarrel with a certain well-known
person (I believed a statement regarding him which his friends imparted to
me, and which turned out to be quite incorrect). To his dying day that
quarrel was never quite made up. I said to his brother, 'Why is your brother's
soul still dark against me? It is I who ought to be angry and unforgiving: for
I was in the wrong.'"

1340. FROM THACKERAY, DICKENS, AND FORSTER TO THE FRIENDS OF LADY BLESSINGTON 24 DECEMBER 1857

Published by Dr. Rosenbach, *Widener Catalogue*, II, 50.

Confidential   24th December, 1857

Dear Sir

We have ascertained from Miss Power that a present of £200, would be of very great service to her at this time, and would be gratefully accepted by her, if it were the result of a private subscription among old and confidential visitors at Gore House. We have made a private list of twenty old friends of Lady Blessington and Count D'Orsay, who may make up the required sum among themselves by a contribution of Ten Pounds each.

Such private list contains your name. If you should desire to contribute your Ten Pounds, any one of us will be happy to receive your donation, and the names of the subscribers shall be forwarded to you on the close of the subscription

Faithfully yours

W M Thackeray. 36 Onslow Sq^{re} Brompton.
Charles Dickens Tavistock House
John Forster 46 Montagu Square

1341. TO MRS. CARMICHAEL-SMYTH 25 DECEMBER 1857

Extracts published, *Biographical Introductions*, IX, lvii.

I must send my dear old Mother & G P a line of Xmas greeting, and tell them how well & happy the young ones are and poor little Amy whom I left a couple of hours ago at Walton, in the midst of such lavish splendours and magnificence as I have never seen the like of in the finest houses here — all w^h splendors, Christmas trees loaded with presents fountains of Champagne &

Hock drives in coaches and four & I dont know what more are lavished upon 8 or nine young girls and 2 or 3 gentlemen — One of them was busy all ⟨. . . spee⟩ch [84] w^h he is to let off in an hour or two at the City of London Tavern in behalf of the Commercial Travellers school. Anny to whom I dictated the speech remembers all the points, and the very words deuce a one of w^h can I recal verbally. I should not be sorry to fail, for then people wont ask me again and I shall be rid of a very severe tax w^h is laid on men in prominent positions — We are to have more holiday making at the Pollocks, and I cant resist for I can't bear that the girls should lose any pleasure, and meanwhile how is No IV to be got out? Well, other folks have their drawbacks and their encumbrances — let us bear our's without too much grumbling. Good accounts from poor Isabella. Her fever is over. Amy brought back the very best report of her and of the care taken of her. I dont know what the French pills are, but they certainly are the most effectual boluses I ever swallowed. I think they have kept off an attack of spasms. They must contain some dreadful strong ingredient but they give no pain and perform to a wonder. I should be glad to hear that they contained nothing wicked. Does Mrs Colmache know anything about their character and does a respectable D^r recommend them? Your heart would have melted over a little boy of 2 [85] last night trolling round the Xmas tree and cry[ing] o Crissamy Tee Crissamy Tree! He looked like a little cherub just peeping into Heaven: & he didn't like even to take away his own share of toys from the general splendor. O dear. I should like very much to stop at home alone for 3 days and get on with that No IV! It was kind of the Sturgiss to ask Amy and as much is made of her as of any one. and very well she looks too and so does Miss Anny who has got thinner & is a comfort to look at especially to her father & to your son my dear old Mother. God bless both of you he says and now let us rehearse that speech.

[84] About five words have here been torn from the letter.
[85] Howard Sturgis (Mrs. Warre-Cornish, *Some Family Letters*, p. 24).

1342. TO DR. JOHN BROWN
25 DECEMBER 1857–2 JANUARY 1858

My text is taken from *Letters of Dr. John Brown*, pp. 326–327.

My Dear Doctor — Xmas day must not pass away without a shake of the hand between Rutland Street and Onslow Square. What a many letters the Square owes you, how kind you are to it, sending *Culverwells, Scotsmen, Medical Reforms,* notices laudatory of *Virginians,* and good wishes always. Accept these in turn, Doctor and Madam, from one of the biggest, busiest, laziest of your friends. We are all on a Xmas visit to Mr. Russell Sturgis, a Merchant Prince. We are feasting in splendour; we have brought down new dresses; our Papa is going to London to-morrow though, to preside at the Bagmen's dinner.[86] He hopes his speech will come better off than at Edinburgh. He wants to be at No. IV.[87] very much, but calls on his time are so constant that he can scarcely get to work unless he flies from house and home. And how go away when the girls are invited to hospitalities? They are so happy and pleased that I must be so too; and ma foi *The Virginians* must wait for a day or two.

A Scotchman here tells me that nobody at Edinburgh spends more than a thousand a year. Hadn't I better come and live there? Hadn't I better come and see you all? Well, I long to do so.

28. — The letter stopped here on Xmas day and ever since I have had so much fish a-frying that I have not been able to finish the good wishes. We had a stupid dinner enough of the bagmen, and yesterday I came back to the Merchant Prince's, and to-day we are going through a sweet calm, many-elmed, gable-ended country, to pay a visit to a neighbour or two. I think I have no news positively. It was breakfast time not long since, and hark there goes the gong to lunch!

Jan. 2. — Is this absurd letter never to go away? Now it is

[86] Thackeray's speech at the Commercial Travellers' Dinner on December 26 is reprinted in Hotten's *Thackeray*, pp. 219–223.
[87] Chapters 13 to 16 for February, 1858.

written from the Garrick Club. I am just back from the Merchant Prince's (I ran away on the 29th and only went back yesterday). Our holiday is over, and I am grappling with No. IV. You will see at any rate, though I don't write, I think of you and Rutland Street. I hope you had no shares in the Western Bank.[88] My acquaintance Captain Reddie tells me that the desolation in Edinburgh is awful, and that 7 old ladies were carried to Asylums two days ago. . . .

I read no new books, only Newspapers and Magazines of 1756, get out my numbers with extraordinary throes and difficulty — am as one distraught while the process is going on, and if I don't do that, am for days without ability to do anything else. I think I am no richer this day than I was on the 1 January last. Yes, Doctor, the Oxford election cost £850. It was a cowardly robbery of a poor, innocent, rightly-served man. And if I had won — that is the beauty of it — I should have been turned out, my agents, in spite of express promises to me, having done acts which would have ousted me. May the present be a luckier year to me, and a happy one!

1343.   TO WILLIAM HOWARD RUSSELL 1857 [89]

Address: W. H. Russell Esq? Hitherto unpublished.

Saturday m͞g

Mon cher Confrere.

Yesterday I had the misfortune to forget that I was engaged to you on Sunday, & to ask some Scotch friends of mine the Blackwoods who were most ineffably hospitable to me whilst I was in Edinburgh to dine here on that day — and somebody else to meet them of course. Pray don't be angry with me. Eat drink & be merry without me. 'Go it my boy' as a noble creature said when

[88] See above, No. 1335, note 80.

[89] This note appears to have been written late in 1857, when Thackeray had at last ceased to lecture on *The Four Georges*.

she sent her husband the door-key to the Club: and believe me
Ever yours

W M T.

Ex-lecturer at the T. R. Almack's

I break my note open — just hearing of Mrs Russells invitation
to the girls but you see they must stop at home as well as their
Papa to meet our unlucky friends.

1344.   TO WILLIAM DUER ROBINSON
             23 JANUARY–25 FEBRUARY 1858

Published in part, *Thackeray in the United States*, I, 354–357.

Saturday . Jan 23. 1858.   36 Onslow Sq^{re}

A sudden gust of friendship blows from this boosom in the direction of Houston Street and my Wobinson. The fact is, Sir, I was
in the drawing room just now, and out of a portfolio on one of
the elegant rosewood tables, there peeped a photograph, w^h represented the honest old mug of W. D. R. How is he? Can he
afford to drink Claret still? are there any cocktails about 604? I
would give a guinea to be there — and now and then get quite
a bust of feeling towards folks on your side. Davis's marriage [1]
came upon me quite inopportunely; I have had to give presents to
no less than 4 brides this year and I can't positively stand no more.
The last was Libbie Strong, whose votive teapot is at this present
moment in my house, waiting for an opportunity to X the water.
What can I tell you about myself? Nothing very good, new, or
funny. That complaint you wot of is never cured quite, and I have
the doctor always about my hydraulic engine. Virginians are doing
pretty well thank you, but not so very well as we expected so that
I only draw 250£ per month instead of 300£ as the agreement is.
But I like everybody who deals with me to make money by me
so I cede those 50£ you see until better times. I have just paid

[1] J. C. Bancroft Davis married Frederica Gore, daughter of James Gore
King, on November 19, 1857.

the last of the Oxford Election bills, and got how much do you think out of 900£ — 13£ is the modest figure returned. Then you know J. G. King's Sons have somehow forgotten to send me any dividends upon Michigan Centrals & N Y Centrals. So I am not much richer in Jan 58 than I was in Jan 57. that's the fact. But then in compensation I live very much more expensively. Charles, much injured by going to America, has been ruined by the company he keeps next door. Next door has a butler and a footman in livery. Charles found it was impossible to carry on without a footman in livery: so when the girls dine off 2 mutton chops they have the pleasaure of being waited on by 2 menials who walk round & round them. We give very good dinners. Our house is full of pretty little things. Our cellar is not badly off. Sir I am going in a few days to pay 100£ for 18 dozen of '48 Claret that is not to be drunk for 4 years. That is the price Wine has got to now. 'Tis as dear as at New York. No wonder a fellow can't afford to send a marriage token to his friend when he lives in this here extravagant way. I fondly talk of going to America in the autumn and finishing my story sur les lieux. I want to know what was the colour of Washingtons livery — Where the deuce was George Warrington carried after he was knocked down at Braddock's defeat. Was he taken by Indians into a French fort? I want him to be away for a year and a half, or until the siege of Quebec. If you see Fred. Cozzens or George Curtis, ask them to manage this job for me, and send me a little line stating what really has happened to the eldest of the 2 Virginians [2] (This is genteeler paper than the other, wch I use for my "copy" paper.) I only got my number done last night, and am getting more disgustingly lazy every day. I *can't* do the work until it's wanted. And yet with all these attacks of illness w^h I have, I ought, you know I ought. Sir I came up stairs now to do a little work before dinner; only I thought how much pleasanter it would be to have a chat with old Robinson! Do you see in the Times this morning the death of Beverley Robinson late a Captain of the R. Artillery?

---

[2] For Cozzens's reply to these queries, see below, No. 1350.

He must be one of you. And now it is 5 minutes to 7: and it is time to go dress for dinner. Hark at the Brougham-horse snorting in the frost!

Not that W is grown any fatter wearing still the same coat waistcoat & britches w^h he sported in N. *York*

This is Wednesday 27. What do you think I did yesterday? gave one of the old 51 lectures in a suburb of London. It was quite refreshing. Went there with my (hydraulic) doctor who attended me all last year

HE DRESSES FOR DINNER

without a fee — gave him the 25£ cheque w^h they gave me for the lecture. It was easily earned money wasn't it? How shall I fill up the rest of this thin paper? Ever since the Georges I have been in disgrace with the Bo Monde. My former entertainers the Earls and Marquises having fought very shy of me. This year they're beginning to come back.

Thursday 25th Yes, but the 25th February. What a time this letter has been a-composing! I have written a number, two numbers [3] since I began have had 3 confounded attacks of spasms have spent ever so much money grown ever so much older and not a bit wiser — am just at my desk again after attack No. 3. Yes, Claret drunk not wisely, but too well,[4] an immoderate use of the fleshpots are beginning to tell upon the friend of W. D. R. If I don't write this letter off now I shall never send it that's flat. It must go, Robinson, and I want you to ask Duer THIS IS THE ONLY IMPORTANT PART of the letter, whether (I cannot spoil my own mug on the other side) [5] whether the Michigan Centrals and New York Centrals are ever going to pay, and what becomes of

---

[3] Numbers IV for February and V, chapters 17 to 20, for March.

[4] *Othello*, V, ii, 344.

[5] This part of the letter is written overleaf from the drawing reproduced above.

the absent dividend of last year? [6] What are my Michigan Bonds
worth now? Will you get me a philosophic answer to these questions please? What more? I often look at your beauteous image.
Next week I am going to Macready in the country to read one of
those demd old Georges. He offers me 50£ to read in 2 little
towns close by and I won't. Why do for nothing what I wont
do for 50£? because I am sick of letting myself out for hire — I
have just bought a famous little cob that carries me to perfection.
Adieu Robinson, Davis, Duer.

1345.   TO WILLIAM CHARLES MACREADY
19 FEBRUARY 1858

Hitherto unpublished. *Endorsed:* Thackeray February 20.

Friday

A thousand thanks my dear Macready. This is not to answer
your note w$\underline{^h}$ I have left on my study table at home: but to say
I have not quite made up my mind about the two other lectures.
I have but the Georges: and dont want to give the IVth of them.
Let me have 24 hours to think please, and tomorrow I will ap-
prise you whether it shall be yea or nay.

Ever yours
(Waiting for the proofs of No V. w$\underline{^h}$ I got up at 6 this m^g to finish)
W M Thackeray.

1346.   TO WILLIAM CHARLES MACREADY
22 FEBRUARY 1858

Hitherto unpublished.

Monday. Feb 22.

My dear Macready   Instead of writing to you on Saturday,
I was sent to bed with one of those fits of spasms that assail me

---

[6] See above, No. 988, note 175.

about a dozen times a year, and am still on my back though I hope to be up & stirring tomorrow.

I think that difficulty I spoke of is fatal against lecturing at Yeovil & Bridport and so I will only give my one little performance at Sherborne under your auspices I hope I'll come down on Monday stay Tuesday with you & Wednesday return to my work. Thank you for thinking of that kindly harmless way of putting 50£ in my pocket. It seems absurd to refuse them, doesn't it? But I believe the moderation is the better policy, & so, Sir, won't take your money.

But I shall gladly shake you by the hand this day fortnight & meanwhile am

> — Yours dear Macready always
> W M Thackeray.

1347.   TO JOHN REUBEN THOMPSON
               25 FEBRUARY 1858

Hitherto unpublished.

> 36 Onslow Sq^{re}
> Brompton.
> Feb 25.

My dear Thompson

I was away from home when your melancholy news came last year, and have left a longer interval than I intended before writing to you and begging you to tell Mrs Stanard how sincerely I deplore her loss ⁷ and esteemed and respected the friend who has been called away from among you. I have been much in Virginia since as you know who have followed my books, and that friendly kind honest good Stanard has been constantly in my mind as I thought of your dear little friendly place. I have all his hospitality in my recollection the pictures on his walls, the flavour of his wine, the tone of his voice, and the generous welcome.

Mrs Stanard knew how much I like him. I counted on more

⁷ Robert Craig Stanard, Mrs. Stanard's husband, had died in June, 1857.

than one other pleasant meeting with him — Your City will hardly be the same to me without him. And to you others who lived with him every day — to the wife whom he cherished with such extraordinary tenderness, and who knows his intimate and sacred good qualities a thousand times better than we do, what must his loss be! No stranger has a right to speak in the presence of such a great domestic affliction, but we may say an honest word of regard and respect for a good man departed, and I beg you my dear Thompson to tell Mrs Stanard and her boy how very warmly and gratefully I think of Robert Stanards kindness to me, and how heartily I liked and respected him.

I am myself so constantly unwell now that I begin to think my turn to be called cannot be delayed very long. These Virginians take me as much time as if I was writing a History. I often hope that I may come over and finish it on the ground itself, and certainly mean to do so if health & circumstance will let me. I would give a guinea to sit in the Rocking Chair [8] again, and shake a few hands in Richmond. Give my regards to any who remember me to Gibson and Myers and your good father; [9] and please to tell Mrs Stanard how very sincerely I am hers

and yours my dear Thompson
W M Thackeray.

We are in a great political excitement here, but I was cured of my political fever by the bleeding I had at Oxford last year. I can't spend 1000£ at every election.

[8] See above, No. 972.

[9] John Thompson, a native of New Hampshire, who had some years earlier established a store in Richmond (*Poems of John R. Thompson*, ed. John S. Patton, New York, 1920, p. xi).

FILBY FECIT.   Dr Goldsmith's New Coat.

From a sketch by Thackeray

DR. JOHNSON AND DR. GOLDSMITH.

Goldsmith in the new Plum-coloured Coat. Mr. Filby looking anxiously after it.

From a drawing by Thackeray

1348.   TO DR. JOHN BROWN
3 MARCH 1858

Extract and facsimile of the drawing published by Dr. Brown and Henry Hill
Lancaster, *North British Review*, February, 1864, p. 256. My text is taken
from *Letters of Dr. John Brown*, p. 327, where the drawing is also reproduced.

Kensington, Wednesday, March 3

My Dear Brown — Behold a drawing [10] instead of a letter.
I've been thinking of writing you a beautiful one ever so long, but,
etc. etc. And instead of doing my duty this morning I began this
here drawing, and remembered I owed Madam one, and will pay
your debt some other day — no, *part* of your debt. I intend to owe
the rest and like to owe it, and think that I'm sincerely grateful
to you always, my dear good friends.

W M T.

The Novel gets on pooty well — well, I think the last week [11]
very well.

A *marquis* and a *lord* had twice of the pudding last week, Mrs.
Brown.

P.S. — Am afraid I shall try Parliament again if a dissolution.
Glad you liked the Nymphs and the misogyny.[12] κάρδος is a thistle:

[10] "Goldsmith, to divert the tedious minutes [while waiting for a late-
comer to dinner], strutted about, bragging of his dress, and I believe was
seriously vain of it, for his mind was wonderfully prone to such impressions.
'Come, come, (said Garrick,) talk no more of that. You are, perhaps, the
worst — eh, eh!'— Goldsmith was eagerly attempting to interrupt him, when
Garrick went on, laughing ironically, 'Nay you will always *look* like a gentleman; but I am talking of being well or ill *drest*.' 'Well, let me tell you, (said
Goldsmith,) when my tailor brought home my bloom-coloured coat, he said,
"Sir, I have a favour to beg of you. When anybody asks you who made your
clothes, be pleased to mention John Filby, at the Harrow, in Water-lane." '
JOHNSON. 'Why, Sir, that was because he knew the strange colour would
attract crowds to gaze at it, and thus they might hear of him, and see how well
he could make a coat even of so absurd a colour.' " (Boswell, *Life of Johnson*,
ed. Hill and Powell, II, 83)

[11] During which Thackeray had begun number VI of *The Virginians* for
April, chapters 21 to 24.

[12] See *Works*, X, 148–149.

looked it out in Lexicon. Tremendously busy. Don't report well of my health, often knocked over... Best regards to Madam.

1349.   TO LADY STANLEY
                    11 MARCH 1858

Hitherto unpublished.

                    36 O. Square.   Thursday 11 March
                              S. W

My dear Lady Stanley.

Hip Hip Hurray. I shall be delighted to come on the 20th and think its very kind of you to ask me, and hope you'll go on.

Returned home last night from a very pleasant excursion to Sherborne. Handsome old house of Queen Anne's time — Wonderful good old wine. Macready the man — even better than Macready the actor — a good scholar and gentleman — very nice in his family — His hobby is education and he has a school of 150 young rustics whom he teaches himself 3 times a week. Honest country families with gig lamps came into the lecture: got 25£ for the benefit of the Institution. Everybody pleased. Isn't it pleasant to be able to give pleasure to country folks with gig lamps and put 30£ worth of books on the shelves of a country Institution? The Benevolent Heart says Yea.

                    Always yours most sincerely
                    W M Thackeray

1350.   FROM FREDERICK SWARTOUT COZZENS
                    21 MARCH 1858

My text is taken from *Thackeray in the United States*, I, 357–359.

                    Chestnut Cottage
                         Sunday night Mch., 21st, 1858.

My dear Thackeray, — Your friend Mr. Robinson was good enough to leave your letter to him on my desk yesterday during my absence, and I have employed this blessed day in hunting up data for your queries.[13]

First, as to the Washington livery. Of Mrs. Washington at the camp before Boston in Irving's "Life of Washington," Vol. 2, page 121, it says (incidental mention is made of the equipage in which she appeared there) a chariot and four with postilion in scarlet and white liveries. It has been suggested that this was an English style of equipage derived from the Fairfaxes: but in truth it was a style still prevalent at that time in Virginia. I see you say "blue and white."

Next, as to the disposition of George Warrington after the defeat of Braddock & Co.

You can by no means fulfil the dreams of Madam Esmond by making G. W. a prisoner in the hands of the Indians. The Indian does not know anything of prisoners of war, except to roast them afterwards.

There have been some few instances, where prisoners have been kept for a short time by the red men as menials, but in the end they were either tomahawked or served up in the usual style, or escaped, instances of which are familiar, scattered throughout frontier story or the earlier histories of New England.

But at Braddock's defeat, we have certain evidence upon this very point. The returns were; killed 456, wounded 421, safe 583 exclusive of women and black servants killed; 3 women only were saved alive — one was retained by the French Commander at Benango the other two sent as slaves to Canada.

My dear old Thackeray, I am delighted to hear that you think of coming here in the autumn.

Your "Virginians" have surprised and pleased all your intimate friends. We all think your pictures of Virginia life are perfect and wonder how you are able to do it. "Oh!" said Irving to me the other day in that sweet, husky, honeycomb voice, "What a fine book he will make of that!" "Have you read it Mr. Irving?" I asked. "No, I have so much to do, but I know Thackeray. I know

[13] See above, No. 1344.

what he is capable of doing, a man of great mind, far superior to Dickens. Dickens's prejudices are too limited to make such a book as Thackeray is capable of making of the 'Virginians.' "

Well, well, for my part, I am surprised at the faithful delineation you have given of old "Virginny."

I must except to your making George Washington use language unbecoming an officer and a gentleman, as you do.[14] If you look at the courteous language of old "Virginny," you will see nothing there but pure and polite English. Even Patrick Henry, the most illiterate of all his contemporaries, uses the most courteous phrases in debate. Where did he get this? Surely, from familiar intercourse with well-bred people for [15] otherwise we had no education.

. . .

Frederick S. Cozzens.

1351.   TO MRS. CARMICHAEL-SMYTH
                2 APRIL 1858

Hitherto unpublished.

Good Friday.

If I dont send this off now, I shall get muddled with the Virginians in a few days, and too bothered and nervous to write to any body including my dear old Mother — so she must have the little budget whilst the month is yet young: and hear what will be much more amusingly told by the girls who do all the fun and observation of the family now. Their talk is capital: it is delightful to hear the prattle, as they come home from their parties. Yesterday we went to Watford and thence to an advertized country house at Kings Langley, upon one of those excursions w^h I make in the newspaper every day, and now and then on the railroad. But I think one quarter of an hour at K. Langley, though it was a pretty lively place, was enough. Minny was the eagerest

[14] See chapter 10 of *The Virginians*.
[15] General Wilson reads *or*.

to come out of it. As for Anny, she seems determined to be happy anywhere, and good tempered always.

I was shocked not surprised to find the other day, that Colonel Newcome of Hyndford House has been speculating unluckily, that his Gutta percha company has already swallowed a thousand up and is calling out for a thousand more. He wrote me desiring me to buy all his wine — 100£ worth that is, consisting of Madeira Sherry Port Hermitage & Lunel — I wanted him to take the money without sending me the wine: but this he utterly refuses, declining to have anything but a bargain between us for what I dont want to buy. However we have agreed to take the Sherry & the Madeira — as for the others I mistrust his Port, & hate Lunel, and tasted the Hermitage wh I found to be a nauseous liquor.[16] O dear me, he was very kind when I was in the money scrape in old days, and bought our wine readily enough. This gave me an opportunity of seeing Mary & Julia Parker, and the Baby [17] wh is the most beautiful baby really I ever saw, and Cheri, and of being formally introduced to two young gentlemen who were about to dine. Charles says he is going to let the house at Midsummer: and is frightened by the menaced call of his bankrupt Company. All Scotland is ruined in the same way I hear by the failure of the joint stock banks Old maids and orphans and widows and half-pay officers by hundreds and thousands, robbed of their all, by banks wh were declaring nine per cent dividends six months ago. I hope the New York & Michigan Centrals will serve us better, and have just made a new little purchase in the former, believing the Railway to be as good as anything in Europe.

Mr Pearman has given me warning and I have engaged a Frenchman in his place, with a good character for honesty and so forth. I find time to ride my little Cob about once a week. Last ride I had he was a great deal too lively to be pleasant: but the

[16] Colonel Carmichael had even less luck in trying to dispose of his wines to the Oriental Club, of which he was a member. "The Committee tried samples of burgundy at 15*s.* per dozen," writes Baillie (*Oriental Club and Hanover Square,* p. 71), "and of port at 28*s.*, and they informed the Colonel that they did not approve of them."

[17] Florence Graham Carmichael.

truth is that the ride is good & wholesome whenever I do take it, better than walking w^h tires and doesnt strengthen much.

Look at this Summary of 3 months in & outgoings & Tremble!

	£
Spent in 3 months	792.
of w^h last years bills	250
Horse, plate, books, gimcracks, property,	100.
Mr Bakewell & Charles in advance	25
Charitable disbursements	25
Left for actual money expended	392
Received B & E. Virginians	750
Lectures 75 (25 to Thompson)	50
Harpers from New York — 3 no^s	60
Railway Dividends (a quarter)	90
Copyrights a quarter	140
	1090
Surplus of gross receipts over gross expences —	300£.

Theres a pretty little sum totele isn't it? These 3 months I have been living at the rate of more than 3000 a year and making 4500. But I want to get it down to 2000 and wonder whether I shall. How did we manage when we hadnt 2? we lived quite as well upon 1. My personal expences have been about 25£ out of this — no say 35. I have bought 1000£ more 8 per cent American Railway stock — So I may be considered as the present possessor of a house and 650£ a year (my copyrights are yielding 600 but I only put 'em at 200) We could live on this if the worst came to the worst and as soon as necessity ordered — Meanwhile we are not good managers thats the fact and make less show with 3000 a year than many people with 1800.

Why Lady Rodd in her great family Coach doesn't spend as much as I do. But I wonder whether she has any bowels of compassion? There is Sims, Coachman. He is so good honest active good-humoured and willing that I cant find it in my heart to part from him when the season is over — Enter the young ladies —

They come and smile upon their pa, as I sit up here alone and glum. You see though I am writing to you I am thinking about No VII [18]— can't help myself — and am very happy thinking about No VII after all — only silent and solitary. Tomorrow I am going into hospital at Thompsons for a couple of days: and hope I shall come out all the better for the discipline. Meanwhile out with you No VII! — let us see if we can do a page or two — and so God bless my dearest old Mother & G P.

W M T.

1352.   TO THOMAS FRASER
3 APRIL 1858

Hitherto unpublished. My text is taken from a transcript supplied by Mr. Blatner.

36 Onslow Sq. S. W.
Saturday

My dear Fraser.

Heres an extract from my mothers letter just come in. I've such a sad letter from Maria Hamerton: She says 'The dark mysterious stranger is closing round me: one or two more folds of his mysterious mantle, and the worlds strife must end. For my poor Bess, and my poor Marie my desire is for longer life. When she thought I was dying, Bess would have her sleep beside her, and then she would creep into my room, & put her arms round my neck & say softly 'Bess is so kind to little 'Cozy' but I love you in the deep deep corner of my little heart.' I believe the only thing for her is to be able to go to the seaside without the attendant fatigue of putting her apartment in order for letting'

I hope you'll put this in your pipe and smoke it

Yours
W M T.

[18] For May, chapters 25 to 28.

1353.   TO MRS. CARMICHAEL-SMYTH
9 APRIL 1858

Published in William Harris Arnold's *Ventures in Book Collecting* (London, 1923), pp. 78–80.

Friday. April 9.

My dearest Mother. Cant make out the Paris journey just now. Have to lecture on the 20th (Mind the proceeds of the lecture are for your ivories) have promised Lord Palmerston to dine at the Literary Fund [19] on the 25th & am rather anxious to repair my defeat at the Dramatic dinner. want to show on the 1 of May at the Royal Academy dinner, and to get time to go into hospital with Thompson, being a good deal bothered at present by my old enemy. Am pretty well on with my work this month, and have found it go easier: am better in general health too I think and this is all my bulletin. For isn't there the days work before me and ought I not to tackle it? When it is done and I am tired, I dont like to write letters; you will fancy I am unwell: when it is not Done and to be done, I don't like to write letters. It reproaches me & says 'Come, Sir do me or nothing else.' And so we go on toiling & devising and tumbling and getting up again. I think it is good fun to hear the girls singing & humming down stairs, and though silent and solitary & preoccupied myself, and seeming very melancholy, am not the least so — but in a pleasant bearable grave grey frame of mind — considering life very tolerable. To be sure it ought to be, with prosperity and good children.

Don't, in the kindness of your heart, propose the open carriage to Mary. I can't have any intimacy. I don't respect her, or regard her, or forgive her. She has been rude to my daughters, and rude to my mother. I dont harbour a pennyworth of ill feeling and will do anything in my small power to serve the young ones & old ones at Hyndford House — But friendship is impossible: why it's a perpetual hypocrisy not to laugh at that astounding — hullo!

[19] For Thackeray's speech on this occasion and at the Royal Academy dinner, see Melville's *Thackeray*, II, 110–116.

Stop! Better go on with the Virginians No VII, than abusing your neighbour.

I copied an extract of your Maria's letter to the girls and sent it to your favorite Tom. Fraser — with the injunction 'Put that in your pipe and smoke it' He says 'there will be no difficulty' and I told him to write to Maria and send her some money w^h he promises to do. My adorer John Brown writes me that they will put me up for Edinburgh. Think I had best leave it alone: am afraid I am too old to speak now: but, never having had a purpose in life, or known what I was going to do until I was doing it, cant tell whether I shall refuse, or accept, or covet, or dont care for this honour if it comes. Come let us get to

Chapter

These feats of agility being over, the four gentlemen quitted the Bowling Green and [20]

The rest is no VII, page 16 of the The Virginians by

W. M. Thackeray.

1354. TO MRS. BAXTER
10–23 APRIL 1858

Published in part, *American Family*, pp. 160–164.

April 10, 23.

36 Onslow Sq^re

My dear Mrs Baxter. Isn't it a horrible thing that Libbies tea pot is still in the cupboard yonder under Washington's bust? Is it a year since she was married? A set of weeks become a month and a set of months a year before I know where I am now. and every day of the year has its turmoil, trouble, illness, parties, letters, printers'-devils, duns botherations, and so we go on and on until the end of troubles and pleasures — Do you know heres the 10th of the month and only 3 pages of my number done? [21]

---

[20] From chapter 26 of *The Virginians* (*Works*, X, 218).

[21] "[Thackeray] says he cannot get ahead with the 'Virginians'," John Blackwood wrote to Lewes on May 23, 1858, "and was desperately pushed

I have had 2 attacks within the last fortnight of my enemy: each attack throwing me back a week or so. I have been with the girls to a deal of parties and dinners. That graceless Charles Pearman has left my service after five years, but has left a remembrance of himself behind with the house maid who has been with me 12 years a respectable honest ugly elderlyish person who must forsooth forget 35 years of decent life and respectable parentage, in order to read the old story with Mʳ Charles. O fie! — But to return to Libbie's tea pot, Captain Comstock wrote to me some time ago that he was coming to London and would take it with him — I not liking to trust the precious article to the common carriage or possible miscarriage of a steamer Hence the delay in the transmission of this domestic little article. Have I ever written to you before on this ugly paper? I find it pleasanter far to the pen than your beautiful cream-laids and gilt edges.

23. And here the letter again stopped 12 days ago; and, on Friday night after awful trouble, I only got my number done, just in time to send it by post to Liverpool & America. The book's clever but stupid thats the fact. I hate story-making incidents, surprises, love-making, &c more and more every day: and here is a third of a great story done equal to two thirds of an ordinary novel — and nothing actually has happened, except that a young gentleman has come from America to England — I wish an elderly one could do 'tother thing, and have the strongest wish to come and see you all. Are there any more Hamptonkins come or coming? What have we been about these 10 days? tramping the round of parties, giving dinners, and eating brandy peaches from New York — quite plain dinners, not ostentatious, but O dear me how much pleasanter the men's parties are than those with ladies, that's the fact. — Tomorrow Miss Anny gives her first drum — I have set my face hitherto against these entertainments from the peculiar nature of Our Society — we know great people & small, polite & otherwise: the otherwise are not a bit comfortable in company of the others but get angry if they are not asked. I

---

with the last No., having written the last 16 pages in one day, the last he had to spare" (Mrs. Porter, *John Blackwood*, p. 42).

know this horrible teafight will bring down all sorts of odium upon the givers: but they will have it, and though I'm not quite such a soft Papa as G B of 2ᵈ Avenue, if my young women set their hearts on anything they are pretty sure to get it. I am afraid the 2 Lambert girls in the Virginians are very like them, but of course deny it if anybody accuses me.

We have been in the midst of immense political fluster. I have seen my name as a candidate for no less than 4 places in event of a dissolution of parliament, but dont want one now for a while. Let us have some more lectures and some more money first. My expenses (have I ever grumbled to you about them?) are awful. I have a one horse chay and spend 2600£ a year *at least*. Two families each with a carriage could live for that money — but they dont give away 500£ as somebody somehow does. Also at the end of the month when the number is done, I go and buy pooty things — 6 such byootiful spoons as I brought home yesterday! And what do you think? I have had a new coat the first in four years. I have a famous little horse to ride and get on him once a fortnight. I have good daughters, good wine in the cellar, easy work, plenty of money in my pocket, a fair reputation — I ought to be happy oughtn't I? Eh bien! I dont think I am above 4 days in the month. A man without a woman is a lonely wretch. Hark at the bells dingdonging for Church! Shall I go? No I forgot — Mʳ & Mʳˢ Blackwood, Mʳ & Mʳˢ Pollen (O Sally Hampton such a pretty woman!) 4 Selves, Lord John Hay,²² Sir Charles Taylor,²³ Mʳ Bid-

---

²² Fourth son (1827–1916) of the eighth Marquess of Tweeddale and later Admiral of the Fleet.

²³ Sir Charles Taylor (1817–1876?), second Baronet, was Thackeray's most frequent companion during the last four or five years of his life. Taylor owned an estate at Hollycombe in Sussex and was a magistrate for that county. It was around this "rich, clever, sarcastic man about town", writes Escott (*Trollope*, p. 145), that the leading Thackerayans at the Garrick Club grouped themselves; he was "a figure prominent in the society of his time, as well as filling a position especially conspicuous and authoritative in all cricketing circles . . . Wherever, indeed, manly sports of any kind were popular, there Sir Charles Taylor was a personage. . . . Taylor's shrewd, bitter social estimates and aphorisms were remembered in the club long after he was forgotten." Yates (*Recollections and Experiences*, I, 237) reports that Trollope

well, Mr Motley [24] (of U.S.A) Mr Creyke, and Mr Edwards [25] are coming to dinner at 7. A Frenchman is my butler and valet, in the place of the seductive Charles — and poor Eliza went away

---

said of Taylor: "A man rough of tongue, brusque in his manners, odious to those who dislike him, somewhat inclined to tyranny, he is the prince of friends, honest as the sun, and as openhanded as Charity itself." He married a Mrs. Rose in 1867, but left no children.

[24] John Lothrop Motley (1814–1877), the American historian, who was well known in England through his *Rise of the Dutch Republic* (1856). Describing a dinner in London on May 17, at which both he and Thackeray were present, Motley wrote to his wife: "I believe you have never seen Thackeray. He has the appearance of a colossal infant, smooth, white, shiny ringlety hair, flaxen, alas, with advancing years, a roundish face, with a little dab of a nose upon which it is a perpetual wonder how he keeps his spectacles, a sweet but rather piping voice, with something of a childish treble about it, and a very tall, slightly stooping figure — such are the characteristics of the great 'snob' of England — nothing original, all planed down into perfect uniformity with that of his fellow-creatures. There was not much more distinction in his talk than in his white choker or black coat and waistcoat. As you like detail, however, I shall endeavor to Boswellise him a little, but it is very hard work. Something was said of Carlyle the author. Thackeray said, 'Carlyle hates everybody that has arrived — if they are on the road, he may perhaps treat them civilly.' Mackintosh praised the description in the 'French Revolution' of the flight of the King and Queen (which is certainly one of the most living pictures ever painted with ink), and Thackeray agreed with him, and spoke of the passages very heartily. Of the Cosmopolitan Club, Thackeray said, 'Everybody is or is supposed to be a celebrity; nobody ever says anything worth hearing and everyone goes there with his white choker at midnight, to appear as if he had just been dining with the aristocracy. I have no doubt,' he added, 'that half of us put on the white cravat after a solitary dinner at home or at our club, and so go down among the Cosmopolitans.' " (*Correspondence*, ed. Curtis, I, 229–230)

[25] Henry Sutherland Edwards (1828–1906), a journalist and foreign correspondent who had recently met Thackeray through the Russian novelist Turgenev. "Thackeray had just been reading 'Madame Bovary'," Edwards (*Personal Recollections*, p. 36) writes, "and told me that he very much disliked the book. I confessed that I had read it with interest and admiration, mentioning particular chapters and scenes, such as the brilliant description of the banquet, the dialogue between Madame Bovary and the priest who mistakes her moral malady for a physical one, and so on. I asked the great writer whether they possessed no merit.

" 'The book is bad,' he said. 'It is a heartless, coldblooded study of the downfall and degradation of a woman.' "

3 days ago — going into the room and giving a last fond look at her young ladies, whom she has faithfully and affectionately tended since Childhood. It's pitiable, isn't it? Meanwhile, comme à l'ordinaire I know who will have to pay the Doctor — Last year the lady with whom my wife lives, made a great outcry because her house was robbed of goods to the value of 25£ & her plate. I gave her 25£ and 6 table spoons 6 tea ditto 6 forks — So it was *I* in fact who was robbed; but she goes on crying about it to this present day. Here have I been chattering till it is time for dinner! My dear kind old friend — once and again it is a pleasure to come and sit down and talk to you — Give my best regards to all, & God bless you — Perhaps you'll let S S H have this and my dooty to her. You see I dont like to stop but keep chattering on till I'm in the hall, down the steps and actually out of doors — Good bye.

W M T.

1355.   TO JAMES WILSON [28]
                MAY 1858 [29]

Hitherto unpublished.

Private.

                                        36 Onslow Sqᵉ Sunday evᵍ
My dear Wilson.

You may remember some conversation wʰ occurred at the table where we met on Tuesday. I have a note from Mʳ Dickens on the subject of a common report derogatory to the honor of a young lady [30] whose name has been mentioned in connection with his.

---

[28] Wilson, Thackeray's neighbor at 19 Onslow Square, was later the father-in-law of Walter Bagehot.

[29] This note appears to have been written not long before Dickens's separation from his wife on May 21, 1858 (*Letters*, ed. Dexter, III, 21).

[30] Ellen Lawless Ternan, daughter of the well-known actress Mrs. Frances Eleanor Ternan (1803?–1873). For an account of Miss Ternan's relations with Dickens, see chapters 15 and 16 of Thomas Wright's *The Life of Charles Dickens* (London, 1935).

He authorizes me to contradict the rumour on his own solemn word and his wife's authority.

Faithfully yours

W. M. Thackeray.

My daughter and I dine with you on Tuesday s. v. p.

1356. TO LADY STANLEY
24 MAY 1858

Hitherto unpublished.

My dear Lady Stanley

If you please may I bring with me tomorrow my disciple M⸢r⸣ Creyke, who was with Lord Carlisle in Ireland and whom I wish to hear the lecture as it praises the Carlisle family — and M⸢r⸣ Motley the American historian a very agreeable presentable gnlmn-like man.[31] At 5.30 PRECISELY is the word.

Very faithfully yours

W M T.

[31] Motley (*Correspondence*, ed. Curtis, I, 241) wrote to his wife on May 30: "The lecture was in the back drawing-room of a very large and elegant house, and the company — not more than fifty or sixty in number — were all comfortably seated. It was on George III.— one of the set of the four Georges, first delivered in America, and which have often been read in England, but have never been printed. I was much impressed with the quiet, graceful ease with which he read — just a few notes above the conversational level — but never rising into the declamatory. This light-in-hand manner suits well the delicate, hovering rather than superficial, style of the composition. He skims lightly over the surface of the long epoch, throwing out a sketch here, exhibiting a characteristic trait there, and sprinkling about a few anecdotes, portraits, and historical allusions, running along from grave to gay, from lively to severe, moving and mocking the sensibilities in a breath, in a way which I should say was the perfection of lecturing to high-bred audiences. I suppose his manner, and his stuff also, are somewhat stronger for larger and more heterogeneous assemblies, for I have no doubt he left out a good deal which might jar upon the ears polite of his audience on this occasion. Still, I was somewhat surprised at the coolness with which he showed up the foibles and absurdities of kings, and court, and court folks in a former but not remote reign, before a small company, which consisted of the cream of London cream.

1357. TO MRS. CARMICHAEL-SMYTH
MAY 1858 [32]

Hitherto unpublished.

My dearest Mother. My letter wont be as neatly written as usual, for I write all askew lying on my back these 4 days under Thompson's inevitable operations. The first 2 days to add to the pleasure I had the spasms as well as the other malady But the last 3 attacks have been decidedly lighter, and I sleep through most part of 'em. So the poor girls' drum went off, and the people who are not asked are all angry as I expected and they agree now that it will be wise never to drum again. The rooms looked very pretty the fire places being crammed with 20/ worth of lurid flowers and I delighted Lady Airlie by telling her M[rs] Fladgates artless compliment who is that handsome woman in the door with the black lace Behind? Everybody praised Pauline but but BUT, I know she's not tall enough for the place.

In spite of the pain & bother, the rest up here has not been unpleasant. When do I ever get 4 days to myself without printers devils engagements petitions for money — O stop Ive forgotten

---

They seemed to enjoy it, and to laugh heartily at all the points without wincing." For another account of the occasion, which includes a list of the persons present, see a letter of Lady Stanley's daughter Katherine, published in *The Amberley Papers; the letters and diaries of Lord and Lady Amberley*, 2 vols., ed. Bertrand and Patricia Russell (London, 1937), I, 49–51.

[32] This letter was written several days after the Thackerays' evening party of Monday, May 24, which Motley describes to his wife in a letter of May 30 (*Correspondence*, ed. Curtis, I, 239–240). On the day before the party a dinner was given at Thackeray's home, of which Motley writes (I, 235): "I sat between Thackeray's two daughters. They are both intelligent and agreeable. The youngest told me she liked 'Esmond' better than any of her father's books. Thackeray, by the way, evidently considers that kind of thing his forte. He told me that he hated the 'Book of Snobs,' and could not read a word of it. 'The Virginians', he said, was devilish stupid, but at the same time most admirable; but that he intended to write a novel of the time of Henry V., which would be his *capo d'opera*, in which the ancestors of all his present characters, Warringtons, Pendennis's, and the rest would be introduced. It would be a most magnificent performance, he said, and nobody would read it."

poor Mr Langley ³³ to whom I give 1£ a week for a sham job! I must ring and ask about Mr Langley — yes he has been here sure enough poor fellow yes he is coming again. We pack him up his sovereign. May we always have one to spare for a poor fellow!

Well what to say? Here is sad news in the literary world — no less than a separation between M.^r & Mrs Dickens — with all sorts of horrible stories buzzing about. The worst is that Im in a manner dragged in for one — Last week going into the Garrick I heard that D is separated from his wife on account of an intrigue with his sister in law. No says I no such thing — its with an actress — and the other story has not got to Dickens's ears but this has — and he fancies that I am going about abusing him! We shall never be allowed to be friends that's clear. I had mine from a man at Epsom the first I ever heard of the matter, and should have said nothing about it but that I heard the other much worse story whereupon I told mine to counteract it. There is some row about an actress in the case, & he denies with the utmost infuriation any charge against her or himself — but says that it has been known to any one intimate with his family that his and his wifes tempers were horribly incompatible & now that the children are grown up — it is agreed they are to part — the eldest son living with her the daughters &c remaining under the care of Miss Hogarth who has always been mother governess house-keeper everything to the family. I havent seen the statement ³⁴

³³ S. Langley, Thackeray's secretary, who lived at "Mr R. Emersons Heath St Hampstead" according to an entry in Thackeray's address-book for 1858.

³⁴ The notorious "Violated Letter", a defence of his conduct which Dickens sent on May 25 to Arthur Smith, the manager of his readings. Smith was empowered to show this document, in which Dickens expresses himself much more freely than in the "Address" on the same subject published on June 8 in *The Manchester Guardian* and on June 12 in *Household Words*, to anyone whom it might "really concern". In view of the elasticity of this restriction, it is not surprising that a copy of the letter should have found its way into the columns of *The New York Tribune* of August 16. The passage concerning Miss Ternan, who was, like her mother, an actress, reads: "Two wicked persons [Dickens's mother-in-law and her youngest daughter] who should have spoken very differently of me, in consideration of earned respect and gratitude, have (as I am told, and indeed to my personal knowledge) coupled with this separation the name of a young woman for whom I have a great attachment

but this is what is brought to me on my bed of sickness, and I'd give 100£ (if it weren't true.) To think of the poor matron after 22 years of marriage going away out of her house! O dear me its a fatal story for our trade.

1358.   TO ADELAIDE PROCTER
                    4 JUNE 1858

Published in part, *Biographical Introductions*, XIII, xxii-xxiii. My text is taken from a transcript given Lady Ritchie by George Murray Smith.

36 Onslow Square.
June 4th.

My dear Adelaide,

Thank you for the little book [35] with the kind little inscription on the first page. There will always be a .... between us, won't there? and we shall like each other out of our books and melancholies and satires and poetries and proses. Why are your verses so very very grey and sad? I have been reading them this morning till the sky has got a crape over it — other folks' prose I have heard has sometimes a like dismal effect, one man's especially I mean with whom I am pretty intimate, and who writes very glumly though I believe he is inwardly a cheerful wine-bibbing easy-going person, liking the wicked world pretty well in spite of all his grumbling. We can't help what we write though; an unknown something works within us and makes us write so and so. I'm putting this case *de me* (as usual) and *de te*. I don't like to think you half so sad as your verses. I like some of them very much indeed: especially the little tender bits. All

and regard. I will not repeat her name — I honor it too much. Upon my soul and honor, there is not a more virtuous and spotless creature than that young lady. I know her to be innocent and pure, and as good as my own dear daughters. Further, I am quite sure that Mrs. Dickens, having received this assurance from me, must now believe it, in the respect I know her to have for me, and in the perfect confidence I know her in her better moments to repose in my truthfulness."

[35] *Legends and Lyrics* (1858).

the allusions to children are full of a sweet natural compassion-
ateness: and you sit in your poems like a grey nun with three or
four little prattlers nestling round your knees, and smiling at
you, and a thin hand laid upon the golden heads of one or two
of them: and having smoothed them and patted them, and told
them a little story, and given them a bon bon the grey nun walks
into the grey twilight, taking up her own sad thoughts and leaving the *parvulos* silent and wistful. There goes the Angelus!
There they are lighting up the chapel. Go home little children,
to your bread and butter and teas: and kneel at your bedside in
crisp little nightgowns.

I wonder whether this has anything on earth to do with Adelaide Anne Procter's poems? I wish the tunes she sang were
gayer: but *que voulez vous?* The Lord has made a multitude
of birds and fitted them with various pipes, (there goes *my* Anny
singing in her room, with a voice that is not so good as Adelaide
Sartoriss but which touches me inexpressibly when I hear it) and
the chorus of all is Laus Domino.

I am writing in this queer way, I suppose (because I went to St
Paul's yesterday — Charity Children's day,[36] Miss, and the sight
and sound immensely moved and charmed,

Yours affectionately, dear Adelaide,
W. M. Thackeray.

[36] Thackeray rarely missed the annual meeting of the children from the
Charity Schools of London, an event which is described in Blake's "Holy
Thursday" and in his own lecture on George III (*Works*, VII, 676). "It is
the finest thing in the world —", he said to Motley (*Correspondence*, ed. Curtis, I, 253), whom he found in Dean Milman's pew at St. Paul's on June 3,
"finer than the Declaration of Independence." This picturesque ceremony,
we learn from Wheatley (*London*, III, 52), "has been discontinued since
1867, in consequence of the interruption to the service rendered necessary by
the erection of a huge gallery round the dome area."

1359. ## TO EDMUND YATES
13 JUNE 1858

Published in *Garrick Club: Correspondence*,[37] p. 2. My text is taken from a draft in Thackeray's hand owned by Mrs. Fuller.

36 Onslow Square
June 13.

Sir

I have received 2 numbers of a little paper called 'Town Talk', containing notices respecting myself of w^h, as I learn from the best authority,[38] you are the writer.

In the first article of Literary Talk you think fit to publish an incorrect statement of my private dealings with my publishers.[39]

In to days number appears a so called 'Sketch'[40] containing a description of my manners person & conversation and an account of my literary works w^h of course you are at liberty to praise or condemn as a literary critic.

But you state with regard to my conversation, that it is either 'frankly cynical or affectedly benevolent & good natured': and of my works (lectures) that in some 'I showed an extravagant adulation for rank and position w^h in other lectures — 'as I knew how to cut my coat according to my cloth' — 'became the object of my bitterest attack'.

As I understand your phrases, you impute insincerity to me when I speak good-naturedly in private; assign dishonorable motives to me for sentiments w^h I have delivered in public, and

[37] A rare four-page pamphlet distributed among the members of the Club shortly before the General Meeting of July 10.

[38] Yates (*Recollections and Experiences*, II, 13) identifies Thackeray's informant merely as "a well-known *littérateur*, whom I at that time believed to be a friend of mine", and in a marginal gloss, more vindictively, as "Judas".

[39] "LITERARY TALK . . . Mr. Thackeray is said to receive £200 a month from Messrs. Bradbury and Evans for the 'Virginians'." (*Town Talk*, June 5, p. 51).

[40] See the facsimile reproduction opposite page 90. This article was the starting-point of what later came to be known as "The Garrick Club Affair".

charge me with advancing statements w^h I have never delivered at all.

Had your remarks been written by a person unknown to me, I should have noticed them no more than other calumnies: but as we have shaken hands more than once, and met hitherto on friendly terms, (You may write to one of your employers, Mr Carruthers of Edinburgh,[41] & ask whether very lately I did not speak of you in the most friendly manner) I am obliged to take notice of articles w^h I consider to be, not offensive & unfriendly merely, but slanderous and untrue.

We meet at a Club where, before you were born I believe, I & other gentleman have been in the habit of talking, without any idea that our conversation would supply paragraphs for professional vendors of 'Literary Talk', and I don't remember that out of that Club I ever exchanged 6 words with you. Allow me to inform you that the talk w^h you may have heard there is not intended for newspaper remark; & to beg, as I have a right to do, that you will refrain from printing comments upon my private conversation; that you will forego discussions however blundering, on my private affairs; & that you will henceforth please to consider any question of my personal truth & sincerity as quite out of the province of your criticism.

                                        W. M. Thackeray.

E. Yates Esq^e [42]

[41] Yates succeeded Shirley Brooks in 1855 as London correspondent of the *Inverness Courier*, which was edited by Dr. Robert Carruthers. See above, No. 1309.

[42] Mrs. Fuller owns three drafts of this letter. The second does not differ materially from the final version printed above, but the last paragraphs of the first draft (dated June 12) offer interesting variants:

"In todays number [of *Town Talk*] appears a so-called 'Sketch' of me, containing a description of my manners and person, announcing that certain works of mine have been 'dead failures', that in some lectures I showed 'an extravagant adulation of birth and position' w^h in others became 'the object of my bitterest attacks' and attributing to me motives, base enough if real, but respecting w^h I trust my critic is even more at fault, than he is regarding my pecuniary dealings.

"Had your statements been made by an unknown person, of course I should have let them pass: but we have shaken hands together often, and been on civil

1360.   FROM EDMUND YATES
                  15 JUNE 1858 [43]

My text is taken from *Garrick Club: Correspondence*, p. 3.

General Post Office,
June 15th, 1858.

Sir,

I have to acknowledge the receipt of your letter of this day's date, referring to two articles of which I am the writer.

You will excuse my pointing out to you, that it is absurd to suppose me bound to accept your angry "understanding" of my "phrases;" I do not accept it in the least; I altogether reject it.

I cannot characterize your letter in any other terms than those in which you characterized the article which has given you so much offense. If your letter to me were not both "slanderous and untrue" I should readily have discussed its subject with you, and avowed my earnest and frank desire to set right anything I

---

nay friendly terms (I protest without any hypocrisy on my part) at a Club where we constantly meet, and where gentlemen {are or have hitherto been} have been in the habit of speaking unreservedly, without any idea that their conversation is to supply paragraphs for professional vendors of 'Literary Talk'

"Out of that Club I don't believe I ever exchanged 6 words with you: and read therefore with surprise that my 'conversation is openly cynical, or affectedly good natured and benevolent'. Allow me to inform you that the talk w^h you may have heard there, and could not elsewhere, is supposed to take place between gentlemen, and never intended for newspaper remark — and to beg, for one, — as I have a right to do — that you will refrain from printing remarks or opinions respecting my private conversation; that you will forego public discussion, however blundering, of my pecuniary affairs; and that you will henceforth please to consider the question of my truth and sincerity as quite out of the province of your criticism.

Your ob^t
W M Thackeray."

[43] According to Yates's narrative in *Recollections and Experiences* (II, 15–18) he originally intended to answer Thackeray's letter by detailing the personalities of which the novelist had been guilty in his own writings. Dickens (see *Memoranda*), to whom he turned for advice, found his reply "too flippant and too violent", and this note was sent in its place.

may have left wrong. Your letter being what it is, I have nothing
to add to my present reply.

Edmund Yates.

1361.   FROM GEORGE WILLIAM CURTIS
                        17 JUNE 1858

My text is taken from *Thackeray in the United States*, I, 361–362.

North Shore, Staten Island, June 17,
1858.

(This day eighty-three years ago, we had a tussle on Bunker Hill)

My dear Thackeray, — I have received all your kind messages,
and we have a hundred times conceived a round robin to you which
flew away before we caught it — and oh! there's no end of
reasons why I haven't written to a man I love dearly. Then I've
been fighting for you in papers, &c., for of course you know how
you've been abused by us for "The Virginians" and especially the
Washington.[44] It is curious that I have seen a copy of a MS. letter
from Edward Mason to Routledge (I think) after the Lee difficulty
at the battle of Monmouth,[45] out of which, it was thought by the
indiscreet, personal difficulty might grow, in which Mason says,
"Have no fear, for I have known W. from boyhood, and he
never had but one opinion of the duels, &c." It has been the most

[44] The Washington that Thackeray drew in the early chapters of *The Virginians* aroused much resentment among his American readers, who had
expected a heroic cartoon rather than a realistic portrait. Curtis came to his
friend's defense both in *Harper's Weekly* ("Thackeray's Washington", February 20, 1858, pp. 114–115) and in *Harper's Magazine* (March, 1858,
pp. 558–559).

[45] The stupidity or treachery of General Charles Lee, who engaged the British before Washington's arrival, nearly lost the Battle of Monmouth in 1778.
Washington appeared in time to turn defeat into victory, but his reproof of
Lee was not temperate, and in the court martial that he ordered, Lee was
suspended from his command. Lee's subsequent abuse of Washington brought
no direct reprisal, but it did lead to a duel between the cashiered general and
John Laurens, one of Washington's aides.

tempestuous teapot you ever heard. Meanwhile I have been as happy as a king, with my queen and prince imperial under the trees here on the island.[46] We are all well, and you would not think it was all vanity, this writing, if you could see the eager circle of children and old men and maidens to whom I read the monthly "Virginians," with shouts of merriment and sometimes even a tear. We wonder if you will ever come back again, or if we are henceforth to shake hands with you at this long stretch; but your kindest memory does not go away. I am a sinner never to have sent you a solitary line before now. I give it an edge by two extracts — the one from Philadelphia, the other from New Orleans. — Good-bye. Think of us sometimes who often think of you.

Yours affectionately,
George W. Curtis.

1362.   TO THE COMMITTEE
          OF THE GARRICK CLUB
          19 JUNE 1858

My text is taken from *Garrick Club: Correspondence*, p. 1.

36, Onslow-square,
Gentlemen,   June 19, 1858

The accompanying letters [47] have passed between me and Mr. Edmund Yates, another member of the Garrick Club.

Rather than have any further personal controversy with him, I have thought it best to submit our correspondence to you, with a copy of the newspaper which has been the cause of our difference.

I think I may fairly appeal to the Committee of the Garrick Club, to decide whether the complaints I have against Mr. Yates are not well founded, and whether the practice of publishing such articles as that which I enclose will not be fatal to the com-

[46] Curtis was living with his wife and son at the home of his father-in-law on Staten Island.
[47] Thackeray's letter of June 13 and Yates's note of June 15.

fort of the Club, and is not intolerable in a Society of Gentlemen.

Your obedient Servant,
W. M. Thackeray.

The Committee of the Garrick Club.

1363.   FROM EDMUND YATES TO THE COM-
MITTEE OF THE GARRICK CLUB
19 JUNE 1858

My text is taken from *Garrick Club: Correspondence*, p. 3.

43, Doughty Street, W.C.
June 19th, 1858.

Gentlemen,

I have just heard from Mr. Thackeray, that he has thought proper to lay before you the details of a personal difference between us.

This course has come upon me utterly unexpectedly, and I therefore beg you to suspend your judgment until I have consulted my friends, and been able to prepare my own version of the matter for submission to you.

Your obedient Servant,
Edmund Yates.

To the Committee of the Garrick Club.

1364.   FROM ALEXANDER DOLAND
TO EDMUND YATES
19 JUNE 1858

My text is taken from Yates's *Mr. Thackeray, Mr. Yates, and the Garrick Club* (1859), p. 7.

Garrick Club, 19th June, 1858.

Sir, — I have the honour, by the direction of the Committee, to acknowledge the receipt of your letter of 19th June.

I am further directed to inform you that a Special Meeting of the Committee is called for Saturday next, at half past three o'clock, to take the subject of Mr. Thackeray's complaint into consideration.

> I have the honour to be, Sir,
> Your most obedient servant,
> Alexander Doland,
> Secretary.

E. H. Yates, Esq.

1365.   FROM EDMUND YATES TO THE
COMMITTEE OF THE GARRICK CLUB
23 JUNE 1858

My text is taken from *Garrick Club: Correspondence*, pp. 3–4.

> 43, Doughty Street, W.C.,
> June 23, 1858.

Gentlemen,

I have received an obliging intimation from the Secretary of the Club, that the Committee will assemble on Saturday next, for the purpose of taking into consideration a complaint made against me by Mr. Thackeray.

With the greatest respect I beg to submit that Mr. Thackeray's grievance is not one to be submitted to the Committee. His grievance is a certain article written by me in a certain newspaper: that article makes no reference to the Club, refers to no conversation that took place there, violates no confidence reposed there, either in myself or any one else.

This article may be in exceedingly bad taste, but I submit, with great deference, and subject to the Committee's better judgment, that the Committee is not a Committee of taste. This article may be most unintentionally incorrect in details, but unless I had so far forgotten the honour and character of a gentleman as wilfully to distort the truth, I still venture to submit that its inaccuracy is not a question for the Committee's collective decision.

Mr. Thackeray's course in laying this matter before the Committee I hold to be unprecedented. Unless I am mistaken, there are members of the Committee's own body, who have been the subject of very strong remarks in print by fellow-members of the Club, but who have no more thought of laying their personal injuries and resentments before a Committee of the Club, than before a Committee of the House of Commons.

Once again, I take this position with the greatest respect. If the Committee think otherwise, then I readily submit myself to the correction of the Committee, and recognize as fully as the Committee can, that Mr. Thackeray lays the correspondence before them in the legitimate and customary way.

In this case, but not otherwise, I strongly entreat the attention of the Committee to the terms of Mr. Thackeray's letter of the 14th instant, and when the Committee have heard that letter read, I ask whether Mr. Thackeray rendered it possible for me to express my regret for having given him offense.

I am, Gentlemen,
Your obedient Servant,
Edmund Yates.

To the Committee, Garrick Club.

1366.   FROM ALEXANDER DOLAND
TO THACKERAY AND YATES
26 JUNE 1858

My text is taken from *Garrick Club: Correspondence*, p. 4.

Garrick Club,
26th June, 1858.

Sir,

I have the honour, by the direction of the Committee, to acknowledge the receipt of your letter of the 23rd instant, and to make the following communication to you.

At a Special Meeting of the Committee, on Saturday, the 26th June, 1858, it was unanimously resolved:

1st. That it is competent to the Committee to enter into Mr. Thackeray's complaints against Mr. Yates.

2nd. That it is the opinion of the Committee that Mr. Thackeray's complaints against Mr. Yates are well founded, and that the practice of publishing such articles, being reflections by one Member of the Club against any other, will be fatal to the comfort of the Club, and is intolerable in a Society of Gentlemen.

3rd. That in the opinion of the Committee, Mr. Yates is bound to make an ample apology to Mr. Thackeray, or to retire from the Club; and if Mr. Yates declines to apologize or retire, the Committee will consider it their duty to call a General Meeting of the Club to consider this subject.

4th. That copies of these resolutions be sent to Mr. Thackeray and Mr. Yates.

Lastly. That this Special Meeting of the Committee do stand adjourned to Saturday the 3rd of July.

I have the honor to be, Sir,
Your most obedient, very humble servant,
Alexr. Doland, Secretary.

To W. M. Thackeray, Esq., and
To E. H. Yates, Esq.

1367.   TO MRS. BECHER
                        28 JUNE 1858

Hitherto unpublished.

My dear M⁣ʳˢ Becher. 1000 pardons — If you knew how busy and bothered I've been! And now having been ill in bed for 3 days I find 7 money applications on my table! I cant send more than 5 this time, as much at Michaelmas if need be. I say this because I am portioning out money to a certain purpose, & oughtn't to dispose of more. Cut this [48] with scissors for the papers almost untearable.

Ever yours

1368.   FROM EDMUND YATES TO THE
COMMITTEE OF THE GARRICK CLUB
1 JULY 1858

My text is taken from *Garrick Club: Correspondence*, p. 4.

Doughty Street, W. C.,
July 1st, 1858.

Gentlemen,

I have the honour to acknowledge the receipt of your Secretary's letter of the 26th ultimo, making me acquainted with the Resolutions you passed on that day, in reference to "Mr. Thackeray's complaints against Mr. Yates."

With all respect and deference, I beg to state to you, that I will not retire from the Club, and that I cannot apologize to Mr. Thackeray.[49] I would very gladly do the latter, if the terms of

---

[48] A draft for five pounds on Sir John Lubbock, which Mrs. Becher did not use, forms the bottom part of this letter.

[49] Yates (*Recollections and Experiences*, II, 23) notes that before he wrote this letter, he read Thackeray's veiled allusion to him in number IX of *The Virginians* (chapters 33 to 36) for July, his implication being that by such a stroke Thackeray had closed all avenues to an apology. Chapter 35 of the novel begins with a paragraph on marriage, in which Thackeray develops the proposition that "there are few better ways of securing the faithfulness and admiration of the beautiful partners of our existence than a little judicious ill-treatment, a brisk dose of occasional violence as an alterative, and, for general and wholesome diet, a cooling but pretty constant neglect." "Women will be please with these remarks," he continues (*Works*, X, 293), "because they have such a taste for humour and understand irony; and I should not be surprised if young Grubstreet, who corresponds with three penny papers and describes the persons and conversation of gentlemen whom he meets at his 'clubs', will say 'I told you so! He advocates the thrashing of women! He has no nobility of soul! He has no heart!' Nor have I, my

Mr. Thackeray's letter to me were less offensive, but I conceive that if I made an "ample apology" to the writer of that communication, I should myself deserve that portion of it which you adopt in your second resolution, and should be "intolerable in a society of gentlemen." I therefore desire to appeal from your opinion to a General Meeting on the two questions:

Firstly, whether the cause between Mr. Thackeray and myself is a case to be submitted to you at all.

Secondly, whether if it be, Mr. Thackeray has any right to claim an apology from one whom he has so very arrogantly and coarsely addressed.

With great regret that I cannot defer to your decision, and with much esteem and consideration,

I have the honour to be, Gentlemen,
Your obedient Servant,
Edmund Yates.

To the Committee, Garrick Club.

1369.   FROM CHARLES DICKENS
TO EDMUND YATES
6 JULY 1858

Published in part by Yates, *Recollections and Experiences*, II, 24–25. My text is taken from Dickens's *Letters*, ed. Dexter, III, 28–29.

Gad's Hill Place
Tuesday Sixth July 1858.

My dear Edmund, — I have been thinking about the General Meeting.[50] My considerations and reconsiderations thereupon induce me to recommend you *not* to attend it in person.

---

eminent young Grubstreet! any more than you have ears." A glance at the caricature of Yates reproduced below (opposite p. 102) will explain Thackeray's reference to young Grubstreet's ears.

[50] Dickens summarizes the situation before the General Meeting, from the point of view of Yates's adherents, in a letter to William Howard Russell of July 7: "The Garrick is in convulsions. The attack is consequent on Thackeray's having complained to the committee (with an amazing want of dis-

Firstly, I think it pretty certain that Thackeray will stay away. If he should do so, it would be regarded as an act of delicacy in him; and your doing the reverse would be regarded as an act of *in*delicacy in you.

Secondly, though he should come; still your staying away, would shew well by the side of his presence.

Thirdly, it is very difficult indeed for any one, even though practised in public meetings and appearances, to keep quiet at such a discussion, the said "any one" being a principal therein.

Fourthly, you could do nothing if you were there but deny that you ever intended to abide by the Committee's decision. That, I will say for you, if necessary.

In case you should be staggered by this advice of mine, ask one or two men of experience and good judgment, whom you can trust, what they say. I am pretty sure that on careful consideration they will agree with me.

I suppose the meeting is not to take place so soon as next Saturday, seeing that I have not yet received any circular. — Ever Faithfully.

[Charles Dickens.]

---

cretion, as I think) of an article about him by Edmund Yates, in a thing called Town Talk. The article is in bad taste, no doubt, and would have been infinitely better left alone. But I conceive that the committee have nothing earthly, celestial, or infernal to do with it. Committee thinks otherwise, and calls on E. Y. to apologise or retire. E. Y. can't apologise (Thackeray having written him a letter which renders it impossible) and won't retire. Committee thereupon call a General Meeting, yet pending. Thackeray *thereupon*, by way of showing what an ill thing it is for writers to attack one another in print, denounces E. Y. (in Virginians, as Young Grubstreet). Frightful mess, muddle, complication, and botheration, ensue — which witch's broth is now in full boil." (*Letters*, ed. Dexter, III, 31–32)

1370.   TO THE CHAIRMAN OF THE GEN-
ERAL MEETING OF THE GARRICK CLUB
10 JULY 1858 [51]

Hitherto unpublished.

Friday
Garrick Club.   July 9. 1858.

To the Chairman of the General Meeting convoked for Saturday
July 10.

Sir

The debate, as between me and the writer of the newspaper-
article w^h has given me offence, is over. I have expressed my
opinion of his conduct in terms of at least no 'feigned bonhommie'.
He has replied. The natural consequences have ensued, & our
little Society has been plunged for weeks past in a turmoil, in w^h
I regret sincerely I should have had any part.

Holding that no gentleman will be safe or intercourse possible
if this practise of commenting upon motives or conversations be
continued, I submitted my case to the Committee of the G. C.
asking protection not only for myself but the whole society. I
accept and am thankful for the Committee's opinion; and of
course it is not I who appeal from their decision.

I presume the effect of tomorrows meeting will be to confirm
or to reverse that sentence. In the latter case, it may be that the
next gentleman attacked will be more patient than I have been;
and, for the sake of a quiet life, will suffer, without complaint
or protest, indignities put upon him, hints thrown out against
his honor and sincerity, & liberties taken with his name. When
mine, unfortunately for me, was selected for comment, more than
one of my friends advised me to say nothing. My duty, perhaps
my temper, caused me to follow a different course: but I shall
grieve sincerely if my indignation at the injury w^h I conceive has

[51] This letter was never sent, probably because Thackeray felt that any move
toward self-justification would weaken his position.

been done me shall have superadded any unnecessary annoyance to the doubt, distrust, division, recrimination, & heart burning, w^h conduct like that of w^h I complain, must bring upon our or any Society!

Taking leave therefore of the case, and with a sincere wish for the prosperity of the Club, I am your most obdt Servt

W M Thackeray

I hear that an eminent Counsel is going to cover Mr Yates with his silk in the discussion next Saturday, whose eloquence no doubt will go to prove that Mr Yates's wrong towards me is very trifling, that I had no right to bring the matter before the Club, that I am thereby creating quarrels and dissensions in a friendly Society — nay I can fancy that a ready eloquence may show that I ought to apologize because Mr Yates has maligned me. I shall not be present at Saturdays discussion or vote at its conclusion, and hope to be out of the region of the little Club where such a storm has been raging.[52]

[52] In another manuscript in Mrs. Fuller's possession Thackeray has recast this postscript and set down his further reflections on the Yates affair, apparently to relieve his own mind and without thought of showing what he had written to anyone else:

"I hear that an eminent gentleman of 'the long robe' proposes to cover Mr Yates with his garment and I have little doubt that the eloquence of the learned gentleman will go to prove, that Mr Yates's wrong towards me is very trifling, that I had no right to bring the matter before the Club, that I am exaggerating a small offence, that I ought to have taken the trifling injury in silence, that I am creating dissensions and quarrels in an amiable society, and that possibly I ought to apologize to it because the gentleman maligned me.

"Except on one night at Mr Dickens's I do not remember that I ever met the gentleman out of the Garrick Club. Here I have talked with him in the most free & friendly manner A little while ago in his Character of 'The Lounger at the Clubs' he expressed an unfavorable opinion of one of my works Not caring a pennypiece about the criticism I did not allow it to alter our amicable relations. He may have thought on this occasion that it was impossible for any writer to keep his good humour after such a critic as the Lounger at the Clubs had expressed his dissatisfaction, & hence that I had adopted an affected 'bonhomie'— w^h is usually spelt with two ms, and under w^h I was concealing the anger 'rankling' within.

"Can he declare upon his honour that his observations upon my affected benevolence open cynicism and conversation *suave* but forbidding were founded

"The smiler with the knife" (Yates and Thackeray in the Garrick Club)

From a drawing by Thackeray

While Lady Ritchie owned this drawing, it was so framed as to cut off Yates's body entirely, and his forearm was erased in order to conceal the fact that there was more to the sketch. In this form it was exhibited as a "Drawing of Thackeray by himself" at the Victorian Exhibition of 1891–1892 at the New Gallery and reproduced in *Centenary Biographical Introductions*, XV, xxxvii. Not till it passed to the present owner, Mr. Craig Wylie, was the frame removed and Yates revealed.

EDMUND YATES IN 1865

From a photograph

1371.   FROM EDMUND YATES TO THE
GENERAL MEETING OF THE GARRICK CLUB
10 JULY 1858

My text is taken from Yates's *Mr. Thackeray*, p. 9.

Gentlemen, — You will this day have laid before you a correspondence between Mr. Thackeray and myself, certain Resolutions of your Committee affecting me, and such few representations as I have thought it becoming to offer to your Committee in writing.

I beg to assure you that although I consider Mr. Thackeray to have placed it out of my power to apologise to him, I am perfectly willing to apologise to you for any unpleasant feeling that I may

---

upon comments w^h he had heard out of doors and not in a hundred amicable conversations w^h we have had together in King S^t? Does a person who signs himself the Lounger at the Clubs and writes about gentlemen whom he meets every day, mean that he carefully gets his information out of the Clubs where he lounges? If so why Lounger? Suppose he were to bring out in one of his papers an article against a brother clerk of the Post Office whom he never met elsewhere with whom he was in the constant habit of laughing talking and shaking hands at the office. Would not the other gentlemen in the room say that it is all very well for Edmund to say this attack on Tom Bags or Bob Knox (I am only putting a hypothetic name) — resulted from remarks w^h Ned had gathered about Tom from other people out of doors — No no Edmund that wont do my boy — Its in this room you met Tom — and never out of it. He is an Islington or Pentonsville or Lambeth cove (the place is also hypothetical) you are amongst the swells, you were taken into the Garrick Club quite young out of regard for your father who was a favorite actor, a Doughty Street party. You go to the Garrick Club, you might as well swear it was there you heard about Tom and not here in Aldersgate St I say that if Yates maligned a brother clerk in one of his newspapers, the 'room' would have a right to be offended and that gents would have a right to say to one another, 'W^h one of us is that *terrific* Edmund a going to pitch into next? Move the venue from St. Mary Ate to Covent Garden and a society of gentlemen who are in the habit of meeting and talking freely together have a right to take cognizance of a libel written against one of them — I have a right to say It is here & here only that you have known me — It is here that I whom you accuse of dissimulation in conversation have treated you on terms of an entire unreserve and good-nature. I have feelings 'rankling' within have I? I am treacherous am I? What are you, who have shaken hands with me a score of times, and to whom I never said a word that was not good-natured?"

have awakened in the Club by the publication of the unfortunate article in question. I have no hesitation whatever in expressing to you (but not to Mr. Thackeray) my sincere regret that I ever wrote it, and put you to the pain and inconvenience of having to take it into your consideration.

Your obedient servant,
Edmund Yates.

1372.   TO N. CLAYTON
                    10 JULY 1858 [53]

Published in *The Critic*, XV (1889), 274.

Onslow Sq^e July 10. 1858.

Dear Sir

I think you have caught Mr Pendennis in a scrape from w^h there is no escaping — unless indeed we suppose that a large passing Cloud obscured the moon at the very moment when that little transaction between Pen and Fanny may have occurred. But did it? I assure you I am on that subject quite in the dark and your very faithful Servt

W M Thackeray

[53] Thackeray is replying to the following note, written from 9 Merrick Square on July 6:

"Sir

"I trust you will pardon a boy's mentioning what appears to him a trifling error in your novel 'Pendennis'.—

"In the 46th Chap.— (Pendennis at Vauxhall Gardens) I read, 'Poor Foker sate alone on one of the highest benches, his face *illuminated by the moon*', again a few lines further on Pendennis is saying 'look how beautiful the moon & stars are, and how calmly they shine', and almost immediately afterwards it is insinuated that Pen kissed Fanny for 'In the first place, it was dark; and nobody could see him',— now if the moon 'illuminated Foker's face', if the moon & stars 'shone calmly' how could it be 'dark' Pen kiss Fanny & 'nobody see him'?

"It may be said the sky became suddenly cloudy but such an explanation gives rather cloudy satisfaction. Should you think this note worthy acknowledgement, a line from you would give more pleasure than can be told by

Your respectful admirer
N. Clayton."

1373.   **FROM ALEXANDER DOLAND**
TO EDMUND YATES
17 JULY 1858

My text is taken from *Garrick Club: Report of the Committee,*[54] p. 2.

Sir,

I had the honor to forward you on Monday last a copy of the Resolutions [55] which were passed at the Special General Meeting held on the 10th instant.

[54] A rare three-page pamphlet issued shortly after July 20.

[55] These Resolutions, which were passed by a vote of seventy to forty-six, read as follows:

"1st. That is was competent to the Committee to enter into Mr. Thackeray's complaints against Mr. Yates.

"2nd. That it is the opinion of this Meeting that Mr. Thackeray's complaints against Mr. Yates are well founded.

"3rd. That the practice of publishing such articles, being reflections by one Member of the Club against any other, will be fatal to the comfort of the Club, and is intolerable in a society of Gentlemen.

"4th. That this Meeting is at once prepared to support the Committee in any step they may consider necessary for the suppression of this objectionable practice.

"5th. That this Meeting trusts that a most disagreeable duty may be spared it, by Mr. Yates making such ample apology to Mr. Thackeray as may result in the withdrawal of all unpleasant expressions used in reference to this question.

"6th. That with this expression of opinion the Meeting refers the whole question back to the Committee." (*Garrick Club: Report of the Committee,* p. 1)

The Committee's note proved no more effective than the Resolutions of the General Meeting in persuading Yates to apologize to Thackeray. At their meeting on July 20 the Committee accordingly had Yates's name erased from the Club's list of members. Dickens does not appear to have expected this step, though it is not easy to suggest what other action the Committee could have taken. He wrote to John Palgrave Simpson, another of Yates's supporters, on July 23: "The committee seems to me to have gone perfectly mad. I really never met with such ridiculous assumption and preposterous imbecility in my life before.

"Like Fox, I should 'boil with indignation' if I had not a vent. But I have. Upon my soul, when I picture them in that back-yard, conceiving that they shake the earth, I fall into fits of laughter.... — But this is not to the purpose concerning Edmund Yates. Before I received your note last night, I had

I am directed by the Committee to express to you their surprise that you have not noticed this communication by complying with either of the Requisitions of the General Meeting.

Bound, as the Committee feel themselves, to carry out with the least possible delay the strongly expressed feeling and Resolutions of the General Meeting, they are still unwilling to adopt the extreme measure if they can possibly avoid so doing; and although quite aware that the sense of the Meeting in reference to the apology in question was, that it should not only be ample but immediate, they look to the fact that no exact time is specified within which it must be made.

They adjourn this day's Meeting to Tuesday, the 20th instant, at Three o'Clock, for their final decision, trusting that the Club will pardon, for the sake of the motive, what might, strictly speaking, be considered a blameable tardiness.

I have the honor to be,
Sir,

Garrick Club,   Your most obedient and very humble Servant,
    17th July, 1858.   Alexander Doland,
To Edmund H. Yates, Esq. Secretary.

---

recommended him to ascertain, from good sound legal authority, the exact state of the legality of the question.

"This he is now doing." (*Letters*, ed. Dexter, III, 33)

Yates learned from his counsel that he had not yet been legally ejected from the Club. It was necessary that he get himself forcibly removed from its premises, and this he succeeded in doing on his second attempt. Since the London season was over and Dickens was away on a reading tour, no further action was deemed advisable for several months. (*Recollections and Experiences*, II, 28–30) Yates did not institute his suit to try the right of the Committee to drop him from the Club until December 5, when a writ was served on Doland, the Club's secretary.

1374.   TO BRADBURY AND EVANS
                    25 JULY 1858

Address: Messrs Bradbury & Evans | 11 Bouverie S^t. Fleet Street — | London |
England. *Postmarks:* BERNE 27 JUIL 1858, LONDON JY 30. Hitherto
unpublished.

> Berne   Sunday 25 July
>
> These pooty little cuts, my worthy friends,
> Titmarsh to the engraver recommends.

Send proofs directly to Lucerne.

1375.   FROM FRANK FLADGATE
                    27 JULY 1858

Address: à Monsieur W. M. Thackeray | Poste Restante | Lucerne. *Postmarks:*
27 JY 1858, LUZERN 30 JUL. Hitherto unpublished.

My dear Thackeray,

Finding from your second letter that you have not yet received
the information which the paper [56] upon which I write these few
lines contains, I send it at once to you.

The *matter* has long since ceased as between you and the ex-
member — It became a question between *him* and the *Club* only
— and it is settled — Some one wrote to me the other day "Y's
conduct has been very un Y's. I can add nothing to all this,
save my best regards to you and to your 'belongings'— health &
happiness.

> your sincere Friend,
> Frank Fladgate.

G. C.
27th July 1858

[56] A copy of *Garrick Club: Correspondence.* See above, No. 1359, note 37.

1376.   TO ?
                        18 AUGUST 1858

Hitherto unpublished.

                                        36 Onslow Sqᵉ S. W.
                                        August 18.

Dᵣ Sir

— I have to acknowledge your kind note wʰ I just found next
door last night on my return from Switzerland. Since you wrote,
you no doubt have heard that the difference between me & the
author of the article in 'Town Talk' has come to an issue — I
never once thought of attributing the article to *you*: and am sorry
that you should have been subject to misrepresentation by news-
paper-writers, as *well* as
                    Your *obliged* Servᵗ
                    W M Thackeray.

   Of course I've not seen the O. C's letter in the papers you allude
to, & hear of ever so many others who seem equally well informed.

1377.   TO THE BAXTERS
                        25 AUGUST 1858

Published in part, *American Family*, pp. 164–167.

                                   36 Onslow Sqᵉ August 25.

   I wonder whether I shall have the energy to get through this
sheet — this sheet? this page. But try we wool though I owe ever
so many people letters before you Madam, and this is safe to be
dreadfuly stupid. Dont you see that I cant even spell? — I am
constantly unwell now — a fit of spasms — then get well in about
5 days; then 5 days grumbling and thinking of my work; then
14 days work and spasms da capo — and what a horribly stupid
story I am writing! Dont tell me. I know better than any of you.
No incident, no character no go left in this dreary old expiring

carcass — There Miss Sally — you howl on your sea-shore and I will roar from mine. Come let us placidly take leave of our friends (not telling them anything I mean) go each to the top of a rock, and jump over and end our troubleoubleoubles in the midst of the sad sea waves' bubbleubblubbles — I am serious — You fancy I am joking. I tell you I am done, & I don't care. My dear it is all liver. We have been away on a (for the girls) jolly little Swiss tourkin of 5 weeks and I find the kind letters among the heap on my return home. As for my dear Mʳˢ Baxters, it steps silently into the room, and soothes me like a sweet refreshing calming anodyne — Fact is I'm quite beat and unwell and can scarce see the paper on wʰ I write.

Is Libbies teapot ever going? Yes Andrew Arcedeckne Esqᵉ (the original of Mʳ Foker [57] dont say so though) will take it over in a foo days. It has got black and is so small & shabby that I am ashamed to send it. But O my dear Libbie — Times are dark and will be dark so dark that no man shall be able to work [58]— Make haste and get married Lucy my dear, if you want a sillivyer tea pot or you will have none from your unfortunate W. M. T. My dear kind mothers heart, I am so glad it is elated at Wylly's getting such honours. When he comes to England he will talk to 2 orphans in a shabby genteel house about their maniac father. Nobody in the least is coming to marry them — and nobody I am sure is wanted, by their selfish parent — Annys happiness makes almost me happy — *unblases* me when I am under the influence over it — When I am lying up stairs in bed you know dreadfully ill with those spasms, and yet secretly quite contented and easy, I say to myself 'Good God what a good girl that is! Amen.

I have nothing to tell you as usual — I went away having got into trouble with a young fellow who told lies of me in a news-paper, wʰ I was obliged to notice as we are acquaintances, and meet together at a little Club [59] — You have read something about

[57] See above, No. 736.
[58] *St. John*, 9, 4.
[59] That the Yates affair was still on Thackeray's mind is shown by a sentence in number XI of *The Virginians* (chapters 41 to 44) for September: "there

it in the papers I daresay — The little papers are still going on abusing me about it I hear — and dont care as I never read one. The public does not care about the story nor about the Virginians nor I about either — nor do I know what there is in these 3 pages, nor whether I shall send them. Yes I think I shall send them because I can pay the post you know, and because once and away I like to growl out that I love you ever so many of you very sincerely — I think taraxacum might do something for Sally who is still (comparatively) young. If I wanted to see the children I would say so: but I don't. I suppose for form's sake I must send my love to them though. There. Bless you bless you my little dears. Take em away Nurse. Wowwowow Rawwawwaw. Chickaly Chickaly Chickaly. O zoo pooty little darlings — O you unfeeling Broo-oo-oot! says Aunt Lucy walking out of the room quite haughty. Well — he is really unwell that is the fact Grandmamma sayes. I think I'm ever so little better now I am got to the end of this absurd paper. God bless you all — Papa and the boys and the gals and Uncle Oliver says

Your Affte
W M T.

1378.   TO LADY STANLEY
                 20–23 SEPTEMBER 1858

Hitherto unpublished.

Hotel Bristol. Place Vendome.
Paris.
Tuesday. 20 Sep^r

My dear Lady Stanley

You must not think me more ungrateful than the generality of mankind for not having answered your kind note w^h I found at

---

is a *modus in rebus*: there are certain lines which must be drawn: and I am only half pleased, for my part, when Bob Bowstreet, whose connection with letters is through Policeman X and Y, and Tom Garbage, who is an esteemed contributor to the *Kennel Miscellany*, propose to join fellowship as brother literary men, slap me on the back, and call me old boy, or by my Christian name" (*Works*, X, 359).

home 6 weeks ago on my return from Switzerland Five of those weeks were spent in being perpetually ill — I dont know what is the matter with Brompton in September but its the most deadly place to me at that time and I think at all — dismal reflection for a man who has bought a house and made it pretty and comfortable. When you said Alderley was damp I shuddered — its in the damp places that my precious health suffers most — whereas the air here is like perpetual Champagne. I am living in this hotel in boy, my daughters hard by with their G mother who is delighted to have them: and I have done more work in a week than I do in 2 months at home.[60] How is it I come to write to you? D'abord there was your unanswered letter on my conscience and that very curious packet of bills from White's w[h] your husband sent me — most characteristic singular & pleasant they are — and then a fellow was smoking in my room last night (we had been to dine with Sir Fitzroy & Lady Kelly [61] if you plaise, about whom there is some mystery) — I say Fletcher Norton [62] was a smoking here last night,

[60] John Pendleton Kennedy, in Paris on his second visit to Europe, wrote on September 26, 1858: "Thackeray calls to see me, and sits for an hour or two. He is not looking well. He tells me he has need of my assistance with his Virginians,— and says Heaven has sent me to his aid. He wants to get his hero from Fort Duquesne, where he is confined as a prisoner after Braddock's defeat, and to bring him to the coast to embark for England. 'Now you know all that ground,' he says to me, 'and I want you to write a chapter for me to describe how he got off and what travel he made.' He insists that I shall do it. I give him a doubtful promise to do it if I can find time in the thousand engagements that now press upon me on the eve of our leaving Paris." (Tuckerman, *Kennedy*, p. 296) Though the narrative of George Warrington's escape from Fort Duquesne in chapter 52 of *The Virginians* (the last chapter of number XIII for November) is patently by Thackeray, it may be based in part on Kennedy's suggestions. See Professor Jay B. Hubbell's "Thackeray and Virginia," *Virginia Quarterly Review*, III (1927), 76–86.

[61] Sir Fitzroy Kelly (1796–1880), who had married Ada Cunningham in 1856, was at this time Attorney-General and M. P. for East Suffolk. He remained in parliament until 1866 when he became Lord Chief Baron of the Exchequer, a post which he retained for the remainder of his life.

[62] Fletcher Cavendish Norton (1829–1859), oldest son of Mrs. Caroline Norton, became First Paid Attaché at the English Embassy in Paris on February 9. Lady Stanley's oldest son, the Hon. Henry Edward John Stanley (1827–1903), later (1869) third Baron Stanley of Alderley, was also in the diplomatic service. (*Foreign Office List*, 1859)

and praising Henry very cordially for talents [honesty and many good qualities de coeur et d'esprit. Surely a mother likes to know that her son has friends who speak well of him I thought, and on this hint sent off my little letter to Alderley

Yes: but it was begun 4 days ago from the mark [only it is wrote this morning — at 'talents' I was interrupted had to go away to dine in the country with old & young folks next day was knocked over by one of my attacks of illness [63] (dry air or moist it seems

[63] "Returning to Paris, after a short tour in Switzerland and North Italy," writes William Allingham at about this time, "I found Thackeray in the Hotel Bristol with his two daughters. He is not well — often in bed till mid-day or later — struggling with [*The Virginians*], but in the evening recovering himself.

"I told him I had been with the Brownings (who were then in Paris staying in the Rue Castiglioni, No. 6).

" 'Browning was here this morning,' Thackeray said, 'what spirits he has — almost too much for me in my weak state. He almost blew me out of bed!'

" 'A wonderful fellow, indeed!'

" 'Yes, and he doesn't drink wine.'

" 'He's already screwed up to concert pitch.'

" 'Far above it. But I can't manage his poetry. What do you say?'

"(I spoke highly of it).

" 'Well, you see, I want poetry to be musical, to run sweetly.'

" 'So do I'—

" 'Then that *does for* your friend B.!'

"I spoke of Browning's other qualities so splendid as to make him, as it were, a law in himself. But Thackeray only smiled and declined further discussion.

" 'He has a good belief in himself, at all events. I suppose he doesn't care whether people praise him or not.'

" 'I think he does, very much.'

" 'O does he? Then I'll say something about him in a number.'

"Thackeray took me to dine with him in the Palais Royal. He noticed with quiet enjoyment every little incident — beginning with the flourish with which our waiter set down the dishes of Ostend oysters. After tasting his wine Thackeray said, looking at me solemnly through his large spectacles, 'One's first glass of wine in the day is a great event.'

"That dinner was delightful. He talked to me with as much ease and familiarity as if I had been a favourite nephew.

"After dinner Thackeray proposed that we should go to the Palais Royal Theatre, but on issuing forth he changed his mind, and said we would call up Father Prout. . . .

"In a narrow street at the back of the Palais Royal, in a large lowish room on the ground floor, we found the learned and witty Padre, loosely arrayed, reclining in front of a book and a bottle of Burgundy. He greeted us well,

to be all the same) Bon Dieu was ever a man so buffeted? and am only today sur pied again. Worse still, my dear old Mother, coming to see her son in his illness and walking for the first time these many months, was knocked down by some gamins close to her own door, has broken a bone in the hip somewhere and is to be lame for life. So in decrepitude and ill health, and straitened circumstances ends one who began beautiful & brilliant with a world of admirers round about her — Of these all are gone except one her faithful old husband on whose affection and fidelity I look with more admiration than on H. E. Aimable Jacques Duke of Malakoff or any Grandee I ever set eyes on. And between ourselves, (this is a little bit of sentiment such as my cynical spirit sometimes loves to indulge in) it was worth being ill to have 2 such nurses as my girls to take care of me. How good they were how watchful silent & tender! Here they come in new dresses * for wh I know who will pay: and he sends very kind greetings to all of you and is

Yours dear Lady Stanley very sincerely
W M Thackeray.

* They have left the elders and taken up again with their papa.

---

but in a low voice and said, 'Evening boys, there's a young chap asleep there in the corner.' And in a kind of recess we noted something like bed-clothes. Thackeray was anxious to know who this might be, and Prout explained that it was a young Paddy from Cork or thereabouts, who had been on a lark in Paris and spent his money. Prout found him 'hard up,' and knowing something of his friends in Ireland had taken him in to board and lodge, pending the arrival of succour.

"This piece of humanity was much to Thackeray's taste, as you may suppose. Thackeray said the Burgundy was 'too strong', and had brandy and water instead.

"We talked among other things of Dickens, I said how much a story of Dickens might be improved by a man of good taste with a pencil in hand, by merely scoring out this and that.

"Says Thackeray (with an Irish brogue), 'Young man, your threadin' on the tail o' me coat!'

"I did not understand at first.

" 'What you've just said applied very much to your humble servant's things.' " (*William Allingham: A Diary*, ed. H. Allingham and D. Radford, London, 1907, pp. 76–78)

1379.   TO PATRICK KENNEDY [64]
                      18 OCTOBER 1858

Address: The Author of | 'Legends of Mount Leinster' | Kennedy's Library.
Angelsea St. | Dublin. Hitherto unpublished.

                                          36 Onslow Sq^r
                                          Monday. October 18.

My dear Sir

I shall gladly accept the Xtian Hero [65] from you, and wish your
shop were nearer that I might poke about among your old books.
I am living 100 years ago at this present moment and read in
scores and scores of old volumes so as to make me au courant with
the times.

I wish I could help you with your Wexford Story [66]— but I
daren't recommend any more books to any publishers here of my
acquaintance. I have wearied them quite out with applications —
and have almost every day of my life to acknowledge my inability
to help some aspirant who sends me his MS.

                          Very faithfully yours
                          W M Thackeray.

1380.   TO DR. JOHN BROWN
                      4–10 NOVEMBER 1858

Published in part, *Biographical Introductions*, X, xli-xlii. My text is taken
from *Letters of Dr. John Brown*, pp. 327–330.

                          Hôtel des 2 Mondes, Rue d'Antin,
                          Paris, November 4.

My dear Dr. John — Your kind note has followed me hither.
I have many a time thought of you and of writing to you, but
it's the old story, work, dinner, and *da capo*. I have nothing spe-

---

[64] A Dublin bookseller (1801–1873), who had published his first book,
Legends of Mount Leinster (1855), under the pseudonym of Harry Whitney.
[65] Sir Richard Steele's tract, which appeared in 1701.
[66] Possibly *The Banks of the Boro; a chronicle of the county of Wexford*
(1867). Kennedy was a Wexford man.

cially cheerful to say about myself and don't like *The Virginians* half as much as you do. Very good writing, but it ought to have been at its present stage of the story at No. X.[67] I dawdled fatally between V. and X; ... I am old, or I am tired, or some other reason. All remains yet doubtful about my poor mother. She has had more than six weeks bed, but we don't know yet whether the fracture is to join or what is quite the nature of it. Poor dear, it was in returning from coming to see me that some boys ran against her near her own door and occasioned the mishap. She bears it wonderfully; her health has rather improved, and neither she nor her husband quite know how serious the accident is. I send no condolements about the departure of your good old Father.[68] He was ready I suppose, and had his passport made out for his Journey. Next comes our little turn to pack up and depart. To stay is well enough, but shall we be very sorry to go? What more is there in life that we haven't tried? What that we have tried is so very much worth repetition or endurance? I have just come from a beefsteak and potatoes 1 f., a bottle of Claret 5 f., both excellent of their kind, but we can part from them without a very severe pang, and *nota* that we shall get no greater pleasures than these from this to the end of our days. What *is* a greater pleasure? Gratified ambition? accumulation of money? What? Fruition of some sort of desire perhaps; when one is twenty, yes, but at 47 Venus may rise from the sea, and I for one should hardly put on my spectacles to have a look. Here I am snarling away on the old *poco curante* theme. How good-natured you are not to be tired of me.

The girls and I have been to Versailles to-day. We rather liked it. They went to my mother afterwards, I to solitude and beef-steak before mentioned ... Have never heard Dickens,[69] but hope

[67] For August, chapters 37 to 40. Thackeray was currently at work on number XIV for December, chapters 53 to 56. Number V included chapters 17 to 20.

[68] Dr. John Brown the elder died on October 13, 1858 (*Dr. John Brown*, p. 122).

[69] Dickens had given a series of readings from his books in Edinburgh between September 27 and 30 (*Letters*, ed. Dexter, III, 59).

and believe he will make a great bit of money for the 8 children.

O how cold my back is! How cold the weather is! How stupid the letter is! How much better it would be to be sitting by the fire reading that stupid book than writing this stupid note! From the tone of this note don't you think I had better take a grain of blue pill to-night? Good-night, Doctor; good-night, Madam; good-night, children.

Wednesday Morning. — But *is* Miss Mackenzie going to marry Milor? Bath House will be restored to us in that case. Since her death I have never been within the door.[70] Have been sleeping in the most innocent manner for 10 hours; have got such beautiful apartments here, am living at an awful expense, though. £1 a day for rooms is nothing here. It is the dearest capital in Europe. How respectable folks in your Athens would tremble at the extravagance here! Come, there is no more room in the paper.

P.S. — My mother goes on remarkably well, so well that I think I may soon go home.

1381.　　　FROM CHARLES DICKENS
24 NOVEMBER 1858

My text is taken from Yates's *Mr. Thackeray*, p. 13.

Tavistock House, Tavistock-square, London, W. C.
Wednesday, 24th November, 1858.

My Dear Thackeray, — Without a word of prelude, I wish this note to revert to a subject on which I said six words to you at the Athenæum when I last saw you.

Coming home from my country work, I find Mr. Edwin James's[71] opinion taken on this painful question of the Garrick

[70] Thackeray's friend the first Lady Ashburton had died on May 4, 1857. Lord Ashburton married Louisa Mackenzie, who had inherited the Mackenzie estate of nearly 30,000 acres in county Ross, on November 17, 1858.

[71] Edwin John James (1812–1882), a very successful barrister though even at this time of sinister reputation. He was disbarred three years later for malpractice extending back to 1853. When he departed for New York in July, 1861, his liabilities were said to exceed £100,000. (*Annual Register*, 1862,

and Mr. Edmund Yates. I find it strong on the illegality of the Garrick proceeding. Not to complicate this note or give it a formal appearance, I forbear from copying the opinion; but I have asked to see it, and I have it, and I want to make no secret from you of a word of it.

I find Mr. Edwin James retained on the one side; I hear and read of the Attorney-General [72] being retained on the other. Let me, in this state of things, ask you a plain question.

Can any conference be held between me, as representing Mr. Yates, and an appointed friend of yours, as representing you, with the hope and purpose of some quiet accomodation of this deplorable matter, which will satisfy the feelings of all concerned?

It is right that, in putting this to you, I should tell you that Mr. Yates, when you first wrote to him, brought your letter to me. He had recently done me a manly service I can never forget, in some private distress of mine (generally within your knowledge),[73] and he naturally thought of me as his friend in an emergency. I told him that his article was not to be defended; but I confirmed him in his opinion it was not reasonably possible for him to set right what was amiss, on the receipt of a letter couched in the very strong terms you had employed. When you appealed to the Garrick Committee and they called their General Meeting, I said at that meeting that you and I had been on good terms for many years, and that I was very sorry to find myself opposed to you; but that I was clear that the Committee had nothing on earth to do with it, and that in the strength of my conviction I should go against them.

If this mediation that I have suggested can take place, I shall be heartily glad to do my best in it — and God knows in no hostile spirit towards any one, least of all to you. If it cannot take place, the

---

pp. 140–143) Thackeray appears to have had James's *débâcle* in mind when he described the later phases of Dr. Firmin's career in *Philip*.

[72] Sir Fitzroy Kelly.

[73] This can only be a reference to Dickens's intimacy with Miss Ternan. According to Mr. Wright (*Life of Charles Dickens*, p. 282) Yates was one of the few persons who knew the details of this story.

thing is at least no worse than it was; and you will burn this letter, and I will burn your answer.

Yours faithfully,
Charles Dickens.

W. M. Thackeray, Esq.

1382.   TO CHARLES DICKENS
                        26 NOVEMBER 1858

My text is taken from Yates's *Mr. Thackeray*, p. 14.

36, Onslow-square, 26th November, 1858.

Dear Dickens, — I grieve to gather from your letter that you were Mr. Yates's adviser in the dispute between me and him. His letter was the cause of my appeal to the Garrick Club for protection from insults against which I had no other remedy.

I placed my grievance before the Committee of the Club as the only place where I have been accustomed to meet Mr. Yates. They gave me their opinion of his conduct and of the reparation which lay in his power. Not satisfied with their sentence, Mr. Yates called for a General Meeting; and, the meeting which he had called having declared against him, he declines the jurisdiction which he had asked for, and says he will have recourse to lawyers.

You say that Mr. Edwin James is strongly of opinion that the conduct of the Club is illegal. On this point I can give no sort of judgment: nor can I conceive that the Club will be frightened, by the opinion of any lawyer, out of their own sense of the justice and honour which ought to obtain among gentlemen.

Ever since I submitted my case to the Club, I have had, and can have, no part in the dispute. It is for them to judge if any reconcilement is possible with your friend. I subjoin the copy of a letter which I wrote to the Committee, and refer you to them for the issue.

Yours, &c.,[74]
W. M. Thackeray.[75]

C. Dickens, Esq.

[74] Protesting against Forster's description of Dickens's difference with

1383.   TO THE COMMITTEE OF THE
                        GARRICK CLUB
                    28 NOVEMBER 1858

Published by Yates, *Mr. Thackeray*, p. 14. My text is taken from a draft in Thackeray's hand owned by Mrs. Fuller.

36 Onslow Sq^e November 28. 1858.

Gentlemen

I have today received a communication from Mr Charles Dickens relative to the dispute w^h has been so long pending, in w^h he says

'Can any conference be held between me as representing Mr Yates, and any appointed friend of yours as representing you, in the hope and purpose of some quiet accommodation of this deplorable matter, w^h will satisfy the feelings of all parties?'

I have written to Mr Dickens to say that since the commencement of this business I have placed myself entirely in the hands of the

---

Thackeray as an "estrangement . . . hardly now worth mention even in a note" (*Life of Dickens*, ed. Ley, p. 697), Yates writes that "at the time no one was more energetically offended with Thackeray than John Forster himself. I perfectly well remember his rage when Dickens showed him the letter of 26th November, and how he burst out with 'He be damned, with his "yours, &c."!'" (*Recollections and Experiences* II, 36)

75 To a first draft of this letter in the possession of Mrs. Fuller Thackeray has added the following comments: "On the 28 November I wrote to the Committee of the G. C. enclosing the paragraph A in Mr Dickens's letter and saying that if they could come to a pacific ending no one would be more glad than myself.

"The Committee did not meet till the ensuing Saturday Decr 5, and on that day Mr Yates served a Writ on the Secretary of the Club, & this article appeared in the Illustrated Times.

"'THE THEATRICAL LOUNGER
THE "HISTRIONIC BARONET."

"My personal experience of baronets, limited though it be, does not inculcate a belief in them as a class. Perhaps I have not been fortunate, but of the half-dozen with whom I have been brought into contact, one is a cynic, one a stupid nincompoop, one a spiteful fool, one an antiquated fogey, one a harmless chip-in-porridge, and only one a real gentleman. Two of these live on their estates, two on the reputation of their ancestors, one by bedabbling

Committee of the Garrick, and am still, as ever, prepared to abide by any decision at w̲ḥ they may arrive on the subject. I conceive I cannot, if I would, make the dispute once more personal, or remove it out of the Court to w̲ḥ I submitted it for arbitration.

If you can devise any peaceful means for ending it, No one will be better pleased than,

Your obliged faithful Ser̲ṭ
W M Thackeray.

The Committee of the Garrick Club.

1384.   TO ANNE AND HARRIET THACKERAY
4 DECEMBER 1858

Hitherto unpublished.

Saturday.   Dec̲ṛ 4.

Young women. You may depend on it your dear Papa is not very comfortable in mind nor pens nor paper when he begins at

---

his "bloody hand" in coal dust and retailing Yorkshire "slack" to London merchants, and one by his wits — and, heaven knows, he has but a slight subsistence! My estimate of the order was not heightened by witnessing the performance of Sir William Don, on Monday evening, at the Haymarket. This gentleman, who stands six feet and a-half in height, relies apparently upon his grotesque appearance, and his very comic face, for his success as an actor. All that man can do in the way of gagging and fun-forcing he did, and he certainly succeeded in "hammering a hoarse laugh from a coarse throng;" but of the lights and shades of acting, of the accurate representation of character, he has no more idea than Mr. M. F. Tupper has of poetry, or than I have of what the editor of the "Musical World" means by the word "perfunctory". Holding the mirror up to nature is all very well; but what is the result when, from physical conformation, you are compelled to hold the mirror so high above nature's head that she cannot get a glimpse at herself, or but sees herself in a grotesque and distorted medium? No, no! brevity is the soul of wit, and in Sir William Don's case, certainly the exception does *not* prove the rule!' "

In this clipping Yates is of course guilty of the same offence that gave rise to Thackeray's initial protest to the Committee of the Garrick Club. His information about most of the "half-dozen" Baronets whom he describes must have come chiefly from conversations within the Club's walls. No doubt Sir William Henry Don (1828–1862), seventh Baronet, who in 1850 sold his estates to pay his creditors and went on the stage, was also a member of the Club.

you in this hand writing.[76] He got up this morning at 7 quite
cheerfully and well, and lighting the candle on the mantel-piece
saw before him

'The pills immediately the Draught two hours after the pills.'
Like a good boy he took the pills instantly at 7. the Draught at 9.
It was Rhubarb, w^h your dear Father hates like poison. But que
voulez vous? He was committed already by having swallowed
the pill, dont you see? It is now 12 o'clock He is nauseated, uncomfortable all over, with the dreadful idea that the pill will
have its effect about 5 o'clock, and at 7 he is to be at dinner at M^r
Heath's at Richmond. Fancy having to get up abruptly, and leave
the table! Yesterday I only got 5 letters asking me for money.
One from poor Eyre 5£: one from Mrs Beckwith 5£: and then
when I was settling to work comes your Uncle Arthur who informs
me that he is about to be arrested for a bill of 235£ — w^h I shall
end by paying. Isn't it jolly?

The Yates and Thackeray affair still roars on bravely. Three
articles this week. Two against me and accusing me of persecuting
Yates — private letter from Higgins to tell me that I am utterly
in the wrong, that Yates's article *wasn't* malicious, and that I had
best beware of Edwin James and the scarifying w^h I shall get in
the Witness box. Having done me some services, H takes them
out in the most confounded ill-conditioned letters, with a sort of
savage mischief I suppose in thinking that I can't resent them.

I begin to like Mrs Martin [77] more and more. There's a very

[76] This letter is written in Thackeray's slanting hand.
[77] The former Helena Saville Faucit (1817–1898), one of the most famous
actresses of her time, who had married Theodore Martin (1816–1909),
K. C. B. (1880), in 1851. While Thackeray lived in Brompton, the Martins
were his near neighbors at 31 Onslow Square. "All our recollections of Thackeray were delightful," writes Sir Theodore (*Helena Faucit Lady Martin*,
Edinburgh and London, 1900, p. 258). "He used to pay us long visits at

genuine sweetness and kindness about her. Sorry I cant go and dine there tomorrow. Engaged to the Procters. Adelaide going to be married: [78] it was time: she has lost her front tooth *my* tooth. but looks very much happier & comfortabler. Haven't seen JOB nor my German correspondent. Dined at Forster's with Elwyn. Forster was admirably grotesque and absurd. I was glad to get out of the house without touching on the Dickens affair. John Brown writes from Edinburgh to day, that C D is a miscreant. He is 1/2 mad about his domestic affairs, and tother 1/2 mad with arrogance and vanity. O Mr Haden! [79] Mr Haden! y, y, did you give me that confounded rewbarb?

Yesterday I gave Shirley Brooks dinner at the Reform Club Que c'etoit une curiosité a le voir. Yesterday Mr Yates presented himself at the Garrick Club for the purpose of being again turned out.[80] Fladgate is sublime on the great question. Poor Mrs Russell is ill with erisypelas. Alice Corkran has the typhus fever: but is going on pretty well. Did you see w^m Conyngham's nice girl is dead of dyphtheria? My God what a blow! And Macready's eldest son is come home to England doomed to die. Here's a merry letter I am writing to you!

Here I break off to write a line to poor W. Coningham, and no

---

breakfast, and then he talked with frankness and unreserve, more like those of a large-hearted boy than of a man who had seen life in so many phases, many of them of a kind to induce the *pensieri stretti*, for which strangers thought he was peculiar. His nature was obviously one that yearned for sympathy. It was full of tenderness, and showed it, where he was sure that it would be understood. In fact, of all men I have known he was the most tender-hearted; in this respect, indeed, almost womanly. He always showed a marked respect for my wife's opinion in all matters of literature and art. What he thought of her we learned from a note which came into my hands many years after his death. It was addressed to Lady Knighton, inviting her to meet the well-known Helen Faucit at dinner, in which he spoke of her as 'one of the sweetest women in Christendom'." Martin was the author with Aytoun of *The Bon Gaultier Ballads* (1842–1844), and he later wrote the official *Life of the Prince Consort* (1875–1880).

[78] Miss Procter never married.

[79] Francis Seymour Haden (1818–1910), knighted (1894), a prominent London surgeon, now remembered chiefly for his etchings.

[80] See above, No. 1373, note 55.

XV [81] of the Virginians if you please? Come Come Sir it is pouring with rain Had you not best set to work? — I was afraid Granny's news was too good to be true. How philosophical it is to say the months are long but that they pass! G. B. all.

W M T.

1385.   TO LADY MORGAN
DECEMBER 1858 ?

Hitherto unpublished.

    My dear Lady Morgan. I send you a little present of small beer for this Christmas drinking: and, just on the point of departure for Paris, wish your ladyship a happy New Year.

Believe me dear Lady Morgan
Yours ever

Nicholas. Cardinal.

[81] For January, chapters 57 to 60.

1386.   TO CAPTAIN ATKINSON [82]
               27 DECEMBER 1858

Published in facsimile, *The Leisure Hour*, 1883, p. 561.

Hotel Bristol. Place Vendome.
December 27. 1858.

My dear Captain Atkinson

I received your beautiful book [83] whilst I was in London, but was in such a state of bewilderment and botheration with my own little volume that I hadn't heart to perform the proper duties of gratitude and society and thank you for your present and dedication. It was very interesting to me to see what my native country is like now — I have far off visions of great saloons and people dancing in them, enormous idols & fireworks, rides on elephants or in gigs, and fogs clearing away and pagodas appearing over the trees, yellow rivers and budgerows &c — I'm always interested about the place, and your sketches came to me as very welcome, besides being exceedingly pretty cheerful & lively. I hope the book will succeed: it must have been an awful bill to pay.

[82] George Francklin Atkinson (1822–1859), who served in the East India Company's army from 1841 till his death and published several volumes of sketches from Indian life (*Leisure Hour*, 1883, p. 560).

[83] *Curry and Rice, on forty plates; or, the ingredients of social life at our station in India* (1858), which is dedicated to Thackeray.

As for that little hint about Printing House Square, I know the Editors and most of the writers; and, knowing, never think of asking a favor for myself or any mortal man. They are awful and inscrutable, and a request for a notice might bring a slasher down upon you, such as I once had in the Times for one of my own books (Esmond) of w.ʰ the sale was absolutely stopped by a Times article.[84] I wish your volume every success, and thank you for putting my name on its first page.

Ever yours
W M Thackeray.

1387.　　　TO ROBERT CHAMBERS
27 DECEMBER 1858

Published in *Chambers's Journal*, Sixth Series, XIV (1897), 710. My text is taken from Lady Priestley's *The Story of a Lifetime* (London, 1908), pp. 70–71.

Paris, December 28th, 1858.

My Dear Chambers,

Will you send the above scrap to Mr. Payn,[85] as I don't remember where he lives? and, in asking you to perform this kind office for me, will you permit me to seize the opportunity afforded me of expressing to you, Mrs. Chambers, and your somewhat numerous family, my wish that you may enjoy many happy recurrences of a season which Christians venerate, but which you do not, I believe, acknowledge in Scotland, and the assurance of the profound consideration with which I have the honour to be, Sir, Madam, and your kind, merry, pretty young ladies,

Your faithful servant,
W. M. T.

[84] See above, No. 935, note 25.
[85] James Payn (1830–1898), the novelist, a regular contributor to *Chambers' Journal*.

1388.   TO MADAME LE VERT
                    1858? [86]

My text is taken from *Thackeray in the United States*, I, 292.

Wednesday.

My dear Madame Le Vert, — I am very sorry that I am engaged on Thursday evening. I am only just returned from Paris, or I should have acknowledged your invitation sooner.

Very faithfully yours,
W. M. Thackeray.

1389.   TO SIR HENRY KNIGHT STORKS [1]

              22 JANUARY 1859

Address: Major General Sir H Storks &c | War Office | Pall Mall. *Postmark:* LONDON JA 22 59. My text is taken from a facsimile in Henry Sayre Van Duzer's *A Thackeray Library* (New York, 1919), opposite p. 133.

36 Onslow Sq^r S. W.
                              Saturday

My dear Stork

Can you dine here tomorrow at 7. No party: but I want you very much to give me some military information for the Virginians. [2]

Yours ever
The Author.

[86] General Wilson gives this year as the date without stating his authority. Thackeray made several trips to Paris during 1858.

[1] Storks (1811–1874) was made a K. C. B. in 1857 but according to *The Dictionary of National Biography* did not become a Major-General until 1862.

[2] Number XVI for February, chapters 61 to 63.

1390.   FROM ANNE THACKERAY TO
                  DR. JOHN BROWN
                  26 JANUARY 1859

My text is taken from *Letters of Dr. John Brown*, pp. 330–331.

                              36 Onslow Square, January 26

Dear Dr. Brown — You who have written so many kind letters
to the above address about my father and about his books must
let my father's daughter try and tell you all the pleasure your
book [3] has given there.

Coming back from Paris the other day and going my rounds
over the house, I thought I saw a new face smiling freshly down
from among all the old and seedy ones on Papa's book-shelf. And
when I pulled it out I found it was Dr. John Brown I was saying
how d'ye do to, whose handwriting we know so well.

I thought it would be very easy when I began my note to tell
you how delightful I have found that handwriting in print, and
how it seems to say all the things one has been looking about for,
and to say them so charmingly and truthfully that it is the greatest
pleasure to listen, only now I begin to feel rather foolish and
inclined to stammer, and don't quite know how to go on. But
though I stop now talking, it is not that I am going to leave off
reading I assure you, and the still fresh cover is rapidly getting
shabby, as it travels about after me up and down stairs.

We are all very cheerful and thankful to be at home and together
again. Papa finished his No. last night about 2 1/2 o'clock. To-day
we have been out on our monthly lark, and he felt so fresh and
eager for work that the lark was cut rather short so that he might
rush into *March*, [4] at least a couple of pages before dinner. Don't
you think that looks as if he was much better than he has been
for a very long, weary time? Except a one-day attack on Xmas
day he has not been ill for nearly six weeks. One doesn't like to

[3] *Horæ Subsecivæ. Locke and Sydenham, with Other Occasional Papers*
(1858).
[4] Number XVII, chapters 64–67.

boast about it yet, one can only hope and long for things to have taken a better turn. You see I write just as if I knew you, but I haven't read your books and heard Papa talk about Edinburgh, without learning to count you as a friend.

Please say how d'ye do to Mrs. Brown and to Jock for us, and believe me, very truly yours,

Anne Thackeray.

1391.   TO MRS. CARMICHAEL-SMYTH
FEBRUARY 1859 [5]

Hitherto unpublished.

I am in for a second bout of Thompson — an accident rendered the first inefficacious, & left almost all the ground to be gone over again. But the pain is very momentary & trifling, I sleep quite well, and except that in the recumbent posture I can't think very brilliantly I actually enjoy the quiet & leisure, the visits of the girls, the look out of the cheerful ⟨win⟩dow & so on. I would write with a pen but that it blots my ⟨sheet⟩s and counterpane. I knock off arrears of letters. Providence w^h poor Minny impugns is very tolerably kind to me. She didn't seem to be aware that she had used such rebellious expressions when I took her to task. I asked her why the natural laws were to be interrupted in my particular case? Did Heaven send the little boys out of the shop to knock you down and give you 100 days of pain, & years of lameness? Was it specially concerned in punishing chastising trying blessing, smashing saving those Jews, who were under the tower of Siloam when it fell? [6] A brick may have knocked a just man's brains out: and a beam fallen so as to protect a scoundrel who happened to be standing under. The bricks and beams fell according to the laws w^h regulate bricks in tumbling — So with our diseases, we die because we are born; we decay because we grow. I have a right to say O Father give me submission to bear cheerfully (if possible)

[5] This letter was written shortly after February 19, 1859.
[6] See *St. Luke*, 13, 4–5.

& patiently my sufferings but I cant request any special change in my behalf from the ordinary processes, or see any special Divine *animus* superintending my illnesses or wellnesses. Those people seem to me presumptuous who are forever dragging the Awful Divinity into a participation with their private concerns. In health, disease, birth, life, death, here, hereafter, I am His subject & creature He lifts me up and sets me down certainly — so He orders my beard to grow. Yonder on my table in the next room is a number of the Earthen Vessel — Brother Jones writes of Brother Brown how preciously he has been dealt with. Brown ⟨has bee⟩n blessed by an illness: he has had the blessing of getting better; he has relap⟨ses, p⟩ains and finally has the blessing of being called out of the world altogether. I dont differ with Brown essentially — only in the compliments as it were w^h he thinks it proper to be for ever paying. I am well. Amen. I am ill. Amen. I die Amen always. I can't say that having a tooth out is a blessing or a punishment for my sins — I say it's having a tooth out.

Bout no 2 is over, and Im sorry to say has done me the smallest amount of good. I wish I had had the heroic remedy applied: w^h must come sooner or later. a little touch of the knife w^h is hardly felt and appears to be the only effectual treatment in my case. There's little or no risk in it. But Thompson who would apply it without hesitation in an ordinary case, is afraid to employ it upon such a well-known public character. In his book[7] there is an amusing account of old Sir Everard Horne, applying the instrument more than 2000 and caustic more than 500 times to one poor gentle ⟨. . .⟩[8] old Pillans who is not rich has sent them 200£, and their brother who is poor 100£ besides being security for the pomes! And think of Charles insisting upon these poor people

[7] Thompson's *Pathology and Treatment of the Stricture of the Urethra* (1854) was in Thackeray's library at the time of his death (*Catalogues*, ed. Stonehouse, p. 154). See Appendix XXVIII.

[8] About thirty-five words have here been cut away from the letter. The passage appears to have concerned the financial troubles that beset the Corkrans (see below, No. 1417, note 56), for Mrs. Corkran was the adopted daughter of Professor Pillans (1778–1864), a noted teacher of the classics at the University of Edinburgh.

going to the Marquis del Riso's lectures who charges them 3, 4, 5, I dont know what guineas for their attendance. I havent seen him since I gave him the 400 — I fear it has not proved sufft.[9] I think Mary gave two 20's or two 30£ for poor Isabella — She may have those too ere long. And he'll take it. And lucky it is that the money comes in so plentifully. Have you got your surgeons bill? You know thats my affair. I shall receive 600£ this month: & have a good little lump in hand besides — And 8500 in the next 2 years from Smith & Elder [10] — prodigious! — besides 800 or 900 of income & no rent. One talks of stopping, but how

[9] For Colonel Carmichael's financial problems, see above, No. 1351.

[10] Early in 1859 George Smith had determined to establish a new magazine. Each number was to contain an installment of a novel by Thackeray and a variety of other good reading. The price was to be one shilling, which the public was accustomed to pay for the monthly parts of Thackeray's novels alone. These details fixed, Smith gave Thackeray the following memorandum, saying " 'I wonder whether you will consider it, or will at once consign it to your wastepaper-basket!' "

"Smith, Elder, & Co. have it in contemplation to commence the publication of a Monthly Magazine on January 1st, 1860. They are desirous of inducing Mr. Thackeray to contribute to their periodical, and they make the following proposal to Mr. Thackeray:

"1. That he shall write either one or two novels of the ordinary size for publication in the Magazine — one-twelfth portion of each novel (estimated to be about equal to one number of a serial) to appear in each number of the Magazine.

"2. That Mr. Thackeray shall assign to Smith, Elder, & Co. the right to publish the novels in their Magazine and in a separate form afterwards, and to all sums to be received for the work from American and Continental Publishers.

"3. That Smith, Elder, & Co. shall pay Mr. Thackeray 350£. each month.

"4. That the profits of all editions of the novels published at a lower price than the first edition shall be equally divided between Mr. Thackeray and Smith, Elder, & Co.

"65 Cornhill: February 19th, 1859."

"Thackeray read the slip carefully," Smith writes, "and, with characteristic absence of guile, allowed me to see that he regarded the terms as phenomenal. When he had finished reading the paper, he said with a droll smile: 'I am not going to put such a document as this into my wastepaper-basket.' " Shortly afterward he accepted Smith's proposal. (*George Smith, A Memoir*, pp. 106–108)

stop with such fees? Went to see Mrs Dickens yesterday. The row appears to be [about] not the actress, but the sister in law — nothing against Miss H [11]— except that she is the cleverer & better woman of the two, has got the affections of the children & the father — thank God for having a home where there is nothing but sunshine! the Pillans benefaction is a secret — mind — dont allude to it in writing to M^rs ⟨C.⟩ C.[12] The Yates trial is abandoned and he is going to issue a pamphlet [13] doubtless full of compliments to me — w^h I hope I shant have to an⟨swer . . .⟩ [14]

[11] Miss Georgina Hogarth. See above, No. 1357.

[12] Mrs. Charles Carmichael.

[13] For some time after December 5 Yates's legal proceedings moved slowly, but he continued to snipe at Thackeray in the "Lounger" column of *The Illustrated Times*. His rancorous parody of Thackeray's "Ballad of Bouillabaisse" in the issue of January 29 very nearly resulted, indeed, in the resignation of a large part of the magazine's staff. (Vizetelly, *Glances Back through Seventy Years*, II, 14–15) On the same day Charles Lever, in London on one of his periodical visits, wrote to his wife and daughter: "The Dickens, Yates & Thackeray row comes on at the Law Courts on Wednesday — I heard that they were most anxious to summon me as a witness to prove that when imitated by Thackeray in his prize Novelists — I did not feel any sense of anger — or wounded pride — in fact, the object being — to show that Thacker[a]y — least of all men should protest again[st] any quizzing personality." (Rolfe, *Huntington Library Bulletin*, Number 10, p. 167) At the last moment, however, Yates found it necessary to abandon his suit, for "the Committee pleaded virtually that the whole property of the Club was absolutely vested in trustees, the only persons responsible on its behalf to anybody for anything; that the secretary was a name, and the Committee were a name; that nobody but the trustees had legally incurred, or could legally incur, any responsibility arising out of what had been done to me" (*Recollections and Experiences*, II, 30). His only remedy against the trustees was an action in Chancery, the expenses of which were beyond his means. On March 11 he wrote to a friend (in an unpublished letter owned by Mr. Carlebach): "By a series of Jew-lawyer-like tricks, unprecedented I should hope, the Committee of the Garrick have got the best of me in my legal proceedings, and my only resource . . . has been the publication of a pamphlet, a copy of which I have sent you.

"I trust the facts there set forth, in a temperate, gentlemanly, and withal unvarnished manner will have due weight." This pamphlet was, of course, *Mr. Thackeray, Mr. Yates, and the Garrick Club*.

[14] The final lines of this letter have been cut away.

1392.   TO MR. LEEMING
                         2 MARCH 1859

Hitherto unpublished.

                                     36 Onslow Sq.ʳ S. W.
                                          March 2. 1859
Sir

I have just found your note. I presume Mͬˢ Leeming's maiden
name was Thackeray, of whom there are many in the North, and
doubtless we all come from the same stock. My progenitors [15] are

              * Elias Thackeray .—. buried in Yorkshire
                   Thomas Thackeray D D. xɪ760

7 daughters & 7 sons of whom Wͫ Makepeace Thackeray Esqᵉ
† 1814 7 daughters & sons one being Richmond Thackeray †
1815 who was father of Your most obdt Servᵗ W M Thackeray
b. 1811.

* Elias Thackeray & an epitaph commemorating him are to be
found in I forget whose history of Yorkshire.

1393.   TO FREDERIC CHAPMAN
                         MARCH 1859 [16]

Address: F. Chapman Esqᵉ. Hitherto unpublished.

Dear Chapman

If you have a copy of the Yates pamphlet wont you lend it to
                         Yours in bed
                         W M T.

Send by messenger if you can.

[15] See *Genealogy*. The Thackerays were a clan of Yorkshire farmers, and
Elias, who went to Cambridge and held the living of Hawkshurst in Yorkshire, was the first member of the family to distinguish himself. But he was
the uncle, not the father, of Thomas Thackeray, who was descended from
Elias's farmer brother Timothy. See *Biographical Introductions*, XIII, xxxvi.
[16] Yates's pamphlet was issued shortly before March 11. See above, note 13.

1394.   # TO CHARLES KINGSLEY
12 MARCH 1859

Hitherto unpublished.

March 12.

36 O. S.

My dear Kingsley

Thank you for your letter. I have no doubt in my own mind that I was right to be indignant in the matter, and to call the offender before the Club, w^h is a social Institution quite unlike other clubs, and where men have been in the habit of talking quite freely to one another (in a little room not 15 feet square) for this 1/4 of a century or more. If the penny-a-liner is to come in to this sanctum, and publish his comments upon the conversation there held and the people he meets there, it is all over with the comfort and friendliness of our Society. I never exchanged a word except of kindness with this Mr Yates until the appearance of this article against me. What pains me most is that Dickens should have been his adviser: and next that I should have had to lay a heavy hand on a young man who, I take it, has been cruelly punished by the issue of the affair,[17] and I believe is hardly aware of the nature

---

[17] Thackeray can hardly have realized quite how severe Yates's ordeal was. It is described in the following letter (which I transcribe from the unpublished original in the Berg Collection of the New York Public Library) sent by Yates to Herman Merivale on May 25, 1889, when the latter was collecting material for his *Thackeray*:

"I am much obliged by the kind feeling which has prompted you to write the letter wh. I have just received. Most certainly do I desire that the episode of my controversy with Thackeray sh^d not be 'passed over', but rather entered into with as much detail as you can give to it. To enable you to do this, I send you, not merely the *World* article of last week, which you ask for, but a copy of my *Reminiscences*, in which, at p. 232, you will find the whole story, honestly, fairly, and unemotionally narrated.

"Please bear in mind, first, the circumstances under which the offending little article was written. While the press waited, to supply 'short copy', at a desk in a printing office, with the master-printer at my elbow, urging me on, slip by slip being carried off to the compositors, as it was written. Think that I was then only 27 years old, with wife & three children, supplementing

of his own offence, and doesnt even now understand that a gentleman should resent the monstrous insult w^h he volunteered. Scores
of the pennyaline fraternity have written on his side, and a great
number of them are agreed that it's the description of *my nose* w^h
makes me so furious — Not one of them seems to understand that
to be accused of hypocrisy of base motives for public & private

---

a small Post Office salary by journalistic labour, sitting down at my desk, three
or four nights a week, after my day's official grind, sitting down at 8 pm. &
steadily writing till midnight. Remember what the social degradation inflicted
upon me at Thackeray's instance, not the fury of a moment but deliberately
insisted on through six weeks, meant to an unknown man, who had not made
any mark then, but was merely pulling the devil by the tail, in a struggle for
bread. Think of being 'expelled' from a club, as tho' one had been a card-
sharper, a cheat, a thief, a braggart about women! 'He was expelled from
the Garrick': for 30 years that has been the cry, no one caring to ask why
or wherefore, the kindest among the speakers allowing that it must have
been for printing revelations of what I had heard in the club circle! It has
been thrown in my teeth by five hundred drunken leprous ruffians in the rags
for which they wrote: it has been always brought forward if any friend knowing
the real state of affairs ventured to nominate me for any respectable *cenacle*:
and it is only within the last six weeks that my selection for the Carlton, over
the heads of 2000 waiting candidates, has relieved me from this frightful
opprobrium, this shameful stigma which I have borne for 30 years, and
enabled me to breathe freely, & to walk with my head erect, in the regions
of Clubland. Then, taking the article on the ground of its 'personality', the
huge stone with which I was smashed to earth, compare it not merely with
W M T's own early writings, but with the articles of now-a-days. In my
wretched nonsense, there is no single reference to Thackeray's home-life, no
mention of his Club, no 'gossip' of any kind, no hint — God forbid! — at his
domestic trouble, no word of anything that was not thoroughly patent & well
known at the time. Then, look at the persistent malignity with which I was
hunted down! all offer of compromise rejected, nothing but bitter insatiable
revenge. I am, by constitution & fibre, a strong man, & I 'lived it down': but
in those days I too was sensitive, & it nearly broke me down: what was suffered by my wife and my mother, I shall never forget.

"Throughout all these 30 years, Thackeray, as author, has had no more
devoted worshipper: even now, I w^d go through a stiff examination paper, with
innumerable quotations from his works: do your paper without any reading
Vanity Fair, Pendennis, The Newcomes: & constantly dipping into the *Miscellanies* & the Ballads. But for Thackeray, the man, I shall think, & say, to my
dying day, that his treatment of me was one of the wickedest, cruellest, & most
damnable acts of tyranny, ever perpetrated.

Always yours
Edmund Yates."

conduct & so forth — are the points w^h make me angry — and I
look for more press libels immediately showing how I have ruth-
lessly persecuted an excellent & harmless young man, and how
Dickens has exhausted every possible means to make peace —
Dickens who dictated Yates's letters to me, who made him submit
to the Committee, then call a general meeting, & then go to law.
Well. I know we are in a minority, and I know we are right — and
I am very glad you think so.   et voila.

Yours ever
W M Thackeray.

1395.   TO WILLIAM DUER ROBINSON
                29 MARCH 1859

Hitherto unpublished.

March 29.

My dear W D. I got your letter this morning. I wrote how
many pages do you think in reply? 8 — I have just torn those 8
pages into 164 pieces — because they related to the Yates Thackeray row, and because I think (though now nothing prevents me
from speaking) that the more dignified and I may say sweller
course is to hold my tongue, and let the pennyaliners fire away
their abuse till the subject dies out. Somebody at last has said
something like the truth about the business in a paper w^h I send
to you, & my dear good Baxters, & to Fields at Boston, & Mac-
michael at Philadelphia — But the paper was written without any
previous knowledge of mine, and I never saw it until yesterday —
Well, I wish I was coming to N. Y. but you see at one period of
my story I was so ill and dawdled so that the American part w^h
was to have been in 12 numbers now has dwindled to 6 — the con-
struction the story must perforce be altered, and a study of it
sur les lieux is impossible. Besides I should have got out of my
depth in the military details and must describe them in quite a
difft way to that w^h I had first intended.

Then, for next year, I am engaged to write a story [18] in 16 numbers for w. I am to receive — well, more than I have ever received yet by 100£ a number. Think of that! and then after a little pause another story. I may want to give up novel-writing but how refuse when I am paid such prodigious sums? Why didnt they buy me at 30, not the tired old horse at 50?

I have done pretty well this last year — am much better I think in health — have had my water-works retinkered and the cisterns & pipes put into good working order, and am very happy with my family thank God: and always remember afftly my dear old W. D — O I should like to come over & see you all that I should!

Come. I'll pay another shilling for this — I can afford it. I made 5000£ last year and spent only half I wish you'd come over. I have 300 bottles of '41, & 48 claret paid for. Shall I go on with another [19]

1396.   TO WILLIAM BRADFORD REED
                      2 APRIL 1859

My text is taken from Reed's *Haud Immemor*, p. 25.

Maurigy's Hotel, 1 Regent Street, Waterloo Place,
April 2, 1859.

My Dear Reed:

This is the best place for you, I think. Two Bishops already in the house. Country gentlefolks and American envoys especially affect it. Mr. Maurigy says you may come for a day at the rate of ten guineas a week, with rooms very clean and nice, which I have just gone over, and go away at the day's end, if you disapprove.

The enclosed note is about the Athenæum, where you may like

[18] *Philip*, the writing of which Thackeray deferred until after the publication of *Lovel the Widower* and *The Four Georges*. As it was finally published, the novel required twenty numbers. It appeared in *The Cornhill Magazine* from January, 1861, to August, 1862.

[19] This letter, which was apparently not sent, breaks off here.

to look in. I wrote to Lord Stanhope,[20] who is on the committee, to put you up.

I won't bore you by asking you to dinner till we see how matters are, as of course you will consort with bigger wigs [21] than yours, always,

W. M. Thackeray.

1397.   TO ?
2 APRIL 1859

Hitherto unpublished.

36 Onslow Sq. S. W.
April 2.

Dear Sir

Many thanks for the trouble you take. My death of Wolfe is not in print yet,[22] and I would gladly read any documents regarding Canada and Wolfe w.h might help me to give one or two touches of reality to the little picture. If your friend will part with his papers I will take good care of them.

The book-post has not yet brought me the volumes w.h you

[20] Thackeray's friend Lord Mahon, who had become fifth Earl Stanhope in 1855.

[21] "No 'bigger wigs' came between us," Reed writes (*Haud Immemor*, pp. 25–26). "During my fortnight in London — for I was hastening home after two years' absence — we saw him nearly every day. He came regularly to our quarters, went with me to the Athenæum — that spot of brilliant association — where he pointed out the eminent men of whom I had heard and read; and then he would go to his working-table in the Club Library, and write for the 'Cornhill', to which he said he had sold himself to slavery for two years. He would carry my son, a young man just of age, off with him to see the London world in odd 'haunts' I dined with him twice. once at his modest house No. 36 Onslow Square, where we had the great pleasure of seeing his daughters; and once at Greenwich, at a bachelor's dinner.... I left London on the 30th April, 1859. Mr. and Miss Thackeray were at the Euston Square station to say farewell. He took my son aside, and to his infinite confusion handed him a little *cadeau*. ... We parted with a great deal of kindness, please God, and friendly talk of a future meeting."

[22] It occurs in chapter 74 of *The Virginians*, part of number XIX (chapters 72 to 75) for May.

have confided to it. The order of Cincinnati was a failure in America & in the pictures of many of the republican leaders they appear with that little decoration.

Very faithfully yours
W. M. Thackeray

1398.   TO DR. JOHN BROWN
3-4 APRIL 1859

My text is taken from *Letters of Dr. John Brown*, p. 331.

April 3 and 4.

My Dear J. B. — There is something artless in the accents of the enclosed youth [23] which inclines my heart towards him. Will you and Madam send him a line and see him, and if he is not a humbug, lend him this bit of paper. If he is not a fit subject, burn the cheque, please. I hope you are both quite well and jolly. . . .

Heard Dean Milman ordering *Horæ Subsecivæ* at the Athenæum the other day. A publisher, who was it? in Edinburgh wrote me some weeks back asking me to review it in the *Quarterly*, but I couldn't make such a good review of it as some person long familiar with Edinburgh Society; and I can't write to ask a favour, but if ever I lay my eyes upon Elwin I will speak of the matter, — not of my doing it, but his getting some fit man.

I send my very best regards to Madam and the children, and am yours, my dear Brown, as always,

W. M. Thackeray.

[23] The enclosure is not described in *Dr. John Brown*.

1399.   TO WILLIAM HEPWORTH DIXON
20 APRIL 1859

Hitherto unpublished. Endorsed: April 20, 1859.

Dear Dixon

We have a dinner [24] on the 23 here [*here a hand is sketched pointing to the letterhead of the Garrick Club, above*], and my name has been down ever so long. Otherwise I should have gladly accepted your hospitality at Our Club.[25]

Yours ever
W M Thackeray.

1400.   TO FRANCIS ST. JOHN THACKERAY
6 MAY 1859 [26]

My text is taken from Francis Thackeray, *Temple Bar*, July, 1893, p. 376.

May 6.

My dear St. John,

I thought all that hankering about Brompton meant something. I congratulate you with all my heart, and promise you my benediction and a teapot. What can I say more, but that I am yours and your wife's,

Affectionately always,
W. M. Thackeray.

Am just out of bed, having been ill. Am going to work again

[24] The annual Shakespeare dinner on St. George's Day.

[25] A dinner club for literary men which was founded by Douglas Jerrold and continued to flourish for some time after his death. It met every Saturday evening from November to May on an upper floor of Clunn's Hotel, next door to Evans's Hotel, in the north-west corner of Covent Garden. Jeaffreson (*Book of Recollections*, I, 216–245) describes "Our Club" in detail and gives a list of its members when Thackeray joined it in November, 1861. See also Masson's *Memories of London in the Forties*, pp. 211–256.

[26] Francis Thackeray (*Temple Bar*, 1893, p. 376) writes that he received this note in 1859, shortly after he was engaged to be married. His marriage to Louisa Katharine Irvine took place on August 10, 1860 (*Memorials*, p. 496).

immediately. Too busy to come to Oxford to see you billing and cooing.

1401.   TO ?
                        14 MAY 1859

Hitherto unpublished.

                              36 Onslow Sqʳ May 14. 1859.
                                    S. W.
Sir

My General was killed ²⁷ when your letter came upon the authority too of a bystander who professed to have seen him wounded, carried to the rear, and dying.

But I thank you for thinking of helping me in the matter — and for the token of your kindness & good will.

                    Your obliged faithful Servᵗ
                              W M Thackeray.

1402.   TO MRS. THERESA HATCH
                        15 MAY 1859

Hitherto unpublished.

                              36 Onslow Sqᵉ S. W.
                              May 15, 1859.

Dear Madam

I have been ill and very busy, or I should sooner have acknowledged your note.²⁸ I am very thankful to have such testimonies

²⁷ See above, No. 1397.
²⁸ Mrs. Hatch's letter, the original of which is owned by Mr. Carlebach, reads as follows: "The intense delight caused by the perusal of each successive book of yours & more especially by that of the Virginians has been raised this morning to such a height by the reading of this that I cannot help laying before you a humble tribute of gratitude & esteem, not to the genius only, but to the man, by whose tenderness & pathos all our best feelings are roused & we are forced to own the power & sometimes, nay often to regret the perspicacity which reads the bad side of our characters with as much ease as the good, who portrays both with equal fidelity & truth making us at one moment ashamed & at another proud to be called 'women'.

"But in the number before me you have more especially spoken to my

of good will as your letter contains, and am occupied this early Sunday morning in answering no less than four w̱ʰ the last number of my story ²⁹ has brought me. I have been called misanthrope and cynic so long and so often, that I can't help being pleased when people find out that my heart is not altogether stone. The truth is I think in art as in life that Sentiment should be most carefully and sacredly used: and mistrust the man who is always crying in his books or in his daily dealings. That I can give my readers comfort or pleasure is a sincere pleasure and comfort to me: and the thought of being able sometimes to do so, is one of the most precious rewards w̱ʰ my profession brings me. I am glad that you & Theo are both out of your troubles, and am yours dear Madam very faithfully W M Thackeray

1403. TO MRS. DICK
27? MAY 1859 ³⁰

Hitherto unpublished.

36 O S. S. W
Saturday.

My dear Mʳˢ Dick. I am trying to reconstruct that dinner for Friday. June 3. at 7.45. Do you & John please be disengaged and come to

Yours always
W M Thackeray.

_____

feelings in the beautiful & touching description of poor Theo's trial, which by its truthfulness brought before me a trouble of my own so similar that I was forced involuntarily to exclaim to my husband 'He might have known us some years ago.' This I think is a sufficient proof of the masterly way in which you have depicted the emotions of such a time of misery. Men feel equally your power but are not perhaps so willing to own it.

"Pray excuse the liberty I have taken in thus addressing you & accept my thanks for the many delightful hours you have allowed me to spend in your society. May I & all your readers often have the opportunity of looking forward with anxiety & longing for your welcome monthly visit."

²⁹ XIX for May, chapters 72 to 75. Theo's ordeal is described in chapter 75.

³⁰ During the years Thackeray lived at Onslow Square, June 3 fell on Friday only in 1859. This note was probably written the previous Saturday, May 27.

1404.   TO MRS. BLACKWOOD
                           28 MAY 1859

My text is taken from Sotheby's catalogue of November 10, 1931.

                                    Onslow Square, May 28,
Madam,

On Friday 3 June can you and Monsieur Blackwood come and
dine if you please with W. M. T. & Co.

O what a narrow escape I have had this month

        Twice ill. 4 days each time. obliged to
            come out without my plates.[31]

                What a national calamity!
                    only down at 6
                        yesterday
                           ev'g.
                        Hip Hip
                        Hurray

1405.   TO MISS COLE
                           28 MAY 1859 [32]

Reproduced in facsimile in *The Orphan of Pimlico*, "Gore House." *Endorsed:*
Miss Cole.

                                    36 Onslow Sq. S W.
                                    Saturday. 28 May.

Mr Thackeray presents his compliments to the Council, Secretary,
Treasurer, and Members of the Trap club,[33] and, in reply to their
obliging invitation, has the honor of saying that he most heartily
wishes they may catch him.

[31] See number XIX of *The Virginians*, chapters 76 to 79.
[32] During the years Thackeray lived at Onslow Square, May 28 fell on a
Saturday only in 1859.
[33] "Trap and ball have been croqueted away," writes Lady Ritchie in *The
Orphan of Pimlico*, "and croquet is in turn rolling off disconsolate, since certain fine summer afternoons a great many years ago, when some young people
used to play at their innocent games, and sit under the trees in the gardens of
Gore House. On one occasion the Miss Coles, the owners of the trap, sent a
formal invitation, to which came an answer."

1406.   **TO CHARLES LEVER**
1859 [34]

Hitherto unpublished.

36 Onslow Sq[r] S. W. Tuesday

My dear L.

Can you send us your Adventure out of hand *and immediately?* I suppose we may have the authors name? If you can let us have the article — 10 pages — by the 8th or so, You may draw next day on Smith & Elder for 50£.

I am puzzled about your affair, being on quite friendly terms with the Chapmans, and not liking to act privily with one of their writers.

Send us the paper, and believe me

Always yours
W M T.

[34] This letter was presumably written a short time before No. 1407.

1407.   TO CHARLES LEVER
                27 JUNE 1859

Hitherto unpublished.

36 Onslow Sq.ʳ S. W.
June 27. 1859.

My dear Lever

You ought to have had a letter 2 days at least sooner. But — O that number! [35] It was only done, after a fearful struggle, on Saturday night.

I have heard from Smith & Elder who are quite willing to treat with you, but are afraid that your terms may be too high. They don't know what they are, nor does your humble Servant.

And Bradbury & Evans dined with me on Friday and *they* also are willing to treat. You dont know perhaps that I leave them, (we remain perfect good friends) and go over to Smith & Elder.

But B & E having room for a monthly periodical might be your best market. Cant you run over and treat yourself personally? Or send me your terms and I will go to one or other. Smith I must tell you is a splendid fellow and a clever Tradesman, as everyone tells me: indeed I have had every reason to be satisfied with both firms.

Yours laconically but sincerely
W M Thackeray.

I saw Fred Chapman just now. I didn't say a word about your letter to me of course.

[35] XXI for July, chapters 80 to 83.

1408. TO JOHN ELLIOT JR.[36]
28 JUNE 1859

Address: John Elliot Esq⁹ J͟r | Temple. *Postmark:* LONDON JU 28 59.
Published by Mr. Wilson, *Boston Transcript,* July 31, 1920.

36 Onslow Sq⁹ S. W.

June 28 —

—There is at the present moment, somewhere in the West
End of London, a young barrister, who is highly connected,
but in a dreadful dilemma owing to his recent marriage.

My dear J. E.

This letter, so far as the printed extract, was begun who knows
how many days ago? — Whilst you were in the bliss of your
honeymoon.

The delicate subject of early and imprudent marriages is touched
also in the ensuing number of a periodical w͟h you read.[37] I made
such a marriage myself. My means being

8 guineas a week (secured on a newspaper w͟h failed 6 months
after.) My wifes income 50£ a year promised by her mother,
and paid for 2 quarters, since w͟h (1837) I have received exactly
10£ on account.

And with this fortune, I have done so well, that, you see, I am
not a fair judge of early marriages, but always look upon them,
and upon imprudent young people *qui s'aiment* with a partial eye.

In the first 6 months, *I saved money.*

I hope J. E may do likewise; and as to the struggles and ups
and downs of life that are before him, that he may bear them with
a cheerful heart. How to set to work? How to confront the baker
and the butcher with unconcerned face? How to pay that Doctor's
fees at that period when he must be called in? These, and a hundred other such questions, you will have to solve. As I think of
my own past, and what happened, I say Laus Deo with a very

---

[36] Elliot was admitted to the bar on January 26, 1855, and went on the
Oxford Circuit, Worcester and Gloucester Sessions. He had chambers at 11
Crown Office Row. (*Law List,* 1858)

[37] Thackeray is referring to chapter 81 of *The Virginians,* "Res Angusta
Domi," which formed part of the number for July.

humble grateful heart. May your voyage end prosperously too, I sincerely hope and — I am going to say, pray, — for I cant see a friend and his young wife setting forth on a journey w^h I have made myself, and in w^h I have undergone disaster, grief, and immense joys and consolations, without the most serious thoughts and a prayer to God Almighty for his welfare.

I hope we shall see Mrs Elliot when you come to town (the only address on your letter was IVORY and I dont know where that is & so write to the Temple) and am yours my dear Elliot

Very sincerely always
W M Thackeray.

1409.   TO LADY MOLESWORTH
24 JULY 1859

Hitherto unpublished.

Sunday
36 Onslow Sq^r

My dear Lady Molesworth

I have been away with my books at a romantic village (Gravesend by name) and only find your kind note upon my return.

On the 22 August D. V. we shall come to pay our visit. I say D. V. for I hope D will be V that my last (double) number [38] will be done by the 22, and the writer of the Virginians a free man. the present number [39] isn't done yet I grieve to say and O dear me it is the 24th! Never mind let us work hard and hope for the best. I wont offer ourselves for a fortnight as you hospitably propose for we have relations whom we must go to and I MUST go and drink some water thats certain.

But before that I will take a little of your wine if you please and am

Always yours very faithfully
W M Thackeray.

[38] *The Virginians* did not conclude with a double number. Part XXIII for September, chapters 87 to 90, appeared on August 31; and part XXIV for October, chapters 91 and 92, appeared on October 1 (*Spectator*, 1859, pp. 892 and 1012).

[39] XXII for August, chapters 84 to 86.

1410.   TO THOMAS CARLYLE
                          3 AUGUST 1859 [40]

                                         August 3. 36 O. Sq^{re}

Dear Carlyle

Perhaps this small present may be useful to you — It is the only
steel-pen with w^h I could ever write comfortably, and if it suits
your hand as it does mine, why it will save you much pen-knife
work and may make your life easier

                          Yours ever (just on the point of
                                    starting somewhither)
                          W M T.

It writes better the 2^d day & following than the 1st This I'm
writing with is a week I sh^d think in use. Its much best on a smooth
paper. Note the number Gillotts 353.

1411.   TO THE REV. WILLIAM BROOKFIELD
                      3? AUGUST 1859 [41]

Hitherto unpublished.

       What do you think, most hard-to-please of men,
       Of William Mitchell's patent broad-nibbed pen?
       I've bought a box — three shillings for the gross —
       At Mitchell's Stationer's in Charing Cross.
       Try these: and if you like the pens, I'll trouble you
       To write to 36. O. Square. S. W.
       Where Somebody is found, who'll gladly spend
       Three Bob to be of sarvice to a friend.

    PS.   I think they seem to suit better for the upright, than the
slantingdicular writing.[42]

P.S. 2. A gentleman has just passed my table with a sweet smile
on his face, and in his hand the last number of THE V.RG.N..NS

    [40] Thackeray's reference to *The Virginians* in the companion note to Brook-
field which follows determines the year in which this note was written.
    [41] It seems likely that this note was written at the same time as the preceding
note to Carlyle.
    [42] This sentence is written in Thackeray's slanting hand, the rest of the
letter is in his upright hand.

[For fragments of a letter to Kate Perry 4 August, 1859, see letter 55, Appendix XXVI.]

1412.   TO ANNE AND HARRIET THACKERAY
23 AUGUST 1859

Hitherto unpublished.

XXXVI. O.S. S.W.
XXIII. VIII. MCCCCCCCCLXIX [43]

Once more I'm out again, and going about again, should be sorry to have such another bad bout again. Only think of that unlucky Charles whom I told to stop at Haden's on his way saying that he rang 3 times & couldn't get in. Hence I wasted 6 hours. The sickness came on the medicine wouldnt stay in my stomach — and I'm only better this morning. Also. The brandy w^h Cole gave me & w^h I had 1 glass had leaked to a glass & a half: he says 'some one must have another key to the cupboard; also the once-round ties about w^h I made a hubbub have come back into residence in my drawers. I'm afraid the poor fellow is a roguypoguy. But then the poor fellow took an excursion train 5/ there & back and only spent 8^d for his dinner.

Nothing has happened except that I have a letter from an anonymous gentleman in Germany who says that unless I can help him to something to do, he shall shoot himself on the night of the 8th September next in St James's Park! — a German evidently, but writing excellent English.

The news with Smith & Elder is this.[44] For the new Magazine we are going to turn the Comedy into a story in 6 numbers to be

[43] A mistake, of course, for 1859.

[44] Smith had for some time tried without success to find a suitable editor for his new magazine, when it at length occurred to him that Thackeray might be willing to accept the post. Thackeray was engaged at £1,000 a year, and after the immense success of the first number (see below, No. 1432), his salary was doubled. Laden with this new burden, Thackeray thought it unwise to begin his long novel immediately, and consequently set about turning *The Wolves and the Lamb* into *Lovel the Widower*. (*George Smith*, pp. 108 and 114)

followed by the 4 Georges in 4 numbers — and not begin the long story until July. Haden strongly recommends me to try Harrogate or Aix les Bains — And Im at a loss between the 2. It will be late for the latter when my next number is done.

And tell Mʳˢ Southern with my compliments that I hope the married couple will go out of my room tomorrow as we shall scarcely be comfortable three in a bed.

And give Sir Wᵐ 45 an old man's blessing for taking care of my daughters — I shan't make any promises about coming down *à cause*: but I hope tomorrow will be the happy day & shall have spent 6 days in London, on only the first of wʰ any work was done. Perhaps it mayn't be tomorrow after all. There are still 12 pages to do.

And so farewell my sweet young creatures says

Your respectable père
W M T.

Of course give the poor boys anything you like.

1413. TO GEORGE SMITH
7 SEPTEMBER 1859

My text is taken from a facsimile in Sir Leslie Stephen's terminal essay, "The Writings of W. M. Thackeray", in the "De Luxe" edition of Thackeray's *Works*, XXVI (1886), after p. 360.

Pavilion. Folkestone
Wednesday. 7 Sepʳ

My dear Smith

I only finished my number 46 at 2 o'clock this mᵍ and now D. V. propose to do nothing till the end of the month. I will be in London D.V. on Monday mᵍ October 3. If you want me on Saturday 1, a letter will find me at Bordeaux Poste Restante.

Sir H. Rawlinson has promised me some short papers: and

---

45 Lieutenant-Colonel Sir William Plunkett de Bathe (1793–1870), third Baronet, a Garrick Club crony of Thackeray's.

46 XXIV.

Charles Dunn one or two upon the Old Actors and Talma and Mars during the Army of Occupation in France. Hannay might do a set of Salt-water heroes. Collingwood. Van Tromp. Jean Bart, a Buccaneer or so. If he will do them as well as that noble paper in the Quarterly, and I think he will for an old friend. As I think of the editing business I like it. But the Magazine must bear my *cachet* you see and be a man of the world Magazine, a little cut of Temple Bar, or Charles I on the outside? We will have further talk October 3. I am surprised I have finished the Virginians so well — O what a load is off my mind!

Never mind, we will lay another on soon.

Always yours,
W M Thackeray.

G. Smith Esq^e

1414.   TO MRS. PROCTER
                    10 SEPTEMBER 1859 [47]

Hitherto unpublished. My text is taken from a transcript given Lady Ritchie by George Murray Smith.

Saturday.

My dear Mrs Procter,

The dinner is ON again. Three men accepted yesterday, one very handsome, one very interesting, two like the Calenders in the Arabian Nights with one eye apiece [48] (we will make them narrate their adventures) and at dinner last night I met little Fields and his wife who has never actually been to Greenwich.[49]

[47] It appears from Fields's story below that this letter was written on September 10, the Saturday intervening between Thackeray's completion of *The Virginians* on September 7 and his departure for the continent about September 15.

[48] See "The History of the Three Calendars".

[49] "I happened to be one of a large company," writes Fields (*Yesterdays with Authors*, pp. 17–18), "whom [Thackeray] had invited to a six-o'clock dinner at Greenwich one summer afternoon, several years ago. We were all to go down from London, assemble in a particular room at the hotel, where he

Now please let me withdraw my letter of yesterday, and if my Contributor [50] will come too she will give great pleasure to my other Contributor and to,

Yours always,
W. M. Thackeray.

1415. TO ALFRED TENNYSON
? SEPTEMBER–16 OCTOBER 1859 [51]

My text is taken from the second Baron Tennyson's *Alfred Lord Tennyson* (London, 1897), I, 444–446.

Folkestone, September.
36 Onslow Square, October.

My dear Old Alfred,

I owe you a letter of happiness and thanks. Sir, about three weeks ago, when I was ill in bed, I read the "Idylls of the King,"

---

was to meet us at six o'clock, *sharp*. Accordingly we took steamer and gathered ourselves together in the reception-room at the appointed time. When the clock struck six, our host had not fulfilled his part of the contract. His burly figure was yet wanting among the company assembled. As the guests were nearly all strangers to each other, and as there was no one present to introduce us, a profound silence fell upon the room, and we anxiously looked out of the windows, hoping every moment that Thackeray would arrive. This untoward state of things went on for one hour, still no Thackeray and no dinner. English reticence would not allow any remark on the absence of our host. Everybody felt serious and a gloom fell upon the assembled party. Still no Thackeray. The landlord, the butler, and the waiters rushed in and out the room, shrieking for the master of the feast, who as yet had not arrived. It was confidently whispered by a fat gentleman with a hungry look, that the dinner was utterly spoiled twenty minutes ago, when we heard a merry shout in the entry and Thackeray bounced into the room. He had not changed his morning dress, and ink was still visible upon his fingers. Clapping his hands and pirouetting briskly on one leg, he cried out, 'Thank Heaven, the last sheet of The Virginians has just gone to the printer.' He made no apology for his late appearance, introduced nobody, shook hands heartily with everybody, and begged us all to be seated as quickly as possible. His exquisite delight at completing his book swept away every other feeling, and we all shared his pleasure, albeit the dinner was overdone throughout."

[50] Adelaide Procter, from whom Thackeray had already secured the promise of a contribution to the *Cornhill Magazine*.

[51] This letter was begun shortly before Thackeray left for the continent on September 15 and completed on October 16.

and I thought, "O I must write to him now, for this pleasure, this delight, this splendour of happiness which I have been enjoying." But I should have blotted the sheets, 'tis ill writing on one's back. The letter full of gratitude never went as far as the post-office and how comes it now?

D'abord, a bottle of claret. (The landlord of the hotel asked me down to the cellar and treated me.) Then afterwards sitting here, an old magazine, *Fraser's Magazine*, 1850, and I come on a poem out of "The Princess" [52] which says, "I hear the horns of Elfland blowing blowing," no, it's "the horns of Elfland faintly blowing" (I have been into my bedroom to fetch my pen and it has made that blot), and, reading the lines, which only one man in the world could write, I thought about the other horns of Elfland blowing in full strength, and Arthur in gold armour, and Guinevere in gold hair, and all those knights and heroes and beauties and purple landscapes and misty gray lakes in which you have made me live. They seem like facts to me, since about three weeks ago (three weeks or a month was it?) when I read the book. It is on the table yonder, and I don't like, somehow, to disturb it, but the delight and gratitude! You have made me as happy as I was as a child with the *Arabian Nights*, every step I have walked in Elfland has been a sort of Paradise to me. (The landlord gave *two* bottles of his claret and I think I drank the most) and here I have been lying back in the chair and thinking of those delightful "Idylls," my thoughts being turned to you: what could I do but be grateful to that surprising genius which has made me so happy? Do you understand that what I mean is all true and that I should break out were you sitting opposite with a pipe in your mouth? Gold and purple and diamonds, I say, gentlemen and glory and love and honour, and if you haven't given me all these why should I be in such an ardour of gratitude? But I have had out of that dear book the greatest delight that has ever come to me since I was a young man; to write and think about it makes me almost young, and this I suppose is what I'm doing, like an after-dinner speech.

[52] "The Splendour Falls", one of the songs added to the revised edition (1850) of *The Princess*.

P.S. I thought the "Grandmother" [53] quite as fine. How can you at 50 be doing things as well as at 35?

October 16th. (I should think six weeks after the writing of the above.)

The rhapsody of gratitude was never sent, and for a peculiar reason; just about the time of writing I came to an arrangement with Smith and Elder to edit their new magazine, and to have a contribution from T. was the publishers' and editor's highest ambition. But to ask a man for a favour, and to praise and bow down before him in the same page seemed to be so like hypocrisy, that I held my hand, and left this note in my desk, where it has been lying during a little French-Italian-Swiss tour which my girls and their papa have been making.

Meanwhile S.E. and Co. have been making their own proposals to you, and you have replied not favourably I am sorry to hear: but now there is no reason why you should not have my homages, and I am just as thankful for the "Idylls," and love and admire them just as much, as I did two months ago when I began to write in that ardour of claret and gratitude. If you can't write for us you can't. If you can by chance some day, and help an old friend, how pleased and happy I shall be! This however must be left to fate and your convenience: I don't intend to give up hope, but accept the good fortune if it comes.[54] I see one, two, three quarterlies advertized to-day, as all bringing laurels to laureatus. He will not refuse the private tribute of an old friend, will he? You don't know how pleased the girls were at Kensington t'other day to hear you quote their father's little verses, and he too I daresay was not disgusted. He sends you and yours his very best regards in this most heartfelt and artless (note of admiration)!

Always yours, my dear Alfred,

W. M. Thackeray.

[53] "The Grandmother's Apology", which was published with an illustration by Millais in *Once a Week*, July 16, 1859. It was reprinted as "The Grandmother" in *Enoch Arden* (1864).

[54] See below, No. 1432.

1416.   TO GEORGE SMITH
                     29 SEPTEMBER 1859

My text is taken from Lady Ritchie's "The First Number of 'The Cornhill' ",
Cornhill Magazine, New Series, I (1896), 3.

Coire, Switzerland, September 29, 1859.

Have you found a title? St. Lucius, *who founded the church of
St. Peter, Cornhill,* is buried here.[55] Help us, good St. Lucius!
and I will be your faithful W. M. T.

1417.   TO MRS. CARMICHAEL-SMYTH
                     1 OCTOBER 1859

Published in part, *Biographical Introductions*, XI, xv, xvii; additions in *Thackeray and his Daughter*, pp. 121–123.

Chur. Saturday. 1 October

My dear old Granny

We have not been in Paradise for the last week, but, please God,
Anny's difficulties are near over; and now I want to be in town or
near a good surgeon, for my botherations are annoying me a good
deal. There is good however out of all these mishaps, Min has
been a famous nurse for her sister and has borne her hard times
very well: and if she repents of having had her way, and somewhat
in opposition to her Papa's, I shall not be sorry for the circumstances. Anny thinks now that if she had had a dose of medicine
in the good old British fashion, her illness might have been spared
her. But who can calculate the might-have-beens? My own old
enemy gives me rather serious cause for disquiet — not the spasms
— the hydraulics — a constant accompaniment of those disorders
is disordered spirits — and well they may be: but mine will rise

[55] Thackeray and his daughters had come to Chur by way of Boulogne,
Tours, Milan, Como, and the Via Mala. Annie's illness delayed them for
some time in the Swiss village, which is described in *The Roundabout Papers*
(*Works* XII, 167–169), and they did not return to England until mid-October.
See *Thackeray and his Daughter*, p. 121.

again when my gal is all right — and I am within reach of my bed-room and Doctor.

We could not have had a prettier prison than this dear little old town: nor, I am sure, a more patient prisoner. If I could but have had pluck enough to do some work, I might have turned the imprisonment to some account: but I tried and hadn't the heart thats the truth — though I recollect having to work when poor Nan had the same complaint as a baby twenty years ago, and it was necessary to find a guinea for the Doctor. If I can work for 3 years now, I shall have put back my patrimony and a little over — after 30 years of ups and downs. I made a calculation the other day of receipts in the last 20 years and can only sum up about 32000£ of moneys actually received — for w^h I have values or disbursements of 13000 — so that I havent spent at the rate of more than 1000 a year for 20 years. The profits of the lectures figure as the greatest of the receipts 9500£ — Virginians 6 — Vanity Fair only 2. 3 years more please the Fates — and the girls will then have the 8 or 10000 a piece that I want for them: and we mustn't say a word against filthy lucre, for I see the use & comfort of it every day more and more. What a blessing not to mind about bills! — The expenses of this journey for the first 18 days were prodeegious: and who cares? I, for my part, should have liked no journey at all, or not farther than Hombourg or Baden — but the young folks willed otherwise, or seemed to will — and I like them to have their holyday. All along the road they have worked the prices up to be pretty like England — the inn at Milan where they charged us 12 francs for rooms 8 years ago, they make you pay 25 now, and so on and so on. I wonder what your resolves have come to by this time, and whether you'll stay on in England or have gone back to Paris, or will try Bath or Brighton? I have been living at Bath for the last 10 days in Miss Austen's novels w^h have helped me to carry through a deal of dreary time — they and the Times newspaper w^h the landlord of this out of the way Inn luckily takes in for the English who *don't* come. How dismal I should have been without the Times Newspaper! Well, I have been dismal enough with it: but my dear Nan is better please God;

and her Pa's spirits rise accordingly. Now let us go and get some money at the Banker's, and tomorrow D V. let us be on our way home to work and printers devils. I have dreamed constantly that the number wasn't ready & here was the end of the month! It shows how the care weighs upon one: but Law bless us, who hasn't cares at 50 of some shape or other? As I think about the poor Corkrans and *their* cares,[56] I'm ashamed of my own good fortune. Heres my paper full Goodbye my dear G P and my dear old Mother.

W M T.

1418.   TO GEORGE SMITH
                       4 OCTOBER 1859

My text is taken from Lady Ritchie, *Cornhill Magazine*, New Series, I, 3.

Zürich, October 4, 1859.

I see Macmillan's advertisement, and am glad he appears in November.[57] The only name I can think of as yet is "The Corn-hill Magazine." It has a sound of jollity and abundance about it.

---

[56] "In my father's time of trouble," writes Henriette Corkran (*Celebrities and I*, p. 109), "Mr. Thackeray was much more than a brother to him. I am sure that he fully appreciated my father's nature — a proud oversensitive man, full of intellect, but shy and unobtrusive. My mother told me that when he heard for the first time of my parents' pecuniary loss he was most agitated, and turning to my mother he asked her what she was going to do.

" 'I mean to trust to the ravens,' she answered.

"An expression of pain flitted over the great man's face, but after a few seconds of silence he put his large hand over hers, and in a husky voice said, 'And so you may; the ravens are kind friends.' "

[57] The first number of *Macmillan's Magazine*, which like *The Cornhill Magazine* sold for a shilling, appeared in November. It was edited by Thackeray's friend David Masson.

1419.   TO JOHN HOLLINGSHEAD [58]
               19 OCTOBER 1859

My text is taken from an Anderson Galleries catalogue, May 26, 1909.

Dear Sir:

Thank you for your volume, in which I have been reading with
much pleasure last night and this morning. I had already spoken
to Messrs. Smith & Elder about my anxiety to have the services
of the author of the Paper City.[59] I cannot offer you such a post as
you desire on the new magazine, and I fear, can only beg you to
write more and more. Can you oblige me with a visit some morning? say this day week (any other will do) the 26th before 12
o'clock? You will find that we are good paymasters for good work.

Very faithfully yours,
W. M. Thackeray

I want some articles done which can be better discussed by
talk than by letter.

1420.   FROM THOMAS CARLYLE
               20 OCTOBER 1859

My text is taken from Lady Ritchie, *Cornhill Magazine*, New Series, I, 4.

October 20, 1859.

Dear Thackeray, — Right gladly I would, if only I could, but
I can yet bethink me of nothing in the least likely. Indeed I am
so crushed to death amid Prussian rubbish,[60] these long years past,

[58] Hollingshead (1827–1904), who had turned to journalism after working
as a bagman and a cloth merchant, was at this time on the staff of *Household
Words*. From 1868 to 1880 he was manager of the Gaiety Theatre, where
in 1880 he was the first English producer to stage a play by Ibsen.

[59] "The City of Unlimited Paper", an article inspired by the accommodation
bill crisis of 1857, which appeared in *Household Words* on December 19 of
that year (pp. 1–4). Hollingshead describes his connection with *The Cornhill Magazine* in *My Lifetime*, I, 161–165.

[60] Carlyle had begun his *History of Friedrich II of Prussia, called Frederick
the Great* in 1851. The first two volumes were published in 1858, the sixth
and last in 1865.

I have nearly lost the power of thinking in any form, and am possessed by one sad futile ghost of a thought. How am I to get out of this cursed thing alive? If ever I do live to get out of it and find the Thackeray Magazine and Editor still lively, then!

Meanwhile I do not quite give the matter up, your matter I mean, as desperate. And if any possibility do offer, be sure I will lay hold of it. With prayers for the new periodical and you,

Yours ever,
T. Carlyle.

1421.   TO ANTHONY TROLLOPE [61]
                28 OCTOBER 1859

My text is taken from Trollope's *Autobiography* (Stratford-upon-Avon, 1929), p. 99.

36 Onslow Square, S. W.,
October 28th.

My dear Mr. Trollope, — Smith & Elder have sent you their proposals; and the business part done, let me come to the pleasure, and say how very glad indeed I shall be to have you as co-operator in our new magazine.[62] And looking over the annexed programme,[63] you will see whether you can't help us in many other ways besides tale-telling. Whatever a man knows about life and its doings, that let us hear about. You must have tossed a good deal about the world, and have countless sketches in your memory and your portfolio. Please to think if you can furbish up any of these besides a novel. When events occur, and you have a good lively tale, bear us in mind. One of our chief objects in this magazine is the getting out of novel spinning, and back into the world. Don't understand me to disparage our craft, especially *your* wares. I often say I am like the pastry-cook, and don't care for tarts, but prefer bread and cheese; but the public

---

[61] See *Memoranda.*

[62] Trollope's *Framley Parsonage* appeared serially in *The Cornhill Magazine* from January, 1860, to April, 1861.

[63] A printed copy of the next letter.

love the tarts (luckily for us), and we must bake and sell them. There was quite an excitement in my family one evening when Paterfamilias (who goes to sleep on a novel almost always when he tries it after dinner) came up-stairs into the drawing-room wide awake and calling for the second volume of *The Three Clerks*.[64] I hope the *Cornhill Magazine* will have as pleasant a story. And the Chapmans, if they are the honest men I take them to be, I've no doubt have told you with what sincere liking your works have been read by yours very faithfully,

W. M. Thackeray.

1422.   TO "A FRIEND AND CONTRIBUTOR"
1 NOVEMBER 1859

My text is taken from *George Smith*, pp. 109–111.

'The Cornhill Magazine,' Smith, Elder & Co.
65, Cornhill, November 1, 1859.

A LETTER FROM THE EDITOR TO A FRIEND AND CONTRIBUTOR.

Dear —. Our Store-House being in Cornhill, we date and name our Magazine from its place of publication. We might have assumed a title much more startling: for example, 'The Thames on Fire' was a name suggested; and, placarded in red letters about the City, and Country, it would no doubt have excited some curiosity. But, on going to London Bridge, the expectant rustic would have found the stream rolling on its accustomed course, and would have turned away angry at being hoaxed. Sensible people are not to be misled by fine prospectuses and sounding names; the present Writer has been for five-and-twenty years before the world, which has taken his measure pretty accurately. We are too long acquainted to try and deceive one another; and were I to propose any such astounding feat as that above announced, I know quite well how the schemer would be received, and the scheme would end.

---

[64] Which Trollope had published in 1858.

You, then, who ask what 'The Cornhill Magazine' is to be, and what sort of articles you shall supply for it? — if you were told that the Editor, known hitherto only by his published writings, was in reality a great reformer, philosopher, and wise-acre, about to expound prodigious doctrines and truths until now unrevealed, to guide and direct the peoples, to pull down the existing order of things, to edify new social or political structures, and, in a word, to set the Thames on Fire; if you heard such designs ascribed to him — *risum teneatis?* [65] You know I have no such pretensions: but, as an Author who has written long, and had the good fortune to find a very great number of readers, I think I am not mistaken in supposing that they give me credit for experience and observation, for having lived with educated people in many countries, and seen the world in no small variety; and, having heard me soliloquise, with so much kindness and favour, and say my own say about life, and men and women, they will not be unwilling to try me as Conductor of a Concert, in which I trust many skilful performers will take part.

We hope for a large number of readers, and must seek, in the first place, to amuse and interest them. Fortunately for some folks, novels are as daily bread to others; and fiction of course must form a part, but only a part, of our entertainment. We want, on the other hand, as much reality as possible — discussion and narrative of events interesting to the public, personal adventures and observations, familiar reports of scientific discovery, description of Social Institutions — *quicquid agunt homines* [66] — a 'Great Eastern,' a battle in China, a Race-Course, a popular Preacher — there is hardly any subject we *don't* want to hear about, from lettered and instructed men who are competent to speak on it.

I read the other day in 'The Illustrated London News' (in my own room at home), that I was at that moment at Bordeaux, purchasing first-class claret for first-class contributors, and second class for those of inferior *cru.* [67] Let me adopt this hospitable simile;

[65] Horace, *Ars Poetica*, l. 5.
[66] Juvenal, *Satires*, I, 85.
[67] "TOWN AND TABLE TALK ON LITERATURE, ART, &C. . . .

and say that at our contributors' table, I do not ask or desire to shine especially myself, but to take my part occasionally, and to invite pleasant and instructed gentlemen and ladies to contribute their share to the conversation. It may be a Foxhunter who has the turn to speak; or a Geologist, Engineer, Manufacturer, Member of the House of Commons, Lawyer, Chemist — what you please. If we can only get people to tell what they know, pretty briefly and good-humouredly, and not in a manner obtrusively didactic, what a pleasant ordinary we may have, and how gladly folks will come to it! If our friends have good manners, a good education, and write in good English, the company, I am sure, will be all the better pleased; and the guests, whatever their rank, age, sex be, will be glad to be addressed by well-educated gentlemen and women. A professor ever so learned, a curate in his country retirement, an artisan after work-hours, a schoolmaster or mistress when the children are gone home, or the young ones themselves when their lessons are over, may like to hear what the world is talking about, or be brought into friendly communication with persons whom the world knows. There are points on which agreement is impossible, and on these we need not touch. At our social table, we shall suppose the ladies and children always present; we shall not set up rival politicians by the ears; we shall listen to every guest who has an apt word to say; and, I hope, induce clergymen of various denominations to say grace in their turn. The kindly fruits of the earth, which grow for all — may we not enjoy them with friendly hearts? The field is immensely wide; the harvest perennial, and rising everywhere; we can promise competent fellow-labourers a welcome and a good wage; and hope a fair custom from the public for our stores at 'THE CORNHILL MAGAZINE.'

W. M. Thackeray.

New Year's Day is to give us No. 1 (one of many, we trust) of an unnamed magazine under the control of Mr. Thackeray. . . . Thackeray is at Bordeaux, ordering first-class claret for his first-class contributors and second-class claret for his second-class contributors. Michael Angelo Titmarsh, fie, for shame!"
(*Illustrated London News*, October 15, p. 369)

1423. ## TO GEORGE SMITH
NOVEMBER 1859 [68]

My text is taken from *Centenary Biographical Introductions*, XVIII, xxv-xxvi.

My dear S. — Do do the other announcement yourself. I am so horribly nervous at this minute I can't.

It will be the greatest of pities if we give up the accounts of good books. Here is a letter from Captain Galton [69] regarding one book the Engineer accnt. of the Siege of Sebastopol of which I wanted a good acount and you will see who was ready to do it. Twelve good articles on twelve good books I maintain would be as readable, pleasant, and useful as any we could furnish in the shape of tales, sketches, etc.

Send me back letters of Galton & Wrottesley;[70] we must take Sir John and his name used in paragraphs hereafter will be very useful.

I have been with Mr. Keene [71] and pressed him in vain. His hands he says are quite too full. I spent a great part of yesterday at the Museum trying if I could devise a title page myself but this morning bethought that my friend Mr. Cole at the Boilers might find an artist to my purpose. He introduced me to a gentleman there of the very highest skill to whom I explained the design we wanted, who took immediately my view of it and will bring me a drawing as soon as done.[72]

Yours,
W. M. T.

[68] This note was written shortly after Thackeray's letter of November 1, the "other announcement" mentioned below.

[69] Captain Douglas Strutt Galton (1822–1899), later (1887) K. C. B., civil servant, writer, and inventor.

[70] Sir John, second Baron Wrottesley (1798–1867), an eminent scientist who was President of the Royal Society from 1854 to 1858.

[71] Charles Keene (1823–1891), cartoonist for *Punch* from 1851 to 1890.

[72] Smith writes that "The cover of the magazine, designed by Mr. Godfrey Sykes, a young student at the South Kensington Schools of Art [popularly known as the 'Brompton Boilers'], had the good fortune to strike the popular taste, and I still think it most effective. When I showed the sketch of the

1424.   TO THE REV. WHITWELL ELWIN
                    9 NOVEMBER 1859

Extract published by Warwick Elwin, *Some Eighteenth Century Men of Letters*, I, 240.

36 Onslow Sq: S. W. 9 Nov.

In happier times the owner of the umble name signed to this prospectus used occasionally to have an honoured visit and remembrance from the Reverend Doubleyou E.

That divine has however made *ascertained visits to London*,[73] where he has been locked up without being allowed to communicate with acquaintances of ahappier ayears. Flere tacere is my motto: has this pockethandkercher (the writer uses it) been so utterly wrung with grief that it can't mop up a pint or two of hagony more? O Elwin O rector of Boo-ooo-ooo-hoo-hooton!

But no more of my private griefs w^h are those of *the man*: on the other page [74] Sir, my brother, I address you as the Editor and am

de votre Majesté Trimestrielle
le Bon Frère
Cornucopiosus I

1425.   TO ?
                    10 NOVEMBER 1859

Hitherto unpublished.

36 Onslow Sq^re S. W.
November 10. 1859.

Sir

The accompanying note [75] will show you the tone of the periodical we are about to publish: and you will be able to judge from

---

cover to Thackeray, he said: 'What a lovely design! I hope you have given the man a good cheque!' " (*George Smith*, p. 111)

[73] During these visits Elwin appears to have stayed with Forster, who sided with Dickens in the Garrick Club Affair.

[74] This note is written on the second leaf of Thackeray's printed letter of November 1.   [75] A copy of Thackeray's printed letter of November 1.

your own experience in what you are most likely and able to help us. I shall be glad to look at short readable and suggestive articles from the Manufacturing Districts, if you can furnish me with a specimen or two, and to use them if suitable for the Cornhill Magazine. Please to keep copies of all you send me as I cannot undertake to return all unacceptable articles.

Your obdt Servt
W M Thackeray

1426. TO HENRY WADSWORTH LONGFELLOW
16 NOVEMBER 1859

Published in part by Samuel Longfellow, *Henry Wadsworth Longfellow*, II, 346. My text is taken from a facsimile in *Thackeray in the United States*, II, 6–7.

36 Onslow Sq^{re} S. W. London
Novr 16. 1859.

My dear Mr Longfellow,

Has Hiawatha ever a spare shaft in his quiver, w^h he can shoot across the Atlantic? How proud I should be if I could have a Contribution or two from you for our Cornhill Magazine! [76]

I should like still better to be driving to Cambridge in the snow, and expecting a supper there and 2 or 3 months ago actually thought such a scheme was about to come off. I intended to shut up my desk for a year.— not write a line — and go on my travels. But the Gods willed otherwise. I am pressed into the service of this Magazine, and engaged to write ever so much more for the next 3 years. *Then*, if I last so long, I shall be free of books & publishers: and hope to see friends to whose acquaintance I look back with I can't tell you how much gratitude and kind feeling.

I send my best regards to Tom Appleton and beg him to back my petition to his brother-in-law.[77]

Always Sincerely yours
W M Thackeray

[76] Thackeray was not successful in securing a contribution from Longfellow.
[77] Longfellow had married Frances Elizabeth Appleton.

P.S.   If you see Sumner,[78] will you, please, tell him that his books were forwarded to Mr Ivor of Liverpool and went out in the Canada with the Senator himself.[79]

1427.   TO MR. CUPPLES
                    18 NOVEMBER 1859

Hitherto unpublished.

                                November 18. 1859
                                36 Onslow Sq^r S. W.

Dear Mr Cupples

I wrote a note many days ago in reply to yours, but cleverly directed it to St Leonard's whence it was returned to me.

I am full of continuations at this present minute and cant afford to take in 35 pages of Ghost Story. I rather want fact than fiction. You've seen our address I daresay — Cast about in your mind whether there is anything you know, or have seen, to w^h you can help us.

                        Very faithfully yours
                        W M Thackeray.
Brevity is best — 6, 7, 8 pages.

1428.   TO ROBERT BROWNING
                    19 NOVEMBER 1859

My text is taken from a Sotheby catalogue, May 1–8, 1913, lot 298.

A friend of Robert Browning and Elizabeth Barrett, his wife, has agreed to become Editor of A Magazine w^h is to appear with the New Year.

He wishes to provide for the public as much amusement, as much instruction, as much knowledge, pleasure, poetry, pathos,

[78] Charles Sumner, Longfellow's intimate friend, had recently left England for the United States.

[79] James Murray Mason (1798–1871), United States Senator from Virginia, with whom Sumner was at feud. Mason was later (1861) a Confederate Diplomatic Commissioner to Europe.

fun, as can be procured for love or money. He has a great deal of
the first and a liberal portion of the latter to offer such contributors
as R. and E. B. B. Have one or both of you a short poem w^h you
can give for an early number of the *Cornhill Magazine*?

(Private.) Two young ladies named Thackeray send very kind
remembrances to the above-mentioned lady and gentleman.

1429.   TO ?
                      28 NOVEMBER 1859

Hitherto unpublished.

                                     36 Onslow Sq^r S. W.
                                     November 28, 1859.

Dear Sir

The Magazine is open to all comers; and because you thought
I was curt and discourteous ever so long ago, and because I thought
you made me a proposal w^h had been better left alone, there is no
ill-blood I trust, and no earthly reason why you should not write
me a good Article for the Cornhill Magazine. I have not followed
your papers of late years, and dont know what your *spécialité* is.
I don't want stories unless perchance they are short and very
remarkably good; nor London Sketches, having 2 or 3 artists
already engaged upon such works. You had best think of some
subjects that you would like best and know best how [to] write
about, and call some morning before 12 on

                                     Yours faithfully
                                     W M Thackeray.

Next week will be better than this.

1432.   TO THOMAS HOOD [80]
                          6 DECEMBER 1859

Hitherto unpublished.

                                        December I mean
                                        {November} 6. 59
                                        36 Onslow Sq. S. W.

My dear Mr Hood

   Pyrrha [81] is charming, and I shall hang up her yellow tresses
grato antro, and I shall keep Spring s. v. p for Spring time. I
don't say I'll take the Remarkable Dream: & dont say otherwise.
Let the author write some more for me. The writer of the Dream
can do better than that: Its very lively & pleasant though.
                          Faithfully yours
                          W M Thackeray

1431.   TO A. ANDERSON
                          15 DECEMBER 1859

Hitherto unpublished. In the hand of Anne Thackeray, but signed by Thackeray.

                                        36. Onslow Square
                                        Dec. 15, 1859.

Dear Sir,

   I regret that I am too busy to attend your Fête on the 29th I
can only wish every prosperity to your Institute and remain
                     Your obliged faithful servant
                          W M Thackeray.

A. Anderson Esq
   &c. &c.

---

[80] Son (1835–1874) of the poet and humorist of the same name.
[81] "To Goldenhair", Hood's imitation of the fifth ode of Horace's first book,
which begins:
                   Quis multa gracilis te puer in rosa
                   perfusus liquidis urget odoribus
                   grato, Pyrrha, sub antro?
"To Goldenhair" and "Spring" appeared in *The Cornhill Magazine* of
February and April, 1860, respectively, but Thackeray did not use "The
Remarkable Dream".

1432.　　　　　　　TO MRS. TENNYSON
　　　　　　　15 DECEMBER 1859

Address: Mrs Tennyson | Faringford | Isle of Wight. *Postmark:* LONDON
DE 15 59. Hitherto unpublished.

Pathological Society of London.
53, Berners Street.
36 Onslow Sq^e S. W. Decr 15.

My dear Mrs Tennyson.

Hip Hip Hurray. Our number is gone to press [82] but the poem
will be still more welcome for February,[83] for a reason w^h I wonder
whether Alfred will guess when he buys (as I trust he will do)
No 1 of the Cornhill Magazine. I am so glad he has thought of

[82] It was successful beyond Thackeray's most sanguine expectations. "The
announcement by his publishers," writes Fields (*Yesterdays with Authors*, pp.
30–31), "that a sale of a hundred and ten thousand of the first number had
been reached made the editor half delirious with joy, and he ran away to
Paris to be rid of the excitement for a few days. I met him by appointment
at his hotel in the Rue de la Paix, and found him wild with exultation and
full of enthusiasm for excellent George Smith, his publisher. 'London,' he
exclaimed, 'is not big enough to contain me now, and I am obliged to add
Paris to my residence! Great heavens,' said he, throwing up his long arms,
'where will this tremendous circulation stop! Who knows but that I shall
have to add Vienna and Rome to my whereabouts? If the worst comes to
the worst, New York, also, may fall into my clutches, and only the Rocky
Mountains may be able to stop my progress!' Those days in Paris with him
were simply tremendous. We dined at all possible and impossible places together. We walked round and round the glittering court of the Palais Royal,
gazing in at the windows of the jewellers' shops, and all my efforts were
necessary to restrain him from rushing in and ordering a pocketful of diamonds
and 'other trifles', as he called them; 'for,' said he, 'how can I spend the
princely income which Smith allows me for editing the Cornhill, unless I begin
instantly somewhere?' If he saw a group of three or four persons talking
together in an excited way, after the manner of that then riant Parisian
people, he would whisper to me with immense gesticulation: 'There, there,
you see the news has reached Paris, and perhaps the number has gone up
since my last accounts from London.' His spirits during those few days were
colossal, and he told me that he found it impossible to sleep, 'for counting up
his subscribers.' "

[83] Tennyson's "Tithonus" duly appeared in *The Cornhill Magazine* for
February, 1860, pp. 175–176.

me. And I am writing from my Doctors [84] and my fingers are, o so cold!

Always faithfully yours
W M Thackeray

1433.   TO MRS. IRVINE
                    16 DECEMBER 1859

Hitherto unpublished.

December 16. 1859.

Dear M[rs] Irvine

We sent S[t] John [85] away yesterday with a box of sweets to the sweet [86] — and here I find, on my study table, A Pie presented to me by the same indefatigable giver of good things (an American) who brought us the sweetmeats.

As for this pie, he gave me one the other day, and it made me so sick that I daren't attack another. It is pisonous to me this pie is.

But S[t] John is young, has I hope a fine appetite, and a good digestion, and mayn't be afraid of foie gras for breakfast: (I suppose he breakfasts?) Do put this delicacy down before him, as a savory token of his kinsman's benevolence.

Always yours
W M Thackeray.

1434.   FROM RICHARD MONCKTON MILNES
                    27 DECEMBER 1859

My text is taken from Lady Ritchie, *Cornhill Magazine*, New Series, I, 3–4.

Broadlands: December 27.

My dear T. — Obliged for and pleased with No. 1. It is almost too good for the public it is written for and the money it has to

---

[84] Henry Thompson, who was an honorary secretary of the Pathological Society of London (*Post Office London Directory*, 1862).

[85] Francis St. John Thackeray.

[86] *Hamlet*, V, i, 266.

earn. How you, the contributors, and the publishers are to be paid out of it is economically inconceivable! I send you some verses [87] as you desired; I should like to see a proof at No. 16 U. B. Street, W., whenever you think fit to use them.

I like the Leigh Hunt [88] very particularly. I heartily wish you would employ Macdonald,[89] the author of "Phantastes" and "Within and Without." He is a man of very fine fancy, high education, and good taste. He would write you some poetical prose that would be sure to be good. The old Premier [90] here looks so hearty, I believe he would write you an article if you asked him. He sat five hours at the farmers' dinner at Romsey, and then they said "looked quite disappointed to have to go."

I am, yours ever,
R. M. Milnes.

1435.   TO SAMUEL LUCAS [91]
1859

Hitherto unpublished.

My dear Lucas —

Milnes says he has got a poem printed in America but not here — will that do for you? Scarcely I suppose for the first number.

I did not consider myself authorized to mention Tennyson, whose name might have induced the other bard to sing like-

---

[87] "Unspoken Dialogue," *Cornhill Magazine*, February, 1860, pp. 194–197.

[88] "A Man of Letters of the Last Generation," *Cornhill Magazine*, January, 1860, pp. 85–95.

[89] George MacDonald (1824–1905), author of *Within and Without. A Poem* (1855), *Phantastes: A Faerie Romance for Men and Women* (1858), and many other poems and novels.

[90] Lord Palmerston, Prime Minister from 1859 to 1865, at whose country seat Milnes was staying.

[91] A minor Victorian journalist (1818–1868) who was for some years literary reviewer for *The Times*. He appears from this letter to have been employed by Smith, Elder during the months when the first number of *The Cornhill Magazine* was in preparation.

wise. Forster will try to prevent Tennyson from writing for you: if I'm not mistaken.

Yours

W M T.

1436. TO WILLIAM ALLINGHAM
4 JANUARY 1860

My text is taken from *Letters to William Allingham*, p. 282.

36 Onslow Square, S. W.,
January 4, 1860.

My dear Allingham, — Your note arrived when I was at Paris.

In reply I beg, Sir, to refer you to the yellow cover of *The Virginians*: on which two gentlemen are represented in an attitude [1] which I trust will always be maintained between you and — Yours,

W. M. T.

1437. FROM ROBERT BROWNING
17 JANUARY 1860

Hitherto unpublished. My text is taken from the *Howe Proofs*, p. 403.

Rome, Via del Tritone, 28
Jan. 17. '60.

Dear Thackeray:

Your note proved to be one of the Roundabout papers, — reaching us after a stoppage in Florence, besides: and now it is here, we feel embarrassed by everything but your kindness in the matter — for, what do you think? On this table are two other requests from Editors to try our luck & test their liberality. As for me, I really know exactly the way to treat such compliments as they deserve, & yet do the Editor no harm, — have so often taken it, indeed, in my capacity of *pianiste* when pressed to contribute to the enjoyment of an evening-party — but my wife's performances have a different effect & need cause nobody to repent of their good

[1] Shaking hands.

nature. May we have it *so* — that if she finds herself at any time provided with what is likely to suit your book, she may send it & be sure of the most benignant inclination of your brow?

In whatever the event, take our truest thanks & best wishes. We received the extravagant gift of two copies, — or was the publisher's intent that we should not fight for *first read?*

Give our kind regards to your Daughters and tell them the boy, they & you were so good to, rides like a man.

Ever yours faithfully,
Robert Browning

1438.   TO GEORGE SMITH
          23 JANUARY 1860

Hitherto unpublished. My text is taken from a transcript supplied by Mrs. Fuller.

January 23.

My dear S.

I was on my back yesterday treating myself for my old malady and unable to move, and remembered too late that 'the enclosed' from Merivale was not enclosed at all. Here it is. You have the pull over me in the argument, that you have read the paper, and I have not.

BUT it is written by an eminent scholar and practised writer, whose works are received with welcome by the old reviews; and I should have accepted it, as you have accepted others, upon the character of the author.

We agreed that both of us should have a veto upon articles, and in this case I can't complain if you exercise yours. We shall lose Merivale. I am sorry.

Colonel Fuller's book about England I read and found hopelessly dull. Papers from him about France would be no good. Life in Louisiana would be dull from his pen, and he is committed to Slave-advocacy which is not our side at all.

Yours,
W. M. T.

1439. TO KATE PERRY AND MRS. CRAWFURD? [2]
26 JANUARY 1860

My text is taken from a facsimile in a Sotheby catalogue, May 28–30, 1934.

Athenæum. Thursday. 26 Jan. 1860 5 p. m.

Ladies

This is the present attitude of your elderly brother, and the title of the elegant work w^h he is reading is Les Victimes de l'Amour.

Yours affectionately
J. Crawfurd.

[2] Horatia Perry, the sister of Kate and of Mrs. Elliot, married Walter Crawfurd. John Crawfurd (1783–1868), F. R. S., a distinguished Indian civil servant and geographer, appears to have been her brother-in-law.

1440. TO THE REV. SAMUEL REYNOLDS HOLE [3]
26 JANUARY 1860? [4]

Published in Hole's *Memories* (London, 1892), p. 83.

January 26.
36 Onslow Sq^e

My dear Hole

Did I ever write and comply with your desire — To have a page of autograph? You're welcome to a quire. Tell your friend the lady [5] I have no pleasure higher than in writing pretty poetry and striking of the lyre in compliment to a gentleman whom benevolence did inspire to send me pheasants and partridges killed with a shot or wire (but whatever the way of killing them I equally admire) and who of such kind practices I trust will never tire. May you bring your birds down every time you fire This, my noble sportsman, is the fond desire of W. M. Thackeray Editor and Esquire.

[3] Hole (1819–1904) was Vicar of Caunton from 1850 until 1887, when he became Dean of Rochester. An able clergyman and an agreeable writer who was passionately fond of hunting, he was intimate with that other ardent sportsman John Leech, at whose home he first met Thackeray. "He arrived in high good humour," writes Hole (*Memories*, pp. 78–79), "and with a bright smile on his face. I was introduced by our host, and for his sake he gave me a cordial greeting. 'We must be about the same height,' he said; 'we'll measure.' And when, as we stood *dos-a-dos*, and the bystanders gave their verdict, 'a dead heat' (the length was six feet three inches), and I had meekly suggested 'that though there might be no difference in the size of the cases, his contained a Stradivarius, and mine a dancing-master's kit,' we proceeded to talk of giants. . . . As we were conversing, Leech's boy entered the room, and was immediately welcomed by Thackeray with 'Come here, my young friend. You're my godson. Come here and be tipped.'" In the last years of his life Thackeray saw much of his new friend, than whom he had no more faithful admirer. See *Memories of Dean Hole*, pp. 79–85.

[4] It seems likely that this note was written in 1860. In the following years Thackeray would not have bothered to mention his editorship.

[5] Mrs. Mansfield Parkyns, one of Hole's parishoners at Caunton.

1441.   TO THE REV. ALEXANDER MAC EWEN [6]
7 FEBRUARY 1860

Address: A. McEwen Esq^e | Parsick | Glasgow. *Postmark:* FE 8 1860.

36 Onslow Sq^r S. W.
Feb. 7. 1860.

Sir

I ought earlier to have acknowledged your note of the 27th I will bear the subject of it in mind and if I can see a prospect of success in the course you propose will gladly adopt it. But to fail would be much worse than not to attempt at all, and I very much fear we should not get up a satisfactory response to our appeal

Your obdt Servt
W M Thackeray

[6] MacEwen (1822–1875) was minister of the Claremont United Presbyterian Church in Glasgow from 1856 until his death.

1442.   FROM SIR EDWIN LANDSEER
20 FEBRUARY 1860

Published by Lady Ritchie, *Cornhill Magazine*, New Series, I, 8. My text is taken from a facsimile in *Biographical Introductions*, XI, xxvi–xxvii.

Monday 20 Feb

My dear Thackeray

Old Rams look wicked sometimes, *Sheep* usually *innocent* What am I to do? If you will let me know what kind of sheep

you really want I will do my best to illustrate a page for *the* mag

Yours sincerely,
E. Landseer.

1443.   ## TO HENRY THOMPSON
FEBRUARY? 1860 [7]

My text is taken from *Centenary Biographical Introductions*, XVIII, xxxvi.

The leg is found.

W. M. T.

1444.   ## TO GEORGE SMITH
MARCH 1860

My text is taken from *Centenary Biographical Introductions*, XVIII, xli–xlii.

My dear S. — You will see by the annexed that Landseer [8] is a worthy and grateful Knight.

Along with him comes a paper by Oliphant [9] 'Campaigning in

[7] "Before the *Cornhill* came out," Sir Henry Thompson wrote to Lady Ritchie (*Centenary Biographical Introductions*, XVIII, xxxvi–xxxvii), "your father told me that he intended to develop a new principle — that he thought every man, whatever his profession, might be able to tell something about it which no one else could say, provided the writer could write at all: and he wanted to utilize this element. 'So,' said he, 'I want you to describe cutting off a leg as a surgical operation, and do it so that a ship's captain at sea, who had not a doctor on board, would be able to take a sailor's leg off by reading your description.' Having heard in a letter from your father signed 'Yours in trouble', that the article was lost, I was very glad to learn by an envelope addressed to me with the following words, 'The leg is found. W. M. T.' that the manuscript had come to light. The article finally appeared [in *The Cornhill Magazine* of April, 1860, pp. 499–504] with a new title. When your father had read it, it struck him that the paper he had asked for might be somewhat painful, so he wrapped it up in something sweet for the British public to take, and called it 'Under Chloroform.' I had brought the anaesthesia to the front for the same purpose "

[8] No doubt Landseer's drawing of a black sheep, reproduced beneath the initial letter to chapter 4 of *Lovel the Widower*, *Cornhill Magazine*, April, 1860.

[9] Laurence Oliphant (1829-1888), novelist and special correspondent of *The Times*, was private secretary to Lord Elgin in China from 1857 to 1859. His "Campaigning in China" appeared in *The Cornhill Magazine* of May, 1860. Later in the year he visited Italy, where he met Cavour and plotted with Garibaldi.

China,' which I should like to use as we may have another valuable paper by the same hand about Savoy, and secret negotiations there which may make folks' hair stand on end. He is going to Savoy straightway.

Higgins will write a telling article about Public Schools [10] from the man-of-the-world point of view, dealing with expenses and so forth, and asking why gentlemen's schools and education are not improved now that so much is done for schools of lower degree? The philosophical part of the question might be treated by others afterwards.

I am getting on with Lovel [11] and hope to astonish you by its speedy completion.

Always yours,
W. M. T.

1445.   TO C. W. JONES
                          6 MARCH 1860

Hitherto unpublished.

36, Onslow Sq. London.
March 6, 1860.

Dear Sir,

I am glad that the receipts of the Lecture leave a small overplus to cover your expenses. My Bankers are Sir John Lubbock & Co. Will you have the kindness to forward me a cheque crossed to them and believe me

Your very faithful servant
W M Thackeray.

C. W. Jones Esq

[10] "Paterfamilias to the Editor of the 'Cornhill Magazine' ", *Cornhill Magazine*, May, 1860.
[11] Presumably chapter 5 for May.

1446.   **TO SIR EDWIN LANDSEER**
MARCH 1860 [12]

Address: Edwin Landseer. Hitherto unpublished.

Black Sheep Black Sheep Have you any Wool?
Yes, of course I have, you stoopid old Fool.
'Black Sheep, black Sheep, Will you come and dine?
'Wery homely wictuals, wery decent wine.
If you'll come and try-'em on Saturday the Tenth
My master vill velcome you vith all his soul and strenth.
Saturday the Ten[h] is the day vich ve fix
Vich my little number is number Thirty Six.

I'll send tomorrow.

[12] This note was written a few days before Saturday, March 10.

1447.   TO GEORGE SMITH
                      8 MARCH 1860

My text is taken from *Centenary Biographical Introductions*, XVIII, l–li.

                                          March 8, 1860

I have taken at last the house on Kensington Palace Green,[13] in which I hope the history of Queen Anne [14] will be written by yours always,

                      W. M. T.

[1448. See No. 1496A.]

1449.   TO SIR EDWIN LANDSEER
                      13 MARCH 1860

Hitherto unpublished.

                              36 Onslow Sqᵣ S. W.
                              March 13.

You cant work after 7.30 can you? And will you at that hour on Thursday 22 come dine with

                  Your obleeged
                  W M Thackeray.

In the number of the C H wʰ will contain a fine vignette of a Black Sheep: there will be a few words about Leslie [15] (introduced apropos of another subject) wʰ I hope will please you.

---

[13] We learn from Lady Ritchie (*Centenary Biographical Introductions*, XVIII, li) that "the old house which [Thackeray] had intended to alter and to live in was found to be tumbling to pieces and not safe to knock about. After some demur it was pulled down, and the Queen Anne building was erected, in which he took so much pleasure." Thackeray moved into 2 Palace Green, Kensington, on March 31, 1862. See Appendix XXIII.

[14] See above, No. 626, note 171.

[15] In the opening paragraph of "The Last Sketch" (*Works*, XII, 186–187), Thackeray's introduction to a fragment of a story by Charlotte Brontë published in *The Cornhill Magazine*, April, 1860.

1450.   TO HENRY THOMAS BUCKLE [16]
15 MARCH 1860

Hitherto unpublished.

March 15. 36 O. Sq[re]

Dear Buckle

It is agreed. I am yours for Wednesday. You are mine for Thursday. But I cannot give you such a feast as Lucullus prepares for us. Can you? I hope you do rather.

Always yours
W M Thackeray

The fault of the delay is here & not at the Post Office. I am wofully irregular about my papers: and have an Irish amanuensis who is *woefullier* so.

1451.   FROM SIR EDWIN LANDSEER
18 MARCH 1860

My text is taken from Lady Ritchie, *Cornhill Magazine*, New Series, I, 8.

March 18, 1860.

Dear Thackeray, — My used-up old pencil worked with friendly gladness for an old friend, and was richly rewarded by the reception you gave the black sheep. I now feel under an avalanche which really embarrasses me. The magnificent gift now before me so startled me that a state of prostration has set in with its usual severity! It is from your large heart the pretty ewer comes.

---

[16] On February 9, 1860, Thackeray dined with Buckle (1821–1862), who was already famous through the first volume of his *History of Civilization in England* (1857), at the home of their common friend Priaulx. On the following day Buckle lent Thackeray a copy of Comte Arthur Auguste Beugnot's *Histoire de la destruction du paganisme en Occident* (1835) from his magnificent library. (Alfred Henry Huth, *Life and Writings of Henry Thomas Buckle*, New York, 1880, p. 292) The delay of which Thackeray writes no doubt occurred in returning this book.

I am willing to believe, and do hope that you never intended me to feel under obligation; some such feeling mingles with my thanks. Spite of which I shall always have great pleasure in the bottle, which is in perfect taste, quite lovely. Only I do feel ashamed of accepting anything so precious for a speck of scribbling done in neighbourly eagerness for a good fellow, with whom I am proud to share a page. What am I, or you, to say to Messrs. Smith & Elder? The impression of our vignette comes very well, nicely engraved.

My dear Thackeray, faithfully and sincerely yours,

E. Landseer.

1452.   TO ADELAIDE PROCTER
MARCH 1860

My text is taken from *The Memories of Dean Hole*, p. 84, where the drawing reproduced on the opposite page appears in facsimile.

The Editor of the Cornhill Magazine presents his compliments to the Author of the Carver's Lesson [21] and requests the honor of her company at dinner on Thursday 22. March. at 7.30. to meet her Mamma.

[21] Published in *The Cornhill Magazine*, May, 1860, p. 560.

THE CARVER'S LESSON

The Editor of the Cornhill Magazine presents her
Compliments to the Author of the Carver's Lesson and
requests the honor of her company at dinner on Thursday
22. March. at 7. 30. to meet her Mamma.

DRAWING IN THACKERAY'S LETTER TO ADELAIDE PROCTER

1453.   ## FROM THOMAS HOOD
31 MARCH 1860

Hitherto unpublished.

Saturday, 31st

My dear Mr Thackeray.

I have sent off by this post a short essay, with an initial letter, which I hope will be held admissible for the Cornhill. Every number delights me more than its predecessor — with an Essay without End I am very much struck. As for the illustrations Millais' last is very fine, and Sir Edwin's Black Sheep is really a *Capital* letter. As for the first illustration it is from a pencil that I admired when a boy as illustrating the Fat Contributor, and which though the Critics say it has mightily progressed lately will never to my mind be able to surpass the Pendennis pictures, or the Irish Sketches. I am pleased to hear from Lady Molesworth that she comes to Pencarrow on Monday — when she was last here she spoke of your probable visit — I hope you will come down now and have a peep at our Cornish Lent-lilies & violets.

If the "Remarkable Dream" be not suitable for the Cornhill may I trespass on your kindness by asking its return.

I am going to trespass still more on your kindness by a request which I am obliged to make because I have tried to obtain the pamphlet it refers to everywhere & have failed — It is the pamphlet Concerning Thunder and Small Beer, which I have long wished to obtain — for I think that is almost the only one of your acknowledged works which I have not read — and re-read — not to mention unacknowledged ones, which I have recognised, just as a port wine drinker detects the flavor of the '37 vintage whatever be the cut of the decanter that contains it.

Believing that if you have a spare copy by you, you will kindly make me the happy possessor of it, I remain

Yours very truly
Tom Hood

1454.   FROM MRS. BROWNING
                              13 APRIL 1860

Hitherto unpublished. My text is taken from *Howe Proofs*, p. 404.

Dear Mr. Thackeray,

   You asked me too long ago for a contribution to your magazine
— too long ago in every sense perhaps — for here is my husband
who suggests that, being in very ill odour with you all in England
just now (scarcely bettered by a misstatement in the Athenæum)
I may not be welcome between the wind[22] & your nobility at
Cornhill.

   But in that case you will return my verses enclosed, & no harm
will be done — if indeed it is no harm to send love to dear Annie
& Minnie, whom I never forget —

   Yes, — and don't I remember Mr. Thackeray's kindness to
little Penini? — who grows big, & is learning Latin, & riding a
poney, & is not much changed otherwise.

   With my husband's regards, I remain,
                                   Most sincerely yours
                                   Elizabeth Barrett Browning

28, Via del Tritone
Rome — April 13 —
   where we shall be till the end of May — then we return to
Florence.

1455.   TO GEORGE SMITH
                              APRIL 1860

My text is taken from *Centenary Biographical Introductions*, XVIII, xlii.

   I wrote to ask if Landseer was disengaged, and here[23] is the

   [22] The *Howe Proofs* read *mind*, but Mrs. Browning is obviously echoing
I Henry IV, I, iii, 45.
   [23] "Dear T. — The Black Sheep will be most happy to cut the Cornhill
mutton on the day kindly proposed.
                                   Yours truly,
April 25, 1860.   E. L."

Knight's reply. Send him a card please to remind. I've not heard
from Leighton;[24] have you?

1456.   TO THORNTON HUNT? [25]
                 29 APRIL 1860

Hitherto unpublished.

                                                36 O. Sq.
                                                April 29.

Can you air the Order of Britannia project [26] in the Telegraph? *
I am sure such an order would be most popular in the Mercantile &
I dont see y not in the Royal Navy.

                        Yours W M T.

   * The last article in the CornHill.

1457.   TO SIR HENRY DAVISON
                 4 MAY 1860

My text is taken from Francis Thackeray, *Temple Bar*, July, 1893, p. 377.

                                                4 May.

How dy do, my dear old Davus? Read the Cornhill Magazine
for May; the article Little Scholars is by my dear old fat Anny.
She sends you her love, so does Minny. We're going out to drive.
We've got two hosses in our carriage now. The Magazine goes
on increasing, and how much do you think my next twelve months'
earnings and receipts will be if I work? £10,000. Cockadoodle-
oodloodle. We are going to spend 4,000 in building a new house
on Palace Green, Kensington. We have our health. We have

   [24] Frederic Leighton (1830–1896), later (1896) first Baron Leighton of
Stretton, the painter.
   [25] Editor of *The Daily Telegraph* from 1855 to 1872.
   [26] See "On Ribbons" (*Works*, XII, 200–201), which was published in
The Cornhill Magazine, May, 1860, pp. 631–640.

brought Granny and G. P. to live at Brompton Crescent,[27] close
by us, and we are my dear old Davus's

Faithful,

W. M. A. I. & H. M. T.

1458.   TO THE BISHOP OF ST. DAVIDS
18 MAY 1860 [28]

Published by John Connop Thirlwall Jr., *Connop Thirlwall* (London, 1936),
pp. 152–153. My text is taken from a photostat in the Columbia University
Library.

36 Onslow Sq. S. W. Friday

My dear Lord Bishop

Ought I to thank you for speaking so kindly of me on Wednesday? My mother and daughters I am sure do, and are proud to
have your good opinion. That is among the prizes w^h have lately
fallen to men of my calling — to have the goodwill and apprecia-
tion of men like you. Think of poor Smollett (an honest hard-
working man) dying a pauper at Leghorn; of Fielding leaving
England without a friend to shake him by the hand; & of poor
Goldsmith's dismal end. I'm afraid the last two were dishonest
about money: but what a blessed difference between their time
and our's! I for one am rather ashamed of my luck. Some of us

---

[27] "My grandmother," writes Lady Ritchie (*Biographical Introductions*,
XII, xv), "lived for a couple of years in Brompton Crescent, and remained
there until my grandfather's death, when she came home to us. My father
paid her a daily visit on his way into town."

[28] Connop Thirlwall, Bishop of St. Davids, served as chairman at the dinner
of the Literary Fund on Wednesday, May 16, 1860. During the course of
his speech on that evening he said: "Think of our admirable friend Mr.
Thackeray. I am sorry that I cannot ask you to look at him. We must all
deplore his absence on this occasion; but see, what an immense amount of
ecclesiastical patronage he has at his disposal! What a number of sees *in parti-
bus* are in his exclusive nomination. I have never been ambitious of being
translated to any of them, but I believe there are few clergymen to whom
it can be a matter of indifference what position they occupy in Mr. Thackeray's books." (*Letters Literary and Theological of Connop Thirlwall*, ed. by
the Revs. J. J. Stewart Perowne and Louis Stokes, 2 vols., London, 1881, I,
241–242)

are paid like tenor opera-singers: and I hang down my head when I hear of a scholar toiling for bread, whilst Fortune has put such a heap of butter on mine. I must bear the inequality without re-pining however; and now if I could but get that laudable virtue of the other Thackerays, the resolute saving and getting of money: how respected I should be in the family! Meanwhile, to have your good will and good word is no small instalment of good fortune. I pray God Almighty I may continue to deserve them; and feel immense thankfulness for the fair hope w^h I have now that I may leave my children a competence and a good name. Let him who stands take heed to be sure ... Pardon this egotism: it is occasioned by your own extreme kindness and sympathy.

I was annoyed at not being able to come to the dinner (never supposing such sweetmeats were to be served to me for dessert) but I had been confined to my bed for 60 hours before, and was so weak and ill that I could not face the chance of an after-dinner speech. Thank you for your's and believe me

Your very grateful & sincere
W M Thackeray

1459. FROM THOMAS CARLYLE
24 MAY 1860

My text is taken from *Chapters*, p. 139.

Chelsea, 24th May 1860.

Alas, dear Thackeray, I durst as soon undertake to dance a hornpipe on the top of Bond Steeple, as to eat a white-bait dinner in my present low and lost state! Never in my life was I at such a pass You are a good brother man; and I am grateful. Pray for me, and still hope for me if you can. — Yours ever,

T. Carlyle.

1460.   FROM THOMAS CARLYLE
                    26 MAY 1860

My text is taken from *Chapters*, p. 139.

Chelsea, 26th May 1860.

Dear Thackeray, — The thing I contemplated just now (or the nucleus of the thing) was a letter concerning that anecdote about *Fontenoy*. "*Faites feu, Messieurs,*" on the part of the English, with answer from the *Gardes Françaises*, "Begin you, gentlemen; wouldn't do such a thing for the world!" My letter is from Lord Charles Hay, Captain of the Scots Fusiliers, main actor in the business; it was sent me last year by Lord Gifford; and I could have made a little story out of it which would have been worth publishing.

But on applying to Lord Gifford, he (what he is himself, I believe, truly sorry for) cannot at present give me permission. So the poor little enterprise falls to nothing again; and I may be said to be in a state of ill-luck just now!

If I ever in the end of this book have life left, you shall have plenty of things. But for the time being I can only answer *de profundis* to the above effect.

Fair wind and full sea to you in this hitherto so successful voyage, for which the omens certainly are on all sides good. Your people do not send me a copy (Since No. I.); but we always draw our purse upon it to the small extent requisite. — Yours ever truly,

T. Carlyle.

1461.   TO ERNEST JONES [29]
2 JUNE 1860

Hitherto unpublished.

36 Onslow Sq? S. W.
Saturday June 2.

Dear Sir

I am glad to be able to lend you the money w^h you require, and hope with yourself that your difficulties will only be temporary.

I wonder could you do a Chartist Article? — not opinions — but facts — organizations — imprisonment — personal adventure?

Faithfully yours
W M T.

Put a grey stamp on the cheque. & scrawl any thing on it.

1462.   TO GEORGE SMITH
JUNE? 1860

My text is taken from *Biographical Introductions*, XII, xvii.

My dear S., — I have been lying awake half the night about that paper [30] in a sort of despair; but I think I have found a

---

[29] Jones (1819–1869) was a poet and former Chartist agitator. Thackeray knew him at the Middle Temple, where he was admitted to the bar in 1844, and reported his speech at a Chartist meeting for *The Morning Chronicle* of March 15 1848. See above, No. 457, note 68.

[30] "On Screens in Dining Rooms", published in *The Cornhill Magazine* for August. This essay was Thackeray's answer to "Echoes from the London Clubs", which Edmund Yates contributed to *The New York Times* of May 26. "In literary matters we are all alive," Yates writes, "but the success of the *Cornhill Magazine* in already showing symptoms of being on the wane. That notable periodical went up like a rocket, and is beginning to come down like the stick; it is certain that its first number sold nearly a hundred thousand, and that its second reached seventy thousand, but ever since then it has been declining, and now I should think forty thousand was about the mark. With a less circulation it would not — could not pay, for it receives comparatively few advertisements, and its expenses are enormous. There have been already four tremendously heavy dinner parties given by SMITH, (of SMITH & ELDERS,) at his residence in Gloucester-terrace, at which all the principal

climax dignified and humourous enough at last, Heaven be praised,
and that our friend won't sin again. — Yours ever, W. M. T.

---

contributors have been present. THACKERAY is, of course, the great gun
of these banquets, and comes out with the greatest geniality in his power,
speaking of G. H. LEWES as 'Mr. BEDE' (Mrs. L. is the author of *Adam
Bede*,) and drawing each man out to the extent of his ability. But there is one
very funny story which will bear repetition: SMITH, the proprietor of the
Cornhill, and the host on these occasions, is a very good man of business, but
totally unread; his business has been to sell books, not to read them, and he
knows little else. On the first occasion of their dining there, THACKERAY
remarked to those around him, 'This is a splendid dinner, such an one as
CAVE, the bookseller of St. John's Gate, gave to his principal writers when
Dr. JOHNSON'S coat was so shabby that he ate his meal behind the screen;'
then calling out to his host, who was at the other end of the table, THACK-
ERAY said, 'Mr. SMITH, I hope you've not got JOHNSON there behind
that screen?' 'Eh?' said the bibliopole, astonished; 'behind the screen?
JOHNSON? God bless my soul, my dear Mr. THACKERAY, there's no
person of the name of JOHNSON here, nor any one behind the screen —
what on earth do you mean?' A roar of laughter cut him short; poor MR.
SMITH had probably never heard of DR. JOHNSON and his screen dinner.
... The paper called 'Little Scholars,' in the current number [of *The Cornhill Magazine*], was written by THACKERAY'S eldest daughter — her
first attempt at literary composition; it is pretty, but bears traces of being
touched up by the parental hand, — as THACKERAY himself once said to
PETER CUNNINGHAM, who was proudly pointing to some anonymous
article as his writing: 'Ah! I thought I recognized your *hoof* in it!' "

This gossip was given circulation among English readers by an article in
The Saturday Review of June 23 (pp. 799–800), the avowed purpose of
which was to reprove the license of American journalism. Yates's personalities
about Thackeray and Smith were reprinted, "because it is impossible otherwise
to estimate what we should come to here if society and the higher portion of
the press did not constantly keep newspaper gossip in decent bounds." There
can be no question that the editors of *The Saturday Review*, whose consistent
hostility to Thackeray Professor Wells has demonstrated in the notes to his
edition of *The Roundabout Papers* (see particularly pp. 361–362), took a
malign pleasure in spreading Yates's slanders under the pretence of upholding
journalistic morality.

Any doubts that Thackeray may have had as to the identity of the writer
in *The New York Times* was dispelled when Trollope confessed to Smith
that he had given Yates the information on which his description of the contributors' dinner was founded. Urged particularly by Mrs. Smith, who was
much disturbed by Yates's sneer at her husband, Thackeray wrote "On Screens
in Dining Rooms", in which he reproved his old enemy for scandal-mongering
and took *The Saturday Review* to task for tale-bearing. See *George Smith*,
pp. 120–121.

1463.　　　　TO SAMUEL ALLIBONE [31]
　　　　　　　　8 JULY 1860

Hitherto unpublished.

　　　　　　　　　　　36 Onslow Square. S. W. London.
　　　　　　　　　　　　　　July 8. 1860.

Dear Sir

　I think I am bound to tell you in reply to your present of last year, and to several notes w[h] I have since received that the cause of my silence regarding the Dictionary was an idea that the Author intended to publish my note among the testimonials favorable to his work. And though I might have a very high opinion of the book, it seemed to me unfair that this opinion should be in a manner demanded from me in return for a present w[h] I had not solicited. In the only *public* way in w[h] it was in my power to notice the Dictionary of Authors I did so, in a brief note appended to an article on Washington Irving in the Corn Hill Magazine.[32]

　I have since had the pleasure of conversing with a mutual friend, M[r] Winthrop of Boston, and I am sure I break no confidence in saying that his account of you was so friendly, so highly creditable to your character of gentleman and man of letters — that I felt anxious to explain to you how and why it is, I thought it my duty to be silent when thanks were assuredly deserved and would have been pleasant and easy.

　After my taciturnity I shan't expect the good luck of the present of the second volume, and frankly say that I intend to buy it. I hope you may live to complete it with the fullness & accuracy w[h], as far as I have looked into it marks Volume I. And when you come to the T's there is an author (whose lax morality you repre-

---

[31] An American scholar and librarian (1816–1889), who is remembered for his *Critical Dictionary of English Literature and British and American Authors*, 3 vols. (Philadelphia, 1858–1871).

[32] In a footnote to "Nil Nisi Bonum", which appeared in *The Cornhill Magazine*, February, 1860, p. 129, Thackeray mentions "the most remarkable *Dictionary of Authors*, published lately at Philadelphia, by Mr. Alibone."

hend—v. Fielding. Henry.) [33] who believes that your wish is to speak justly of all authors, who admires your industry very much and who is

Your obliged faithful Serv[t]

W M Thackeray.

1464.   TO HENRY C. PENWELL [34]
10 JULY 1860

Address: H. C. Pennell Esq[re] | Admiralty. | Whitehall. *Postmark:* LONDON JY 10 60. Hitherto unpublished.

Sir   I regret that the enclosed clever verses will not suit us: but I am too old-fashioned to let rhymes like 'wrath' & 'North' appear in our Magazine. Your obliged Serv[t] W M Thackeray.

1465.   TO WILLIAM DUER ROBINSON
11 JULY 1860

My text is taken from *Thackeray in the United States*, II, 10.

36 Onslow Sq[r] S. W. July 11. 1860

My dear W. D.: — This will be handed to you by my young friend Mr. Gore [35] son of Mrs. Gore, who is going to Bluenosia to look after property left by his *loyalist ancestors* — this will be a recommendation to him with somebody whose name I shall

---

[33] To Allibone's mind the apology offered for Fielding's "loose manners and dissipated habits" in Thackeray's *English Humourists* is indefensible. "We have often listened with pleasure — indeed, with edification — to Mr. Thackeray's moral reflections upon the Lives and Works of the departed great, but we soon found that the summing up of the learned judge leaned not always 'to virtue's side;' and if the literary offender happened to be a three-bottle man, we entertained no apprehensions for his safety, and felt quite confident that a gentle rebuke, hardly calculated to depopulate the tables of Lucullus, would be the extent of his punishment." (*Critical Dictionary*, I, 592)

[34] Chief Clerk of the Naval Department of the Admiralty (*London Directory*, 1862).

[35] Captain Augustus Wentworth Gore, one of Mrs. Gore's two surviving children.

write presently on an envelope. Gore has been in India with his regiment and served there like a man. He is also as you will see one of the Crem-ornaments of our young society. Please show him what you think pretty and profitable for him at New York, of w̱ʰ I never think without a wish to see my trusty kind old W. D. Think of a letter to *You!* going to N. York & coming back to me! [36] Was n't it too bad? It was a stupid letter, but dull or lively, I am always WD's WT.

1466. TO ROBERT DALE OWEN [37]
18 JULY 1860

Hitherto unpublished. *Endorsed:* Robt Dale Owen.

36 Onslow Sqᵣ S. W.
July 18. 1860.

Dear Sir

The little article [38] is printed, and contains only the private experiences of a single observer. I may possibly have another article containing the testimony of another eye witness to the same *séance*. But there I think we shall stop for the present, as — but never mind giving reasons

I shall order your book [39] at the Athenæum and read it without delay.

Believe me very faithfully yours
W M Thackeray

[36] This letter has not been preserved.
[37] Son (1800–1877) of the famous socialist Robert Owen.
[38] Robert Bell's "Stranger than Fiction", which appeared in the *Cornhill Magazine* in August, 1860, pp. 211–224. See below, No. 1471.
[39] *Footfalls on the Boundary of another World* (1859), of which Thackeray wrote in *The Cornhill Magazine* of November, 1860, "My dear sir, it will make your hair stand quite refreshingly on end" (*Works*, XII, 244).

1467.   TO THE REV. WHITWELL ELWIN
                      28 JULY 1860

My text is taken from Elwin's *Some Eighteenth Century Men of Letters*, I, 240–241.

July 28th, 1860

My dear Primrose, — What is this that I read in the I.L.N. about your laying down the sceptre? [40] I have been away in the distant solitudes of Tunbridge Wells, and only came to town for a day, when I read this dismal announcement.

Whether you are a King or a country Primrose, my dear Elwin, you must please remember that I am affectionately * yours,

W. M. Thackeray

* This is rather a strong term, you see, nor do I use it on many occasions, but in this I can't help myself, and when I likes a man I likes him.

1468.   TO ADELAIDE PROCTER
                      JULY 1860

My text is taken from a facsimile in the Grolier Club's *Catalogue of an Exhibition Commemorating the Hundredth Anniversary of the Birth of William Makepeace Thackeray*, New York, 1912, p. 94. *Endorsed:* Thackeray to A. A. Procter July 1860.

My dear A. Why shouldn't we keep both those pretty poems? [41] Indeed I dont. know. w^h I like best. I have this minute come up

[40] It is stated in *The Illustrated London News* of July 28, 1860, that "the editorship of the *Quarterly Review* has changed hands . . . and the learned and acute Mr. Aylwin has laid down the sceptre of command."

[41] "Fate and a Heart" and "Sent to Heaven", which appeared in the September and November issues of *The Cornhill Magazine* for 1860.

from Tunbridge Wells,[42] and have been staying there a whole
week.

Your obedient editor

1469.   TO MRS. GORE
                      27 AUGUST 1860

Hitherto unpublished.

Rock Villa. Tunbridge Wells
August 27.

My dear Mrs Gore.

Thank you for your note, to w^h I reply with my usual dilatori-
ness and brevity. I cant write about Scheffer [43] for I dont care

---

[42] " 'Tunbridge Toys' was written in the summer of 1860," Lady Ritchie
(*Biographical Introductions*, XII, xvi–xvii) relates, "when we were staying
at Turnbridge Wells in an old wooden house at the foot of Mount Ephraim.
The drawing-room windows looked across a garden towards the common. 'De
Juventate' was also written there. I remember my father showing me the
manuscript at the time, and as I read it now everything comes back. The
grandparents were living in the ground-floor sitting room; we were established
overhead, with a couple of puppies, whose antics were the chief events of those
peaceful days. The puppies were called Gumbo and Saidie, after the two nigger
boys in 'The Virginians'. Gumbo had a fine time of it, driving vast herds of
sheep before him across Rustington Common. Saidie was of a meeker disposition.
When we went abroad later in the year, Saidie returned to Onslow Square, and
Gumbo was sent away to live with our friends the Synges, a present for . . .
Bobby Mistletoe. I cannot help describing here the little story my father
told us of Gumbo's behaviour when they met again on our return from abroad.
Gumbo in his black-and-tan coat, was quietly passing the time on the pavement in front of the house in Pimlico, when he saw the hansom-cab driving
up the middle of the street with my father inside; and with one wild leap
from the curb-stone he sprang into the advancing cab and landed safe on
my father's knees, knocking off his spectacles and licking his face all over."
For "Bobby Mistletoe", see below, No. 1473.

[43] Henry Scheffer (1798–1862), like his better known brother Ary (1795–
1858), was a painter of the French romantic school.

much for him. I think he is a poor genius and draftsman, though a neat workman — Leslie's genius I loved and admired sincerely, and was glad when I heard from the good mans family that they were pleased with my little say about him.⁴⁴ Have you read the Memorials of Hood? ⁴⁵ I may speak about that some day, having read few books wʰ have touched me more. All those wonderful puns and jokes & all that sickness and misery — all that genius and that very very scanty reward — I feel ashamed almost of my own luck when I think of his small earnings.

I have my old folks and young folks here at Tunbridge Wells — where it rains sweetly, and where I am as glum as possible. What is this about a Preface to a Certain 'Banker's Wife' ⁴⁶ the author of wʰ novel, the girls tell me, hints that I took Colonel Newcome from one of her characters? Half of Colonel Newcome is down stairs now — the other half is in London ⁴⁷ and as for the Banker's wife, Madam, I would have you to know that I have no more read it than I have read Newton's Principia. That is one of the blessings for wʰ you, sure, may be thankful; that you read novels. I cant any more, not even those of

Your humble servant to command,

W M Thackeray.

⁴⁴ In "The Last Sketch", *Cornhill Magazine*, April, 1860 (*Works*, XII, 186–187).

⁴⁵ F. F. Broderip and Thomas Hood, Jr., *Memorials of Thomas Hood* (1860). See "On a Joke I once Heard from the late Thomas Hood", *Cornhill Magazine*, December, 1860 (*Works*, XII, 261–270).

⁴⁶ This novel by Mrs. Gore was first published in 1843. The preface to which Thackeray refers appeared in the reissue of 1859.

⁴⁷ "When 'The Newcomes' was coming out," writes David Freemantle Carmichael (Baillie, *Oriental Club and Hanover Square*, p. 75), "I said to Thackeray, 'I see where you got your Colonel.' 'To be sure you would,' he replied, 'only I had to *angelicise* the old boys a little.' By this he meant, his stepfather, Major Henry Carmichael-Smyth, and *his* younger brother, General Charles Carmichael."

1470.   TO WILLIAM S. WILLIAMS
27 AUGUST 1860

Hitherto unpublished.

Rock Villa. Tunbridge Wells
27 August.

My dear Mʳ Williams.

I think Mʳˢ Browning is quite good enough for us and has some very fine lines [48] — but Peter Cunningham wont do at all.

I read and had at home Mʳ Hoods 2 articles 'A Very Singular Dream', and a 'Lay Sermon', with the latter was a block. Did the papers go back to CornHill? If not will you please have this sentence copied and sent to Mʳ Langley 36 Onslow Sqʳ — and tell him to find the papers and take them to Mʳ Hood. I suppose from Mʳ Smith's note that he wrote to Mʳ H. about his poems.[49]

I fear greatly Dʳ Doran [50] won't do.

Yours very truly
W M Thackeray.

[48] Mrs. Browning's contribution was "A Forced Recruit at Solferino", which appeared in *The Cornhill Magazine* for October, 1860, pp. 419–420. Neither of Hood's articles was published.

[49] Hood wished to republish the poems which he had contributed to *The Cornhill Magazine*, a proceeding contrary to Smith's policy.

[50] John Doran (1807–1878), a miscellaneous writer who served on the staff of the *Athenæum*, a magazine which he later (1869–1870) edited.

1471.   TO ROBERT BELL
                 AUGUST 1860

Hitherto unpublished.

The angel Gabriel presents his compliments to M⸢r⸣ Bell and
sends him the likeness of the spirit who stood the watch.⁵¹

⁵¹ "Il y a quelques années," writes Louis Blanc (*Lettres sur l'Angleterre,
II⸢e⸣ Série*, Paris, 1866, II, 253–25); "les journaux de Londres annoncèrent
qu'un Français, dont il est inutile que je vous dise le nom [Blanc himself],
allait donner en anglais, dans le quartier de Saint-John's Wood, ce qu'on
appelle ici une *lecture*.. Au nombre de ceux qui, mus par un sentiment de
bienveillance délicate et de curiosité hospitalière, songèrent à aller l'encou-
rager de leur presence, Thackeray fut des plus empressés. La lecture finie,
l'administrateur (*manager*) de l'institution littéraire de l'endroit crut devoir,
je ne sais à quel propos, recommander aux assistants de ne pas sortir sans
prendre garde à leurs poches, la foule étant très-serrée aux portes. Cette
recommandation, adressée à un auditoire composé de personnes très-respec-
tables, dont quelques-unes très-distinguées, fit un fort mauvais effet.
    "Il y en eut qui réclamèrent, et nul n'éleva la voix avec plus d'éloquente

1472. TO WILLIAM SMITH WILLIAMS
AUGUST? 1860

Hitherto unpublished.

65, Cornhill.
London,
E. C.

Dear Mr Williams

I suspect you are at Taffy's house, whilst he is at your's. Please to send this drawing to Swaine [52] for the Roundabout w^h I now

---

vivacité qu'un inconnu très-bien couvert, qui était assis à côté de M. Robert Bell. Non content de parler, l'inconnu gesticulait, et cela d'une manière étrangement animée: 'N'est-ce pas, monsieur, disait-il a M. Bell, qu'un pareil avis est indécent, insultant? Pour qui nous prend-on? etc..., etc..., etc...' Après avoir exhalé de la sorte son indignation, le susceptible inconnu s'éclipsa; et lorsque M. Robert Bell, voulant savoir combien de temps la *lecture* avait duré, consulta sa montre, il se trouva qu'elle lui avait été volée. Thackeray apprit de son excellent ami Robert Bell, séance tenante, cette triste aventure, et l'invita à diner pour un des jours suivants. Le jour venu, autour d'une table égayée par la présence de plusieurs hommes d'esprit, M. Robert Bell alla prendre place, et ne tarda pas à avoir un joyeux assaut à soutenir relativement à un article de lui, très-remarqué et très-remarquable, qui avait paru dans le *Cornhill Magazine*, alors sous la direction de M. Thackeray, — article contenant un exposé fidèle, sériux et philosophique des faits de *spiritisme*, dont l'auteur avait été témoin dans une séance donnée par M. Home. M. Robert Bell est un admirable causeur, plein de bon sens britannique et de verve irlandaise. Les questionneurs trouvèrent donc à qui parler, et chacun fit merveille. Le lendemain, un messager mystérieux arrive chez M. Robert Bell, et lui remet sans pouvoir dire qui l'envoie, une boîte dans laquelle était un billet ainsi conçu ou à peu près: 'Les esprits présentent leurs compliments à Robert Bell, et, pour lui témoigner leur gratitude, ils ont l'honneur de lui faire tenir la montre qu'on lui a volée.' C'était effectivement une montre que la boîte contenait, mais une montre beaucoup plus riche que celle qui avait disparu.

"M. Robert Bell pensa tout de suite à Thackeray et lui écrivit, sans s'expliquer davantage: 'Je ne sais si c'est vous .... Mais cela vous ressemble bien!' " Thackeray's reply was the note printed above.

Thackeray appended to "Stranger than Fiction," Bell's *Cornhill* article, a note vouching for the "good faith and honourable character of our correspondent, a friend of twenty-five years' standing." Bell's continued interest in the occult is testified by "Spiritualism", an article which he wrote for *The Cornhill Magazine* of June, 1863, pp. 706–719.

[52] Joseph Swain, manager of the engraving department of *Punch* from

send. 2 other designs will be also sent for it — and a letter if it is used, as a paper by itself. If printed along with the other no initial will be wanted and the paper can be called *De juventute*.[53]

Send me a proof if poss of George & the Dragon by to nights post to Tunbridge Wells.

1473.   TO LORD ?
                          1 SEPTEMBER 1860

Hitherto unpublished.

                                        36 Onslow Sq^e S. W.
                                        September 1. 1860.

My Lord

Hearing that a considerable addition is speedily to be made to the number of Foundation-Boys at Charter House, I take leave as an old Carthusian to address your Lordship, & beg you if not engaged to give your nomination to the son [54] of my old friend W. Follett Synge Esqre of the Foreign Office.

Mr Synge has just returned from Central America whither he went as Secretary to Sir Gore Ouseley's Mission.[55] His character and services can be authenticated by all his chiefs. His boy (7 years old) is the eldest of many children. I entreat your good offices for the little boy as a most worthy candidate for the benefits of our school and am

                          Your lordships very humble Servt
                          W M Thackeray.

1843 to 1890, who had a large corps of assistants and did much work for other magazines.

[53] Published in *The Cornhill Magazine* for October, 1860.

[54] Robert Follett Synge (b. 1853), the "Bobby Mistletoe" of "Round About the Christmas Tree" (*Works*, XII, 271–278), who entered Charterhouse in 1865.

[55] Synge was made Secretary to the special mission to Central America of Sir William Gore Ouseley (1797–1866) in July, 1858 (*Foreign Office List*, 1859).

1474.   TO LADY ELIZABETH THACKERAY
                27 SEPTEMBER 1860

Hitherto unpublished.

36 Onslow Sq^e S. W.
September 27.

My dear Lady Elizabeth.

Anny has written to tell you how we have been abroad [56] and only returned on Tuesday night, when first we heard of your affliction.[57] You have treated me and mine with such kindness and friendliness always, that you may be sure we feel sympathy at anything w^h causes you pleasure or grief; and at this sad time as at all others I am sure you will believe that I am

Most sincerely yours
W M Thackeray.

1475.   TO LORD ?
           SEPTEMBER 1860 [58]

Hitherto unpublished.

36 Onslow Sq^r

My dear Lord. I passed you this moment, as I was on my way to your house (after going to see a poor neighbour of your's in affliction) in order to thank you for your prompt kindness to the little Synge. He is one of ever so many dear little children with the best little mother, and your kind help was never better bestowed than in his case. Thank you again for your goodness and believe me

Your very faithful and obliged
W M Thackeray

[56] Thackeray's tour on the continent is described in "Notes of a Week's Holiday" (*Works*, XII, 242–260).

[57] General Thackeray, Lady Thackeray's husband, had died on September 19, 1860.

[58] This note was written shortly after Thackeray's note of September 27 to Lady Elizabeth Thackeray, who is the "neighbour . . . in affliction."

1476.   TO WILLIAM DUER ROBINSON
                  28 SEPTEMBER 1860

Published in part, *Thackeray in the United States*, II, 10–11.

XXXVI Onslow Sq.ʳ S. W.
28 Sept.ʳ 1860

My dear old W. D R.   I fancy *you* write anything against me?
What next?   The culprit was my old friend M.ʳ Yates [59] who was
turned out of the Garrick because after agreeing to submit the
difference between us to the Club, he would not consent to the
apology w.ʰ they ordered him to make.   And in consequence of
the last business even Dickens has cut him.[60]   We dont like men
writing about our privacies on this side of the water.

And what the dickens has happened to Davis?   I found on my
return home a notkin beginning 'dear Sir' and enclosing yours.
He was here for some time, and never told me he had come.   As
soon as I heard it, I went to look for him.   He never came to look
for me.   I thought nothing of it, but that he was busy engaged
in some tremendous railroad transaction some one told me — too
busy to come after me — and went away out of town with my
young folks, and my parents, and my Magazine on my back, and
my stricture in my bladder, in dreary health, spirits, condition.
We had a little trip to Holland from w.ʰ I have just returned —
and find your note.   Well, surely, I've written since my last letter
was sent back   I know I have — but that I have sent the letter
is another paire de bottes — I find letters lying about weeks &
months after and be hanged to me — I not only am lazy in
writing 'em, but incorrigibly irregular in sending 'em.   I have
done those things w.ʰ I ought not to have done I have left undone
those things w.ʰ I ought to have done, and there is little health
in me.[61]

[59] See above, No. 1462.
[60] In this Thackeray was mistaken.   On September 23 Dickens (*Letters*,
ed. Dexter, III, 178–179) wrote Yates a warm letter of condolence on the
death of his mother.
[61] "General Confession," *Book of Common Prayer*.

But if I dont write to my friends they'll remember what heaps of letters I have to write and forgive me, wont they? I have a Magazine once a month, a fever attack once a month, the charge of old folks and young folks whom I have to take to the country or arrange for at home — a great deal of business & bad health, and very little order. *I* offended with my friends? I have been looking out for my dear good Baxters, who wrote in the Spring, and here's winter almost and no sign of 'em.

What news for you? I am making and spending a deal of money have outlived my health, popularity, and inventive faculties as I rather suspect — am building a fine house and wonder whether I shall ever be able to live in it, and am yours my dear Robinson as always.

W. M. T.

1477.   TO GEORGE AUGUSTUS SALA
SEPTEMBER? 1860 [62]

My text is taken from Hodder's *Memories of my Time*, p. 367.

Dear S., — No! Who tells these lies? — W. M. T.

[62] Not long after his last paper on Hogarth appeared in *The Cornhill Magazine*, Sala accepted the editorship of *Temple Bar*. It was rumored, perhaps by Yates, that Thackeray was irritated by his contributor's defection, and Sala accordingly wrote to justify himself. (Hodder, *Memories of my Time*, pp. 366–367) The line printed above is Thackeray's reply. When the first issue of *Temple Bar* was published in December, Thackeray wrote in *The Cornhill Magazine* (p. 760): "Our course has been so prosperous, that it was to be expected other adventurers would sail on it, and accordingly I heard with no surprise, that one of our esteemed companions was about to hoist his flag, and take command of a ship of his own. The wide ocean has room enough for us all."

1478.   TO ?
                            3 NOVEMBER 1860

Hitherto unpublished.

                                                65, Cornhill,
                                            November 3, 1860.
Sir

The lectures were printed in my absence in America and contain
many errors — For Jervas read Richardson — the letter [63] is dated
June 10. 1733. My edition is rather a shabby one. the booksellers
Edition of 1812. Vol 7. p. 112.

                        Your obdt Serv.ᵗ
                        W M Thackeray

1479.   TO LADY ELIZABETH THACKERAY
                        8 NOVEMBER 1860

Address: The Lady Elizabeth Thackeray | The Cedars | Windlesham.
Postmarks: LONDON NO 10 60, BAGSHOT NO 10 60. Hitherto unpublished.

                                        36 Onslow Sqᵉ S. W.
                                            November 8.
My dear Lady Elizabeth.

As ill luck will have it, I have just knocked at the door of
the Colonial Office in behalf of an old acquaintance, a Surgeon
who wants an appointment in the Colonies. And I could give this
gentleman very little hope, because, also as ill luck will have it,
I made an unfortunate speech at Edinburgh some years ago, wʰ
I know was read by the Duke of Newcastle, who had previously

---

[63] Thackeray sent with this note a copy in his secretary's hand of the letter
of Pope's which he describes. In the first edition of *The English Humourists*
(London, 1853, p. 207) the recipient of this letter is identified as Jervas.
Actually Pope was writing to Richardson, as Thackeray's correspondent could
have ascertained, had he glanced at the notes to *The English Humourists*
where Pope's letter is reprinted.

been particularly kind and friendly to me & who had a right not to be pleased by what I said.[64] I am a sad blunderer and in a dreadful panic whilst speaking — I omitted the very point w.ʰ I wished to make (and w.ʰ was intended to be a compliment to him and Lord Elgin) and, I fear, justly offended him. He has never said anything to me on the subject; but his manner has not been so cordial to me, as it used to be.

I will go to the Home Office where Waddington the Under Secretary is my friend and see if he can help us — I should think his father's son and yours will be sure of goodwill — You know you have it from your young friends here and

Yours most sincerely always
W M Thackeray.

[64] Thackeray defended himself against the charge of radicalism that *The Four Georges* had caused to be brought against him at a dinner given by his Edinburgh admirers on April 2, 1857. The Duke of Newcastle, who had been from 1852 to 1854 Secretary for War and Colonies in Lord Aberdeen's cabinet and was again from 1859 to 1864 Secretary for the Colonies in Lord Palmerston's second cabinet, may have been offended by the following passage in Thackeray's speech. "I do not hold any dangerous revolutionary opinions. . . . I belong to the class that I see around me here, the class of lawyers, and merchants, and scholars, and men who are striving on in the world, of men of the educated middle classes of this country. And, belonging to them, my sympathies and my desires are with them. If it happened that we were all here an assembly of noblemen and earls, we should no doubt form a Viscounts' Government, and think it the best of all Governments possible. (Cheers.) If a difficulty arose in China, for instance, we should look for my Lord Duke A. to go out and settle the difficulty, or we should ask Earl B. to go if my Lord Duke A. were not inclined." (*Times*, April 4, 1857) As Thackeray had predicted, the Duke of Newcastle not being available, the eighth Earl of Elgin was appointed Her Majesty's High Commissioner and Plenipotentiary on a Special Mission to the Emperor of China on April 17 (*Foreign Office List*, 1859).

1480.   FROM ANTHONY TROLLOPE
                  15 NOVEMBER 1860

Extracts published by Mr. Parrish, "Adventures in Reading and Collecting
Victorian Fiction," *Princeton University Library Chronicle*, III (1942), 39.

Waltham Cross.

November 15, 1860

My dear Thackeray,

I trust you to believe me when I assure you that I feel no
annoyance as against you at the rejection of my story.[65] An im-
partial Editor must do his duty. Pure morals must be supplied.
And the owner of the responsible name must be the index of the
purity. A writer for a periodical makes himself subject to this
judgement by undertaking such work; and a man who allows
himself to be irritated because judgement goes against himself is
an ass. So much I say, that I may not be set down by you as
disgusted, or angry, or malevolent. But a few words I must say
also in defence of my own muse.

I will not allow that I am indecent, and profess that squeamishness — in so far as it is squeamishness and not delicacy — should
be disregarded by a writer. I of course look back for examples to
justify myself in alluding to a man with illegitimate children, and to
the existence of a woman not as pure as she should be. I think first
of Effie Deans.[66] Then coming down to our second modern great
gun — Observe how civil I am to you after the injury you have
done me — I reflect upon the naughtiness of Miss Beatrice,[67] all
the more naughty in that they are told only by hints; — and also
of the very wicked woman at Tunbridge Wells who was so surprised because young Warrington did not "do as others use" with
her — I forget whether it was her daughter, or her niece or her
protegee.[68] Then there is that illegitimate brat in Jane Eyre with

---

[65] "Mrs. General Talboys," published in *Tales of All Countries. Second
Series* (1863).

[66] In *The Heart of Midlothian*.

[67] In *Esmond*. See particularly the preface (*Works*, VII, 8).

[68] See chapter 29 of *The Virginians*.

the whole story of her birth; and Hetty Sorrel [69] with almost the whole story of how the child was gotten. I could think of no pure English novelist, pure up to the Cornhill standard, except Dickens; but then I remembered Oliver Twist and blushed for what my mother and sister read in that very fie-fie story. I have mentioned our five greatest names and feel that I do not approach them in naughtiness any more than I do in genius.

But in such cases, you will say, the impurities rest in the heads of the individual authors, — and that you must especially guard the Cornhill. Well... But how have we stood there? History perhaps should be told even to the squeamish, and therefore the improprieties of the improper Georges must be endured. But how about the innuendoes as to the opera dancers [70] which made the children of Terpsichore so mad thro' the three kingdoms?

You speak of the squeamishness of "our people". Are you not magnanimous enough to feel that you write urbi et orbi: [71] — for the best and wisest of English readers; and not mainly for the weakest?

I of course look forward to bringing out my own story in a magazine of my own. It will be called "The Marble Arch", and I trust to confound you by the popularity of Mrs. Talboys.

Joking apart I must declare that I disagree with your criticism. But at the same time I assure you that I am quite satisfied that you have said your own judgement impartially and with thoroughly good intention.

Always yours,
Anthony Trollope.

[69] In *Adam Bede*.
[70] See chapter 1 of *Lovel the Widower* and "Thorns in the Cushion" (*World*, XII, 214–215).
[71] From the Pope's blessing.

1481.   TO ANTHONY TROLLOPE
                17 NOVEMBER 1860

Hitherto unpublished.

                                    Nov.ʳ 17. 1860.
                                    36 O. Square

My dear Trollope.

I am just out of bed after one of my attacks, wʰ leave me very nervous and incapable of letter writing or almost reading for a day or two. So, as your letter came, and upon a delicate subject too — I told one of the girls to read it.

I give you her very words — I can't help it if they are not more respectful. She says after reading the letter "He is an old dear and you should write him an affectionate letter."

Then I had courage to have your letter read. I am another, am I? I always said so.

'The Marble Arch' is such a good name that I have a months mind to take it for my own story.

                                    Always yours
                                    W M T.

1482.   TO THOMAS COLLEY GRATTAN [72]

                5 DECEMBER 1860

Address: M. T. C. Grattan. | 30 Place de Meir | a Anvers. *Postmark:* LONDON DE 5 60. Hitherto unpublished.

                                    36 Onslow Sqᵉ S. W
                                    Dec.ʳ 5. 1860.

My dear Mʳ Grattan.

We strongly object to early republications from the Magazine, and this may not suit you. Bearing this in mind, you may be

---

[72] A prolific miscellaneous writer (1792–1864), known chiefly for his three series of *Highways and Byways* (1823–1827).

sure any contribution you may send will have the very best attention of

Yours sincerely

W M Thackeray

1483.   TO JOHN SKELTON
     14 DECEMBER 1860

My text is taken from Sir John Skelton's *Table Talk of Shirley*, pp. 27–28.

36 Onslow Sqare, S. W.,

Dec. 14, 1860.

Dear Sir, — I ask pardon for delaying to answer your note. Frequent illness, constant business, and want of system send my letters often deplorably into arrear, and I lose even more time in finding them than in answering them.

Queen Anne has long been my ambition; but she will take many a long year's labour, and I can't ask any other writer to delay on my account. At the beginning of this year I had prepared an announcement stating that I was engaged on that history; but kept it back, as it was necessary that I should pursue my old trade of novelist for some time yet to come. Meanwhile her image stands before St Paul's for all the world to look at, and who knows but some one else may be beforehand with both of us and sketch her off while we are only laying the palette?

Is all your spare time given to *Fraser*, and have you any subject which you think would suit us at Cornhill? I should be glad to have any suggestions from you. —

Truly yours,

W. M. Thackeray

1484.   FROM JOHN SKELTON
                    19 DECEMBER 1860

Hitherto unpublished.

                                            Dec. 19. 60.

Dear Sir,

I have to thank you for your note — I am sorry that you mention "illness" — I trust that it is nothing very serious, & that it has now passed away.

Should you try Queen Anne any materials I may then have will be very heartily at your service.

In the meantime I will continue to spend an hour sometimes among the dusty treasures of our Library — which is very rich in political & historical matter.

Since my poor friend John Parker's death I do not feel so much "engaged" to *Frazer*, & sh.ᵈ be happy if any subject offered to do some little thing for you. I have been meditating for some time an article on "Fishing in Scotland & the North" — which perhaps might suit you. The House of Lords has been "sitting" upon our fisheries & has issued a report containing a great deal of curious matter, & one or two rather interesting questions about fishing-rights in the North have been agitated. A *Scotchy* article on this subject, with a little information about some features of our system not much known south of the Tweed, might be made, I think, pleasant & picturesque.

Do not trouble to answer this note, unless you think the subject suitable.

                              Believe me, with thanks,
                                    Truly yours
                                    John Skelton

1485.   FROM JOHN RUSKIN [73]
           21 DECEMBER 1860

Published in Lady Ritchie's *Records of Tennyson, Ruskin and Browning* (London, 1893), pp. 159–161.

Denmark Hill

21st December.

1860.

Dear Mr Thackeray.

I think — or should think if I did not know — that you are quite right in this general law about lecturing: though until I knew it, I did not feel able to refuse the letter of request asked of me.

The mode in which you direct your charity puts me in mind of a matter that has lain long on my mind: though I never have had the time — or face — to talk to you of it. In somebody's drawing-room, ages ago, you were speaking accidentally of M. de Marvy. I expressed my great obligations to him: ⟨on⟩ which you said that I ⟨might⟩ now prove my gratitude if I chose — to his widow. Which choice I, not then accepting, — have ever since remembered the circumstance as one peculiarly likely to add — so far as it

---

[73] Though Thackeray and Ruskin were not intimate, they had been in frequent communication for some months past. "In the summer of 1860," Ruskin writes in the preface to *Munera Pulveris* (*Works*, 39 vols., ed. E. T. Cook and A. D. O. Wedderburn, London, 1902–1912, XVII, 143), "perceiving then fully, (as Carlyle had done long before), what distress was about to come on the said populace of Europe through these errors of their teachers [the orthodox political economists], I began to do the best I might, to combat them, in the series of papers for the *Cornhill Magazine*, since published under the title of *Unto this Last*. The editor of the Magazine was my friend, and ventured the insertion of the first three essays [in the issues of August, September, and October]; but the outcry against them became too strong for any editor to endure, and he wrote to me, with great discomfort to himself, and many apologies to me, that the Magazine must only admit one Economical Essay more.

"I made, with his permission, the last one [published in November] longer than the rest, and gave it blunt conclusion as well as I could — and so the book now stands."

went — to the general impression on your mind of the hollowness of peoples sayings — and hardness of their hearts.

The fact is I give what I give almost in an opposite way to yours; I think there are many people who will relieve hopeless distress, for one, who will help at a hopeful pinch; and when I have choice — I nearly always give where I think the money will be Fruitful, rather than merely helpful. I would lecture for a school — when I would *not* for a distressed author: and would have helped de Marvy to perfect his invention, but not — unless I had no other object — his widow after he was gone. In a word, I like to prop the falling — more than to feed the fallen.

This, if you ever find out anything of my private life — you will know to be true; but I shall never feel comfortable, nevertheless about that Marvy business, unless you send to me for ten pounds for the next author, or artist, or widow of either, whom you want to help.

— And with this weight at last off my mind, I pray you to believe me always

Faithfully & respectfully Yours
J Ruskin

All best wishes of the season to you & your daughters.

1486.   TO THE BAXTERS
          25 DECEMBER 1860

My text is taken from *American Family*, pp. 168–170

36 Onslow Square, Brompton
Christmas, 1860

The autumn has passed away in which you were to have come to England and here is a bitter cold Christmas day and no news of you. I am unwell. I am hard at work trying to get the new story [74] on a head. I have been quill-driving all the morning,

---

[74] *Philip*, the first installment of which appeared in *The Cornhill Magazine* for January, 1861.

but I must say a word of God bless you to my dear kind friends at Brown House Street and wish you a Christmas as merry as may be. Aren't you in a fright at the separation? [75] Is Sally going to be a country-woman of yours no longer, and will her children in arms fight Libby's? It's a horrible thing to me to read of. Have you ever seen a coloured print called the Belle of the West I have it hanging up because it is like a young woman whom I used to admire very much. (perhaps other little partialities are hung up too and are now only so many painted memorials on a wall) Is it this horrid Separation that has prevented your all coming to Europe. Or are you waiting till next year when my fine new house will be built — at Palace Green, Kensington — opposite the old palace. If I live, please God, I shall write the history of Queen Anne there. My dear relations are furious at my arrogance, extravagance & presumption in building a handsome new house, and one [76] of them who never made a joke in his life said yesterday to me "You ought to call it Vanity Fair."

I wonder whom you have got at dinner today? Our house is all hollyfied from bottom to top. We have asked a poor widow from India with her *five* children, and two or 3 men friends, and we have got a delicate feast consisting of

> *Boiled Turkey*
> *Roast Goose*
> *Roast Beef.*

and I am going to make a great bowl of punch in the grand silver bowl you know — the testimonial bowl.

No one has come to marry either of my dear girls. I am surprised they don't. But I hardly know any men under fifty, and cant be on the lookout for eligible bachelors as good dear London mammas can. I have not made their fortunes as yet, but am getting towards it and have saved a little since I wrote last; but

[75] Abraham Lincoln was elected President of the United States on November 20, and in protest South Carolina, where Mrs. Hampton was living, adopted an Ordinance of Secession on December 20.

[76] Charles Carmichael.

I am free-handed, have to keep my wife, to help my parents, & to give to poor literary folks — in fine my expenses are very large. I am supposed to make 10,000£ a year. Write 5 and it is about the mark. Health very soso. Repeated attacks of illness. Great thankfulness to God Almighty for good means, for good children. And thats all. Hadn't I better go on with Philip? Here is the very last sentence I wrote:

"When I was a girl I used always to be reading novels, she said but la! they're mostly nonsense! There's Mr. Pendennis, I wonder how a married man can go on writing about love and all that stuff!" [77] And indeed it is rather absurd for elderly fingers to be still twanging Don Cupid's toy bow & arrows. Yesterday is gone, yes — but very well remembered. And we think of it the more now we know that Tomorrow is not going to bring us much.

Goodbye my dear Yesterdays. And believe me affectionately yours.

1487.   TO GEORGE SMITH
                      1860

Hitherto unpublished.

                                             Friday.
My dear S.

Shant we have you for Thursday? We have Milnes, Donnelly, Miss Procter, Landseer Contributors and Buckle — who might do something for us.

                                   Yours
                               W M T.

[77] From chapter 6 of *Philip* (*Works*, XI, 156).

THE BELLE OF THE WEST.

"The Belle of the West"
From the Currier Lithograph

1488.   TO GEORGE SMITH
                        1 JANUARY 1861

My text is taken from George Smith's "Our Birth and Parentage," *Cornhill Magazine*, New Series, X (1901), 17.

                        36 O. S., S. W.: Jan. 1, 1861.
My dear S., —
H. N. Y. to all Smiths.
I am afraid we can't get Loch.[1] He has been advised not to write except his own book, whatever that may be.
Stephen [2] can't do anything for Feb.
Wynter [3] says he will do Bread.
This is all the present news from

                        Yours ever,
                        W. M. T.

[1] Henry Brougham Loch (1827–1900), later (1895) first Baron, who had been imprisoned and tortured by the Chinese in 1860 while private secretary to Lord Elgin on the latter's special mission to China.

[2] James Fitzjames Stephen (1829–1894), later (1891) first Baronet, took his B. A. degree at Trinity College, Cambridge, in 1851 and was called to the bar in 1854. He wrote for *The Saturday Review* from its inception in 1856. He contributed two articles to *The Cornhill Magazine* in 1860 and eight or nine during each of the next three years. "His connection with the 'Magazine'," writes his younger brother Leslie (*Life of Sir James Fitzjames Stephen*, London and New York, 1895, p. 177), "led to very friendly relations with Thackeray, to whose daughters he afterwards came to hold the relation of an affectionate brother."

[3] Dr. Andrew Wynter (1819–1876), editor of *The British Medical Journal* and essayist.

1489.   TO DR. JOHN BROWN
                     JANUARY 1861 4

My text is taken from John Skelton's *Table-Talk of Shirley*, p. 30.

                              The Cornhill Magazine,
                              Smith, Elder, & Co.

My dear J. B., — I see Mr Skelton has been saying kind things about me in *Fraser*. Is he full of work? Could he do something for [*Here a hand is drawn, pointing to "The Cornhill Magazine" above.*] If you know his address will you send him this line on from yours,

                                        W. M. T.

1490.   TO GEORGE SMITH
                     JANUARY 1861? 5

Hitherto unpublished.

My dear S.

Ainsworth who is sitting by me, wants to know about America. What arrangements have we made and with whom? and what would be the best plan for him to adopt?

I'm glad you like Philip. Long life to him

                    Yours
                    W M T.

4 This note was written shortly after the publication of Skelton's "On the Propriety of Abolishing the Writing of Books" (*Fraser's Magazine,* January, 1861, pp. 92–97), in which there are complimentary allusions to Thackeray.

5 It seems likely that this note was written shortly after the publication of the first installment of *Philip* in *The Cornhill Magazine* for January, 1861.

1491.   FROM DR. JOHN BROWN
13 JANUARY 1861

Hitherto unpublished.

23 Rutland Street
Edinburgh
Jan 13ᵗʰ

My dear Thackeray — Thanks for your two noticles — short
as they are, they let me know, what indeed I did not need to
be assured of, that you are what you used to be. There are some
people — not many, about whom I never concern myself as to
manifestations of what they are. I have settled the matter as to
them, & never need to be forever pulling up my plant of friendship to see if it is growing — I send John Skelton your last — &
he writes to say how pleased he is & that he will cast about for
something for the Cornhill I am ashamed of my shabbinesses to
you — but the truth is I must be forced to write — if you were to
make your printer Command me to have something ready by a
certain day, I would do it but if it is left to my own sweet will —
it is left forever — I am thinking of giving you an additional
member of "Our Dogs" [6] Birkie — a real dog — & the best successor I have ever known, to "Crab" "the sourest-natured dog that
lives" as his master said —

As to your health — I still think that you might have been
materially the better by seeing Syme,[7] & I am sure Thompson
would have been pleased to get his counsel — but as I said there
is an end of it — & I am rejoiced at your spasms being better —
what a pleasure, a perpetual pleasure it is to me to see & hear
everywhere the world's gratitude & praise to "Theophilus Wagstaff" [8] — I have been finding out your beginnings in Punch. Miss

---

[6] Brown's sequel to "Our Dogs" was not written for many years. It is
reprinted under the title "More of 'Our Dogs' " in the third series of *Horæ
Subsecivæ*.

[7] James Syme (1799–1870), the eminent Edinburgh surgeon.

[8] Brown evidently means Lancelot Wagstaff, an early pseudonym of Thack-

Tickletobys Lectures & the cuts — more history & philosophy & sense in them than in Mess.ʳˢ Kingsley Froude & Co ⁹ —

I was up two days ago seeing M.ʳˢ Krum. I cannot help hoping she is a little better & in such a case, one comes to be very grateful for any small mercies — she is happy & sleeps soundly — & enjoys external nature & is full of simple lore & tenderness & though childish in many of her ways — they are the ways of a wise child. About religion, this is especially the case — she seems to have got back to the immediate instincts of a pious nature, with all the depth, experience that her woman life has given her — you would be quite surprised at this. but why do I go on at this 'rate'? She was speaking of you, & giving such a clear, simple account of how truly she liked such a nature as yours — The lonely place where she is, was when I last was there, resounding with cuckoos — & I asked her if they were gone — "Oh yes & I am very glad — I don't like that *egotistical* bird" —

Is that house with 3 windows on each side of the door the Kensington Mansion? — Thackeray House? ¹⁰ Goodbye & God bless & keep you & the girls & us all —

Yr ever Affect
J. Brown

---

eray's over which he wrote four articles for *The New Monthly Magazine* in 1844 and 1845. "Miss Tickletoby's Lectures on English History" appeared in *Punch* from July 2 to October 1, 1842.

⁹ Charles Kingsley's *Westward Ho! or the Voyages and Adventures of Sir Amyas Leigh, Knight, of Burrough, in the County of Devon, in the Reign of her most Glorious Majesty Queen Elizabeth* appeared in 1855, and the first two volumes of James Anthony Froude's *History of England from the Fall of Wolsey to the Death of Elizabeth* were published in 1856.

¹⁰ See below, No. 1504.

1492. TO FREDERICK WALKER [11]
21 JANUARY 1861

My text is taken from John George Marks, *Life and Letters of Frederick Walker* (London, 1896), p. 20.

36 Onslow Square, S. W.
Jan. 21, 1861.

Dear Sir, — Can you copy the face on this block [12] as accurately as may be on to another block, improve the drawing of the figures,

[11] Walker (1840–1875), the seventh child of a working jeweller, was born and brought up in London. After three years of study in an architect's office and various drawing academies, he apprenticed himself in 1858 to the wood-engraver Josiah Whymper. By the beginning of 1861 he was proficient not only as an engraver, but also as a painter in water-colors and oils, and he was eager to secure work. He managed with some difficulty to bring his drawings to the attention of George Smith. "It happened just then," Smith relates (Huxley, *House of Smith, Elder*, pp. 142–143), "that Thackeray was beginning to find it troublesome to draw on wood. His last two or three drawings for the 'Adventures of Philip' were made on paper, and these had to be redrawn on wood by an artist, and the result, so far, had not been very satisfactory. It occurred to me that my youthful visitor was precisely the man to re-draw on wood Thackeray's sketches, and I proposed the task to him, and understood that the idea was acceptable. But Walker's nervous agitation while I was speaking to him was almost painful, and, though I did my best to set him at his ease, he left my room without my being sure that he understood the arrangement I wished to make with him. The plan was to be subject to Thackeray's approval, and I explained to him how painfully nervous his new assistant was. 'Can't you bring him here,' said Thackeray, 'and we can soon prove whether he can draw.' I wrote to Walker, and said I would call and drive him to Thackeray's house on a given day.

"The drive was almost a silent one, Walker's agitation being very obvious. When we reached our destination, Thackeray set himself in a most genial fashion, but with very partial success, to put Walker at his ease. At last he said, 'Can you draw? Mr. Smith says you can.' 'Y-y-yes, I think so,' said — in a hesitating fashion — the artist, who, within a few years, was to excite the admiration of the world by the excellence of his drawings! 'I am going to shave,' said Thackeray; 'would you mind drawing my back?' Thackeray went to his toilet glass and commenced shaving, while poor Walker took a sheet of paper and began sketching his subject's broad back. The sketch [which is reproduced in *Biographical Introductions*, XI, xlv] is a proof at once of his artistic skill and of his nervous state of mind.

"I looked out of the window while Walker worked, in order that he might

furniture, and make me a presentable design for wood engraving?

Faithfully yours,

W. M. Thackeray.

The less work the better. The two tumblers touching each other — the old man red-nosed and a wig. The young man light hair, large whiskers, moustache.

---

not feel he was being watched. Thackeray's idea of giving his back to Walker as a subject, was as ingenious as it was kind; for I believe, if Walker had been asked to draw Thackeray's face, instead of his back, he would hardly have been able to hold his pencil.

"Walker made two or three drawings from Thackeray's designs, and the work, it is needless to say, was done well. Then he came to me one day in some excitement, and said, without a word of preface, 'I am not going to do any more of this work!' I naturally inquired what was the matter; was he dissatisfied with the payment he received? No, he replied, he was quite satisfied with the payment, but the work offended his artistic self-respect. It was not original work, and his friends, he said, told him he could do original work, and he ought to do it, and not copy other people's designs; 'a task,' he added, 'which any fool could do who could draw!' I said I would talk the matter out with Thackeray, and asked if he would be willing to make the original illustrations for the story himself, and would listen to verbal suggestions made by Thackeray, either directly, or through me, as to the subjects to be illustrated, and their treatment. This I explained to my sensitive interlocutor, would not detract from the originality and independence of his work. Walker consented, and Thackeray, who had conceived a high opinion of Walker's ability as an artist, was glad to accept the arrangement, which saved him very much trouble."

Beginning with "Nurse and Doctor" in *The Cornhill Magazine* for May, Walker executed all the remaining illustrations for *Philip* with only the slightest hints from Thackeray. Thus introduced to public notice, he became very successful not only as an illustrator but also as a painter in oils and watercolors. At the time of his death he was one of the best known of Victorian artists.

[12] "The Old Fogies" in *The Cornhill Magazine* for March.

1493.   TO FREDERICK LOCKER [13]
                              JANUARY 1861

My text is taken from Augustine Birrell's *Frederick Locker-Lampson* (London, 1920), pp. 106–107, where the date is also recorded.

Garrick Club

My dear Locker,

I hope you bear your   •   of Saturday equanimiously. I ought to have been here to prevent it, for you was only b-k b-ll-d because there was nobody to speak for you, and there should have been such a friend. But I was in bed, Thursday, Friday, and 1/2 Saturday, with one of my spasm fits, & too sick to think of anything but the basin. I had to go out on Saturday to see Fred Elliot, & just as I was driving away, his sister-in-law, poor Miss Perry said she would like to see me. When I arrived here, all was over. Bear up like a man. You are none the worse and 28 guineas the richer.

Yours
W. M. T.

[13] Locker (1821–1895), who later (1885) took the additional surname of Lampson, is still remembered for his engaging *vers de société*. After his marriage to Lady Charlotte Bruce in 1850, he was a familiar figure in London society. He made his literary reputation with *London Lyrics* (1857). Among his recollections of Thackeray, recorded in *My Confidences* (London, 1896), pp. 297–307, there is the following little story: "I remember calling in Palace Gardens, and, while talking with all gravity to Thackeray's daughters, I noticed that they seemed more than necessarily amused. On looking round, I discovered that their father had put on my hat, and, having picked my pocket of my handkerchief, was strutting about flourishing it in the old Lord Cardigan style. As I was thin-faced, and he, as a hatter once remarked of Thomas Bruce, was 'a gent. as could carry a large body o' 'at,' you may suppose he looked sufficiently funny." (p. 305)

1494.   TO FREDERICK LOCKER
                    11 FEBRUARY 1861

My text is taken from Birrell's *Locker-Lampson*, pp. 106–107.

36 Onslow Square
Febr. 11. 1861.

My dear L,

Might we say *Joy* go with her & not God? the name of Allah jars rather in the pleasant little composition,[14] & I never like using it if it can be turned or avoided. If I don't hear from you I shall therefore print "Joy" instead of —— when I use the poem. Not this month however.

Yours always
W. M. T.

1495.   TO FREDERICK WALKER
                    11 FEBRUARY 1861

My text is taken from Marks, *Walker*, pp. 20–21, where the date is recorded.

Dear Sir, — The Blocks you have executed for the *Cornhill* Magazine have given so much satisfaction that I hope we may look for more from the same hand. You told me that the early days of the week were most convenient for you, and accordingly I sent last Monday, or Tuesday, a couple of designs which, as you would not do them,[15] I was obliged to confide to an older and I grieve to own, much inferior artist. Pray let me know if I may count upon you for my large cut for March.

Believe me, very faithfully yours,
W. M. Thackeray.

[14] "My Neighbour Rose," which is printed (with the alteration that Thackeray suggests) in *The Cornhill Magazine* of September, 1861, pp. 319–320.
[15] See above, No. 1492. The older and inferior artist was, of course, Thackeray himself.

1496.   ## TO WILLIAM DUER ROBINSON
FEBRUARY 1861

My text is taken from *Thackeray in the United States*, II, 12.

February, 1861.

My dear old W. D. Russell [16] is going to you with this, and I wish I was a going too

1496A.   ## TO JOHN FREDERICK BOYES
10–19 MARCH 1861

Hitherto unpublished.

March 10. 1861

My dear F. B.

Only 2 days ago, in one of my own attacks of illness w[h] are now so frequent, I was lying in bed thinking of old times and my illness at School and your Mother's dear kind face standing over me — and when I got up I thought I would go and see her, and shake a hand with the kind old times w[h] are now ended.[17] I only found your note amongst my heap of letters this morning, Sunday, when I'm able to read — not quite to remember and arrange — for the first time these 5 days — Im so weak and nervous now from illness (and other circumstances w[h] become immensely annoying when the corpus is not yet quite sanum) that I can only write you a word of hearty condolence and sym-

---

[16] Russell departed for America in March, 1861, to report the Civil War for *The Times*. His faithful description of the Battle of Bull Run on July 21 brought him into extreme disfavor with his northern hosts, and he was forced to return to England in April, 1862.

[17] Mrs. Boyes had recently died.

pathy and promise you that I retain always a warm tender recollection of old kindness, old days, old *youth* — now gone whither? Are we young people still walking about at this minute with your dear mother, or sitting round the old supper-table? Why shouldn't the good old Father be walking down to the New River with us boys now? Perhaps we are all kneeling down somewhere, and hearing Pritchard [16] praying away — What a turn it gave me, when I went to see you, to recognize the old books. Thalaba,[17] Martyr of Antioch and so on! — Those recollections were not dead, only sleeping — and so, pray God, nothing dies love least of all — w^h your dear Mother assuredly has for you in Heaven, as you here below have for her. So we all hold on by love to the past, and by just a little turn of the circle, it becomes the future. All the way up the countless ages preceding us, Mother and Children reach in wonderful tender tradition, and off our earth pass into the world beyond — I have had a child there for 20 years now, and love her still. Good bye. I am writing with such horrible ink, pens, paper, disturbance, desk, conversation (just after Church) going on, and weakness of illness, that I scarce know how my sentences begin or end — but I am yours my dear old friend always

WMT.

March 19. This incoherency you see is more than a week old. It was scarce done when I had to struggle to my unfinished months work [18] and get it done somehow or other — and looking at this paper thinks I — it is all about myself and not about my old friends. Never mind — the meaning is, that I sympathize with your grief, and kindly remember old times. Our best regards

[16] Probably William Amon Gee Pritchard (b. 1812), who entered Charterhouse in 1826, went to St. John's College, Cambridge, and in later life was Rector of Brignall, Yorkshire.

[17] Southey's *Thalaba the Destroyer* (1801) and Milman's *Martyr of Antioch* (1822).

[18] Chapters 8 to 10 of *Philip*, which appeared in *The Cornhill Magazine* for April, 1861.

to your wife. We hope to come and see you ere long and I am always yours

WMT.

But that point is odd to speculate about, isn't it? The soul being immortal — The have been is eternal, as well as the will be. We are not only elderly men, but young men, boys, children.

1497.   TO THE MISSES JONES
1 APRIL 1861

Hitherto unpublished.

36 Onslow Sqᵉ S. W.
April 1.
The Editor of the CornHill Magazine

I must inform the authors of 'a No' [19] that two tearful stars bedimmed my spectacles on reading their very very tender and pathetic verses.

The verses are so good that they ought to be better. Why leave careless and loose rhymes such as those marked? Why not polish the verses more and more and make them as bright as they possibly can be? Indeed they are worth all the trouble, I hope to have them back at an early day, and am the writers'

Obliged faithful Servᵗ
W M Thackeray

vows so dear and
Not hear the passionate words so fondly told

[19] Published in *The Cornhill Magazine* of November, 1861, pp. 599–600.

(2)
> For all my soul goes sorrowing to behold
>> How much &c.

5 x grasping pen? & mine & thine are but poor rhymes

7 *stars, futurity*

10. sea, me, see, be. The whole stanza is obscure. earthly sea specially obscure.

17 Go then! & take with thee &c

7 Dimmed with a mist of tears my eyes I raise
> Two tearful stars are all my eyes can see   ?
> But thine into futurity should gaze

1498. ## TO MRS. BROWNING
2 APRIL 1861

Published by Lady Ritchie, *Cornhill Magazine*, New Series, I, 12–13.

36 Onslow Sq^r· April 2. 1861.

My dear kind Mrs. Browning

Has Browning ever had an aching tooth w^h must come out (I don't say Mrs Browning, for women are much more courageous) — a tooth w^h must come out and which he has kept for months and months away from the dentist? I have had such a tooth a long time, and have sate down in this chair, and never had the courage to undergo the pull.

This tooth is an allegory (I mean *this* one). Its your poem [18] that you sent me months ago — and who am I to refuse the poems of Elizabeth Browning, and set myself up as a judge over her? I cant tell you how often I have been going to write, and have failed.

You see that our Magazine is written not only for men and women, but for boys, girls, infants, sucklings almost, and one of the best wives, mothers, women in the world, writes some verses, w^h I feel certain would be objected to by many of our readers — Not that the writer is not pure, and the moral most pure chaste and right — but there are things my squeamish public

[18] Lady Ritchie identifies Mrs. Browning's contribution as "Lord Walter's Wife" (*Cornhill Magazine*, New Series, I, 12).

will not hear on Mondays though on Sundays they listen to them
without scruple. In your poem you know there is an account of
unlawful passion felt by a man for a woman — and though you
write pure doctrine and real modesty and pure ethics, I am sure our
readers would make an outcry, and so I have not published this
poem.

To have to say no to my betters is one of the hardest duties I
have — but I'm sure we must not publish your verses — and I go
down on my knees before cutting my victims head off, and say
'Madam you know how I respect and regard you, Brownings wife
and Peniny's mother: and for what I am going to do I most
humbly ask your pardon.'

My girls send their very best regards and remembrances: and
I am, dear Mrs. Browning

Always yours

W M Thackeray

1499.   FROM JAMES FITZJAMES STEPHEN
18 APRIL 1861

My text is taken from Lady Ritchie, *Cornhill Magazine*, New Series, I, 7.

April 18, 1861.

My dear Thackeray, — Smith told me that you had been very
unwell, which I was sorry to hear. Your not answering my note
was of no consequence, as I took the liberty of forwarding the
article which it proposed, and I suppose from Smith's having
sent the proof that you do not object to it.

I have a variety of articles which I could propose to you if you
would let me know when I could call on you to talk over them.
I always used to find with Cook [19] that it saved a deal of trouble,
and made the articles better, to have a stock on hand.

Ever sincerely yours,

J. F. Stephen.

Would you be at home some time after four on Saturday?

[19] John Douglas Cook (1811–1868), editor of *The Morning Chronicle*
from 1852 to 1855 and of *The Saturday Review* from 1856 to 1868.

1500.   FROM MRS. BROWNING
                      21 APRIL 1861

Published by Lady Ritchie, *Cornhill Magazine*, New Series, I, 13–14.

April 21. Rome.
126 Via Felicè.

Dear Mʳ Thackeray   Pray consider the famous "tooth" (a wise tooth!) as extracted under chloroform, and no pain suffered by anybody.

To prove that I am not sulky I send another contribution [20] — which may prove too much perhaps, — and, if you think so, dispose of the supererogatory virtue by burning the ms, as I am sure I may rely on your having done with the last.

I confess it, dear Mʳ Thackeray, never was anyone turned out of a room for indecent behaviour in a more gracious and conciliatory manner!   Also I confess that from your Cornhill stand:point, (paterfamilias looking on) you are probably right ten times over. From mine, however I may not be wrong — and I appeal to you as the deep man you are, whether it is not the higher mood which on Sunday bears with the 'plain word', so offensive on monday during the cheating across the counter — ?   I am not a 'fast woman' — I dont like coarse subjects, or the coarse treatment of any subject — But I am deeply convinced that the corruption of our society requires, not shut doors and windows, but light and air — and that it is exactly because pure & prosperous women choose to *ignore* vice, that miserable women suffer wrong by it everywhere. Has paterfamilias, with his Oriental traditions and veiled female faces, very successfully dealt with a certain class of evil?   What if materfamilias, with her quick pure instincts and honest innocent eyes, do more towards their expulsion by simply looking at them & calling them by their names —

See what insolence you put me up to by your kind way of naming my dignities, — "Browning's wife, and Penini's mother"

[20] "Little Mattie", which appeared in *The Cornhill Magazine*, June, 1861, pp. 736–737.

— And I, being vain, (turn some people out of a room and you dont humble them properly) retort with — "materfamilias"! —

Our friend Mr Story has just finished a really grand statue of the "African Sybil" — It will place him very high.

Where are you all, Annie, Minnie — why don't you come and see us in Rome?

My husband bids me give you his kind regards, and I shall send Pen's love with mine to your dear girls —

most truly yours

Elizabeth Barrett Browning.

We go to Florence in the latter half of May.

1501. FROM ANNE THACKERAY TO MRS. BAXTER
25 APRIL 1861

Hitherto unpublished.

36. Onslow Sq. April 25

How do you do My dear Mrs Baxter after all these years that we have known you and talked about you and this is indeed not nearly the first time that I have written to you and burnt my letter. We know you all I think a great deal better than you know us for Papa has been talking about you these 5 6 7 years I dont like to count up it seems such a life time and you don't know how much we liked getting the pictures. Only we cried out first *where is Mrs Baxter* & she had stopped behind in America — We have 3 faded little old tin daguerreotypes w^h my Father brought home when he first came back & as we look at them we think everybody very much changed — I dont think you w^d regret this if you could see our old friends — Miss Libby has lost her nose (the old picture is Miss Libby still) And Lucy an eye and her sister is faded away altogether and so these seem quite fresh new friends come to see us again after a long absence. When are we going to see you all really? Only three days before your letter came Papa & I were saying we can put Mrs Baxter into the big front room & Lucy into the back & the boys up above when the new house is finished. Everybody here says O what dear little children — I am quite foolish abt the little girl she has a sweet little face of her own w^h quite touches me but I think the little boy is the general favourite. (I am meandering off from y^r children to your grand children) and in short you must come to us or we must go to you for I know it is fated that we shall meet one day. There are very few people to whom we can even talk about you — Mr Mildmay used to tell us abt Miss Sallie sometimes but I think we were never very partial to him & scarcely knew him. We saw him with his wife [21] the other night: she has been very handsome   I remember her at certain French classes a lovely young creature — We have seen very few Americans lately the last we cared for were some charming Miss Fishes [22] or Fishs or Fish and since then only some very odd queer people from y^r country have been to see us. When your son comes to see us we will be very stupid & we shall be very glad to know him & I am afraid he will be dreadfully bored & I know he will be very welcome. Do you know what our household consists of 1. a little dog with a curly tail. 2. 3. Jack & Jill two puppies that squeak a good deal 4 a little cat passionately attached to Papa, & she purrs & jumps on his knee & wont be turned off. 5 a certain kind gentleman whose picture I send you — tho' to me it is not him a bit. 6 Miss Anny 7 Miss Minny. Im nearly 24 & Minny nearly 21 and absurdly young for her age for she still likes playing with children and kittens & hates reading & is very shy tho' she does not show it & very clever tho' she does not do any thing in particular and always helps me out of scrapes w^h I am always getting into. Then there is Amy Crowe who has lived with us these 7 years & who is one of the best and gentlest & kindest of women and then there is a faithful but tearful & affected cook, a pretty little maid called Fanny who is literary and quotes the Cornhill Magazine; and a gawky housemaid; and also a faithful reckless youth who breaks the china & tumbles down stairs & is called the Butler. And now good night for tonight dear M^{rs}

[21] Henry Bingham Mildmay married Georgiana Frances Bulteel (d. 1899) on July 24, 1860.
[22] See below, p. 392.

ANNE THACKERAY

From a painting by G. F. Watts

HARRIET THACKERAY
From a painting by G. F. Watts

Baxter here is a message from Minny to say I must go & dress as we are going to fetch Papa at the club & on to some tea-parties — I have not written you a letter at all but a very silly little domestic history — (two days after) and all this while you in America are hearing guns thundering and canon & speeches and seeing a good deal of smoke as I sincerely & every body here sincerely hopes The news of the Fort-battle [23] came in after I began my letter and now I am almost ashamed to send such twaddle when you must be think & talking of wars & politics and presidents — and anything but puppies and kittens Papa gets letters f^m Mr Russell of the Times by whom he sent you a token w^h was never delivered. I dont think you will find him a bit changed when you do come & see us, he is always ill but rallies and cheers again in the wonderfullest way — When his attacks come we are as I need not tell you very wretched and anxious & when they go away we forget all about them as he does himself he is up in his room now at work & he will wonder at my coolness in writing you such a letter as this only as I know you are the Mrs Baxter I'm sure you are I am not afraid that you will be angry. We have been reading some charming books [24] from y^r country lately Mr Holmes' I sat up half the night over — Mr Motley is hardly an American — I hope it is true what people say & that Miss Motley will marry Ld Dufferin [25] — All our trees are green with spring but the east winds are still blowing & make us shiver & parch until they are gone. In the new house there is a garden where we can sit in summer-time & pleasant rooms opening into it & windows looking over Kensington Gardens & the Rooks & the Elm trees — That is what I hope you will see some day & meanwhile I am Your very sincerest

A I Thackeray

[23] The Confederate bombardment of Fort Sumter on April 12–13.

[24] Holmes's *The Professor at the Breakfast-Table* was published in 1860, and the first two volumes of Motley's *United Netherlands* were published in 1861.

[25] The fifth Baron Dufferin (1826–1902), later (1888) first Marquess of Dufferin and Ava, married Georgina Hamilton in 1862.

1502.   TO WILLIAM WEBB FOLLETT SYNGE
2 MAY 1861

Address: W. W. Synge Esqre | 3 Cumberland S^t | Pimlico. *Postmark:* LONDON MY 2 61. Extracts published, *Thackeray in the United States*, I, 105.

I take another sort of paper to see if I can make it more cheerful. Why the deuce shouldn't I be? Morgan John always is — and you know by rights ought to hang himself — I have no doubt he was at Paddy Green's [26] last night, and as happy with those old songs and that tepid gin and water, as Lord Overstone [27] with his (tell me if I put the figures right) 10,000,000£. Anny is always cheerful too — Amy ditto — so I daresay am I, only I moan and grumble. My chief companions now are Bob Bell and Fladgate, and our amusement is to go dine tête à tête at Greenwich or Blackwall. We did so yesterday — and our enjoyment was to speculate upon Mr Lovegrove's speedy and certain suicide — for the river stinks fitfully — (though quite pleasant yesterday) the Company has left off coming: the rent must be awfully heavy: the provision must rot, *faute de mangeurs,* and RUIN must ensue. When will you be back? In time enough to welcome the Liberator of Italy [28] (from the Alps to the Adriatic) when he comes to give freedom to the oppressed nationalities at present groaning in these islands. The South of your dear Ireland will receive him with open arms — small doubt of that. Armstrong says if he will wait for two years: we can wap him: and a gentleman at the G (where the political information is usually very fine) said last night, he has been spending during the war at the rate of 200000£ a day —

[26] Evans's Hotel, the proprietor of which was John ("Paddy") Green.
[27] Samuel Jones Loyd (1796–1883), first and last Baron Overstone, one of the richest men in England. His annual rent-role in 1883 was £58,098 (Bateman, *Great Landowners,* p. 348), and on his death his personal estate was sworn under £2,100,000. He owned the great banking house of Jones, Loyd, and Company.
[28] Napoléon III, whose aid had been instrumental in establishing the Kingdom of Italy on March 26, 1861.

And Abbott [29] was talking about you then and wondered whether I would be ready for the 17th — as I have promised to be these months past: and Crawfurd is going to marry Miss Ford (30000£) and me and the gals is a going to Cornwall to Lady Molesworth next month if our work is done — and if our elders will let us. who have taken lodgings at Hythe and are expected to day there. My mother has wonderfully recovered from her accident: but I suppose she inherits from me rather a gloomy temper, & the prospect of a summer at Hythe does not add much to my cheerfulness. We have made one or 2 new acquaintances whom we like, and who like us — at first. I have not fallen in love with anybody all the year. I went t'other night to Cremorne,[30] and found even that melancholy. And the Sherry Cobler — O l'infamie! I have bought 12 new forks 6 new teaspoons. We have got a puppy. He fell down the area & broke his leg. Lady Palmerston has only asked me & 1 girl once the whole season. At Harrow speeches I was cheered more than anybody except the Prince of Wales. I am prodigiously popular in Russia. We are going to have only one more little dinner this season. We keep a boy now, in loo of a boy and a butler, and do just as well. The swells have almost entirely left us off. My hydraulic apparatus continues to be disorganized. And now, sir, I must go back to my plate and to my work: and, having told you all the news (Jo Crowe has been Times Correspondent & was close to the Emperor of Austria at Solferino) — I present my cordial respects to your beloved Chief,[31] and quick Charles! Send somebody with this to M[r] Abbott at the F. O.

Adieu. Yours

W M T.

[29] Charles Stuart Aubrey Abbott (1834–1882), later (1870) third Baron Tenterden, who was at this time a clerk in the Foreign Office. He afterwards became Permanent Under-Secretary for Foreign Affairs.

[30] Cremorne Gardens. See above, No. 963.

[31] Lord John Russell, who was Foreign Secretary in Lord Palmerston's second cabinet.

1503.   FROM MRS. BROWNING
                        21 MAY 1861

Address: Editor of the CornHill Mag. | (Mess.rs Smith & Elder.) | Cornhill. |
London — | Angleterre. *Postmarks:* 21 MAG., 23 MAI 61 MARSEILLE.
Published by Lady Ritchie, *Cornhill Magazine*, New Series, I, 14.

Dear M.r Thackeray

I hope you received my note & last poem —

I hope still more earnestly that you wont think I am putting
my spite against your chastening hand, into a presumptuous &
troublesome fluency —

But Hans Christian Andersen is here, — charming us all, & not
least, the children — So I wrote these verses.[32] — Not for Cornhill
uses this month of course, — though I send them now that they
may lie over at your service (if you are so pleased) for some
other month of the summer. We go to Florence on the first of
June, — and lo' — here is the twenty first of May —

With love to dear Annie & Minny, I remain

                         Most truly yours
                         Elizabeth Barrett Browning

Rome — 126. Via Felice.

1504.   TO MRS. BAXTER
                         24 MAY 1861

Published in *American Family*, pp. 171–175.

                              24 May. 36 Onslow Sq.e

I think you hardly know me in this hand-writing [33] I return to
it by fits and starts and when I write with quill pens. Your little
package of photographs [34] came and touched us all — How I
should like to see the originals, and the one who *isn't* represented,

[32] Mrs. Browning's last poem, "The North and the South".
[33] Thackeray's slanting hand.
[34] Mrs. Fuller tells me that these photographs have not been preserved.

Madam. Why is there not one of you? I suppose Papa did not care to have his wife shown with a wrinkle in her face, and always thinks of her as that young lady in white muslin and a frill, who to my mind is not half so good looking as the Mrs Baxter I knew. How the boys have grown! Wyllys moustache is quite elegant. I daresay George has one by this time on his solemn face. Do you know, but then I should not like to tell her, I think Sarah has grown handsomer: and we are divided here about w^h of the children we like best — the dark little maiden with the round eyes or the little man with the Saxon face. There's a very fine kind melancholy letter from Sarah Hampton w^h I have been reading. It is stretching a hand out into the past and shaking hands with a ghost there. I suppose you wont have the courage to leave home now that it is made so comfortable to you by war. If Wylly doesn't come till December or so we shall most likely be able to house him in Vanity Fair House. If he comes sooner we must get him a lodging round the corner. At the pastry cook's you know, there are very decent rooms: and it's not farther off than the brown house from the Clarendon. That wretch W. H. Russell! On the night before he left London we dined at the Garrick Club: and what did I do but cut off a beautiful lock of snowy hair and write in an envelope Be kind to the bearer of this. And he never bore it to you: though he went to the Clarendon. And I dont at all envy him the errand upon w^h he is gone to the states.[35]

Awful Reprisals. Thackeray invested the money w^h he received for his lectures in America, in American railway stocks.[36] If they cease to pay dividends, he threatens to come back to America, and give more lectures.

I wonder shall I go and call upon your Minister?[37] I have well nigh broken with the world the grand world and only go to the people who make my daughters welcome. The fine ladies won't: or is it that the girls are haughty, and very difficult to

---

[35] See above, No. 1496.
[36] See above, No. 988, note 175.
[37] Charles Francis Adams (1807–1886), American Minister to Great Britain from 1861 to 1868.

please? They won't submit to be patronized by the grandees at all, that's the fact: and I think I rather like them for being rebellious and independent — more so than their Papa, who is older and more worldly.

I think I kept back this notekin in order to sketch the new house at Kensington — but fond memory supplies the place of actual survey: and this is what you will see when you come to London —

the reddest house in all the town. I have already had 1000£ offered me for my bargain: but I want if I can afford health & time to write the life of Queen Anne in that room with the arched window w^h has a jolly look out on noble Kensington Garden Elms, and is no farther from the centre than what? than 25th Street let us say. But the house is very dear. It costs 6000£ and 100£ a year ground rent. Where we are now only costs 3000 — But its a famous situation & will be a little competency to the girl who inherits it. Anny has been ailing of late, and has gone to the country for change of air.

I think Trollope is much more popular with the Cornhill Magazine readers than I am: [38] and doubt whether I am not going down hill considerably in public favor. It doesn't concern me very much Were I to let yonder red house We could live almost without writing but then you know Wife and parents are expensive. They

[38] The concluding installments of Trollope's *Framley Parsonage* were appearing in *The Cornhill Magazine* concurrently with the early chapters of *Philip*.

want more money here than at Paris: and Thank God up to the present there's no lack. But my mother gets very rebellious and wants to go back. There's a little clique of old ladies there who are very fond of her and with whom she is a much more important personage than she is in this great city. If anything happens to the Major she will go to Paris and give us the slip and grumble when she is there and presently come back.

Well. This is not much to tell is it? To write twopenny news of domestic gossip to people enjoying a revolution. I have never got to believe in it as serious as yet: and my impression of the U. S. is so incurably friendly that I can't fancy you quarrelling and hating each other. I cant think the fight will be a serious fight. In what will it benefit the North to be recoupled to the South? In the old wars wc used to talk of the ruin of England as ensuing on the Separation of the Colonies — and aren't both better for the Separation?

Come let me shut up this little twaddling letterkin, and pay a shilling for it w^h is 11 1/2 more than its worth, and send it with a handshake to dear friends from their faithful

W M T.

1505.   TO THE REV. WHITWELL ELWIN
24–31 MAY 1861

My text is taken from Warwick Elwin's memoir of his father in *Some Eighteenth Century Men of Letters*, I, 158, and from a Sotheby catalogue of November 12, 1928.

24 May, ever so many days after birth

My dear Primrose

I think I have just been proposed and *refused* as a member of the Literary Club .. Walpole [39] proposed me: and I told him that an adverse fate w^d very likely befal me. All people don't like me as you do. I think sometimes I am deservedly unpopular, and in some cases I rather like it. Why should I want to be liked by Jack and Tom? Not long ago I went to the Stalls at Drury

[39] Spencer Horatio Walpole (1806–1898), the politician and historian.

Lane with Robert Bell, and to us came in the next stalls Dickens and Wilkie Collins. Dickens & I shook hands and didn't say one single word to each other. And if he read my feelings on my face as such a clever fellow would he knows now that I have found him out. Forster is the man who cut me because he fancied I meant him in one of the Roundabout Papers [40]. . . . I know the Thackeray that those fellows have imagined to themselves — a very selfish, heartless, artful, morose, and designing man. — What gall and wormwood is trickling from my pen! Well, there's no black drop in *you*, Mr. Parson; but, mind you, primroses are very rare flowers by the side of Thames. . . . My old friend James White has been in London several weeks and at 200 yards from this and never let me know of his being here. He has a great alliance with Dickens and Forster. But why should that prevent him from seeing an old friend. Ah if I dared but put all those fellows into a book! And suppose they put me into another — giving their views of your humble servant? Those books would be queer reading.

I wonder shall I have life and health to write Queen Anne? I long to get at it in my old age, feeling that the days of novels & romances and love making are over . . . what about books? You know we dont read 'em in London. I admire but cant read Adam Bede and the books of that Author. Motley and the Spanish Armada amused me very much: and sure Buckle is very diverting . . .

This scrap was written a week ago: don't you think it were best

[40] Forster had in mind the following passage from "On a Joke I Once Heard from the Late Thomas Hood", which appeared in *The Cornhill Magazine* for December, 1860: "There is my friend Baggs, who goes about abusing me, and of course our dear mutual friends tell me. Abuse away, *mon bon*! You were so kind to me when I wanted kindness, that you may take the change out of that gold now, and say I am a cannibal and a negro, if you will. Ha, Baggs! Dost thou wince as thou readest this line? Does guilty conscience throbbing at thy breast tell thee of whom the fable is narrated? Puff out thy wrath, and, when it has ceased to blow, my Baggs shall be to me as the Baggs of old — the generous, the gentle, the friendly." (*Works*, XII, 264–265) Thackeray's first draft of this passage, in which Baggs is described as absurd as well as generous, friendly, and gentle (*Roundabout Papers*, ed. Wells, p. 394), suggests Forster even more unmistakably.

burned? Many letters were best burned; for example, love letters, and especially *hate* letters. But if I don't send this one off to you, how on earth shall I communicate with my Vicar of Wakefield? You know I am too lazy to begin a new page. . . . A gossiping letter! Well, upon my word, this is a rarity! Good-bye, my dear Vicar. Mind and come and see us when you come up.

1506.   TO FREDERICK WALKER
                    MAY? 1861 [41]

My text is taken from Marks, *Walker*, p. 24.

Then you must be hungry, and shall have my piece of cake.

Dear Mr. Walker, I think this will make as good a subject as another. The three or four children *ad libitum*, Mrs. Pendennis, Bandeaux, Madonna; Mr. P. round face, no moustache; Mrs. Pendennis making breakfast, two or three children, Pendennis reading newspaper. Philip just come into breakfast-room.

[41] In chapter 15 of *Philip* (*Works*, XI, 269) the gift is of bread and jam, but in Walker's drawing for the July number of *The Cornhill Magazine* it is unmistakably cake.

1507.   TO MISS CAMPBELL [42]
                         13 JUNE 1861

Address: The Honorable Miss Campbell | Stratheden House. *Postmark:*
LONDON JU 13 1861. Hitherto unpublished.

36 Onslow Sq[re]
Thursday.

Dear Miss Campbell.

I go down on my knees to you and beg you to read my queer
petition. The writer of the accompanying [43] was curate when I
used to live at Kensington and go to 8 o'clock morning church with
that unostentatious piety (w[h] perhaps you dont know) distinguishes
me. He was a good simple gentlemanlike moderate and modest

[42] John, first Baron Campbell (1779–1861), Lord Chancellor of England,
had two unmarried daughters, both of whom lived with him at Stratheden
House, Kensington Road. They were Mary Scarlett Campbell, who married
in 1869, and Cecilia Campbell, who married in 1862.

[43] Thackeray's enclosure has been lost.

man and I heard from him one of the three best sermons I have ever heard in my life.

There is, it appears, a young woman who wants to be married to this worthy man — and as I know by your face you have a kind heart — what can I say more?

Yours most faithfully

W M Thackeray

1508.   TO THE REV. WHITWELL ELWIN
JUNE 1861 [44]

Published in facsimile by Warwick Elwin, *Some Eighteenth Century Men of Letters*, I, 246–247.

Dear Dr Primrose

Lest I should be too much elated by your praises the other day

---

[44] " 'Won't you come to London,' Thackeray wrote, May 24th, 1861, 'and see the new house I am building? — such a good, comfortable, cheerful one, all built out of Cornhill money.' Accordingly Elwin lunched with him when he was in town in June, and went to look at the house. As they were going over it, Thackeray said, 'An uncle of mine [Charles Carmichael] annoyed me

see what a wholesome corrective [45] was in store for me in that heap of letters w^h you saw.

Yours in pretty good spirits nevertheless

1509.   TO DR. JOHN BROWN
                          1 JULY 1861

My text is taken from *Letters of Dr. John Brown*, p. 332.

36 O. Sqr., July 1, 1861.

My dear J. B.—Thanks for your constant kindness to W. M. T., who is indolent and disorderly but not ungrateful. . . .

---

by saying, "It ought to be called *Vanity Fair*".' 'Why should that annoy you?' asked Elwin. 'Because it is true,' replied the other; 'the fact is, it is too good for me.'

"Elwin, on the same occasion, praised the Adventures of Philip, which was then coming out in the Cornhill. Thackeray knew wherein its weakness lay. He said, 'I have told my tale in the novel department. I can repeat old things in a pleasant way, but I have nothing fresh to say. I get sick of my task when I am ill, and think, Good heavens! what is all this stuff about?' Miss Thackeray asked him at lunch whether he was going to dine at home or 'at a house by a river'. 'At a house by a river, to be sure,' he answered; 'I shall go to Greenwich and write a bit of Philip.' 'Write Philip at a tavern at Greenwich!' exclaimed Elwin. 'Yes,' he replied, 'I cannot write comfortably in my own room. I do most of my composition at hotels or at a club. There is an excitement in public places which sets my brain working.'

"Miss Thackeray brought out some pen-and-ink sketches which her father had been making for a charity bazaar. Elwin asked if she would sell him one by private contract. 'No,' interposed Thackeray, 'you cannot afford to buy gimcracks, now you are a dethroned editor. I will draw something for you, and give it to you." (Elwin, *Some Eighteenth Century Men of Letters*, I, 245–246) A few days later this drawing and note arrived.

[45] A note by an anonymous critic, which reads: "It is with great regret I write the following letter,—regret that cause should have arisen for the writing of it. I will not trespass much on your valuable time, and will at once come to the subject. That subject is the great degeneration in your writings since you published your last great work, the Newcomes. The Virginians was a great falling off, but even that was immensely superior to the portion which has appeared of the Adventures of Philip. Surely, as an admirer of your genius, I have a right to appeal to you (even at an immense pecuniary sacrifice) to consult your future fame, and to keep it intact by

What a fine memoir that is of your father! [46] What a fine patriarchal figure! The book is all good reading. I wish you a good heart, fortunes and misfortunes, and am always, my dear Brown, yours,

W. M. T.

1510.

TO THOMAS FRASER
31 JULY 1861

Address: Thomas Fraser Esqre | Reform Club | Pall Mall London. *Postmarks:* FOLKESTONE JY 31 61, LONDON JY 31 61. Facsimile published in Van Duzer's *Thackeray Library*, p. 8.

Pavilion. Folkestone. Wednesday

My dear T. F.

Now that our dear old Lord Mayor is beaten,[47] couldn't we get up some testimonial to him? All sides would join in it, and though I'm economical enough in paper [48] I should be very glad to put my name alongside of a penny stamp. Think if you can't agitate the matter

Yours W M Thack.

writing no more novels, if you cannot improve on Lovel the Widower. Perhaps this letter is written to no purpose. Maybe, blinded by the flattering incense offered by the world to a great man and a successful one like you, you will set me down as a presumptuous fool. Anyhow, I have done what I consider my duty in writing and telling you the truth, even at the risk of irretrievably offending you. It is written in the best wish both for your future fame and happiness. . . . P. S. I send my address, and hoping you will not lug my humble epistle into a Roundabout Paper." (Elwin, *Some Eighteenth Century Men of Letters*, I, 246–247)

[46] "Letter to John Cairns, D. D." in the second series of Brown's *Horæ Subsecivæ* (1861), the dedication of which Thackeray shared with Gladstone, Ruskin, and Andrew Coventry Dick.

[47] In 1861 Lord John Russell, M. P. for London, accepted the Chiltern Hundreds previous to becoming a peer. Two candidates presented themselves for his place in parliament, William Cubitt (conservative), Lord Mayor of London in 1861 and 1862, and Western Wood (liberal). On July 30 Wood was returned by a vote of 5,747 to 5,241. (*Times*, July 30–August 1)

[48] Thackeray's note is written inside the flap of an envelope.

1511.   TO ?
                          6 AUGUST 1861

Hitherto unpublished.

                                              Folkstone.
                                              August 6.

Dear Sir

The very good verses you sent to me are I think on a subject
that will scarce suit our public. I once wrote a story myself in w.^h
an elderly woman fell in love with a young man; [49] and it was
the old women who were angry. I shall be very glad to hear from
you again and if you have prose as good as your verse, to give it
my best attention.

                              Faithfully yours
                              W M Thackeray.

1512.   TO FREDERICK WALKER
                          AUGUST? 1861 [50]

My text is taken from a facsimile in Marks's *Walker*, p. 22.

                        For Mr Walker

Lord Ringwood on his sofa in the gout. Philip puts on his hat
& makes him a bow

Lord Ringwood dressed in an old fashioned tail coat of 1824
date High stock & collar.

___

[49] Lady Maria Castlewood and Harry Warrington in *The Virginians*. See
particularly chapter 18.

[50] Thackeray is describing "A Quarrel", which appeared in *The Cornhill
Magazine* for October.

A Quarrel

1513. TO GEORGE SMITH
3 SEPTEMBER 1861

My text is taken from *Biographical Introductions*, XI, xxxi, where the drawing is reproduced in facsimile.

36 Onslow Square, September 3, 1861.

Some people think long faces very becoming. Mine will lengthen; but it is because your speculation is not so good as it might be, not for the personal loss to yours always, W. M. T.

1514. TO JOHN FREDERICK BOYES
1 OCTOBER 1861

Address: J. F. Boyes Esqre | 10 St James's Terrace, | Bomfield Terrace | W. *Postmark:* LONDON 3 OC 61. Published in part, *The Bookworm*, IV (1891), 49; the whole letter by Mr. Wilson, *Boston Transcript*, July 31, 1920.

36 Onslow Sq^e October 1.
S. W. 1861

My dear J. F. B.

I dont know how long your packet has been lying here. I thought it contained old books purchased by me, and only opened it yesterday, when I recognized the little old Lives w^h I remember reading when we were boys in CharterHouse Square. Now we are half a century old and the kind hand w^h wrote the name in the books in that fine well-remembered writing is laid under the grass w^h will cover us old gentlemen too ere long, after our little life journey is over. And the carriage is going down the hill, is n't it? Mine is: after having had some pleasant travelling, after being well nigh upset, after being patched up again, after being robbed by footpads &c &c. The terminus can't be far off — a few years more or less. I wouldn't care to travel over the ground again: though I have had some pleasant days and dear companions.

I have just come back from Scotland where I have been burying my good old step-father;[51] who had but a few hours illness, and was quite well and cheerful the night before he was sent for. So they pass away. And now comes the turn of our generation: and Amen. We send our best regards to your wife and thank you for the little books.

Yours always
W M T.

1515.　　　　　TO MISS THACKERAY
3 OCTOBER 1861

Hitherto unpublished.

36 Onslow Sq^r S. W.
October 3.

My dear Cousin

About that photograph — why it is weeks and weeks since I owe you a letter. Yours came to me at Folkestone and I had no means of getting you a photograph other than one of those ill favoured pictures w^h you have seen and dont like. Then I went to Paris tempted by a very fine day and smooth sea and was ill there. Then I came home and had to hurry off to Scotland to my mother whose dear old husband died there. As soon as I can I

---

[51] Major Carmichael-Smyth died on September 9, 1861.

will get a more pleasing likeness of your humble servant and send it to Bath. Meanwhile he is

Yours sincerely always
W M Thackeray

Have you seen me done as the Literary Gorilla?[52] A very hairy and hideous baboon.

1516.   TO THE MISSES JONES
14 OCTOBER 1861

Address: The Misses Jones | 3 Bedford Terrace | Bedford. *Postmarks:* LON-DON OC 14 61, BEDFORD OC 15. Hitherto unpublished.

36 Onslow Sq.ʳ S. W.
October 14. 1861.

I have been away, and in the midst of many troubles, forgot the verses [53] — and mislaid the corrections wʰ you made. Will you kindly look at the proof again, and oblige

Your very faithful Servᵗ
W M Thackeray.

1517.   FROM FRANCIS D. FINLAY[54]
17 OCTOBER 1861

Hitherto unpublished.

Northern Whig Office
Belfast. 17 Oct 1861

Dear Mʳ Thackeray,

We had a talk — some of us — the other evening, on the pos-sibilities of getting you to make a public appearance in Belfast. I was requested very urgently to bell the cat. You may not have

[52] In *The Cornhill Magazine* for September Thackeray had written: "walk-ing down St. James Street yesterday, I met a friend who says to me, 'Rounda-bout, my boy, have you seen your picture? Here it is!' And he pulls out a portrait, executed in photography, of your humble servant, as an immense and most unpleasant-featured baboon, with long hairy hands, and called by the waggish artist 'A Literary Gorilla'." (*Works*, XII, 324)

[53] See above, No. 1497.

[54] No doubt the son of Francis Dalzell Finlay (1794–1857), who founded *The Northern Whig* in 1824.

forgotten that once I was very near succeeding on this point, and that it fell through partly through fear of the sea and partly through apprehension of Mulligan and C̣o I cannot undertake to rule the waves but I will undertake to manage Mulligan. At least I will put it out of Mulligan's power to make your appearance a pecuniary loss. You told me once you got £25 a lecture for the Georges and were therewith contented. I am authorised to say that I will get you £150 for three nights reading if you will come to Belfast. Dublin ought to be good for double that, and Cork for as much. Say £500 clear of all expenses inside a fortnight. I think you might count on that. Would it be worth taking? all things considered.

Personally I have long wished to see you in Belfast where success is certain. The Mulligans don't flourish and abound here.

Will you take the idea into consideration?

Yours very truly
Francis D. Finlay

W. M. Thackeray Esq

Little Bruce,[55] whom you saw ("Classic & Historic Portraits") is dead.

1518. TO MISS GASSIOT
20 OCTOBER 1861 [56]

Hitherto unpublished.

Miss Gassiot. I cannot find my fine pens, or I could have made a much finer crown and 3. But I think you beat me, and that your little hand is more legible than that of your most respectful

humble Servant
W M Thackeray

---

[55] James Bruce (1808–1861), author of *Classic and Historic Portraits* (1853) and editor of *The Northern Whig*, had died on August 19.

[56] This note, written the day before, accompanied Thackeray's letter of October 21 to Lady Olliffe.

1519.   TO LADY OLLIFFE
              21 OCTOBER 1861

Address: Lady Olliffe | Mansion House | E. C. *Postmark:* LONDON OC 21
61. Hitherto unpublished.

For
The Lady Mayoress.[57]
These.

My dear lady olliffe but the fact is we have been engaged
this ever so long to dinner with my cousin mrs bayne in regent's
park otherwise i should have been delighted to come you know i
should and as i prepared this for miss gassiot yesterday i may
as well kill two birds with one stone and address myself to the
lady mayoress in this manner and its very difficult to read and
very witty isn't it?

p s if you turn over youll see a picture of the lord mayor killing
master jack cade opposite smith and elders shop

1520.   TO FRANK FLADGATE
              OCTOBER? 1861

Hitherto unpublished.

36 Onslow Sq[e]
Saturday

Dear Fladgate

The time for completing my number [58] is awfully near. If
you have read Philip in yesterdays holyday, please send me the
proof back — as I want to go on with the story.

Or can you come and dine tomorrow? I wont have the shivers
D. V. nor too much brandy & bitter beer. and with a sober bottle
of Claret we will talk over the matter.

[57] Lady Olliffe was the daughter of Thackeray's friend William Cubitt, at
this time Lord Mayor of London.
[58] Chapters 23 and 24 of *Philip*, which appeared in *The Cornhill Magazine* for November, 1861.

For

The Lady Mayoress.

These.

My dear lady ————— but the fact ——— bird been engaged these ever so long to dine with my cousin at so & so in Regent's park otherwise should have been delighted to come you know I should and as I prepared this for miss gassiot yesterday may as well kill two birds with one stone and address myself to the lady mayoress in this manner and it is very difficult to read and very witty is it?

P.S. if you turn over you see a picture of the lord mayor taking a master jackadee opposite Smithaus aldermans shop

THACKERAY'S LETTER OF 21 OCTOBER 1861

from an MS. temp. Ric.? II.

A DRAWING SENT WITH THACKERAY'S LETTER OF 21 OCTOBER 1861

Morgan John O'Connell & another friend of mine may be here but they are friends of the house and interested in the progress of the story.

I can no more attempt to do intricate law-business than to play the piano — a very brief few lines rightly put must be all I can venture upon.

very faithfully yours
W M T.

1521.　　　　　　　TO FRANK FLADGATE
　　　　　　　　　　2 NOVEMBER 1861

Hitherto unpublished.

G.
November 2.

Dear Fladgate.

I have been very ungrateful in not thanking you sooner for the Wicked Earl.[59] We shall be able to reward Virtue and confound Vice famously now at the end of Vol III. How I wish I had got so far! It was most kind of you to take all this trouble for

Yours very sincerely
W M Thackeray

1522.　　　　　　　TO MR. HOLL
　　　　　　　　　　19 NOVEMBER 1861

Hitherto unpublished.

November 19.
36 Onslow Sq^r S. W.

My dear Mr Holl.

The Article is very lively, well-written, and pleasant BUT (now it's coming out!) — but the plot I think won't do for us.

---

[59] Fladgate appears to have told Thackeray the story of the Lowther inheritance, for which see *Biographical Introductions*, XI, xliii.

So I fold up your Corazza and return it with many thanks, and not a little regret to send back such a merry little paper.

very faithfully yours
W M Thackeray.

1523.   TO LADY OLLIFFE
30 NOVEMBER 1861

Hitherto unpublished.

Saturday. Novr 30.

My dear Lady Telegraph.

I was obliged to go away from Caulfields [60] tother night immediately after dinner unwell — and I'm no better and in such a dismal way that I can't hope to come to you tomorrow; although I am

Yours always respectfully

1524.   TO GEORGE VIRTUE [61]
13 DECEMBER 1861

My text is taken from a facsimile published by Mr. Wilson, *Boston Transcript*, July 31, 1920.

Decr 13. 1861.

Dear Mr Virtue

I {gave} lent Maginn 500£ in his life time and he paid me 20£ back. I think I have done enough in giving him bread — let other philanthropists give him a stone.

Faithfully yours
W M Thackeray

---

60 Colonel James Montgomery Caulfield, F. R. G. S., 23 Bruton Street, Berkeley Square (*London Directory*, 1862).
61 George Virtue (1794–1868), a London bookseller and publisher.

1525.   TO MR. AND MRS. MARTIN
24 DECEMBER 1861

My text is taken from Sir Theodore Martin's *Helena Faucit*, p. 258.

Dec. 24/61.

Many thanks for Fuchs.[62] I write in the twilight, wishing all neighbours a merry Xmas. Off in half an hour to Boulogne. 'For all travellers by water, for all *sick persons*,' [63] please see the Litany. — Adieu, *mes bons voisins*!

1526.   TO JOHN SKELTON
1861

My text is taken from Skelton's *Table Talk of Shirley*, p. 30.

Wednesday, 36 Onslow Square.

My dear Mr Skelton, — Many thanks to Shirley. I like his writing so much, that I long to know whether we can't have some of it in the *C. H. M.*? About that Winter article? Will Winter stay if you don't hold it by the beard? If you have it, do send it to Cornhill, and write a line to my house warning, — Yours very faithfully,

W. M. Thackeray.

1527.   TO ADELAIDE PROCTER
1861

Hitherto unpublished.

Miss

A friend is a friend. A man's word is his word. Take this little paper.[64] Ah if you knew the agony it has cost me to make it! 3

---

[62] No doubt a copy of Goethe's *Reinecke Fuchs* (1794).
[63] See above, No. 879.
[64] "A Leaf out of a Sketch Book", published in *The Victoria Regia* (1861), which Miss Procter edited.

days I give you my word. I can't write unless — unless I am paid.

I will write to Mʳ Swain the wood engraver to do 2 blocks of Jim and Sady to be printed along with the article and am

Yours

WMT.

On the sketch under the figures is some writing wʰ I took down at the time and for wʰ directions are left in the MS.

1528.   TO ? 1861 [65]

Hitherto unpublished.

We had read the Telegraph with much edification in this house, and I knew the writer of the article [66] as well as if I had seen his hand and blue ink. I hope we may both of us live so long as to outlive all chances of paragraphs in large print: decent prosy people comfortable under our vine and fig-tree: [67] playing at whist of nights: looked up to in the parish: respected by the neighbouring tradesmen. And I don't think I shall read any novels then: shall you? But who can say? You see Madame Saqui [68] has resurged on the tight-rope — Perhaps I shall be wanting to perform again when I am an old woman.

[65] This letter was written in the late autumn of 1861, when Yates (*Recollections and Experiences*, II, 64–65) had a severe attack of gastric fever while travelling in Switzerland with his wife and Alfred Austin.

[66] I have not seen a file of *The Daily Telegraph* for 1861.

[67] *Micah*, 4, 4.

[68] A celebrated tightrope dancer (1786–1866), supposed to have made her début before the outbreak of the French Revolution as the infant child of the heroine in *Geneviève de Brabant*. Napoléon I called Mme Saqui the "première acrobate de France", and she enjoyed a career of unbroken success for fifty years. She made her final appearance in a benefit performance at the Hippodrome in 1861.

So poor Yates has been having gastric fever. I all but died of it 12 years ago in the middle of Pendennis. I am thankful I tided over that bad time, so as to save a little for the young ones. Laus Domino. Amen

Yours very truly
W M Thackeray.

1529.   TO FREDERICK WALKER
JANUARY? 1862 [1]

My text is taken from Marks, *Walker*, p. 24.

[*sketch*]

Children laughing at school-room door. Philip and Charlotte reading the letter.

1530.   TO FREDERICK WALKER
FEBRUARY? 1862 [2]

My text is taken from Marks, *Walker*, p. 24.

Dear Mr. Walker, Will this do?

[*sketch*]

Old gentleman in thick shoes scratching a pig's back over a pigstye railing in his garden. Philip disgusted. Background, trees, cottages, villas, Hampstead Heath.

---

[1] Thackeray is describing "A Letter from New York," which Walker drew for *The Cornhill Magazine* of March, 1862.

[2] See "Mugford's Favorite" in *The Cornhill Magazine* of April, 1862.

1513.   TO GEORGE AUGUSTUS SALA
                    1 MARCH? 1862 [3]

Hitherto unpublished. My text is taken from a draft in Thackeray's hand on the back of p. 409 of the manuscript of *Philip* in the Huntington Library.

36 Onslow Sq. S. W.
Saturday.

Dear Mr. Sala

I will with great pleasure be your backer.

Always yours
W M Thackeray

1532.   TO GEORGE SMITH
                    4 MARCH 1862

My text is taken from a facsimile published by Lady Ritchie, "The First Editor: and the Founder," *Cornhill Magazine*, New Series, XXVIII (1910), opposite p. 4.

36 Onslow Sq.^e S. W.
March 4. 1862

My dear Smith.

I have been thinking over our conversation of yesterday, and it has not improved the gaiety of the work on w.^h I am presently busy.

Today I have taken my friend Sir Charles Taylor into my confidence, and his opinion coincides with mine that I should withdraw from the Magazine. To go into bygones now is needless. Before ever the Magazine appeared, I was, as I have told you, on the point of writing such a letter as this: And whether connected with the Cornhill Magazine or not, I hope I shall always be

Sincerely your friend
W M Thackeray

[3] Page 424 of the manuscript of *Philip* is written on the back of a letter of March 7, 1862, from the Secretary of the Reform Club to Thackeray, announcing that on March 13 Mr. Sala "seconded by you will be balloted for". It is possible that this note was written on Saturday, March 1.

1533. ## TO GEORGE SMITH
6 MARCH 1862

My text is taken from a facsimile published by Lady Ritchie, *Cornhill Magazine*, New Series, XXVIII, opposite p. 5.

36 Onslow Sq^e
March 6. 1862

My dear S.

I daresay your night, like mine, has been a little disturbed: but *Philip* [4] presses and until this matter is over, I can't make that story so amusing as I would wish.

I had this pocket pistol [5] in my breast yesterday but hesitated to pull the trigger at an old friend. My daughters are for a compromise. They say 'It is all very fine Sir Charles Taylor telling you to do so and so. Mr Smith has proved himself your friend always.' *Bien.* It is because I wish him to remain so, that I and the Magazine had better part company. Good bye and God bless you and all yours

W M T

[4] Chapters 33 and 34, which appeared in *The Cornhill Magazine* for April.
[5] Thackeray's note of March 4, which was sent with this letter. Drafts of both are included in Thackeray's diary for this year.

1534.   TO JOSEPH SWAIN
MARCH 1862

Address: M![r] Swain | Bouverie S![t] Hitherto unpublished.

Dear M![r] Swaine

Can some of your young men do me a pretty ◯ 2 beehives
in a garden, & a moon behind.[6] Mind the bees mustn't be out.

W M T

1535. TO CONTRIBUTORS AND CORRESPONDENTS
THE CORNHILL MAGAZINE
18 MARCH 1862 [7]

My text is taken from Lady Ritchie, *Cornhill Magazine*, New Series, I, 14–15.

March 25, 1862

Ladies and Gentlemen (who *will* continue, in spite of the standing notice below, to send papers to the Editor's private residence)

---

[6] The vignette initial letter of chapter 33 of *Philip*, which appeared in
The Cornhill Magazine in April, 1862.

[7] This letter is in the form of a yellow slip, which was laid into copies of
The Cornhill Magazine for April, 1862.

— perhaps you will direct the postman to some other house, when you hear that the Editor of "The Cornhill Magazine" no longer lives in mine.

My esteemed successor lives at Number ——, but I will not intrude upon the poor man's brief interval of quiet. He will have troubles enough in that thorn-cushioned editorial chair [8] which is forwarded to him this day by the Parcels (Happy) Delivery Company.

In our first number, ladies and gentlemen, I, your humble servant, likened himself to the captain of a ship, to which and whom I wished a pleasant voyage. Pleasant! Those who have travelled on shipboard know what a careworn, oppressed, uncomfortable man the captain is. Meals disturbed, quiet impossible, rest interrupted — such is the lot of captains. This one resigns his commission. I had rather have a quiet life than gold-lace and epaulets: and deeper than did ever plummet sound I fling my speaking trumpet.[9] Once in a voyage to America I met a Sea-Captain who was passenger in the ship w^h he formerly had commanded. No man could be more happy, cheerful, courteous than this. He rode through the gale with the most perfect confidence in the ship and its Captain; he surveyed the storm as being another gentleman's business: and his great delight was to be called at his watch to invoke a blessing on the steward's boy who woke him, and to turn round in his crib and go to sleep again. Let my successor command the *Cornhill*, giving me always a passage on board; and if the Printer's boy rings at my door of an early morning with a message that there are three pages wanting or four too much, I will send out my benediction to that Printer's boy and take t'other half-hour's doze.

Though Editor no more, I hope long to remain a contributor to my friend's Magazine. I believe my own special readers will agree that my books will not suffer when their Author is released

---

[8] See "Thorns in the Cushion" (*Works*, XII, 209–216).
[9] An echo of *The Tempest*, V, i, 56–57:
> Deeper than did ever plummet sound,
> I'll drown my book.

from the daily tasks of reading, accepting, refusing, losing and finding the works of other people. To say No has often cost me a morning's peace and a day's work. I tremble *recenti metu*.[10] Oh, those hours of madness spent in searching for Louisa's lost lines to her dead Piping Bullfinch, for Nhoj Senoj's mislaid Essay! I tell them for the last time that the (late) Editor will not be responsible for rejected communications, and herewith send off the Chair and the great *Cornhill Magazine* Tin-box with its load of care.

Whilst the present tale of *Philip* is passing through the press, I am preparing another,[11] on which I have worked at intervals for many years past, and which I hope to introduce in the ensuing year; and I have stipulated for the liberty of continuing the little Essays which have amused the public and the writer, and which I propose to contribute from time to time to the pages of *The Cornhill Magazine*.

W. M. T.

1536.   TO FREDERICK MULLETT EVANS
APRIL 1862 [12]

Hitherto unpublished. My text is taken from a transcript supplied by Mr. Scheide, who owns the original.

Palace Green,
Kensington, W.
Note the address & tell them
about it for Wednesday you know.

Dear Evans

If you please that little account for Lady Day —

Yours

W M Thackeray

[10] Horace, *Odes*, II, xix, 5.

[11] Thackeray originally intended that "The Knights of Borsellen" (see above, No. 193, note 4) rather than *Denis Duval* should succeed *Philip*.

[12] Lady Day, the Feast of the Annunciation, occurs on March 25. Thackeray did not move into his new home at Palace Green until March 31. This note was therefore written early in April.

1537.   TO ANNE AND HARRIET THACKERAY
21 APRIL 1862

Hitherto unpublished.

Easter Monday.

A fair passage. just enough not to be sick and to feel sick all the way in the train. No room at Bristol. Excellent quarters here. Sorry we didnt all come. Just come from R. Godot. Jane & Charlotte all right. Very good about William [13] Very glad I came, I mean I am. The children like children. All gone to the grandes eaux at Versailles. Now I must and will go to work. So hot here dont know what to do with my great coat. I take it off and send my benediction.

W M T.

1538.   TO STEPHEN SPRING RICE
APRIL? 1862

My text is taken from Francis Edwards's catalogue 620 (1938).

Cornhill Magazine

My dear S. S. R.,

I am no longer Editor yonder and MSS. sent to me must rely on their own merits and not on my advocacy w^h is powerless.

Yours in a flurry
W. M. T.

I forward the MS with a private note to S. & Elder, doing my little possible.

[13] William Ritchie, brother of Jane and Charlotte, had died on March 22, 1862.

1539.   TO ?
                    1 MAY 1862

Published in *The Athenæum*, June 20, 1891, p. 800.

                              Palace Green Kensington
                                    May 1. 1862

Madam.

I dont know where the packet has been delayed, but I have
only this moment found your note, dated Feb. 27, enclosing the
most welcome autograph of Bishop Heber [14] w[h] I regard with
the very greatest interest and affection. He is one of the (literary)
friends of my youth, when one likes people better than in later
days — I used to read his book [15] when it appeared first, and recal
my native Country. I was born; and my father and many of his
brothers died in India; and please God that some of them too
have left a name w[h] is remembered affectionately there still.

                    Believe me
              Your obliged faithful Serv[t]
                    W M Thackeray.

1540.   TO WILLIAM WEBB FOLLETT SYNGE
                    MAY 1862 [16]

My text is taken from *Thackeray in the United States*, I, 105.

My Dear Doubleyou Doubleyou,

I have just met a Trojan of the name of Trollope in the street
(your ingenious note of last night kept me awake all night, be

[14] Reginald Heber (1783–1826), Bishop of Calcutta from 1822 to 1826,
whose career Thackeray sketches in his lecture on George IV (*Works*, VII,
707–708).

[15] *Narrative of a Journey through India, 1824–1825* (1828).

[16] This note was written shortly before May 13, 1862, when Thackeray
noted in his appointment book that he had paid Synge £600. From a further
entry on May 15, it appears that Thackeray lent Synge £1,000 in all, which
was to be repaid in monthly installments. The transaction is explained by

hanged to you), and the upshot is that we will do what you want between us. My dear old Synge, come and talk to me on Friday before twelve.

1541. TO MR. AND MRS. BAXTER
6?–9 MAY 1862

Published in *American Family*, pp. 175–178.

Palace Green,
Kensington. W.

Friday. May 9.

My dear friends. I am glad to have a word of news of all of you, and that you should have wished to hear of me. I didn't write though I have thought of you many a time; and feared for you, lest the war should have brought it's calamity down upon you. Before that grief w^h I know must be in your house: what to say or to do? I know what your feelings are; loyal Northerns though you may be, with the daughter and grandchildren in the South who look at us out of our photograph book so innocent & pretty and then there's the bread winner, the warehouse — does the warehouse bring any rent now? I know & and feel that trying times are come on you all.

Some one called me away the other day when I wrote those last words and then I have been ill for 2 days and I was called away

---

Trollope (*Thackeray*, p. 60): "I heard once a story of woe from a man who was the dear friend of both of us. The gentleman wanted a large sum of money instantly — something under two thousand pounds — had no natural friends who could provide it, but must go utterly to the wall without it. Pondering over this sad condition of things just revealed to me, I met Thackeray between the two mounted heroes at the Horse Guards, and told him the story. 'Do you mean to say that I am to find two thousand pounds?' he said angrily, with some expletives. I explained that I had not even suggested the doing of anything — only that we might discuss the matter. Then there came over his face a peculiar smile, and a wink in his eye, and he whispered his suggestion, as though half ashamed of his meanness. 'I'll go half,' he said, 'if anybody will do the rest.' And he did go half, at a day or two's notice, though the gentleman was no more than simply a friend. I am glad to be able to add that the money was quickly repaid."

just as I was going to say something — Now tell me my dear kind good Baxter and wife — there may be troubles at home — no dividends — the deuce to pay. I know a fellow who is not rich, for he has spent all his money in building this fine house: all but a very little — but who knows? Draw on me for 500£ at 3 months after date: and I am your man. You wont be angry? You may be worth millions; and laugh at my impudence: — I dont know but I dont mean no harm. Only I remember and shall all my life the kindness and hospitality of the dear old brown house.

This one is delightful. I have paid 5000£ on it in 2 years out of income — but theres ever so much more to pay I dont know how much. When done however it will be a little income to the girl who inherits it and do you know I dont much care when she does.[17] I am constantly ill — A Doctor told me at Paris t'other day that I had a fatal complaint and I wasn't very sorry. It turns out not to be true — but, but, but . . . Well upon my word it is one of the nicest houses I have ever seen — as good as Mr Haight's[18] let us say — there is an old green and an old palace and magnificent trees before the windows at w^h I write. I have the most delightful study, bedroom, and so forth; can get 10£ for as much writing as there is on these 4 little sides, have a strong idea that in the next world I shan't be a bit better off — Well — since her husband's death my poor old mother is wandering about happy no where. I inherit from her this despondency I suppose — but have the pull over her of a strong sense of humour w^h gets plenty of cheerful laughs out of your glum old friend. Nobody

[17] James Hannay (*Brief Memoir of the Late Mr. Thackeray*, pp. 29–30) relates that an Edinburgh friend who called on Thackeray in the summer of 1862, "knowing of old his love of the Venusian, playfully reminded him what Horace says of those who, regardless of their sepulchre, employ themselves in building houses: —

'Sepulchri
Immemor, struis domos.'

'Nay,' said he, 'I am *memor sepulchri*, for this house will always let for so many hundreds (mentioning the sum) a-year.'"

[18] Thackeray is no doubt referring to the home at Fifth Avenue and Fifteenth Street of Richard K. Haight (*New York Directory*, 1853–1854), whose name appears on Mrs. Baxter's visiting list.

comes to marry the daughters. Every body is fond of them. I think they have been the happier for my having gone to America, where a good father & mother I know of used to tell me they liked their children to have 'a good time'

I saw the Bigelows at Paris last week — he as jolly as ever. Good bye God bless you Never mind if I dont write I may be lazy or moody but always affectionately yours

W M T.

1542.   TO FREDERICK CLAY [19]
MAY 1862

Hitherto unpublished. *Endorsed:* Thackeray to Fred. Clay. 1862.

Palace Green,
Kensington, W.

Dear Clay.

Since I got your note, I have been ill and 1/2 mad with work. There's no ballot at the Garrick until Saturday 31, when I can put up M. Gautier [20] if he remains.

I daresay he quite forgets that he and I were acquainted in '48.

Ah, if you knew how difficult it is to make those verses! [21] — I tried and got only so far.

Boys
Doctor G. the Learned Warden
Of the College Covent Garden
Sends us little boys to greet you
And with cheery concinnation

[19] Clay (1839–1889) was a composer of operettas who achieved his first success in 1862 with *Court and Cottage.* His best known score, which includes the ballad "I'll sing thee songs of Araby", he wrote for *Lalla Rookh* in 1877.

[20] Théophile Gautier (1811–1872), who was in England writing a series of articles on the "Exposition de Londres" for the *Moniteur universel.* They were published between May 4 and June 11, 1862.

[21] Thackeray's verses appear to have been written for an entertainment at Evans's Hotel in Covent Garden. Dr. G. is Paddy Green, the proprietor; the College, his supper rooms; and the little boys, the lads he had trained to sing glees and madrigals.

And with hearty gratulation
Bids us meet you *Hoc in situ.*

?

Pupils we *something be*   Chorus
Of the learned DOCTOR G.   Doctor G &c
Men

We Professors of this college
And Academy of knowledge
Commiscentes seria joco.
Bid all people hearty welcome
Who to Doctor G's hotel come.
Bid you welcome hoc in loco!   (Chorus)
Welcome all the world, says he

Doctor G, Dont you see?

To the Hall of *Doctor G.*

Fiddle diddle diddledee.

But dont you see it's too long because the point is to come (w^h I have not made yet) and this gives them 64 lines to sing — Thence the delay —

Yours ever
W M Thackeray.

1543.   TO GEORGE SMITH
MAY 1862 [22]

Hitherto unpublished. My text is taken from a transcript supplied by Mrs. Fuller.

My dear Smith,

I can only find this scrap of paper. I grieve for the meagreness of two of the pages of Philip;[23] and am most vexed at the lateness of the whole thing. I began early enough at Paris where I was forced to go, and fell ill — came home and fell ill again, and after these attacks can't write for 2 days, forget the sentence I put down

[22] Thackeray's diaries show that he was in Paris in April, 1862, but not in April, 1861, the only other year during which he was writing *Philip*.
[23] Chapters 37 and 38 for June.

on paper, grow awfully nervous. Chester was misled about computing the MS. I thought all was done when I went down to the printing office yesterday. My stars what a state I was in, when I found there were 3 pages wanting!

It is seven o'clock in the morning and I vow I'll go to work on July,[24] as soon as I have had a cup of tea.

Yours,

W. M. T.

1544. TO SIR WILLIAM WELLESLEY KNIGHTON[25]
31 MAY 1862

Address: Sir W. Knighton Bart | 38 Gloucester Place | Portman Sq^{re}. *Postmark:* LONDON MY 31 62. Hitherto unpublished.

Dear Knighton

I take up my pen (a new gold one price 2/6^d) to say that on our return home, I went to the Ballet and asked for Mr Orrid, w^h he was absent on leave. Our best regards to Lady K & respects to George IV.

---

[24] Chapters 39 and 40.
[25] Second Baronet (1811–1885), son of Sir William Knighton (d. 1836), keeper of George IV's privy purse. He had married Clementina Jameson in 1838.

My dear Knighton.[26] This is why my letters dont go. I write and keep 'em in my pocket I am so glad you are coming and am always your friend and condisciple

W M T.

1545.   TO FREDERICK WALKER
        15 JUNE 1862

My text is taken from a facsimile in Marks's *Walker*, p. 25.

Palace Green,
Kensington. W.
June 15.

Dear Mr Walker

For August I mean.

Philip, the Little Sister, and the 2 Little Children saying their prayers in an old fashioned church pew not Gothic.[27]

The Church is the one in Queen Square Bloomsbury, if you are curious to be exact.

The motto

PRO CONCESSIS BENEFICIIS.

and that will bring the story to an end. I am sorry its over. And you?

Always yours
W M T.

[26] This paragraph and Thackeray's signature are written in the flap of the envelope.

[27] Walker's final illustration for *Philip*, and one of the best known of all his drawings, is "Thanksgiving", which appeared in *The Cornhill Magazine* for August, 1862.

1546.   ## TO MR. DURHAM
30 JUNE 1862 [28]

Hitherto unpublished. *Endorsed:* June | 62.

Monday

Dear Durham

Am I coming or not? I *am* engaged 2 deep but one is an evening party to hear Levassor [29] w^h my girls can go to without me, one a concert & supper at Twickenham, the Duke d'Aumale's [30] at 10–1. Now I can come or not to you as you will. I mean if you have filled my place say so at once. Better for my health perhaps not. Send a line upstairs to say YES or NO to

Yours
W M Thackeray

1547.   ## TO GEORGE SMITH
1 JULY 1862

My text is taken from *Centenary Biographical Introductions*, XVIII, liii.

Palace Green, July 1, 1862.
The Cornhill Magazine,
Smith, Elder & Co.

My Dear S. — I think 'Philip' *tout court* is better than the 'Adventures of &c.' and that a running title on every other page as in 'Esmond' will give a little freshness to the reprint. I shall have done D. V. to-day or to-morrow.

[28] The party at Twickenham took place on Saturday, July 5. This note was written the previous Monday.

[29] Nicolas Prosper Levasseur (1791–1871), a famous basso whom Thackeray had often heard at Paris in the operas of Meyerbeer and Rossini.

[30] Henri d'Orléans (1822–1897), Duc d'Aumale, fifth son of Louis Philippe, who passed most of his time in England between 1848 and 1870. The large fortune he had inherited from the Prince de Condé enabled him to entertain lavishly, and he was very popular in London society.

Sitting in this beautiful room, surrounded by ease and comfort and finishing the story, I stop writing for a minute or two, with rather a full heart.

Will you let Lawrence make another drawing of you? I should like to hang it here.

Always yours,
W. M. Thackeray.

1548.   TO MRS. CARMICHAEL-SMYTH
                    5 JULY 1862

Published in part, *Biographical Introductions*, XI, xli, xlvi; additions in *Thackeray and his Daughter*, pp. 125–127. My text is taken from a transcript supplied by Mrs. Fuller.

Palace Green, Kensington.
July 5th, 1862.

My dearest old Mother gets the budget from the girls and the history of all our doings. On Thursday at 6.15 p.m. after working all day I wrote Finis to Philip: rather a lame ending. Yesterday I spent all day in great delectation and rest of mind making a very bad drawing. Young Walker who is twenty does twice as well: and at twenty you know we all thought I was a genius at drawing. O the mistakes people make about themselves! Then at 5 we drive down like persons of quality in our pretty new (paid for) carriage with our "gens" on the box to the Aumale Fête at Twickenham where I daresay the Dukes and Duchesses would have admired my new lavender gloves (price 2/–) very much, only I forgot 'em and left them in my great coat pocket. Never mind it was a beautiful fête and I am all the better this morning because I could only get a crust to eat and a scrap of galantine left in a lady's plate and a bottle of excellent claret. And did the girls tell you, how I had no dinner the day before, having to take them to the Barbiere [31] (a new opera by Mr. Rossini) and where I had

---

[31] *Il Barbiere di Siviglia* was given at the Royal Italian Opera House on July 3, with Adelina Patti as Rosina (*Times*).

a most refreshing sleep in the back of the box. And this is our life: and now there is a little lull after a constant care and occupation. No, by the way, not yet quite. Mr. Smith says "Do, pray write a Roundabout paper." And that,[32] you see, is churning in my brain, whilst I am writing off a scrap to my dear old Mother. Mesdemoiselles who were up actually till 12 last night, could not be ready for prayers, so I was parson and I can tell you one person of the Congregation was very thankful for our preservation and all the blessings of this life which have fallen to me.

Think of the beginning of the story of the little Sister in the Shabby Genteel Story twenty years ago and the wife crazy and the Publisher refusing me 15£ who owes me £13.10 and the Times to which I apply for a little more than 5 guineas for a week's work, refusing to give me more and all that money difficulty ended, God be praised, and an old gentleman sitting in a fine house like the hero at the end of a story! [33]

The actual increase of health and comfort since we got into the Palazzo is quite curious. I am certainly much better in body. I think the novel-writing vein is used up though and you may be sure some kind critics will say as much for me before long. Anny's

---

[32] "*De Finibus*", which appeared in *The Cornhill Magazine* for August, 1862.

[33] This contrast came frequently to Thackeray's mind in later years. William Holman Hunt (*Pre-Raphaelitism and the Pre-Raphaelite Brotherhood*, 2 vols., New York, 1906, II, 195–196) relates that not long after he sold "The Finding of Christ in the Temple" for 5,500 guineas in 1860, he met Thackeray in the Cosmopolitan Club and was warmly congratulated on his good fortune. When he replied that the picture had taken him years to complete and that he was burdened with heavy obligations to his family, Thackeray said: " 'then you know what it is to have claims upon your harvestings before they are gathered in perhaps, and I daresay you know something of other than blood relations who say 'Give, give, give, but count not me the herd' — the thought of them makes me wince . . . Yes, I know them all . . . with their constant remindings of your 'lucky star,' and that they were not born with your golden spoon, and how everything has been against them. Well, well,' he said with a half-amused sigh, 'they are a dispensation of Providence by which we are brought to reflect upon poor human nature, but then 5500 guineas at thirty-three, that is a good turning point in a man's fortune; I remember when I was about the same age I had been writing for some months for [*Fraser's Magazine*], and the magazine had, in consequence of my contributions, been restored from a state of near collapse to increasing

style is admirable [34] and Smith and Elder are in raptures about it.
But she is very modest and I am mistrustful too. I am sure I
shan't love her a bit better for being successful. They are both of
them beginning to bewail their Virginity in the mountains: [35] and
seem to be much excited because Ella Merivale who is only 17
has had 3 or 4 lovers already and is doubting between 2 who are
imploring her. Here comes Mr. Langley with the proofs which
must be read and there is a good morning's work over them. And
then that Roundabout Paper — a plague on it.

"Mr. Langley, where is the Cicero? in 2 volumes quarto. I
want a quotation out of it". Mr. Langley maunders along the
room helplessly. He wont find it: I shall: and he will be persuaded that he found it and that I cant possibly get on without him.

I wonder shall we make out the Petersburg journey? I have a
fancy for it because it will pay itself in a couple of papers that will
be as easy to write as letters and wont wear and tear the brains.
Then we must do some more work. I think the Story which I
began 20 years ago [36] and then, and then, On — Did you read
about poor Buckle when he got the Fever at Damascus crying out
"O my book, my book!" [37] I dont care enough about mine to be

stability; at that juncture my wife fell ill, and the doctors assured me that
she must be taken for a month to the sea-side. I had no funds for this, and
thinking it not unreasonable, I wrote to the editor: 'Dear Sir, I am in severe
need of ready money, I shall be sending the usual copy for the end of the
month, could you oblige me by advancing me £20 on the forthcoming contribution to your magazine, and thus greatly oblige, W. M. T.'

" 'The reply was prompt, it was to the effect that the editor had made a
rule never to pre-pay his writers, and that he was obliged to adhere to his
regulation. *You* needn't, my dear fellow, be any longer thus driven from
pillar to post to get such a sum, and I am sincerely glad of it. . . . But you are,
after all, a lucky dog, for you have something more than a miserable remnant
or salvage of a life in which to do your work.' "

[34] In *The Story of Elizabeth*, her first novel, published in *The Cornhill
Magazine* from September, 1862, to January, 1863. Thackeray never read
this story. "I couldn't," he told Fanny Kemble (*Records of Later Life*, p. 627).
"It would *tear my guts out!*"

[35] *Judges*, 11, 38.   [36] "The Knights of Borsellen".

[37] Buckle reached Damascus on May 18, 1862, and died there of typhoid
fever eleven days later. He was thinking of the volumes of his *History of
Civilization* (1857–1861) that he was never to write.

disquieted when that day comes. Shall I live to do the big history? Who knows? But I think I shall live to work on it, if the time is left me. God bless you, dear old Mother, I don't write to you by post, but I am writing through the printer all day long and the song is always Ego, Ego, God bless us all — and now come Mr. Langley and let us go through those proofs and all the blunders.

W. M. T.

1549.   TO MRS. CARMICHAEL-SMYTH
20 JULY 1862 [38]

Hitherto unpublished. My text is taken from a transcript supplied by Mrs. Fuller.

My dear old Mother ought to have had a line on that celebrated anniversary but my birthday has occurred so often now that I am almost ashamed of it, at least wont look at it as any day more fortunate or wonderful than the rest. I went to a dinner of painters in honour of the Belgian artist M. Gallait;[39] and had to speak and strange to say came away without a headache. Anny was unwell, Minny was away in the country with the Coles or we might have gone to Lady Harrington's[40] ball in our street. I awoke at 3 with the noise of the carriages and looked out of the window and saw the dandies tripping home. On Saturday Mr. Leech gave us a feast at Richmond. We shall break up suddenly now I think and I fancy Folkestone as lovely a place as any for us but who knows it may be Scarborough or Malvern or Petersburgh or Devonshire.[41] I should like to see the dismal old country again but then the air is depressing and you get no good from your holyday.

[38] This note was written the Sunday after Friday, July 18, 1862.

[39] Louis Gallait (1810–1887), an historical painter of some repute whom Thackeray may have known in the eighteen-thirties when both were young men in Paris studying art.

[40] The former Elizabeth Green (1811–1898), who had married Leicester Fitzgerald Charles Stanhope (1784–1862), fifth Earl of Harrington, in 1831. The Harringtons lived at 13 Kensington Palace Gardens (*Post Office London Directory*, 1862).

[41] See below, Appendix XXII.

1550.   TO ALBANY FONBLANQUE
                      AUGUST 1862

Hitherto unpublished. My text is taken from a transcript supplied by Mr. Parrish, who owns the original.

                                        (Palace Green,
                                            Kensington, W.)

Dear Fonblanque

    Please to answer this and oblige

                        Your faithful W M T.

Who are your favourite heroines in novels? [42]

1551.   TO MRS. PROCTER
                        AUGUST 1862

My text is taken from *Centenary Biographical Introductions*, XX, xxiii.

                                    Palace Green,
                                        Kensington, W.

    Please answer this and oblige
                    Your faithful
                        W. M. T.

Who are your favourite heroes in Novels? [43]

[42] "How do you like your heroes, ladies?" Thackeray writes in "On a Peal of Bells" (*Cornhill Magazine*, September, 1862; *Works*, XII, 381). "Gentlemen, what novel heroines do you prefer? When I set this essay going, I sent the above question to two of the most inveterate novel-readers of my acquaintance. The gentleman refers me to Miss Austen; the lady says Athos, Guy Livingstone, and (pardon my rosy blushes) Colonel Esmond, and owns that in youth she was very much in love with Valancourt." Guy Livingstone was the hero of the novel of that name published in 1857 by George Alfred Lawrence (1827–1876).

[43] Part of Mrs. Procter's reply is printed by Lady Ritchie (*Centenary Biographical Introductions*, XX, xxiii–xxiv): "This subject, Heroes, is one that interests me greatly. Some years ago, when Sir Cornwall Lewis was Editor of the *Edinburgh Review*, I wrote an article on 'Novels written by Women.'

MRS. PROCTER IN OLD AGE

From a photograph

1552.   TO DR. ELLIOTSON
                    22 SEPTEMBER 1862? [44]

Hitherto unpublished.

                                    Palace Green. Monday 22

Mʳ & the Misses Pendennis request the honor of Doctor Goode-
noughs company to dinner tomorrow as ever is at 7 o'clock. Dont
send an answer Come if you can — saw you going to Collins's
just now.

The object being to show how poorly all women had drawn men. That one
looked to their works for the perfect hero — and that they all failed — he
was either a milk-sop or a bully. . . . See Miss Brontë, Mrs. Gaskell, Miss
Muloch [Dinah Maria Muloch, later Mrs. Craik, author of *John Halifax,
Gentleman* (1856)], Mrs. Lewes. It is not necessary to say how admirably
it was written — or that my article was returned. The concluding sentence
was:—
     'Esmond, the truest hero that the world ever saw.'
     Did not this article deserve printing?
     Athos — Guy Livingstone — George Warrington.
     I saw a short time since some papers filled up in a game, [where] you
mentioned your favourite book, colour, flower, hero, &c., &c. The greater
proportion of women named Dobbin.
     Adelaide says Claverhouse.
     When I was young Valancourt was my hero.
                         Yr. affect. old friend,
                              Anne B. Procter.
                                   Friday,
                                        32 Weymouth Street, W.
     Hazlitt has written an article on heroes — in which he says how one gen-
erally prefers the second man in a book — the author pressing the first one
too much on you."
[44] Elliotson figures as Dr. Goodenough in *Pendennis*, *The Newcomes*, and
Philip. This note was probably written on Monday, September 22, 1862,
shortly after the conclusion of the last of these novels.

1553.   TO MRS. WILLIAM RITCHIE
3 NOVEMBER 1862

Hitherto unpublished.

Palace Green. Kensington
Monday. Nov.ʳ 3.

My dear M.ʳˢ Ritchie.

I have been to see M.ʳ Foley,[45] who indeed is as distinguished a sculptor as any we have, and have talked to him about the marble for your dear William. I told him the state of the case and the plan proposed by your friend M.ʳ Hogg. For 300£ very little indeed can be done: for 500£ a handsome monument with a bust, or head in very high relief, and on the slab beneath an allegorical sculpture. The smaller monument would be more especially inappropriate on account of its high position over the door where the sculpture details would hardly be visible. M.ʳ F. showed me a very handsome and effective monument for India of an officer who fell in an assault on Lucknow, the likeness overhead, the epitaph and name following

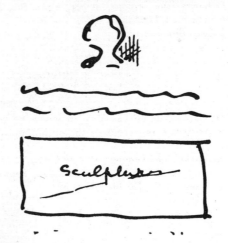

[45] John Henry Foley (1818–1874), R. A., a Victorian sculptor particularly admired for his equestrian statues and sepulchral monuments.

and then the sculpture. I should like to hear of the scholarship too to perpetuate his name. But if some 200£ more are wanting could not some of us make it up? My purse is not long but I can find 30, 40, or 50£ there to help raise a fitting record of that good man.

I am for making up the 200£ at home, taking the 300 from Calcutta: and *not* diminishing the Charitable foundation.

We ought to have a photograph of the arch & door of the Calcutta Cathedral: or a drawing.

It is very likely I shall come and see you all before many days are over. Anny is going to the Isle of Wight with some friends She is not very well: and is very modest, thank God, whilst everybody is praising her.

1554.   TO GEORGE CRUIKSHANK
                 17 NOVEMBER 1862

Hitherto unpublished.

                              Palace Green. Kensington
                              Monday 17 Nov.ʳ

My dear Cruikshank

I have been laid on my back for three days and am only just out of bed. So I couldnt come to the private View on Saturday but wish every success to the public ditto.

                              Yours
                              W M Thackeray

1555.   TO ?
                 NOVEMBER 1862?

Hitherto unpublished.

                              Palace Green,
                              Kensington. W.
                              Thursday. Nov.ʳ ?

My dear Sir

Your volume and the kind note accompanying it were put into a room of the house w.ʰ I seldom frequent and only discovered after many days. I didn't want to write and thank you for the book until I had read again many pieces w^h I liked and remember. Your second note came to me just as I was in labour with some verses of my own;⁴⁶ and, when I'm in that condition, and until the little bantling is born, I neglect my duties my letters, even my invitations to dinner.

My baby finally made its appearance last night, and I have leisure to thank you for sending me yours, and am

dear Sir faithfully yours
W M Thackeray.

1556.   TO THE BAXTERS
25 DECEMBER 1862

My text is taken from *American Family*, pp. 178–180.

Palace Green
Kensington, W.
Christmas Day, 1862

My dear Friends. The sad letter has been here for many days. I had the news ⁴⁷ before from Mr. John Dillon,⁴⁸ who has friends in the South. I have not had the courage to write to you about it. I know there is no consolation. I lost a child myself once, that's enough to say that I understand your grief. That journey of Lucy and her father is the saddest thing I have read of for many a long day. I look at Sarah's face in the photograph book and then at a print w^h I have had for many years because it was like her when I first saw her. My friend Miss Perry was telling me how she had just read an old letter of mine to her dear sister (who is dead ⁴⁹ too, and who was one of the dearest

---

⁴⁶ Probably "Mrs. Katherine's Lantern", which Thackeray wrote for the album of Dickens's daughter, Mrs. Perugini. These lines were first published in *The Cornhill Magazine* of January, 1867, pp. 117–118.

⁴⁷ Of Mrs. Hampton's death. See *Memoranda,* The Baxters.

⁴⁸ John Blake Dillon.

⁴⁹ Mrs. Elliot had died on January 4, 1859.

friends I ever had) and how there was a description of this New York girl. What a bright creature! What a laugh, a life, a happiness! And it is all gone; and you dear people sit bewailing your darling. The letters she sent to me at rare times were awfully sad. In that photograph how sad she looks! As for those little children, those two we know — we three in this house love them both. Ever since they came to us they have been in the girls' sitting room, and the Belle of the West [50] is yonder in mine. How well I remember that first look of her, with the red ribbon in her hair! and next is that sad matron, and next your letter. What a warm welcome, what a kindly fireside, what kind faces round it — and hers the brightest of all! Amen. Dear mourning father, mother, sister we can only shake you by the hand, and pray God comfort you. . . . I have been thinking in this pause of that hospitable table in your dining room, and the Spirits moving about; and looking up wistfully in this big lone room, lest a form should make itself visible.

This morning I was lying awake in the grey looking out at the elms, and thinking of your dear Sarah. God be with us. I dont feel much care about dying. As we love our children, wont our Father love us? Dear friends I have been so happy in my home, and in yours that I can feel for the grief which now bears you down. God bless you all.

Yours affectionately always
W. M. Thackeray

I dont talk a word of politics to you. I was touched by Young saying kind words of me in his paper.[51]

[50] See above, No. 1486 and illustration opposite p. 216.
[51] *The New York Albion.*

1557.   TO DR. ELLIOTSON
12 JANUARY 1863

Extract published, *Notes and Queries*, Sixth Series, IV (1881), 507.

> Palace Green,
> Kensington, W.
> Monday 12. January.

My dear Doctor

Charles Collins [1] and his pretty wife John Leech and his ditto ditto have promised to dine here on Sunday next 18th being the 2^d Sunday after Epiphany. Won't you come and meet them at 7 o'clock? You shall have spinachi patati and cavolfiori, or roast beef if you like, or anything you shall please to go for to order, and you will give pleasure to

> Your grateful
> W M Thackeray.

P. S. Just as you went away the other day, I thought of a merry jape, w^h I would have played on you but you were gone.
Q. Why is John Elliotson M. D. (Camb) like a whalebone rod with the lump of lead at each end?
A. Because he is a Life Preserver.

1558.   TO SIR FREDERICK POLLOCK?
21 JANUARY 1863

Hitherto unpublished.

> Kensington. January 21.

My dear Sir

I should have liked extremely the dinner & the fireside and the company enjoying them: but I have promised my mother to go to an early tea-party with her: and sacrifice myself accordingly.

> very faithfully yours
> W M Thackeray.

---

[1] Charles Allston Collins (1828–1873), brother of Wilkie Collins, a former member of the "Pre-Raphaelite Brotherhood" who had given up painting for literature. He married Kate Dickens in 1860.

If you & the L.C.B.[2] will drink my health, I will ruefully drink your's in a bumper of bohea.

1559.　　　　　　　　TO ?
　　　　　　　4 FEBRUARY 1863

Hitherto unpublished.

> Palace Green.
> Kensington.W.
> Feb 4. 1863

Madam.

L. Fardel when he lived with me was a very honest sober & respectable man, and I am glad to hear that his health has mended

> Your obdt Servt
> W M Thackeray

1560.　　　TO THE REV. WHITWELL ELWIN
　　　　　　　9 MARCH 1863

Hitherto unpublished.

> Palace Green.Kensington W.
> March 9. 1863

My dear Primrose.

I forget the name of the Bath gentleman who lent me Sterne's lying M S journal to Mrs Draper.[3] One of the most curious lies I think I told you. He writes to Eliza that he was dreadfully ill had ever so much blood taken from him but neverthless was ever and ever his Eliza's. In the printed letters there is one (a plague on the people I have been looking for 1/4 hour in vain for my Sterne) addressed from the Mount Coffee House to a Lady C. without any date but he makes tremendous love to her blasphemes about the Lords prayer & being led into temptation and winds up by saying

---

[2] If this note is indeed to Sir Frederick Pollock, "L. C. B." is probably Thackeray's facetious way of referring to his wife, the "Lady Chief Baroness".

[3] See above, No. 795.

if she wont let him come to drink tea he will go to Miss C's benefit that night.

I looked out in the Theatrical Register (pardon forgetting dates names & so forth) on what day in 176+ whatdyecallem — a Miss C had a benefit. I found it was on the very day when Sterne was writing to Mrs Draper to say he was so dreadful ill.

Then there is the lie in Dutens memoirs w^h I quoted in a Roundabout paper[4] — all w^h doesn't prevent the scamp from being a great man

I should like to see your old countenance again   We have a snug little bachelors room remember when you are minded to try it.

Always yours
W M T.

P. S. Letter XCII. dated Mount Coffee House Tuesday
    91 is dated April 9. 1767.
    The actress is only mentioned as Miss ***   I looked out
to see what actress had a benefit on Tuesday in April or March 67.

---

[4] Thackeray omitted the passage of "Notes of a Week's Holiday" (*Cornhill Magazine*, November, 1860) in which this story is told when he published *The Roundabout Papers* as a book. Professor Wells reprints the excised paragraphs in his edition of *The Roundabout Papers* (pp. 384–386).

1561.   TO LORD GRANVILLE
17 MARCH 1863

Hitherto unpublished. My text is taken from a facsimile in Tregaskis's catalogue 857 (1922).

Palace Green. Kensington

Feast of St Patrick. 1863.

Dear Lord Granville

Pardon me for not answering your kind note yesterday. I was at work the whole day, and forgot everything but my task. I am engaged to a literary confrère, and am very sorry that I cannot dine with you on Saturday 21st

most faithfully yours
W M Thackeray

1562.   TO MRS. WILLIAM RITCHIE
18 MARCH 1863

Hitherto unpublished.

Palace Green. K^n
March 18. 1863

My dear Mrs Ritchie

Since the royal marriage w^h you know all about I have been like a mad man over an article [5] in w^h I didnt know what on earth to say. It is just done and I am on my way to the Printer's — and send you a line en route.

I saw Mr Foley on Wednesday. He had begun nothing: but we concluded for the medallion portrait [6] &c as described before and 500 £.

1563.   TO MRS. MARTIN
24 MARCH 1863

My text is taken from Waugh's *Athenæum Club*, p. 59.

March 24th.

My dear Neighbouress, — I am so pleased to hear about T. M.'s election [7] that I must spend a penny and congratulate his wife. You remember my name don't you? The tall man in Spectacles who used to live in the Square,

[5] "On Alexandrines," a Roundabout Paper concerning the marriage of Princess Alexandra of Denmark to the Prince of Wales on March 10 which appeared in *The Cornhill Magazine* for April.

[6] Under *medallion portrait* Thackeray has written *the photograph*. Foley's bust of William Ritchie now stands in Calcutta Cathedral. For the inscription carved upon it, see *Ritchies in India*, p. 245.

[7] Theodore Martin's election to the Athenæum Club.

1564.   TO THOMAS JAMES THACKERAY?
                    MARCH 1863

Address: M⸳ Thackeray | Girard House. Hitherto unpublished.

                              Palace Green,
                                   Kensington. W

My dear Thackeray

We are going into Yorkshire at Easter [8] and have a mind to visit the birth place of the Thackerays. Where is it? Will you tell

                              Yours
                              W M T.

[8] Thackeray's diary for 1863 shows that he and his daughters visited the Milnes at Fryston Hall from April 6 to 13 and then went on to Hampsthwaite, near Harrowgate, the native town of the Thackeray family. They found "a distinguished party assembled at Fryston," writes Sir Edmund Gosse (*The Life of Algernon Charles Swinburne*, New York, 1917, pp. 95–96); "it included Venables, James Spedding, [and] the newly appointed Archbishop of York (William Thomson) . . . Lady Ritchie recalls for me that the Houghtons stimulated the curiosity of their guests by describing the young poet [Swinburne] who was to arrive later. She was in the garden on the afternoon of his arrival, and she saw him advance up the sloping lawn, swinging his hat in his hand, and letting the sunshine flood the bush of his red-gold hair. He looked like Apollo or a fairy prince; and immediately attracted the approval of Mr. Thackeray by the wit and wisdom of his conversation, as much as that of the two young ladies by his playfulness. On Sunday evening, after dinner, he was asked to read some of his poems. His choice was injudicious; he is believed to have recited 'The Leper'; it is certain that he read 'Les Noyades'. At this the Archbishop of York made so shocked a face that Thackeray smiled and whispered to Lord Houghton, while the two young ladies, who had never heard such sentiments expressed before, giggled aloud in their excitement. Their laughter offended the poet, who, however, was soothed by Lady Houghton's tactfully saying, 'Well, Mr. Swinburne, if you *will* read such extraordinary things, you must expect us to laugh.' 'Les Noyades' was then proceeding on its amazing course, and the Archbishop was looking more and more horrified, when suddenly the butler — 'like an avenging angel,' as Lady Ritchie says — threw open the door and announced, 'Prayers! my Lord!' "Lady Ritchie dwells on Swinburne's 'kind and cordial ways' during this amusing visit to Fryston. She had never seen anybody so disconcerting or so charming, and when Thackeray and his daughters had to take their leave, while Swinburne remained at Fryston, the . . . author of *The Story of Elizabeth* burst into tears. The friendship so begun continued until the day of the

1565.   TO LADY LONDONDERRY
                    1 MAY 1863 [9]

Facsimile published in *Thackeray in the United States*, I, 129–130.

Palace Green,
Kensington. W.

Dear Lady Londonderry

I shall be delighted, if you will promise not to put me next to Mrs Strange Jocelyn. The last time I met her at your house (and goodness mercy knows why) she cut me as dead as ever she could cut. Now suppose, in your kindness and innocence, you were to say 'Mr &c take the Honble Mrs Strange Soandso to dinner,' and she were to begin cutting me over again? What a painful repast all of us would have, especially poor W M T! T.o.s.v.p.[10]

I am just going out after my day's work, to buy myself a gold shirt button, and prevent the painful necessity of being *sown up* as I was at London House last night.

Yours very sincerely.
W M Thackeray

 Suppose it had been a poor curate anxious to make a favorable impression on his bishop? What a state the poor fellow would have been in when obliged to ask to be sown up by the housekeeper!

---

poet's death, though they met rarely. It appears from Lady Ritchie's recollections that Thackeray must have been shown some of Swinburne's MS. poems by Lord Houghton, for he expressed his admiration of them. He died, as we know, a few months later, too soon to see any of them in print, except those which were printed in the Spectator in the course of this year, 1862."

[9] Thackeray dined at London House on April 30, 1863. This note appears to have been written the next day.

[10] Turn over *s'il vous plait*.

1566.   **TO MRS. JAMES**
                      MAY 1863 [1]

Hitherto unpublished.

> Palace Green,
> Kensington. W.
> Saturday (but I own too late
> for post)

My dear Mrs James

I wish I could accept your kindness but I have been stopping at 3 country houses in the last 2 months, have got into awful arrears with my work, and must go away somewhere alone where I shall be forced to work. I know what it is. A Study & a Bedroom won't do. I should go to sleep on the bed and write nothing. I have done nothing for a WHOLE YEAR and I MUST go to my horrible pens & paper.

Aha. What has W M J been writing about to the Times? I am his and

> Yours always
> **W M T.**

The infantas are under agreement to go to the I of Wight, I am going to separate from them & be alone alone alone.

1567.   **TO CHARLES HEATH**
                      13 JUNE 1863

Hitherto unpublished.

> Palace Green,
> Kensington. W.
> June 13. 1863.

My dear Heath.

I have had such kindness from you and your's that I can't but sympathize with any sorrow w^h befals your family. My girls and

---

[1] This letter was written shortly after Thackeray began *Denis Duval*, for which see below, No. 1574.

I tender you our most sincere condolences. We have lost one of the kindest friends we have ever had. I write but half a dozen lines to say how I feel for your grief, and am always my dear Heath

Gratefully & truly yours
W M Thackeray

1568.   TO ?

21 JUNE 1863

Hitherto unpublished.

Palace Green Kensington
June 21.

Gentlemen

I am engaged to dine at the Mansion House on the 5 of July, or I should have had great pleasure in attending at your dinner.

Believe me very faithfully yours
W M Thackeray

1569. TO SIR WILLIAM AND LADY KNIGHTON

20 JULY 1863 [11]

Hitherto unpublished.

Palace Green,
Kensington. W.
July 20.

My dear Sir and Madam

My foot was actually uplifted to quit the shore of Albion, when the morning's post brought your obliging invitation which instantly caused me to turn back again. We shall be delighted to come to you for Goodwood. As for the cup, your best Claret I daresay is good enough for me, though if you hear of any better, I don't wish you not to send for it. My name it is needless to add. It is that of a man

---

[11] Thackeray's diary for 1863 shows that he visited the Knighton's country house at Blendworth, near Horndean, in Hampshire on July 29 of that year.

Palace Green,
Kensington. W.

July 20.

My dear Sir and Madam

My foot was actually uplifted to quit
the shore of Albion, when the ——— post
brought your obleeging invitation which instantly

THACKERAY'S LETTER OF 20 JULY 1863 TO SIR WILLIAM AND LADY KNIGHTON

caused me to turn back again. We shall be delighted to come to you for
Goodwood. as for the Cup. your best Claret I daresay is good enough for me
though if you hear of any better. I don't wish you not to send for it. My name
it is needless to add It is that of a man who has his faults I daresay (though I
never found 'em) and who is yours & lady knighton's always etcetgrabedu
P.S. clin Dieu what a quantity of aerial perspective I have given you for the money !!!

THACKERAY'S LETTER OF 20 JULY 1863 TO SIR WILLIAM AND LADY KNIGHTON

who has his faults I daresay (though *I* never found 'em,) and who is yours & Lady Knighton's always etcetera &c &c

P. S. Mon Dieu what a quantity of aerial perspective I have given you for the money! ! !

1570.   TO MRS. PROCTER
                     AUGUST 1863 [12]

Hitherto unpublished. My text is taken from a transcript given Lady Ritchie by George Murray Smith.

The Athenaeum.

Milnes has got his peerage — says a little bird
Ain't you very glad of it — Yes upon my word.
Pretty little Robin? [13] — now there is no doubt on
Is the eldest son of Richard M Lord Houghton.

1571.   TO MRS. CASPAR WISTAR [14]
                4 SEPTEMBER 1863

Hitherto unpublished.

                          Palace Green. Kensington.
                          S. W. September 4. 63

Dear M[rs] Wister

The publisher (M[r] Chapman & Hall) and your faithless correspondent have both been out of town, hence a delay in the matter of your story.[15]

When I left him a month ago, he said the story would make 2

---

[12] Milnes was created Baron Houghton on August 20, 1863.

[13] Robert Offley Ashburton Milnes (b. 1858), later second Baron Houghton (1885), first Earl of Crewe (1895), and first Marquess of Crewe and Earl of Madeley (1911).

[14] See above, No. 949, note 75.

[15] This note is written on the back of a sample page for a novel, headed "From Dan to Beersheba" and dealing with Yankee and Confederate characters.

volumes and he would give 100£ — w^h is little, but w^h is a very good beginning. Now, I am sorry to say the news is not so good.

It would make 550 pages printed like this, and this is not enough. If we had a proper-sized page viz 1000 letters in a page — your story would want 204 pages of the requisite 640.

It can only make one volume: and for this 40£ is as much as can be given. Will you take £ 40?

We had such a pleasant visit to your Aunt in her new kingdom in Hampshire. How I wish I had not sold my American Shares until now.[16] I am ashamed of not having written before. Yours always

W M Thackeray.

1572.   TO MR. ALEXANDER
                         SEPTEMBER 1863

Hitherto unpublished.

My dear Alexander

Now that the milk is spilt there is no use crying. When I heard that Mr Gladstones [17] man withdrew, I wrote to him, said I wasn't authorized: that you would not ask yourself; that you were a trump; (w^h Admiral Fitzroy [18] says so too) and without a word of complaint, hinted that the place ought to be your's: but its all no use. I couldnt write to the Duke: because I knew him once & he has forgotten me — and so he has a much more deserving man than

Yours
W M T.

[16] See above, No. 988, note 175.

[17] This note is written on the last page of a letter of September 21, 1863, from Gladstone to Thackeray, stating that the latter's recommendation of Alexander had been passed along to Edward Adolphus St. Maur (1804–1885), twelfth Duke of Somerset, then First Lord of the Admiralty.

[18] Admiral Robert Fitzroy (1805–1865), author with Darwin of the *Narrative of the Surveying Voyages of H. M. Ships Adventure and Beagle* (1839).

1573.   TO DR. JOHN BROWN
                        23 SEPTEMBER 1863

Published in part, *Biographical Introductions*, XII, xxviii. My text is taken from *Letters of Dr. John Brown*, p. 332.

Palace Green, Kensington, September 23.

My dear J. B. — I am very glad you like my little Min. With her and her Sister I have led such a happy life, that I am afraid almost as I think of it, lest any accident should disturb it. She seems to be enjoying herself greatly; but when she has done with the Lows, I think she ought to come back to her Papa and sister. We three get on so comfortably together, that the house is not the house, when one is away. I know how kind you and your children would be to her. But Anny wants her companion, and a month will give her as much change of air as, please God, will be good for her. I have done no work for a whole year and must now set to at this stale old desk, or there will be no beef and mutton. I have spent too much money on this fine house, besides gim-cracks, furniture, China, plate, the deuce knows what. . . . If I don't mistake there was a man who lived at Abbotsford overhoused himself. I am not in debt, thank my stars, but instead of writing to you why am I not writing the history of Denis Duval, Esq., Admiral of the White Squadron? Because I don't know anything about the sea and sea-men, and get brought up by my ignorance every other page; above all, because I am lazy, so lazy that a couple of dozen would do me good. Good-bye, my dear J.B. — My love to the children from your grateful old friend,

W. M. T.

1574·   TO GEORGE SMITH
                  SEPTEMBER? 1863

My text is taken from Frederick Greenwood's "Notes on Denis Duval",
Cornhill Magazine, IX (1864), 657.

My dear S., —

I was born in the year 1764, at Winchclsea, where my father was
a grocer and clerk of the church.[19] Everybody in the place was a
good deal connected with smuggling.

There used to come to our house a very noble French gentleman,
called the COUNT DE LA MOTTE, and with him a German,
the BARON DE LUTTERLOH. My father used to take pack-
ages to Ostend and Calais for these two gentlemen, and perhaps I
went to Paris once and saw the French queen.

The squire of our town was SQUIRE WESTON of the Priory,
who, with his brother, kept one of the genteelest houses in the
country. He was churchwarden of our church, and much respected.
Yes, but if you read the *Annual Register* of 1781, you will find, that
on the 13th July, the sheriffs attended at the TOWER OF LON-
DON to receive custody of a De la Motte, a prisoner charged with
high treason. The fact is, this Alsatian nobleman being in difficulties
in his own country (where he had commanded the Regiment Sou-
bise), came to London, and under pretence of sending prints to
France and Ostend, supplied the French Ministers with accounts of
the movements of the English fleets and troops. His gobetween
was Lutterloh, a Brunswicker, who had been a crimping agent, then

---

[19] Thackeray is writing in the character of Denis Duval, the hero of his last
(unfinished) novel. It appears from a letter of May, 1863, to Mrs. William
Ritchie — the original of which I have not traced — that *Denis Duval* was
begun during that month: "If I haven't written to you sooner, be pleased to
know that for the last ten days I have been almost *non compos mentis*. When
I am in labour with a book I don't quite know what happens. I sit for hours
before my paper, not doing my book, but incapable of doing anything else,
and thinking upon that subject always, waking with it, walking about with
it, and going to bed with it. Oh, the struggles and bothers — oh, the throbs
and pains about this trumpery!" (*Centenary Biographical Introductions*, XXI,
xiv)

a servant, who was a spy of France and Mr. Franklin, and who turned king's evidence on La Motte, and hanged him.

This Lutterloh, who had been a crimping agent for German troops during the American war, then a servant in London during the Gordon riots, then an agent for a spy, then a spy over a spy, I suspect to have been a consummate scoundrel, and doubly odious from speaking English with a German accent.

What if he wanted to marry THAT CHARMING GIRL, who lived with Mr. Weston, at Winchelsea? Ha! I see a mystery here.

What if this scoundrel, going to receive his pay from the English admiral, with whom he was in communication at Portsmouth, happened to go on board the *Royal George* the day she went down?

As for John and Joseph Weston, of the Priory, I am sorry to say they were rascals too. They were tried for robbing the Bristol mail in 1780; and being acquitted for want of evidence, were tried immediately after on another indictment for forgery — Joseph was acquitted, but George capitally convicted. But this did not help poor Joseph. Before their trials, they and some others broke out of Newgate, and Joseph fired at, and wounded a porter, who tried to stop him, on Snow Hill. For this he was tried and found guilty on the Black Act, and hung along with his brother.

Now, if I was an innocent participator in De la Motte's treasons, and the Westons' forgeries and robberies, what pretty scrapes I must have been in?

I married the young woman, whom the brutal Lutterloh would have had for himself, and lived happy ever after.

1575.   TO ALBANY FONBLANQUE
              SEPTEMBER? 1863

Published in part by Greenwood, *Cornhill Magazine*, IX, 657–658. My text is taken from a transcript supplied by Mrs. Fuller.

Palace Green, Kensington
W.

My dear Fonblanque. I am a little boy born in the year 1763 at Winchelsea where my parents lived, having been expelled from

France after the Revocation Edict of Nantes, which I suspect brought the Fonblanques to England too.

My Grandfather was Precentor and Elder of the French Church at Winchelsea, a perruquier by trade, but a good deal engaged in smuggling. I went upon various smuggling expeditions; but as I don't know the difference between a marling spike and a binnacle, I must get information from somebody as does. And who knows better than you?

Three or four sentences will be enough to tell me and write them like a bold sea man as you are for

Yours ever

W. M. Thackeray.

My Grandfather's name was Duval, he was a barber and perruquier by trade, an Elder of the French Protestant Church at Winchelsea. I was sent to board with his correspondent a Methodist grocer at Rye.

These two kept a fishing boat but the fish that they caught were many and many a barrel of Nantz brandy which we landed — never mind where — at a place to us well known. In the innocence of my heart, I a child got leave to go out fishing. We used to go out at night and meet ships from the French coast.

I learned to scuttle a marling spike

       reef a lee-scupper

       keelhawl a bowsprit

as well as the best of 'em. How well I remember the jabbering of the Frenchmen the first night! as they hawled the kegs over to us. One night we were fired into by His Majesty's revenue cutter Lynx, I asked what those balls were fizzing into the water?

I wouldn't go on with this smuggling being converted by Mr. Wesley who came to preach to us at Rye — but that is neither here nor there.

What I want is a few sentences about sailing, smuggling and so forth — how we went out at night, what we did, how we came back.

1576. ## TO MRS. BENZON [20]
16 NOVEMBER 1863 [21]

Address: Mrs Benzon | 10 Palace Gardens | Kensington. *Postmark:* LON-
DON NO 17 63. Hitherto unpublished.

Monday

Dear Mrs Benzon

I am glad to find Friday is quite free, and I shall be delighted
to pay a second visit to your beautiful house.

Very faithfully yours
W M Thackeray

I came to town very envious and coveting a number of my neighbours goods but the pang is quite over now.

1577. ## TO GEORGE SMITH
17 DECEMBER 1863

My text is taken from *Centenary Biographical Introductions,* XXI, xxiv-xxv.

Palace Green.

Dear Smith, — I was just going to be taken prisoner by Paul
Jones when I had to come to bed. If I could get a month's ease
I could finish the eight numbers handsomely with the marriage of
Denis and Agnes, after the capture of Toulon by the English. 'The
Course of True Love' [22] I thought of as a pretty name. . . .

Yesterday BURGLARS entered our house, and robbed my poor
mother and girls of watches, trinkets, diamonds — all my little
presents, lockets, bracelets, to poor Annie since she was fifteen.

[20] Mr. and Mrs. Ernest Leopold Benzon were Thackeray's nearby neighbours. It was with them that he and his daughters were engaged to dine on
December 24, the evening of his death. (Lady Priestley, *Story of a Lifetime,*
p. 72)
[21] The day before Tuesday, November 17.
[22] *A Midsummer Night's Dream,* I. i, 134.

1578.   TO MRS. JOHN LESLIE
                        20? DECEMBER 1863 [23]

Hitherto unpublished. My text is taken from a transcript given Mrs. Fuller
by Mr. Shane Leslie, who owns the original.

Dear Mrs. Leslie

Since I wrote and said yes, I have been in bed 3 days and Fate
and the doctor says No.

Indeed I am unfit to come (I have only this minute crawled
down to my sofa) and nobody can be more sorry than

> Yours Very faithfully,
> W. M. Thackeray.[24]

[23] Sir Algernon West (*Recollections*, I, 299) writes that Thackeray "was a
great friend of [Mrs. John Leslie], and spent many hours in her company.
His death was very sudden, as he was engaged to dine with her on the Sunday
before his death; his letter saying Fate and the Doctor prevented him from
keeping his engagement was the last he ever wrote."

[24] Thackeray's last days are described by Charles Allston Collins in a letter of
February 17, 1864, to his brother Wilkie, which I transcribe from the original
in the Berg Collection of the New York Public Library: "Thackeray . . . was
in this house on the Monday before the Thursday on which he died and was
in famous spirits and full of fun. On the Tuesday he dined at the Garrick
and those who saw him then saw almost the last of him. He came home
that night and went to bed as usual. On the next day — Wednesday — he
was so poorly as to keep his bed all day. His eldest daughter went into his
room about the middle of the day and saw him. His servant looked after him
the last thing at night. At mid-night his mother who slept in the next
room heard him retching violently, and when we were at breakfast the next
morning a servant came to us from the house to say 'that Mʳ Thackeray was
dead'. I never shall forget the day which we passed at the house — we went
there of course — or the horror of seeing him lying there so dreadfully
changed. It was apoplexy after all, and I don't think that what he had suffered
from so long had much, if anything, to do with it."

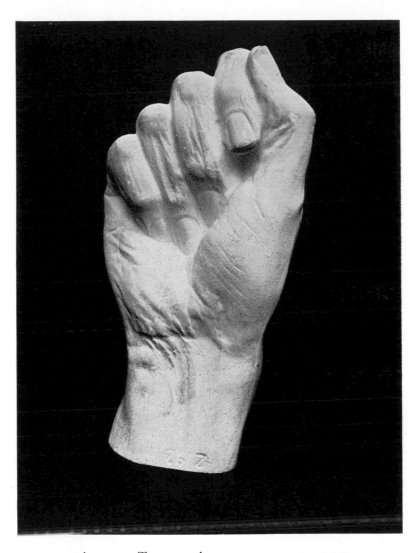

A cast of Thackeray's hand, made after death

1579. TO WILLIAM BRADFORD REED
1863

My text is taken from a facsimile in Reed's *Haud Immemor*, p. 28.

At sight pay any kindness you can to the bearer, Major F. Goldsmid,[25] and debit the same to

Your old friend,

W M Thackeray

Hon.ble W. B. Reed   Philadelphia

Permission to use the Reading Room will be withdrawn from any person who shall write or make marks on any part of a printed book or manuscript belonging to the Museum.

Press Mark.	Heading and Title of the Work wanted.	Size.	Place.	Date.
	At sight Pay any kindness you can to the Bearer Major F. Goldsmid and debit the same to Your old friend			

(Date)   W M Thackeray   (Signature).

_____ (Number of the Reader's Seat).

Please to restore each volume of the Catalogue to its place, as soon as done with.

Hon.ble W. B. Reed   Philadelphia

[25] Shortly before leaving on a trip to the United States in the summer of 1863, Major Goldsmith (*Athenæum*, 1891, p. 475) had encountered Thackeray in the British Museum. Learning of his plans, Thackeray wrote this note on one of the library's printed call slips.

1580.   TO HENRY THOMPSON
1863

My text is taken from a facsimile in *Centenary Biographical Introductions*,
XVIII, opposite p. xxxvi.

Palace Green. Kⁿ
Tuesday

My dear Thompson   Is it true about the 100000£ & the Grand
Cross? [26]   Hip Hip Hooray.

I don't want to borrow money, & am almost as pleased as if
I had received it myself.

1581. FROM ANNE THACKERAY TO MRS. BAXTER
30 APRIL–1 MAY 1864

Hitherto unpublished.

Putney Heath. Sunday May 1 —

Dear Mrs Baxter. I must write you one line tonight before I go
to bed. I have not written before because I can only write about
Papa & sometimes I *cant* — When I am worried & troubled about
other things then it seems a sort of desecration. I thought of you
often & often when I was in his study burning & putting away
papers in a sort of dream — There were one or two letters to you
begun there was a packet of Sally's letters — I burnt them too and
kissed them before I put them into the fire — The scraps to you I
will send one day but they are with much more of his writing in big
boxes locked & I cannot get at them. There is a little picture of
Mrs Hampton we put into a pretty frame for him. He was touched
when he found it & said I shall send this to her Mother — & I think
you will like to have it. Forgive me for speaking of your daughter
as I speak. To me the dead are dearer than the living and more

[26] Thackeray playfully exaggerates the rewards given Thompson for his
successful operation on Leopold I, King of the Belgiums, in Brussels during
1863.

alive at times. I think Papa knows perhaps I am writing to you now. Our home where you were once to have come is sold — We have only kept enough furniture for a small house where we are going to live with my Grandmother we believe — Friends are kindness itself there is money enough because Papa was always working for us, and our pain is far far less than it has been — It seems to us that sorrow at first is not sorrow but a terrible physical suffering. It seems to us that we could bear anything with only Papa to talk to about it, but to go stumbling & falling without him is weary work. My little Minny is asleep now too sad to keep awake tonight — But she is much better thank God & the aching leaves off for a while now & then — Only she looks thin and so wan at times that I can't bear it, but thank God she is much better. Granny has gone to Paris for a little change — perhaps we should have gone with her — but we could not bear it, & there was so very much to see to that it was decided we sh^d stay. We are in a little cottage on Putney Heath all the gorse is coming out & the green trees; & the birds are singing, & it is much better than London lodgings. Papa had not been very ill this last year — We had the happiest little Journey together — we did not see one other soul. We were with him all day long, & we thought we had never been so happy in our lives — *Next morning* Minny & the little dog are standing at the garden gate. Here come some children with flowers who tell us it is Mayday —

What we like to think about is a little expedition with Papa a week before Christmas — We went to the Temple Church together & then walked in the garden with all the sun setting — And he was so well & in such good spirits — Just the last week he was very sad & he said to me that if it was not for us he did not want to live much longer. But he was not near so ill as we had often often seen him & Monday he was well again we thought, and Tuesday it seems so very hard he went out & we missed him twice in the day — once he came back on purpose to see us — & we thinking he had gone out for the day as usual, had gone out too, so we only saw him for a minute, and at night I remember thinking how I c^d not bear two days to pass without seeing him more often. It is almost more dreadful to think of these last days than of those w^h came after. A little time ago we dined out somewhere & met a violent little American woman who spoke unkindly of you all — she did not know you, it was only some political madness. Papa turned upon his heel, — he said he was in such a rage he could scarce contain himself — he strode across to the other end of the room and desired us never to speak to that little Devil again. He never c^d hear her name with patience any more — Yours he never mentioned without many a word of affection and regard — The last time I remember his speaking of you was in the long green study, perhaps a month before & he said — "Poor dears. I am afraid they are very sad & lonely. It is quite different from old days I am afraid people suspect them of Southern leanings — My poor dear Mrs Baxter. Do you remember his kind voice when he loved people?

We are going to live in some new houses near Onslow Square. *8. Onslow Gardens Brompton.* if ever you write to us, please write there   My sister & I have bought the house & my grandmother is to rent it of us & we are to live with her. We try not to look forward much & to get thro each day as it comes. Granny is very kind, but very ill & feeble & every thing seems uncertain and dim. But we have had so much sunshine in our lives such a measure of love that we must not complain now if the light is hidden for a while. I know some day we shall all find our way to the Dearest & Brightest who love us still pray God

Good bye dear Mrs Baxter. Give our love to Lucy — We wish she had not been ill. Are you pretty well once more — You have not thought me familiar, I write as we think of you always.

Your sincere

A I Thackeray

1582. FROM ANNE THACKERAY TO MRS. BAXTER
24 OCTOBER 1864

Hitherto unpublished.

8 Onslow Gardens — Brompton
October 24. 1864

My dear Mrs Baxter   Your kind letter came to us when we
were still abroad — Thank you for it & for telling us about Papa —
When I write to you I almost feel as if all the years had gone back
& he was with you — only a few days journey off — and when I
read your letters it seems as if you were writing to give us news of
him & to tell us not to be afraid & though we fail & stumble so & go
so wrong without him yet he loves us all the same & knows what
weary work it is. I think I may go on complaining to you because
you will know that it is not all ingratitude & discontent. Everyday
we say Thank God for all his great mercy — But to have had Papa
to go to always, only makes it more lonely now. And yet we did not
think that such quietness as this would ever have come to us again.

I have been thinking about the letters of w^h you write — I can
only tell you that we ourselves must not publish one word that he
has ever written home. He told us that he did not wish it & said to
me one day when we had been speaking of a memoir of a friend of
ours *Mind this* there is to be nothing of the sort published about me
when my time comes.[1] And so we have been firm though many
people have spoken to us on the subject. Dear Mrs Baxter if it is
not too late I cannot help hoping that you too will keep what he
has written. I forget if I told you. We had a wretched anxious
time tracing some old letters of his w^h had been — so they said —
sold by mistake in an old table — The man into whose hands they
got began by asking £ 100 & then £ 200 for them   Our kind
friend Mr Smith frightened him into giving them back to us at
last — but it was most miserable work at the time — We heard of
them in one place & in another — some of them had been lent to a

[1] See above, I, lxvii.

poor little cripple artist to whom Papa had been kind, & he it was
who gave us warning of what was going on.[2]

But this is all over now & we are in this little house w^h does not
look very unfamiliar   Grannie was to have come immediately
but she has put it off for a fortnight & I think it will perhaps seem
less dreary when she is here. Everybody is still so very kind, but
London is empty now & so we seem to see scarcely anyone & each

---

[2] "Shortly after Mr. Thackeray's death his house in Palace-gardens and its
furniture were sold, the latter by auction. Among the articles was an old-
fashioned bureau, or writing table, that used to stand in its owner's bedroom,
and being somewhat shabby-looking, was knocked down without competition
to a neighbouring broker for a few shillings. As soon as the broker had got
his purchase home, he began furbishing it up and overhauling it, when, to
his surprise, either in some secret drawer or an ordinary drawer, which not
even the auctioneer's man who lotted the goods had troubled himself to open,
he discovered heaps of letters, including those written by Thackeray to his
mother in his schoolboy days, copies of a few important letters he had written
to other people, and numerous letters that had been addressed to him by
individuals of some note, such as well-known public men and the more distinguished among his brethren of the pen and pencil.

"The broker, elated with his 'find', and desirous of turning it to profitable
account, in the full belief that having purchased the writing table at public
auction he had acquired a property in the contents of the drawers, took the
parcel of letters to Julian Portch, the artist, who lived close by, and with
whom he had previously had some dealings. After consulting with Portch
he came to the conclusion that the letters were worth a considerable sum —
either one or two hundred pounds, I forget which — and asked Portch if
he would ascertain for him whether Thackeray's family would like to purchase them for that amount. Portch agreed to do so, and the letters being
left with him, he submitted them to Mr. Frederick Greenwood, who was
then editing 'the Cornhill' and the 'Pall Mall Gazette', and with whom
Portch was intimate through the former connection of the two with the 'Illustrated Times'.

"Greenwood at once recognised the importance of the discovery and submitted the broker's offer. Unluckily for the man the family solicitors were
consulted, and at once pooh-poohed the claim. They insisted on the letters
being retained, and the broker being left to prove his title to them in a court
of law. Irritated beyond measure at the turn affairs had taken, the latter
threatened proceedings against everybody concerned for the illegal detention
of his property. Eventually, however, he calmed down and accepted some
moderate compensation in lieu of enforcing his imaginary rights, and the
Thackeray correspondence was secured to the family." (Vizetelly, *Glances
back through Seventy Years*, II, 110–111)

day passes in a strange dull way only — I dont think we should have liked it to be less sad

I am glad you are in the country & pray God the peace & the greeness & the children above all will restore you & comfort you a little. We had the dear little children [3] framed long ago, & they hung in the pretty morning room & everybody said 'O what a dear little pair" when they looked at them.

I know Papa was tired & that he did not want to live except for us & yet my heart sickens & aches & I feel that he might have been with us now — But no words mean anything & even last night I woke up with a start saying to myself It has only been a dream & it is not true. It makes one so humble & so ashamed to hear of his tender goodness & to remember his unceasing love & partiality — & it is like a sort of torture now to remember how little we understood it   Though indeed we did care very very much, I was never happy or easy until I had gone to him about everything. Just a week before Christmas a thief got into our house & stole all my pretty trinkets that he had given me at one time or another When Papa came home & said "Poor Nan" I remember thinking it was worth while losing them for him to look so kind. I will send you the best picture of him I can find — There have been so many but we seem to like the old ones that he has seen & that we are used to best. There is a little picture he told me he should send to you one day — It is only one that you sent us, of Mrs Hampden — years ago — It became discoloured & faded & then we cut away the faded part & had it framed in a little chapel w^h seemed to fit it — It was in Papas study, when I went to put away his papers & I packed all the familiar little belongings away — Sometimes Minny looks very like Papa & sometimes she says things so like him that it is a wonder. She can remember things he said & liked & his words, & she has all his tenderness — I mean it is like his — Shall we ever come and see you? I know we should like it some day, — if you were to come — Even in this little house we could make room. Dear Mrs Baxter some day perhaps we may meet. — Did Papa ever talk to you about

³ See above, No. 1501.

M[rs] Brookfield? She has taken us under her kind wing she is coming to live close by only to be near us. All this terrible year she has been so good to us all three that I do not know how we could have dragged through without her.

Eyre Crowe is an artist still but he has also got a good place at the Sth Kensington Museum where he is an inspector — do you know that his sister who lived with us married our cousin Edward Thackeray & went to India with him. We hardly ever see M[r] Crowe — I cannot quite tell you why — He became shy & gradually went away. Sometimes we see M[r] Lawrence he used to come & draw Papa in the dining room at Kensington. We like the drawing very much, but the photograph of the drawing is not like somehow. We too still prefer the first that we have always looked at & w[h] seems to be Papa from long use as much as anything. There is a little drawing by Maclise, done years ago when Papa was quite a young man — I will send you [a] photograph of that, tho perhaps it is only long use, as with the other w[h] makes us like it so much.

Minny is going out for a drive with M[rs] Carlyle this afternoon, — we met old Thomas the other day on his horse & he suddenly began to cry. I shall always love him in future, for I used to fancy he did not care about Papa.[4] Now that the house is in order & we have done with carpenters &ct we must look about I suppose & find something to do & to be interested in — It is very difficult — I try & write a little but I have nothing to say — It is like speaking when one is not thinking of what one says — I suppose we must take to some schools or sick people & do the best we can. Economising is an employment after all & fortunately we have chosen rather too dear a house. But we will always pay our bills every week so that

[4] "Poor Thackeray!" Carlyle wrote to Milnes on December 29, 1863. "I saw him not ten days ago. I was riding in the dusk, heavy of heart, along by the Serpentine and Hyde Park, when some human brother from a chariot, with a young lady in it, threw me a shower of salutations. I looked up — it was Thackeray with his daughter: the last time I was to see him in this world. He had many fine qualities, no guile or malice against any mortal; a big mass of a soul, but not strong in proportion; a beautiful vein of genius lay struggling about in him. Nobody in our day wrote, I should say, with such perfection of style. I predict of his books very much as you do. Poor Thackeray! — adieu! adieu!" (Reid, *Life of Lord Houghton*, II, 113)

do not be afraid that we shall get into debt — And besides I am in hopes that Grannie will get a good pension. We have had much more for Papa's copyrights than he expected. The poor old Kensington red house has sold for £ 10.000. Unfortunately though it is my greatest comfort & shows that he did not expect more what was to come, than we did — papa had been altering his will & had not signed it; and so a third has to be funded & put away for my poor Mama

And now Goodbye dear Mrs Baxter we send all our best greetings to you all — If you will send us the pictures I think we should value them very very much but we do not want to take them from you. Goodbye once more with Minnys love & that of

Your affectionate
A I Thackeray

LETTERS OF UNCERTAIN DATE

1583.   TO LADY AIRLIE
[1855–1862]

Hitherto unpublished.

36 Onslow Square
March 1.

Dear Lady Airlie

You are very kind to come & see my daughters, and to ask me again to dinner. I wish I *could* come: but I dine with the Lord Mayor of England on Saturday.

Always yours
W M Thackeray

1584.   TO MRS. ARABIN
                           [1854–1862]

My text is taken from Madigan's *Word Shadows of the Great*, pp. 208 and 210.

36 Onslow Sq.,
Sunday.

Dear Mrs. Arabin:

I have chosen this black-edged paper to denote my grief, that I am unable and can't go out to dinner. Why, I think I have had to refuse ten friends this week, and believe me, the person who is most sorry of all, is

Yours faithfully,
W. M. Thackeray

1585.   TO MRS. BACON
                           [1854–1862]

Hitherto unpublished.

Friday. 36 Onslow Sq^r

Dear Mrs Bacon

My 'card trick' is one of the cleverest I have ever performed but where can the card be that was written to M^r & Mrs Bacon & Miss Bacon?

It was to beg and pray that you would dine with me at Greenwich on Sunday at the Trafalgar at 6.30. I do so hope that we are still not too late.

very faithfully yours
W M Thackeray.

LUCY BAXTER

From a photograph

Smoking-Room.

Dear Barham.   Reynolds has just raised a wonderful objection to an important article,   (of a few lines) w. I have submitted to him. Would you be good natured and hear the passage read?

It must be in secret   *W.M.T.*

AN UNDATED LETTER FROM THACKERAY TO THE
REV. RICHARD HARRIS BARHAM

1586. TO THE REV. RICHARD HARRIS BARHAM
[1837–1845]

Hitherto unpublished.

Smoking-Room.

Dear Barham. Reynolds has just raised a wonderful objection to an important article, (of a few lines) w^h I have submitted to him. Would you be goodnatured and hear the passage read?

W M T.

It must be in *secret*

1587.   TO MRS. BAYNE
[1854–1862]

Hitherto unpublished.

36 Onslow Square. Tuesday.

My dear Mrs Bayne. I wish I could meet my old college friends — but I have asked two people to dine here on Friday — and am writing in the midst of a fine attack of spasms w^h began last night, w^h will most likely prevent that dinner too. I cant say any more but that I am

Yours very truly
W M Thackeray

1588.   TO MR. BLUNT
                         [1846–1853]

Hitherto unpublished.

Kensington. Monday.

My dear Blunt
    I am transporting my young ones into the Country or I should
have had the greatest pleasure in joining your party on Wednesday.
                         Always yours
                         W M Thackeray

1589.   TO MRS. R. BOYLE [1]
                         [1846–1853]

Address: Honble Mrs R. Boyle. Hitherto unpublished.

                         13 Young St Kensington. Saturday
My dear Madam
    I send you a ragged portfolio full of scraps w^h may amuse you
some afternoon when your own hand is tired of doing much better

[1] Wife of Robert Edward Boyle (1809–1854), fourth son of the eighth
Earl of Cork and Orrery.

things. Liston used to say he was a great tragic actor, and so it's my opinion that I am a painter *manqué*. You have youth time and genius: I hope you will work, and not hide those precious candles of your's — The Line The Line is the thing. When I think of that text, I'm ashamed of this rubbish w^h I ask you to look at.

Thank you for your charming drawings, I shall frame them and look at them often; and am dear Madam

Most faithfully yours
W M Thackeray

1 or 2 of the drawings are in the anastatic ink with that pen.

1590.   TO BRADBURY AND EVANS
                    [1847–1858]

Address: Messrs Bradbury & Evans. Hitherto unpublished.

My dear Sirs

The first plate is done. I etched the second to day, It waits to be bitten in. the title is ready the book is ready. Dammy who s afraid?

Yours
W M T.

1591.   TO MRS. BROOKFIELD
                    [1848–1851]

Published in *Collection of Letters*, p. 138.

My dear Madam. I am always thinking of M^rs C⟨...⟩² W⟨...⟩ H⟨...⟩ with a feeling of regard so intense and incomprehensible that feeble words cannot give it utterance, and I know that only a strong struggle with my interior and a Principle w^h is based on the eternal data of perennial reminiscence can keep this fluttering heart tolerably easy and secure. But what is memory? Memory without Hope is but a negative idiosyncrasy and hope without memory a

² Apart from their initial letters, Mrs. Brookfield has irrecoverably over-scored this and the following names.

plant that has no root. Life has many such: but still I feel that they
are too few. Death may remove or in some way modify their
poignancy: the Future alone can reconcile them with the irrevocable
fiat of yesterday: and Tomorrow I have little doubt will laugh them
into melancholy scorn. Deem not that I speak lightly, or that beneath the mask of satire any doubt any darkness any pleasure even
at foreboding can mingle with the depth of my truthfulness. Passion is but a hypocrite and a monitor (however barefaced) — Action
febrile continuous action should be the pole star of our desolate
being. If this is not reality I know not what is — M^{rs} H⟨...⟩
C⟨...⟩ W⟨...⟩ may not understand me: but you will [3]

1592.   TO MRS. BROOKFIELD
                           [1848–1851]

Hitherto unpublished.

                                                     Monday ev^g
                                                          15.

My dear lady — You who know everything beforehand what
will you say to this sad news ⟨...⟩[4] and oppressed) and the old
wretch of a female said she would come too! — and come she did
and talked to me some confounded vulgar reminiscences of her
stupid existence — whilst the poor old red nose walked by us
meekly.

They will all do in a book so will every[one] do in a book so
would you so would even

                           Your ever tryew friend
                                  W M T.

[3] The original here breaks off in the middle of a line.
[4] Two-thirds of the first page of this letter are here cut away.

1593.   TO MRS. BROOKFIELD
                         [1848–1851]

Hitherto unpublished.

My dear Mⁱˢ Brookfield will see by the enclosed⁵ that *some*
vipers is not very dangerous reptiles.

1594.   TO MRS. BROOKFIELD
                         [1848–1851]

Hitherto unpublished.

My dear Mⁱˢ Brookfield — Yes if you please this very day.

                    always yours —ly
                         W M T.

1595. TO THE REV. WILLIAM AND MRS. BROOKFIELD
                    [1848–1851]⁶

Published in *Collection of Letters*, p. 135.

My dear Sir or Madam

Pax vobiscum ora pro nobis. If you go to the lecture today will
you have the Fly? it will be only ever so little out of the Fly's way
to come for you; and will you fetch me from this place please and
will you send an answer by Coachman today whether you'll come
or no?

I had a gentle ride in the Park and was all but coming to 15,
but thought I wouldn't get off my oss at anyplace save that where

⁵ No doubt a pen-wiper.
⁶ This note cannot concern Thackeray's lectures of May–July, 1851, for
the Brookfields had moved from 15 Portman Street to 64 Cadogan Place in
the early weeks of that year.

I am going to work namely this here ⁷ till Lecture time. Doyle will be in waiting at 4 1/2 o'clock to let the stray sheep into the fold.

I am yours
Makepeace. Bishop of Mealypotatoes.

1596.   TO THE REV. WILLIAM BROOKFIELD
[1842–1851]

Published in *Collection of Letters*, p. 25.

> Had I but ten minutes sooner
> Got your hospitable line
> 'Twould have been delight and honor
> With a gent like you to dine —
> But my word is passed to others
> Fitz he is engagéd too —
> Agony my bosom smothers
> As I write Adieu Adieu.

1597.   TO THE REV. WILLIAM BROOKFIELD
[1846–1851]

Published in *Collection of Letters*, p. 51.

My dear Vieux   Will ye dine with me on Friday at the G. my work will be just over on that day, and bedad we'll make a night of it and go to the play. On Thursday I shall dine here: and Sunday most probbly — or we go to Richmond on Sunday. Make your game and send me word.

Ever yours
W M T.

> Having occasion to write to a man in
> Bloomsbury Place & to Lady Davy I
> mixed up the addresses, & am too
> mean to throw away the envelope so
> give you the benefit of the same.

⁷ The Reform Club, according to Mrs. Brookfield (*Collection of Letters*, p. 135).

1598.   TO THE REV. WILLIAM BROOKFIELD
[1846–1851]

Hitherto unpublished.

Monsieur et Mesdemoiselles Thackeray ont l'honneur de prier
M. L'Abbé Brookfield de venir manger le gigot chez eux Dimanche
prochaine à six heures précises. Monsieur Forster y sera.

J'ai la soussignée & l'honneur d'offrir mes complimens respec-
tueux a Madame Brookfield.

Harite Marion Thackeray [8]

1599.   TO THE REV. WILLIAM BROOKFIELD
[1846–1851]

Hitherto unpublished. *Endorsed:* From W. M. T. To W. H. B.

13 Young St Kensington Friday
Tomorrow at one
Let us meet at *The Garrick*

The Rev^d
W. H. Brookfield

1600.   TO THE REV. WILLIAM BROOKFIELD
[1852–1863]

Hitherto unpublished.

My dear Vieux   The only free day I have this week is Friday
and I should like very much if you would come and dine here. It
would give me a great pleasure to shake hands with you & to smoke
a pipe once more. Gby.

W M T.

[8] The signature is in Minnie's hand.

1601.　　　　TO MRS. CARMICHAEL-SMYTH
　　　　　　　　　[1843–1846]

Hitherto unpublished.

And so God Almighty bless my dear little ones and their mother, and their Granny and all who love them, and bring us all together again; and as for next week why I really *will* write.

　　　　　　　　My dearest Mothers afft
　　　　　　　　　W M T

1602.　　　　　TO EDWARD CHAPMAN
　　　　　　　　　[1840–1863]

Hitherto unpublished.

Dear Chapman

A very deserving young person has sent me the accompanying MS. for w^h she wants a publisher & a profit of course. She has 50 subscribers she says — Will you make an estimate of the lowest price at w^h such a book could be published, and let me write to the author, on the subject.

　　　　　　　　Yours ever
　　　　　　　　　W M T.

I want to see if there is any reasonable way of holding the author harmless, & making the publisher answer. The songs are very pretty some of them.

1603.   TO EDWARD CHAPMAN?
                        [1846–1853]

My text is taken from a facsimile in an American Art Association catalogue,
January 8–9, 1936, p. 226.

Kensington, Friday

My dear Edward   I shall dine at home on Sunday will you
come and see your

Louisa

    6 o'clock

P S You had better get your spectacles to read this

1604.   TO CHAPMAN AND HALL
                    [1846–1853]

Hitherto unpublished. My text is taken from a transcript supplied by Mr.
Sessler, who owns the original.

                        13 Young St Tuesday Morning
Dear Sirs
    Will you please to let the bearer bring away my plate chest — I
thank you for having faithfully kept it through so many years.[9]
                        Yours
                        W. M. Thackeray

1605.   TO EDWARD CHAPMAN
                    [1846–1863]

Hitherto unpublished. My text is taken from a transcript supplied by Mr.
Sessler, who owns the original.

Dear Chapman.
    My oldest daughter rushing down to embrace yours truly, fell
down stairs and shook and hurt herself a little, so that she is gone
to lie down: and I & the other must stay at home tonight — Otherwise we should have all been on the road to Bolton by this time
where I hope you will have a pleasant evening without
                        Yours very sincerely
                        W. M. T.

1606.   TO CHAPMAN AND HALL
                    [1846–1849]

Address: Messrs Chapman & Hall | 186 Strand. Hitherto unpublished.

Dear Sirs
    At last Vizetelly has done his duty & sent me a really good
Cut. Pray urge him to do his very best with these w^h come; and

        [9] See above, No. 182.

(some of the others being altered) we will have a great & worthy & triumphant book for Xmas.

1607.   TO MR. CHESTER
                      [1860–1862]

Hitherto unpublished.

                                          Monday.
My dear C.
    The text is good but much also depends on the Sermon. A lively series of illustrations of the clumsy working of Gov! Offices would be good reading — but a disquisition wouldnt. So about M! Robinson — I cant judge at all till I see the article, and 2

on *aud 2, as I think* as I think would be better than 3.

            Yours
            W M T.

1608.   TO MRS. ARCHER CLIVE [10]
                      [1860–1862]

Hitherto unpublished.

Dear M!! Clive.
    I was so hard at work that I could see nobody, & forgot every thing but my Roundabout Paper w! I have just done (3.30) We should be delighted to dine with you: but I want if I can to make a run to Paris or somewhere as soon as my number is ready; and, if you please, will say No.
    I refused (with thanks) a poem for my present number because of its defective conclusion, and that poem was written by
            Yours always
            W M Thackeray.

[10] Mrs. Clive (1801–1873) was the author of *IX Poems by V* (1840), *Paul Ferroll* (1855), and other volumes of verse and fiction.

1609.   TO MRS. COLE
                        [1854–1863]

My text is taken from *Thackeray in the United States*, I, 329.

                                          31, Saturday.

My dear Mrs. Cole, — I am going to confiscate [11] an American
rocking-chair which has been an eye and shin-sore in my room
for years past since a Yankee Captain gave it to me. The girls
say your children like to rock in this chair very much in spite of
its ugliness and many defects. Will they have it in the nursery,
or shall the Broker ship it off? Please ask Mamma to decide
this most important question.

1610.   TO HENRY COLE
                        [1848–1863]

Address: H. Cole Esqre Hitherto unpublished.

My dear Cole Will you please tell Mr Lascelles that I cant
come out this morning having work to do w^h must be delivered
by 2 o'clock. but that I engage myself for £2.2.0; and if need
be to propose a resolution at the meeting
                        Yours ever
                        W M Thackeray
I wont write to Mr Lascelles because he must be in the midst
of preparations and a messenger such as you is surer than a note.

1611.   TO HENRY COLE
                        [1854–1862]

Hitherto unpublished.

                                          36 O. S. S. W.

My dear Cole I ought to have written before but could not
write till yesterday from illness.

[11] General Wilson reads *confiseoli.*

Put me down for 100£ Debenture please of the Horticultural Society of London.

Yours ever
W M Thackeray

1612.   TO HENRY COLE
                      [1860–1862]

Hitherto unpublished.

We'll talk over that idea of the article.

H. Cole Esqr

1613.   TO HENRY COLE
              14 FEBRUARY [1860–1862]

Hitherto unpublished.

14 Feb.

My dear Cole

S & E write that some verbal changes have been made in your article at Cornhill. I am so busy that I haven't time to collate the papers, so I send you the revised proof, but have made so bold as to pass the article, as the Printer waits to go to press

Yours
W M T.

Your title is too big and we have xtended you by the name I leave unerased.

1614.   TO JOHN PAYNE COLLIER
                      [1837–1840]

Address: J. Payne Collier Esq^e | &c &c &c. Hitherto unpublished.

Tuesday.

My dear Collier   I should have been delighted but I am going out of town next week with my family: for a little recreation at Brighton.

Ever yours
W M T.

1615.   TO DUDLEY COSTELLO
                    [1854–1862]

Hitherto unpublished.

                                        36 Onslow Sq. S. W.
                                                Friday.

My dear Costello.

Have been laid up in bed otherwise should have written earlier
— Send me word or call if you plaise and say how you can
be served by

                        Yours ever
                        W M T.

1616.   TO GEORGE CRUIKSHANK
                    19 NOVEMBER

Hitherto unpublished.

                                        Novr 19.

My dear Cruikshank

Axel's number I dont know but if you will send your drawing
to H. Glynn Esq^e Berkeley Chambers Bruton St saying who is
the author and that you are come from me, you may depend on
having a proof

                        Yours always
                        W M Thackeray

1617.   TO MRS. CUNNINGHAM
                    [1849–1863]

Address: Mrs Cunningham | 2 Madeley Villas. Hitherto unpublished.

Dear Madam.

Could you kindly lend me the Handbook of London [12] if you
have a copy of that interesting book? It shall be safely returned
in the course of the day by

                        Yours very truly
                        W M Thackeray

[12] By Peter Cunningham, first published in 1849.

1618.   TO CHARLES ANDERSON DANA [13]
             2 OCTOBER [1857–1863]

Hitherto unpublished.

36 Onslow Sq? S. W.
October 2.

My dear Dana

I have left a letter at home w^h I ought to have forwarded to you, from S. Lucas (of the Times) who will send you some letters. He edited the Press for some time is a liberal Conservative a very worthy man and a good writer. He has the confidence of the Conservative party. He *wont* write scandal though, or much personalities. He might be lighter but he is the best man I know of just now. He says unless you prefer a Saturday letter very strongly, a Tuesday letter w^d be better, as the party meetings are on Sundays generally, and the gossip comes afterwards My regards to Don Bayardo, and all who remember

Yours ever
W M Thackeray.

1619.   TO HENRY DAVISON
                [1846–1856]

My text is taken from a Sotheby catalogue of November 7, 1927.

My dear Davison,

I am engaged to a lord and a lady, how can you expect me free to go with anything commoner? [14]

Yours,
W. M. Thackeray.

[13] Dana (1819–1897) was editor of *The New York Tribune*.
[14] According to the Sotheby catalogue Thackeray wrote this note "In reply to a suggestion that he should go to the Derby in a hansom cab."

1620.   TO THE SECRETARY OF THE
DEANERY CLUB
[1837–1863]

My text is taken from a facsimile in *Thackeray in the United States*, I, 66.

Mᵣ Thackeray regrets that a previous engagement will prevent him from having the pleasure of dining with the Deanery Club on Thursday next. In making this announcement Mᵣ Thackeray will feel much obliged if the Secretary will
— Thats all.

1621.   TO CHARLES DICKENS
[1836–1858]

Hitherto unpublished.

My dear Dickens
    1000 pardons. Im very sorry Im engaged on Monday 4ᵗʰ
                                                    W M T.

1622.   TO RICHARD DOYLE
[1848–1863]

Hitherto unpublished.

My dear RD.
    Lord Ashburton is coming to dine with me at home on Friday at 7, and I wish you would come too. Let us meet as much as we possibly can in this world, mon ami; and as for the next who knows

but that both MacHale [15] and Sir Robert Inglis may be wrong, and have settled prematurely who is who and who is not —— less?

Yours ever

W M T.

1623.   TO D.
                     [1846–1863]

Hitherto unpublished.

My dear D.   I did not receive your n: until late this e: too late to put the answer into the p here. But as I am going into T to D I hope in this reply to say I will be at the R at 4 and will gladly introduce you to C & H.

Yours my d d

v. t.

W M T.

1624.   TO MRS. ELLIOT
                     [1848–1851]

My text is taken from a facsimile in *Collection of Letters*, opposite, p. 94.

M![r] Jeames de la Pluche presents respeckfle Comps to M![rs] Elliot and I am very sorry that he cannot igsept *your genteal and palight invitation* w![h] he is engaged as you will be *gladd* to hear to meat Miss Virginia Pattle: and afterwoods to go to a *friendly Swoary* where praps a *reverend gent's* lady by name of Br—kf—ld may *cumsoal* me fir his igstreme disapintment in not meeting neither M![rs] E nor *Miss P*

PS. Respeckfl Comps to the young lady who sang like a *Siring*
PS. Genteel regards to Miss K. E. P.

[15] John Machale (1791–1881), Catholic Archbishop of Tuam. Sir Robert Inglis was an ardent Episcopalian.

1625. TO DR. ELLIOTSON
[1846–1853]

My text is taken from *Notes and Queries*, Sixth Series, IV (1881), 507.

Kensington, Tuesday Ev^g

My dear Doctor, — How can you ask such a buck as I am to eat a mere 1/2 buck? — and the worst of it is that I'm going to refuse even that — I want to go out of town for my health's sake, & try Dr Air and Dr Thalatta. You are a good doctor but I want I say to try *the latter* (if I had but written Dr Ether instead of Dr Air, you will perceive I could have made another pun on the subject and said how happy I could be with,[16] &c.).

But so, all things duly weighed, I am obliged regretfully to say no: though I want to dine with you very much, and though I dare say after all I sha'n't get out of town.

Ever your's reminiscently
W. M. Thackeray.

1626. TO THE REV. WHITWELL ELWIN
5 APRIL [1855–1863]

Hitherto unpublished.

Grosvenor Sq^e
April 5.

$\overset{1}{} \qquad \overset{2}{}$
As you have given currency & importance to a very complacent
$\overset{3}{} \qquad \overset{4}{} \qquad \overset{4}{} [sic]$
misrepresentation of the offer we have had the honour to make to
$\overset{6}{}$
the Literary Fund on behalf of a third person you will perhaps favour us with an opportunity of correcting IT.

O Elwin! what a sentence!
My name is needless but it is that of
a true Briton and a lover of his Country.

---

[16] See above, No. 442.

Mr. James de la Pluche presents respectful Comps to Mrs. Elliot and I am very sorry that he cannot igsept your genteel and palight invitation wh he is engaged as you will be gladd to hear to meat Miss Virginia Paille: and afterwards to go to a *friendly Swoary* where *praps* a *reverend genlt lady* by name of Br—kf—ld may *comsoal* mr fer'her igstreme disapintment on not meeting neither Mrs. E nor Miss P

PS. Respectfl Comps to the young lady who sang like a Siren

PS. Genteel regards to Miss K. E. P.

An undated letter from Thackeray to Mrs. Elliot

1627.   TO FREDERICK MULLET EVANS
                    [1846–1851]

My text is taken from a Sotheby catalogue, March 26–27, 1934, p. 31.

My dear Evans.

Can you settle with me — a 1/4 quarter of Punch and the proceeds of that last masterpiece. We expect the young ladies on Wednesday at 3, and then Papa at 6/30.

W. M. T.

1628.   TO FREDERICK MULLET EVANS
                    [1847–1851]

My text is taken from a Sotheby catalogue, February 13, 1928.

Dear Evans

Will you pay in for me my month and 70£ as the Punch quarter.

Yours like Saturday
W. M. T.

R. S. V. P.

1629.   TO FREDERICK MULLET EVANS
                    MAY [1847–1851]

Address: F. M. Evans Esqre   Hitherto unpublished.

My dear Evans.

All that money the other day was paid away, and I am still crying for more. Can you let me have 60 for the no, and 40 on the Punch acc^t that will ease the payment at the end of June w^h w^d otherwise come awfully heavy upon you.

Yours ever
W M Thackeray.

1630.   TO MRS. AND MISS FANSHAWE
                     [1849–1851]

Hitherto unpublished.

My dear f and Miss F.

    You must come to day please: for I want ladies of all things
having 2 or 3 men and only our dear M^{rs} B —

    Send word that you'll come and ease the mind of

                    Your distracted
                    W M T.

1631.   TO MRS. FANSHAWE
                     [1849–1851]

Address: Mrs Fanshawe | 10 Portman Street. Hitherto unpublished.

My dear f

    May I come to night to tea at 8 o'clock? On my way to another
sworry.

                    Your respectful
                    W M T.

    I wish you a very happy New Year indeed.

1632.   TO MRS. FANSHAWE
                     [1852–1857]

Hitherto unpublished.

My dear kind little f.

    Fanshawe writes that you are coming through town and might
like to stay a day or two. Do come for days or for weeks you
know you & Totty will always be welcome by

                    Yours
                    W M T & Co

    I go away to Glasgow on the 12th but the house & the cellar
is still here.

1633.   TO MR. FAULKNER
[1854–1862]

My text is taken from *Thackeray in the United States*, II, 163.

36 Onslow Square, S. W.

My dear Faulkner,

Will you send the wine and the bill to me at ☞ . I am just out of bed after an illness else I would have ⠀⠀⠀ sooner written to you. The girls send with Papa, their very kind regards to Mrs. Faulkner and I am Yours always

With all my ♡ ⠀⠀⠀ W. M. Thackeray.

1634.   TO MRS. JOHN FITZGERALD
[1848–1851]

Hitherto unpublished.

My dear Mʳˢ Fitzgerald

I was on my way to you when the rain descended in a cataract, and I write at this moment from a friends room and dressed in his clothes wʰ are I grieve to say too small for me in fact I am in this situation

and how long the buttons will endure it is impossible for me to
say — My own garments

at the kitchen fire — I blush at the mere notion of these details.

My servant was to come to your house at 6 1/2 for the oss:
will you be so good as to order him to Jones Mews at Portman St
whence he may fetch it.

Are we to meet tomorrow at Doctor Piper's? We are all in
next weeks Punch: and I am always very truly yours

W M Thackeray

1635.   TO JOHN FORSTER
                       [1846–1853]

My text is taken from an American Art Association catalogue, March 25, 1920.

Kensington, Saturday

My dear F.

If not engaged, you will find roast beef and Higgins here tomorrow at 6 o'clock.

Ever thine
W. M. T.

1636.   TO JOHN FORSTER
                            [1846–1856]

Address: J. Forster Esqre | 58 Lincolns Inn Fields. Hitherto unpublished.

My dear Forster

Will Friday do? or Sunday? and can you write as elegant as this? The other day when Minny heard that I had met you at dinner she flushed up and said 'I hope you gave him my love' So I told a falsehood and said I had. I'm engaged unfortunately on Saturday and write so beautifully because I am very busy and ought to lose no time

                              Yours always
                              W M Thackeray

1637.   TO JAMES FRASER
                        1 JULY [1838–1840]

My text is taken from a facsimile in the New York Public Library.

                         13 G^t Coram S^t 1 July.
Dear Fraser

Do make up my account now directly — if you owe me so much the better I am hard up and want money, if you don't, so much the better too, for you that is and I shall know where I am. Sempiternally yours

                         W. M. Thackeray.

                              Impromptu
        In case you owe send what you owe
        In case you don't dont send you know

1638.   TO THOMAS FRASER
                            [1841–1846]

Hitherto unpublished.

The Earl of Malmesbury [17] has arrived in Paris from London [18]
The Marquis of Thackeray has also arrived and passed three
hours *on Sunday* at the apartment of the Correspondent of the
Morning Chronicle: who was absent *at a Steeple Chase*! His
Lordship affably partook of some rhubarb and magnesia at the
correspondent's expense. Up to the time of our Express leaving
Paris, no satisfactory results had ensued from the potion.

1639.   TO MRS. HALL
                          [1860–1862] [19]

Hitherto unpublished.

                                          36 Onslow Sq^e S. W
                                              March 10.

Dear Mrs Hall.
    I am known as a willing horse, and have such a number of live
people on my back that I fear I must not let poor Mrs Hemans's
statue get up and ride. I assure you it is harder to me to say No
than yes; but if you were to see *my* little list of applicants alive
and hungry, you would I think advise me to say No too.
                        Yours very faithfully
                        W M Thackeray.

[17] James Howard Harris (1807–1889), third Earl of Malmesbury (1841),
a well-known statesman.
[18] This sentence, obviously the beginning of a despatch to *The Morning
Chronicle*, is in Fraser's hand. The rest of the note is written by Thackeray.
[19] This note is written on the stationery of *The Cornhill Magazine*.

1640.   TO MRS. HAWES [20]
                         [1846–1856]

Hitherto unpublished.

My dear Mrs Hawes

I will come on Sunday with great alacrity and on Saturday
evening I should like to come very much, but I doubt whether
the distant dinner to w^h I'm engaged will break up time enough
to admit me to Queen Square.

Pax vobiscum
Ora pro nobis
Yours very faithfully
W M Thackeray

1641.   TO LADY HAWES
                         [1856–1862]

Hitherto unpublished.

36 Onslow Sq^e S. W.
Tuesday.

Dear Lady Hawes

I have been unwell and am anxious to go out of town; and
only waited that my daughter might keep her engagement for
Thursday. As your table is too crowded to receive her, will you
kindly let me vacate my place too, and go off with my girls to
Brighton.

Very faithfully yours
W M Thackeray.

[20] The wife of Benjamin Hawes (1797–1862), later (1856) K. C. B.,
Deputy Secretary of State for War and afterwards Permanent Under-Secretary
of State for War from 1851 until his death.

1642.   TO LEIGH HUNT
                        DECEMBER [1846–1859]

Published in *The Cornhill Magazine.* My text is taken from a transcript
supplied by Mrs. Fuller.

My dear Hunt,

> Though we never meet we should
> If you could and if you would
> Will you take your dinner here
> On the last day of the year?
> And believe me Hunt my dear
> Yours for ever and a day
> Doubleyouem Thackeray.

1643.   TO MRS. IRVINE
                           [1848–1863]

My text is taken from a facsimile in *Unpublished Letters by W. M. Thackeray,*
ed. Shorter, p. 6.

Mr Thackeray who is in bed will have great pleasure in dining
with Mrs Irvine this evening.

1644.   TO WILLIAM JERDAN
          [1837–1843]

Address: W. Jerdan Esqre | &c &c &c. Published by Charles Plumptre Johnson, *The Early Writings of William Makepeace Thackeray* (London, 1888), p. 34.

13 G^t Coram S^t
Brunswick Sq^e

My dear Jerdan.

Is it fair to ask whether the Literary Gazette is for sale? I should like to treat: and thought it best to apply to the Fountainhead of w^h I am always the obligated

W M Thackeray

1645.   TO JOHN KENYON
          [1848–1850]

Hitherto unpublished.

13 Young St Kensington

My dear Kenyon

I must go away to Brighton on Sunday with Pendennis: or I should have come to you with pleasure — Farewell! be happy without your melancholy friend

W M T.

1646. TO SIR WILLIAM KNIGHTON
[1862–1863]

My text is taken from Maggs's catalogue 659 (1938), where the drawing is reproduced in facsimile.

Palace Green, Kensington, W.

My dear Knighton

Can you tell me what sort of a place this here is. Someday when you have O to do would you go and look at it? I should so like to have a house, a garden, and a field or two. If the place is marshy or clay soil it won't do for me, and I am, we are, Yours and Lady Knighton's always, W. M. T. and daughters.

1647.   TO JOHN LEECH
                         [1843–1863]

Hitherto unpublished.

Dear Leech. I have been here since yesterday, and if you
dont come in about 10 minutes I think I shall be gone. This is
King of the Garrick Club sitting at my window. He little knew
I was sending him to the great cawickachawist of the Age. But
the *real* reason I have to write is this. I have just been reading an
odd volume of Chambers Journal & find the following pretty lines

  The toddler tyke neer has sic a good byke
   As the bonny gairy bee;
  But of a' the bie-bykes that ever I saw
   The red beltie bears the gree.
    Upon my word its so.

1648.   TO WILLIAM LEIGHTON LEITCH [21]
[1854–1862]

Hitherto unpublished.

Dear M[r] Leitch

Are you in town for yet a little time & could you give a few lessons at your own house & at as early an hour as you like to

Yours very truly
W M Thackeray.

36 Onslow Sq[e] Brompton.

1649.   TO MRS. MAC CULLAGH
[1862–1863]

Hitherto unpublished.

Kensington Thursday

Dear M[rs] MacCullagh.

No 1 of my daughters is unwell and we are obliged to decline evening-parties in consequence; otherwise mesdemoiselles w[d] have had great pleasure in accepting Miss MacCullagh's invitation

Always faithfully yours
W M Thackeray

On the back of my note I see with dismay the picture of a little boy saying his prayers. As the subject is moral and edifying, I don't write a new note, and economize a sheet of paper.

---

[21] Leitch (1804–1883) was the best teacher of landscape painting of his time. He was drawing master to the Queen and the royal family from 1842 to 1864.

1650.   TO MRS. MACREADY
                         [1841–1852]

Hitherto unpublished.

Ah my dear Mrs Macready Mr William Thackeray presents his
compliments to you and is quite grieved that I am engaged to
dinner on Monday. He begs me to state that he is ever

                    Sincerely yours
                    W M Thackeray.

1651.   TO LORD MAHON?
                        [1846–1853]

My text is taken from a facsimile in a Goodspeed Bookshop catalogue.

                                13 Young S.t Thursday Ev.g

My dear Lord   See how differently History is written by different
hands! As I read your version of my conduct I feel I'm a criminal
and monster of ingratitude, so dexterously do you put me in the
wrong. But when I examine my own buzzum I know that it is
quite innocent: I kept away from modesty (upon my word) not
indifference, and thought you would send for me when you wanted
to see me. I didn't know that you had been badly ill, until 2
nights ago, & only heard that you were keeping your room and
did not see people. I'd like to set off this instant and go and see
you: but, failing that, I will come directly, and thank you for
wishing that I should come. On Sunday I am going to Lord
Lansdowne, Wednesday & Thursday am disengaged: may I come
either of those days? I mean not counting the morning visits w.h
I will by the blessing of Heaven pay you. Ever truly yours
                                W M Thackeray

1652.   TO MRS. MARTIN
                        [1856–1858]

Hitherto unpublished.

    Dear M.rs Martin. Would you like to come through the rain &
hear a lecture about George III at 4 precisely. Never mind answer

    36 Onslow Square. Brompton.

1653.   TO MRS. MARTIN
                        [1860–1862] [22]

Address: M.rs Martin | 31 Onslow Square. Hitherto unpublished.

    My dear Neighbour. I have refused 2 dinners for Thursday
already, on the plea of ill health w.h unfortunately is too true:
and mustn't come indeed I mustn't. Always yours.

[22] This note is written on *Cornhill Magazine* stationery.

1654. TO RICHARD MONCKTON MILNES?
[1846–1851]

Hitherto unpublished.

Your reflections about my family are unkyind and unjust. My enjoyment is never greater than when, surrounded by the beings dearest to me, I distribute to them slices of that mutton w^h my industry has enabled me to purchase. The palled epicure sneers at those simple festivals. Luxury has enfeebled his sickened appetites: the Natural ceases to stimulate the flaccid debauchee. Childless but not chaste, you cannot comprehend the raptures of those whose infants draw sustenance from their labours, and in their leisure frolic round their knees. Worldling! these are the daintics w^h render my feasts more delicious than Luculline banquets. Idle moth burning your painted wings in Fashions reeking torch: how can you understand the quiet joys of those who warm themselves at the Hearth of Domestic Love?

But, Wretch, are you so ignorant of the very routine of home-pleasures as not to know the hour when a blessed slumber ends them? Are you unaware that at the time when the revels of the voluptuary are but commencing, the innocent eyes of childhood are sealed in sleep? My honest household is quiet, when your fevered menials are plying the smoking salver or the inebriating corkscrew. The heartless jibe, the indelicate retort, the sneering laugh w^h desecrates all things Holy & Beautiful are echoing in your polluted halls, when only the deep breath of slumbering Innocence interrupts the sacred silence of my cottage.

It was *then*, when the good slept — that I proposed to come to *you*: to touch you perhaps with words of warning: to interpose an element of peace in your carouse: — a life-boat venturing in that storm of dissipation — haply to rescue some stray poor soul that was battling on the waves of perdition.

Now it is too late. I asked two gents to partake of my humble meal. *Our* evening will pass away in philosophical converse. May yours be at least not criminal. Adieu. Though the rains are falling on the gardens of our peaceful village the church bells are ringing their sweet invitation. Farewell then.

1655. TO SIR WILLIAM AND LADY MOLESWORTH
[1846–1853]

Hitherto unpublished.

Sir W & Lady Molesworth. to remind.

13 Young S<u>t</u> Kensington

Friday
21
7½

1656.   TO MRS. MONTGOMERY
                             [1846–1851]

Hitherto unpublished.

                                        Kensington. Friday.
Dear Mrs Montgomery.

If you did but know all or half this weary h& is forced to do
in these days, I am sure you would pardon me for not having
answered your kind note sooner. I am working just now and for
4 or 5 days more to come from morning till long after bread-and-
butter time. But when my business is done I shall have very much
pleasure in coming to you and asking for a cup of the best of teas.

                        Always truly yours
                        W M Thackeray

1657.   TO MRS. MONTGOMERY
                             [1848–1851]

Hitherto unpublished.

Dear Mrs Montgomery

Knowing that I was very anxious to pay a visit to this house
a lady & friend of mine has given me a pretext, and I appear if
you please as Ambassador from Mrs Brookfield in the Bourgeois
as Governess business.

Mrs B who has {housed and sheltered} lunched I think is the
proper word) Mlle Bourgeois, whom I have also seen at her house,
says that her sister at Exeter (Mrs Tinling) gives the most favorable testimony of Madlle B — indeed sent her to London to Mrs
Brookfield

Tho she was obliged to leave the School at Exeter, she is only
one of very many French teachers who have shared the same
fate at the hands of the ojous vulgar cruel & domineering Miss
Morrish — in fact what could a woman be whose name was
Morrish?

The Paris association it appears will take much time before they answer your letter — First they will write to Morrish, next to London to find how Mlle Bourgeois has been spending her time here — to w^h Mrs Brookfield will have to reply — then finally an answer may be sent to Mrs Montgomery by this slow coach of an association.

Meanwhile la Bourgeois languit dans la solitude and the anguishes of deferred hope — I can bear witness that she talks good French is not too good looking and yet not disagreeable: and Mrs Brookfield has bidden me to enclose a letter from Mr Chancelor Martin (who M. le Chancelier is I dont know,) bearing witness to the good beayviour of the lady — A note also is humbly forwarded from the Association of Institutresses to show that Mlle B does actually form one of the number.

At 6 o'clock if you sh^d have returned I myself shall be on my way back into town, and will ask leave to call again and see if there be any answer to this long note for

Yours dear Madam very sincerely
W M Thackeray

P. S. Does anybody want any more drawings in their albums.

1658.   TO ALFRED MONTGOMERY
                    [1848–1863]

Address: Alfred Montgomery Esq^e Hitherto unpublished.

Jeudi avec grand plaisir cher et aimable Montgoméri. Oui je passe trois fois par mois pres de Somerset House mais Jamais avant 3 heurs. — Oui vous avez été bien bon. et de venir et de me pardonner. Nous réconcilierons Jeudi au Coventri Club.

Tout a vous de coeur cher Alfred
Chevalier de Titmarsh.

1659.   TO LADY MORLEY
                      [1846–1855]

Published in *Biographical Introductions*, VI, xxviii–xxix, where the drawing here reproduced opposite p. 344 is reproduced in facsimile.

But, permit me to say dear Lady Morley — Merciful powers! what must have been the astonishment of the reigning Duchess on entering her grand daughters apartment long before daybreak on the bridal morning (with her maids of honour called up from their couches to attend the anxious parent & Sovereign) what I say must have been her H's astonishment to find the Princess's couch deserted! —

Yes deserted! — The virgin night-cap lay crimped and undisturbed on the unruffled pillow, the pillow on the swelling feather-bed — w^h that night — enfin, w^h had not been slep upon that night. The room was vacant. The window was open. The bird had flown.

Dear Lady Morley, Adelgisa had fled!

    With best respects to your family circle believe me ever faithfully yours

                 Samuel Rogers.

1660.   TO LADY MORGAN? [23]
                      [1846–1851]

Hitherto unpublished.

Madam

H. Hallam will tell your ladyship why it is that the Fates prevent me from coming to your party (I would have said your fête but luckily remembered the pun just in time) — to your party I say to night. There are men coming here to day, & the brutes will smoke after dinner. He refused to dine in consequence of that horrid dessert, & in order that he might keep himself pure for you.

I am very glad indeed to hear that you are well again. Is

[23] Lady Morgan lived at 11 William Street (*Royal Blue Book*, 1851).

General Cabrera [24] coming? What man need despair when such a one carries off the great prize.

I hope you enjoyed your dinner yesterday — I rode round your Brougham intending to pay you a visit in it: but, going in to your neighbours house for a moment, you were gone when I came out. I leave this at your door and trust that the evening will pass off brilliantly in William St. w.ʰ it cant do on account of the smoke on the premises of

Your humble servant to command

W M Thackeray

1661. 　　TO GEORGE WILLIAM NICKISSON

[1841–1846]

Hitherto unpublished.

Dover.

Tuesday Evg.

My dear Nickisson

I wish you would look at the accompanying paper — w.ʰ I think exceedingly good and apropos. It is written by one of the best critics on art I know of — not excepting The Titmarsh: and I hope you will have my friends paper & that it will make a figure in the Magazine.

Yrs ever

W M Thackeray

1662. 　　　　TO MRS. OLLIFFE

[1848–1853]

Hitherto unpublished.

Dear Mrˢ Olliffe

Let Tuesday be the happy day to take the dinner and the tay.

Yours very truly

W M Thackeray

[24] Ramon Cabrera (1806–1877), the Carlist General.

But, permit me to say dear Lady Morley — Merciful powers! what must have been the astonishment of the reigning Duchess on entering her grand daughters apartment so long

before day break on the bridal morning (with her maids of honour called up from their couches to attend the anxious parent & sovereign) what I say must have been her H's astonishment to find the Princess's couch deserted! —

Yes deserted! — The virgin night-cap lay crimped and undisturbed on the unruffled pillows, the pillow on the swelling feather-bed — wot that night — enfin, wo! had not been slep upon that night. The room was vacant. The window was open. The bird had flown.

Dear Lady Morley, Adelgisa had fled!

With best respects to your family circle believe me ever faithfully yours
Samuel Rogers.

AN UNDATED LETTER FROM THACKERAY TO LADY MORLEY

1663.   TO LADY OLLIFFE
                       [1853–1863]

Hitherto unpublished.

Dear Lady Olliffe.

The cake wʰ you were so unkind as to send me has made me
very unwell. I could not help eating a great deal too much of it
and I know very well that I shall go on eating and eating as long
as any of it remains. How many enjoyments are there in this life
of wʰ we will partake although we know they are injurious how
many temptations (especially those bits of sweetmeat) wʰ we cannot resist; how many things on the other hand wʰ we are obliged to
digest wʰ are not near so agreeable as Lady Olliffes plum cake!

   I am with sincere regret your most faithful Servᵗ
       Thomas Fraser
      Archbishop of Dublin

1664.   TO LADY OLLIFFE
                       [1853–1863]

My text is taken from a Sotheby catalogue, June 14, 1926.

My dear Lady O.

If you please I will come to you.

    Yours (in the middle of his work)
      W. M. T.

1665.   TO JOSEPH PARKES
                            [1844–1850]

Address: J. Parkes Esqᵉ | 21 Gᵗ George Sᵗ | Westminster. Hitherto unpublished.

My dear Parkes —
    I am always engaged of a Monday at our weekly dinner with Mʳ

1666.   TO KATE PERRY
          [1856–1863]

My text is taken from a facsimile in a Sotheby catalogue of May 30, 1934.

A party who's fond of ladies from Paris has just come
    back
Good heavens how stupid it was! and to crown it all poor
    Thack
Wound up his visit of duty with a twenty-fifth attack —
Then in came Sir Joseph Olliffe with his pills & his
    doses black
And yesterday afternoon I returned (in the Folkestone
    Smack)
And I'm very sorry you're out (and Somebody Else good
    lack)
And I shake you all by the hand, and have no more rhymes
    in my pack

1667.   TO SIR FREDERICK POLLOCK
          1 MAY [1848–1854] [25]

My text is taken from *Works*, XIII, 79.

By fate's benevolent award,
    Should I survive the day,
I'll drink a bumper with my lord
    Upon the last of May.

That I may reach that happy time
    The kindly gods I pray,
For are not ducks and peas in prime
    Upon the last of May?

At thirty boards, 'twixt now and then,
    My knife and fork shall play;
But better wine and better men
    I shall not meet in May.

[25] These verses appear in Thackeray's *Ballads* (1855) under the heading
"The Last of May: in reply to an invitation dated on the 1st."

And though, good friend, with whom I dine,
  Your honest head is grey,
And, like this grizzled head of mine,
  Has seen its last of May;

Yet, with a heart that's ever kind,
  A gentle spirit gay,
You've spring perennial in your mind,
  And round you make a May!

1668.   TO MR. PRIDEAUX
                 27 APRIL [1857–1862]

Hitherto unpublished.

                                    36 Onslow Sq^e S. W.
                                          April 27.

My dear Prideaux
  We have made a law against balls and must not break it for
fear of being *criblé* with balls. Thank you for asking my girls
and believe me
                      Yours gratefully
                      W M Thackeray

1669.   TO MRS. PRINSEP
                 28 MAY [1848–1852] [26]

Hitherto unpublished.

                          13 Young Street à Kensington
                                    le 28 Mai

  Les journaux, Madame, m'ont appris vôtre retour à Londres.
Le printemps il me semble revient avec vous. Pauvre prisonnier,

[26] The Prinseps did not settle at Little Holland House in Kensington, where
the painter Watts lived with them for twenty-five years, until five or six years
after they returned to England from India in 1843 (*Dictionary of National
Biography*).

cloué à ma table de travail, voyant qu'à travers les grilles de mon
cachot les douces fleurs printanières, souvent je me suis dit — que
ne puis-je voir Madam Prinsep? L'infame
n'a-t-elle donc plus de souvenirs? L'amitié
est-elle oublieuse? Dans les tourbillons de la
fashionne, dans les raouts splendides, les bons
coeurs se noyent ils quelquefois? Non, mille
fois non, mon coeur me l'assure. Les hommes
mentent ainsi, mentent et oublient. Les
femmes sont plus fidèles. Doute de toi même,

lâche hérétique — des femmes jamais! Pour elles jadis est au-
jourdhui, elles seules conservent le culte archisaint du passé!
Incrédule! As tu même remis une carte a cette porte autrefois si

hospitalière? — Cours y malheureux! Va faire honte à ta peur prématurée!

Voila donc ma carte, Madame, moi même je la dépose sur votre seuil. Que veux je? vous voir encore une fois — et pourquoi? — pour vous dire que moi aussi je me souviens.

Minuit.

1670.   TO MRS. PROCTER
                          [1841–1843]

Hitherto unpublished. My text is taken from a transcript given Lady Ritchie by George Murray Smith.

                                        Bedford Hotel,
                                        Covent Garden,
My dear Mrs Procter,

You saw how ill I behaved the other day, expectorating like an American. I have been so bad since with cough and influenza that I have been fit to go nowhere, and go off this evening Pariswards. I oughtn't to go, and had much better be in bed. But then my Mother would be in such a terrible fright! What ink they give one at inns! You will hardly be able to see the Good bye all which I send from

                          Yours affectionately,
                          W. M. Thackeray.

1671. TO MRS. PROCTER
JUNE [1844–1863]

Hitherto unpublished.

My dear Mrs Procter

I look in my book and I'm ready to cry I find I'm engaged on the first of July. The fourth and the fifth I am also put by, but some other evening? I hope you will try.

Ever yours
W M Thackeray

1672. TO BRYAN WALLER PROCTER
30 MARCH [1848–1863]

Hitherto unpublished. My text is taken from a transcript given Lady Ritchie by George Murray Smith.

March 30.

My dear old B. C.

I should not wish to have this made public, but I find that if I have been out to a very good dinner, and read a dozen letters on coming home at night I sometimes forget part of them. So I looked at the first lines of your note — cut off the cheque and put it away — and forgot all about the lady of the poems, until yesterday when I read your note through — or again, which was it?

Of course you are welcome to my little subscription. I'm vexed that I had not looked more carefully at your letter.

Always yours,
W. M. T.

1673.
TO R.
[1846–1853]

Hitherto unpublished.

13 Young Street Kensington

My dear R   Friday

   Will you please to remember that you dine with
me at the G on Monday? Bedad we'll make a night
of it. And will you please to keep it in mind that you
are due with me at Richmond most probbly on
Thursday? Make your own game and let me know.

Always most faithfully
W M Thackeray

1674.
TO A. RADCLIFFE
[1854–1862]

Hitherto unpublished.

36 O. Sqᵉ S. W
May 13.

My dear Radcliffe

   I will write to Ritchie, who is my cousin; and your brother in
law shall have all my gigantic influence in his behalf. But his
case seems so good that I should think he may do without me
very well.

   I am very glad to have a line from you, disgusted to gather
from your hints that when you come to London on business, the
business isn't pleasant. So I am never to hear the wind whistle
in the dear old house at Everton [27] again? But I shall always
remember how kind the people were in it. Give my best remembrances to Sir Edward Radcliffe, & the assurance from my daughters

---

[27] Thackeray stayed with Radcliffe at Northumberland Terrace, Everton,
Liverpool, in October, 1852, and in December, 1856. This note may have
been written a year or two after either visit.

of as much affection as is consonant with maidenly modesty. Also
kind regards please to any of your friends at Lpool who remember
Yours always
W M Thackeray.

If Teddy has holyday time about now, couldnt he come to us
for a week? We'll get him a bed round the corner & send him to
all sorts of larks and divarsion.

1675.   TO CHARLOTTE RITCHIE
                              [1849–1854]

Hitherto unpublished.

Sunday. Rue d'Angouleme

My dear Charlotte

We go to dine with Stevens to day at his Tuskulum;²⁸ and I
suppose tomorrow must dine with the elders but on Tuesday if
you will have us, we 3 will be delighted to come. At 6 I suppose
dont mind answering.
Always afftly everybody's
W M Thackeray

1676.   TO SAMUEL ROGERS
                        29 JUNE [1847–1851]

My text is taken from P. W. Clayden's *Rogers and his Contemporaries* (London, 1889), II, 231.

13 ²⁹ Young Street, Kensington: 29th June.

My dear Sir, — The moment I had finished my work yesterday
and had returned to this real world, I thought to myself, "Does
Mr. Rogers remember that he invited me (that is, that I asked
him to ask me and he asked me) to breakfast with him on the
30th?" The transaction took place at Mr. Sartoris's: in the presence of witnesses — and to-morrow is the day. I shall not trouble
Mr. Rogers to write to me (I reasoned with myself), but at 10

---

²⁸ Stevens was a dentist.   ²⁹ Clayden reads 73.

o'clock I will be at his door. I will say, "A gentleman who was invited a fortnight and a day ago comes to claim his breakfast. The host may have forgotten, but the guest has not."

And I give you warning, my dear sir, that this visit is hanging over you, and that unless you fly from London you can't help hearing my knock at your door at 10 to-morrow morning.

Always faithfully yours,
W. M. Thackeray.

1677.   TO LADY RACHEL RUSSELL [30]
[1846–1853]

Published in facsimile in *Thackeray in the United States*, II, 184.

J. Pummell Beadle of Kensington presents his compce to Lady Rachel Russell, and begs to Suttify that the young man is known to me who have put out the Inclosed Andbill.[31]

[30] Youngest daughter (d. 1898) of the sixth Duke of Bedford. She married Lord James Wandesforde Butler in 1856.
[31] The enclosure has not been preserved.

He live in Young S^t: as a Fammly: and pays his taxes reglar. The tradesmen know him and trust him. And though at Church seldom, must say in the Watchus he never Ave been.

Pummell begs his duty to her Grace and as usual lets neat flys & Brooms on Jobbs: and supplies the Nobillaty with fish at exackly double the London Prices.

1678.   TO LAURA SMITH
                      [1848–1863]

My text is taken from a facsimile in Johnson's *Early Writings of William Makepeace Thackeray*, p. 49.

My dear Miss Laura

Words quite fail me. I never saw such a beautiful pen wiper in my life. Receive in lew of it the thanks and blessings of an old man. —

1679.   JAMES SPEDDING
               15 JUNE [1854–1861]

Hitherto unpublished.

                                     36 Onslow Sq^{re}
                                         June 15.

My dear J. S.

Will you and your young friend come and dine here on Sunday at 7?

I send you my first effort in serious verse.[32] And since I composed it — knowing my ancient friend you're undertaking this ever so long a History of Lord Baking — most strongly recommend as greatly fitter at your — advanced old age the light poetic literature.

In the romantic little town of Highbury
My father kep a circulating library.
Mamma was an innabitant of Drogheda,
Where my dear Pa fust met her and enjoyed her.*
I in the famous island of Jamaica
From early youth have been a sugar-baker.

---

[32] Spedding repeated these lines to Trollope, who prints a modified version of them in his *Thackeray* (p. 32), remarking slyly that "There may, perhaps, have been a mistake in a line". The fourth verse, indeed, has become:
     Very good she was to darn and to embroider.
In Mr. Ball's Album there are also the following unpublished stanzas added by Thackeray to an undated note from FitzGerald to Spedding:
                        Impromptu
     On the Viscountess **** at Court this day.
     To court the fair Emily came
     All blazing in pearls and in rubies
     Her stomacher all in a flame
     From her shoulder strap down to her pubis.
     But ah! should her Ladyship strip
     I'd care not for pearls or for rubies
     What ruby's as red as her lip
     What pearl is as white as her boobies!
         Louisa to dear James: with love.

And here I dwell the *Muse's* appy vot'ry ⎫
A-cultivatin every kind of potry ⎬
Under the shadow of the green cocõa-tree. ⎭
* He followed in his youth that man immortle who
Conquered the Frenchman on the field of Warterloo

1680. TO CLARKSON STANFIELD
[1837–1843]

My text is taken from a reduced facsimile in *The Dickensian*, XXII (1926), 204, 217. I have not traced the original, which was owned by Mrs. Walton of Eltham in 1926.

13 Coram S^t
My dear Stanfield.
  By some mistake your kind invitation to dinner does not specify the *day* when I am to have the honour of dining with you I only want to know the date, I have not the slightest doubt but that I shall be disengaged
      ever your faithfully attached
        Wilhelmina

1681. TO MRS. STURGIS
[1848–1863]

My text is taken from an American Art Association catalogue, November 17, 1919.

My dear Mrs. Sturgis:
  I am so very sorry about Monday & humbly beg your pardon. I didn't think any day was fixed for dining with you except the 1 April, when I hope you and Mr. Sturgis will come to dine with me and see one or two pretty Englishwomen.
        Always yours,
          W. M. Thackeray.

1682.   TO WILLIAM MAKEPEACE THACKERAY
SYNGE [33]
[1860–1863]

Published by Merivale and Marzials, *Thackeray*, p. 243. My text is taken from *Thackeray in the United States*, I, 105–106.

My dear William Makcpeace Thackeray Synge, —

I just saw this nice fish in a shop, and thought it would be a nice gift for my godson. Dear boy, when you have some princes to dine give them this, and when they have quite done and the shell is clean, I think you may make boats of the tail and boots of the claws. I wish the man had not cut the claw off. He did it with his great knife, and at the same time hit me on the nose. I did not cry much, and I am your true friend and godpapa. P. S. I cannot eat any of it. I am glad....

1683.   TO WILLIAM WEBB FOLLETT SYNGE
[1853–1863]

Reproduced in facsimile by Madigan, *Word Shadows of the Great*, pp. 212–213.

Sir   I am desired by Lord Palmerston to say that Perhaps you have heard of Miss Simons? She dines at a twopenny Pieman's But when she goes out to a ball or a Rout Her stomach is covered with di'monds. I have the honor to be, Sir,

Your obedient Serv[t]
W M Tomkins

1684.   TO WILLIAM WEBB FOLLETT SYNGE
[1853–1863]

Hitherto unpublished.

I make you and your wife and M[r] Gilbert my compliments. — am just on the way to order dinner at the Garrick with Bob Bell

---

[33] Thackeray's godson, born August 5, 1860.

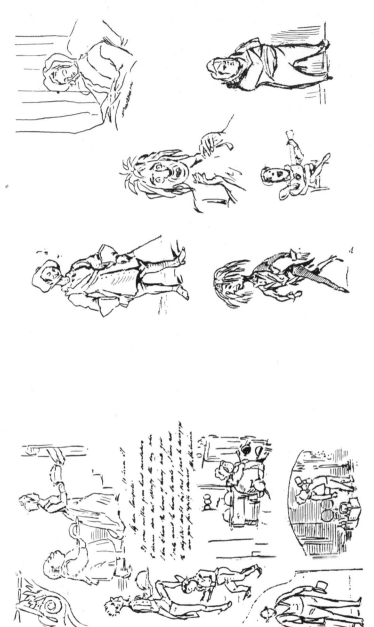

and Tom Fraser at *6.30*. If you can join our party we shall be deloighted.

W. M. T.

Feast of O. B. L.

1685.   TO WILLIAM WEBB FOLLETT SYNGE
[1853–1863]

Hitherto unpublished.

My dear Synge

Here is the answer from Smith & Elder regarding the little scheme w^h you proposed to them —

Your friend Mr Lucas's brother came upon me on Sunday at lunch with a letter from you, asking me for 2 days work and a contribution of money for a charity. I gave him 10£. but declined the dinner and speechifying. So much obliged to you for sending him to

Yours ever
W M T.

1686.   TO WILLIAM WEBB FOLLETT SYNGE
[1860–1863]

Hitherto unpublished.

My dear S

Had nt you better dine here on Sunday? Bring the ladies & Trollope too. 7 o'clock

W M T.

1687. TO ALFRED TENNYSON
[1841–1863]

My text is taken from the second Baron Tennyson's *Alfred Lord Tennyson*, I, 266–267.

My dear Alfred,

I woke at 2 o'clock and in a sort of terror at a certain speech I had made about Catullus.[34] When I have dined, sometimes I believe myself to be equal to the greatest painters and poets. That delusion goes off; and then I know what a small fiddle mine is and what small tunes I play upon it. It was very generous of you to give me an opportunity of recalling a silly speech: but at the time I thought I was making a perfectly simple and satisfactory observation. Thus far I must *unbus'm* myself: though why should I be so uneasy at having made a conceited speech? It is conceited not to wish to seem conceited. With which I conclude,

Yours, W. M. T.

[34] Thackeray and Tennyson "had been dining together," writes the second Lord Tennyson (I, 266), "and my father said, 'I love Catullus for his perfection in form and for his tenderness, he is tenderest of Roman poets,' and quoted the lines about Quintilia's death ending with
'Quo desiderio veteres renovamus amores
Atque olim amissas flemus amicitias' —
lines which he would translate by four lines from one of Shakespeare's Sonnets,
'Then can I drown an eye, unused to flow
For precious friends hid in death's dateless night,
And weep afresh Love's long since cancell'd woe,
And moan the expense of many a vanish'd sight,'
and the stanza from the 'Juliæ et Mallii Epithalamium,'
'Torquatus, volo, parvulus
Matris e gremio suæ
Porrigens teneras manus
Dulce rideat ad patrem,
Semihiante labello.'
Thackeray answered, 'I do not rate him highly, I could do better myself.' Next morning my father received this apology."

1688.   TO ANNE THACKERAY
                    [1848–1851]

Hitherto unpublished.

My dearest Fat.

You must both of you work hard during my absence: and have
the carriage when you like and go to Portman S⸰ and Hampstead
once. And God bless you prays your

                                        Papa.

1689.   TO ANNE THACKERAY
                    [1854–1862]

Address: Miss Thackeray | 36 Onslow Square —. Hitherto unpublished.

I have just remembered LADY GLASGO Order a fresh
horse to be ready with the Brougham against Sims returns at 10.15.
And fetch me with a bag of Clothes from the Athenæum at 10.30.
           May my daughter live 1000 years.
                    W M T.

1690.   TO ANNE AND HARRIET THACKERAY
                    [1849–1856]

Hitherto unpublished.

                                        Monday. 1.

My dearest Shildren.

I have had a good night am all right and the Doctor retiring
with his compliments says to a roast leg of mutton you may go.
How sick you will be of hearing of my being always ill!

Davison read my letter to you on Sunday night but didnt know
it was in verse. I shall be soon back I spose and have a respite
now for 10 days haven't I? but this attack has been quite different
to the others and decidedly choleraic. Good by my dears.

In the Morning Post of yesterday theres an advertisement of a piano to be sold at 86 Gower Street Bedford Sq^re. You might take a fly and go see it.

W M T.

1691.   TO GENERAL THACKERAY
[1854–1860]

Address: General Thackeray. Hitherto unpublished.

36 Onslow Sq^e Friday.

My dear General

Lady Elizabeth has promised to come to a scrambling dinner at 7 *chez moi* and I do hope you will be of the party. It is only made up within 2 hours, and I dont quite know how many there are or if there's enough for dinner.

Yours ever
W. M. Thackeray.

1692.   TO MR. TORNOW
[1846–1863]

Hitherto unpublished.

My dear Tornow

Will you dine en famille with us on Monday at 7. 30. If I can find any pleasant person to meet you I will: if you like pleasure theatres London delights pray dont come to my humdrum quarters: if you have *no* better sport in view, do come and shake by the hand

Your old friend
W M Thackeray

1693.   TO ANTHONY TROLLOPE
              [1861–1862]   ·

Hitherto unpublished.

My dear Trollope.

I haven't a lecture by me except that stale old Humour & Charity w^h I give for literary men in distress *not* for Societies — Otherwise there w^d be no end to the calls on me.

So with the greatest desire to do what you ask — you see I cant. And as for writing a lecture just now I am much too busy preparing my friend Philip.

Yours ever
W M T.

Have you mind to dine here on Monday at 7.30?

1694.   TO HORATIO WADDINGTON?
              [1849–1863]

Hitherto unpublished.

My dear Horatio I am afraid of the eleven o'clock dinner & had better be in bed at that hour. Yours ever. W M Thackeray.

1695.   TO MR. WALLER [35]
              [1854–1862]

My text is taken from a Henkels catalogue, November 12, 1903.

Onslow Square

Dear Mr. Waller

The fire from my chimnies communicates to the Barons [36] walls, and smoke breaks through the panels of his drawing room. Will

---

[35] Robert John Waller, builder, 26 Grosvenor Street West, Pimlico (*Watkins's London Directory*, 1855).

[36] Baron Marochetti.

you send somebody to examine my fire places and my neighbours?
We may all be in ashes if we don't mind.

Faithfully yours,
W. M. Thackeray.

1696.   TO MRS. ELIOT WARBURTON
[1848–1852]

Hitherto unpublished.

Tuesday.

Dear Mrs Warburton Do not Judge harshly of me yet: attribute
my absence to indispensable engagements; my silence to continual
occupation — I've been writing so much that I hate the sight of a
pen; and get so nervous that I tremble before answering an invitation. Dont let Eliot write too much therefore: lest you should
have him in my woful condition: and till I am free in a day or two

Believe me Yours very truly
W M Thackeray

I wanted to come to you on Saturday, but I was beat & broke
down.

1697.   TO SAMUEL WARD
[1853–1863]

Hitherto unpublished.

Saturday.

My dear Ward
    One or 2 friends dine with me at Voisin's at 7 o'clock today. Will
you be des nôtres?

Always yours
W M Thackeray.

1698. TO SAMUEL WARREN
[1857–1862]

Address: S. Warren Esqre | 16 Manchester Square. Hitherto unpublished.

Saturday

My dear Warren.

When I am parturient with one of my numbers, I don't accurately hear what is said to me, or remember what I say or read. It appears that I, the girls, and Edward Thackeray all made an engagement to dine with you — and to this minute I don't recollect it. What are we to do? Will you have the young ones without the old one? You will get me out of a scrape, if you will be generous: and the young folks shall dine with you or not entirely as you think fit to decide.

I am much annoyed by the blunder and pray you to forgive

Yours sincerely
W M Thackeray

1699. TO WILLIAMS AND NORGATE
10 OCTOBER [1848–1852]

Hitherto unpublished.

13 Young St Kensington.
10 October.

Gentlemen

I have been too ill until now to acknowledge your letter. I shall be happy to agree with Mr Tauchnitz's terms, & will thank you to send me the 20£ w^h you have in charge for me.

Yours very faithfully
W M Thackeray

Messrs Williams Norgate.

1700.   TO WILLIAM YARDLEY
                          [1841–1846]

My text is taken from a facsimile in an American Art Galleries catalogue of
April 18, 1923.

    Dear Yardley Having dropped into Hewson's Rooms at 5 o'clock
I found him and Morgan John O'Connell in the following attitude
& costumes. Summers Hartford waited yesterday upon his Sovereign and Frank Murphy has lost his voice Rose is winning as usual
at billiards and we all remain
                      Yours &c —

1701.   TO ?
                          [1837–1840]

Hitherto unpublished.

    Mrs Thackeray made such wry faces at the idea of my going away
for two days, that I must give up the notion I fear. — it is all settled

I believe that I am to be turned off on Tuesday the 23ᵈ so please to receive this in lieu of plumb cake.

ever yours

W. M. Thackeray

1702. TO ?

[1841–1843]

Hitherto unpublished.

Tuesday.

I'm entirely ashamed of what I'm going to say and do. Instead of coming to tea I'm going to Brighton. There are no lodgings to be had in the whole town; and I must be lodged somewhere to night, and at work tomorrow morning. But unless you write to tell me you forgive me, Remorse will pursue me like a fiend to the Chain Pier: and I shall never forgive myself.

the distracted

Titmarsh.

1703. TO ?

[1842–1851]

Hitherto unpublished.

Sir

Mr. Mark Lemon is the Editor of Punch I am only a contributor to that periodical, nor can he return rejected contributions nor answer the innumerable correspondents of the journal wʰ he conducts.

I return your paper & am Sir

Your very obdt Servt

W M Thackeray

I myself have no control over the arrangements of the paper & am only concerned for my own contributions.

1704.   TO LADY ?
                               [1846–1853]

Hitherto unpublished.

                                      Kensington. Wednesday
Dear Madam
    Who can have all the objects of his desire in this life? I should
have liked to meet Mrs Trelawney very much but shall still be very
happy to dine with your Ladyship, and in spite of the misfortune
shall come to dinner with the contentment and appetite of a philosopher
                               Very faithfully yours
                               W M Thackeray

1705.

TO ?
[1846–1853]

Hitherto unpublished.

My dear lady I did not send
the hand-chaise to day for the
reason w^h keeps me at home drawing the vine out of the window,[37]
and thinking of things. But if
you please shall I send it tomorrow? Or wouldnt it be
better to have a very easy going
Brougham from my man
here, whose charges are
moderate, and who will
not jolt you as the chaise
I fear will. And will
you please let me know
which you will have and
whether I shall bring
the carriage tomorrow
if it is fine at 12 o-
clock: And will you
believe that I never
never will
laugh at
you in my
sleeve, but
the contra-
ry: and that I will always be truly and respectfully yours.

[37] At 13 Young Street, Kensington.

1706. TO ?
4 JANUARY [1847–1851]

Hitherto unpublished.

à Kinsington ce 4 Janv.ʳ

Mosieur!

Au jour de l'an nous avons goutè de votre beau cadeau de Rhom de Jamaïque

Ah Mosieur! qu'il est bon, votre rhum de Jamaique! — et que vous méritez une annee bonne et heureuse, comme vous la souhaite.

Votre serviteur dévoué

P. S. I have got such a beautiful pen that I can't help performing exercises of calligraphy

1707.   TO ?
                              [1848–1863]

Extract published by Professor Dodds, *Thackeray*, p. 22.

Sir

My first published book was the Paris Sketch Book in '38 or '39. Part of it had previously appeared in Fraser's Magazine previously, and a Comic story called 'the Professor' was I think my first regular appearance as a paid author, in Bentley's Miscellany 1837 I think, but about dates I am not certain.

Your very obdt Servt
W M Thackeray.

1708.   TO ?
                              [1850–1853]

Hitherto unpublished.

Dear Sir

I promised Miss Power a contribution for the Keepsake,[38] w^h I send and beg you to forward to the Printer. I am going away immediately: but the MS. is so clear that I scarcely need see a proof.

Faithfully yours
W M Thackeray.

1709.   TO ?
                         2 JUNE [1854–1861]

Hitherto unpublished.

Brompton. June 2.

Dear Madam

Indeed I am quite at a loss how to advise you, not knowing the bent of your mind nor the literature w^h you should choose. When

---

[38] Contributions by Thackeray appeared in *The Keepsakes* of 1851, 1853, and 1854.

I was young I read everything I could lay my hands on — and what I wrote was bad and poor stuff for many years — Whereas some people begin to write well young — witness Mr Dickens, and Mr Tennyson who was a great poet at 20. No one can advise another on this score but the more you know, the better for you. For learning the structure of the English language to know Latin is very necessary: but I would no more counsel you to imitate any given person's style than to imitate any one's tone of voice. You should know that there are thousands & thousands of ladies and men too who would like to write stories and to help their families You have first to have the undoubted merit and genius, then to succeed in persuading a publisher; then to succeed in pleasing the public — I trust all these desirable things may happen for you: but who can help you? No instructor — only genius and industry. I wish I had more than these common-places to send in reply to your note, and am

> Your very faithful Servant
> W M Thackeray.

1710.   TO ?
                          [1856–1862]

Hitherto unpublished.

                                   36 Onslow Sq. July 21.
Sir

I can't from the specimen you send me, by any means venture on a prophecy as to your success as a literary man. No man can predict another's fortune in that profession, or help another to much effect: or possibly say after the perusal of 20 pages what a young writer's future development may be. I read your sheet through and was amused — might take an exception or two, but indeed I must not. I am writing by this post to another gentleman who sends a long MS. work, asks an opinion, wants a publisher, and to whom I am obliged to give but disheartening council. I wish this task were not put upon me so often or that in your instance I could offer you direct encouragement to pursue literature. Believe me

Your very faithful Servt
W M Thackeray.

1711.   TO ?
                          [1857–1863]

Hitherto unpublished.

The day after the

When the girls told me that they had written to you to ask whether they might bring partners — their father's usually benevolent countenance looked as black as thunder.

After the ball this morning Minny says 'Well, Papa, I think it was very impudent of us to think of asking to bring partners to such a ball. Why, it was the most beautiful thing I ever saw.'

And I was pretty well for the 1st time this ever so long and thought of going. Lucky I didn't. Had refused Sheriff's dinner on plea of being too unwell to dine out.

I am glad it was such a great success and will sign my name some other day — as that of your most humble Servant.

P. S. Somebody had told the girls that they might ask & I told them they had taken a liberty

1712.   TO ?
                               [1860–1862]

My text is taken from Goodspeed's catalogue 293 (1938).

My dear Sir,

I am just writing to my cousin who has put in an indignant protest too: and if someone will send me a smart and pleasant article, not too long — I shall be delighted to let the public hear the *alteram partem*. Cooksley might do it, might he not? But it won't be in time for the next number.

                         Very faithfully yours,
                              W. M. Thackeray.

APPENDICES

APPENDIX XVIII

THACKERAY IN NORWICH, MAY, 1857

During May, 1857, the Whitwell Elwins spent two days with Thackeray in Norwich, where he was lecturing. The following notes on his visit, which were made by Mrs. Elwin, are reprinted from *Some Eighteenth Century Men of Letters*, I, 177–182.

He speaks very low. I found it needed attention to catch each word. He does not develop his ideas much; he only puts into words just the thought that passes through his own mind. This gives a fragmentary air to his talk. He seems little to care whether it is set off fully and to advantage, or even whether those who hear him altogether take it in. He showed two manners, — one very quiet, very earnest, very deep, almost pathetic; another (a general and much more common manner) is like one who played at ball with every subject, tossing them about with a light, careless, but unerring hand, taking up one thing after another, — serious and gay, trifling or important, — and sporting with them as though he would get pleasantry out of everything. But if any religious subject was spoken of he talked with solemnity and earnestness.

If you did not know who he was, the first thing which would strike you would be that he was a man who looked with a magician's eye through and through everything before him. In five minutes you know he has made a complete inventory of the room, and he has weighed out everybody in it. He sits quietly watching a face for two whole minutes, and then he turns away, having spelt every letter of the character. He is constantly speaking of the sort of face a man has, — "he has a bad face," "a hang-dog face," etc. Badness mars all talent in his eyes. He talks of someone who is clever, and he then adds, "But he is a bad man," as if we had no right to admire a bad clever man. On the other hand, he is always throwing in gentle, considerate excuses for everybody. "So-and-so has this and that weakness." — "Ah, but then remember such and such a reason for his excuse," — "Remember such and such a good quality notwithstanding." He seems to notice the slightest specks of goodness.

As the hour for the lecture got near, he left. I had gone soon after dinner to sit with the children. When Thackeray left the dining-room he opened the door where we were, and said in his grave pathetic voice, "I am come to say good-night," and took each child's hand, and lingered for a moment with their hands in his own. Then he stepped out into the balcony, took out his purse, and threw a shilling to a brass band which had been playing before the window. "Now then for the sermon," he said, turning to me, and went to his own hotel to prepare for the lecture.

He talks quite freely and simply of his own writings — tells a story, and then adds that it suggested such and such a trait of one of his characters. He said, "People tell me such and such a character is not natural; but I *know* it is natural, that it is to the life." [1]

It is evident that he does not set a tremendous price on his own writings. It appears as if he did not, and could not, labour them; and, being the produce of little effort, he cannot believe they are what they are. He replied to some of Whitwell's admiration of him, "Yes, but you rave; you are a maniac." Whitwell asked him how he found out his true vein, as his earliest things were not in it. He said he began to write when his misfortunes began, and then found it.

He said he regretted not having illustrated the Newcomes himself. Whitwell said the conception of the Colonel's face and figure was fine. "Oh yes," he said, "but I gave it Doyle. I drew the Colonel for him."

He laughed at the idea of future fame. He said he could not understand why any should care for fame after they were dead.

His mother he described as having been exquisitely handsome, and as fascinating everyone who came in her way. "When I was a child my mother took me to Exeter to a concert. She looked like a duchess. She came splendidly dressed, in a handsome carriage, and all suitable appurtenances. That was thirty years ago. The next time I went to Exeter it was I who danced on the tight rope. I took the girls down with me. I could see that the waiter at the inn took them for part of the performance, and expected them to put on their trousers and spangles, and come in and sing a comic song. We went and saw the place where Pendennis kissed Miss Costigan,[2] and identified it all quite satisfactorily."

"The first literary man I ever met was Croly. I was a lad of seventeen, on the top of a coach, going to Cambridge. Somebody pointed Croly out to me. I had read Salathiel at sixteen, and thought it divine. I turned back and gazed at him. The person who pointed him out to me said, 'I see that lad is fated!' He knew it by the way I gazed after him as a literary man."

"I once lent a man £300 to get an outfit for India. He lived on the same stairs with me at the Temple. He was to pay me when he could,

---

[1] "I heard a story the other day," Kingsley writes in *Yeast* (New York, 1909), p. 19, "of our most earnest and genial humorist, who is just now proving himself also our most earnest and genial novelist. 'I like your novel exceedingly,' said one lady; 'the characters are so natural — all but the baronet [old Sir Pitt Crawley], and he surely is overdrawn; it is impossible to find such coarseness in his rank of life!'

The artist laughed. 'And that character,' said he, 'is almost the only exact portrait in the whole book.'"   [2] See chapter 6 of *Pendennis*.

and in course of time he did pay me. He came home to England, and I went to see him, and asked him to dine with me that day three weeks, — at all events, my first vacant day. I asked him three times, and he never would come. At last he said, 'The truth is, I *can't* come. If it had been in India, and you had come there, my house would have been open to you, and not to you only, but to all your friends to come and make it a home. And I come to England, and you ask me to dine with you *this day three weeks!*' The truth is, they live in India, and cherish such ideas of England, and a home, and love, that when they come to it they are disappointed. — You remember, Colonel Newcome was invited to dine *that day three weeks* with his brother?" [3]

"I think I shall take the girls, and go to India next year. I should like to see my native country. I have friends in almost all the judgeships. Twelve lectures would pay for it." Whitwell expressed his astonishment at this wish, but said, "I take it, you like a roving life." "Yes," said he, "I like it. I should never be at home if I could help." — "But, can you write away from home?" — "I write better anywhere than at home, and I write less at home than anywhere. I did not write ten pages of the Newcomes in that house at Brompton. I wrote two lectures in it. The last half of the Newcomes I wrote at Paris. This" — meaning an hotel — "is the best place to write in. After a good breakfast, I make one of the girls sit down to write. It is slow work. Sometimes not a sentence for a quarter of an hour. I could not do that with a stranger. With the young ones it is different, and they are delighted. A Scotchman came to me a little while ago, and I tried him as secretary, but he was deaf. I would begin, At this moment Anna entered the room, when the Captain observed to the Countess — What? — *The Captain observed to the Countess.* — But, you know, that couldn't go on."

Talking of the wearisomeness of going about lecturing, he said, "There is something very sweet about it, too. I meet everywhere such kindness and hospitality, — taken into families, and making friends among them, — so that there is quite a little heart-pang at parting." "People bring me autograph books to write my name in, — books full of the autographs of singers, fiddlers — I can't conceive what they want the autograph of a fiddler for. So I wrote my name under Signor Twankeydillo. — Now your address. — But that was too much, I would not write my address."

He said he made £70 by the lecture for ————. "I always have a charity lecture every year. It is so pleasant to feel that I always have twenty pounds in my pocket for a poor man."

"A lady, a blue, at New York, said to me at dinner, I was told I

[3] See chapter 6 of *The Newcomes.*

should not like you, and I don't. — And I replied, I don't in the least care whether you like me or no. — She looked so surprised." [4]

Whitwell said it was delightful to walk with him from Norwich to Thorpe, and see his keen enjoyment of the scene and of the beautiful day. He noticed the quick, artistic eye with which he viewed everything, but Thackeray said that it distressed him to find that he did not observe as much as he formerly did.

He told me it had been a delightful day to him, going over the old city. He said it was "a charming old city." He thought Exeter a very fine city, but Norwich was much better. He thought the beauty of the cathedral cloisters wonderful. He went over the castle.[5] The aspect of it "stifled" him. "The men in the zebra clothes" saddened him. He "panted to be out again." His whole expression of face was disturbed as he talked of them, and he kept shuddering.

He wished to go and see Yarmouth, but Whitwell discouraged him, and told him there was nothing to see there. "I want to see the Great Ocean; I want to see where Peggotty lived." [6]

[4] See above, No. 964.

[5] "Then used as the county gaol" (Elwin, Some Eighteenth Century Men of Letters, I, 182).

[6] During the previous year Thackeray had told a group of friends in Philadelphia "that while he loved Colonel Newcome — and was delighted that other people did — he believed a finer gentleman was Dan'l Peggotty! It was really delightful to hear him sustain this position against many dissenting voices, and with such evident admiration for the character that no one who listened could fail to conceive a warmer regard both for Peggotty and Mr. Thackeray himself, so genuine was the praise of the old fisherman's tender and noble heart." (McMichael, Philadelphia Press, June 12, 1887)

APPENDIX XIX

THE OXFORD ELECTION, 1857

In the general election of April, 1857, Thackeray's friend Charles Neate, leader of the Independent party in Oxford, appeared to have fulfilled a long-standing ambition, the disruption of the Whig-Liberal monopoly of the City of Oxford's seats in parliament. His opponents were Dr. James Haughton Langston, M. P. for the City from 1841 till his death in 1863, and the distinguished statesman Edward Cardwell (1813–1874), later (1874) first Viscount Cardwell of Ellerbeach, who represented the City from 1852 to 1857 and, after a few months' intermission, from 1857 to 1874. When the poll was declared, the results were found to be:

Langston	1,667
Neate	1,057
Cardwell	1,016.[1]

But Neate's triumph was short-lived. He was disqualified for bribery, and in July another election was announced for Oxford's second parliamentary seat.

The Liberal nominee was Viscount Monck, a wealthy Irish peer of little political strength. Neate persuaded Thackeray to be the Independent candidate, arguing that against such opposition his chances of victory were very good. Lady Ritchie writes that Thackeray later told her of

> a charming little speech made by Lord Monck, which gave him great pleasure at the time. . . A sort of catchword, 'May the best man win', was the constant refrain just then.
> My father meeting Lord Monck in the street, shook hands with him, had a little talk over the situation, and took leave of him with the doggerel, 'May the best man win'.
> 'I hope *not*,' said Lord Monck very cordially, with a kind little bow.[2]

Despite the efforts of Lord Monck's supporters to discredit Thackeray by airing his views on the Sabbath Question,[3] he made an excellent can-

---

[1] At this time the population of Oxford was 27,843, exclusive of the University, but there were only 2,818 registered electors. See Dod's *Parliamentary Companion* (1857).

[2] *Biographical Introductions*, X, xxxi–xxxii.

[3] See the handbills opposite pp. 382–383.

didate. His popularity was achieved without assistance from his literary reputation. Dickens relates, indeed, that he received a note from Thackeray in Oxford urging him to "come down and make a speech, and tell them who he was, for he doubted whether more than one or two of the electors had ever heard of him, and he thought there might be as many as six or eight who had heard of me!" [4]

It shortly became apparent that Lord Monck could not hope to win. He accordingly withdrew in favor of Cardwell, against whose heavy artillery Thackeray in turn had little chance. So we find Annie writing in her journal on the evening of July 21:

> Papa came home beaten but in capital spirits and we are very happy again now, but the first news that Papa wasn't elected wasn't at all agreeable.
>
> Thackeray   1005
> Cardwell   1070 . . .
>
> He has been telling us of a fat auctioneer who would call him Thackeray; he says if the poll had been put off a single day more he would have been obliged to kick him. He says he will never go canvassing again, it's too disgustingly humiliating. 'Are you Mr. Neat's friend? Master's h'out, but he said I was to say he would vote for yeou.'
> Papa himself is a Cardwellite he says.[5]

The details of Thackeray's electioneering may be traced in the following manifesto and addresses.

I.

Broadside "To the Electors of the City of Oxford",[6] *July 9.*

Gentlemen,

I should be unworthy of the great kindness and cordiality with which you have received me to-night were I to hesitate to put your friendship to the test and ask you to confirm it at the Poll.

To the Electors of the City who were not present I would repeat briefly the political opinions which I hold, and which agree in the main with those of the valued Representative whose services you have just lost. Would that mine could equal them! or that I could bring to them the aid upon which you could count from his talents, his eloquence, and the just confidence which you placed in a friend so well tried and known!

I would use my best endeavours not merely to enlarge the Constituen-

---

[4] "In Memoriam", *Cornhill Magazine*, February, 1864, p. 130.
[5] *Thackeray and his Daughter*, pp. 113–114.
[6] My text is taken from a copy of this broadside in the Bodleian Library.

Mr. THACKERAY'S.

SENTIMENTS ON THE

Sabbath Question

"I would not only open the Crystal Palace, the British Museum, and the National Gallery but I would go further, and open the CONCERT ROOMS and THEATRES on Sundays."

Vide Report of the Speech delivered by Mr. Thackeray to his Friends at the Mitre Hotel, July 9, 1857.

From a broadside

THE
Sabbath Question,

TO THE
ELECTORS
OF THE
CITY OF OXFORD.

THE Paper which was put forth yesterday by **Mr. Boddington**, and in which my opinions regarding the Sunday Question were stated on my authority not appearing sufficient to you, I gladly give you my sentiments under my own signature.

I am desirous that the people who work hard all the week should have the means of relaxation, amusement, and instruction upon their only day of rest.

I would to this end open to them Picture Galleries, Museums, Scientific Collections, and such places as the Crystal Palace near London, where are to be found Gardens and Flowers, Statues and Pictures, and objects the most harmless and beautiful.

I believe the labouring man would enjoy these sights in company with his family, and that the enjoyment of them would keep him from intoxication, not lead him into it, as opponents of my views fear. Those who have seen our great cities know how the Sunday is often passed, and whether drunkenness is prevented by the present Legislation. Should the opening of such a place as the Crystal Palace be found to occasion drinking and disorder, which I disbelieve, surely a stop may be put to the sale of intoxicating liquors in that place on the Sunday.

I never spoke or thought of opening Theatres on Sunday.—I would try to multiply the means of procuring peace and harmless pleasure for the people on that day, and know that in many Theatrical Pieces there are jests, and allusions, and situations ill-fitted indeed to any, but especially to the Sacred Day.

I would consent to and encourage good Band-Music, which has been played before our Sovereigns for a hundred years past; but would object to Songs, for the same reason that renders me averse to Plays,—because Songs may be made vehicles for jokes and buffoonery, which, on such a day, might justly shock the sense of religious persons. And I believe the relaxation of the present system would make many people friendly to the Clergy whom they now suppose to be hostile to their honest pleasures; would be a means of happiness and union amongst the families of the Poor; and ought not to offend the feelings of any Christian man.

Your very faithful Servant,

W. M. THACKERAY,

Mitre, July, **18, 1857.**

VINCENT, PRINTER, OXFORD.

From a broadside

cies, but to popularize the Government of this Country. With no feeling but that of good will towards those leading Aristocratic Families who are administering the chief offices of the State, I believe that it could be benefited by the skill and talents of persons less aristocratic, and that the country thinks so like wise.

I think that to secure the due freedom of Representation, and to defend the poor voter from the chance of intimidation, the Ballot is the best safeguard we know of, and would vote most hopefully for that measure. I would have the Suffrage amended in nature, as well as in numbers; and hope to see many Educated Classes represented who have now no voice in Elections.

The China War Question, which occasioned the dissolution of the late Parliament, is now settling itself; and that Gun being charged must be fired home. Should the Country have to engage in another and more terrible contest, which even now may be pending, I hope that men of all sides will be as one, and will aid to the utmost of their power the Ministry, whatever it may be, which shall best know how to employ the immense zeal and wealth, and talents, and bravery of the Country for a happy termination of the struggle.

But the usefulness of a Member of Parliament is best tested at home: and should you think fit to elect me as your Representative, I promise to use my utmost endeavour to increase and advance the social happiness, the knowledge, and the power of the people.

I am, Gentlemen,

Your faithful Servant,

W. M. Thackeray.

Mitre, July 9, 1857.

II.

Address at the Town Hall,[7] *July 10.*

Mr. Chairman and gentlemen, I have the hardest task before me; I have to try and answer in some degree for the extraordinary praise with which my friend Mr. Neate has been pleased to speak of me. I have to speak after one of the most eloquent and kind addresses, I can assure you, I have ever heard. (Cheers.) To bespeak your praise, being so little known to any of you at this moment, would be idle; even to say that I possess the power of eloquence — which I wish to Heaven that I had — would be vain, for I shall break down very likely in a sentence or two, and you will have to moralise on the strange fact that a gentleman who can spin off sentence after sentence in his study, is hard put to it to find

---

[7] My text is taken from *The Oxford University Herald*, July 11, p. 10.

words when he is on his legs. (Laughter and cheers.) But very seldom in my life does such an event as this happen to me. On the first occasion on which it happened I think it was in a room about twice as large. There were present some of the most clever orators that have ever spoke, and I had the honour after about two sentences of breaking smash down, stopping in the middle of a sentence and owning I could not continue, and sitting down in the chair which Mr. Spiers is occupying now, and which I shall, perhaps, be obliged to ask him to give up to me. However, the sun rose, the funds did not fall down, and people went about their business just about as usual. (Laughter.) Now, I got up to try again, and do my best. You want business rather than words, so I take it, unless you can get business clothed in such noble words as those of my friend Mr. Neate. I agree with him in the main — in most of the opinions which he uttered in addressing you — and in very many of those which he has expressed in to-night's address. I go with all my heart and soul for the adoption of the ballot (hear and cheers) — and I desire with the utmost of my power the extension of the suffrage. (Cheers.) I do not say for one moment I mean universal suffrage because those of you who have read the papers have seen how universal suffrage obtains in the neighbouring country of France, the Emperor riding cockhorse over the whole country — (laughter) — the press throttled truly and entirely, and one tyrant ruling over the people. With respect to triennial parliaments, if the people are for it I am ready to follow the popular behest. I do not see for my own part how any great good can arise from them. It does not seem to me that if a perpetually recurring system of election was practised it would be conductive of much good. Some time ago I had to say a few words about political matters at a dinner in Edinburgh,[8] to which I was invited, and I got a good deal of illwill in certain very genteel quarters in London when I returned because I said at that dinner that those gentlemen with handles to their names, that the members of great aristocratic families had a very great share of public patronage and government, and that for my part, I heartily desired that men of the people — the working men and educated men of the people — should have a share in the government. I instanced the case of the American Minister who was then wanting — the government had appointed a lord; a minister of China was then wanting, and the selection lay between a Duke and an Earl. Great outcries were made against me when I went back, and people said why do you sneer against Duke A., Lord B., and Earl C.? Why do you speak against men whom you know to be perfectly honourable and able. I did not sneer in the least against Lord Elgin who was appointed ambassador to China, or Lord Napier the

[8] See above, No. 1479.

recently appointed American minister, because at that time few men more honourable, eloquent, able, or experienced could be found. What I complained of was that we are obliged to go to the aristocracy when we were in need of officers. (Hear, hear, and cheers.) There is never any chance for a man of the people to step forward — there seems a sort of absolute necessity that when Lord Palmerston goes out of office Lord John must come in, and when Lord John jumps out of the boat Lord Palmerston must come in and pull stroke oar again. (Laughter and cheers.) Are there not prudent intelligent men whose services the country might profit by but who have no chance to gratify the legitimate object of their ambition, so that an eternal change of the great aristocratic families seems intended to go on for ever? Will it be your will and pleasure that this state of things should continue? (Loud cries of No, no.) If so introduce into the House of Commons men of popular intelligence — the best men that you can bring into it. The popular influence must be brought to bear on the present government of the country, if they flinch remind them that the people is outside and wants more and more. Hold them to the promise given, as a special reform promise next year; if they do not give a sufficient measure, let us screw them and screw them till we get a larger measure. I little doubt as I look to the progress, the general daily progress the people are making, the reforms we desire will more and more satisfactorily be carried into execution. Every day the popular cause will advance, will receive interest and advantage. Mr. Thackeray then proceeded to remark that if on a future occasion he should have the honour of appearing before them, he would explain at large on all public questions which might interest individual electors. He could not hope to please all of course, but he hoped they would understand that as a working man who for 25 years has been labouring not unsuccessfully in his vocation, who has reached that point which must be the ambition of every Englishman who is able to say he is independent — independent of ministers or anybody — (hear hear, and cheers) — he came before them relying at least on his honesty, believing that possibly they might know what his literary career has been, and trusting to their favour the character which he may have obtained from them, and the benefit of a further acquaintance, for obtaining a still further hearing from them. In conclusion he returned his warmest thanks to Mr. Neate for having introduced him to them, and to those present for the patient hearing they had given him. (Much cheering.)

III.

Address at the Hustings,[9] *July 20.*

As I came down to this place, I saw on each side of me placards announcing that there was no manner of doubt that on Tuesday the friends of the Right Hon. Edward Cardwell would elect him to a seat in Parliament. I also saw other placards announcing in similar terms a confidence that there was no doubt that I should be elected to a seat in Parliament for the City of Oxford. Now as both sides are perfectly confident of success — as I for my part, feel perfectly confident, and as my opponents entertain the same favourable opinion in regard to themselves — surely both sides may meet here in perfect good-humour. I hear that not long since — in the memory of many now alive — this independent city was patronized by a great university, and that a great duke, who lived not very far from here, at the time of election used to put on his boots and ride down and order the freemen of Oxford to elect a member for him. Any man who has wandered through your beautiful city as I have done within these last few days cannot but be struck with the difference between the ancient splendour, the academic grandeur that prevailed in this place — the processions of dons, doctors, and proctors — and your new city, which is not picturesque or beautiful at all, but which contains a number of streets, peopled by thousands of hard-working, honest, rough-handed men. These men have grown up of late years, and have asserted their determination to have a representative of their own. Such a representative they found three months ago, and such a representative they returned to Parliament in the person of my friend, Mr. Neate. But such a representative was turned out of that Parliament by a sentence which I cannot call unjust, because he himself is too magnanimous and generous to say so, but which I will call iniquitous. He was found guilty of a twopennyworth of bribery which he had never committed; and a Parliament which has swallowed so many camels, strained at that little gnat, and my friend, your representative, the very best man you could find to represent you was turned back, and you were left without a man. I cannot hope — I never thought to equal him; I only came forward at a moment when I felt it necessary that some one professing his principles, and possessing your confidence, should be ready to step into the gap which he had made. I know that the place was very eagerly sought for by other folks on the other side, entertaining other opinions. Perhaps you don't know that last week there was a Tory baronet down here, walking about in the shade, as umbrageous almost as that under which my opponent, Mr. Cardwell, has sheltered himself.

[9] My text is taken from Hotten's *Thackeray*, pp. 148–152.

Of course you know there came down a ministerial nominee — Lord Monck; but you do not know that Mr. Hayter, who is what is called the Whipper-in for the Ministerial party, came down here also on Saturday week in a dark and mysterious manner, and that some conversation took place, the nature of which I cannot pretend to know anything about, because I have no spies, however people may be lurking at the doors of our committee-room. But the result of all was, that Lord Monck disappeared, and Mr. Hayter vanished into darkness and became a myth; and we were informed that a powerful requisition from the City of Oxford had invited Mr. Cardwell. Mind, Mr. Cardwell has given no note in reply — no mark, no sign. We do not know, even now, whether he accepted that polite invitation; we do not know it even to this day, except that his godfathers have been here and said so. After the manner in which the electors of Oxford have received me, could I possibly have gone back simply because we are told that Mr. Cardwell had received an invitation, which we did not know whether he had or accepted or not? I feel it, therefore, to be my humble duty to stand in the place where I found myself. I do not know that I would have ventured to oppose Mr. Cardwell under other circumstances. I am fully aware of his talents. I know his ability as a statesman, and no man can say that I have, during the whole of my canvass, uttered a word at all unfriendly or disrespectful towards that gentleman. I should have hesitated on any other occasion in opposing him, but I cannot hesitate now, because I know that we have the better cause, and that we mean to make that better cause triumphant. . . . Any man who belongs to the Peelite party is not the man who ought to be put forward by any constituency at the eve of a great and momentous English war. As to my own opinions on public questions, you may have heard them pretty freely expressed on many occasions. I only hope if you elect me to Parliament, I shall be able to obviate the little difficulty that has been placarded against me — that I could not speak. I own I cannot speak very well, but I shall learn. I cannot spin out glib sentences by the yard, as some people can; but if I have got anything in my mind, if I feel strongly on any question, I have I believe got brains enough to express it. When you send a man to the House of Commons, you do not want him to be always talking; he goes there to conduct the business of the country; he has to prepare himself on the question on which he proposes to speak before six hundred and fifty-six members, who would be bored if every man were to deliver his opinion. He must feel and understand what he is going to say, and I have not the least doubt that I shall be able to say what I feel and think, if you will give me the chance of saying it. If any one in the House of Commons talked all he thought upon everything, good God! what a Babel it would be!

You would not get on at all. On the first night I came among you, many questions were put to me by a friend, who capped them all by saying, 'Now, Mr. Thackeray, are you for the honour of England?' I said that that was rather a wild and a wide question to put, but to the best of my belief I was for the honour of England, and would work for it to the best of my power. About the ballot we are all agreed. If I was for the ballot before I came down here, I am more for the ballot now. As to triennial Parliaments, if the constituents desire them, I am for them.

IV.

Address after the Declaration of the Poll,[10] July 21.

Give me leave to speak a few words to you on this occasion, for although the red, white and blue are my friends, I hope to make the green and yellow my friends also. Let me tell you a little story, but a true one. Some years ago, when boxing was more common in this country than it is at the present time, two celebrated champions met to fight a battle on Moulsey Heath. Their names were Gully and Gregson. They fought the most tremendous battle that had been known for many long years, and Gregson got the worst of it. As he was lying on his bed some time afterwards, blinded and his eyes closed up, he asked a friend to give him something to drink. A person in the room handed him some drink and grasped him by the hand. 'Whose hand is this?' asked Gregson. ' 'Tis Jack Gully's,' was the reply. Now Gregson was the man who was beaten and Gully was the conqueror, and he was the first man to shake him by the hand, to show him that he had no animosity against him. This should be the conduct of all loyal Englishmen, to fight a good fight, and to hold no animosity against the opposite side. With this feeling I go away from Oxford. With this feeling I shall have redeemed one of the promises I made you yesterday; the other I cannot by any possibility answer, because, somehow or other, our side has come out a little below the other side. I wish to shake Mr. Cardwell by the hand, and to congratulate him on being the representative of this great city. I say it is a victory you ought to be proud of; it is a battle which you ought to be proud of who have taken part in it; you have done your duty nobly and fought most gallantly. I am a man who was unknown to most of you, who only came before you with the recommendation of my noble and excellent friend Mr. Neate, but I have met with many friends. You have fought the battle gallantly against great influences, against an immense strength which have been brought against you, and in favour of that honoured and respected man, Mr. Cardwell. (Hisses.) Stop, don't hiss. When Lord Monck came down here and addressed the

[10] My text is taken from Hotten's *Thackeray*, pp. 153–156.

electors, he was good enough to say a kind word in favour of me. Now, that being the case, don't let me be outdone in courtesy and generosity, but allow me to say a few words of the respect and cordiality which I entertain for Mr. Cardwell. As for the party battle which divides you, I am, gentlemen, a stranger, for I never heard the name of certain tradesmen of this city till I came among you. Perhaps I thought my name was better known than it is. You, the electors of Oxford, know whether I have acted honestly towards you; and you on the other side will say whether I ever solicited a vote when I knew that vote was promised to my opponent; or whether I have not always said — 'Sir, keep your word; here is my hand on it, let us part good friends.' With my opponents I part so. With others, my friends, I part with feelings still more friendly, not only for the fidelity you have shown towards me, but for your noble attachment to the gallant and tried whom you did know, and who I hope will be your representative at some future time. (Cry of bribery.) Don't cry out bribery; if you know of it, prove it; but as I am innocent of bribery myself, I do not choose to fancy that other men are not equally loyal and honest. It matters very little whether I am in the House of Commons or not, to prate a little more; but you have shown a great spirit, a great resolution, and great independence; and I trust at some future day, when you know me better than you do now, you will be able to carry your cause to a more successful issue. Before I came to Oxford, I knew that there was a certain question that would go against me, and which I would not blink to be made a duke or a marquis tomorrow. In March last, when I was at a dinner at Edinburgh, some friend[s] of mine asked me to stand for the representation of their city. My answer was this — 'That I was for having the people amused after they had done their worship on a Sunday.' I knew that I was speaking to a people who, of all others, were the most open to scruples on that point, but I did my duty as an honest man, and stated what my opinion was. I have done my duty honestly to this city, and I believe that this is the reason why I am placed in a minority; but I am contented to bow to that decision. I told you that I was for allowing a man to have harmless pleasures when he had done his worship on Sundays. I expected to have a hiss, but they have taken a more dangerous shape — the shape of slander. Those gentlemen who will take the trouble to read my books — and I should be glad to have as many of you for subscribers as will come forward — will be able to say whether there is anything in them that should not be read by any one's children, or by my own, or by any Christian man. I say, on this ground I will retire, and take my place with my pen and ink at my desk, and leave to Mr. Cardwell a business which I am sure he understands better than I do.

APPENDIX XX

DIARY 3 JANUARY–23 SEPTEMBER 1858

Hitherto unpublished. Original owned by Mrs. Fuller.

January   3   Spasms — beginning at 3. a. m
           4   not relieved until 4 p. m.
           5   Hamley
           9   C. Baron [1]
          14   Forster [2]
          15   Roberts 7.
          21   Home.
          26   Lecture.
          27   Ld Cork.[3] 7.30
          29   Merivale. 7.
          30   Bidwell

[1] Sir Frederick Pollock.

[2] Thackeray also dined with Forster on January 6, when their common friend Whitwell Elwin was a guest. "He did not know [Thackeray] was to be there, and on seeing him in the room, he exclaimed, and ran up to greet him before he had spoken to Mrs. Forster. Forster remonstrated, and said it was not like him to do it. 'Oh! yes, it is,' said Thackeray, and then turning to him added, 'Never mind, *I* forgive you.' At dinner Elwin told Thackeray that his best poem was that on his pen. 'I cannot give you the pen with which I wrote it,' Thackeray replied, 'for I let it fall at Naples, and broke it, but I will give you the pencil-case.' Thereupon he took a silver pencil-case, with a gold pen, from his pocket, and put it into Elwin's hands. It was the pencil-case which the novelist had used for years, and it was the pen with which he had written many of his works. Elwin was so rapturous over the gift that Forster declared indignantly he would never invite him and Thackeray together again. The pen was treasured at Booton for the rest of Elwin's life as his most valued possession.

"After the dinner at Forster's Thackeray and Elwin left together. On their way home Thackeray talked of the Virginians, which was then in its early stages. He said he meant to bring in Goldsmith, — 'representing him as he really was, a little, shabby, mean, shuffling Irishman,' — Garrick — whose laugh he was positive he should be able to identify from the look in his portrait — Dr. Johnson, and the other celebrities of the reign of Queen Anne. He thought that he should find this easy, but he afterwards told Elwin that he had discovered he could not do it. The failure of his design threw him out, and the second half of the novel dragged for lack of materials." (Elwin, *Some Eighteenth Century Men of Letters*, I, 168–187)

[3] Richard Edmund St. Lawrence Boyle (1829–1904), ninth Earl of Cork and Orrery.

February	1	L. Clanricarde.
	2	Lecture
	4	Sir W de Bathe.
	5	Spasms coming on very gradually after breakfast took 12 grains Calomel. Acme about 2 p. m pretty severe for 24 hours when relief came gradually
	8	Lady Molesworth.
	9	Dean Trench.
	11	Sir B. Hawes 7.[4] 3/4.
	16	Dean S.t Pauls.[5]
	18	Priaulx
	20	Spasms beginning at 6. p.m.
	23	Fladgate. M.rs Ford. T. M.rs Elliot
	24	Waddington.
March	2	Eyre Arms Week Day Preachers.
	9	Macready at Sherborne
	11	x Lady Astley.[6] M.rs Mansfield.
	13	x 6. 3/4 Bacon.
	19	Lady Molesworth
	20	Lord Stanley of Alderley.
	22	M.r Harcourt.
	29	Theatrical Fund.
April	9	Merivale 7.
	10	11 Deans yard 7.30.
	11	Baron L. Rothschild
	13	G. Smith 7.
	14	Sturgis.
	18	Do.
	20	Eyre Arms. George III.
	21	Lady Waldegrave. Mem. Sir R Murchinson [7] 16 Belgrave Sq.e Lady Derby.[8]
	22	L.d Stanley.
	23	Garrick Spasms coming on at night.

[4] Sir Benjamin Hawes, see above, No. 1640.
[5] Dean Milman.
[6] The former Emma Lethbridge (d. 1872), who had married Sir Francis Dugdale Astley (1805–1873), second Baronet, in 1826.
[7] Sir Roderick Impey Murchison (1792–1871), later (1866) first Baronet, a distinguished geologist.
[8] The former Emma Caroline Bootle-Wilbraham (1805–1876) had in 1825 married the fourteenth Earl of Derby, who was thrice conservative Prime Minister.

	24	{Bishop of London}.[9] not relieved till late in afternoon.
	25	Heath.
	26	Home.
	27	Th. Martin.
	29	Bates.[10]
	30	E. Ellice.
May	1	R Academy.
	4	Higgins 7.45 More spasms beginning about 9 and
	5	{L. Fund.} lasting till 11 night.
	6	{Rothschild} People at home. Mrs Phelps & Mrs Owen Americans. General. Lady Eliz. Selina Thackeray Meriwether very good fun. Friday that is
	8	Went with girls to Windsor. Stough. Reading. Henley. pleasant trip but cost 4£
	9	Home. F. Elliot. Synge. Dickens. Maclise. Landseer Ld Broughton. Ld Stanley. Tourgueneff [11]
	12	declined Miss Thackeray.
	13	Priaulx. 7
	14	declined Dillon. M. Thackeray. O. Clayton.
	17	Mackintosh [12] 7.30 2 Hyde Pk Terrace K. Gate
	18	Ld Londonderry.
	22	K. Macaulay
	26	declined Sir W. Clay.[13]
June	3	2 Knights 2 Forsters 2 Ardens.[14] 2 Denmans 2 Blackwoods. Motley. Phinn. Maurice.
	7	4 Fishes.[15] 3 Selves, 2 Moffatts.[16] 2 Sartoris. 2 Halle

[9] Archibald Campbell Tait (1811–1882), who was Bishop of London from 1856 until 1868, when he became Archbishop of Canterbury.

[10] Joshua Bates (1788–1864), an American merchant who became a partner in Baring Brothers in 1826.

[11] Ivan Turgenev (1818–1883), the Russian novelist, who, Thackeray told Henry Sutherland Edwards (*Personal Recollections*, p. 37), "had called upon him without any introduction, simply in the character of a foreign admirer of his works, and without saying a word about his own literary position."

[12] Robert James Mackintosh, who was still living at 2 Hyde Park Terrace in 1862 (*Post Office London Directory*).

[13] Sir William Clay (1791–1869), first Baronet, M. P. for Tower Hamlets from 1832 to 1857.

[14] Joseph Arden (1799–1879), who had become Principal of Cliffords Inn in 1855.

[15] For Fish's impressions of this dinner, see Allan Nevins, *Hamilton Fish* (New York, 1936), p. 70.

[16] George Moffat (1810–1878), a wealthy wholesale tea-dealer who was in parliament without interruption from 1845 to 1868. He had married Lucy Morrison in 1856.

2 Wilson. Meriwether. Ainsworth, Elliot, Trench, Swinton.

9   Gordon.[17] Greenwich 6.

11 Lady Harding.[18] Cockburn. Halle. M.r & Miss Belli

14 Venables. Brunswick Blackwall 6. 3/4

15 Waddington 7.30.

16 Stationers Compy 6 1/2

20 Trafalgar. 2 Procters. M.rs Baird, Sir W de Bathe. 2 Taylors. Cayley. Mansfield.

24 Spasms at 6 in the morning relieved at night Moffatt 7.30.

25 but leaving me in cold sweat almost shiver

26 and very languid next day.

July   12. From home to Pavilion Hotel Folkestone

         13. Dover. Calais. Ghent. Hotel Royal.

         14   Cologne. Rolandseck.

         15   Up Rhine to Biberich. Melancholy Nassau's garden.

         16   To Heidelberg Hotel Schrieder

         17. Wolfsbrunn in the evening

         18   ditto. Wrote beginning of XI.[19]

         22   T.h Wrote XI. drive at evening

         23   F. to Berne. Faucon. Sent 2 Chap XI to England Tuesday from Berne to Lucerne, having felt for 2 or 3 days great drowsiness languor low spirits violent cold & oppression of chest Worked in spite. Wednesday Thursday ill. slight spasms beginning on Tuesday night took 10 grains did not operate till Thursday after I had called in Doctor. Salivated by 10 grs. more. Faneon at Berne very comfortable but bill 2£ per day.

August   3   From Lucerne to Olten. Bill at Lucerne rather more than 2£ per day. Bill at dirty Olten 38 francs with 1 dinner.

         4   To Zurich Hotel Banc au Lac. much better in health. excellent hotel. No 31 room.

         5   Finished No XI, and sent off to London.

---

[17] No doubt Sir Alexander Duff-Gordon.

[18] The former Lady Emily Jane Stewart (1789–1865), wife of Viscount Hardinge of Lahore.

[19] Chapters 41 to 44 of *The Virginians,* published for September.

8   From Schaffhausen over the lake of Constance to Fredrichshafen. 6.30–1. To Augsburg 2.40.8 3 Mohren.

9   To Munich 4 Saisons.

10   Saw Picture Galleries. Bavaria — Drove round the town at night. Cobham. Prall Essex S! [20]

11   Palace — delightful old rooms — brilliant Ancestor-Hall dreary Nibelungen.

12   Awake at 12 in order to be able to get up at 4 — to Stuttgart. pretty little kindly town. drive to Schloss-garten Cannstat.

13   To Frankfurt. Hotel d'Angleterre

14.   To Cologne. Disch.

15   Cathedral in the morning — to sleep at Ghent. Hotel Royal.

16   To Bruges in the middle of the day, & then to Ostende whence a capital passage to Dover & the Ship.

17   Home. Laus Deo. Dine with Fladgate at the Reform Club.[21]

20   Spasms on Friday about 6. p.m.

21.   lasting till 2 p.m. when relieved, but I think without medicine; for that w^h Douglas gave me would not stay 10 minutes in the stomach.

September 9   Slight spasms at 7 o'clock

10   Sickness all day, but relieved

13   From Folkestone to Paris H. du Louvre

16   Hotel Bristol. Wrote XII [22] in these days.

22   Spasms in the morning lasting 4 or 5 hours not severe. sickness all day & part of next day.

23   no medicine.

[20] Richard Prall lived at 19 Essex Street, Strand, in 1862 (*Post Office London Directory*).

[21] On August 21 Dickens wrote to Yates: "I re-open this to tell you that I encountered Thackeray and Fladgate on the steps of the Reform Club. We spoke as if nothing had happened, — except that Fladgate's eyebrows went up into the crown of his hat, and he twisted himself into extraordinary forms." (*Letters*, ed. Dexter, III, 41)

[22] Chapters 45 to 48 of *The Virginians* for October.

APPENDIX XXI

DIARY FOR 1861

Hitherto unpublished. Original owned by Mrs. Fuller.

W. M. Thackeray. 36 Onslow Sq^re S.W.

January 1 12.5 Mr Thackeray out
2 12.30.
17 Sickness &c beginning at 6 as usual, relieved at 4, but renewed on Friday in consequence of repetition of medicine.
26 New firm of Robarts & Lubbock [1] very civil gave me discount & lunch called at Mansion House.[2] Champagne tasting dinner at the G. No work done.
29 Mr Hollond
31 Ld Mayor 6.30 precisely.

February 1 2 FitzRoys 2 Troubridges [3] 1 Oliffes. Bigge. Ld Tenterden. Major Ramsay. 2 Hattons.
2 Ld J. Russell.
7 Sickness beginning at 6. a.m. not relieved till Friday.
11 Mrs Bayne
14 Unwell all Wednesday with sensation of sickness occasioned by repetition of pills on Tuesday night — dined at Willis's sate till 2 — obliged to go to bed on Thursday afternoon sent for Elliotson who arrived on Friday at 1 1/2 relieved on Friday.
22 Mr Robarts.[4]
26 C. Justice.[5]
27 Ld Stanley of Alderley. 7 3/4.

[1] Robarts, Lubbock, and Company, bankers, of 11 Mansion House Street, had replaced the firm of Lubbock, Forster, and Company, with which Thackeray was accustomed to do business (*Post Office London Directory*, 1862).
[2] To see his friend William Cubitt, Lord Mayor of London.
[3] Colonel Sir Thomas St. Vincent Hope Cochrane Troubridge (1815–1867), third Baronet, who had fought in the West Indies, Canada, and the Crimea, losing his right leg and left foot at Inkerman. He married Louisa Jane Gurney (d. 1867) in 1855.
[4] Abraham John Robarts, the head of Robarts, Lubbock, and Company.
[5] Sir Alexander James Edmund Cockburn (1802–1880), tenth Baronet, Lord Chief Justice of England.

	28	L de Chatret du Rieux of Levourne draws for 268 fr. 7s. Commissioner Rangel Woollett & Co.[6]
March	1	2 Higgins 2 Marochetti 3 Edens. Ebers. Venables Lady Eastlake. Van de Weyer.[7] Sir W. Fraser.[8] 3 Selves.
	2	Ld Airlie.
	5	Mr Robarts declined Spasms beginning after dinner on Tuesday
	7	and with partial relief on Wednesday, continued till Thursday ev^g
	8	Ellison. Ship & Turtle
		Lady Stanhope
		Lady Lyell [9]
	12	Loch 7.30
	14	Master of the Rolls.[10]
	18	Lady Olliffe.
	20	Chatret de Rieux of Levourne will draw for 90 francs. Lord Mayor.
	21	Milnes. 7.30
	25	Bacon, Arden Taylor 2 Fladgates, Bence Jones.[11] Shawe. G. Russell. St John Thackeray.
	27	Delane
	28	W. Fladgate.
	30	Bence Jones. 7
April	3	Mrs Ford
	4	Cold fit (without actual shivers not fit &c) and sleep almost all day
	5	On titles. (Magazines, novels &c) Streatham. (Mrs Thrale, Thrale. Johnson) on bread & butter. Joseph Gillott's patent 225.[12]
	6	Stirling 7.30

[6] Indian agents and shipbrokers of 1 Lime Street (*Post Office London Directory*, 1862).

[7] Sylvain Van de Weyer (1802–1874), Belgian Envoy from 1831 to 1867.

[8] See above, No. 754, note 44.

[9] The former Mary Elizabeth Horner, wife of Sir Charles Lyell (1797–1875), later (1864) first Baronet, who was famous for his *Principles of Geology* (1830–1833).

[10] Thackeray's friend Sir John Romilly was Master of the Rolls from 1851 to 1873.

[11] Dr. Henry Bence Jones (1813–1873), F. R. S., physician to St. George's Hospital from 1846 to 1862.

[12] A kind of pen; Gillot was steel pen manufacturer to the Queen (*Post Office London Directory*, 1862).

   10 L. F.[13] D[r] Jones.

   26 2 Stanleys, 2 Prinseps, 2 Caufields, 2 Curzons,[14]
      Landseer. Osborne, Low, Buckle. 3 Selves, 2 Leslies.

May 4 Royal Academy

   5 Synge, 3 Folletts, 2 Collins, Comyn, 4 Selves, Craigie,[15]
      Miss Russell, Trollope,

   6 R. A. Club Greenwich

   7 D[r] Wynter proposes on Forbes Winslow [16] & submarine
      cables.

   10 M[r] Dickson [17] 28 Upper Brook S[t] 7 3/4

   11 Stirling

   13 Taylor Albion.

   15 L. F.

   16 Holland.

   22 Waddington 7. 3/4.

   29 40 Grosvenor St.[18]

   30 1815 European Magazine. 471. 'At Brighton in the
      89th year of her age that celebrated character Martha
      Gunn.'

   31 Promise to make a payment to J & G.[19]

June 1 103 Eaton Sq [20]

   6 Declined Marybone Institution dinner Sickness &
      spasms partially relieved on Friday.[21]

[13] The annual dinner of the Royal Literary Fund.

[14] Thackeray's friend Robert Curzon had married Emily Julia Horton (d. 1866) in 1850.

[15] John Livingstone Craigie, F. R. C. S. (*Post Office London Directory*, 1862).

[16] Wynter evidently wished to write an article for *The Cornhill Magazine* on Dr. Forbes Benignus Winslow (1810–1874), editor of *The Quarterly Journal of Psychological Medicine* and a distinguished specialist in insanity.

[17] Peter Dickson, F. R. G. S., lived at 28 Upper Brook Street (*Post Office London Directory*, 1862).

[18] Miss Wyatt Edgell lived at 40 Grosvenor Street in 1862 (*Post Office London Directory*).

[19] Jackson and Graham, contractors for Thackeray's house at 2, Palace Green, Kensington.

[20] Where lived George Mullatt.

[21] "Yesterday I spent a pleasant afternoon with Thackeray," John Blackwood wrote to his wife on June 4, 1861. "He carried me off bodily to see the new house he is building in Kensington Gardens. It is very nice indeed, and I have named it the Palazzo Thackeray. It is very pleasant to see old Thack., as delighted as a child, showing me all over it. He wishes me to rollick down to Greenwich with him, he having declined four other invitations on the plea of illness. I was going to dine at Warren's, but he made an appointment to dine with me at the Rag. or Greenwich, and doubtless the fun will be great." And on the following day Blackwood wrote that Thackeray's dinner was given at the Blue Posts, where

	7	Belli 7.30.
	10	J Coningham at Ascot.
	12	Bacon.
	18	Sickness & spasms relieved at night without medicine Took some at night.

July   4   4 p.m. Donne.[22] 40 Weymouth S^t

18   Sickness began on Wed^y ev^g relieved with podoph. on Thursday ev^g

August   15   After taking compound colocynth followed attack of cold, hot fit, & perspiration.

27   Sonty. R du Louvre 8 frames and glasses. Mrs Russell. Arran Lodge. St John's Wood. Grove End Road.

29   Sickness and spasms accompanied with diarrhœa this time beginning in the morning, and lasting until Saturday. Took no medicine at all but the languor remained over Sunday. Inserted by mistake. the attack was on Thursday Sepr 5.

September 9   † On this day, as I was returning from Paris, my dear old G P died at Ayr in Scotland after only a few hour's illness.

18   More sickness &c. commenced on Tuesday ev^g relieved on Wednesday Thursday by Citrate of Magnesia only.

October   1   T. Hood 43 Grove Place Brompton.
J. Payn [23] 11 Gloster Crescent Hyde Park.
F. Michel 38 Bloomsbury S^t

10   Brunel 27 Margaret St.

15   Call of 100 on Universal Marine.

24   Pay Mrs Bakewell.

26   Mr Corkran

November 16   Sickness beginning 9 a.m. took no medicine till Sunday beginning with a calming p. and then colocynth

---

he seemed "a sort of king, and we got a dinner and wines such as I never saw in the house before. The fun was undeniable, and in the passages between Hamley and Thack. there was much greater cordiality than formerly." (Mrs. Porter, *John Blackwood*, p. 64)

[22] Fitzgerald's friend William Bodham Donne was living at 40 Weymouth Street (*Post Office London Directory*, 1862).

[23] James Payn (1830–1898), a novelist and miscellaneous writer who edited *The Cornhill Magazine* from 1883 to 1896.

APPENDIX XXII

DIARY FOR 1862

Hitherto unpublished. Original owned by Mrs. Fuller.

January	10	Leech
	24	Haringtons. Sterling. Phinn.[1] 2 Sandwiths Taylor 2 Caulfeild
February	11	Sickness & spasms lasting 2 days.
	12	Sir C Russell.[2] 7
	13	Sir J Harington.
	17	A quiet morning's work. Chimney sweep. Ball party. Angry contributor. Unhappy do. Coachman & Van
	24	Play 8.
	25	Play
March	4	36 O. Sqᵉ A

36 O. Sqᵉ   A

My dear S. I have been thinking over our conversation of yesterday and it has not improved the gaiety of the work on wʰ I am presently busy. Today I have taken my friend Sir Charles Taylor into my confidence, & his opinion coincides with mine that I should withdraw from the Magazine. To go into bygones now is needless. Before ever the Magazine appeared, I was, as I have told you on the point of writing such a letter as this. And whether connected with the C H M or not I hope I shall always be Sincerely your friend W. M. T.[3]

6   To Smith. My dear S. I daresay your night, like mine, has been a little disturbed, but *Philip* presses, & until this matter is over, I can't make that story so amusing as I could wish.

I had this pocket pistol (A) in my breast yesterday but hesitated to pull the trigger at an old friend. My daughters are for a compromise. They say 'it is all very fine Sir C. Taylor telling you to do so & so Mʳ

---

[1] Thomas Phinn (1814–1866), a barrister and politician who in 1854 had become a Q. C. and bencher of the Inner Temple.

[2] Sir Charles Russell (1826–1883), later M. P. for Berkshire and Westminster and a Lt.-Col. in the Grenadier Guards.

[3] The drafts of this and the following letter that Thackeray sent are printed above, Nos. 1532 and 1533.

Smith has proved himself your friend always' Bien. It is because I wish him to remain so that I & the Magazine had better part company Goodbye & God bless you & all yours.   W M T.

	11	Wrote 2 pages in the New House for the first time.
	25	Coningham. 7.30
	31	Came to Kensington.
April	11	Miss Cottin.
	18	The May number [4] not finished till today, after repeated stomach derangements, sickness, ague, fever &c.
	26	Ill at Paris on these days. Chipmell finds M. B.[5]
	28	L. Mayor [6] 6.3/4.
May	3	R. Academy
	7	Sir J. O.[7]
	8	F. Grant.[8] 87 3/4 27 Sussex Place Regents P^k
	9	Mr Dickinson
	11	Trollope at Star & Garter
	13	At Bankers 4640. Paid Graham 1000£ Synge 600£
	15	L. F.[9] Gordon Halyburton. Mrs Pollock. Synge agrees to make 9 half yearly payments of 100£ each beginning from October 1 and a 10th payment of 112.10 to close the transaction.[10]

	16	W. Russell	2 Simeons.	Bigge.
		G W Cooke.[11]	Wolowski	2 Bullers [12]
		Count Waldstein.	Landseer.	4 Selves.

[4] Chapters 35 and 36 of *Philip*.   [6] William Cubitt was still Lord Mayor.
[5] Perhaps Mrs. Beckwith.   [7] Sir Joseph Olliffe.
[8] Francis Grant (1803–1878), R. A., later (1866) knighted, lived at 27 Sussex Place, Regent's Park (*Post Office London Directory*, 1862). He was a painter of portraits and sporting scenes.
[9] The annual dinner of the Royal Literary Fund.
[10] See above, No. 1540.
[11] George Wingrove Cooke (1814–1865), barrister, legal writer, and *Times* correspondent. William Holman Hunt (*Pre-Raphaelitism and the Pre-Raphaelite Brotherhood*, II, 240) writes that Cooke, who was a very rapid writer, asked Thackeray in 1862 to join him in a party celebrating his return from abroad, but Thackeray refused on the ground that he had his month's work to finish. Returning from his party, Cooke passed by Thackeray's house where he found the lights still on in the novelist's study. "There was the writing-pad with some sheets of notepaper on the table, and the upper sheet had about twelve lines of his neatest small writing, with a blank space at the bottom. I held it up before Thackeray. 'Tell me,' I said, 'is this all that you have written this blessed evening?' "'Alas!' he replied quite sadly, 'that is all.' "
[12] Arthur Buller and his wife, who were living at 20 Queen's Gate Terrace at this time (*Post Office London Directory*, 1862).

17 Col. Challoner.[13]

18 Ld Lansdowne.

21 Mr Heywoods [14]

22 James 7.30

23 Mrs Senior [15]

26 Lady Stanhope. London House.

28 Mrs M. G. Lady Clay

29 Garraways [16] will send Port on Thursday m^g P G K
May 30. Sir I propose thoroughly to paint and repair my house 36 O. S. B: and will be glad to have an estimate from you of the expense. But it must be understood that I do not pay anything for the survey and do not bind myself to accept your contract If you show this to the people in charge of the house they will let you see it.

30 Mr Smetham. 33 Palace St Pimlico. refers to Jordan [17] Ebury S^t and Miss Blackman 4 Pembroke Cottages
Mrs Senior
Lady Eastlake.

31 B. R.
Chiswick House 3.7

June   1 Tenison 54 Grosvenor S^t 8.

      2 Mr Macaulay.

[13] Colonel Thomas Bisse Challenor, 11 Charles Street, Berkeley Square (*Post Office London Directory*, 1862).

[14] James Heywood (1810–1897), a wealthy scholar living at 26 Kensington Palace Gardens (*Post Office London Directory*, 1862).

[15] The wife of Nassau William Senior.

[16] Garraway's Coffee House, 3 Change Alley. Thackeray was extensively acquainted with the contents of the cellars of obscure London inns. "I once brought a smile to his face," relates John Cordy Jeaffreson (*A Book of Recollections*, I, 288), "by telling him, that a Lincoln's Inn barrister, struck by seeing him on several occasions walking eastward in Holborn, when the barristers of the Inns were walking westward after work, from pure curiosity turned about on a certain afternoon, and tracking him to the Gray's Inn coffee-house, saw him dine there in the coffee-room without a companion.

" 'Ah!' said Thackeray, with enjoyment of the story, and of the good wine which it recalled to his memory, 'that was when I was drinking the last of that wonderful bin of port. It *was* rare wine. There were only two dozen bottles and a few bottles over, when I came upon the remains of that bin, and I forthwith bargained with mine host to keep them for me. I drank every bottle and every drop of that remainder by myself. I shared never a bottle with living man; and so long as the wine lasted, I slipped off to the Gray's Inn coffee-house with all possible secrecy short of disguise, whenever I thought a dinner and a bottle by myself would do me good.' "

[17] Henry Jordan, tailor, 60 Ebury Street (*Post Office London Directory*, 1862).

3   Lady Glasgow [18]
    Sir Roderick Murchison
4   Derby.
    Mʳ Gladstone
5   R. Gurney [19] 7.30
    Lady Harrington
6   Mʳˢ Gardner Mʳˢ Senior. Mʳˢ Robarts
8   2 Martins. 2 Kennys. 2 Knightons. Goldsmid Murc.
    2 Ellisons. Gautier. Wolowski
10 Dn of Westminster [20] 7 1/2
    Mʳˢ Sartoris Home ch:
    Lady Harding.
11 Lᵈ Airlie. 1/4 Athenaeum
12 Lady Harrington
13 Lady Langdale [21] 10 Lowndes Sᵗ 7. 3/4
    Mʳˢ Bayne
    Mʳˢ Senior
14 Dufferin Lodge.[22]
16 J. Coningham at Bracknell for M. T. W.
17 Sir R Murchison
    Home Ch:
18 Mʳ Bacon [23] 7.30 1. K. G. Terrace
19 T. Martin.
    Lady Harrington
20 Mʳˢ Senior
    Play
    Paid Jackson & Graham 932.15.9
    Making price of house 6433.
    Chimney pieces   250
    Grates &c Feetham   317 say (265.15.6)
                            7000
21 Moffat 7.45.

[18] The dowager Countess of Glasgow (1796–1868), widow of the fourth Earl.
[19] Russell Gurney (1804–1878), Recorder of the City of London from 1856 to 1878.
[20] Dean Trench.
[21] The former Lady Jane Elizabeth Harley (1796–1872), daughter of the fifth Earl of Oxford and widow of the first Baron Langdale.
[22] Dufferin Lodge, Fitzroy Park, Highgate, was the town house of the fifth Baron Dufferin and Clandeboye.
[23] James Bacon (1798–1895), later (1871) knighted, was a Q. C. and bencher of Lincoln's Inn who afterwards became Vice-Chancellor.

22   For dinner for 18 people

    4 Sherry   20
    2 Sauterne   21   Wine for a
    4 Champagne   32   dinner for 18.
    1 old Sherry   10   about 8£
    1 Port   10
    4 Claret   40
    1 Brandy 1 Malaga 15   148/

23   2 Blackwoods. Browning. V. Prinsep. 3 Thompsons. 2 Story Ellison Ormsby. 2 Monroes. Bunbury. Wynne. 3 Selves

    7000
     800   Jackson & Graham for painting & decoration (5 paid)
     200   Verity Gas fittings & lamps.
    8000

24   Edwards. 57 Eaton Sq. 7.30
    Mʳˢ Sartoris

25   Mʳˢ Bates. 7.30

26   Mussy [24] 7 1/2

27   A. Buller 7.45
    Mʳˢ Senior

28   Mʳˢ King 7 3/4
    Lady Dufferin
    Lady Shelley [25]

29   2 Higgins 2 Seniors Mᵐᵉ Mohl.[26] Fonblanque. 5 Selves Pichot.

30   Bevan 6

July   1   E. Curzon

2   Lord Russell Mʳˢ Lysley Lʸ Mildred Hope
    Mʳˢ Wyndham.

3   6.15 p. m. Finis Philippi
    Lady Harrington

4   Orleans House.[27]

5   Heatley. Fulham.

[24] Henri Guéneau de Mussy (1814–1892), physician to the Orleans family, who came to England with Louis Philippe in 1848 and built up a large London practice.

[25] Probably the former Louisa Elizabeth Knight (d. 1895), who had married Sir John Shelley, seventh Baronet, in 1832.

[26] The former Mary Elizabeth Clarke (1793–1883), who had married the orientalist Julius Mohl in 1847. The receptions that she held at her house in the Rue du Bac in Paris were popular for forty years.

[27] Where lived the Duc d'Aumale.

     6　　Including J & G's extra bill 3062
         I make out that I have spent 2062 of capital
         Including loan to S.　　　900
         To L　　　　　　　　　　200
         I owe my estate　　　　1962
     7　　H. Corry 71a Grosvenor S.t M.rs Prescott [28]
     8　　on Wednesday. Evans, Lemon, Leech, Lucas, May-
         hew, Brooks, Tenniel, Keene. Silver,[29] Taylor, Ed-
         wards. M.rs Sartoris
    10　　Lady Harrington
    18　　Gallinot Dinner
    19　　Leech at Richmond.
    24　　M.rs Sartoris

August　　8　　23 Portland Place. Sale Chandeliers.　Dresden　65
         Lowndes Sq.　Round table
    14　　Canterbury
September 10　　3 days sickness at Folkestone
    13　　Home after Paris and Folkestone GBAITH
    26　　2 Whitmores. Watts.[30] Col. Fladgate. M.rs Cameron
October　　1　　Synge's Dividend
November 28　　Christie's Q. Ann dish & Ewer
December　1　　Kensington Vestry 8.[31]
    10　　Lucas
    16　　Sir E. Perry.
    17　　Phinn?
    19　　Delane

[28] The wife of William George Prescott.

[29] Henry Silver, a contributor to *Punch* during the eighteen-fifties and eighteen-sixties, whose diary forms the basis of E. V. Lucas's "Thackeray at the Punch Table" (*Loiterer's Harvest*, New York, 1913, pp. 18–41).

[30] George Frederic Watts (1817–1904), the celebrated painter, who lived with Thackeray's friends the Prinseps at Little Holland House.

[31] Thackeray's appointment with Archdeacon Sinclair was no doubt to make final arrangements for the wedding of Edward Thackeray and Amy Crowe, which took place on December 2. "So grieved was he at the thought of parting from [Miss Crowe]", writes John Guille Millais (*The Life and Letters of Sir John Everett Millais*, I, 276), "that on her wedding-day he came for consolation to my father's studio, and spent most of the afternoon in tears."

APPENDIX XXIII

NUMBER 2, PALACE GREEN, KENSINGTON

The following reckoning of Thackeray's assets and inventory of the furnishings of his last house at 2 Palace Green, Kensington, is here published for the first time from the early pages of his diary for 1862.

Study.

Italian Sofa & 6 chairs	30
3 Inlaid chairs	9
Louis XVI inlaid table	10
2 Easy chairs	4
Study table	10
Do	8
Do small	3
Looking Glasses	40
Prints & frames	6
Pictures	25
Jars	5
Candlesticks	5
Fender & Irons	1
Paper Case	4
Books	150
Chintz Sofa	1
Small do.	1
Lamp	10
Carpet	10
Clock	10
	340

Drawing-Rooms

Chandeliers	40
Piano	40
Round table	10
Long do	10
Library do.	5
Bookcase and contents	100
Looking glasses	60
Sofas	5
Chairs	25

Drawings   50
Curtains   10
Carpets   20
China   40
Candlesticks   20
Clock   40
Watch   10
                              515

Hall

Glass   10
China   10
Pictures   20
Marble Tables   30   70
Hat Stand &c.

Dining Room

19 Chairs   35
Table   10
Small table   5
Gold table   15
Looking Glass   35
Do   5
Chandliers   15
Turkey Carpets   30
Sideboard   20
Stand.   5
                              170

Morning Room.

China & Cupboard   40
Pictures   25
Glasses   20
Chairs   10
Tables   5
Sofa   5   105

Annys Room.

China & Cupboard   60
Pictures & Prints   10
Cabinet   6
Table   5   81

5 Best bed rooms & furniture		165
2 Bath rooms		40
5 Attics		100
China & Glass (say)	100	
Plate (say)	200	
Wine (say)	400	2286
Onslow Sq^e		2600
Copyrights		4000
Moneys owing (?)		1200
Kensington		8014
		18100 [1]

[1] On the page of Thackeray's 1862 diary opposite these final figures Lady Ritchie has added the following "Estimate with Mr Fladgate 25 Feb^y", which presumably dates from 1864:

	Min.	—	Max.
[Furnishings:]	2320		2500
[Onslow Sq.:]	say 2500	to	2600
[Copyrights:]	4000	—	6000
[Moneys owing:]	400	—	400
[Kensington:]	8000	—	10000
	17,200		21,500
		Say 20,000£.	

APPENDIX XXIV

DIARY FOR 1863

Hitherto unpublished. Original owned by Mrs. Fuller.

January   3   Praed [1] 7.30
4   Leech 6.30
5   Home. 2 Leeches, 2 Leslies, Ellison Goodlake 6 Selves
7   Mr Heath
9   Fladgate
15   Priaulx 7.
16   Roberts
18   3 Selves, 2 Caulfields, 2 Cottins, 2 Edwards, Elliotson Wyndham Smith, Leech, Sothern, H. Merivale J^r Dillon 3 Sherry 3 Champ. 3 Claret 51. 1 Port
20   Dyce [2] 33 Oxford Terrace. 7
21   Phinn
25   C C [3] 7.
26   Mentmore
31   7 1/2 G S.

February   2   Waddington 7.30
3   143 Regent S^t 10.15
4   Mrs Trollope. Arch^d [4] Kerrich J^r [5] 2 Denmans. Metcalfe. Merivale. Senior. 7.30
     3 Claret 54 2 Champagne. 2 Sherry.
5   Mrs Ford. 7.45
6   Stephen [6]
14   Mem. to send 5 for Mrs Sleap. Sickness & Spasms not severe for 2 days.
17   Offer to see Miss Roberts Tuesday or Wednesday

---

[1] Charles Tyringham Praed (1833–1895), a partner in Praed and Company, bankers.
[2] The Rev. Alexander Dyce (1798–1869), editor of Shakespeare, Beaumont and Fletcher, Middleton, Shirley, and other Elizabethan dramatists.
[3] Probably Charles Collins.
[4] Archdeacon Sinclair.
[5] FitzGerald's nephew.
[6] James Fitzjames Stephen.

18   30 N. Brook S!̠ [7] 6.30
19   M[rs] Mansfield T.
21   2 Collins 3 Fanshawes, Sterling, Buller, Ormsby, Percy [8] 3 Selves
24   L[d] Russell 7 3/4
25   Millais

March 1   T. Taylor
2   Heatly 8
3   Reeve 7.30
5   Mussy 7.30
6   Sartoris.
8   3 Selves J J. 2 Leeches. Gordon. 2 Colvilles.[9] Phinn Stirling. Landseer. Hills. M[rs] Ford. 3 Sherries 1 Old Sherry. 3 48 Claret. 3 Champagne. 1 Port. 1 ordinaire 4. 6. 0
9   Coulson [10] 1 Chester Terrace R P.
10   M. Temple [11]
11   Bryant 8.
      M[rs] Sartoris's ball
      M[rs] Gopits
12   Priaulx 7.15
13   Dutton 1/4 8
16   Merivale 7.30
      Ford. I shall make a point of going W M T.
17   D[r] r[t] Beaumont
21   Bageot [12] 7.30
23   Sir James Colville 7.30
24   Coningham 7.45. D[r] Marg. Beaumont
25   M. Thackeray. 7
26   Ly Molesworth.
27   Dr Bence Jones 6.30

[7] Where was located the White Hart, an inn managed by Thomas John Pope (*Post Office London Directory*, 1862).

[8] Dr. John Percy (1817–1889), an authority on metallurgy and a contributor to *The Times, The Athenæum*, and *The Saturday Review*, who was, like Thackeray, a member of "Our Club".

[9] Sir James William Colvile (1810–1880), who returned to England in 1859 after a distinguished career as an Indian judge. He had married Frances Eleanor Grant in 1857.

[10] William Coulson (1801–1877), Senior Surgeon of St. Mary's Hospital, Paddington, lived at 1 Chester Terrace (*Post Office London Directory*, 1862).

[11] A dinner at the Middle Temple.

[12] No doubt Walter Bagehot (1826–1877), the eminent economist and man-of-letters, who was the son-in-law of Thackeray's friend James Wilson.

28   Wingrove Cook. R. C.
29   2 Cayleys 2 Collins Gregory Swinton
      3 Claret 2 Champ. 2 Sherries 1 Port
           21   14   8   7   £2 10
30   Fairbairn 23 Qs Gate

April 2   Heath.
       6   Mr Milnes?
      13   From Frystone to Hamsthwaite Harrogate York
      14   To Lord Galway's [13] at Bawtry
      16   Home.
      17   Clayton 7.30
      18   Col Stanley [14] 8
      25   O. C. Shakespear dinner [15]
      26   2 Russells 2 Wilsons 2 Curzons Doyle Twyford [16] 3
            Selves Taylor

[13] George Edward Arundell Monckton-Arundell (1805–1876), sixth Viscount Galway, who had married Henrietta Eliza Milnes (d. 1891), the sister of Thackeray's friend, in 1838. The Galways' country seat was Serlby Hall, Bawtry, Nottinghamshire.

[14] Colonel John Stanley, a younger son of the Stanleys of Alderley.

[15] Thackeray's last appearance at "Our Club" was to preside at this dinner, a burdensome duty rendered doubly disagreeable by the circumstances under which he spoke. In *The Athenæum* of April 25 had appeared a malicious review of his daughter's *Story of Elizabeth*. The novel is "undeniably clever", the critic admits (pp. 552–553), but it "turns on a subject which is, or ought to be, quite inadmissable for a novel: the antagonism of a mother and a daughter, both rivals for the love of the same man." Moreover, it "is told in a mocking, sarcastic spirit, which is very unpleasant, and which degrades all characters alike." Thackeray attributed this notice to John Cordy Jeaffreson, whom he found among those present at "Our Club". It is not surprising that in his speech on Shakespeare, as Jeaffreson (*A Book of Recollections*, I, 308) relates, "he spoke of the atmosphere of rivalry and contention which Shakespeare breathed, while he 'was doing his appointed work and making his imperishable fame, — of the tatlers who talked saucily about him from mere mental flimsiness, and of the malicious detractors who from spiteful jealousy magnified the defects, and disparaged the excellences of his writings and character. Observing how the tattlers and detractors were remembered only by the few persons who remembered them with contempt, and how all their ineffectual efforts to defame their great master had failed to influence the world's judgment, he remarked how tenderly time and fate had dealt with the poet, in causing him to be known to us only by his writings." After Thackeray had left "Our Club" early in the evening, he described Jeaffreson as "a man who, in order to give him pain, had slapped his daughter's face". Though the offending review of *The Story of Elizabeth* was written, on Jeaffreson's showing, by Geraldine Jewsbury (1812–1880), the novelist and friend of Mrs. Carlyle, Thackeray was not wrong in sensing a cabal against him among certain members of *The Athenæum's* staff. See Appendix XXV.

[16] Augusta Small Twyford, 24 New Street, Spring Gardens (*Post Office London Directory*, 1862).

27   G. general meeting.
28   St James's Theatre. Lady Audley's Secret [17] & Effie Deans.
29   Sir J. Simeon
      Lady Rothschild.
30   London House. 10 Mrs Halle.

May   1   H. Wilson
       3   Leech at Richmond
       5   Norman.
       6   Archbishop of Y.[18]
       8   F. Chapman. G. 6.30
      10   Gordon 2 Cayleys 2 Trollopes. 2 Stephens 3 Selves.
      12   R Bell S.
      13   Colvile 7. 3/4
      14   2 Troubridges. Col. Greathed [19] 2 Milnes 2 Lows. Heatly. Baring Ld Stanley. 3 Selves. Venables. 2 Thackerays. Ellison. Lady Cullum.   18.
           Breakfast with Mr Gladstone [20] 10. 4 Champagne 2.48 4.47
           1 Port 4 Sherry 1 Old Sherry. 28 3.3 8 16 10 = 6.5
      15   Arden. Cliffords Inn:
           Lady de Grey [21]
      16   Mr J. Crow Horseferry Road Taxes 2.12.4
      19   Lady Taunton [22]
      20   Mrs Gladstone.
      21   Miss Thackeray. 7.30.
      22   Mr Gurney.
      24   Clarence.

[17] A drama by George Roberts from the novel of the same name by Miss Braddon, first presented at St. James's Theatre on February 28, 1863. *Effie Deans, The Lily of St. Leonards* (1863) was adapted by Shepherd from *The Heart of Midlothian.*

[18] Archbishop Thomson. See above, No. 1564.

[19] Lt.-Col. Edward Harris Greathed (1812–1881), later (1865) K. C. B. and a General.

[20] The other guests at Gladstone's breakfast were the Duchess of Sutherland, the Bishop of Brechin, the Bishop of Montreal, Cobden, and "Mr. Evarts, the new U. S. coadjutor to Adams" (John Morley, *Life of William Ewart Gladstone*, 3 vols., London, 1903, II, 189).

[21] The former Henrietta Ann Theodosia Vyner, who had married George Frederick Samuel Robinson (1827–1909), third Earl de Grey and later (1871) first Marquess of Ripon, in 1851.

[22] The former Lady Mary Howard (d. 1892), daughter of the sixth Earl of Carlisle, who had married Henry Labouchere (1798–1869), first Baron Taunton, in 1852.

25 H. James 6 3/4

28 2 Duttons. 2 Higgins. 2 Mussys. 2 Galways. 2 John-
sons. Swinton F. Elliot. 3 Selves. Clifford Bigge
4 Cham. 4 Claret. 1 Port. 3 Sh. 1 O.S. 2 Claret 5. 12.0

29 Lady Stanhope Mrs Halle. Lady Lyell

June 1 Leech. Lady Lyell

3 Sir T. Troubridge 7. 3/4. 8 Queen's Gate.

5 M^r & Mrs James 7.30
Lady Eastlake Mrs Gardner

6 Lady Essex [23]

9 Dined with girls at Star & Garter.

10 Clifford. Trafalgar.

15 Lady Troubridge Mr Roderick Murchison

17 Mr Grant Duff.[24]

18 Bevan. Mr Pennethorne [25] at 10.1/2 here

19 Mr Walter [26] 7.30
M^r & Miss Donne

20 Mr Merewether June 22.

> Sir. A div^d of 100£ was due from S [27] to me on the
> 1 April w^h was not paid. The quarters interest at 5 per
> cent is 1.2.6 the discount on w^h will be 1.2.6 on 1 July.
> By paying me 200£ now the interest & disc^t will balance
> each other.
>
> A dividend will be due on 1 Ap. 64 from w^h take 9
> months disc^t 3.15. A div^d on 1 October from w^h take
> 15 m^{ths} disct 6.2.6.
>
> If you can give me a cheque for 400 minus 9.17.6
> I shall be very glad to get it & not trouble S for some
> time to come
>
> G. B. Gregory Esq

21 2 Knightons 3 Pollens Mrs Leech. Heywood. Hicks.
3 Selves 2 Duffs. Clark 14.

24 Mr^s Lysley [28] Mr^s Walter 10.30 Mr^s Th: Hankey [29]

[23] Louisa Boyle (1833–1876), daughter of Viscount Dungarvan and grand-
daughter of the eighth Earl of Cork, who had married Arthur Algernon de Vere
Capell (1803–1892), sixth Earl of Essex, three days earlier.
[24] Mountstuart Elphinstone Grant Duff (1829–1906), later G. C. S. I., the
politician and colonial administrator. [25] James Pennethorne (1801–1871), later (1870) knighted, a well known
architect. [26] John Walter (1818–1894), proprietor of *The Times*. [27] Synge.
[28] The wife of William John Lysley (1791–1873), barrister and M. P. for
Chippenham from 1859 to 1865.
[29] Thomson Hankey (1805–1893), political economist and liberal M. P. for
Peterborough from 1853 to 1868 and 1874 to 1880.

25   Mʳˢ Longman
26   Miss Thackeray Mʳˢ Foley [30] at 4
27   Mʳˢ Prescott Lady Pollock
29   Orleans House. Mʳˢ Kirkman Hodgson [31]

July   1   R. C.[32] 4 p.m.
2   Harrow School
3   Slight attack only lasting a day
7   Moffatt. Tuesday. Wednesday.
22   Evans, Leech, Lemon, Brooks, Keane, Tenniel, Tay-
     lor, Silver Becher, Self,
26   Drove to Richmond to Dʳ Owen [33] & Mʳ Heath. asked
     to dinner by Phinn, Owen, Heath.
27   Fonblanque at 2. A slight attack of sickness at 5 am.,
     went off and ate at 5 pm.
29   Knighton. Blendworth.[34] Horndean Waterloo to Row-
     lands Castle

August   1   Sartoris.
3   To Ryde.
4   To London.
7   Lubbocks loan
16   Left home by L. C & D. slept at Dover Lᵈ Warden.[35]
17   To Calais. Quillacq.
18   Brussels Hotel de Suede.
20   To Dinan by Namur
21   To Paris by Givet & Rheims. H des 2 Mondes. nice
     little apartment. 78.
22   Hotel Cluny. Dine at Café Anglais. Theatre du
     Chatelet Secret de Miss Aurore.[36]
23   Dine at Café Gaillon
24   Bois de Boulogne. Dine at Hotel
     Excellent Drama of Sorciere at Amb. Com.

[30] Wife of the sculptor John Henry Foley.
[31] The wife of Kirkman Daniel Hodgson (1814–1879), who had been Thackeray's schoolfellow at Charterhouse. Hodgson was a partner in Baring Brothers,
a director of the Bank of England, and M. P. for Bridport from 1857 to 1868.
[32] The Reform Club.
[33] Dr. Richard Owen (1804–1892), later (1884) K. C. B., the eminent natural-
ist.
[34] See above, No. 1569.
[35] Thackeray was friendly both with Lord Palmerston, Lord Warden of the
Cinque Ports, and the fifth Duke of Newcastle, Lord Warden of the Stanneries.
[36] A five act drama by Lambert Thiboust (1826–1867) and Bernard Derosne,
first presented at the Théâtre du Châtelet in July, 1863.

25   Gaité Dreadfully stupid piece of Peau d'Ane [37]

27   To Folkestone. Denibas's buggy hotel

28   Home by 11.30

September 21   Slight attack beginning 5 am. yielding to 9 gr. Colocynth in a few hours.

24   2 Collins. Dyce. Schmidt. Smith 2 Taylor. 3. 47. 2
Sherry. 2 Champagne.

October 14   2 Normans, Mc Gregor. 1 Hock. 1 Sherry 2 Latour.

19   2 Lows 2 Troubridges. 2 Collins. Taylor. Russell 5
Selves. M. Irvine. G. Duff. 3 Claret (48. 51. 54)
2 Taylor's Claret. 3 Sherry. 3 Champagne. 1 Brandy.
4 0 0

29   c.m.a.

November 1   2 Heaths 2 Collins Hamstede [38] Corbyn.

5   Gresham. 6

6   2 Harness. 2 Collins. Stephenson. Follett. 2 Mussy.
Hills 3 Selves 2 Harness Stocken.

11   Mme de Mussy

12   Mrs Harness. Liberal 7.

13   Willis's 2.30 p.m.
Archdeacon. 7.15

15   3 Thackerays. 3 Selves. 2 Benzons. Landseer. 1 Shawe
O'Dowd. Phinn. 2 Collins's Woodford.[39]

19   Mem to send Mrs Bakewell 12.10. Phinn.

20   Mr Benzon

22   Heath.

26   Sir J. Colvile 7.

December 3   Millais 7.15

4   Mrs Mansfield

7   Charter house.

[37] A four act play by Clairville and Paul Aimé Chapelle (1806–1900), called
Laurencin, based on the fairy tale of Charles Perrault. It was first presented at the
Théâtre de la Gaîté on August 14, 1863.

[38] Frederick William Hamstede, a retired city-clerk of little education who
served as secretary for "Our Club". He regarded professional authors with reverence and thought it a great privilege to be allowed to associate with them. He
was not prepossessing in appearance. "Besides being a small man," writes Jeaffreson (*A Book of Recollections*, I, 224), "he was a hunchback, and so crippled in
his limbs that he could not move across a room without the help of a stick."
Thackeray became very fond of Hamstede, whom he took under his protection
when banter at "Our Club" became rough. See Masson's *Memories of London in
the Forties*, pp. 250–256.

[39] General Sir Alexander Woodford (1782–1870), later (1868) Field-Marshall.

9 J. Merivale 9.30
10 Priaulx
11 Forsyth
12 C. H.[40]
16 D. R.
17 Forsyth.

[40] Charterhouse.

APPENDIX XXV

THACKERAY AND THE NATIONAL SHAKESPEARE COMMITTEE

Among Thackeray's papers are the two clippings reproduced on the next two pages, which he cut from newspapers during the last week of his life. Did they not exist to testify that the National Shakespeare Committee was a matter of some concern to him, it would hardly be necessary to describe the proceedings of that organization.[1] "I wish to — well Jupiter or Thor," Shirley Brooks wrote to Dallas on November 13, 1863, "that Thackeray would leave off caring about the snarls of these little Bohemian curs. They *know* he writhes, & therefore snap whenever they can. But there is no persuading a man out of his sensations."[2]

The journalistic allies of Edmund Yates, whose abuse of Thackeray by no means terminated with the failure of his action against the Garrick Club in 1859, included William Hepworth Dixon and John Cordy Jeaffreson of *The Athenæum*. As we have seen, these men first showed their hand in *The Athenæum* of April 25, 1863, by a virulent review of Anne Thackeray's *Story of Elizabeth,* a blow which was calculated to hurt Thackeray even more than his daughter.[3] During the following summer Dixon was chiefly responsible for the foundation of a National Shakespeare Tercentenary Celebration Committee. Aware that the management of this Committee was unfriendly to him, Thackeray ignored two circular-invitations to join it that he received. When Dickens, Tennyson, and Bulwer-Lytton became committeemen and Vice Presidents of the Shakespeare Association, however, Thackeray's friends injudiciously sought to secure a similar honor for him. Their proposal was brought before the Committee on December 7, and Dixon had the malign satisfaction of procuring its rejection by a considerable majority.

This direct and intentional affront to Thackeray, for such it was despite the arguments which Dixon and Jeaffreson later offered in palliation of their offence, was brought to the notice of the public by Henry Vizetelly in the "Lounger at the Clubs" column of *The Illus-*

---

[1] In what follows I have depended chiefly on Vizetelly's narrative in *Glances back through Seventy Years*, II, 105–110, though I have not ignored Jeaffreson's presentation of the case for the defence in his *Book of Recollections*, I, 316–322.

[2] From an original letter owned by Mr. Wells.

[3] See above, Appendix XXIV, note 15.

The Shakespear M C in London is acquiring for itself a very injurious notoriety by its capricious and utterly embarrassing like proceedings. The nominal list of the committee & V.Ps is numerous and imposing but none of those distinguished persons ever attend & the management is left in the hands of a very small clique of men, distinguished literary cliques. admits none of the others &c &c their jealousies

jealousies and antipathies that mark their conduct by glancing at a scene which took place there recently. Colonel Sykes (who has nothing to do with the clique) was in the chair when Mr. Thackeray was proposed as a vice-president, a similar distinction having been recently conferred on Mr. Dickens and Sir Bulwer Lytton. "So natural a proposition," says the writer, " did this seem to Colonel Sykes that he was about to put the resolution as an unopposed motion when one of the honorary secretaries of the committee, the well-known editor of a certain literary journal famous for puffing the books of its contributors, rose and objected that, as Mr. Thackeray was not already a member of the committee, he was ineligible for the office of vice-president. Attention, however, having been drawn to the fact that nearly the whole of the other vice-presidents had been solicited to accept the position conferred upon them without being previously called upon to join the committee, another writer in the journal spoken of—a novelist of feeble powers—took upon himself to say that he had reasons for believing Mr. Thackeray thought himself so immeasurably superior to the individuals composing the general committee, that he would decline to join it, and he begged the committee not to demean itself, &c. &c., and so forth. This appeal to the self-dignity of a clique of little men, who, for the most part, take their cue from the one honorary secretary—the other never opens his lips, but for ever 'sits like patience on a monument, smiling at grief'—at once settled the question, and it was resolved — the contributors and hangers-on to the particular journal constituting of themselves a majority—that one of the greatest of living writers should not be vice-president of a movement which professes to have at heart the honouring of the literary calling, symbolised in the person of its most distinguished representative—'the poet of all time.'" We take it for granted that at a future meeting, when the contemptible clique shall be outnumbered, this disgraceful resolution will be reversed, if, indeed, the "movement" do not go off the rails altogether. In the meanwhile the distant reader may be curious to know who the literary potentates are who have determined that Mr. Thackeray shall not participate in the Shakespeare celebration. The "well-known editor" is Mr. Hepworth Dixon, and the journal he edits is the 'Athenæum'; the "novelist of feeble powers" is one Mr. Cordy Jeafferson; and the honorary secretary who "never opens his lips" is Mr. J. O. Halliwell, a gentleman very much out of place in such a situation.

THACKERAY AND THE NATIONAL SHAKESPEARE COMMITTEE

THE "LOUNGER AT THE CLUBS."

TO THE EDITOR OF ' THE DAILY TELEGRAPH."

SIR—It having been very frequently stated, in metropolitan and provincial newspapers, that the article " The Lounger at the Clubs" in the *Illustrated Times* is written by me, I shall be much obliged by your giving publicity to the fact that, as statements implicating individuals by their names have been introduced into that article without my sanction, I have relinquished my connection with the *Illustrated Times*, and protested against a practice which any respectable journal in England would hold to be unwarrantable.—I am, Sir, yours, &c.,

EDMUND YATES.

Mayesbury House, Willesden, Dec. 19.

THACKERAY AND THE NATIONAL SHAKESPEARE COMMITTEE

trated Times for December 12.[4] Other London magazines and news-papers that concerned themselves with literature were not slow to take up the cry against the *Athenæum* clique. And Thackeray's death on December 24 made the affair a major scandal.

On Christmas Day Shirley Brooks speculated that: "Perhaps [Thackeray] is now explaining to Shakespeare why he was not on the Committee — and why Dixon is, and they laugh good-naturedly",[5] but neither Brooks nor the rest of Thackeray's journalistic friends were inclined to let Jeaffreson and Dixon off scot free. The two were severely censured at the meeting of the Committee on January 11, 1864, and later in the month Vizetelly published a pamphlet called *The National Shakespeare Committee and the Late Mr. Thackeray*, which is made up of excerpts from articles in the London press about the affair.[6] The prestige of the Committee was by this time irretrievably damaged, and the visions of a £30,000 monument to Shakespeare that Dixon had entertained, writes Jeaffreson, "resulted in nothing more important than a modest sum of funded money, which may be serviceable to Shakespearian celebrants in 1964, and the planting of a small oak on Primrose Hill, which has hitherto declined to grow much bigger."[7]

[4] The greater part of Vizetelly's article is quoted in the first of the clippings reproduced opposite pp. 416–17. Thackeray found the second clipping interesting because Yates in it offers public assurance to Dixon and Jeaffreson that he has had no hand in the exposure of their manoeuvres.

[5] From an original letter to Percival Leigh in the Berg Collection of the New York Public Library.

[6] On the cover of this pamphlet are quoted some Elizabethan or pseudo-Elizabethan verses, one line of which reads "Crocodiles weep tears for thee". To these words the note is appended: "See Mr. Edmund Yates's letter to the *Belfast Northern Whig*; report of Mr. Hepworth Dixon's speech, *Daily Telegraph*, Jan. 5th; Mr. Cordy Jeaffreson's letter, *Daily News*, Jan. 7th."

[7] *A Book of Recollections*, I, 316.

APPENDIX XXVI

EXCERPTS FROM THACKERAY'S UNPUBLISHED
LETTERS TO MRS. BROOKFIELD, MRS. ELLIOT, AND
MISS PERRY

For reasons given in the preface it has proved impossible to publish a number of Thackeray's letters to Mrs. Brookfield and to Mrs. Elliot and Miss Perry. The excerpts from these letters in the *Lambert* and *Goodyear* catalogues are so extensive and important, however, that this appendix has been devoted to reprinting the texts and descriptions there first made public. A few additional fragments of letters to Mrs. Elliot and Miss Perry are included from a Sotheby catalogue of May 28–30, 1934, here called the *Elliot Catalogue*.

1.   TO MRS. BROOKFIELD
                          25? FEBRUARY 1848

Lambert Catalogue, p. 42. One page, 12mo. "Written immediately after the revolution of February 22, in France."

                        13 Young St., Kensington, Friday

. . . Paris is so tranquil from all accounts that we need fear no danger for any of our friends there. I have a letter from my mother written the day after the fighting (some of which had taken place under her window) and all were safe and well. . . .

2.   TO MRS. ELLIOT AND KATE PERRY
                         30 JUNE 1848

Lambert Catalogue, p. 52; *Goodyear Catalogue*, lot 321. Two pages, 12mo.

                              June thirty, Friday

D—r l—d—s!

[*Thackeray omits many of the vowels in this letter, hoping that the*] C—l—nial Off—ce won't c—nc—l any more d—sp—tches. . . . [*The rainy weather, which he deplores, prevented him from coming to them, lest he should have appeared*] w—t to the sk—in and my c—at w—stc—t and p—nt—l—ns all dr—pp—ng! After that I was in s—ch an ag—ny with V—n—ty F—r [1] that it was imp—ss—ble to st—r. I only f—n—sh'd y—st—r—day and was too f—t—gued to wr—te then. . . . But I am alw—ys, Your w—ll w—sher,

W. M. Th—ck—r—y

3.
TO MRS. BROOKFIELD
OCTOBER 1848

Lambert Catalogue, p. 43; *Goodyear Catalogue*, lot 320. Incomplete. Two concluding pages, 8vo.

. . . [*Writing of doctors:*] What can be said of a man who says one day lie flat on the peril of your life, and the next, get up, walk, run, drink porter at mid-day and quinine all the afternoon. They know nothing; they grope about in the darkness and hit or miss — everybody does. . . . [*Of his mother:*] I look at her character, and go down on my knees as it were with wonder and pity. It is Mater Dolorosa, with a heart bleeding with love. Is not that a pretty phrase? I wrote it yesterday in a book,[2] whilst I was thinking about her — and have no shame somehow now in writing thus sentimentally to all the public; though there are very few people in the world to whom I would have the face to talk in this way tete-a-tete. To you I can because you are made of the same soft stuff . . .

W. M. T.

4.
TO MRS. BROOKFIELD
22 DECEMBER 1848

Lambert Catalogue, p. 49; *Goodyear Catalogue*, lot 320. One page, 12mo.

Friday

. . . The weather is 'Eavenly. I am going on with III [3] pretty well. I wish my gals was here. I am at the Bedford, but whether I shall come to London to-day or tomorrow Lauramussy only knows. This morning I could do no work because of the abomnanable brass bands. . . . I have been in love, but am restored to my usual state.

[1] The final number (chapters 64 to 67), published for July.
[2] In chapter 2 of *Pendennis* (*Works*, II, 19), which with chapters 1 and 3 forms number I of that novel, published for November, 1848.
[3] Chapters 7 to 10 of *Pendennis*, published for January, 1849.

5.   TO MRS. BROOKFIELD
                      31 JANUARY 1849

Goodyear Catalogue, lot 320, facsimile of first page. Two pages, 8 vo.

                                        Ship. Dover.
                                Just before going away

My dear lady, How long is it since I have written to you in my
natural handwriting? *but having just completed another very sentimen-
tal letter to you in the other penmanship I think best to cancel it* and
tell you simply that I am so far on my road to Paris Meurice's Hotel
Rue Rivoli and that I had made up my mind to this great I may say
decisive step when I came to see you on Saturday before you went to
Hither Green. I didn't go to the Sterling [4] as it was my last day and
due naturally to the family We went to bed at 9 1/2 o'clock. To day
I went round on a circuit of visits, including Turpin at your house
— it seems as if I was going on an ever-so-long journey — Have
you any presentiments? I know some people who have — Thank you
for your note of this morning and my dear old W^m for his regard for
me — Try you, and conserve the same — As I get older I will grow
so polite calm and elegant in my behaviour that I will never at least
offend you by too much abandon Shall I begin and call Mrs. Brookfield
again? Ah no. I have not got to that, dear lady. You shall be my
dear lady always to me and I will be your affectionate Grandfather . . .
                              W. M. T.

6.   TO KATE PERRY
                      JULY 1849

Lambert Catalogue, p. 61; *Goodyear Catalogue,* lot 321. One page, 16mo.
"Thackeray writes for news of Mrs. Brookfield, who was at this time in South-
ampton with Mrs. Fanshawe. The latter was very ill."

Dear Miss
    . . . I am alarmed at not hearing. All yesterday I was in a panic
thinking that something had happened there, and came home with a
perfect certainty that ill news would be waiting for me . . .
                              W. M. T.

    [4] The Sterling Club. See above, No. 677.

7. ## TO MRS. BROOKFIELD
11 SEPTEMBER 1849

Lambert Catalogue, p. 44. Four pages, 12mo.

Hotel Bristol

... Mrs. Errington in a slouched Spanish hat with a black feather, and real cheeks as red as roses looked uncommonly handsome, handsomer than the portrait Lawrence painted of her as Miss Macdonald more than twenty years ago. We used to have prints of it, when boys, in our rooms at College. What a bore to be a beauty famous enough to be engraved, and have the register of your birth always against you! If you have your picture done Madame, don't have an engraving of it, so that interested people may know your age and expose you. . . . Altogether it was a pleasant scene and a cheery evening. I wound it up with the amusement of smoking at the Embassy with one of the attaches, and my lord Douglas who had been with the President on a railway excursion. He will be Emperor before long, that you may communicate to my lords of the Council; and then I suppose he will have to fly like other potentates out of this uneasy kingdom. . . . I have still been reading the Vicomte de Bragelonne and am angry that there are only 12 volumes as yet to read . . .

8. ## TO MRS. BROOKFIELD
18 SEPTEMBER 1849

Lambert Catalogue, p. 45. Two pages, 12mo.

... I was in such hag'nies at dinner that though they got me a slipper (by which I had the advantage of showing a neat stocking to Lady Rodd) I was obliged to go home and send for a doctor. He put me to bed, where I am to stop today and perhaps tomorrow working at Pendennis. . . . My leg is to be amputated tomorrow, but I shall be well on Thursday, and shall come to see you with my leg in my hand. I suppose one only gets to simplicity a force d'artifice, and gradually casts off the skin of fine writing. Is it honesty or only consumate roguery? Both I think — honesty and policiy —

9.   TO MRS. BROOKFIELD
                              3 NOVEMBER 1849

Lambert Catalogue, pp. 44–45. Four pages, 12mo. Mentions the rainy day and
the state of Thackeray's health.

                                                    Saturday, 8 [5]

... And what do you think else I should like to do? To see you, I
dare say you think, but that's not what I meant you vain woman — I
meant that the paper looks so nice and white, I should like to write a page
of Pendennis. Doesn't all this prove I am getting stronger? ... I saw
Albert Goldsmid's weak aquiline beak and purple hair on the pier, and
we greeted each other without the least cordiality.... I feel as if I was
never going to smoke again, and to lead an altogether new life — who
knows? perhaps I shall turn historian or divine.... What makes you
so frightened of my mother. It is only her figure-head which is awful;
her guns are never shotted....

                                W. M. T.

10.   TO MRS. BROOKFIELD
                              8 DECEMBER 1849?

Lambert Catalogue, p. 45; *Goodyear Catalogue*, lot 320. One page, 12mo.

... As I thought your beautiful countenance wore an igspression of
alarm when I went away last night and you looked as if you thought
I was going to be ill again this to inform you that I had a famous sleep
of 12 hours and am this morning igseeding cheerful ...

                                W. M. T.

11.   TO MRS. BROOKFIELD
                                    1849

Collection of Letters, p. 67; *Lambert Catalogue*, p. 45. Incomplete. One page,
12mo.

                                                    Wednesday. 1849.

    What have I been doing since these many days? I hardly know. I
have written such a stupid number of *Pendennis* in consequence of not

    [5] A mistake for Saturday, November 3, 1849.

seeing you, that I shall be ruined if you are to stay away much longer. K. Perry, her name is K. (I don't call her by her Xtian name but am very fond of her because she loves you and pities me) found me out — Says she to me . . . 'It is clear to me that you are always thinking of something else; your soul's not in your work; you go about to parties but don't take any heed of 'em. Your heart's in the Highlands,'. . .

12. TO MRS. ELLIOT AND KATE PERRY
5 MARCH 1850

Lambert Catalogue, p. 52; *Goodyear Catalogue,* lot 321. One page, 12mo. Thackeray explains his sudden departure for Paris.

Paris, Mar. 5

. . . I got sick of waiting outside a certain door in P--rtm--n St. . . . I am engaged to Lady Molesworth to dinner tomorrow. Do send excuses. . . . Well, I'm not near so miserable as I try and make myself out to be and I intend to be jolly for 10 days or so here. Aren't you coming at Easter too? I have got such nice rooms. Come and let us go and have little larks together. We may be happy yet. I don't know why I wrote you this, for as you see very well it is all nonsense. . . .

13. TO MRS. ELLIOT AND KATE PERRY
12 MARCH 1850

Lambert Catalogue, p. 60; *Goodyear Catalogue,* lot 321, where the last page is given in facsimile. Three pages, 8vo.

Hotel Bristol, Place Vendome, Tuesday

My dear young ladies (for so by courtesy you still may be called)
. . . Makepeace is still staying on at Paris trying to get his wounds healed. He had a visit from Miss Smith yesterday who communicated conjugal intelligence to him; he did not say what he thought of the gentleman who is going to be married. He hates every man who is going to marry a nice girl. . . . He has been to a party in the Faubourg St. Germain, and has noted the manners of the inhabitants; making some remarks upon Anglo-French and American Snobs which may serve him in future publications of a satirical nature. He made acquaintance in the railway with Caradoc Baron Howden who asked him to

dinner, where as usual he ate and drank a great deal too much. . . .

. . . (not that he has used it to any purpose for this confounded French paper drinks in the ink and wont let the pen run) what struck and pleased him most was a Suisse in the hall, who when the guests entered rose from his seat seized a halbert and brought it to the ground with a prodigious clink w^h astonished and terrified Makepeace very much. He says he has eaten of many dinners but never tasted a Swiss before.

He cannot describe to you one of the plays w^h he has seen because you would blush so and say 'O for shame you naughty wretch.' He blushed for this country in beholding the piece of Daphnis and Chloe. Perhaps he would like to see it again (so attractive is Vice) but if he does he will say nothing to nobody.

He hears from home that the Miss Berrys have asked him to an entertainment. He begs his good friends Mrs J. E. & Miss KP. to tell those ladies that he is in foreign parts, and to assure them that his heart is in London.

Yes his heart is in London. Some of it on one side of the Park but some on the tother, a great deal at Kensington thank God and a good bit at Thuttysevincheshimplacelown-square:[6] where he hopes everybody is quite well, and whither (for he is grammatical in the midst of all his errors) he sends a benediction

Why dont you come here if you please? I give my best regards to everybody and am your friend and well wisher

Blanche Foker.

14.   TO MRS. BROOKFIELD
                         JUNE 1850?

Lambert Catalogue, p. 46. Two pages, 12mo. Thackeray promises to get a box at the theatre for Mrs. Brookfield.

. . . I am going to dine with C. B.[7] again, at an early family party, and will come in the evening to pay my respects at the theatre. . . .

[6] The Elliots and Miss Perry lived at 37 Chesham Place, near Lowndes Square.
[7] Charlotte Brontë.

15. ## TO MRS. BROOKFIELD
11 JULY 1850

Lambert Catalogue, p. 46. One page, 12mo.

Dieppe, July 11

...I was so sick and ill this morning that I determined on instant flight. And I write one word to say God bless you and little baby and his reverence, and I've been working at Punch for the dear life ever since I've been here — and now, now, I go upon the blew, blew sea....

W. M. T.

16. ## TO MRS. BROOKFIELD
21 AUGUST 1850

Lambert Catalogue, p. 45; *Goodyear Catalogue,* lot 320. Three pages, 8vo.

From the old shop, 21.

...At the train whom do you think I found. Miss ⟨Gore⟩ who says she is Blanche Amory, and I think she is Blanche Amory,[8] amiable (at times) amusing, clever and depraved. We talked and persifflated all the way to London; and the idea of her will help me to a good chapter, in which I will make Pendennis and Blanche play at being in love, such a wicked false humbugging love, as two blase London People might act, and half deceive themselves that they were in earnest.[9] That will complete the cycle of Mr. Pen's worldly experiences, and then we will make, or try and make, a good man of him. O! me, we are wicked worldlings most of us, may God better us and cleanse us. ... I wonder whether ever again I shall have such a happy peaceful fortnight as that last? How sunshiny the landscape remains in my mind, I hope for always; and the smiles of dear children and the aspect of the kindest and tenderest face in the world to me. God bless you, God bless you my sister. I know what you'll do when you read this — well, so am I. I can hardly see as I write for the eye-water. ... How happy your dear regard makes me! How it takes off the solitude and eases it. May it continue pray God till your head is as white as mine ... O Love and Duty — I hope you'll never leave us quite. Instead of being unhappy because that delightful holiday is over or all but over, I intend that the thoughts of it

---

[8] But see *Memoranda,* Theresa Reviss.
[9] See chapters 63 and 64 of *Pendennis* in number XX for September and XXI for October, 1850.

should serve to make me only the more cheerful and help me, please
God, to do my duty better . . .

17.   TO MRS. BROOKFIELD
                          OCTOBER 1850

Lambert Catalogue, p. 47; *Goodyear Catalogue*, lot 320. Three pages, 12mo.

. . . We went to breakfast at 9 1/2 when I amused the company by
making many and bad puns, they serve like Jeux de societe to carry the
hours through, and had a pleasure in practising them on Rawlinson and
on the kind and sublime Henry Taylor. Familiarity has the zest of
irreverence almost before that angelic man — he smiles sadly under
jokes: and says he's capable of making them under strong pressure, but
though I asked him to make a joke on the instant he couldn't [10] do one.
Honest Rawlinson is a good brave fellow. . . . At eleven we went to
the school to see Wm's school-mistress whom they've been exalting here
as a merrycle of beauty. She was very neat and lives in the dearest little
school house with a kitchen and parlor like the rooms of the heroine of a
novel, and she had 30 children to instruct, and Mr. Salmon the parson
is always coming to see her in the hours when the children are NOT
there. . . . But I had time to think about other things as we plodded over
the turnips and ploughed lands: about you, O my sister, though I know
you think that I drop you when I'm away from you: whereas, whereas
— the manner in which a man manages to accomodate 2 thoughts into
his mind is curious. You're never away from me — from waking to
nightcap time. Will you always be there my dear and let your name and
my young ones' go together in that last small prayer? It must have
been about this time last year that I was just out of the Valley of the
Shadow of Death . . . [11]

                          W. M. T.

18.   TO MRS. BROOKFIELD
                              1850?

Lambert Catalogue, p. 48. One page, 12mo. Thackeray asks if he may leave his
daughters with Mrs. Brookfield while he is at Hampstead.

[10] *Lambert Catalogue* reads *could'nt*.
[11] *Psalms*, 23, 4.

19. TO MRS. BROOKFIELD
JANUARY 1851?

Lambert Catalogue, p. 46. Four pages, 8vo.

... I went to dine with my aunt on Thursday and to the Presidents soiree at night. There must have been thousands of people there, the whole street was full of cabs and coaches. To get up to make your bow to the great man, you had to shoulder through a little covered gallery and hot ballroom crammed with folks. I met the Ambassador elbowing through the crowd, 'Sir,' said I, 'my shoestring is untied. Do you think the President of the Republic will notice it?' At which Lord Normanby said, 'The President will look up at you — not down.' And the fact is he gave me a shake of the hand through a little naval officer over whose head I made an elegant bow.... But you should have seen Lord Normanby's puzzled face when I put the question about the shoe-string, with that inveterate flippancy which Mr Wilkins remarks and deprecates in your most obedient servant. I know its disrespectful, but I can't help myself...

20. TO MRS. BROOKFIELD
17–20 JANUARY 1851

Lambert Catalogue, p. 47. Four pages, 12mo.

... When I tell you ma'am that there were TRADESMEN and their wives present [*at the President's Ball*]! I saw one woman pull off a pair of list slippers and take a ticket for them at the greatcoat repository; and I rather liked her for being so bold. Confess now would you have the courage to go to court in list slippers and ask the footman at the door to keep 'em till you came out? Well, there was Lady Castlereagh looking uncommonly 'andsome, and the Spanish Ambassador's wife blazing with new diamonds and looking like a picture by Velasquez, with daring red cheeks and bright eyes. And there was the Princess what-d'you-call-'em, the President's cousin, covered with diamonds too, superb and sulky.... The children went to church yesterday and Minny sat next to Guizot, and Victor Hugo was there — a queer heathen. Did you read of his ordering his son to fight a duel the other day with the son of another literary man? Young Hugo wounded his adversary and I suppose the father embraced him and applauded him — and goes to Church afterwards as if he was a Christian.... I am going again to

Gudin's tonight being tempted by the promise of meeting Scribe,[12] Dumas, Méry, and if none of them are there what am I to do ...

21.   TO MRS. BROOKFIELD
                        1851

Goodyear Catalogue, lot 320. One page, oblong.

... I am on a ride for my health's sake, and in the midst of the commencement of my work. I must do it, I mustn't go on idling and ogling and drinking tea and dining and so forth — What would you say if I made a fiasco in June? [13] But I like just to pass by and say that I am yours as usual: and should be glad to know that you were well . . .

22.   TO MRS. BROOKFIELD
                     14 MAY 1851

Lambert Catalogue, p. 48. One page, 12mo.

... I can't help sending you a line to say that the night's proceedings [14] are over; that the speech went off very well (I don't in the least know what occurred) and that Peel made a pointed and handsome compliment at the end of his address. ...

23.   TO MRS. ELLIOT AND KATE PERRY
              23 SEPTEMBER 1851

Goodyear Catalogue, lot 321. One page, oblong 12mo.

... The affair is at an end and the rupture complete. Monsieur [15] has spoken out like a man ... There is nothing more to be said or done ... There have been very high words between me and Monsieur in consequence of something I said to him that was quite unjustifiable ... But they'll probably leave London and the affair will end. I am going out of town and I don't know where.[16] God bless you all.

[12] Eugène Scribe (1791–1861), the famous playwright; Joseph Méry (1798–1865), poet, playwright, and novelist.
[13] That is, in his lectures on *The English Humourists*, the first of which was given on May 22, 1851.
[14] See above, No. 777.
[15] Brookfield.
[16] Thackeray left London on September 24 for Matlock Bath.

24.   TO MRS. ELLIOT AND KATE PERRY
                26 SEPTEMBER 1851

Lambert Catalogue, p. 53; *Goodyear Catalogue*, lot 321. Four pages, 12mo.

Friday, Chatsworth [17] if you please

Ladies

... You will see into what quarter I am got ... I came down to
Matlock, made a sketch at Haddon Hall, and a very bad sketch too,
wrote, read, worked hard, but it wouldn't do to drive dull care away,
and yesterday I ... came to a famous inn here, wrote and read, and,
ah! the devil was with me still ... And this morning [I] wrote to Mr.
Paxton [18] ... and the answer was Paxton in a carriage to fetch me ...
and a gracious reception from the Duke ... I've been round the house,
and seen the interior splendour — pictures, and state-rooms, and manu-
scripts in the library ... and oh! but the Devil is with me still gnawing
away ... I had a great mind to say 'Show me the Bluebeard Closet
where the dead wives and the murdered secrets are: you must have
a Bluebeard Closet — everybody has one.[19] Let me go and sit in that
— it's that I'd like best. I write because I'm unhappy. If I write my
book [20] in this frame of mind it will be diabolical. I wrote a bit yesterday
that was quite Satanic and raged about with a dreadful gaiety. Can you
do anything to soothe and ease that poor lady? Mrs. Fanshaw sent me
a letter of hers about me and at me, and what do you think I did? I
wrote back to Mrs. F. to inform her principal that even this roundabout
correspondence oughtn't to be; that her husband acting at this moment
nobly and gently must be nobly and gently used, and until he authorized
a correspondence none such must be. And now, and now, if she's in
torment take her a drop of water with you from another soul in purga-
tory. I know it will soothe her to know that I'm unhappy ... the only
thing is Duty Duty Duty. Her husband is a good fellow and does love
her: and I think of his constant fondness for me ... and how cruelly
I've stabbed him and outraged him with my words ...

[17] Chatsworth House, "The Palace of the Peak", a great country mansion built
chiefly by the first Duke of Devonshire between 1688 and 1706. Haddon Hall was
a medieval house nearby,
[18] Joseph Paxton (1803–1865), later (October 23, 1851) knighted, the famous
horticulturalist who designed the plan of the Great Exhibition of 1851. He had
been superintendent of the gardens at Chatsworth since 1826.
[19] Compare *Works*, VIII, 118–119.
[20] *Esmond.*

25.   TO KATE PERRY
                       SEPTEMBER 1851

Goodyear Catalogue, lot 321. Two pages, 12mo.

... Je disais je l'aime je l'aime je l'aime ... Que je voudrais les
baiser ces chere pieds de ma douce maitresse ... Je tremble d'amour
quelquefois devant elle ... Bon dieu que ses yeux me poursuivent ...

26.   TO MRS. BROOKFIELD AND KATE PERRY
                       SEPTEMBER 1851

Lambert Catalogue, p. 53; *Goodyear Catalogue*, lot 321, where the second page
is given in facsimile. Four pages, 12mo. "All correspondence ceased, for the
time, between Thackeray and Mrs. Brookfield, but he could not refrain from
committing his thoughts to paper, and, writing this letter, sent it to Miss Perry,
who undoubtedly showed it to Mrs. Brookfield."

My dear lady
    ... In October I shall go to Oxford and Cambridge; then in Novem-
ber to Liverpool and Edinburgh, then in January to America most
likely ...
    I shan't see much of my dear Sister, and wherever she is I think my
heart will go too. The misfortune of poor W^{ms} mood is that it makes
perforce hypocrites of you and all who approach him — We've before
talked of these 'lies' pardonnez moi le mot — they are called virtues
in women — they are part of the duty w^h my dear has set herself, and
in w^h I say God speed her — The fact of your position makes it impossible to write almost — I am not to show that I feel you are miserable.
I am not to show that I think your husband is wicked and cruel to you.
I am not to show that I think you know you are unhappy, and are
treated with the most cruel tyranny — Nobody is to know anything
of your misery. We are to go on grinning as if we were happy, because William's cough is certainly very bad, and he should not be disturbed in exercising his temper. The children are very well; kiss yours
for me. When I see blue eyes and round faces I look wistfully after
them — when I see tall women in black I feel queer — But I've got
my work to do and I must do it ... I lay awake for a long hour last
night thinking of you: and will tonight, and would to God I could
think of you happy. God bless you.
                    W. M. T.

[*A note at the end to Miss Perry reads in part:*] You will see by
this letter which I didn't send because I thought I should only bring
more tears to her eyes, what my sentiments were regarding my poor
lady. . . . After his letter by which I saw how much the poor soul had
given me up, I . . . checked all correspondence through that dear good
Mrs. F. There can be no harm in a message between friends now and
then. . . . What hasn't she given up for that man? Youth and happiness
and now her dearest friend — what a friend — and to what a man —
a fellow that says to her face he ought to have married a cook, and
treats her like one. He'll do better now after this great shock, and
shows a great generosity on a great occasion. Good by; don't mind my
cries and my rage. I shall be better soon . . .

27.   TO KATE PERRY
                          SEPTEMBER? 1851

Lambert Catalogue, pp. 53–54; *Goodyear Catalogue*, lot 321. Incomplete. Two
concluding pages, 12mo.

. . . I don't see how any woman should not love a man who had
loved her as I did J.; I don't see how any man should not love a woman
so beautiful, so unhappy, so tender; I don't see how any husband, however he might have treated her, should be indifferent at the idea of losing
it. But that I knew I was safe (I mean that any wrong was out of
the question on our children's account) I suppose I should have broken
away myself. I'm sure that one or the other on their side were wrong in
not dismissing me. But a part of poor Brookfield's pride of possession
was that we should envy him and admire her, and of all the weakness,
goodness, love, generosity, vanity, playing with edged tools, we are now
paying the penalty . . . I wish that I had never loved her. I have been
played with by a woman, and flung over at a beck from the lord and
master — that's what I feel. I treet her tenderly and like a gentleman:
I will fetch, carry, write, stop, what she pleases — but I leave her . . .
I was packing away yesterday the letters of years. These didn't make
me cry. They made me laugh as I knew they would. It was for this
that I gave my heart away. It was 'When are you coming dear Mr.
Thackeray,' and 'William will be so happy,' and 'I thought after you
had gone away how I had forgot, etc.' and at a word from Brookfield
afterwards it is — 'I reverence and admire him and love him with not
merely a dutiful but a genuine love' — Amen. The thought that I
have been made a fool of is the bitterest of all, perhaps . . . I have loved
his wife too much to be able to bear to see her belong even to her hus-

band any more — that's the truth ... Good bye. I wish it was my novel
I'd been writing on all these pages.

W. M. T.

28.   TO KATE PERRY
OCTOBER 1851

Goodyear Catalogue, lot 321. One page, 12mo.

... Allez, je vous prie voir ma Dame, ma seule Dame, embrassez
la, dites qu'en donnant cette affreuse *lecture* je ne pensai qu'a la voir:
que toute la semaine (excepte un seul jour mercredi) j'ai rode autour
de sa maison esperant la voir — que de pres ou de loin je ne suis qu'a
clle toujours. Consolez, la chere amie et croyez en toute ma reconnais-
sance — C'est pour derouter le domestique j'ecri ce mauvais jargon.
Brulez ma lettre ...

29.   TO KATE PERRY
30 OCTOBER 1851

Goodyear Catalogue, lot 321. Two pages, 12mo.

My dear K. E. P.

... We have not had a reconciliation but a conciliation. Lady Ashburton was nobly kind ... The morning was spent in parleys and the
Inspector and I shook hands at the end and I'm very thankful that her
dear little heart is made tranquil on the source of our enmity at least.
Friends of course we're not; but bear each other, and in six months
things may be better. I think it is not he who is ill it is she, God bless
her. It gave me a pang to take his hand too so lean it has grown. But
thank God I've shaken it, and now Heaven speed her. . . .

W. M. T.

30.   TO MRS. ELLIOT AND KATE PERRY
NOVEMBER 1851

Lambert Catalogue, p. 54; *Goodyear Catalogue,* lot 321. Two pages, 12mo.
Thackeray meets Brookfield half-way when he attempts to apologize.

... It is not she who has been a traitress as I thought, nor has she
said more than she ought, and she's suffering more than I dare to think,

God bless her. He is full of queer ceremonies, punctilios unheard of amongst men of a franker sort. He clings to the fancy that nobody knows anything about his interior; and I shall of course hold my wagging tongue and speak of his affairs as little as possible. . . . The poor fellow likes mysteries, and when his wife was you know in what a condition insisted that nobody knew or saw the circumstance. God help him. I shall suffer the least of the three. But will it soothe my dear to know that I'm always here, and that I admire her, bless her, love her? I'll keep that light . . . though she mayn't be there to see it: and who knows but some day she may come again & knock at the door . . .

W. M. T.

31. TO KATE PERRY
DECEMBER 1851

Lambert Catalogue, p. 52; *Goodyear Catalogue*, lot 321. Two pages, 12mo.

. . . . [I] met a niece of Lady Scott's, a Mrs. Gregory who began sotto voce to deplore the state of the dear old ladies' minds, and their worldliness & fear about kingdom come. I said God made birds to sing in all sorts of ways, and we must not quarrel with the kindly old note of these — at w'ch Mrs. Gregory said 'Yes but there's one thing we ought all to sing.' So I didn't say why? as I could and perhaps should — But one hasn't the courage of one's opinions. And just before I went to see Walter Scott's old house, and the famous back parlour who should there be with his writing before him too, tranquilly scribbling away but little Doctor Simpson, the obstetrician, you understand who had brought a little girl into the world just 10 minutes before and was settling down to his work quite calmly . . . So you see how life is agoing on ladies, how the old folks are bowled out and the grown pursue their business, and the young come squalling into the globe and so on & so on . . . The place is dangerous for flattery, that's the truth. Well, thank God there are some kind people who are pleased with my twopenny laurels: and God bless two of them . . .

W. M. T.

32. TO MRS. ELLIOT AND KATE PERRY
JANUARY 1852

Goodyear Catalogue, lot 321. Two pages, 12mo. Thackeray condoles with his friends on the death of Eliot Warburton, who had just lost his life on a burning ship.

33.   TO MRS. BROOKFIELD
                         OCTOBER 1852

Lambert Catalogue, p. 48; *Goodyear Catalogue*, lot 320. One page, 12mo.

Liverpool, Wednesday

...I cannot come to London till Sunday, when my dear dear sister
will be gone; for dear and sister she is to me however she may think it
her duty to style me, and I love and bless her always whether I am far
away or near...

W. M. T.

34.   TO MRS. ELLIOT AND KATE PERRY
                   8–10 NOVEMBER 1852

Lambert Catalogue, pp. 54–55. Two pages, 12mo.

...Now the greater part of the voyage is over, and we are within
70 miles of Cape Race; and we are not sick any more, and we talk to
one another pretty freely, everything is pretty nearly possible indeed
but writing. The ideas stagger about, all the desks and glasses jingle and
rattle; the sea-scape out of the window is now so [*sketch*] and then so
[*sketch*] (its not the least like the sea or the cabin window, or the
boat or anything) and I'm half sick in bending with my head over the
confounded quivering creaking table.... There is an awful superior
woman aboard, Mrs. Lowell with a clever husband, very pleasant....
Tell Higgins that canvas backed Dux cost 5 dollars a brace at Boston,
and that I wont pay so much, that's flat...

W. M. T.

35.   TO MRS. ELLIOT AND KATE PERRY
                    7 DECEMBER 1852

Lambert Catalogue, p. 55; *Goodyear Catalogue*, lot 321. Three pages, 8vo.

New York, Dec. 7, 1852

...It's nothing here but dollars and flattery; but I do not think it
harms my head as I keep in constant view that the people are always
exaggerating, and that I am not half such a swell in my own country
as they make me out here.... I don't intend to make a book. No. No.
The goose is much too good a goosey to be killed. In fact I'm looking

ahead, and my dear friends must help me. I've been here and there in the 'Upper Ten' world [21] but not much. It's the most curious varnish of Civilization. The girls are dressed like the most stunning French actresses, the houses furnished like the most splendid gambling houses. It's all gold and yellow brocade and the little dandies are like little French shop boys, and the houses are all so new that the walls are not even papered, and on the walls in the midst of the hangings of brocade and the enormous gold frames and mirrors you see little twopenny pictures and colored prints. . . . The jolly manner answers here very well, which I have from Nature or Art possibly, and the Press and I, with the exception of the Herald which abuses me like anythink, are the best of friends. You should have heard how Bancroft flattered them all at a Press Dinner the other day. There were 30 present, and they made as many speeches, in every one of which they fired a great thundering compliment point blank at me. I didn't flatter a word in reply actually, nor do the cordial business like Dickens . . . God bless you my d. k. f. and kiss a dear sweet lady for me. . . .

36.   TO MRS. ELLIOT AND KATE PERRY
            13–15 JULY 1853

Lambert Catalogue, p. 56; *Goodyear Catalogue*, lot 321. Eight pages, 16mo.

Baden Baden, Wednesday, July 13
. . . I don't remember the day these 10 years when I have felt so much at ease. And this helps me write too. Three days ago I broke ground with the new book and have done 2 days work ever since upon it. . . . I know who I wish was with me. God almighty bless her and make her happy, dearest, fondest, & truest women. . . . It's a great comfort to want no books & nothing but fresh ink and a good pen & paper. . . . [The Newcomes] goes pretty well . . . not so high-toned or so carefully finished as Esmond but that you see was a failure besides being immoral. We must take pains and write careful books when we have made the 10000 for the young ladies . . . Lord, Lord, how much better this is than being in London! We have a little wickedness here too. I have already lost 5 Napoleons at roulette. . . . I have been reading Don Quixote and Tacitus in French and part of the latter in Latin — the deuce is in it if my style does not improve from the study of these great authors. . . . This is Friday morning, and by all the powers I am waiting for breakfast again. Haven't I got a sweet temper? Mustn't the girls be very insubordinate. Well, they and I get up when we wake.

[21] See above, III, 684.

A deal of sleep seems to suit the family; and of all God's gifts I doubt whether that isn't one of the best . . .

W. M. T.

37. TO MRS. ELLIOT AND KATE PERRY
28–31 JULY 1853

Lambert Catalogue, p. 56; *Goodyear Catalogue*, lot 321. Four pages, 12mo.

Vevey, Switzerland, July 28–31

. . . There was a corner of the carriage that of course I often filled up with Somebody, who has a place in her coach too I know for me, whether I fill it or not, and there may be a dozen of children in that carriage, and a poor old Inspector too . . . yet I know there's always a place in it occupied by one W. M. T. . . . The novel is getting on apace, and I shall have done a couple of numbers by the end of the month. Anny is amused, who writes a good deal of it to dictation, a good sign. Mr. Pendennis is the author of the book, and he has taken a great weight off my mind, for under that mask and acting, as it were, I can afford to say and think many things that I couldn't venture on in my own person, now that it is a person, and I know the public are staring at it. I can't talk to folks in Inns, etc. for that reason of my uncontrolable modesty, and wish to the deuce I were not a public character. The Americans have quite conquered Switzerland and the Rhine districts, and the Hotels are as the Astor House. How pretty almost all of the women are; and the men how awful! . . . I think I have spent as pleasant a fortnight as ever I have had in my life, plenty of work, play, health, money, good children. What could man ask for more? Only one thing that he can't have. That one thing everybody hankers after, no doubt . . .

W. M. T.

38. TO THE REV. WILLIAM BROOKFIELD
24 SEPTEMBER 1853

Lambert Catalogue, p. 49; *Goodyear Catalogue*, lot 320. Two pages, 12mo. Thackeray sends a box of cigars.[22]

Sept. 24

. . . When I was ill the other day I made a sort of will in which I begged you and Fitzgerald to act as a sort of guardians to the children,

---

[22] In the box of cigars which accompanied this letter Thackeray enclosed the following note: "My dear Wm. I send you these for the sake of old and constant friendship" (*Goodyear Catalogue*, lot 320).

and that you'd have them every year to stay with you and your dear
wife. . . . God bless you both now after 2 years asunder, when there
are no more rages on my part, I pray you to forget savage words as I
do (for I don't remember what I said or wrote only that a great deal
of it was furious and unjust). Forget all this if you can and remember
the friend of old days. I shant say anything more, and don't want you
to say anything. . . .

W. M. T.

39.   TO MRS. ELLIOT AND KATE PERRY
                    OCTOBER 1853

Lambert Catalogue, pp. 56–57; *Goodyear Catalogue*, lot 321. Four pages, 12mo.
Thackeray notes that he has settled for the time in Paris and writes at some length
of his mother before turning to the Brookfields.

Paris, Thursday

. . . Dear J. whom I have seen in London, but always with the
children & in the company of the poor Inspector who tries his best to
smother his hatred of me — only Jack in the box comes rushing out
again . . . I remember a passage of a novel called Esmond w'ch says
when E. thought of the splendour and purity of his dear mistress's love,
the thought of it smote him on to his knees.[23] I Behold that beautiful
constancy with wonder & thanks to God — with such a feeling as one
looks at the Alps or the stars in Heaven. . . . I admire human nature
in thinking of her. I think I am nearer to her when away than when
sitting by her, talking of things we don't feel — with poor Tomkin's
restless eye ever and again trying not to look at us. It's happier that
we should love each other in the grave, as it were, than that we should
meet by sham-chance, and that there should be secrets or deceit. When
you see her preach this to her again and again. Many and many a time
a friend of mine whispers me (he is represented in pictures with horns
and a tail), 'My good friend *a quoi bon* all this longing and yearning
and disappointment; yonder gnawing grief and daily nightly brooding?
A couple of lies and the whole thing might be remedied. Do you suppose other folks are so particular?' Behold there are 4 children put
their innocent figures between the devil and me; and the wretched old
fiend shirks off with his tail between his hoofs. Go and wipe away her
tears, you dear kind sisters of charity. My girls I suppose see all about
it; but they love her all the same. . . . When I was in England I went
and reconciled myself with Mrs. Procter (only those pitchers when

[23] Thackeray is apparently alluding to *Works*, VII, 195.

mended wont hold water any more) and with Higgins who had been offended too, at my not going to him; and paid dutiful visits to all my step-father's relatives and my own; and bought a pretty house, 36 Onslow Square, Brompton, next door to Marochetti; and am to pay for it in 3 years, £700 a year or thereabouts. Whether we go to Rome or not is now undetermined, most likely not. I had some talk with another publisher about doing another kind of work, editing Walpole and writing a life of him. It rains money with me. I may make £5000 in the next year, think of that! . . .

40.   TO MRS. ELLIOT AND KATE PERRY
                          16 FEBRUARY 1854

Lambert Catalogue, p. 57; *Goodyear Catalogue*, lot 321. Four pages, 8vo.

Naples, Feb. 16

. . . For the last 6 weeks, ill as I was, I worked every day, getting up before light, think of that, and scribbling till mid-day. I want to get the book finished. Who knows what may happen. One, two three, severe attacks of my old complaint, and not from any excess this time. . . . If I could shake off the Newcomes I think I should be all the better. But they pursue me: and bother — Stop — thou blabbing egotist! I wonder if by taking to the upright hand I shall write in a better humour . . . ah, me — perpendicular or slantingdicular all comes to the same thing. . . . I must take to politics when I have done Newcomes and the next set of lectures for America; and then in 1855, give up rambling. If I last 2 or 3 more years they will be provided against the day of departure. . . . I made the acquaintance of no ends of converts at Rome, but I don't think they did much to convert the present miserable sinner who writes. How wonderful the works of nature are, which provides men with a traitte that can swallow all those enormous legends! I have been reading various new works. Lockhart's Life of Scott, Boswell's Life of Johnson, Rome under Augustus,[24] and Saint Paul's Epistles. I have done the best part of a Child's Fairy Tale for next Xmas, and the Newcomes up to almost June next. . . . I had nobody at Rome that I care for except Adelaide Sartoris, who is one of the best of creatures, but you know there must always be a little comedy in any intimacy in that quarter. I learned to admire but not to endure Fanny Kemble . . .

W. M. T.

[24] *History of the later Roman Commonwealth from the end of the Second Punic War to the Death of Julius Caesar; and of the Reign of Augustus: with a Life of Trajan* (1845) by Thomas Arnold (1795–1842), republished from *The Encyclopædia Metropolitana*.

41.   TO KATE PERRY
                       25 MARCH 1854

Lambert Catalogue, pp. 57–58, where the date is given, apparently from the postmark; *Goodyear Catalogue*, lot 321. Four pages, 8vo.

My dear K. E. P.

... It has been the decree of Allah that the writer of this his slave should undergo many tribulations in this region. I had two severe attacks of illness at Rome and have been visited here with [an]other two. Add to which the girls have had the scarletina, and I leave you to fancy how pleasant our sojourn here has been. ... Two days since, in the early, early morning, looking out of the window on Capri yonder [*watercolor sketch*] and the beautiful, beautiful rosy-tinted nature; I was thinking of the girls convalescing, and asleep close by; and of that day 15 years ago when their little sister died at sunrise. O you sweet and bitter thoughts. ... All my private art business at Rome was an utter failure. ... Art turned away her countenance or I did not dare to interrogate her. But there is very little Art thats the fact — not that great blustering hulking Colosseum for instance, nor those simpering Canovas, sickly Guidos, swaggering Caracci — only bits here and there. I went yesterday to see the Farnese Hercules made by Glykon the Athenian as he announces at the foot of the Statue and Glykon has been passed as you know, as well as the Statue, for a stunning fine fellow. O the great coarse bumptious old braggart! Playing a smart piece on the piano, or cutting a neat figure of 8 on the Serpentine, or writing a Review, are really as good as that thumping piece of Skill. There are avenues of worthless marble and canvass here and at Rome. ... I have bought some old English paper marked 1837, made when we were tolerably young people, and its such a comfort to write on, with an old fashioned quill. But I ought to be writing No. XI and XII of the New-comes,[25] Miss — and though the first volume is rather slow, I promise you the second shall have plenty of interesting business in it ...

                       W. M. T.

[25] Chapters 33 to 38, published for August and September, 1854.

42.   TO KATE PERRY
                       19 JULY 1855

Lambert Catalogue, p. 58; *Goodyear Catalogue*, lot 321. Three pages, 8vo.

Hombourg, July 19, 1855

... The dear old soul [*Thackeray's mother*] made me pass thirty miserable hours, and kept me awake a night and gave me a headache — What, won't this other, wise saint of a woman ever cease to stab and wound me? ... When you are married, when you have a beautiful only son, when you are a widow, why then, take care and don't marry again — for you can't hold the son & the husband too; & from wishing to have too much love at a time, you may lose what once was secure. If I married a widow I don't think I could be heartily fond of her children, and these, if good little dears, ought never to forgive their mother for loving their step-papa. No if ever I marry I will have an artless young virgin — who doesn't know the ways of the world, who never flirted with any other party, whose character is all simplicity, and whose young affection should be all mine. ...

Miss, very few pictures or statties are worth a pin. After dangling for hours about the Exposition at Paris I came to that conclusion irrevocably. So and so, this portrait or that landscape is very nice; but apres? Bon Dieu what's the use of doing them? Say you can copy trees or human faces skilfully, well? Say you can black boots, or make puddings, or turn gimcracks at a lathe, why not? Nothing is so overrated as the Fine Arts. ... Its pleasant though, in Sidney Smith,[26] to get glimpses of the old Whig society — of the folks only just dead and gone. That book would make a good lecture wouldn't it? to repeople Holland House, to revivify the old Edinburgh Review clique, to light up again the poor dear old dead lights in Curzon Street and set the kind old souls talking round the hissing silver cauldron. Rise up again out of limbo ye three old bodies! Lift up the grave stone with thy nose Foley! Pluck the sword out of thy ribs and come from behind the arras old Polonius! ...

[26] Lady Holland's *Memoir of Sydney Smith* (1855).

43.   TO MRS. ELLIOT AND KATE PERRY
                     22 OCTOBER 1855

Elliot Catalogue, p. 88. Two pages, 8vo.

                                        Oct. 22, 1855

... This day week I think it was we passed Cape Clear — The
week has seemed about a year. It has been awfully stupid; it has blown
every way, soft, hard, very hard, in our teeth, in our stern;[27] the sea
has been mountings high; it has not been sick that is the present heroic
Nelson has not except once a very little in the midst of a very little shiv-
ering fit....[28]

Shall I give you sarcastic accounts of my fellow passengers. Of that
confounded old Massachusetts? ex-lady school mistress who talks platitudes all dinner and breakfast and tea and lunch too only I don't go
there ... No, we won't make fun of the passengers — we are too old
to care for those jokes — what do we care that some of the Americans
are not over refined; the Germans very greedy especially that broot
who sits opposite and I declare has taken pork and currant jelly, cucum-
bers and oil and vinegar, all with the same knife. There are Jews of
Poland and Almayne who are both odious and amusing — but at our
age with our matured politeness, these details become insignificant and
disagreeable even. Heaven bless the man! Why has he nothing to
say? ...

What a comfort it is that women in our country are unlike the women
of this and are comfortable and pleasant to look at [for] years — this
is suggested by a wizened old American hag of 35 who passes — she was
a beauty 15 years ago (suppose the wind should blow this paper to her
and her husband or she pick it up and read it? Lor!) We remain
quite good looking up to 50, 60, 70 don't we? Time doesn't hurt the
dear kind old faces....

                     W. M. T.

[27] *Elliot Catalogue* reads *starn.*
[28] *Elliot Catalogue* reads *bit.*

44.   TO MRS. ELLIOT AND KATE PERRY
                      30–31 OCTOBER 1855

Elliot Catalogue, p. 88. Four pages, 8vo.

                                    Clarendon Hotel, N. Y.
                                    30–31 October, 1855

. . . won't you like to hear that all the seats are taken for the lectures
— and that we shall repeat them D. V. about 4 times in and about
New York in the month of November. Mesdames the dollars will begin
to rain again — the way in wh they go on here about the Newcomes
makes my eyes wink with surprize I mean. You have no idea what a
big dog I am voted by some. Doctor Kane [29] who is come back from
his Arctic expedition says he watched one of his sailors for hours poring
over a book in the endless night and lo it was Pendennis. . . .

    O but last night I had such a narrow escape from awful danger!
I tremble now when I tell you — I live on the 3rd floor — came in
late from a remarkably good dinner at Delmonico's, took my key and
went to my sitting-room, pulled off my boots and began to undress.
When lo and behold — a voice from the bedroom within sweetly cried
out Georgey! I had got into the second floor room by mistake — I
dashed out of the place gathering my garments together — it's a mercy
I'm here upon the third floor. How kind people are here; I am affected
by their friendliness and affte. welcome. Sunday dining with Mrs.
Baxter — the good soul brings out a bottle of brandy peachs wh I
had liked and eaten on the last day I was here — and she put them
away and kept them till my return — they choked me somehow . . . An
old gentleman at dinner yesterday told me a story about George III wh
made me cry. Willis [30] his Dr. took charge of him on the express condition that his remedy was never to be divulged.[31] He said to Q. Charlotte he would kill her if she told what had passed — what had passed
was that he was flogged like a nigger. . . .

                                    W. M. T.

[29] *Elliot Catalogue* reads *Kahn.*
[30] Dr. Francis Willis (1718–1807), who attended George III during his first
attack of madness.
[31] *Elliot Catalogue* reads *devulged.*

45.   TO MRS. ELLIOT AND KATE PERRY
20 NOVEMBER 1855

Elliot Catalogue, p. 89. Three pages, 8vo.

Clarendon, New York,
Nov. 20

. . . The lectures are going better and better — the people like them better as they begin to understand about them. Papers that were hostile are now pretty complimentary. What matters provided the dollars pour in and the knowing ones are satisfied?

. . . The war news from England has set us all in a fine flurry. Something tells me I shan't be so very long away from that island. O to go back again, and see folks, won't it be pleasant?

. . . The girls I hear from my mother are well and busy and happy. I dare say rest for his brain will do their old father good — this turmoil in wh one lives perforce here occupies the body but not the head; and please God the 5 or 6 months holy day will refresh the present giant and set him going for another good spell of work, the Georges will make a pretty 2 volumes of easy occupation and tittle-tattle gathering wh I can do when I come home. O home, how sweet you'll be!

W. M. T.

46.   TO MRS. ELLIOT
1? JANUARY 1856

Elliot Catalogue, p. 90. One page, 8vo. "From New York, with New Years greetings, thanks for a letter, and a newspaper cutting about himself."

. . . Thank you for yours my dear kind J. E. I hear your kind voice and others tollarollably well remembered and are they not sweet to the wandering youth? Here we are flourishing just as elsewhere — prodigious audience last night. . . . and such a night to come to lectures! I could hardly get to my cab so slippery was it across the pavement. . . .

W. M. T.

47.   TO MRS. ELLIOT AND KATE PERRY
                        NOVEMBER 1856

Elliot Catalogue, p. 92. Two pages, 8vo. "About his lectures which were being
very successful at Glasgow."

                                        3, Randolph Crescent, Edinburgh
. . . It isn't a bad profession is it? to be feasted every day to have to
work an hour per diem and get £150 or £200 at the end of the week!
. . . I see I must play this play out and take in the odd harvest wh. seems
springing up every day at my feet. Why the girls will be little heiresses
if we go on in this way. Let us not be vain nor over proud, but be
thankful for what God sends us. . . .
                              W. M. T.

48.   TO MRS. ELLIOT AND KATE PERRY
                        2 DECEMBER 1856

Lambert Catalogue, p. 59. Eight pages, 12mo.

                              Station Hotel, Hull, Monday, Dec. 2, 1856
. . . I finished at Dumfries on Saturday night in a funny little theatre
crammed full of kind people, the night before I had more than 3000
people in the City Hall at Glasgow (but a miscreant society makes all
the profits), the night before that was in a church at Paisley, the night
before that farewell at Edinburgh — and perhaps I am going [on] a
fresh Scottish campaign. It agrees with me wonderfully, the ceaseless
racket. Don't you see how I am going back to my natural old handwriting, and giving up that mean literary man's fist? Let this go on,
and one more novel, and we absolutely shall be INDEPENDENT.
Hip Hip Hurray. . . . All the time at Edinburgh was spent at J. Blackwood's house — the most hospitable and magnificent inn I ever put up
in — the company not altogether so polished as Sir Charles Grandison
or David Dundas,[32] but good shrewd fellows, the 4 Blackwood brothers
liking each other hugely and sitting jovially together night after night
over bottle after bottle of the most prodigious good claret. . . . At Paisely
Mr. Peter Coats, the great thread-maker, entertained me. You never
saw such splendor. The Duchess of Sutherland's room was nothing to

---

[32] Sir David Dundas (1799-1877), liberal statesman, Privy Councillor, Q. C.,
and bencher of the Inner Temple.

the best bed room. We had 16 to dinner at 6, and eighteen to supper at 10, none of your kickshaws but regular ham and turkey, and all this splendid succession of victualing administered by one maid and a hired waiter to whom Charles graciously condescended to give a little aid. These kind simple people are worth a million of money I daresay and keep 1100 girls working in their factory at thread. I saw the girls, and healthy, jolly, kindly girls they looked. All with good characters, so says Mr. Peter Coats, and why should I doubt about 1100 virgins? ...

W. M. T.

49.   TO MRS. ELLIOT
               6 DECEMBER 1856

Lambert Catalogue, pp. 59–60. Eight pages, 12mo. Thackeray "devotes three pages to a description of his aged mother and querulous stepfather, another to a humorous idea of a funeral pile for Mrs. Elliot."

Hull, Saturday, 6 December

. . . I am glad I am roaming about, and seeing new people, and new aspects of the world. This is a mean ugly petty place but there's very good company in it. The ceremony dinner of 20 was awfully bad to be sure and John upset a glass of Port accurately into my sleeve, but the dinner of leg of mutton with Dr. Cooper (Sir Henry Cooper he is called, having been mayor and knighted last year) was pleasant, and there was a very pleasant and well educated Jew, who has some '20 port which we are going to drink on Sunday . . .

W. M. T.

50.   TO MRS. ELLIOT AND KATE PERRY
               DECEMBER 1856

Lambert Catalogue, p. 60. One page, 12mo.

...With the deepest grief I take my new scissors and cut out [of] my paper at breakfast the following awful SMASHER for yours truly. [*Clipping*] I am picked up again, however, wiped clean and set on my feet by the Bradford paper. [*Clipping*] But the Manchester paper has the most luminous and elegant account of all. [*Clipping*] ...

51. TO KATE PERRY
1856?

Lambert Catalogue, p. 59; *Goodyear Catalogue,* lot 321. Four pages, 12mo.

Saturday

Mademoiselle

... By going to call on my friends in Chesham Place and by the easy pace of the cabman afterwards I was exactly 1/2 a minute too late for the train yesterday, so, after letting off a quantity of the steam of wrath (I mean wicked oaths, cusses at cabmen and naughty igspressions which relieve anger) I concluded to come by a later train. . . .

[*Mrs. Brookfield had evidently threatened to become a Catholic, and of this Thackeray writes:*] She is a woman quite capable of skipping into a Chapel, popping into a confessional before a priest who would hear her, sooth her, absolve her, baptise her and send her home engaged to Catholicism before she knew where she was; and then she would tell her husband; and then it would be bon jour; and away would go Magdalene and Arthur and the Inspector in one cab; and she in another to Our Lady of Sorrows and two guineas a week for her board; and good-by to the children, and to friends whom she loves as a sister, and to those who have loved her as women are not loved every day. I can see Aubrey de Vere [33] coming in with his sanctified smirk to visit her afterwards and the rest of the shavelings coaxing and squeezing her hand and giving her precious conversation and dainty little penances, and making much of her. . . .

W. M. T.

52. TO MRS. ELLIOT AND KATE PERRY
8 MARCH 1857

Elliot Catalogue, pp. 92 and 94. Four pages, 8vo.

March 8, 1857

... This dissolution will play havoc with my money schemes and nobody will care for lectures when there will be so much spouting at General Elections. Never mind we shall only be a little longer amassing the money — And the consciousness of this quack profession oppresses me daily more and more. Haven't I got enough? Can't I come off the

[33] Aubrey Thomas De Vere (1814–1902), the Catholic poet.

stage and write a book with perfect ease of mind? Well — But that is no excuse, my profession is honester than other folks — honester than you partizan-shouters on the Lorcha question [34] — whose unanimity on one side and the other shocks me — And Lord John's opposition shocks me too. I see personal motives actuating all of them — and — well this is as you say uncommonly stupid, . . .

53.   TO KATE PERRY
              24 MARCH 1857

Lambert Catalogue, p. 61; *Goodyear Catalogue*, lot 321. One page, 12mo.

                                        Inverness, 24th

  . . . If there is anyone Miss Perry knows who wishes to know about anybody Else and Anybody else remembers Anyone this is to say that Anybody else is in pretty good health and spirits and always thinks about Anyone at this season of the year [35] . . .

54.   TO MRS. ELLIOT AND KATE PERRY
                    MARCH 1857

Elliot Catalogue, p. 92. One page, 8vo. "Apologizing for not keeping an engagement — he had to stay and be feasted in Edinburgh, having had one of his attacks and been unable to keep a prior appointment."

  . . . Goodbye, mes bonnes — and its O but I am getting tired of this wandering work.

                      W. M. T.

[34] The lorcha *Arrow*, commanded by a British master and possessing a colonial register, was anchored off Canton on October 8, 1856, when she was boarded by a party of imperial soldiers, who seized twelve of the fourteen Chinese members of her crew. The British Consul being unable to secure redress from the Viceroy, a ship of the Royal Navy on October 27 bombarded Canton, and part of the city was soon in British hands. The question of whether Lord Palmerston's colonial representative had been too hasty in his recourse to force, as the conservatives and Lord John Russell charged, became an important parliamentary issue early in 1857. (*Times*, January–February, 1857)
[35] Mrs. Brookfield's birthday was on March 25.

55.
TO KATE PERRY
4 AUGUST 1859

Lambert Catalogue, p. 60; *Goodyear Catalogue,* lot 321. Two pages, 12mo.

36 Onslow Sq., 4 August

. . . All day to-day I have been taking a spell at the Virginians, and now it's late, isn't it? and I must dress and go out with the girls. . . . You must know that we go to Brighton where I have taken a house, 126 Marine Parade, for the old folks and the young ones. I shall come backwards and forwards, and be here chiefly I think being bent upon doing a great stroke of work, and having all my books and appliances here about me. . . .

W. M. T.

56.
TO MRS. BROOKFIELD
[1846–1851]

Lambert Catalogue, p. 49. One page, 12mo.

. . . I have got a ticket for the National Concerts . . . and am going to take the young ones to hear the Berlin Singers . . .

W. M. T.

57.
TO MRS. BROOKFIELD
[1848–1850]

Goodyear Catalogue, lot 320. Four lines. Thackeray sends Mrs. Brookfield a seal by Harry Hallam.

. . . I wished to say God Almighty bless the wearer and keep the giver in his love and his duty . . .

58.
TO MRS. BROOKFIELD
[1848–1851]

Lambert Catalogue, p. 49. One page, 12mo.

. . . It is very good for some people to scold servants, and make pickles and puddings, and a woman may be very good and charming who does the latter; but there's a fitness of things, and I hope you won't be too much of a housekeeper as yet . . .

59.   TO MRS. BROOKFIELD
[1848–1851]

Lambert Catalogue, p. 49. One page, 12mo. Thackeray informs Mrs. Brookfield that he cannot take her to the Roman Paragon because he must be at a club to vote for a man he has seconded.

60.   TO MRS. BROOKFIELD
[1848–1851]

Lambert Catalogue, p. 49. Two pages, 12mo. In French. Thackeray expresses in most affectionate terms his love for Mrs. Brookfield's *"sainte figure".*

61.   TO MRS. BROOKFIELD
[1849–1851]

Lambert Catalogue, p. 49. Two pages, 12mo. In French. Thackeray asks Mrs. Brookfield to accompany him on a visit to Lady Ashburton.

62.   TO MRS. ELLIOT
[1847–1859]

Goodyear Catalogue, lot 321. One page, 12mo. Thackeray declines an invitation to dinner.

My dear, no, I beg your pardon, Dear Mrs. Elliot

 . . . But I wonder whether you would give me a cup of tea tonight. I shall ride by. A signal in the window, a flower-pot in the balcony, a scarf waved from a casement would suffice to confer hope and happiness . . . on one who is now disappointed and desolate indeed. . . .

63.   TO MRS. ELLIOT
              24 JANUARY [1848–1859]

Goodyear Catalogue, lot 321. One page, 12mo. *Endorsed:* The last I ever received
from my dear friend W. Thackeray.

Madame.

   . . . I have the honour to inform you that there will be read this
evening at the Geographical Society a paper on 'THE ISTHMUS OF
KRAW'. As a man I have long known and esteemed him; [36] that he
laid claim to be an Isthmus I never knew before. I beg you to accept my
sincere congratulations upon this additional honour w'ch has been conferred on your distinguished relative, and am Your most humble servant,
Turn Over.
   [*On the other side of the sheet Thackeray has written:*] Now please
turn back again.

64.   TO MRS. ELLIOT AND KATE PERRY
                   [1847–1859]

Lambert Catalogue, p. 61. One page, 12mo. Thackeray writes of the illness of
his maid.

65.   TO KATE PERRY
                   [1847–1863]

Goodyear Catalogue, lot 321. One page, 8vo.

My dear K. E. P.
   . . . I have got all Mr. Punch to dinner today: isn't it pleasant? . . .
                   W. M. Thack

  [36] Presumably John Crawfurd, a voluminous writer on geographical and eth-
nological subjects. See above, No. 1439.

APPENDIX XXVII

FORGED THACKERAY LETTERS

For many years a forger operated in London who made a remunerative specialty of Thackeray autographs. Since he had access to channels through which authentic letters passed and since, as Lady Ritchie remarked, his simulation of Thackeray's writing was "distressingly clever", his work has generally been accepted as genuine. There are few large collections of Thackerayana that do not contain at least one letter from his hand.[1]

Yet his forgeries should not deceive any careful student of Thackeray's correspondence. His imitation of Thackeray's writing, which is confined to the upright hand, is nearly perfect letter by letter, but his letters are smaller and more crabbed than their prototypes, and his lines are run more closely together than is Thackeray's custom. Thackeray's letters appear to be (as they nearly always were) first drafts; the forger's efforts are laboriously careful copies of texts set before him. If the reader will compare the facsimile of a characteristic forged autograph which appears opposite the next page with the reproduction of Thackeray's letter of 29 February–4 March 1856 which serves as the frontispiece to Volume III of this edition, he should acquire a sense of the difference between the two hands.

The forger also betrays himself in other ways. He had no clear conception of the years during which Thackeray lived at his several London residences, and he consequently dates letters from Kensington when Thackeray was living in Brompton, and vice versa. Not knowing that London was divided into postal districts only in 1858, he employs such anachronistic dates as "Kensington, W. Wednesday, December 9, 1841" and "Kensington, W., August 7th, 1850". He appears to have been ignorant of the existence of perpetual calendars, for he rarely makes the day of the month in his chosen year correspond to the proper day of the week.

But the forger gives himself away most completely in the content of his letters. His facetiousness is painful, his sentiment is inane, and his general observations are invariably the most insipid platitudes. Having no real knowledge of Thackeray's life, he exercises such care in avoiding specific references to persons and events as to make many of his shorter

---

[1] Attention was first called to his activities in "Thackeray's Autographs", *Saturday Review*, LVIII (1884), 692–693.

notes almost unintelligible. He was apparently aware of these deficiencies, for most of his longer letters are made up of quotations or summaries of historical data, a device that allows him to evade (however implausibly) the insuperable difficulty of imitating Thackeray's thought and style.

There are photostats of some twenty examples of the forger's work in the Harvard College Library.

Saturday

Dear Ned

I am positively surprised at you. I am indeed. What do you mean by "they are so common", and "only buttercups and red clover to see"? I suggest a ramble over our delightful Surrey hills, and you throw cold water on the suggestion. Only buttercups, only clover! That confounded little adverb was never invented before the fall of man, I will affirm. There is nothing "common" in nature, my friend: be sure of that.

Common! Yes (and you in a sense are right, I must own) that is just the wonder of it, that such dazzling brilliancy, such richness of colour should be spread, poured even to waste where there were none to value or even admire! I have seen a distant meadow on a cloudy day, which appeared to be basking in a flood of golden sunshine — wh. was, in fact, basking in a sunshine of golden buttercups — an "effect" more exquisite than any picture ever painted by the hand of man; and wh. was only ~~equalled~~ equalled by a patch of deep, pure rose-colour, looking as though a sunset cloud had fallen on the steep brown side of the rugged hill where it lay, and would fade away again when morning came. It was not a sunset cloud: it was "only clover", as you would say. Get rid of such ideas as quickly as you can, for they are as absurd as they are untrue.

I am glad — very glad — to learn that "you two" have "made a match of it: and happy to think you are so fond of each other. Buttercups are very beautiful: —

Sweet are those flowers I despair to describe,
Beauteous their bright hue, in springs bright sun;
Yet not so sweet, or beauteous, as the dream.
Of love that melts two spirits into one!

Ever thine,
W M Thackeray

A FORGED THACKERAY LETTER

APPENDIX XXVIII

THE MEDICAL HISTORY OF WILLIAM MAKEPEACE THACKERAY

A perusal of Thackeray's voluminous correspondence reveals a series of nervous and physical complaints that complicated and at times dominated the greater part of his life. These ranged from ordinary accidents and minor illnesses to chronic organic diseases of major importance. That his life should have been exceedingly full of literary and social activity merely emphasizes the capacity of his genius and the intensity of a spirit that could override so many disabilities. He was by nature temperamental, like most artists; his bodily ailments were aggravated by anxiety and emotional pressure and by uncontrolled conviviality. His letters reveal with rather amazing insight and frankness the influence of his habits and tensions on his somatic (physical) complaints and provide a colorful background for an analysis of his numerous symptoms. In turn, there can be little doubt of the effect of his symptoms in influencing his moods and his work. Although serious organic disease was an almost constantly recurring accompaniment of the latter third of his life, an equally important component of Thackeray's ill health can be attributed to intemperate eating and drinking and neurotic disturbances. Interest in the exact diagnosis of his various ailments must remain somewhat speculative, because of the lack of precise information, but, for the most part, detailed descriptions of various symptoms gleaned from his letters render a fairly adequate analysis quite within the realm of possibility.[1]

As a young man he seems to have been endowed with good general health and of normal physical build. His habits, even while

[1] See Index under "Health" and especially I: 17, 21n., 24, 26, 79, 81, 126, 191, 468; II: 40, 97, 112, 148, 346, 677, 678; III: 426, 469; IV: 25, 78, 142. Significant information appears in the recollections of contemporaries, e.g., John Cordy Jeaffreson, *A Book of Recollections*, I, 258–259, 299–301; and Richard Bedingfield, in *Cassell's Magazine* II, vol. 30, p. 105.

at Charterhouse School, where he was described as a rosy-faced, stout, broad-set boy, were sedentary. A suggestion as to future tendencies is to be found in the statement that he was "gustative." As a boy he had erysipelas, and throughout his life had numerous upper respiratory infections, sore throats, and at least one attack designated as "illfluelza." Dental caries and abscesses common to his generation were frequently noted, and are not surprising in view of the prevailing lack of good dental hygiene and his intemperate eating habits. Eventually dentures were necessary at the age of forty-eight, but not until he had suffered from many toothaches and "swelled chops" which at times prevented him from chewing properly.

While at Charterhouse School (aet. 14–17) he first describes severe headaches which were undoubtedly of nervous origin and seem to have been directly associated with the persecutions of a rigid headmaster, who treated him "with manifest unkindness and injustice," and with examinations. These headaches at times were so severe as to require the application of leeches. In later years headaches appear to have frequently accompanied overwork or overindulgence. Thus he mentions headaches due to prolonged writing and a severe attack "after Dickens's ball" (1848). At times his headache was a "cursed" one, which prevented him "from working to any advantage." Associated visual disturbances are suggested at times, and the possibility of migraine is not particularly unlikely.

More prominent, however, is the complaint of "bowowels" or frank digestive disturbances that runs throughout his communications to family and friends like a constant theme. These stomach and intestinal difficulties seem to have been due, in large part, to extreme dietary indiscretions and intemperance in the use of alcohol. Constant reference is made to these two habits, and at times Thackeray flagellates himself for his indiscretions and resulting physical unhappiness but without any lasting success in correcting his acknowledged faults.

Purgation followed innumerable digestive upsets, and the frequent use of calomel, salts, colocynth, magnesia, podophyllin, and similar drugs, recalls the popular remedies of the time and emphasizes the fact that Thackeray's normal functions were constantly upset by irregular habits, overeating, overdrinking, anxiety, and fatigue. At seventeen he first records that he felt very ill and took calomel and salts for relief. In 1832 (aet. 21) he notes a merry party after which he went to bed with "a couple of pills in my internals" while others finished up the feast. In 1842 (aet. 31) he is sorry "as how shouldn't a man be who has a taste for Portwine and good company?" A year later he comments that he went out to dinner every day in the week and adds, "This racket agrees better with me than a quieter life." But remorse returned with physical discomfort, and he noted the "usual feverish symptoms in the morning," following a dinner at Parke's, and remarked, "Can't I for Heaven's sake, be moderate?" In 1850 he left "town and its fleshpots" for the Continent, and saw Dieppe "only . . . with such bilious eyes as a man deserves who dines out every day of his life." "I had exactly 4 times as much wine as was good for me and woke sick and ill and have been ill & sick ever since." He affirmed later that he was wrong in drinking too much and keeping too late hours, yet his awareness of this fault did not keep him from repeatedly landing in a "bed of sickdess" as he did in 1855 after the Lord Mayor's dinner and "the whiskey & water afterwards." He described himself as a "two bottle man" and as one who behaved "like a schoolboy at a Christmas feast, eating everything that is offered to me, everything that comes my way. The season plays the devil with me, because I dine out a great deal, and I am in no sense my own master at any dinner-table but my own, and even at my own table I can't control my wicked appetite, when I am entertaining a lot of people." After a severe attack of cramps and "spasms" in 1857 (aet. 46), he was asked if he had taken the best medical advice. Thackeray said that he had, "but what is the use of advice if you don't follow it? . . . They tell me not to drink, and I *do* drink. They tell me not to smoke, and I *do* smoke. They tell me not to eat, and I *do* eat. In short, I do everything that I am desired not to do, and, therefore, what am I to expect?"

It is highly probable that this lack of control was in part due to a sense of insecurity and intense loneliness following his wife's mental deterioration, which completely deprived him of her company and affection only four years after their marriage. This terrible calamity must have driven him to seek solace in food, drink, and social pleasures to escape from that which "makes my heart sick to be parted from her." His grief at times overwhelmed him, and "every now and then," writes Thackeray, "turns up something . . . which knocks me quite down and makes me cry like a child. I get melancholy, too, being with the children." As his acquaintance Jeaffreson wrote, "In truth, everything that was gravely irregular and hurtful in Thackeray's way of living, from the close of 1840 to the year of his death was mainly referable to his conjugal bereavement. Had his marriage afforded him for twenty-five years the same measure of felicity which it yielded him before the first manifestations of his wife's nervous failure, Thackeray might and doubtless would still have been rather too fond of gaiety and good cheer, but his wife's influence would have preserved him from the habits of gustatory self-indulgence, which resulted in the physical disorders that eventually deprived the world of his splendid genius."

At the age of thirty-eight he suffered from an acute febrile episode that very nearly caused his death. It was variously diagnosed as "cholera," "gastric fever," "bilious fever," and "intermittent fever," and for a month he was critically ill. Following a long convalescence at Brighton he recovered, but it may be said that his health was definitely impaired from then on. An exact diagnosis is not possible, but it is highly probable that this illness was caused by typhoid fever, a malady that was all too common at this particular period.

As early as 1840 (aet. 29) Thackeray wrote of a condition which caused him untold suffering until his death in 1863. He mentioned that "As soon as I see myself decently in the way of making money & have had my stricture cured I will insure my life." Lacking any evidence to the contrary, it is logical to assume that such a urethral stricture was due to an earlier venereal infection, although serious local injury could have produced such a condition. Whatever the cause, the result was a constantly recurring set of symptoms of discomfort, pain, partial obstruction requiring painful instrumentation, local infection, and possibly kidney infection with chills and fever.

In 1843 he was laid up for six weeks as the result of an abscess in relation to the stricture. He refused the aid of doctors, undoubtedly preferring to avoid the suffering caused by treatment without anesthesia, and ended by "curing it" himself. A few years later he "staved off the old complaint." Bladder irritation caused intermittent trouble, and in his closing years he was compelled to go so frequently to Sir Henry Thompson for surgical treatment that at times he dared not leave London. In 1859, four years before his death, he writes bitterly, "My own old enemy gives me rather serious cause for disquiet — not the spasms — the hydraulics — a constant accompaniment of those disorders is disordered spirits."

Added to these difficulties was another chronic condition acquired in Rome in the latter part of 1853. Again an accurate diagnosis cannot be assured, but there can be little doubt that this malady was due to a severe malarial (tertian) infestation, at that time common in Italy. Characteristically relapses occurred so that he writes from England in September, 1855, "Since my visit to Italy 20 months since about every month I have had 2 days illness sometimes spasms, sometimes aguish fever." Two years later he felt it necessary to travel with a servant on account of "obstinate attacks of Roman (bilious) fever w^h has had hold of me these 4 years past, and seizes me and prostrates me every month or so." Quinine and purges were used freely, but gave only temporary control of the attacks.

To this long list of bodily ailments may be added that of joint troubles. At the age of seventeen he writes of his "gout" but gives no details except that he obtained relief by using hot water "for my foots." "Rheumatism" involving shoulder joints and face was noted in a letter to his mother two years later, of such severity that "I could not use my arms, & afterwards for a considerable period I could not use my teeth!" In 1840 he again wrote his mother,

"I think I have a touch of the gout really & truly, for 3 months there has been a regular ceaseless pain in my great to [*sic*], not sewere but steady & he looks red, this is the beginning of gout all my friends inform me, & I suppose that 1 day or other I must look for the completion of it." On numerous occasions he sprained his ankle, which may have been easily traumatized, and one such accident immediately preceded his nearly fatal illness in 1849. Whether he actually suffered from true gout is a question that cannot be answered. It is more probable that he had recurrent attacks of rheumatoid or infectious arthritis, possibly in association with serious dental sepsis, inasmuch as there is no mention of gouty (joint) symptoms in the closing years of his life when overeating and overdrinking were constantly repeated events.

During the last ten years of his life one encounters a constantly recurring theme of "spasms," vomiting, diarrhea, purgation, pain, chills, and fever. In spite of his disabilities, Thackeray wrote, traveled, and lectured continuously. During an American tour in 1855–1856 he "overworked, overdined, oversupped, overvisited." From Boston he writes, "three days ago I fell ill and have passed two since in great pain and comfort in my bed room." As early as 1853 (aet. 42) his mixture of melancholy and elation is summed up in the note that, "I don't think my course is to be a long one. — I've no reason why. My health is famous but when mayn't it drop? — If I last another year there will be £300 a year for you *young* ones." Thus he lived, worked, and suffered. Because of overindulgence in his "flesh pots" he became stout and admitted a weight of fifteen stone (210 lbs.). As a result of prolonged illness, however, his appearance was much altered for some time before his death, and he was thin at fifty.

On December 20, 1863, he wrote what was probably his last letter, but he was said to have been "well and full of fun two days later." He dined out on December 23rd, retired, and after midnight had a violent retching attack which resulted in the rupture of a cerebral vessel and death. A friend wrote, "It was apoplexy, after all, and I don't think that what he had suffered from so long had much, if anything to do with it." The genius of the great novelist had finally succumbed to his insatiable need for good company and good cheer.

CHESTER M. JONES, M.D.
Physician, Massachusetts General Hospital
Clinical Professor of Medicine, Harvard
University

A THACKERAY GENEALOGY

The following tables are compiled for the most part from *Memorials* and *Ritchies in India,* though some information has been added from other sources:

TABLE I (1–26): Archdeacon Thomas Thackeray (1693–1760) and his Descendants.

TABLE II (27–49): The Descendants of Thomas Thackeray of Cambridge (1736–1806).

TABLE III (50–76): The Descendants of William Makepeace Thackeray (1749–1813).

TABLE IV (77–97): The Descendants of John Talbot Shakespear (d. 1825).

TABLE V (98–107): The Descendants of Richmond Thackeray (1781–1815).

TABLE VI (108–115): The Descendants of John Ritchie (d. 1849).

(3) Thomas Th
    (1736–1806
    m. (1763)
(4) Lydia Whish
    (1737–1830

(27) Thomas (1767–1852) m. first (1795) (28) Fanny Ward (d. 1800)	(30) William Makepeace (1770–1849) m. (c. 1803) (31) Mrs. John Jones	(32) Elias (1771–1854) m. (c. 1802) (33) Rebecca Hill (d. 1846)	(34) Frederic (1774–18 m. first (1 (35) Mrs. Will Francis (d. 1820)
(43) Thomas James (1796–1877) m. second (29) Miss C. E. Prior	(44) Frederick (1797–1831) two children		one child (36) m. second Mary Eliz (1793–18
(45) Joseph (1805–1880)	(46) George (1806–1875)	three other children	(47) Frederick

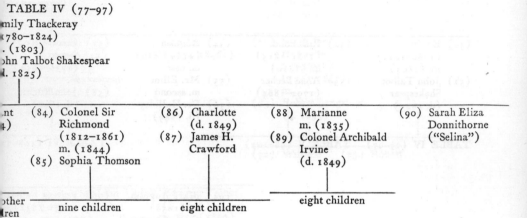

TABLE IV (77–97)

mily Thackeray
(780–1824)
. (1803)
ohn Talbot Shakespear
d. 1825)

| | (84) Colonel Sir Richmond (1812–1861) m. (1844) (85) Sophia Thomson | (86) Charlotte (d. 1849) (87) James H. Crawford | (88) Marianne m. (1835) (89) Colonel Archibald Irvine (d. 1849) | (90) Sarah Eliza Donnithorne ("Selina") |
| other ren | nine children | eight children | eight children | |

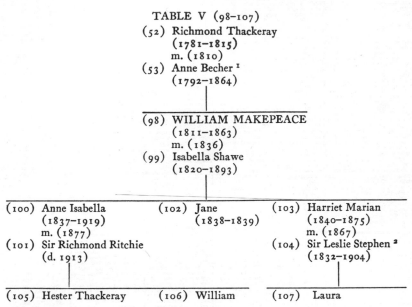

TABLE V (98–107)

(52) Richmond Thackeray
    (1781–1815)
    m. (1810)
(53) Anne Becher [1]
    (1792–1864)

(98) WILLIAM MAKEPEACE
    (1811–1863)
    m. (1836)
(99) Isabella Shawe
    (1820–1893)

(100) Anne Isabella	(102) Jane	(103) Harriet Marian
(1837–1919)	(1838–1839)	(1840–1875)
m. (1877)		m. (1867)
(101) Sir Richmond Ritchie		(104) Sir Leslie Stephen [2]
(d. 1913)		(1832–1904)

| (105) Hester Thackeray | (106) William | (107) Laura |

[1] In 1817 Mrs. Thackeray remarried, her second husband being Captain Henry Carmichael-Smyth.

[2] Stephen remarried in 1878, his second wife being Mrs. Herbert Duckworth. One of his children by this marriage was Virginia Woolf.

TABLE VI (108–115)

(57) Charlotte Sarah Thackeray
(1786–1854)
m.
(58) John Ritchie
(d. 1849)

(108) William
(1817?–1862)
m. (1844)
(109) Augusta Trimmer
(1817?–1888)

(110) Charlotte
(1820?–1878)

(111) Jane
(1822?–1865)

(112) John
(1824?–1847)

(113) Emily
(1828?–1842)

(114) Augusta   (115) Blanche   six other
children

INDEX OF CORRESPONDENTS

IN VOLUME IV

INDEX OF CORRESPONDENTS

IN VOLUME IV

AINSWORTH, WILLIAM HARRISON
    From Thackeray: pages 9, 10
AIRLIE, LADY
    From Thackeray: page 305
ALEXANDER, MR.
    From Thackeray: page 290
ALLIBONE, SAMUEL
    From Thackeray: page 191
ALLINGHAM, WILLIAM
    From Thackeray: page 171
ANDERSON, A.
    From Thackeray: page 167
ARABIN, MRS.
    From Thackeray: page 306
ATKINSON, CAPTAIN FRANCKLIN
    From Thackeray: page 124
BACON, MRS. JAMES
    From Thackeray: page 306
BARHAM, RICHARD HARRIS
    From Thackeray: page 307
BAXTER FAMILY
    From Thackeray: pages 55, 108,
    212, 278
BAXTER, GEORGE
    From Thackeray: page 263
BAXTER, MRS. GEORGE
    From Thackeray: pages 79, 234,
    263
    From Anne Thackeray: pages 229,
    298, 301
BAYNE, MRS.
    From Thackeray: page 307
BECHER, MRS.
    From Thackeray: page 97
BELL, ROBERT
    From Thackeray: page 198
BENZON, MRS. ERNEST LEOPOLD
    From Thackeray: page 295
BLACKWOOD, MRS. JOHN
    From Thackeray: page 142

BLESSINGTON, LADY, THE FRIENDS OF
    *From Thackeray, Dickens, and
    Forster:* page 61
BLUNT, MR.
    From Thackeray: page 308
BOYES, JOHN FREDERICK
    From Thackeray: pages 223, 246
BOYLE, MRS. ROBERT EDWARD
    From Thackeray: page 308
BRADBURY AND EVANS
    From Thackeray: pages 58, 107,
    309
BROOKFIELD, JANE ELTON
    From Thackeray: pages 309, 310,
    311, Appendix XXVI
BROOKFIELD, WILLIAM
    From Thackeray: pages 147, 311,
    312, 313
BROWN, DR. JOHN
    From Thackeray: pages 48, 63,
    71, 114, 138, 216, 291
    From Anne Thackeray: page 127
    To Thackeray: page 217
BROWNING, ELIZABETH BARRETT
    From Thackeray: pages 184, 226
    To Thackeray: pages 228, 234
BROWNING, ROBERT
    From Thackeray: page 165
    To Thackeray: page 171
BUCKLE, HENRY THOMAS
    From Thackeray: page 181
CAMPBELL, MISS
    From Thackeray: page 240
CARLYLE, THOMAS
    From Thackeray: pages 147, 157
    To Thackeray: pages 187, 188
CARMICHAEL-SMYTH, MAJOR HENRY
    From Thackeray: page 3
CARMICHAEL-SMYTH, MRS. HENRY
    From Thackeray: pages 3, 5, 7,

12, 61, 74, 78, 85, 128, 154, 270, 273, 314

CARRUTHERS, ROBERT
From Thackeray: page 36

CHAMBERS, ROBERT
From Thackeray: page 125

CHAPMAN, EDWARD
From Thackeray: pages 314, 315, 316

CHAPMAN, FREDERICK
From Thackeray: page 132

CHAPMAN AND HALL
From Thackeray: page 316

CHESTER, MR.
From Thackeray: page 317

CLAY, FREDERICK
From Thackeray: page 265

CLAYTON, N.
From Thackeray: page 104

CLIVE, MRS. ARCHER
From Thackeray: page 317

COLE, HENRY
From Thackeray: pages 318, 319

COLE, MRS. HENRY
From Thackeray: page 318

COLE, MISS
From Thackeray: page 142

COLLIER, JOHN PAYNE
From Thackeray: page 319

CORNHILL MAGAZINE, THE CONTRIBUTORS AND CORRESPONDENTS OF THE
From Thackeray: page 258

COSTELLO, DUDLEY
From Thackeray: page 320

COZZENS, FREDERICK SWARTOUT
From Thackeray: page 16
To Thackeray: page 72

CRAWFURD, MRS. WALTER
From Thackeray: page 173

CRUIKSHANK, GEORGE
From Thackeray: pages 277, 320

CUNNINGHAM, MRS. PETER
From Thackeray: page 320

CUPPLES, MR.
From Thackeray: page 165

CURTIS, GEORGE WILLIAM
To Thackeray: page 92

DANA, CHARLES ANDERSON
From Thackeray: page 321

DAVISON, SIR HENRY
From Thackeray: pages 185, 321

DEANERY CLUB, THE SECRETARY OF THE
From Thackeray: page 322

DICK, MRS. WILLIAM FLEMMING
From Thackeray: page 141

DICKENS, CHARLES
From Thackeray: pages 58, 59, 118, 322
To Edmund Yates: page 99
To the Friends of Lady Blessington: page 61
To Thackeray: page 116

DIXON, WILLIAM HEPWORTH
From Thackeray: page 50

DOLAND, ALEXANDER
To Edmund Yates: pages 94, 96, 105
To Thackeray: page 96

DOYLE, RICHARD
From Thackeray: page 322

DURHAM, MR.
From Thackeray: page 269

EDMONSTON, A.
From Thackeray: page 24

ELLIOT, JOHN, JR.
From Thackeray: page 145

ELLIOT, MRS.
From Thackeray: page 323, Appendix XXVI

ELLIOTSON, DR.
From Thackeray: pages 275, 280, 324

ELWIN, REV. WHITWELL
From Thackeray: pages 15, 163, 194, 237, 241, 281, 324

EVANS, FREDERICK MULLETT
From Thackeray: pages 260, 325

FANSHAWE, MISS
From Thackeray: page 326

FANSHAWE, MRS.
From Thackeray: pages 27, 326

FAULKNER, MR.
From Thackeray: page 327

FINLAY, FRANCIS D.
    From Thackeray: page 248
FITZGERALD, MRS. JOHN
    From Thackeray: page 327
FLADGATE, FRANCIS
    From Thackeray: page 250, 251
    To Thackeray: page 107
FONBLANQUE, ALBANY
    From Thackeray: pages 274, 293
FORSTER, JOHN
    From Thackeray: pages 328, 329
    To the Friends of Lady Blessington: 61
FRASER, JAMES
    From Thackeray: page 329
FRASER, THOMAS
    From Thackeray: pages 77, 243, 330
GARRICK CLUB, COMMITTEE OF THE
    From Thackeray: pages 93, 101, 119
    From Edmund Yates: pages 94, 95, 98, 103
GASSIOT, MISS
    From Thackeray: page 249
GORE, MRS.
    From Thackeray: page 195
GRANVILLE, LORD
    From Thackeray: page 283
GRATTAN, THOMAS COLLEY
    From Thackeray: page 208
HALL, MRS.
    From Thackeray: page 330
HATCH, MRS. THERESA
    From Thackeray: page 140
HAWES, LADY
    From Thackeray: page 331
HAY, LADY
    From Thackeray: pages 31, 41
HEATH, CHARLES
    From Thackeray: page 287
HOLE, REV. SAMUEL REYNOLDS
    From Thackeray: page 174
HOLL, MR.
    From Thackeray: page 251
HOLLAND, LADY
    From Thackeray: page 50

HOLLINGSHEAD, JOHN
    From Thackeray: page 157
HOOD, THOMAS [THE YOUNGER]
    From Thackeray: page 167
    To Thackeray: page 183
HOPKINS, A. I.
    From Thackeray: page 54
HUNT, LEIGH
    From Thackeray: page 332
HUNT, THORNTON
    From Thackeray: pages 41, 185
IRVINE, MRS.
    From Thackeray: pages 169, 332
JAMES, MRS. WILLIAM MILBOURNE
    From Thackeray: page 287
JERDAN, WILLIAM
    From Thackeray: page 333
JONES, C. W.
    From Thackeray: page 178
JONES, ERNEST
    From Thackeray: page 189
JONES, THE MISSES
    From Thackeray: pages 225, 248
KENNEDY, PATRICK
    From Thackeray: page 114
KENYON, JOHN
    From Thackeray: page 333
KINGSLEY, CHARLES
    From Thackeray: page 133
KNIGHTON, SIR WILLIAM
    From Thackeray: pages 267, 288, 334
KNIGHTON, LADY
    From Thackeray: page 288
LANDSEER, SIR EDWIN
    From Thackeray: pages 176, 179, 180
    To Thackeray: page 187
LEECH, JOHN
    From Thackeray: page 335
LEEMING, MR.
    From Thackeray: page 132
LEITCH, WILLIAM LEIGHTON
    From Thackeray: page 336
LESLIE, MRS. JOHN
    From Thackeray: page 296

LEVER, CHARLES
From Thackeray: pages 143, 144
LE VERT, MME.
From Thackeray: page 126
LOCKER-LAMPSON, FREDERICK
From Thackeray: pages 221, 222
LONDONDERRY, LADY
From Thackeray: page 286
LONGFELLOW, HENRY WADSWORTH
From Thackeray: page 164
LOW, S., AND SONS
From Thackeray: page 60
LUCAS, SAMUEL
From Thackeray: page 170
MacCULLAGH, MRS.
From Thackeray: page 336
MACREADY, WILLIAM CHARLES
From Thackeray: pages 53, 68
MACREADY, MRS. WILLIAM CHARLES
From Thackeray: page 337
MacEWEN, REV. ALEXANDER
From Thackeray: page 175
MACKINNON, WILLIAM ALEXANDER
From Thackeray: page 47
MAHON, LORD, see STANHOPE
MARTIN, THEODORE
From Thackeray: page 253
MARTIN, MRS. THEODORE
From Thackeray: pages 253, 284,
338
MILLAIS, SIR JOHN EVERETT
From Thackeray: pages 25, 26
MILNE, J. D.
From Thackeray: page 34
MILNES, RICHARD MONCKTON
From Thackeray: pages 169, 339
MOLESWORTH, SIR WILLIAM
From Thackeray: page 340
MOLESWORTH, LADY
From Thackeray: pages 49, 146,
340
MONTGOMERY, ALFRED
From Thackeray: page 342
MONTGOMERY, MRS.
From Thackeray: page 341
MORGAN, LADY
From Thackeray: pages 123, 343

MURRAY, LADY
From Thackeray: page 39
NICKISSON, GEORGE WILLIAM
From Thackeray: page 344
OGILVY, LADY JANE
From Thackeray: page 37
OLLIFFE, LADY
From Thackeray: pages 54, 250,
252, 344, 345
OWEN, ROBERT DALE
From Thackeray: page 193
PARDON, GEORGE FREDERICK
From Thackeray: pages 42, 46
PARKES, JOSEPH
From Thackeray: pages 53, 346
PENWELL, HENRY C.
From Thackeray: page 192
PERRY, KATE
From Thackeray: pages 173, 347,
Appendix XXVI
POLLOCK, SIR FREDERICK
From Thackeray: pages 280, 347
PRIDEAUX, MR.
From Thackeray: page 348
PRINSEP, MRS.
From Thackeray: page 348
PROCTER, ADELAIDE
From Thackeray: pages 87, 182,
194, 253
PROCTER, BRYAN WALLER
From Thackeray: page 351
PROCTER, MRS. BRYAN WALLER
From Thackeray: pages 150, 274,
289, 350, 351
RADCLIFFE, A.
From Thackeray: page 352
READ, THOMAS BUCHANAN
From Thackeray: page 51
REED, WILLIAM BRADFORD
From Thackeray: pages 44, 136,
297
RITCHIE, CHARLOTTE
From Thackeray: page 353
RITCHIE, MRS. WILLIAM
From Thackeray: pages 276, 284

ROBINSON, WILLIAM DUER
From *Thackeray:* pages 65, 135, 192, 202, 223
ROGERS, SAMUEL
From *Thackeray:* page 353
ROTHSCHILD, LADY DE
From *Thackeray:* page 29
RUSKIN, JOHN
To *Thackeray:* page 211
RUSSELL, LADY RACHEL
From *Thackeray:* page 354
RUSSELL, WILLIAM HOWARD
From *Thackeray:* page 64
SALA, GEORGE AUGUSTUS
From *Thackeray:* pages 203, 256
SKELTON, JOHN
From *Thackeray:* pages 209, 253
To *Thackeray:* page 210
SMITH, GEORGE
From *Thackeray:* pages 149, 154, 156, 162, 172, 177, 180, 184, 189, 214, 215, 216, 246, 256, 257, 266, 269, 292, 295
SMITH, LAURA
From *Thackeray:* page 355
SPEDDING, JAMES
From *Thackeray:* page 356
SPRING-RICE, STEPHEN
From *Thackeray:* page 261
STANFIELD, CLARKSON
From *Thackeray:* page 357
STANHOPE, PHILIP HENRY, 5TH EARL
From *Thackeray:* page 338
STANLEY, HENRIETTA DILLON-LEE, LADY
From *Thackeray:* pages 72, 84, 110
STEPHEN, JAMES FITZJAMES
From *Thackeray:* page 227
STORKS, SIR HENRY KNIGHT
From *Thackeray:* page 126
STURGIS, MRS. RUSSELL
From *Thackeray:* page 357
SWAIN, JOSEPH
From *Thackeray:* page 258
SYKES, COLONEL WILLIAM HENRY
From *Thackeray:* page 52

SYNGE, HENRIETTA WAINWRIGHT
From *Thackeray:* page 52
SYNGE, WILLIAM MAKEPEACE THACKERAY
From *Thackeray:* page 358
SYNGE, WILLIAM WEBB FOLLETT
From *Thackeray:* pages 38, 232, 262, 358, 359
TAYLOR, BAYARD
From *Thackeray:* pages 46, 47
TENNYSON, ALFRED
From *Thackeray:* pages 151, 360
TENNYSON, MRS. ALFRED
From *Thackeray:* page 168
THACKERAY, ANNE
From *Thackeray:* pages 19, 20, 22, 23, 26, 28, 30, 32, 35, 40, 49, 120, 148, 261, 361
To *Dr. John Brown:* page 127
To *Mrs. Baxter:* pages 229, 298, 301
THACKERAY, LADY ELIZABETH
From *Thackeray:* pages 201, 204
THACKERAY, FRANCIS ST. JOHN
From *Thackeray:* page 139
THACKERAY, GENERAL FREDERICK
From *Thackeray:* page 362
THACKERAY, HARRIET
From *Thackeray:* pages 19, 20, 22, 23, 26, 28, 32, 35, 40, 49, 120, 148, 261, 361
THACKERAY, MISS
From *Thackeray:* page 247
THACKERAY, THOMAS JAMES
From *Thackeray:* page 285
THIRLWALL, CONNOP
From *Thackeray:* page 186
THOMPSON, SIR HENRY
From *Thackeray:* pages 177, 298
THOMPSON, JOHN REUBEN
From *Thackeray:* page 69
TORNOW, MR.
From *Thackeray:* page 362
TROLLOPE, ANTHONY
From *Thackeray:* pages 158, 206, 208, 363

VIRTUE, GEORGE
  From Thackeray: page 252
WADDINGTON, HORATIO
  From Thackeray: page 363
WALKER, FREDERICK
  From Thackeray: pages 219, 222,
239, 244, 255, 268
WALLER, ROBERT JOHN
  From Thackeray: page 363
WARBURTON, MRS. ELIOT
  From Thackeray: page 364
WARD, SAMUEL
  From Thackeray: page 364
WARREN, SAMUEL
  From Thackeray: page 365
WILLIAMS AND NORGATE
  From Thackeray: page 365

WILLIAMS, WILLIAM SMITH
  From Thackeray: pages 197, 199
WILSON, JAMES
  From Thackeray: page 83
WISTAR, MRS. CASPAR
  From Thackeray: page 289
YARDLEY, WILLIAM
  From Thackeray: page 366
YATES, EDMUND
  From Thackeray: page 89
  To Thackeray: page 91
  From Alexander Doland: pages
94, 96, 105
  From Charles Dickens: page 99
  *To the Committee of the Garrick
Club:* pages 94, 95, 98, 103
YOUNG, JAMES REYNOLDS
  From Thackeray: page 42

INDEX

CUE TITLES

AM	*Ainsworth's Magazine*
A.T.	Anne Thackeray
B	*Britannia*
B., Mrs.	Mrs. Brookfield
BFR	*British and Foreign Review*
CM	*Cornhill Magazine*
C-S	Carmichael-Smyth
DN	*Daily News*
E	*Examiner*
ER	*Edinburgh Review*
FG	Edward FitzGerald
FM	*Fraser's Magazine*
FQR	*Foreign Quarterly Review*
G.	Genealogy
GP	Major Carmichael-Smyth
H.T.	Harriet Thackeray
I.T.	Isabella Thackeray
K	*Keepsake*
LWR	*London and Westminster Review*
MC	*Morning Chronicle*
NBR	*North British Review*
NMM	*New Monthly Magazine*
NS	*National Standard*
P	*Punch*
PT	*Pictorial Times*
QR	*Quarterly Review*
S	*Spectator*
S.B.	*Sketch Book*
SLM	*Southern Literary Messenger*
T.	Thackeray
TL	*Times*, London
V.F.	*Vanity Fair*

NOTE ON THE INDEX

This index comprises two parts; the first is a general index which includes all names mentioned in the text and footnotes, the second is an index of Thackeray's works.

In the general index, there is no entry on Thackeray himself; subjects such as Thackeray's health have been indexed under Health. All titled people have been indexed under the highest title they attained; where the family name is better known than the honor, the family name is indexed. Wives usually follow their husbands in order of arrangement. In some cases more or less tenuous references have been indexed, for example, a reference to "Eugenie Crowe's husband" will be found indexed under Robert Wynne, while there is no direct reference to his name on the page. Because of space limitations modifications have been omitted wherever possible; in extensive entries, such as those covering the Thackeray children, modifications have been arranged at the head of the entry, with all other page references following.

In general place names have been omitted, since the chronology in Volume I shows where Thackeray was at any given time. The place names which are included indicate a direct comment by Thackeray.

The general index also includes all books and periodicals cited in the text, and those which have been quoted extensively in the footnotes. These titles will be found under their author's names.

The second index includes all Thackeray's works mentioned in the letters or in the footnotes. Characters from the works have been indexed under the book in which they appear. There are also some general headings, such as Projects (works and ideas for works which Thackeray never followed out), Poetry, and Reviews.

GENERAL INDEX

A.A., *Letter to:* III, 412

ABBOTT, CHARLES STUART AUBREY, *see* TENTERDEN, 3rd Baron

À BECKETT, GILBERT ABBOTT, II: 105n., 247n. III: dead 617, 622; 685

À BECKETT, MRS. GILBERT ABBOTT, II: 247, 248

À BECKETT, GILBERT ARTHUR, III: 617. IV: 15

ABD EL-KADER, III: 137

ABEL, MR., II: 333

ABERDEEN, GEORGE HAMILTON GORDON, 4th Earl of, III: ministry 181, 317n., 455n. IV: cabinet 205n.

ACHILLI, GIOVANNI, III: trial 66

ACLAND, SIR THOMAS DYKE, III: 560

ACT, FORBES MACKENZIE, IV: 31

ADAMS, CHARLES FRANCIS, IV: 235

ADAMS, HENRY, *Education*, quoted I: xc

ADAMS, JOHN, III: 551, 552

ADAMSON, MR., I: 187

ADDISCOMBE, I: 12. II: 357, 360n., 361. III: 667

ADDISON, CHARLES GREENSTREET, I: 513

ADDISON, JOSEPH, II: 763. III: 389–
90, 438, 589. "Roger de Coverly,"
I: 294; II: 279, 821
ADELAIDE, QUEEN, II: 629
ADMINISTRATIVE REFORM SOCIETY,
III: 416n.; T. joins 454; 455,
456n., 457, 461
ADOLPHUS, JOHN LEYCESTER, II:
378n.
Letter to: II, 377
Africa, The, III: 479, 583
AGASSIZ, JEAN LOUIS RODOLPHE, III:
"delightful" 239
AGÉNOR, ANTOINE, see GRAMONT,
Duc de
AILESBURY, CHARLES BRUDENELL-
BRUCE, 2nd Earl and 1st Marquess
of, III: 508n.
AILESBURY, LADY [Maria Elizabeth
Tollemache, m. 2nd Earl], III:
508
AINSWORTH, BLANCHE, II: 124, 212,
293n.
AINSWORTH CHILDREN, III: 391
AINSWORTH, WILLIAM HARRISON, I:
328. II: 54, 133, 212, 230, 232,
253; "hates" T. 308; 366, 485,
581n.; T. on 583; Mrs. B. on 585.
III: 117, 363, 391, 434. IV:
"coolness" toward T. 13; 216, 393
Crichton, I: 326, 327. Jack
Shepherd, I: 395, 437. Lanca-
shire Witches, II: 343n., 344
Letters to: I, 326; II, 40, 124,
132, 160, 198, 224, 293; IV: 9,
10
Ainsworth's Magazine, II: 54, 107,
109, 232
AIRLIE, DAVID GRAHAM DRUMMOND
OGILVY, 7th Earl of, II: 805n.,
822, 823. III: 70, 135n., 338,
342, 343, 449, 478, 672. IV: 396,
402
AIRLIE, LADY [Henrietta Blanche
Stanley, m. 7th Earl], I: clxxi. II:
700, 756; to marry 805; 807,
815, 816, 822, 823, 824. III: 39,

40, 70, 82, 135, 178, 338, 342,
343, 478. IV: 85
Letter to: IV, 305
ALBANY, NEW YORK, see also chro-
nology, III: 508
ALBERT, MME., I: 204
ALBERT, PRINCE CONSORT, I: 416n.,
430; anecdote on drinking 434.
II: 396n., 703, 768. III: P and
432; 588
ALBONI, MARIETTA, II: 310. III:
160
ALCIATI, ANDREA, Emblems, quoted
III: 112
ALDERLEY, see STANLEY family
ALDRIDGE, IRA, I: 260n.
ALEXANDER, CAPTAIN, II: to put I.
T. with 171, 173; 321n.; chil-
dren with 404, 417
ALEXANDER, MISS, II: 321, 373, 379,
381, 382, 393, 409
ALEXANDER, MR., Letter to: IV, 290
ALEXANDRA, PRINCESS, of Denmark,
IV: 284
ALEXIS THE SOMNAMBULIST, see
DIDIER
ALFORD, HENRY, Dean, I: 107n.,
108n., 493, 494, 497
ALFORD, MRS. HENRY [Fanny Al-
ford], Dean Alford, quoted I:
108n.
ALINE, Sultane d'origine Mogole, II:
733
ALISON, SIR ARCHIBALD, III: 46.
History, II: 821. Marlborough,
III: "blunders" in 446
ALLEN, CAPT. BIRD, II: 43n.–44n.
ALLEN FAMILY [John], I: 419, 440.
II: 131
ALLEN, GEORGE JOHN, I: 495
ALLEN, JOHN, I: biographical lxxxi–
lxxxiv; 107n., 173, 174, 198,
292, 391; education inspectorship
399; "perfect saint" 413; 420,
421, 424, 440; diary excerpts 493–
98. II: 43n.; book 101–02; and
Brookfield 279–80. III: 30

Letters to: I, 185; II, 137, 273, 277; III, 419, 641

ALLEN, MRS. JOHN, I: 292, 391, 428, 441, 446, 449. II: 275. III: 419, 641

ALLEN, MAY, III: 419, 641

ALLEN, WILLIAM, I: 497

ALLENDALE, WENTWORTH BLACKETT BEAUMONT, 1st Baron, III: 274

ALLIBONE, SAMUEL, *Critical Dictionary*, IV: 191; quoted 192n.
Letter to: IV, 191

ALLINGHAM, H., and D. Radford, ed. *William Allingham*, quoted IV: 112n.–13n.

ALLINGHAM, WILLIAM, IV: 112n.–13n. *Poems*, II: T. on 710–11, 723
Letters to: II, 710; III, 65, 476; IV, 171

Amazon, The, III: lost 18

AMERICA, *see* UNITED STATES

AMERICANS, III: 224, 270, 282, 289–90, 293, 295, 553, 575, 580, 587, 589, 592, 653. IV: 435

AMES, SAMUEL, III: 530

ANAXAGORAS, II: 92

ANCELOT, JACQUES, II: 747n.

ANCELOT, MME. VIRGINIE, II: 747

ANDERSEN, HANS CHRISTIAN, II: "wild about him" 263. III: 338n. IV: E. B. Browning and 234

ANDERSON, A., *Letter to:* IV, 167

ANDERSON, JAMES ROBERTSON, II: 663

ANDERSON, MRS. GARRETT, III: 201n.

ANGELO, MR., I: 449

ANGELO, MRS., I: 429, 449

ANSTEY, THOMAS CHISHOLM, III: 393

Antar, a Bedoueen Romance, II: 157

Anti-Corn-Law Circular, I: T. to illustrate 385n., 386n.; 455n.

APPLETON AND CO., III: 158, 278

APPLETON, THOMAS, III: 496, 503, 614. IV: 164

APPLETON, WILLIAM HENRY, III: 121
Letter to: III, 129

ARABIAN, COLONEL, I: 31

Arabian Nights' Entertainment, I: Alnaschar's story 297, 439, 459. II: 15. IV: 150, 152

ARABIN, MRS., *Letter to:* IV, 306

ARCEDECKNE [or Archedecne], ANDREW, II: as "Foker" 721; 722n., 777n. IV: 109

ARCHENHOLTZ, JOHANN WILHELM VON, *Geschichte des siebenjahrigen Krieges*, I: 219

ARCHER FAMILY [of Wicklow], II: 75, 77

ARCHIBALD, MR., II: 417

Arctic, The, III: 399n.

ARDEN, JOSEPH, IV: and wife 392; 396, 411

ARETZ, M., I: *Paris S. B.* dedicated to 453

ARLINCOURT, CHARLES VICTOR PRÉVOT, Vicomte d', *The Three Kingdoms*, II: 737

ARMSTRONG, MR., IV: 232

ARNAL, ETIENNE, I: 233. II: 140

ARNDT, ERNST MORITZ, *Lied von Feldmarschall*, I: T. translation 179–80

ARNOLD, DR. RICHARD DENNIS, III: 665

ARNOLD, THOMAS, *Rome*, IV: 438

AROUET, FRANÇOIS MARIE, *see* VOLTAIRE

ARTHUR, MR., I: 5, 7. II: "odious blackguard" 669

ARTHUR, MRS., I: 5, 7
Letters from: I, 6, 7

ARTHUR'S SCHOOL, *see also* Education, I: T.'s description of 5n.; 9. II: 669

ASHBURTON, WILLIAM BINGHAM BARING, 2nd Baron, I: biographical lxxxiv–lxxxvi; xcix. II: 660, 672n., 694, 777, 808n., 824. III: 3, 89n., 99, 317, 390, 391, 404,

608, 641n., 667, 685. IV: 116, 322

ASHBURTON, LADY [Lady Harriet Mary Montague, 1st w. of 2nd Baron], I: biographical lxxxv-lxxxvi; xcix, cv. II: 459, 470, 475, 481, 647, 653, 654, 658, 660, 662, 663, 684, 694, 695n., 696n., 698, 699, 808n., 824n. III: 39, 72, 89n., 90n., 123, 150n., 184, 369, 391, 404, 460, 641n., 685. IV: 116, 432, 449

ASHBURTON, LADY [Louisa Mackenzie, 2nd w. of 2nd Baron], IV: 116

ASHURST, WILLIAM HENRY, II: 21, 49, 372, 379, 382, 401
    Letter to: II, 399

ASKELL, MR., I: 87, 88, 89

ASTLEY, SIR FRANCIS DUGDALE, IV: 391n.

ASTLEY, LADY [Emma Lethbridge, m. Sir Francis], IV: 391

ASTON, SIR GEORGE, II: 363

ASTOR, WILLIAM BACKHOUSE, III: 227, 614

Athenæum, I: 280, 456n., 457. II: 7, 111, 307n., 311; quoted 360n.–61n. III: 121. IV: 17, 18n., 50n., 184, 197n., 409n.; reviews A. T. 410n., 416, 417

ATHENÆUM CLUB, II: Hallam backs T. 271n.; 441; backers 635; T. blackballed 636–37; T. elected 754; 815. III: 201, 291, 321, 351, 367, 385, 419, 687. IV: 54, 55, 116, 136, 137n., 138, 173, 193, 284n., 289, 361, 402

ATKINS, JOHN BLACK, Russell, quoted III: 455n.–56n.

ATKINSON, GEORGE FRANCKLIN, Curry and Rice, IV: 124
    Letter to: IV, 124

ATKINSON, MR., II: 217

AUBER, MRS., II: 292

AUBIGNÉ, JEAN HENRI MERLE D', III: 94

AUBIGNÉ, THÉODORE AGRIPPA D', Mémoires, II: 148

AUGIER, ÉMILE, Gabrielle, II: 656

AUGUSTA, GEORGIA, see also chronology, III: 563; "quaint" 567

AUMALE, HENRI D'ORLÉANS, Duc d', IV: 269, 270, 403, 413

AUROY, MRS., I: 227, 230

AUSTEN, JANE, II: 562. IV: 155, 274n.

AUSTEN, MR., I: 218

AUSTIN, ALFRED, IV: 254n.

AUSTIN, CHARLES, III: 609n.

AUSTIN, MRS. CHARLES [Harriet Jane Ingilby], II: 286n., 335, 362, 381, 416, 643. III: 388, 609

AUSTIN FAMILY, II: 22

AUSTIN, JOHN, I: 203n.

AUSTIN, MRS. JOHN [Sarah Taylor], I: 203

AUSTIN, LUCY, see DUFF-GORDON

AVILLON, F., II: 532n.

AYLMER, LADY, I: 436n.

Aymé Verd, II: 146

AYRE, JAMES, I: 425

AYTOUN, WILLIAM EDMONDSTOUNE, II: 482. III: 46, 408, 686
    Letters to: II, 261, 267, 618

AYTOUN, MRS. WILLIAM EDMONDSTOUNE, III: 687

BACON, FRANK, I: 444

BACON, MRS. FRANK, I: 444

BACON, JAMES, IV: 306, 391, 396, 398, 402

BACON, MRS. JAMES, Letter to: IV, 306

BACON, JOHN, I: 65

BADEN, PRINCESS MARIE OF, II: 593n.

BADGER, ALBERT, I: 43, 50, 52, 53, 66, 76

BAGEHOT, WALTER, IV: 83n., 409

BAGET, JULES, I: cvii

BAGRATION, PRINCESS, II: 649n.

BAILEY, MR., I: 496

BAILEY, PHILIP JAMES, II: 821
BAILLIE, MR., III: 672
BAIRD, MAJ.-GEN. JOSEPH, I: 430n.
BAIRD, MRS. IV: 393
BAIRD, MRS. JAMES [Rhoda Willis],
see ELTON, Mrs. A. H.
BAKER, HENRY, I: 53, 493, 495
BAKEWELL, MR., II: 240, 545. III:
419. IV: 76
BAKEWELL, MRS., I: clxv. II: 172,
217, 231, 243, 306, 844n. III:
69, 388, 419, 537, 596. IV: 13,
83, 398, 414
BALFE, MICHAEL WILLIAM, II: 142.
Bohemian Girl, quoted IV: 49n.
BALFOUR, MR., I: 112
BALLANTINE, SERJEANT WILLIAM,
Some Experiences, quoted I: 507;
IV: 59n.
BALLANTYNE, A., I: Banantyne Con-
troversy 460n.
BALLARD, MR., III: 383
Letter to: III, 382
BALLET, I: 85–86, 202. II: 383,
499
Ballou's Pictorial, III: 533
Baltic, The, III: 601, 603
BALZAC, HONORÉ DE, I: 223n. Chou-
ans, II: 146. Le Peau de Chagrin,
I: 222, 225
"BANATYNE CONTROVERSY," see
LOCKHART AND BALLANTYNE
BANCROFT, GEORGE, III: 119, 123,
133, 190, 661, 662. IV: 435
Letter to: III, 317
BANCROFT, MRS. GEORGE, III: 133,
317, 318
Letter to: III, 125
BANCROFT, MRS. [of London], II:
684
BANDINEL, MR., II: 380
BANKERS, T.'s, see KING, J. G.
and Sons and LUBBOCK, Forster,
and Company
BANKS, PERCIVAL WELDON, I: 199
BANNING, MR., I: 188, 189

BAOUR-LORMIAN, PIERRE MARIE, I:
227-28
BARBER, MRS., II: 291
BARDOLPH, MR., II: 360
BARHAM, RICHARD HARRIS, II: 844n.
Garrick Club, quoted I: 282n.
Letters to: II, 59; IV, 307
BARHAM, RICHARD H. D., Richard
Harris Barham, quoted II: 5n.
BARING COMPANY, III: 154, 173.
IV: 392n., 413n.
BARING FAMILY, II: 647
BARING, SIR FRANCIS THORNHILL,
III: 672
BARING, MR., II: 602n. III: 274,
667, 674. IV: 411
BARING, WILLIAM BINGHAM, see
ASHBURTON
BARLOW, ARTHUR PRATT, III: 158n.
BARLOW, FREDERICK PRATT, Letter
to: III, 157
BARNES, THOMAS, I: 424
Letter to: I, 375
BARNES, WILLIAM MAULE, I: 41
BARNETT, JOHN, II: 248n.
BARNUM, PHINEAS T., IV: 17
BARRÉ, ISAAC, III: 321
BARRÈRE, M., I: cvii
BARROWKNIGHT, MR., I: 383
BARTLETT, WILLIAM HENRY, Jeru-
salem, II: 199
BARWELL, MR., II: 233
BARWICK, MR., I: 271
BARWICK, MRS., I: 271
BASTIDE, JULES, II: 391n.
BATES, JOSHUA, III: 72n. IV: 392
BATES, MRS. JOSHUA [Lucretia
Augusta Sturgis], III: 72, 375,
675. IV: 403
BATH, JOHN ALEXANDER THYNNE,
4th Marquess of, III: "Farintosh"
102, 316
BATH AND WELLS, BISHOP OF, see
LAW, G. H.
BATHE, HENRY PERCEVAL DE, III:
395

BATHE, SIR WILLIAM PLUNKETT DE, III: 395n. IV: 149, 391, 393

BATTERSEA, LADY [Constance Rothschild, m. 1st Baron], II: 524n.

BATTIER, MR., I: 358, 361, 362

BAUGH, MR., I: 441

BAUREL, MME. DE, II: 400, 681, 682

BAUTIER FAMILY, I: 230

BAXTER FAMILY [George], I: biographical lxxxvii-xc. III: 165, 174; and religion 198; 242, 262, 263, 272, 290, 483, 491, 540, 542, 543, 653. IV: 135, 203, 265
    Letters to: III, 268, 279, 474, 488; IV, 55, 108, 212, 278

BAXTER, GEORGE [Sr.], I: lxxxvii. III: 142, 159, 204, 207, 239, 308, 309, 316, 357, 369, 516, 543, 627, 661. IV: 81, 111, 235, 278
    Letters to: III, 258, 319, 520; IV, 263

BAXTER, MRS. GEORGE, I: lxxxvii. III: 142, 148n., 153, 163, 180n., 183, 190, 191n., 206, 207, 215, 232, 259, 284, 285, 311, 312, 314, 319, 368, 484, 540, 652, 654. IV: 442
    Letters to: III, 150, 159, 164, 176, 203, 209, 211, 220, 238, 260, 262, 271, 273, 307, 313, 327, 356, 464, 516, 525, 526, 541, 568, 603, 607, 626; IV, 79, 229, 234, 263, 298, 301

BAXTER, GEORGE [Jr.], III: 207, 211, 309, 312, 370, 570. IV: 56, 235

BAXTER, LUCY, III: 142, 164, 177, 190, 191, 204, 212, 213, 214, 224, 238, 260, 270, 271, 274, 282, 298, 309, 357, 358, 378, 484, 522, 526, 555, 556, 558, 560, 561, 568, 570, 572, 604, 654. IV: 109, 110, 229, 278, 300. American Family, quoted I: lxxxvii-lxxxviii, lxxxix; II: on

Pendennis 437n.; III: 148n., 179n.–80n., 256n.–57n., 569n.
    Letters to: III, 163, 206, 215, 232, 259, 310, 368

BAXTER, RICHARD, Saint's Everlasting Rest, III: 160

BAXTER, SALLY, see HAMPTON, Mrs. Frank

BAXTER, WYLLYS, III: 309, 312, 370, 475. IV: 56, 109, 230, 235

BAYARD, JEAN FRANÇOIS, and Louis Émile Vanderburch, Gamin de Paris, II: 704

BAYFORD, AUGUSTUS FREDERICK, I: 493, 495

BAYFORD, JAMES HESELTINE, I: 493, 495

BAYLEY, FREDERICK WILLIAM NAYLOR, I: 197, 260n.

BAYLEY, HENRY VINCENT, I: 189n.

BAYLEY, MRS. HENRY VINCENT [Miss Pattle], I: 189n. II: 325

BAYLEY, MRS., III: 312

BAYLEY, WILLIAM BUTTERWORTH, II: 287

BAYNE, MRS. WILLIAM JOSEPH [Alicia Pryme, G. 48], II: 670n., 672, 818. III: 674. IV: 250, 395, 402
    Letters to: II, 528, 666, 783, 784; III, 6, 253, 371; IV, 307

BAYNE, MRS. WILLIAM, and Mrs. Richard Pryme, Memorials, quoted I: 107n.–08n.

BEACONSFIELD, 1st Earl of, see DISRAELI, Benjamin

BEADLE, MRS., I: 231, 270, 391

BEALE, THOMAS WILLERT, IV: 10, 15, 17, 27, 39, 42n. Light of Other Days, quoted IV: 10n., 43n.

BEAUCLERK, TOPHAM, II: 371

BEAUFORT, HENRY SOMERSET, 7th Duke of, II: 685n.

BEAUFORT, DUCHESS OF [Emily Frances Smith, m. 7th Duke], II: 685

BEAUMARCHAIS, PIERRE AGUSTIN CARON DE, II: 679
BEAUMONT, FRANCIS, I: 253
BEAUMONT, DR. MARG., IV: 409
BEAUMONT, THOMAS WENTWORTH, I: 324, 346
BEAUMONT, WENTWORTH BLACKETT, see ALLENDALE
BEAUVOIR, ROGER DE, I: cli. II: 588
BECHER, CAPT. ALEXANDER BRIDPORT, II: 129, 195, 204, 399. III: 157. IV: 413[?]
BECHER, ANNE, I: 4, 8, 92, 221, 399, 401, 419, 426. II: 204, 231, 372, 548, 551
    Letter from: I, 4
BECHER, CHARLES, I: 8
BECHER, HARRIET, see GRAHAM, Mrs. Allan
BECHER, HENRY CORRY ROWLEY, III: 675n.
    Letters to: III, 156, 533
BECHER, MRS. HENRY CORRY ROWLEY, III: 534
BECHER, JOHN HARMAN, I: cvi, cxii
BECHER, MRS. JOHN HARMAN, I: cxii, cxiii, 3. III: 293
BECHER, MRS., Letter to: IV, 97
BECKET, THOMAS À, II: 406, 650, 651
BECKWITH, MRS., III: 637, 638, 685, 686. IV: 121, 400
BEDFORD, FRANCIS RUSSELL, 7th Duke of, II: 542
BEDFORD, JOHN RUSSELL, 6th Duke of, II: 683n.
BEDFORD, DOWAGER DUCHESS OF [Lady Georgiana Gordon, m. 6th Duke], II: 683, 684
BEDFORD, MR., II: 561n.
BEDFORD, PAUL, I: 440n.
BEDINGFIELD FAMILY, II: 194, 351
BEDINGFIELD, MRS., II: 195
BEDINGFIELD, RICHARD, I: cx, clxin., 18, 26n. II: writing 129; T.'s advice 136–37; 170; advice 192–

93; 195, 675n. Miser's Son II: 132, 136, 137, 167
    Letters to: II, 136, 167, 192, 325, 328, 329
BEECHER, HENRY WARD, III: 492n.
BEERS, HENRY A., Willis, quoted I: 406n.
BEETHOVEN, LUDWIG VON, I: T.'s description of Battle Symphony 133–34. Fidelio, I: 202, 441
BELHAVEN, ROBERT MONTGOMERIE HAMILTON, 8th Baron, III: 632n.
BELHAVEN, LADY [Hamilton Campbell, m. 8th Baron], III: 632
BELL, CURRER, pseud. see BRONTË, Charlotte
BELL, JACOB, III: 680
BELL, JOHN, Letter to: II, 519
BELL, ROBERT, IV: 199n., 232, 238, 358, 411. "Stranger than Fiction," IV: 193, 199n. "Spiritualism," IV: 199n.
    Letters to: II, 423; IV, 198
BELLI, MR., IV: and Miss 393; 398
BELLINI, VINCENZO, I: 237. La Sonnambula, I: I. T. and 432
BELLOWS, REV. HENRY WHITNEY, III: 122, 143
BELMONT, AUGUST, III: 662n.
BELMONT, MRS. AUGUST, III: 662
BELPER, EDWARD STRUTT, 1st Baron, II: 514, 558
BELPER, LADY [Emily Otter, m. 1st Baron], II: 514
    Letter to: II, 677
BENAND, MISS OR MRS., I: 461
BENEDICT, JULIUS, II: 409n., 621
BENEDICT, MME. JULIUS [Adèle Jean], II: 409, 417, 621
BENESONTAG, SIGNOR, I: 190
BENJAMIN, JUDAH PHILIP, III: 581n.
BENNET, JOHN, III: 276
BENNETT, JAMES GORDON, III: 88n., 652
BENNETT, REV. WILLIAM JAMES EARLY, II: 736, 746. III: 19
BENTINCK, GEORGE, II: account of

Castlereagh-Melci duel 643n.–44n.

Bentley's Miscellany, II: 40; naming of 59n.; 60. III: 434. IV: 371

BENTLEY, RICHARD, II: as "Bacon" 59n.
  Letter to: II, 90

BENZON, ERNEST LEOPOLD, IV: 414

BENZON, MRS. ERNEST LEOPOLD, IV: 414
  Letter to: IV, 295

BÉRANGER, PIERRE JEAN DE, I: FG translation of poems 330–341. III: 124. "Le Grenier," II: 702

BERESFORD, WILLIAM, III: 679, 680

BERKELEY, GRANTLEY, I: 460

BERNARD, CHARLES DE, *Le Pied d'argile*, I: "Bedford-Row Conspiracy" stolen from 433n.

BERRY, AGNES, I: cviii. II: 620, 645, 654, 658, 662, 664, 669, 685, 746, 749, 791n., 826. IV: 424

BERRY, MARIE, Duchesse de, I: 235

BERRY, MARY, I: cviii. II: 620, 645, 654, 658, 662, 664, 669, 685, 746, 791n. III: 25, 55, 127. IV: 424

BERRYMAN, MISS, III: 194, 268

BERTIN, DR., III: 361, 571, 646

BERTRAND, M., I: 235

BERWICK, JACQUES FITZ-JAMES, Duc de, *Mémoires*, III: 446

BEVAN, MR., I: 227, 228, 233

BEVAN, SAMUEL, II: 150. *Sand and Canvas*, quoted II: 157n.–58n.
  Letter to: II, 483

BEVAN, WILLIAM, II: 253. III: 424. IV: 403, 412
  Letters to: III, 424, 426

BEWLEY, JOHN H., III: 380n.

BEYNON, REV. DAVID, I: 114

BEZZI, MR., III: 45

Bible, The, Acts, I: 85; II: 768. Corinthians, II: 591, 716. Ecclesiastes, I: 279, 389; II: 324; III: 30. Exodus, III: 94, 154. Ephesians, II: 309. Isaiah, I: 46; II: 688; III: 639. Job, I: 466; II: 759. Judges, II: 751n.; IV: 272. Kings, I: 383. Micah, III: 114; IV: 254. Numbers, II: 273. Psalms, I: 248, 424, 476, 458; II: 292, 571, 711; III: 30. Revelation, I: 96, 410. Romans, I: 382. St. John, III: 85. St. Luke, I: 97, 403; II: 724; III: 182, 395; IV: 128. St. Matthew, I: 355; II: 100; III: 169, 547, 439. St. Paul, IV: 438

Bibliothèque Nationale, II: bad management of 650–52

BIDDLE, CLEMENT CORNELL, III: 184
  Letter to: III, 186

BIDWELL, MR., I: 447. IV: 82, 390

BIGELOW FAMILY, IV: 265

BIGGE, MR., IV: 395, 400, 412

BILL DISCOUNTING BUSINESS [Birchin Lane], I: 269, 504–05, 508

BINNY, JOHN, Henry Mayhew, and others, *London Labour and the London Poor*, II: 817

BIRCH, MISS, III: 13

BIRD, ROBERT MONTGOMERY, III: 410

BIRKBECK, MR., I: 197

BISSHOPP, REV. SIR CECIL AUGUSTUS, II: 157

BITCHERDEAR, MRS., II: 55

BLACK, ADAM, IV: 36

BLACK, DR., II: 49, 57–58, 97

BLACKBURN, HUGH, III: 423

BLACKBURN, MRS. HUGH, III: 634. IV: 4. *Illustrations of Scriptures*, III: 422, 423
  Letter to: III, 422

BLACKIE, JOHN STUART, III: 687. IV: 40

BLACKMAN, MISS, IV: 401

BLACKWOOD, ALEXANDER, I: 407n., 419n., 489
  Letter to: I, 450

BLACKWOOD, ARCHIBALD, III: 636

BLACKWOOD FAMILY [John], III:

631, 647, 651, 688. IV: 23, 26, 27, 64
BLACKWOOD, JAMES, III: 46
BLACKWOOD, JOHN, II: 263, 801. III: 46n., 406n., 409, 624, 686, 687. IV: 15n., 24, 26, 27, 64; quoted 79n.–80n.; 81, 142, 392; letter quoted 397n.–98n.; 403, 444
    Letter to: III, 406
BLACKWOOD, MRS. JOHN, III: 406n., 407n., 408, 647. IV: 81, 392, 397n., 403
    Letter to: IV, 142
Blackwood's Magazine, I: 39, 196, 412, 419, 450, 462. II: 113, 262, 263. III: 393, 395, 406n., 407, 409, 434. IV: 16n.
BLACKWOOD, ROBERT, I: 419, 421
BLACKWOOD, MAJ. WILLIAM, III: 687
BLAKESLEY, JOSEPH WILLIAMS, I: 194
BLANC, LOUIS, *Histoire de dix ans,* II: 829. *Lettres sur l'Angleterre,* IV: 198. *l'Organisation du travail,* II: 355
BLANCHARD, SAMUEL LAMAN, I: and *Constitutional* 301n., 303. II: 107, 109, 485. *Life and Works,* II: 230
    Letter to: II, 106
BLANCHE, II: 684
BLECHYNDEN, MRS., I: cxiiin., 183, 208, 245. II: 32, 34, 35; daughter of 367, 381
BLEECKER, ANTHONY J., III: 290n.
BLEECKER [or Bleaker], MR., III: 290, 298, 307
BLESSINGTON, LADY [Marguerite Power, m. 1st Earl], II: 139, 316n., 390, 391n., 532n.; sale of Gore house 532, 534; death 593n.; 734. IV: 61
    Letters to: II, 420, 426, 427, 431, 432, 465, 485, 533
BLOCK, MISS, III: 633

BLOMFIELD, CHARLES JAMES [Bishop of London], I: 12n. II: 12, 13
BLUNT, JOHN JAMES, I: 73, 78
BLUNT, MR., *Letter to:* IV, 308
BOCHER, M., III: 16
BODE, BARON WILLIAM HENRY OTTO DE, II: 209
BODISCO [or Bodiski], ALEXANDER, III: 205
BODISCO [or Bodiska], MRS. ALEXANDER, III: 205
BOGGS, MRS., III: 295
BOGUE, DAVID, I: cl. II: and Marvy 608, 613. III: 410n.
    Letter to: II, 610
BOISSY, HILAIRE ROUILLÉ, Marquis de, II: 390n., 391n.
BOISSY, MME. DE [Teresa Gamba, m. Marquis], II: 390, 391n.
BOKER, GEORGE HENRY, III: 536
BOLINGBROKE, HENRY ST. JOHN, 1st Viscount, I: 37, 95, 166, 496. II: 761, 776
BÖLTE, MME., II: 242
BONAPARTE, *see* NAPOLÉON
BONAPARTE, PRINCE JÉRÔME, I: 128n. III: 140
BONIFACE, JOSEPH XAVIER ["Saintine"], II: 829. III: 668
BONINGTON, RICHARD PARKES, I: 285, 287
BONNET, M., II: 139
BONNEVAL, CLAUDE ALEXANDRE, Comte de, II: 800
BONNEVAL, COUNT LIONEL DE, II: 792n., 793. III: 460
BONNEVAL, LADY DE [Caroline Gallwey, m. Count Lionel], II: 792, 793
BOO, LEE, II: 246, 247n.
Book of Common Prayer, II: 628, 769. III: 297, 612. IV: 202, 253
BOONE, JAMES SHERGOLD, I: 311
BOOTT, MRS., III: 601
BOSQUET, PIERRE JEAN FRANÇOIS, III: 403
BOSTON, MASSACHUSETTS, *see also*

chronology, III: papers abuse T. 166, 169; society of 170; 173, 179, 183, 193, 514, 529

Boston Courier, The, III: 174n.

Boston Journal, The, III: 174n.

BOSWELL, JAMES, III: 161n. IV: 438. *Johnson,* quoted III: 574; IV: 71n.

BOUFFÉ, HUGUES-DÉSIRÉ-MARIE, II: 142, 143, 704

BOURGEOIS, MLLE., IV: 341, 342

BOURGUIGNON, ABBÉ, III: 267

BOWDEN, ALBINIA, *see* CHAVE, Mrs.

BOWER, ELLIOT, I: clii

BOWER, MRS. ELLIOT, I: clii

BOWERS, DR. GEORGE HULL [Dean Manchester], III: 97

BOWES, JOHN BOWES, I: biographical xc-xciii; 229, 231, 232, 233, 234, 235, 236, 237, 238, 277, 286. II: 27n.–28n., 29n., 31, 33, 502

BOWIE, MR., *Letter to:* III, 623

BOXALL, WILLIAM, II: 149

BOYD, ROBERT, II: 843, 844

BOYES, BENJAMIN, I: 20n., 23, 30

BOYES, MRS. BENJAMIN, I: 20, 23, 29, 30. IV: death 223–24

BOYES, JOHN FREDERICK, "T.'s School-Days," quoted I: 16n., 20n.–21n., 24n.
Letters to: I, 27; IV, 223, 246

BOYES, MRS. JOHN FREDERICK, IV: 225, 247

BOYLE, RICHARD EDMUND ST. LAWRENCE, *see* CORK

BOYLE, ROBERT EDWARD, IV: 308n.

BOYLE, MRS. ROBERT EDWARD, *Letter to:* IV, 308

BRACEBRIDGE, MRS., II: 422

BRACHMANN, DR., I: 123

BRACY, MR., I: 210

BRADBURY AND EVANS, II: 144, 177, 358, 444, 530, 704, 757, 840, 841. III: 251, 280, 346, 349, 350, 351, 408, 461, 463, 471, 487, 596. IV: 56, 76, 89n., 144
Letters to: II, 82, 162; III, 300, 386; IV, 58, 107, 309

BRADBURY, HENRY, II: 247, 396, 441. III: 641n.
Letter to: II, 284

BRADDOCK, GEN. EDWARD, IV: 66, 73

BRADDON, MARY ELIZABETH [Mrs. Maxwell], *Lady Audley's Secret,* IV: 411n.

BRADENBAUGH, CHARLES, III: 541, 543, 547, 550
Letters to: III, 515, 526

BRAHAM, JOHN, I: 177n.; sketch of 501. II: 703

BRAINERD, CHARLES H., *Letter to:* III, 532

BRANDAUER, MISS, II: 439

BRANDON, 8TH DUKE OF, *see* HAMILTON, 11th Duke of

BRAUN, LILY, *Im Schatten der Titanen,* quoted I: 129n.

BRAY, CHARLES, III: 437, 438n., 439n., 448. IV: 41

BRAY, MRS. CHARLES, III: 437n., 438n., 439n.
Letter to: III, 448

BRETONNE, RESTIF DE LA, *Le Paysan perverti,* I: 213

BRIDGMAN, LAURA, III: 226

BRIGHT, H. S., III: 642, 651, 689

BRIGHT, JOHN, II: 753. III: 76n.

BRIMLEY, GEORGE, III: 130n.

BRINE, JOHN GRANT, I: cxvii, 286, 359, 509, 511

Britannia, I: cxlix. II: 482

Britannic Review, II: 124

British Critic and Quarterly Theological Review, I: 460

British and Foreign Review, I: cxliii, 325, 346, 374, 382, 383, 388, 420

"BRITISH GRENADIERS," I: 169–70

BRODERIP, F.F., and Thomas Hood, *Memorials,* IV: 196

BRODIE, JESSIE, I: 394, 397, 405, 420, 447, 464, 472, 476, 477, 478, 479, 487. II: 88, 101, 102, 131, 193. III: 324, 540. IV: 35

Brohan, Émilie, II: 743
Brome, John, I: 56
Bronson, Miss, III: 399, 400
Brontë, Charlotte ["Currer Bell"], I: biographical xciii-xciv; cxl; and "Becky Sharp" clviii. II: T. and dedication 340; slander about T. and 341n., 697; relationship with T. 420, 611n.–12n., 673, 674n., 784n.–85n.; 675, 755n., 810n. III: "rage scorching her heart" 12; 13; criticizes *Esmond* 15; T. on 19, 67; 231; "poor little woman of genius" 233; 248. IV: 180n., 206, 424. *Jane Eyre*, II: T. on 318–19; 331; dedication quoted 340n.–41n.; 342; identity of author 441, 611n.–12n., 784n. *Villette*, III: 231, 232; T. on 233, 248, 252; 253
Brooke, Miss, I: 275
Brooke, Robert, III: 435n.
Brookfield, Arthur Montagu, III: 127n., 221n., 282. *Chequered Life*, quoted I: cn.
Brookfield, Charles, II: 759, 760
Brookfield, Charles and Frances, *Mrs. Brookfield*, quoted II: 392n., 475n., 560n., 602n.–03n., 695n., 735n., 791n., 824n.
Brookfield family [William], I: T. on cxxvi. II: 448, 572, 701, 717, 809, 812. III: 63, 72, 127, 276, 282, 284, 342, 388, 393. IV: 445
Brookfield, Magdalene, I: xcviii. II: 558; born 638; 640, 641, 642, 644, 646, 647, 648, 650, 653, 655, 658, 659n., 662, 672, 686, 688, 691, 693[?], 699, 710, 716, 719, 723n., 733, 737, 739, 741, 744, 745, 747, 750, 760, 767, 794, 795, 796, 824n. III: 17, 82, 282. IV: 341, 342
    Letter to: II, 639
Brookfield, Rev. William Henry,

I: biographical xcv-c; cxxvii, cxxxiii, 277n. II: T. backs for position 273–75, 277–80; 314n., 322, 326, 331, 391, 397, 402, 429, 434, 439, 440, 454, 461, 462; appointed school inspector 466n.; 467, 468, 469, 475, 476, 478; and T.'s relationship to Mrs. B. 492–93; 497, 498, 502, 503, 507, 509, 510, 511, 514, 515, 516, 520, 521, 524, 528, 530–31, 536, 537, 542, 547, 548, 552; offended with T. 557; 560n., 562, 563, 565, 567, 577, 582, 583, 586, 587, 589, 594, 602, 616, 619, 620, 629, 638, 639, 644, 647, 653, 658, 662, 664, 683, 685n., 689, 691, 698, 701, 705, 706, 710, 715, 717, 719, 731, 733, 735n., 737, 738, 739, 740, 746, 749, 750, 751n., 760, 768, 770, 788, 796; quarrel with T. 798n., 802n.; attempted reconciliation 808; 814, 844. III: 17, 68, 182, 183, 185; "dark spirit" 221; reconciled with wife 284; 306, 508, 582. IV: 21, 22n., 323, 420, 425, 426, 427; break with T. 428, 429, 430; treatment of wife 431; reconciliation 432; "God help him" 433; 436, 437, 446
    Letters to: II, 114, 127, 271, 304, 307, 314, 323, 421, 441, 466, 482, 488, 489, 513, 521, 522, 533, 540, 557, 561, 597, 606, 633, 640, 660, 759; III, 47; IV, 147, 311, 312, 313. *Letter from:* II, 638
Brookfield, Mrs. William Henry [Jane Octavia Elton], I: biographical xcv-c; lxxxviii, cxxvii, cliv; T. letter on cxl; "Amelia" clxv. II: 110; T.'s "beau-ideal" 231; 271–72; 273, 278, 292, 304, 306, 307, 314n., 315, 322, 323; "Amelia" 335; ill 374, 380;

392n., 398, 428, 429; "Miss Raby" 445n.; 466, 488, 489, 516, 533, 544, 547, 558, 567, 605, 629, 638, 639, 640, 659n., 668, 672, 674n., 693; letter to husband 695n.; 696, 701, 706, 717, 760, 798n., 808, 812, 814, 824n. III: 12; and T.'s characters 27n.; 68, 134, 135, 173, 195, 196; "angelical creature" 221; 225, 282; reconciled with husband 284; 306, 388, 495, 531n., 532, 560, 580, 617n., 626, 641n., 673. IV: 29, 122, 304, 313, 326, 341, 342, 429; treatment by husband 431; reconciliation 432; 433, 435, 436, 437; threatening Catholicism 446; 447

   Letters to: II, 269, 326, 389, 391, 394, 396, 403, 410, 411, 422, 425, 434, 435, 438, 445, 449, 451, 452, 461, 462, 467, 469, 472, 486, 492, 493, 500, 505, 508, 513, 524, 530, 540, 547, 552, 556, 557, 558, 559, 561, 564, 569, 578, 586, 590, 592, 597, 600, 601, 602, 606, 614, 615, 619, 620, 621, 638, 641, 646, 649, 652, 654, 657, 661, 677, 680, 681, 684, 689, 697, 709, 714, 718, 723, 729, 733, 743, 747, 760, 765, 767, 788, 792; III, 122, 182; IV, 309, 310, 311, Appendix XXVI. *Letters from:* II, 275, 395, 460, 467, 477, 520, 526, 536, 577, 584, 688, 738, 739, 745

BROOKING, ARTHUR, I: 494, 496
BROOKS, CHARLES WILLIAM SHIRLEY, III: 614n. IV: 36, 90n., 122, 253, 404, 413, 416, 417
BROOKS, PRESTON S., III: 627
BROTHERTON, MR., II: 157. III: crazy 333, 336, 337, 438, 506, 557
BROTHERTON, MRS., III: 336, 337, 338, 438, 506

BROUGHAM, HENRY PETER, Baron, I: 159, 359; T. writes on 388; 431. II: 593n.; "best and wickedest" 685; 741. IV: 56
BROUGHTON, LORD, *see* HOBHOUSE
BROUN, SIR THOMAS, II: 139
BROWN, FORD MADOX, II: 709n.
BROWN, HELEN, III: 3, 47, 409, 640. IV: 49, 116, 128, 138, 291
BROWN, "JOCK," III: 3, 47, 409, 640. IV: 49, 116, 128, 138, 291
BROWN, JOHN, and D. W. Forrest, *Letters of Dr. J. Brown,* quoted II: 818n.; III: 637n., 688n.; IV: 40n.
BROWN, DR. JOHN, I: biographical c-cii; cxlvn., cxxix. II: 483n., 687, 818. III: 4. IV: 79; on Dickens 122; A. T. on 127–28. *Horæ Subsecivæ,* IV: 127, 138, 217n., 243n. "Our Dogs," IV: 217
   Letters to: II, 538, 801, 804; III, 31, 42, 46, 90, 244, 300, 408, 623, 640; IV, 48, 63, 71, 114, 127, 138, 216, 291. *Letters from:* II, 821; IV, 217
BROWN, DR. JOHN, and Henry Lancaster, III: quoted 43n.
BROWN, MRS. JOHN, II: 801, 805. III: 32, 34, 44, 47n., 91, 245, 246, 633. IV: 48, 63, 71, 116, 128, 138
   Letters to: III, 3, 32, 300, 408, 640
BROWN, DR. JOHN [Sr.], IV: 115
BROWN, MRS., I: 15
BROWNE, HABLÔT K. ["Phiz"], I: 326n.
BROWNE, ROBERT WILLIAM, I: 27, 29
BROWNE, WILLIAM KENWORTHY, I: 346, 347
BROWNING, ELIZABETH BARRETT, II: 247n., 821. III: 333; quoted 338n.; 341. IV: 112, 171; solicited for CM 165–66; 197, 234 "A Forced Recruit," IV: 197.

"Little Mattie," IV: 228. "Lord Walter's Wife," IV: T. criticizes morality of 226–27, 228. "North and the South," IV: 234
Letters to: IV, 184, 226. *Letters from:* IV, 228, 234
BROWNING, ROBERT, II: 247n. III: 123n., 328n., 338n., 341, 497. IV: T. on 112n.; 184, 226, 227, 228, 403
Letter to: IV, 165. *Letter from:* IV, 171
BROWNING, ROBERT WIEDEMANN BARRETT ["Penini"], IV: 172, 184, 227, 228, 229
BRUCE, JAMES, IV: 249
BRUCE, LADY CHARLOTTE, *see* LOCKER-LAMPSON, MRS. F.
BRUCE, MISS, III: 318
BRUDENELL, JAMES THOMAS, *see* CARDIGAN
BRUEN, FANNY, III: 191
BRUGNOTI, MISS, I: 202
BRUMMELL, GEORGE BRYAN ["Beau"], II: anecdote 8. IV: 358
BRUNEL, ISAMBARD KINGDOM, II: 384n. IV: 398
BRUNEL, MRS. ISAMBARD KINGDOM, II: 384, 386
BRYANT, MR., IV: 409
BRYANT, WILLIAM CULLEN, III: 124n., 250n.
BUCHANAN, JAMES, III: 264n.
Letter to: III, 463
BUCKINGHAM, JAMES SILK, III: 174, 180
BUCKINGHAM, RICHARD PLANTAGENET TEMPLE-NUGENT-BRYDGES-CHANDOS-GRENVILLE, 2nd Duke of, II: 420n.
BUCKLE, HENRY THOMAS, IV: 214, 238; death of 272; 397
Letter to: IV, 181
BUCKSTONE, JOHN BALDWIN, I: 260n. III: 430

BUFFALO, NEW YORK, *see also* chronology, III: 531
BULL, OLE, III: 514
BULLAR, A., II: 528
BULLAR, JOSEPH, II: 468, 470, 472, 474, 475, 479, 590, 688, 691, 768n.
BULLAR, MR., II: 467
BULLAR, DR. WILLIAM, II: 271n., 422, 479, 670, 689, 690, 768n.
BULLER, MISS A., I: 219
BULLER, ARTHUR WILLIAM, I: ciii, civ, 195, 210, 211, 212, 213, 219, 220, 235, 243, 244, 430. II: 252, 253, 380, 383, 528, 545. III: 636. IV: 400, 403, 409
BULLER, MRS. ARTHUR [Anne Henrietta Maria Templer], I: civ. II: 383. IV: 400
BULLER, CHARLES [Sr.], I: biographical ciii–civ; clvii, clviii, 211, 218, 219, 244, 245, 306, 307n., 308, 321, 347n., 401, 433, 445. II: 163, 380; dead 383. III: 70n.
BULLER, MRS. CHARLES, SR. [Barbara Isabella Kirkpatrick], I: ciii; and Reviss clvii, clviii; 211, 219, 306, 307n., 308, 310, 321, 347n., 367, 401, 412; and Reviss 413; 433, 445. II: 380, 382; husband dead 383; son dead 461; 462
BULLER, CHARLES [Jr.], I: biographical ciii–cv; lxxxvi, 194, 196, 197, 199; T. electioneering for (diary) 210–20; 200, 203, 205, 207, 215; electioneering (letters) 244–49; 308; and politics 382, 383; 385n., 386n., 409n., 458. II: 227n., 252, 293, 380, 383; dead 461, 470, 475
BULLER, JOHN, I: 211
BULLY, EDOUARD ROGER DE, *see* BEAUVOIR, Roger de
BULWER, WILLIAM HENRY LYTTON EARLE [Baron Dalling and Bulwer], II: 486. III: 194n.
BULWER-LYTTON, SIR EDWARD

GEORGE EARLE LYTTON [1st Baron Lytton], I: cxxi, 303n.; T. writes on 395, 412; wife 398, 436n., 438. II: "morbid" 39; 139, 197; attacks Tennyson 225n-26n.; 264; T.'s satire of 270, 271; 296n., 308, 315; T.'s opinion of 485, 486; 543, 554, 780, 821. III: and Catholicism 12, 13; 21, 181n., 184, 370; T. apologizes to 395; 407n., 409, 420. IV: 416

    Caxtons, III: 278. *Devereaux,* I: 95, 98; quoted 98–99. *Disowned,* I: 95, 98n. *Ernest Maltravers,* I: 514. *Eva,* II: 56. *Eugene Aram,* I: "disappointing" 198. *Lady of Lyons,* II: 226, 663; III: 339. *King Arthur,* II: 360. *My Novel,* III: 248, 253; "fresher and richer than any he has done" 288; 298. *Pelham,* I: "dull" 228. *Reign of Terror,* II: 64n. *Sea Captain,* I: 394. *Zanoni,* III: 327n., 331

    Letter to: III, 278

BULWER-LYTTON, LADY [Rosina Doyle Wheeler, m. 1st Baron], I: separated from husband 398; libel suit 435; "graceless, drunken, lying" 438

BUNBURY, MR., IV: 403

BUNN, ALFRED, *The Stage,* I: 451

BUNTING, JOHN, JR., III: letter from quoted 486n.

BUNYAN, JOHN, II: 810n.

BURDETT, SIR FRANCIS, II: 248

BURDETT-COUTTS, ANGELINA GEORGINA, III: 440

BURFORD, ROBERT, I: 26

BURGESS, MR., II: 330

BURGH, ULICK JOHN DE, *see* CLANRICARDE, 14th Earl of

BURGHERSH, FRANCIS WILLIAM HENRY FANE, Baron, *see* WESTMORLAND, 12th Earl

BURNAND, SIR FRANCIS COWLEY, II: quoted 721n.–22n., 777n.

BURNS, ROBERT, I: quoted 234. II: 502. III: quoted 166n.

BURROWS, HENRY NICHOLSON, I: 108n., 495, 496, 497

BURT, DR. JOHN, III: 687

BURTON, HENRY STUART, I: 78

BURTON, JOHN HILL, *David Hume,* II: 234, 235n.

BURTONSHAW, MR., II: 156

BURY, LADY CHARLOTTE SUSAN MARIA, *Diary Relative to George . . . and Caroline,* I: 515; III: 473n. *Eros and Anteros,* I: 515

BUTE, LADY [Lady Sophia Hastings, m. 2nd Marquess], III: 276, 473

BUTLER, I: 11

BUTLER, COL. E. W., I: cvi, cxii

BUTLER, MRS. E. W. ["GM," Harriet Becher], I: biographical cv-cvi; cxii, 15, 145, 271, 273, 274, 275, 289–90, 303, 347, 355, 362, 363, 364, 380, 398, 412, 420, 421, 424, 425, 427, 429, 431, 433, 437, 438, 441, 444, 449, 450, 454, 460, 462, 463, 464, 465, 468. II: 4, 5, 11, 13, 18; M. Carmichael hates 46, 53; 91, 108, 136, 200, 232, 238, 239, 257, 285, 286, 287, 288, 289, 292, 309, 318; dead 323, 324, 325; 328, 372, 401, 418

BUTLER, FRANCES ANN, III: 184, 230, 251

BUTLER, LORD JAMES WANDESFORDE, IV: 354n.

BUTLER, LADY [Lady Rachel Russell, m. Lord James], *Letter to:* IV, 354

BUTLER, MR., I: 89, 90, 92, 99, 101

BUTLER, PIERCE MEASE, III: 184, 230, 251

BUTLER, MRS. PIERCE, *see* KEMBLE, Frances

BUTLER, SARAH, III: 184, 230, 251

BUTLER, WILLIAM O., III: 212n.

BUTT, DR. ISAAC, II: 87
BYNG, FREDERICK GERALD ["Poodle"], II: 657, 750
BYRON, GEORGE GORDON, 6th Baron, I: 131, 166, 511. II: 22, 716. III: 138, 499.
    Childe Harold, I: 112. *English Bards*, I: 90. "Moore," II: 178. *Werner*, I: 349.

CABRERA, GEN. RAMON, IV: 344
CADOGAN PLACE, *see* BROOKFIELD
CAIRD, MR., II: 749
CAIRNES, COLONEL, II: 86
Calcutta Star, see also Hume, II: 97
CALDWELL, COL. HUGH, III: 672
CALDWELL, MR., I: 187, 191, 197, 199, 200, 202, 203
CALLAGHAN, MISS, I: 435
CAMBRIDGE, PRINCE ADOLPHUS, 1st Duke of, I: 389
CAMBRIDGE, GEORGE, 2nd Duke of, III: 363
Cambridge Gazette, The, I: 49
Cambridge Magazine, The, I: 39n., 49, 75n.
CAMERON, MRS., II: 698, 740. III: 73. IV: 404
CAMERON, MRS. CHARLES HAY [Julia Margaret Pattle], I: 189n.
CAMPBELL, CECILIA, IV: 240n.
    Letter to: IV, 240 [?]
CAMPBELL, SIR COLIN, III: 455n.
CAMPBELL, FORBES, II: 726
CAMPBELL, JAMES, II: 427
CAMPBELL, "JOCK," II: 663
CAMPBELL, JOHN CAMPBELL, 1st Baron, II: 666n. III: 667. IV: 240n.
CAMPBELL, MARY SCARLETT, IV: 240n.
    Letter to: IV, 240 [?]
CAMPBELL, MR., I: 187
CAMPBELL, R. B., *Letter to:* III, 504
CAMPBELL, THOMAS, II: 559

Canada, The, III: 99, 106, 107, 122, 127
CANNING, GEORGE, II: 317
CANOVA, ANTONIO, I: 75. IV: 439
CANTERBURY, ARCHBISHOP OF, *see* SUMNER, J. B., and THOMSON, William
CAPEFIGUE, JEAN BAPTISTE HONORÉ RAYMOND, *Empire and Consulate*, II: 146, 147. *Historie*, II: 829
CAPERN, MR., II: 761
CAPPUR, MRS., IV: 27
CARADOC, JOHN HOBART, *see* HOWDEN
CARDIGAN, JAMES THOMAS BRUDENELL, 7th Earl of, I: and Capt. Reynolds 484. IV: 221n.
CARDWELL, EDWARD, IV: and Oxford election 381, 382, 386, 387, 388, 389
CARLISLE, GEORGE HOWARD, 6th Earl of, II: 690n.
CARLISLE, GEORGE WILLIAM FREDERICK HOWARD, 7th Earl of, II: supports Russell on Corn Laws 216; 529, 664, 666. III: 22, 585. IV: 84
CARLISLE, H. E., ed. *Correspondence of Hayward*, quoted II: 202n., 636n.
CARLISLE, MR., I: 81
Carlisle Patriot, The, III: 39
CARLYLE, ALEXANDER, ed. *Letters of T. Carlyle*, quoted II: 824n.
CARLYLE, THOMAS, I: biographical cvi-cix; writes for *Chaos* 155; 184, 196, 247n.; on T. 347n.; 382, 404; "high-minded" 413; likes *Catherine* 421; 451. II: 163; Bedingfield and 167; T. annoyed with 227; 265; opinion of T. 365; "contempt for all mankind" 366; 418, 472, 473, 548, 626; fight with Reeve 628–29; 647, 674n., 699, 777; on T. 824n. III: 126, 179, 317, 404; confused with Car-

lisle 585. IV: T. on 82n.; 211n.; and T.'s death 304

Correspondence with Emerson, quoted I: cviii. *Essays*, I: T. on 396. *Frederick the Great*, III: 91; IV: 157. *French Revolution*, I: FG on 347; IV: 82n. "The Golden Pot," I: translated 214. *Heroes and Hero-Worship*, I: T. hears lecture 445. *Reminiscences*, quoted I: cliii. *Sterling*, I: quoted on T. 304n.; II: "wholly delightful" 808. *Wilhelm Meister*, I: translated 213

Letters to: II, 775; IV, 147, 157. *Letters from:* IV, 187, 188

CARLYLE, THOMAS, and J. A. Froude, ed. *Letters and Memorials*, quoted I: civ, clvii–clix

CARLYLE, MRS. THOMAS [Jane Welsh], I: cviii; on Reviss clvii–clix; 247n. II: 16, 265, 481, 548, 628n., 674n.; quoted on T. Taylor 696n.; quoted 829n. III: 68. IV: 304

Letters to: II, 242, 597, 775

CARMICHAEL, CHARLES HENRY EDWARD ["Chéri"], I: cx. II: sickly 46–47, 726; 738, 762. III: 148, 428. IV: 4, 75

CARMICHAEL, COL. CHARLES MONTAUBAN [before 1842 Carmichael-Smyth], I: biographical cx–cxi; ill 449, 452–53. II: home from India, in love 4; married 9; 11, 13, 21; lends T. money 34; 47, 48, 49, 50, 52, 54, 55, 57, 71; "singular mistrust" of T. 72; 88, 89, 91; in debt 99, 108; 187, 189; dispute with GP 222, 224; 225, 286, 351, 431, 496–501; "stupid generous obstinate devoted" 506; 726, 739; "delusions" 753; 755, 762. III: 9, 148, 276; "strange mania" 306; domestic unhappiness 364, 366, 387, 398, 427–28; 572. IV: 4, 6, 23, 29; "Colonel

Newcome" speculating 75; 129; T. pays back 130; "half of Colonel Newcome" 196; 213, 241n.

CARMICHAEL, MRS. CHARLES MONTAUBAN ["Polly," Mary Graham], I: biographical cix–cxi; 10, 14, 20, 22, 25, 31, 70, 73, 78, 80, 81, 84, 96, 106, 107, 118, 127, 128, 131, 134, 137, 143, 145, 178, 220, 236, 251, 256, 257, 258, 263, 305, 307; keeps house for T. and nurses I. T. 366–67; dispute with Mrs. Shawe 369; 381, 390, 393, 394, 398–99, 428, 429, 441, 447, 449, 453, 454, 468, 473. II: 3; in love 4; married 9; 11, 13, 18, 21; lends T. money 34–35; hates GM 46; jealousy 47; 48, 49, 50; jealousy 52–53; 54, 55, 57, 89, 91, 108, 142, 187, 217, 222n., 225; T. estranged from 231; 240, 258; "a character for Vanity Fair" 292; 310, 334, 409, 431, 494; attempted reconciliation with T. 496; "Becky is a trifle to her" 501; "miracle of deception" 505; 506, 507, 717, 726, 737, 753; "crazy with vanity" 755; 762. III: 8, 9, 17, 276n.; "domestic griefs" 302; break with T. 364–66; 387, 398; unkind to T. children 427; 428, 528, 573, 637, 648. IV: 4, 6, 23; T. children forbidden to see 29; 35, 78, 130, 131

CARMICHAEL FAMILY [Indian branch], II: 184

CARMICHAEL, FLORENCE GRAHAM, I: cx. IV: 75

CARMICHAEL, SIR JAMES ROBERT [before 1841 Carmichael-Smyth], I: cxin., 30, 31, 49, 55, 245, 263. II: 97, 197, 242, 380

Letter to: I, 256

CARMICHAEL, LADY [Louisa Butler, m. Sir James], II: 726, 752

CARMICHAEL, ROSE GORDON, I: cx. III: 387

Carmichael-Smyth, Col. Charles Montauban, *see* Carmichael, C.M.

Carmichael-Smyth, David Freemantle, II: 381

Carmichael-Smyth, Eleanor, III: 388

Carmichael-Smyth, Maj.-Gen. George, I: 45, 141, 144

Carmichael-Smyth, Georgiana Christina, *see* Forrest, Mrs. William

Carmichael-Smyth, Harriet, III: 388

Carmichael-Smyth, Maj.-Gen. Sir James, I: 14, 30n., 426n.

Carmichael-Smyth, Lady [Harriet Morse, m. Sir James], I: 426. II: 97, 197

Carmichael-Smyth, James Doddington, II: 242

Carmichael-Smyth, James Robert, *see* Carmichael, J. R.

Carmichael-Smyth, Maj. Henry ["GP"], I: biographical cxii-cxvi; letter to his wife 31; takes T. to Cambridge 32; and *Constitutional* 301n., 304, 305, 321, 341; plans return to India 361, 362; leaves England because of debts 448n.; and Indian bank crash 508. 4, 8, 9, 12, 17, 20, 22, 44, 45, 47, 48, 49, 50, 54, 55, 56, 57, 62, 64, 66, 69, 70, 72, 73, 76, 78, 80, 81, 84, 88, 89, 92, 96, 106, 107, 118, 123, 128, 131, 134, 137, 143, 145, 151, 153, 161, 176, 178, 183, 186, 187, 188, 219, 226, 245, 256, 257, 258, 263, 265, 268, 271, 291, 292, 307, 311, 346, 356, 360, 382, 383, 389, 390, 397, 401, 428, 429, 431, 435, 438, 442, 449, 454, 465, 479, 482, 484, 500
II: to Italy to meet C. Carmichael 3, 4; his health fetish 36, 38; and *Constitutional* creditors 49, 57; "steadiness of heart" 53; and A.T. 123; T. paying debts of 221, 238; dispute with C. Carmichael 222; alarmed about English riots 358; free of debt 379, 399, 401; returns to England 441; nursing his wife 609; treatment of wife 798. 38, 54, 55, 77, 80, 85, 86, 94, 113, 120, 135, 141, 146, 168, 177, 200, 211, 215, 232, 234, 239n., 240, 247n., 256, 258, 287, 289, 292, 293, 309, 311, 318, 324, 334, 335, 357, 360n., 372, 374, 381, 383, 393, 417, 439, 449n., 522, 523, 525, 536, 551, 558, 559, 564, 568, 574, 599n., 609, 626, 726, 732, 733, 734, 736, 748, 756, 762, 763, 792, 812, 813, 815
III: "noble simple old gentleman" 13; ill with "brain attack" 245, 246; "Colonel Newcome" 464. 9, 18, 24, 25, 40, 48n., 49, 50, 51, 52, 56, 60, 62, 64, 73, 77, 82, 86, 97, 98, 105, 106, 107, 108, 109, 111, 122, 130, 140, 144, 153, 169, 170, 176, 188, 191, 201, 219, 225, 236, 243, 249, 266, 269, 270, 272, 282, 285, 288, 292, 299, 300, 302, 306, 313, 322, 323, 324, 325, 327, 333, 334, 339, 348, 354, 361, 362, 365, 367, 376, 385, 388, 396, 398, 403, 411, 423, 428, 429, 454, 457, 479, 482, 490, 515, 521, 524, 525, 544, 557, 568, 573, 576, 587, 598, 599, 616, 626, 627, 628, 629, 631, 634, 635, 637, 638, 645, 647, 670, 675, 676n.
IV: "half of Colonel Newcome" 196; dead 247, 264, 398. 5, 6, 7, 8, 9, 13, 14, 35, 52, 56, 57, 61, 77, 112, 113, 156, 186, 202, 203, 214, 236, 237, 438, 440
Letters to: I, 175; II, 20, 224;

III, 655; IV, 3. *Letters from:* I, 31; II, 250

CARMICHAEL-SMYTH, MRS. HENRY [Anne Becher (Thackeray), G. 53], I: biographical cxii-cxvi; quoted 9n., 10n.; and *Constitutional* 309. 151, 153, 161, 163, 186, 187, 188, 193, 194, 201, 203, 216, 219, 220, 226, 229, 231, 256, 257, 258, 280, 295, 296, 299, 303, 304, 305, 307, 311, 312, 329, 346, 361, 431, 500, 513, 515, 516

II: to Italy to meet C. Carmichael 3; in *Second Funeral* 4, 8; advises taking I.T. to Germany 31, 32, 33; "angel" 38; and T.'s heterodoxy in writing 209; and illegitimate grandchild 367; half of "Amelia" 394; and Mrs. B. 453; "Mrs. Pendennis" 457; and M. Carmichael 506; "gloomifies" T. 525; and T.'s Literary Fund "smash" 540, 541; her husband nursing her 609; "awfully afraid" of T. 744; T. on 747; relations with husband 798. 20, 21, 34, 36, 64, 110, 145, 146, 147, 168, 173, 178, 183, 187, 195, 196, 210, 225, 240, 257, 324, 350, 360n., 361, 399, 428, 435, 439, 441, 461, 469, 480, 505, 507, 522, 523, 524, 526, 529, 531, 536, 545, 546, 548, 551, 558, 559, 564, 574, 581, 587, 590, 595n., 598n., 599, 602, 605, 607, 621, 624, 626, 654, 661, 672, 693, 717, 719, 732, 733, 734, 735, 736, 739, 745, 748, 749, 784n., 788, 840

III: "so tender so loving so cruel" 13; and religious teaching of T. children 93, 141; T. children nursing her 625, 628, 636, 640, 641; "worn down" by husband 645, 651. 5, 9, 34, 41, 48n., 49, 50, 51, 52, 56, 57, 62, 64, 65, 73, 77, 82, 84, 91, 97, 98, 105, 106, 108, 109, 121, 122, 130, 137, 138, 144, 153, 157, 171, 175, 176, 191, 201, 215, 225, 236, 243, 245, 256, 266, 269, 270, 282, 285, 292, 300, 307, 310, 311, 313, 322, 341, 342, 345, 376, 385, 386, 388, 403, 419, 423, 439n., 454, 464, 468, 474, 482, 490, 503, 505, 506, 511, 513, 515, 521, 522, 524, 534, 540, 555, 556, 557, 565, 566, 568, 571, 573, 576, 587, 604, 613, 616, 626, 627, 629, 630, 631, 632, 635, 637, 638, 639, 642, 643, 644, 647, 648, 649, 653, 656, 675, 676n.

IV: "gloomy temper" 233; husband dead 247; melancholy 264; T. on 378, 419, 440. 19, 21, 23, 28, 34, 35, 39, 40, 56, 57, 111, 112, 113, 115, 116, 123, 186, 196, 202, 203, 214, 236, 237, 280, 295, 296n., 299, 300, 302, 305, 314, 350, 418, 422, 443

Letters to: I, 3, 4, 7, 8, 9, 11, 13, 15, 20, 29, 32, 35, 40, 45, 51, 56, 63, 67, 69, 74, 79, 80, 83, 84, 89, 92, 96, 98, 101, 104, 106, 108, 111, 113, 116, 119, 123, 129, 132, 135, 137, 141, 143, 145, 176, 181, 241, 244, 249, 259, 261, 263, 266, 269, 270, 272, 289, 320, 379, 381, 383, 387, 390, 393, 397, 402, 410, 418, 423, 426, 432, 436, 439, 442, 446, 449, 452, 458, 461, 463, 466, 473, 474, 475, 477, 481, 482, 486; II, 9, 18, 46, 48, 51, 57, 68, 71, 74, 77, 83, 88, 90, 94, 96, 98, 107, 112, 115, 120, 123, 128, 169, 171, 175, 176, 178, 180, 183, 186, 188, 196, 200, 203, 205, 211, 215, 216, 221, 228, 230, 232, 238, 242, 243, 250, 255, 257, 285, 287, 289, 291, 308,

317, 321, 330, 333, 349, 355, 372, 379, 381, 392, 400, 408, 417, 567, 576, 598, 707, 725, 752, 761, 791, 797, 809, 812; III, 15, 23, 38, 58, 109, 148, 168, 187, 198, 216, 246, 287, 301, 305, 323, 324, 325, 332, 336, 346, 352, 361, 364, 365, 374, 396, 414, 427, 437, 479, 496, 527, 543, 598; IV, 3, 5, 7, 12, 61, 74, 78, 85, 128, 154, 270, 273, 314. *Letters from:* I, 10, 258; III, 85, 271, 525

CARMICHAEL-SMYTH, MARIA, II: 762. III: 388

CARMICHAEL-SMYTH, MARIA AGNES, *see* MONRO, Mrs. Alexander

CARMICHAEL-SMYTH, MARK WOOD, II: 47, 762n. III: 375, 388

CARMICHAEL-SMYTH, MRS. MARK WOOD [Marianne Hutton], II: 47. III: 388

CARMICHAEL-SMYTH, MAJ. ROBERT STEWART, I: 189, 259, 383. II: 381, 755, 762. III: 77, 616

CARMICHAEL-SMYTH, MRS. ROBERT [Agnes Rosa Hervey], III: 616, 627, 631

CARMICHAEL-SMYTH, WILLIAM HENRY, I: 274, 421. II: 222, 224

CARNE, JOSEPH, I: 17, 23, 28, 32, 33, 34, 36, 37, 39, 40, 42, 43, 44, 45, 48, 49, 52, 53, 57, 61, 70, 71, 74, 80, 106, 493, 494, 495, 496

CAROLINE AMELIA ELIZABETH, QUEEN, III: 592

CAROLINE, MLLE., II: 359

CARPENTER, WILLIAM BENJAMIN, *Letter to:* II, 368

CARROLL, LEWIS, *pseud. see* DODGSON, C. L.

CARRUTHERS, ROBERT, IV: 90
  Letter to: IV, 36

CARTER, MR., *Letter to:* III, 656

Carthusian, The, I: 17

CARTWRIGHT, MR., I: 30

CASATI, M., I: 277, 282

CASH, MR. AND MRS. JOHN, III: 448

CASTLEREAGH, *see* LONDONDERRY

CATHERINE [a servant], III: 306

CATHOLIC EMANCIPATION, I: 34, 38; petition against 42, 47, 50; 51, 52; Lords pass 55; King signs bill 57; 58, 70n. III: 682

CATOR, CAPT. JOHN FARNABY, *see* LENNARD

CATTERMOLE, GEORGE, I: 283, 287, 329, 413

CATULLUS, GAIUS VALERIUS, II: 554. IV: 360

CAULFIELD, COL. AND MRS. JAMES MONTGOMERAY, IV: 252, 397, 399, 408

CAVE, MR., IV: 190n.

CAVENDISH, GEORGE, *Wolsey*, I: 51

CAVENDISH, WILLIAM GEORGE SPENCER, *see* DEVONSHIRE

CAY [or Kay], MR., I: 197, 202, 203, 231, 233, 237, 269

CAYLEY, CHARLES BAGOT, IV: 393; and wife 410, 411

CENTURY ASSOCIATION, III: 121n., 296n., 666. IV: 16, 18

CERCLET, ANTOINE, I: 358, 359, 360

CERVANTES, MIGUEL DE, *Don Quixote*, I: 105, 383; II: 249, 597; III: 304, 668; IV: 435

CHALLENOR, COL. THOMAS BISSE, IV: 401

CHALMERS, MR., IV: 29

CHAM, *pseud. see* NOÉ

CHAMBERLAYNE, EDWARD AND JOHN, *Magnae Brittanniae Notitia*, III: 447

Chambers Journal, IV: 125n., 335

CHAMBERS, ROBERT, II: 247n., 771n. III: 387. IV: 40n.
  Letters to: III, 265; IV, 125

CHAMBERS, MRS. ROBERT, II: 247, 248. IV: 125

CHAMPMARTIN, CHARLES ÉMILE
CALLANDE DE, I: 280
Chaos, Das, I: 154, 155, 180n.
CHAPMAN AND HALL, I: clxvii; contract with T. 459; T. sells guide
book to 463; 468; agreement about
Irish S. B. 470, 473, 475, 480.
II: 55, 74, 120, 163, 172n., 177,
218, 219, 330, 829n., 841. IV:
143, 159, 289, 323
    Letters to: I, 470; II, 42, 50,
64, 65, 66, 92, 98, 111, 126, 161,
174, 178, 185, 199; IV, 316
CHAPMAN, EDWARD, I: 459. II: 404,
460
    Letters to: II, 201, 218, 219,
258, 290, 321, 326, 399, 444,
455, 466, 480, 481, 482, 613,
614, 687, 723; IV, 314, 315,
316
CHAPMAN, FREDERICK, IV: 144, 411
    Letter to: IV, 132
CHAPPELL, JOHN C., II: 166
CHARLEMONT, LADY [Anne Berming-
ham, m. 2nd Earl], II: 645
CHARLES [a servant], IV: 148, 233
CHARLESTON, SOUTH CAROLINA, *see
also* chronology, III: 587, 588
CHARLESWORTH, ELIZABETH, *see*
COWELL
CHARLOTTE AUGUSTA, PRINCESS, I:
3n.
CHARLOTTE SOPHIA, QUEEN, IV: 442
CHARLTON, *see* FORREST, Col. and
Mrs.
CHARTERHOUSE SCHOOL, *see also*
Education, I: T. at 11–26; 58;
T.'s adult view of 59; 189. II:
"sad experience" at 284. III: 406,
435. IV: 200, 414, 415
CHARTISM AND CHARTISTS, I: T.
proposes article on 407; uprising
410–11; 421, 425, 458. IV: 189
CHASLES, PHILARÈTE, II: 460n.,
502; T.'s letter to 503n.–04n. III:
411
CHATEAUNEUF, AGRICOLA DE LA

PIERRE DE, I: "amused and bored
by" 277
CHATHAM, *see* PITT
CHAVE, MR., I: 429, 432
CHAVE, MRS. [Albinia Bowden], I:
429, 432
CHESHAM PLACE, *see* ELLIOT family
[Thomas]
CHESTER, MR., IV: 267
    Letter to: IV, 317
CHESTERFIELD, GEORGE STANHOPE,
6th Earl of, II: 359, 362
CHESTERFIELD, LADY [Anne Eliza-
beth Forester, m. 6th Earl], II:
784n.
CHESTERFIELD, PHILIP DORMER
STANHOPE, 4th Earl of, III: 358
Chimæra, I: 49, 76, 93; T.'s essay
in 98
CHIPMELL, MR., IV: 400
CHISWICK SCHOOL, *see also* Educa-
tion, I: 3, 9, 10, 16
CHITTY, JOSEPH, I: 181
CHOLERA, I: in Paris 240. II: 438
CHORLEY, HENRY FOTHERGILL, I:
456–57. II: 12, 13, 22, 25. III:
381
    Letter to: I, 457
CHRISTIE, CHARLES CLAYDON, I:
108n., 494, 495, 497
CHRISTIE, MRS., III: 669
CHURCH, MR., II: 60
CHURCHYARD, THOMAS, III: 29
CHURTON, REV. EDWARD, I: 25
CICERO, MARCUS TULLIUS, IV: 272.
Life and Letters, III: 536, 537,
538
CIST, LOUIS J., *Letter to:* III, 597
CIVIL WAR, *see* UNITED STATES
CLANRICARDE, ULICK JOHN DE
BURGH, 14th Earl and 1st Mar-
quess of, II: and T.'s application
for P. O. appointment 427, 431,
432, 433n. IV: 391
CLANRICARDE, LADY [Harriet Can-
ning, m. 14th Earl], II: 784n.
III: 667

CLAPHAM, MISSES, III: 288

CLARENCE, MR., IV: 411

CLARENCE, WILLIAM HENRY, Duke of, II: 363

CLARENDON, GEORGE WILLIAM FREDERICK VILLIERS, 4th Earl of, III: 401. IV: 44

CLARK, MR., IV: 412

CLARK, MRS., III: 662

CLARKE, EDWARD WILLIAM, *Library of Useless Knowledge*, I: 373–74; II: 44–45

CLARKE, MARY KING, III: 250n.

CLARK[E], MISS, III: 194, 358

CLARKE, MRS., I: 103

CLARKE, WILLIAM, I: 203, 228

CLAY, FREDERICK, *Letter to:* IV, 265

CLAY, SIR WILLIAM, IV: 392

CLAY, LADY [Harriet Dickason, m. Sir William], IV: 401

CLAYTON, N., *Letter to:* IV, 104

CLAYTON, O., IV: 392, 410

CLEMENTS, MR., I: 420

CLEVEDON COURT, *see* ELTON

CLIFFORD, CHARLES CAVENDISH, III: 316. IV: 412 [?]

CLINTON, HENRY PELHAM, *see* NEW-CASTLE, 5th Duke of

CLIVE, MRS. ARCHER, *Letter to:* IV, 317

CLIVE, THEOPHILUS, I: 253

CLOUGH, ARTHUR HUGH, II: 463, 578; "real poet" 580–81. III: 107n. *The Bothie of Taber-Na-Vuolich*, II: T. on 456–57, 463. *Letters and Remains*, quoted III: 109, 166n.
   Letter to: II, 456

COATS, PETER, III: 688. IV: 444, 445

COBBETT, WILLIAM, *History of the Protestant "reformation,"* II: 650, 651, 652

COBDEN, RICHARD, I: 385n., 386n. II: 129, 216, 753

COBHAM, MR., IV: 394

COCHRANE-BAILLIE, ALEXANDER, *see* LAMINGTON, 1st Baron

COCKBURN, SIR ALEXANDER JAMES EDMUND, IV: 393 [?], 395

COCKBURN, HENRY, *Memorials*, IV: 21

COCKBURN, MR., III: 689

"COCKEREL," I: 154

COHEN, LUCY, *Lady de Rothschild*, quoted II: 524n.

COLBERT, JEAN BAPTISTE, *Mémoires*, III: 447

COLBURN, HENRY, II: 59n., 149, 198, 218, 262
   Letters to: II, 167, 169

COLE, CHARLES, III: 440

COLE FAMILY [Henry], III: 276. IV: 142n., 273

COLE, HENNY, III: 626

COLE, HENRY, I: on T. 386n. II: 768. III: 89n. IV: 148, 162
   Letters to: I, 385, 386; II, 377; IV, 318, 319

COLE, MRS. HENRY [Marian Bond], I: 385n. III: 63, 375
   Letters to: II, 377; IV, 318

COLE, TISHY, III: 77, 626
   Letter to: IV, 142

COLERIDGE, SAMUEL TAYLOR, II: 53

COLLIER, JOHN PAYNE, I: 398
   Letter to: I, 281; IV, 319

COLLIGNON, M., II: 44, 139, 141, 142, 143, 830

COLLINGWOOD, STUART DODGSON, *Lewis Carroll*, quoted IV: 43n.

COLLINS, CHARLES ALLSTON, IV: 275, 280; on T.'s death 296n.; 397, 408, 409, 410, 414

COLLINS, MRS. CHARLES ALLSTON [Kate Dickens], *see* PERUGINI

COLLINS, EDWARD K., III: 603

COLLINS, WILKIE, IV: 238, 280n., 296n. *The Lighthouse*, III: 685n.

COLLINS, WILLIAM, *The Passions*, I: 9; T. parodies 39

COLLINSON, HENRY, II: 241

COLLIS, JOSIAH, I: 175

COLLIS, MRS. JOSIAH, I: 175

COLMACHE, LAURA, II: 223, 747.
III: 138, 306, 325, 397, 398

COLMACHE, MRS., II: 223n., 230,
232, 250, 734, 747. III: 138.
IV: 62. "Late Prince Talleyrand," II: 219

COLNAGHI, PAUL AND DOMINIC, III:
32

COLON, MARGUÉRITE ["Jenny"], I:
233

COLSON, JASINT, II: 235

COLVILE, SIR JAMES WILLIAM, IV:
409, 411, 414

COLVILE, LADY [Frances Eleanor
Grant, m. Sir James], IV: 409

Comic Almanack, for 1839 I: 395;
for 1840 I: 489n.

Comic Annual, The, I: 132

COMMONS, HOUSE OF, I: 199

COMPTON, MAJOR, Letter to: II, 327

COMPTON, MR., Letter to: III, 334

COMPTON, MRS., III, 334

COMSTOCK, CAPTAIN, IV: 80

COMYN, MR., IV: 397

CONGREVE, WILLIAM, III: lecture
225

CONINGHAM, J., III: 685. IV: 398,
400, 402, 409

CONINGHAM, WILLIAM [and family],
III: 392. IV: 122

CONSTABLE, JOHN, II: 454

CONSTANT, BENJAMIN, Adolphe,
quoted I: 146–47

Constitutional, The, I: civ; started
301; 303; Major C-S and 305;
306, 308, 309, 315, 320, 321n.,
324, 328, 330n.; appeal for money
343–44; 386n.; in debt 448n. II:
creditors of 20, 21, 49, 57-58, 95,
97, 99, 107, 108, 112. III: 390,
411

  Letter to: Directors of I, 341

CONYERS, MR., II: 245

COOK, REV. FRANCIS CHARLES, II:
497

COOK, REV. JOHN, III: 107, 120

COOK, JOHN DOUGLAS, IV: 227
  Letters to: II, 471, 629

COOK, MR., I: 227, 228, 229, 230,
231, 235

COOKE, GEORGE WINGROVE, IV:
400, 410

COOKE, THOMAS POTTER, I: sketch
of 502

COOKESLEY, HENRY PARKER, I: 38,
497

COOKSLEY, MR., IV: 374

COOPER, SIR HENRY, III: 689. IV:
445

COOPER, JAMES FENIMORE, II: 270.
The Bravo, I: "very poor" 206.
The Prairie, II: 156

COOPER, JOHN, III: 501n.

COOPER, WILLIAM DURANT, ed.
Letters . . . by Sterne, II: 800

COOTE, LADY, I: 310

COPELAND, CHARLES TOWNSEND, ed.
Letters of Carlyle, quoted I: 347n.

COPELAND, MR., III: 594

COPLEY, SIR JOHN SINGLETON, see
LYNDHURST

COPYRIGHT, see INTERNATIONAL
COPYRIGHT

CORBIN [or Corbyn], MR., III: 312,
315, 670. IV: 414

CORCORAN, WILLIAM WILSON, III:
215n.

CORCORAN, MRS. WILLIAM WILSON,
III: 215

CORDIER, JULES, see VAULABELLE

CORK, RICHARD EDMUND ST. LAW-
RENCE BOYLE, 9th Earl of, IV:
390

CORKRAN, ALICE, IV: 122

CORKRAN FAMILY [John], III: 139,
141. IV: 156

CORKRAN, HENRIETTE, Celebrities
and I, quoted II: 140n.; IV: 156n.

CORKRAN, JOHN FRAZER, II: 140.
III: 568, 668. IV: 8n., 156n.,
398

CORKRAN, MRS. JOHN FRAZER, III:
137. IV: 129n., 156n.

Cornhill Magazine, I: cxxv, cxlviii, clxviii; Trollope and clxxi, clxxii. III: 471n. IV: contract 130; 136n., 137n.; T. agrees to edit 148; 149–50, 151n.; soliciting Tennyson 153; naming of 154, 156; and Carlyle 157–58; soliciting Trollope 158–59; prospectus 159–61; contributors 162; 163; soliciting Longfellow 164; soliciting Brownings 165–66; and Hood 167; tremendous success 168; Milnes on 169–70; Browning and 171–72; Landseer illustrates 176, 177; 178–80, 182; Hood on 183; 184; A. T. in 185; Yates' article on quoted 189n.–90n.; 191, 192, 193, 194n., 196n.; contributors 197; 199n., 202, 203; Trollope on morality of 206–07; 208, 209; and Skelton 210; Ruskin in 211n.; 212n.; contributors 215; 216n., 217, 220n., 222; 224n., 225n.; and morality 226–27, 228; 230, 234; Trollope in 236; 238n., 239n., 241n., 242n., 244n., 248n., 250n., 253, 255n.; T. resigning from 256, 257, announcement of resignation 258–60; 261, 268n., 271n.; A. T. in 272n.; 274n., 278n., 282n., 284, 302n., 319, 330n., 338n., 382n., 397n., 398n.; draft of resignation letter 399–400
    Letter to: Contributors and Correspondents IV, 258

CORN LAWS, I: T. illustrating pamphlet against 385. II: 67n.; O'Connell and 129, 130; Russell and 216; 683

CORNWALL, BARRY, *pseud. see* PROCTER, Bryan Waller

CORRY, HENRY THOMAS LOWRY, II: 647. IV: 404
    Letter to: II, 759

Corsair, The, I: T.'s connection with 406n. II: 555

CORSILLES [or Corselles], MR., II: 78–79, 306

COSMOPOLITAN CLUB, IV: 271n.

COSTELLO, DUDLEY, I: 321. II: 151
    Letter to: IV, 320

COTTENHAM, SIR CHARLES CHRISTOPHER PEPYS, 1st Earl of, II: 666n.

COTTIN, ELIZABETH, I: 30n. II: 110. III: 685. IV: 400, 408

COTTIN, MME. MARIE RISTEAU, *Mathilde,* I: 102

COULON, M., I: 85, 262n.

COULSON, WILLIAM, IV: 409

COURIER, PAUL LOUIS, I: 230

COURTIRAS, GABRIELLE A. C. DE, *see* DASH

COURVOISIER, FRANÇOIS BENJAMIN, I: 443n.; T. on hanging of 451, 452n., 453, 454

COUSINS, VICTOR, *Philosophie,* II: 225; quoted 226

COUTTS, II: 162

COWAN, CHARLES, IV: 36, 37, 40n.

COWELL, EDWARD BYLES, III: 115n.

COWELL, MRS. EDWARD BYLES [Elizabeth Charlesworth], I: FG and 293. II: 16, 266. III: poetry quoted 115–17

COWLEY, HENRY RICHARD WELLESLEY, 2nd Baron and 1st Earl, III: 316n.

COWLEY, LADY [Olivia de Ros, m. 1st Earl], III: 316

COWPER, CHARLES SPENCER, II: 505, 506

COWPER, MRS. CHARLES SPENCER, *see* ORSAY, Lady Harriet d'

COWPER, WILLIAM, I: T.'s sketch of summerhouse 162; FG on 166–67; 174. *The Task,* quoted I: 420. *Votum,* quoted I: 241

COZIO, DON TELESFORO DE TRUEBA Y, I: sketch of 265

COZZENS, FREDERICK SWARTOUT, III: 529. IV: 66. *Sparrowgrass Papers,* IV: 17

Letters to: III, 510; IV, 16.
Letter from: IV, 72

COZZENS, MRS. FREDERICK SWART-OUT [Susan Meyers], III: 510

CRABBE, GEORGE, III: 29

CRAIGIE, JOHN LIVINGSTON, IV: 397

CRAMPTON, JOHN FIENNES TWISLE-TON, III: 194, 202, 204, 205, 218, 253, 539, 540, 546; diplomatic incident 548n.–49n.; 658, 664

CRANCH, CHRISTOPHER P., III: 464, 466n. "Reminiscences of T.," quoted III: 466n.

CRAVEN, MAJ.-GEN. HENRY AU-GUSTUS BERKELEY, III: 27n.

CRAVEN, MRS. HENRY AUGUSTUS BERKELEY, III: 27

CRAWFORD, GEORGE MORLAND, *Letter to:* II, 721

CRAWFORD, JAMES H. [*G.* 87], I: 263

CRAWFORD, MRS. JAMES H. [Char-lotte Shakespear, *G.* 86], I: 186, 187, 263, 460

CRAWFORD, WILLIAM CONOLLY, I: 493

CRAWFURD, JOHN, IV: 173, 233 [?], 450

CRAWFURD, WALTER, IV: 173n.

CRAWFURD, MRS. WALTER [Horatia Perry], *Letter to:* IV, 173

CREAGH, BEN, I: 476

CRÉBILLON, CLAUDE-PROSPER JOL-YOT DE, *Sopha*, I: 213

CREIGHTON, MR., III: 312

CRERAR, JOHN, III: 491n., 569
Letters to: III, 593, 600

CRESSWELL, MR., II: 151

CRESWICK, THOMAS, II: 454

CREYKE, ROBERT GREGORY, III: 524, 613. IV: 82, 84

CRICHTON, MR., IV: 24

CRIMEAN WAR, III: 393n., 394, 395, 403, 408, 409, 416n., 455n., 548n.

CRITTENDEN, I: 268

CROHON, GEORGE BIRMINGHAM, I: 494

CROKER, JOHN WILSON, II: backs T. for Athenæum 636n.

CROLY, GEORGE, *Salathiel*, I: 52; IV: 378

CROMWELL, OLIVER, I: 496. II: 83

CROSS, GOVERNOR, *Sterne*, quoted III: 281n.

CROSS, MARY ANN EVANS, *see* ELIOT, George

CROUSTADE, M. DE, II: 825

CROWE, AMY MARIANNE, *see* THACK-ERAY, Mrs. Edward Talbot

CROWE, EDWARD, I: cxvii. III: 622

CROWE, EUGENIE, *see* WYNNE, Mrs. Robert

CROWE, EYRE, I: biographical cxvii, cxix–cxx. II: working for T. 190, 612. III: T.'s secretary 25; 47n., 82, 83, 87, 88, 90, 97; with T. to America 100, 106, 107, 110, 119, 121, 129, 144, 148, 153, 159, 161, 165, 170, 176, 179, 180n., 184, 189, 198n., 207, 213, 214, 222, 225, 233, 235, 238, 240, 241, 243, 248, 256, 261; 264, 276, 358, 477, 556, 613, 622n., 625, 626, 634. IV: 13, 52, 121, 304, 391. *T.'s Haunts,* quoted II: 392n. *With T. in U. S.,* quoted III: 119n., 130n.–31n., 176n., 227n.
Letters to: II, 608; III, 18, 79, 310, 560, 625

CROWE, EYRE EVANS, I: biographical cxvii–cxviii; 283, 286, 325n., 358, 360, 435. II: 47, 64, 164, 314; resigns from DN 811, 815. III: 506, 561, 613n.

CROWE, MRS. EYRE EVANS [Mar-garet Archer], I: cxvii, 317, 388. II: 10, 75, 77, 521, 530, 537, 753, 815, 843. III: 79, 121, 409
Letter to: II, 489

CROWE FAMILY, I: biographical cxvii–cxx; 354, 355, 359, 362. II: 20,

32, 143n., 189, 258, 291, 308,
335, 530, 554, 590, 664, 683.
III: 261, 561n.
CROWE, SIR JOSEPH, I: biographical
cxviii-cxix; 511. II: 753; loses
job 811; 814, 815. III: 82, 264,
562, 622n.; TL correspondent
233; 411. *Reminiscences,* quoted
I: 509–10
CRUCIFIX, MR., II: 49, 57
CRUIKSHANK, GEORGE, I: 132; illus-
trating *Stubbs' Calendar* 365, 369;
395; T.'s article on 438
    Letters to: I, 255, 370, 380,
489, 490; IV, 277, 320
CRUM, JAMES, II: 818n. III: 637n.
CRUM, JESSIE, III: 637n. IV: 40n.
CRUM, MARGARET, *see* KELVIN
CRUM, MARY, IV: 40n.
CRYSTAL PALACE, II: 767. III: the
new 62, 375; plan to sell cards at
386; P abuses 432; 609, 675. IV:
31, 37, 38
CUBITT, WILLIAM, IV: 243, 250,
395, 396, 400
CULLUM, REV. SIR THOMAS, II: 434,
809, 843n.
CULLUM, LADY, II: 481. IV: 411
Culverwell's, IV: 63
CUMMING, REV. JOHN, III: 439
CUNDALL, JOSEPH, *Letters to:* II,
434, 612
CUNNINGHAM, HUGH, I: 461, 489.
II: 136
CUNNINGHAM, MRS., II: 603
CUNNINGHAM, PETER, III: 81, 476,
494. IV: 190n., 197. "Charter
House," II: 283, 284. *Handbook
of London,* IV: 320
CUNNINGHAM, MRS. PETER, *Letters
to:* III, 371; IV, 320
CUPPLES, MR., *Letter to:* IV, 165
CURRY, RAIKES, III: 282, 667
CURTIS, MRS. ALFRED. LEONARD,
see STRONG, Elizabeth
CURTIS, GEORGE, III: 550
CURTIS, GEORGE WILLIAM, III: 359,

490, 493, 496, 503, 662. IV:
17, 18, 66
    Ed. Motley *Correspondence,*
quoted III: 152n. "T. in U.S.,"
III: 280. *Nile Notes,* III: T. on
285–86
    Letters to: III, 529, 550, 602.
Letter from: IV, 92
CURTIS, MRS. GEORGE WILLIAM
[Anna Shaw], III: 359n., 490,
493, 496. IV: 17, 93
CURTIS, MR. [of Springfield], III:
161
CURZON, ROBERT, *see* ZOUCHE
CUSHING, CALEB, III: 549

Daily News, II: Forster editor of
252; 480, 646; the Crowes re-
sign from 811, 815. III: 83,
393n., 472n.
Daily Telegraph, IV: 185, 254
DALY, JUDGE CHARLES PATRICK,
III: 510n. IV: 17, 18
    Letter to: III, 602
DALY, MRS. CHARLES PATRICK
[Maria Lydig], IV: 17
DAMER, COL. GEORGE LIONEL DAW-
SON, II: 646, 825
DANA, CHARLES ANDERSON, *Letter
to:* IV, 321
DANA, RICHARD HENRY, III: 166n.
DANCE, CHARLES, III: 606
DANCE, MRS. CHARLES [Mrs. Ralph
Ingilby], II: 286, 381. III: 388,
398
"DANDO" [the oyster eater], I: 327,
328n., 345–46, 515
DANIEL, RICHARD, III: 492, 494,
540
DARBY, MR., I: 282
DARLEY, WILLIAM, I: cxvii, 359,
362, 450. II: 141
DASH, COMTESSE [Gabrielle de Cour-
tiras, Vicomtesse de Saint-Mars],
Mémoires, quoted II: 588n.
DASHWOOD, MR., II: 512

DAVID, JACQUES LOUIS, I: 91, 100

DAVIDOFF, MAJOR, II: 362, 363

DAVIES, REV. GERALD S., *Charterhouse*, quoted I: 11n.

DAVIS, GEORGE T., III: 530, 531n., 665

DAVIS, JOHN CHANDLER BANCROFT, III: 112, 312, 597, 605, 606. IV: 18, 65, 68, 202

DAVIS, MRS. JOHN CHANDLER BANCROFT [Frederica Gore], IV: 65

DAVIS, MISS, III: 379

DAVIS, MR., III: 152

DAVISON, SIR HENRY, II: 370. III: 385, 426, 572, 636; Indian judgeship 637. IV: 16, 361
　　Letters to: III, 648. IV, 185, 321

DAVY, SIR HUMPHRY, II: 518n.

DAVY, LADY [Jane Kerr (Apreece), m. Sir Humphry], II: 518, 533. III: 70. IV: 312

DEANERY CLUB, The Secretary of the, *Letter to:* IV, 322

DEBATING CLUB, I: 107

DEFOE, DANIEL, II: 215. *Crusoe*, I: 344

DEGEN, MR., III: 109n.

DÉJAZET, PAULINE VIRGINIE, I: 238. II: 23–24, 407, 409

DELACROIX, FERDINAND VICTOR EUGÈNE, I: 100

DELANE, JOHN THADDEUS, II: 126. IV: 396, 404
　　Letter to: III, 319

DELAROCHE, PAUL, I: 276

DELDER, MME., II: 287

DELISLE, M., II: 607

DENMAN, RICHARD, III: 671, 672, 675. IV: 392, 408

DENMAN, MRS. RICHARD, IV: 392, 408

DENNERY, *see* PHILIPPE, Adolphe

DERBY, EDWARD STANLEY, 14th Earl of, III: 679

DERBY, LADY [Emma Bootle-Wilbraham, m. 14th Earl], IV: 391

DERING, MRS., III: 285

DEROSNE, BERNARD, and Lambert Thiboust, *Aurore*, IV: 413

DE VERE, AUBREY THOMAS, IV: 446

DEVONSHIRE, ARTHUR HILL, 2nd Marquess of, II: 645n.

DEVONSHIRE, WILLIAM GEORGE CAVENDISH, 6th Duke of, I: 261. II: 18, 373, 418, 527, 665. III: 316, 429
　　Letter to: II, 375

DEVONSHIRE, GEORGIANA, Duchess of [m. 5th Duke], II: 657n.

DEVRIENT, LUDWIG, I: 141; sketch of 499. III: 443

DEXTER, WALTER, ed. *Dickens's Letters*, quoted I: 327n.–28n; IV: 99n.–100n.

DEXTER, DR. WILLIAM PRESCOTT, *Letter to:* III, 509

DEXTER, MRS. WILLIAM PRESCOTT, III: 509

DICK, ANDREW COVENTRY, *Letter to:* II, 821

DICK, ANNA, II: 689

DICK, MRS. ABERCROMBY, III: 631, 687

DICK, CHARLOTTE HENRIETTA RICHMOND [G. 94], III: 687

DICK FAMILY [William Flemming], I: 186, 187, 188, 194, 198, 200, 201, 202, 204, 415, 419. II: 173, 195

DICK, HARRIS ST. JOHN [G. 92], IV: 141 [?]

DICK, GEN. SIR ROBERT, I: 193

DICK, WILLIAM FLEMMING [G. 78], I: 23n., 187, 192, 193, 199. II: 244

DICK, MRS. WILLIAM FLEMMING [Emily Thackeray, G. 77], I: 23, 413, 419. II: 244
　　Letter to: IV, 141

DICKEN, CHARLES ROWLAND, I: 12, 76
　　Letter to: II, 368

DICKENS, CHARLES, I: Carlyle on

cix; biographical cxx-cxxiii; cxliii, 279n., 346n.; and "Lord Bateman" 380, 381n.; 459. II: returning from America 56, 60, 65; and international copyright 66; 110; likes *Irish S.B.* 113; 132, 133, 186, 252n., 253, 260, 270; and T.–Forster fight 294, 295, 296, 303, 304, 307n.; "mistrusts" T. 308; 322n., 333, 346, 449n., 569, 584, 585, 660, 770; T. on 772–73; 777, 780, 822. III: jealous of T. 37n.; 119, 174, 184; "fecundity of imagination" 288; 317, 379–80, 393n., 405; "genius" 407–09; 433n.; anecdote 455; speech 457, 461; 466n., 471; quoted on B. Sheridan 617n.; 620; and theatricals 643n.; 674, 678, 685, 688n. IV: 74; Ternan affair 83–84; separated from wife 86, 122; and Garrick Club Affair 91n., 99n.–100n., 102n., 105n., 106n.; 113n.; giving readings 115–16; and Yates 119, 133, 135, 163n., 202; 207, 238, 278n., 372, 382, 392; note to Yates 394n.; 416, 435

American Notes, II: 88; III: 226. *Battle of Life*, II: 258n.; T. reviews 262; "wretched affair" 266. *Bleak House*, III: 181; "Mr. Turveydrop" 238, 251n. *Cricket*, III: 576. *Christmas Carol*, II: "charming" 135; T. reviews 141, 165; 184. *Copperfield*, II: "bravo" 531; 533, 535, 537, 588, 648; "Micawber" 694; 704; IV: "Peggoty" 380. *Dombey*, II: 266, 267n., 337, 369, 726n. *Hard Times*, III: 363. *Haunted Man*, II: 467, 469, 478. "Holly-tree," III: 537. *Little Dorrit*, III: 518, 523; "capital" 572; 623. *Martin Chuzzlewit*, III: 591, 595. *Master Humphrey's Clock*, I: 438; "sadly flat" 444; 460. *Nickleby*,

II: 24, 45, 88; "Crummles" 262; III: 190. *Old Curiosity Shop*, II: 178n. *Pickwick*, I: cxxi; illustrations 311n.–12n.; 367; II: 262; "Stiggins" 635; 821; III: 10, 487.

Letters to: II, 299, 300, 303; III, 431; IV, 58, 59, 118, 322.

Letters from: II, 297, 336, 369; III, 433; IV, 61, 99, 116

DICKENS, MRS. CHARLES [Catherine Hogarth], II: 110, 337, 367, 481, 569. III: letter to A. T. 643n. IV: and Ternan affair 84; separation 86, 87, 131

DICKENS CHILDREN, III: 537, 544; theatricals 643. IV: and parents' separation 86; 116; and Miss Hogarth 131

DICKENS, KATE, *see* PERUGINI

DICKENS, MARY, III: 643

DICKINSON, HENRY STRAHAN, I: 495

DICKINSON, MR., IV: 400

DICKINSON, WILLIAM, *Letter to:* III, 149

DICKSON, PETER, IV: 397

DIDEROT, DENIS, I: 166. II: 500

DIDGAR, MR., I: 241

DIDIER, ALEXIS [Alexis the Somnambulist], II: 506–07

DIEBITSCH, GEN. HANS VON, I: 163

"DIGNITY OF LITERATURE CONTROVERSY," I: cxxxv. II: 629–35. III: 389

DILDIE, MME., II: 210

DILKE, CHARLES WENTWORTH, II: 441. III: 685

Letter to: II, 311

DILLON, HENRY AUGUSTUS DILLON-LEE, 13th Viscount, III: 53

DILLON, LADY [Henrietta Browne, m. 13th Viscount], III: 53

DILLON, JOHN BLAKE, III: 228, 668 [?]. IV: 278, 392, 408

DISRAELI, BENJAMIN [1st Earl of Beaconsfield], I: T. and "Young England" 215n. II: 148. III: 327n., 697, 683

Coningsby, quoted I: 82n.; II: satirized by T. 148n.–49n.; 188n. *Endymion*, II: T. in 149n. *Sybil*, II: reviewed by T. 148n.–49n.

DISRAELI, MRS. BENJAMIN, II: 644n.

DIXON, WILLIAM HEPWORTH, IV: T. and the Shakespeare Committee 416, 417
  Letter to: IV, 50

DOBBS, MR., I: 197, 200

DOBSON [or Dobbins], MISS, II: 602n., 740

DODD, MRS., II: 361

DODGSON, CHARLES LUTWIDGE ["Lewis Carroll"], IV: on T. 43n.

DODSWORTH, ROGER, and Sir William Dugdale, *Monasticon Anglicanum*, II: 670

DOLAND, ALEXANDER, *Letters from:* IV, 94, 96, 105

DOLBY, MISS, III: 13

DON, SIR WILLIAM HENRY, IV: 120n.

DONALDSON, MR., III: 665

Doneraile Chronicle, I: 430

DONERAILE, LADY, I: 430

DONIZETTI, GAETANO, *Elisiri d'Amore*, II: 14. *Fille du régiment*, III: 236. *Lucia*, II: 383

DONNE, REV. WILLIAM BODHAM, I: 346, 374. III: 115. IV: 398; and daughter 412

DONNELLY, MR., IV: 214

DONOVAN, MR., I: 274

DON PACIFICO, II: debate 757n.

DORAN, JOHN, IV: 197

DORCHESTER, DUDLEY WILMOT CARLETON, 4th Baron, II: 718n.

DORCHESTER, LADY [Charlotte Hobhouse, m. 4th Baron], II: 718n.

D'ORSAY, *see* ORSAY

DOUDET, III: 439

DOUGLAS, DR. JOSEPH, III: 578, 638. IV: 394

DOUGLAS, MRS. JOSEPH, III: 638

DOUGLAS, MARQUESS OF, *see* HAMILTON, 11th Duke of

DOW, GERARD, II: 118

DOWDEN, EDWARD, "Goethe's Last Days," quoted I: 232n.

DOWLING, MR., I: 449–50

DOWLING, MRS., I: 428

DOWNING, MRS. HARRIET, "Monthly Nurse," I: 351

DOWNSHIRE, ARTHUR BLUNDELL SANDYS TRUMBULL, 3rd Marquess of, II: 69

DOYLE, ANDREW, *Letter to:* II, 354

DOYLE, LADY [Sidney Williams-Wynn, m. Sir Francis], II: 751n.

DOYLE, RICHARD, I: cxi; biographical cxxiii–cxxv; cxlvi. II: 105n., 164, 387, 389, 614, 738. III: 126, 140, 155, 160, 231, 251; illustrates *Newcomes* 300, 302, 304, 305, 308; 340; Catholic convert 342n., 343, 351; T. likes his work 362; 375, 622n. IV: 312, 378, 410. *Rejected Cartoons*, II: 345. *Manners and Customs*, II: 537, 700n., 767n.
  Letters to: II, 374, 773; III, 9, 372, 384; IV, 322

D'OYLY, SIR CHARLES, II: 186n.

D'OYLY, LADY [Elizabeth Jane Ross, m. Sir Charles], II: 186

D'OYLY, REV. GEORGE, and Richard Mant, *Holy Bible*, I: 424

DRANE, MR., IV: 51

DRAPER, MRS. DANIEL, III: Sterne and 153n., 165n. IV: Sterne lies to 281–82

DRUMMOND, HENRIETTA BLANCHE, III: 135, 178

DRURY, HENRY, I: 238

DRURY, MISS, II: 286, 288, 289, 292, 306, 311, 318, 351

Dublin University Magazine, II: 29, 140n.

Dubois, Mémoires du Cardinal, I: 233, 253

DUCHÂTEL, CHARLES, II: 731

DUCHÂTEL, MME., II: 738

DUER, WILLIAM DENNING, III: 497, 498, 606. IV: 67, 68

DUFF, MOUNTSTUART ELPHINSTONE GRANT, IV: 412, 414

DUFFERIN, FREDERICK TEMPLE, 1st Marquess of, IV: 231, 402

DUFFERIN, LADY [Georgiana Hamilton, m. 1st Marquess], IV: 231n., 403

DUFF-GORDON, SIR ALEXANDER CORNEWALL, II: 229n., 264; and T.–Forster fight 295, 297, 298, 303, 304; 578, 740. IV: 393, 400, 409, 411
Letter from: II, 300

DUFF-GORDON, LADY [Lucy Austin, m. Sir Alexander], I: 203n. II: 229n., 264, 304, 351, 604, 685

DUFFY, CHARLES GAVAN, III: 467. *Carlyle,* quoted I: cix; II: 227n., 365n.
Letter to: III, 467

DUGDALE, SIR WILLIAM, and Roger Dodsworth, *Monasticon Anglicanum,* II: 670

DULONG, FRANÇOIS CHARLES, II: 228

DUMAS, ALEXANDRE [fils], III: 676
Demi-Monde, III: 460. *Dame aux Camélias,* III: "wicked" 618. *Quatre femmes,* II: 679–80

DUMAS, ALEXANDRE [père], II: "wonderful" 568; 619, 731. III: 676. IV: 428
Fils de l'emigré, I: 226. *Henri III,* I: 88. *Monte Christo,* III: 304. *Mousequetaires,* II: 588; IV: 274n. *Othon l'Archer,* II: T. parodies 141. *Vicomte de Bragelonne,* II: "delight" 588; IV: 421

Dumfries and Galloway Courier, III: 689

DUNDAS, SIR DAVID, IV: 444

DUNDAS, R.-ADM. SIR JAMES WHITLEY DEANS, II: 665. III: 403

DUNDAS, LADY [Lady Emily Moreton, m. Sir James], II: 665

DUNLAP, ARTHUR, I: 27, 29

DUNLAP, MR., III: 664

DUNLOP, JESSIE, III: 655

DUNLOP FAMILY, III: 505, 507, 515, 527, 531

DUNLOP, MRS., *Letter to:* III, 654

DUNN, CHARLES, IV: 149

DUPIN, ANDRÉ, I: 358

DU PRE [or Dupre], CALEDON GEORGE, I: 146n., 153, 189, 192, 198

DUPREZ, GILBERT-LOUIS, I: 363. II: 165–66

DUPUIS, ADOLPHE, III: 460n., 461

DURAND, MME., I: 273

DÜRER, ALBRECHT, I: 286

DURHAM, JOHN GEORGE LAMBTON, 1st Earl of, I: Buller with civ; dead 458

DURHAM, MR., III: 670
Letter to: IV, 269

DUTENS, LOUIS, *Mémoires d'un voyageur,* IV: 282

DUTTON, MR., IV: 409; and wife 412

DUVERNAY, MARIE-LOUISE, I: 262, 266, 276

DWARKANAUTH, *see* TAGORE

DWYER, MAJ. FRANK, II: 66–67; quoted 86n.

DYCE, REV. ALEXANDER, IV: 408, 414

EAMES, CHARLES, III: 664n.

EAMES, MRS. CHARLES, III: 664

EAST INDIA COMPANY, I: charter 42, 47, 51

EASTERN TRIP, II: diary on 150–57; letters on 176–88

EASTHOPE, SIR JOHN, II: 844

EASTLAKE, SIR CHARLES LOCK, I: 276, 294

EASTLAKE, LADY [Elizabeth Rigby, m. Sir Charles], II: slander on T. and *Jane Eyre* 341n. IV: 396, 401, 412

EASTNOR, VISCOUNT, *see* SOMERS, 3rd Earl

EBDEN, JOHN WATTS, I: 493, 495

EBERS AND CO. [booksellers], I: 178

EBERS, MR. AND MRS., IV: 396

EBRINGTON, VISCOUNT, *see* FORTE-SCUE, 3rd Earl

ECONOMICS AND SOCIAL ORDER, II: 356–57

EDDISBURY, BARON, *see* STANLEY, 2nd Baron

EDEN, MR. AND MRS., IV: 396

EDGELL, MISS WYATT, IV: 397

EDGEWORTH, MARIA, I: 395. *Harrington*, I: 158. *Fashionable Life*, I: 206

EDGEWORTH, MR., II: 545

Edinburgh Review, II: T.'s qualifications to write for 190–91, 201–02; 212, 213n.; article "mutilated" by 214–15; 321, 328, 334, 366. IV: 440

EDMONSTON, A., *Letter to:* IV, 24

EDMONSTON AND DOUGLAS, III: 34

EDUCATION, *see also* Arthur's School and Charterhouse, I: T.'s adult view of his own 137–39. II: in Ireland 89; 266

EDWARD VII, IV: 233; marriage 284

EDWARDS, HENRY SUTHERLAND, IV: 392n., 403, 404; and wife 408. *Recollections*, quoted IV: 82n.

EDWARDS, MR., I: 186, 187, 198, 200, 201, 206

EGLOSSTEIN, LOUISE VON, III: 442

EGYPT, II: 155–56

ELDER, DR. EDWARD, I: 12n.

ELDREDGE, CAPTAIN, III: 562n.

ELGIN, JAMES BRUCE, 8th Earl of, III: 624. IV: 205, 215n., 384

ELGIN, LADY [Elizabeth Oswald, m. 7th Earl], II: 749

ELIOT, EDWARD GRANVILLE, Lord, *see* ST. GERMANS

ELIOT, GEORGE [Mary Ann Evans Cross], II: 353n., 490. III: 437n. IV: 190n. *Adam Bede*, IV: morality in 207; T. "can't read" 238. *Amos Barton*, IV: 16n.

ELIZA [a servant], III: 62, 63, 67, 73, 75, 80, 100, 158, 301, 306, 375, 376, 397, 416, 642. IV: 4, 52, 80, 82

ELLENBOROUGH, EDWARD LAW, 1st Earl of, II: 166

ELLER, MR., I: 240

ELLICE, EDWARD ["Bear"], II: 731, 816. III: 267. IV: 392

ELLIOT FAMILY [Thomas Frederick], II: 525, 629, 642, 644, 701, 735n., 744, 746, 750. III: 63, 81, 183, 256, 342, 492, 518, 667. IV: 22, 29

ELLIOT, REV. GILBERT, II: 715

ELLIOT, HARRIET ANNE GERTRUDE, II: 645. III: 316

ELLIOT, HUGH, II: 516n.

ELLIOT, JOHN, JR., *Letter to:* IV, 145

ELLIOT, MRS. JOHN, JR., IV: 146

ELLIOT, MISS, II: 335

ELLIOT, MR. [G. 55], I: 183n.

ELLIOT, THOMAS FREDERICK, I: cxxv. II: 516n., 715n. III: 25, 53, 55, 63, 135, 495n., 496, 532. IV: 221, 392, 393, 412

ELLIOT, MRS. THOMAS FREDERICK [Jane Perry], I: c; biographical cxxv-cxxviii. II: 508n., 509, 512, 524, 541, 602n., 603, 620, 658, 664, 674n., 745, 768. III: 53, 63, 124, 173, 183, 263, 264, 458, 506, 513, 685. IV: dead 278; 391
   Letters to: II, 516, 555, 819, 825; III, 35, 51, 132, 221, 266, 480, 494, 507, 529, 547, 558, 580, 590, 616; IV, 323, Appendix XXVI

ELLIOT, WILLIAM GERALD, *Anecdotage*, quoted I: clix-clx

ELLIOTSON, DR. JOHN, II: 595n., 597, 600, 602, 610; *Rebecca* dedicated to 614; 644, 717 [?], 780n., 815. III: 47; loses money 127; 303, 437, 674. IV: 280, 395, 408

Letters to: II, 704; IV, 275, 280, 324

ELLIOTT, GEORGE P., I: 13, 149

ELLIOTT, BISHOP STEPHEN, III: 565

ELLISON, CUTHBERT EDWARD, IV: 22, 396, 402, 403, 408, 411

ELLISON, MRS. CUTHBERT EDWARD, IV: 22, 23, 402

ELSSLER, FANNY, II: 160

ELMORE, ALFRED, I: 323

ELMORE, DR. JOHN RICHARD, I: 323

ELPHINSTONE, JOHN BULLER-FULLERTON-ELPHINSTONE, 13th Baron, II: 362

ELTON, ARTHUR HALLAM, II: 436n., 469 [?], 520n., 569n.; criticism of *V. F.* 584–85; 606, 715

ELTON, MRS. ARTHUR HALLAM [Rhoda Willis (Baird)], II: 436, 515, 520, 521, 527, 536, 569n., 606

ELTON, SIR CHARLES ABRAHAM, I: xcvi. II: 436n., 516, 518, 580, 715

ELTON, JANE OCTAVIA, *see* BROOKFIELD, Mrs. William

ELTON, JULIA, *see* PARR, Mrs. Thomas

ELTON, LADY, II: 521

ELTON, LAURA BEATRICE, II: 715, 746

ELTON, MARY AGNES ["Missy"], II: 520, 537, 570, 581, 715
Letter to: II, 605

ELWIN, WARWICK, I: quoted cxxix-cxxx

ELWIN, REV. WHITWELL, I: biographical cxxviii-cxxxi. III: 449, 453, 596. IV: 122, 138. *Eighteenth Century Men,* quoted III: 468n., 619n.; IV: 241n.–43n., 377–80, 390n.
Letters to: III, 413, 465, 468, 551, 587; IV, 15, 163, 194, 237, 241, 281, 324

ELWIN, MRS. WHITWELL [Frances Elwin], I: cxxviii. III: 469. IV: impressions of T. 377–80

EMERSON, EDWARD WALDO, and Waldo Emerson Forbes, ed. *Journals,* quoted III: 142n.

EMERSON, RALPH WALDO, I: cviii. II: 672n. III: 142n. *Essays,* III: "wise and benevolent" 547; 548

ENCKE'S COMET, I: 170

ENGLAND—POLITICS I: Bedchamber crisis 384; 458, 484–85. II: 761–62, 823–24. III: universal suffrage 15–16; Crimean war cabinet 416, 417; 429; war scare 548–49, 588, 608; Appendix XVI. IV: 31–32; U.S. Civil War 213, 231, 263; war scare 443; Appendix XIX

ENGLISH FAMILY, I: 6, 8

ENGLISH MINISTER AT LE HAVRE, *Letter to:* III, 420

"EŌTHEN," *see* KINGLAKE

EPPS, DR., *see* NORRINGTON-EPPS CASE

ERCOLE, SIGNORA, III: 328

Ericsson, The, III: 209, 211

ERLACH, MME. D', III: 669

ERNEST AUGUSTUS, King of Hanover, II: 363

ERRINGTON, JOHN EDWARD, II: 743n. III: 668

ERRINGTON, MRS. JOHN EDWARD, II: 743. III: 668, 670. IV: 421

ERSKINE, MRS., III: 439, 440

ESCOTT, T. H. S., *Trollope,* quoted IV: 81n.

ESPARTERO, BALDOMERO, II: 465n.

ESQUIROL, JEAN ETIENNE DOMINIQUE, I: cxlix. II: 3

ESSAY CLUB, I: 56, 57

ESSEX, ARTHUR ALGERNON DE VERE CAPELL, 6th Earl of, IV: 412n.

ESSEX, LADY [Louisa Boyle, m. 6th Earl], IV: 412

ESTAMPER, CECILE D', *see* HANKEY, Mrs. William

ETHICS AND MORALITY, I: 402–03. II: 282. IV: 206, 226–27, 244

ETTY, WILLIAM, I: 279, 295

Europa, The, III: 270

EVANS, FREDERICK MULLETT, II: 148, 149, 247, 248, 383. III: 384, 614n. IV: 404, 413
  Letters to: II, 530; III, 431; IV, 260, 325

EVANS, MARY ANN, *see* ELIOT, George

EVANS, ROBERT WILSON, I: 493

EVANS, THOMAS, I: 494

Evening Post [New York], III: biography of T. 124n.

EVERETT, EDWARD, III: 194, 202
  Letter to: III, 197

EVERSLEY, CHARLES SHAW-LEFEVRE, 1st Viscount, III: 316

EVERSLEY, GEORGE JOHN SHAW-LEFEVRE, 1st Baron, III: 316

EWBANK, REV. W., I: 24

EWBANK, WILLIAM WITHERS, I: 24, 28, 76

Examiner, The, see also Forster, John, I: cxxi, 132, 400, 453. II: 7n., 106, 164n.; T. writing for 189, 190; "parted company" with 203; 257, 403, 404, 409, 424n.; attacking T. 630–34; 779n., 780n.; and L. Napoléon 814. III: 155n., 363, 389

EXPOSITION DES BEAUX ARTS, III: 460

EYRE, WILSON, III: 261, 666

FAGAN, GENERAL, II: 95

FAGAN, MRS., II: 321

FAIRBAIRN, MR., IV: 410

"FAMILY LIBRARY," I: 84n., 118

FANCOURT, MAJOR, II: 363

FANE, FRANCIS WILLIAM HENRY, *see* WESTMORLAND, 12th Earl of

FANE, JOHN, *see* WESTMORLAND, 11th Earl of

FANE, JULIAN HENRY CHARLES, II: 508n.

FANNY [a servant], IV: 230

FANSHAWE, REV. CHARLES S., II: 276n., 476, 659, 667. III: 77. IV: 326

FANSHAWE, MRS. CHARLES S., II: 275n., 276, 512, 528, 560, 562, 565, 577, 581, 590, 592, 644, 653, 663, 668, 670, 672, 685, 737, 739, 740, 744, 750. III: 17, 72, 626. IV: 429, 431
  Letters to: II, 624, 640, 649, 659, 667, 706; III, 80, 473, 630, 632, 640; IV, 27, 326

FANSHAWE FAMILY [Charles], II: 271n., 558n., 738. III: 77, 276. III: 409

FANSHAWE, ROSA ["Totty"], II: 276, 577, 624, 640, 658, 659, 670. III: 640. IV: 326
  Letter to: IV, 326

FARDEL, L., IV: 281

FARLEY, CHARLES, I: 192, 240

FARQUHAR, GEORGE, II: 38

FARREN, WILLIAM, I: 190

FARRER, MISS, II: 698, 750

FAUCHER, LEON, I: 325

FAULKNER, MR., *Letter to:* IV, 327

FAULKNER, MRS., IV: 327

FAVERSHAM, MR., *see* HABERSHAM

FAWCETT, HENRY EDWARD, I: 33, 34, 55, 58, 69, 81

FAWSETT, MRS., I: 109

FAWSETT, WALTER BARHAM, I: 44, 53, 55, 104, 109, 110

FAY, LEONTINE, I: 91, 93

FÉLIX, ELISA, *see* RACHEL, Mme.

FELT, WILLARD L., III: 111, 119n., 263, 358, 541
  Letters to: III, 45, 92, 382, 469

FELT, MRS. WILLARD L., III: 176

FELTON, CORNELIUS C., III: 166n.

FERDINAND II, King of the Two Sicilies, III: P attacks 364

FERGUSON, COLONEL, II: 569

FERGUSON, DR. ROBERT, III: 398

FERRIER, JAMES FREDERICK, IV: 28

FERRIER, SUSAN EDMONSTONE, *Destiny*, I: 158

FÉVAL, PAUL, *Mystères de Londres*, II: 496–97

FIELD, MAUNSELL B., *Memories*, quoted III: 102n.

FIELDING CLUB, III: 455n., 456n.

FIELDING, HENRY, I: T.'s "model" 108n.; 412; T.'s article on 469n. II: C. Brontë on 341n.; 370; T.'s article on 462; 612n., 633, 637. III: 184, 304, 402, 466n. IV: 186, 192

Amelia, II: 249; "delightful portrait" 416. *Joseph Andrews*, II: "coarse and careless" 416; "Trulliber" 633. *Tom Jones*, II: 424

FIELDS, JAMES THOMAS, I: biographical cxxxi-cxxxii. III: 92, 112n., 260, 458, 507, 514. IV: 135, 150. *Yesterdays*, quoted II: 754n.–55n.; III: 110n.–11n., 113n., 150n., 520n.–21n.; IV: 150n.–51n., 168n.

Letters to: III, 161, 243, 249, 259, 483, 488, 490, 519, 534, 544, 550

FIELDS, MRS. JAMES THOMAS, III: 162, 259, 545. IV: 150

FILBY, JOHN, IV: 71n.

FILLMORE, MILLARD, III: 194, 204, 210, 211, 212, 215, 218, 221, 229, 253, 665

FINCH-HATTON, GEORGE WILLIAM, *see* WINCHILSEA, 10th Earl of

FINDLAY, JOHN RITCHIE, III: 688

FINLAY, FRANCIS D., *Letter to:* IV, 248

FISH FAMILY [Hamilton], IV: 230, 392

FISH, HAMILTON, III: 197n., 202, 208, 548, 664. IV: and family 392

FISH, MRS. HAMILTON, III: 197, 208, 548

FISHER, JOHN HUTTON, I: 43, 69

FITZGERALD, ANDALUSIA, *see* SOYRES, Mrs. Francis de

FITZGERALD, EDWARD, I: lxxxii, ci; biographical cxxxiii; cli, 85n., 108n., 187, 198; T. on their friendship 200; 201, 202, 207, 208, 232, 236, 237, 243, 264, 285; "my crony" 291; 305, 308; his translations of Béranger quoted 331–41; quoted 348n.; 362, 367, 368; I.T. on 388; 394, 411, 420, 421, 422, 430, 453, 493, 496, 497, 498. II: 57, 73, 80; staying with T. 94, 97, 109; 121, 127, 128, 129, 137, 163; "makes" T. "too idle" 166; quoted 169n., 191n.; 453; "always right about men" 542; quoted 563n.; 628; thinks T. snobbish 655n.; 703, 755, 765, 815. III: leaves £1,000 to A. and H.T. 34, 39; 419; married 641. IV: 312, 356n., 436

Letters to: I, 150, 156, 159, 161, 172, 238, 239, 246, 252, 254, 275, 278, 287, 297, 322, 349; II, 3, 8, 16, 35, 43, 61, 227, 365, 472; III, 98. *Letters from:* I, 164, 291, 330, 345, 372; II, 265; III, 29, 114

FITZGERALD, MRS. EDWARD [Lucy Barton], III: 641

FITZGERALD, LORD EDWARD, I: T. on 162; FG on 169. II: 317

FITZGERALD, EDWARD MARLBOROUGH, II: 148, 317n., 340; "villain" 366; 843

Letter to: II, 236

FITZGERALD, MRS. EDWARD MARLBOROUGH, *Letters to:* II, 339, 346

FITZGERALD, JOHN PURCELL, I: 292, 346. II: 310. III: 30

FITZGERALD, MRS. JOHN PURCELL [Mary Francis], I: 346; "selfish and heartless" 389. II: 212, 310, 366. III: 31, 67, 68, 71, 387, 419

Letters to: II, 331; IV, 327

FITZGERALD, PETER, II: 80, 81, 83

FITZHERBERT, MRS., IV: 12n.

FITZJAMES, DUC DE, I: 113

FITZPATRICK, W. J., *Lever*, quoted II: 66n.–67n., 86n.

FITZROY, ADM. ROBERT, IV: 290; and wife 395

FITZWILLIAM MUSEUM, I: 65, 66

FLADGATE, COLONEL, IV: 404

FLADGATE, FRANCIS, II: 528n. III: 158, 518, 606. IV: 122, 232, 391, 394, 396, 408
    Letters to: II, 343; III, 493; IV, 250, 251. *Letter from:* IV, 107

FLADGATE, MRS. FRANCIS, IV: 85, 396

FLADGATE, W., IV: 396

FLAUBERT, GUSTAVE, *Mme. Bovary*, IV: "bad" 82n.

FLAXMAN, JOHN, I: 288

FLEMING, MR., III: 70, 71, 181

FLETCHER, JOHN, I: 253. *Maid's Tragedy*, I: 232. *Wit without Money*, I: 233

FLOWER, ELIZA, II: 246

FOLEY, JOHN HENRY, IV: 276, 284, 413n., 440

FOLEY, MRS. JOHN HENRY, IV: 413

FOLLETT FAMILY, IV: 397

FOLLETT, B. SPENCER, IV: 38n., 397, 414

FOLLETT, SIR WILLIAM WEBB, II: 208

FOLTHORPE, J. W., II: 480

FONBLANQUE, ALBANY, I: 399, 400. II: 189, 229n., 438, 631, 792, 811. IV: 403, 413
    Letters to: II, 270; III, 225, 462; IV, 274, 293

FONBLANQUE, MRS. ALBANY, I: 400

FOOTE, SAMUEL, *Mayor of Garratt*, I: 99n.

FORBES, SIR JOHN, II: 611n.

FORBES MACKENZIE ACT, *see* ACT

FORBES, MR., 15n.

FORBES, WALDO EMERSON, and Edward Waldo Emerson, ed. *Journals*, quoted III: 142n.

FORD, MR., IV: 409

FORD, MISS, IV: 233

FORD, MRS., IV: 391, 396, 408, 409

Foreign Quarterly Review, I: T. wants editorship cxxxiv. II: 51, 54, 56, 64, 68, 70, 92, 100, 135, 161, 162, 178, 829n., 830n. IV: 16

FORESTER, GEORGE CECIL WELD FORESTER, 3rd Baron, II: 410

FORGUES, PAUL ÉMILE DAURAND, III: 410–11. "T. et ses romans," III: 389
    Letter to: III, 389

FORMAN, MR., I: 187, 191

FORREST, COLONEL AND MRS., IV: 20

FORREST, EDWIN, III: and Macready 500n.

FORREST, EMILY, I: 415. IV: 8

FORREST FAMILY [William], I: 199, 200

FORREST, GEORGY, IV: 14

FORREST, JOHN HENRY, II: 318, 380

FORREST, CAPT. ROBERT, I: 22n. IV: 8, 14, 20 [?]

FORREST, LT.-COL. WILLIAM, I: 82, 109, 176, 203, 226, 243, 259n., 465

FORREST, MRS. WILLIAM [Georgiana Carmichael-Smyth], I: 82n., 103, 109, 193, 259. IV: 8, 14

FORSTER, CHRISTOPHER, II: 186

FORSTER, JOHN, see also *Examiner, The*, I: cxviii, cxx, cxxi, cxxiii; biographical cxxxiii-cxxxvii; 378, 400n. II: 7, 64, 68, 111, 143, 148, 163, 186, 189n., 248; "greatest man I know" 252–53; 259, 261; letters of the "false as hell" fight 294–304; 308, 377; "uncommonly kind" 403; 404, 424, 429; reviews *Paris S.B.* 453, 457; 466, 573, 629; article on pensions attacks T. 629–34; 704, 754; conduct gives T. "pain" 779–80; reconciliation 781–82; 789; "trai-

tor and a sneak" 792; 811, 815, 829n. III: 4, 46–47, 127; reviews *Esmond* 155; 175, 223, 226, 231, 250, 341; reviews *English Humourists* 396; 468n., 469, 500, 513, 518; appointed to lunacy commission 552, 564, 583; 591n.; married 620; and Dickens theatricals 643. IV: 58; and Garrick Club Affair 118n.–19n.; 122, 163n., 171; offended at T.'s characterization 238; 313, 390, 392
Letters to: I, 455; II, 56, 114, 241, 257, 295, 297, 301, 370, 660, 670; III, 399, 449, 453, 486; IV, 328, 329. *Letters from:* II, 294, 295, 298, 303; IV, 61

FORSTER, MRS. JOHN [Eliza Anne Crosbie], III: 449, 620. IV: 390n., 392

FORSYTH, MR., IV: 415

FORTESCUE, HUGH, 3rd Earl, III: 680

FOSTER, MISS, II: 702n.

FOSTER, MRS., I: 109, 117

FOSTER, STEPHEN, "Old Uncle Ned," II: 746

FOUBE, MRS., I: 350, 353

FOURNIER, MARC, and Adolphe Philippe, *Paillasse*, II: 737

FOURREAU, M., II: 142

FOWLER, THOMAS, IV: 43n.

FOX, CHARLES JAMES, II: 245, 645n. III: 321

FOX, MRS. GEORGE LANE, II: 363, 364, 452

FOX, HENRY EDWARD, *see* HOLLAND, 4th Baron

FOX, WILLIAM JOHNSON, II: 246

FRANCE — POLITICS, I: 158; tailors revolt 268; 360; July revolution 382n.; 425. II: 355, 358, 444, 495, 653. III: L. Napoléon's *coup d'état* 16; 17; Franco-Russian alliance 544

FRANCIS, DR. JOHN WAKEFIELD, III: 487, 500, 502, 511, 605

FRANKLIN, BENJAMIN, III: 134

FRASCATI'S, *see also* Gambling, I: 90, 96, 237, 506

FRASER, ALEXANDER CAMPBELL, II: 772n.

FRASER, ANNIE, I: 389, 399

FRASER FAMILY, III: 353

FRASER, JAMES, I: xci, cviin., 200, 204, 353, 354, 356, 399, 446, 459–60
Letters to: I, 179, 348, 351, 364, 387, 407, 488; II, 29; IV, 329

Fraser's Magazine, I: cvii, cxlvii, 132, 179n., 191n., 200, 280n., 303n.; T. and Maginn writing for 350, 351; T. drawing for 356; 367, 386n., 437, 469, 488. II: 43, 54, 64; Keane's insulting article in 103–05; O'Donnell's plagiarized papers in 130; 135, 137, 139, 140, 141, 160n., 161, 169, 177, 191n., 263, 264n., 283; reviews *V. F.* 423; 538n.; Kingsley in 725; 840. III: "Free British Negroes" in 247, 252; 429, 434; Goethe and 444, 445n. IV: 15, 152, 209, 210; Skelton in 216; 271n.; A. T. in 272n.; 371

FRASER, PETER, III: 687

FRASER, THOMAS, II: 140, 141, 142, 219, 494, 578, 731, 743. III: "good fellow" 267. IV: 79, 359
Letters to: II, 217; IV, 77, 243, 330

FRASER, SIR WILLIAM AUGUSTUS, II: 750n. IV: 396. *Hic et Ubique*, quoted II: 643n.–44n.

FREAK, CHARLES, IV: 35

FREDERICK THE GREAT, III: 321

FRENCH, MRS., III: 662

FRIAR, MRS., I: 429

FRIEDRICH KARL, Prince of Prussia, I: 127

FRIEDRICH WILHELM III, King of Prussia, I: 158

FRIEDRICH WILHELM IV, King of Prussia, II: 421

FRISWELL, JAMES HAIN, *Houses with the Fronts Off*, III: 402, 404–05 *Letter to:* III, 402. *Letter from:* III, 404

FRITH FAMILY, II: 155

FRITH, ROBERT WILLIAM, I: 19, 111

FROST, CHARLES, III: 698

FROST, JOHN, I: "scoundrel" 411

FROUDE, JAMES ANTHONY, IV: 218

FROUDE, JAMES ANTHONY, and T. Carlyle, ed. *Letters and Memorials*, quoted I: civ, clvii–clix

FRY, ELIZABETH, *Memoirs*, II: Mrs. B. reads 577–78

FRY, MR., II: 578

FULFORD, FRANCIS [Bishop of Montreal], III: 261

FULFORD, ROGER, and Lytton Strachey, ed. *Greville Memoirs*, quoted I: cv; III: 608n.

FULLER, COLONEL, IV: 172

FULLER, MRS. RICHARD [Hester Thackeray Ritchie], quoted I: cxii–cxiv, clxv, 506

FULLERTON, LADY GEORGIANA CHARLOTTE, III: 66

FULLERTON AND RAYMOND, III: 569 *Letter to:* III, 600

FURNESS, HORACE HOWARD, III: quoted 203n.

FURSE AND COMPANY, III: 346

GAGIOTTI, MME., II: 515, 559, 560

GAINSBOROUGH, CHARLES NOEL, 1st Earl of, II: 671

GALE, FREDERICK, II: 692, 697, 735n. IV: 15. "Progress of a Railway Bill," IV: 15 *Letter to:* II, 798

Galignani's Messenger, I: 148, 295n.; T. to write for 358, 359. II: 43, 90, 244, 475, 581

GALIGNANI'S SHOP [Jean-Antoine and Guillaume], I: 102, 225, 251, 358, 359, 361, 363

GALLAIT, LOUIS, IV: 273

GALLOIS, CHARLES ANDRÉ, *France d'Anquetil*, II: 829

GALT, JOHN, *The Radical*, I: "clever but dull" 201. *Stanley Buxton*, I: 187

GALTON, CAPT. DOUGLAS STRUTT, IV: 162

GALWAY, GEORGE EDWARD ARUNDELL MONCKTON-ARUNDELL, 6th Viscount, IV: 410, 412

GALWAY, LADY [Henrietta Milnes, m. 6th Viscount], IV: 410n., 412

GALLWEY, MISS, II: 792

GAMBA, TERESA, *see* BOISSY

GAMBLE, JANE C., III: 609

GAMBLING, *see also* Frascati's, No. 60, No. 64, I: 90–91, 93, 95; T.'s discourse on 96–97; 98, 138n.; debt 175; 186, 187, 191, 197, 198, 199, 200, 201, 202, 204, 205, 207, 208, 225, 228, 229, 230, 237, Appendix IV. II: 414, 415, 416, 419, 421, 735. III: 289, 512. IV: 435

GARDEN, VIRGINIA, II: 602n.

GARDNER, MRS., IV: 402, 412

GARLICK, DR., IV: 19

GARNETT, ROBERT S., ed. *New Sketch Book*, II: 100n., 140n.

GARRICK CLUB, *see also* Garrick Club Affair, I: 263, 264; members 265; 282, 308, 313, 350, 404, 416n. II: 94, 114, 134, 144, 150, 224, 454, 514, 528n., 533, 540, 612n., 665, 766, 843. III: 158, 392, 455n., 464n., 472n., 474, 493, 494, 606, 674. IV: 16n., 18, 64, 81n., 86, 90, 91n., 99n., 107, 109, 116, 117, 118, 131n., 133, 134n., 149n., 202, 221, 232, 235, 251, 265, 296, 312, 313, 335, 352, 358, 391, 395, 411, 416

GARRICK CLUB AFFAIR, *see also*

Yates, Edmund, I: cxx, cxxxvii. IV: 50n.; correspondence of 89–92, 93–97, 98–104, 105–06, 107, 109, 116–120, 121, 122; Yates's pamphlet 131, 132; 133–35, 163n., 202

GARRICK CLUB, COMMITTEE OF THE, *Letters to:* IV, 93, 94, 95, 98, 101, 103, 119

Garrick Club: Correspondence, IV: 107

Garrick Club: Report of the Committee, quoted IV: 105n.

GARRICK, DAVID, III: 304. IV: 71n., 390n.

GARROW, SIR WILLIAM, I: and family 175; 188, 424

GASKELL, MRS. WILLIAM [Elizabeth Cleghorne Stevenson], *Miss Brontë,* I: T.'s feeling against xcivn.

GASKER, ATHANASIUS, *pseud. see* CLARKE, Edward William

GASSIOT, MISS, IV: 250
    Letter to: IV, 249

GATTY, ALFRED, I: quoted 25n.

GAUTIER, THÉOPHILE, IV: 265, 402

GAY, JOHN, II: 645n. *Beggar's Opera,* I: 177; II: 344n.

Gazette des Tribunaux, II: 32

GEORGE I, II: 645n. III: 65, 474, 488, 491, 493, 592, 629n., 675n. IV: 33

GEORGE II, III: 474, 494, 564, 630

GEORGE III, II: 645n. III: 321, 474, 491, 494, 501, 502, 507, 519, 526, 529, 546, 564, 571, 583, 585, 590, 595, 637n., 656. IV: 9, 10, 43n., 53, 84n., 88n., 338, 391, 442

GEORGE IV, I: 57, 64, 109n., 163. II: 317, 724. III: 474, 475, 477, 491, 494, 519, 526; "contemptible imposter" 590; 592, 595, 612. IV: 3, 12, 262n., 267n., 543n.; T.'s lecture on attacked 564; 571, 584

George Cruikshank's Table-Book, II: 198n.

GEORGIA HISTORICAL SOCIETY, Secretary of the, *Letter to:* III, 553

GERMANY — POLITICS, I: revolution 119; 158. II: 444

GERRARD, CAPTAIN, I: 223, 227, 229, 230, 249

GIBBON, EDWARD, I: 47. *Decline and Fall,* I: 228; "entertaining" 229. *Memoirs,* quoted III: 459

GIBBS, HENRY, I: 190, 191

GIBBS, JOSEPH, I: 497

GIBBS, THOMAS WASHBOURNE, *Letters to:* II, 783, 799

GIBSON, DR., III: 666

GIBSON, MR., I: 205, 207

GIBSON, MR. [of Richmond], IV: 70

GIBSON, THOMAS MILNER, II: 843n.

GIBSON, MRS. THOMAS MILNER [Susanna Cullum], II: 843
    Letter to: II, 599

GIFFARD, STANLEY LEES, I: 209; 210, 421

GIFFORD, ROBERT FRANCIS, 2nd Baron, IV: 188

GIGOUX, JEAN FRANÇOIS, II: 732

GILBERT, HENRY, III: 267

GILBERT, MR., IV: 358

GILMAN, ARTHUR DELEVAN, III: 520

GILMAN, DR. SAMUEL, III: 665

GIRALDON, M., II: hires T. for translating 139, 141, 841
    Letter to: II, 159

GIROT, BLANCHE, III: 138

GLADSTONE, WILLIAM EWART, III: 388n., 457n. IV: 290, 402, 411

GLADSTONE, MRS. WILLIAM EWART [Catherine Glynne], IV: 411

Glasgow Argus, I: 464

GLASGOW, DOWAGER COUNTESS OF [Julia Sinclair, m. 4th Earl], IV: 402

GLASS, JAMES, III: 512

GLASS, MRS. JAMES, III: 536

GLEIG, GEORGE ROBERT, *Waterloo*, II: 294

Globe, The, I: T.'s possible connection with 409. III: 138

GLOYNE, MRS., II: 215, 216, 231, 240, 243, 287, 288, 289, 305. IV: 4

GLUCK, CHRISTOPH WILIBALD, *Orpheus*, I: "sublime" 363

GLYN, MRS. ISABELLA DALLAS, III: 293

GLYNN, HENRY, II: 148, 362. III: 380. IV: 320

"GM," *see* BUTLER, MRS.

GODERICH, *see* RIPON

GODWIN, GEORGE, *London Shadows*, III: 360
    Letter to: III, 360

GOETHE, ALMA VON, III: 444

GOETHE, AUGUST VON, I: 125n., 134

GOETHE, FRAU AUGUST VON [Ottilie von Pogwisch], I: 125, 131, 153n. II: 798n. III: 443, 445
    Letters to: I, 153, 184

GOETHE, JOHANN WOLFGANG VON, I: 125; T. meets 130; 136, 137, 140; "old rogue" 148. II: 133, 262, 772. III: T.'s reminiscences of 442–45; Lewezow affair 522, 523
    Faust, I: 124n., 133; III: quoted 266; IV: 48. *Wilhelm Meister*, I: Carlyle translation "wretched" 213. *Reinecke Fuchs*, IV: 253. *Werther*, I: 312; III: 150n., 412

GOLDIE, MRS., I: 103

GOLDSHEDE, MR., I: 190, 197

GOLDSMID, ALBERT, IV: 422

GOLDSMID, FRANCIS HENRY, II: 515

GOLDSMID, MRS. FRANCIS HENRY, II: 515
    Letter to: III, 441

GOLDSMID, SIR ISAAC LYON, II: 645

GOLDSMID, LADY [Isabel Goldsmid, m. Sir Isaac], II: 645

GOLDSMID, MR., IV: 402

GOLDSMITH, MAJ. FREDERICK J.,

II: 361. IV: 297. "Reminiscences of T.," quoted I: 259n.; II: 360n.
    Letters to: II, 259, 355, 398

GOLDSMITH, OLIVER, I: cxxxvi. II: 312; Forster's book on 370–71; 781. III: 124n., 151. IV: anecdote 71n.; 186, 390n. "Deserted Village," II: 663. *Vicar of Wakefield*, I: and Elwin cxxix

GOLDWORTHY, JOHN, I: 31, 257, 259, 352, 393n., 412, 419, 420, 425, 427, 438, 443, 452, 472, 473, 484. II: 91, 99, 193, 260, 319, 373. III: 125

GOLDWORTHY, MARTHA, I: 31, 257, 427. II: 193

GOODCHILD, JOHN, II: 763

GOODCHILD, MISS, I: 392, 399. II: 763–64

GOODLAKE, MR., IV: 408

GOPITS, MR., IV: 409

GORDON, ALEXANDER, 4th Duke of, II: 683n.

GORDON, GEORGE HAMILTON, *see* ABERDEEN

GORDON, O., III: 672

GORE, CAPT. AUGUSTUS WENTWORTH, IV: 192, 193

GORE, CECILIA ANNE MARY, *see* THYNNE, LADY

GORE, MRS. CHARLES ARTHUR [Catherine Moody], II: 585, 695n., 697, 699. III: 285. IV: 192
    Banker's Wife, IV: 196. *Cecil*, II: 13. "Congress of Vienna," II: 162. *Hamiltons*, II: 724. *Mayfair*, I: 203. *Sketches of English Character*, II: 724n.
    Letters to: II, 694, 724; III, 27, 73, 74; IV, 195

GORE HOUSE, *see* BLESSINGTON

GORHAM CONTROVERSY, II: 662

GORHAM, GEORGE CORNELIUS, II: 662n.

GOSSAINT, M., III: 94

GOSSE, EDMUND, *Swinburne*, quoted IV: 285n.–86n.

GOURDIN, MR., III: 666

Gownsman, The, I: 85n.

"GP," *see* CARMICHAEL-SMYTH, Maj. Henry

GRAHAM AND JACKSON, *see* JACKSON and Graham

GRAHAM, CAPT. ALLAN, I: cx

GRAHAM, MRS. ALLAN [Harriet Becher], I: cx, 4

GRAHAM, MISS, I: 25

GRAHAM, MARY, *see* CARMICHAEL, Mrs. Charles

GRAMONT, ANTOINE AGÉNOR, Duc de, II: 593n., 750n.

GRAMONT, ANNE DE GRIMAUD, Duchesse de, II: 593n., 750

GRAMP, MR., II: 52

GRANGE, THE, *see* ASHBURTON

GRANT, FRANCIS, IV: 400

GRANT, JAMES, *Paris and its People*, II: 126, 139

GRANT, MR., I: 193, 200

GRANTLEY, *see* NORTON, Thomas Brinsley

GRANVILLE, GEORGE, *see* SUTHERLAND, 2nd Duke of

GRANVILLE, GRANVILLE GEORGE LEVESON-GOWER, 2nd Earl, II: 359, 814
　Letter to: IV, 283

GRANVILLE, LADY [Lady Marie Louisa Joseph, m. 2nd Earl], II: 374, 683, 685. III: 369, 674

GRATTAN, THOMAS COLLEY, *Letter to:* IV, 208

GRAY [a cook], III: 69, 376, 562, 565, 656n., 657. IV: 13, 52

GRAY, THOMAS, *Elegy*, I: 129n.

GREAT EXHIBITION OF 1851, *see also* Crystal Palace, II: 702, 767–68, 769, 771, 786

GREATHED, LT.-COL. EDWARD HARRIS, IV: 411

GREELEY, HORACE, III: 662

GREEN, JOHN ["Paddy"], IV: 232, 265, 266

GREENHOW, MISS, III: 210, 213

GREENHOW, ROBERT, III: 210n.

GREENHOW, MRS. ROBERT [Rose O'Neil], III: 210n., 213

GREENWOOD, FREDERICK, IV: 302n.

GREGORY, G. B., IV: 410, 412

GREGORY, MRS., IV: 433

GREIG, MR., I: 219

GRENVILLE, RICHARD PLANTAGENET TEMPLE-NUGENT-BRYDGES-CHANDOS, *see* BUCKINGHAM, 2nd Duke of

GRESHAM, MR., IV: 414

GRESSET, JEAN-BAPTISTE-LOUIS, *Vert Vert*, II: 236

GREVILLE, CHARLES, *Memoirs*, quoted I: cv; III: 608n.

GREY, CHARLES, 2nd Earl, I: and reform bill 188n. III: 25n.

GREY, 3RD EARL DE, *see* RIPON, 1st Marquess of

GREY, WILLIAM GEORGE, III: 25, 670

GRIER, R. M., *John Allen*, quoted I: lxxxiii.

GRIEVE, THOMAS, I: 241

GRIMSHAW, JAMES G., III: 581n.

GRISI, MME. GIULIA, I: 266. II: 335; Castlereagh duel 643, 644n.

GROOME, ROBERT, I: 107n., 495

GROTE, MR., I: 301n.

GROTE, MRS., III: 70n.

GUDIN, THÉODORE, II: 731, 732, 736, 743. III: 670. IV: 428
　Letters to: II, 741, 745

GUDIN, MRS. THÉODORE [Louise Gordon Hay], II: 736, 743

GUERARD, JOHN M., III: 665

GUILD OF LITERATURE AND ART, II: 770

GUILLEMARD, JAMES, I: 27, 29. II: 245

GUIZOT, FRANÇOIS PIERRE GUILLAUME, I: 457. III: 138n. IV: 427

GUIZOT, MLLE HENRIETTE, *see*
　WITT
GUNNELL, MR., I: 190, 191, 207,
　208, 209
GUNNING, HENRY, I: 52, 67, 189
GUNSTEN, CAPTAIN, III: 482
GUNTER, II: 95
GURNEY, RUSSELL, IV: 402, 411
GWILT, JO, II: 124, 150, 160

HABERSHAM [or Faversham], ROB-
　ERT, III: 241, 665
HADEN, FRANCIS SEYMOUR, IV: 122,
　148
HAHNEMANN, SAMUEL CHRISTIAN
　FRIEDRICH, I: I.T. with 356
HAIGHT, RICHARD K., IV: 264
HAILSTONE, JOHN, I: 53, 56, 493,
　494, 495, 496, 497
HAINES, WILLIAM CLARK, I: 495
HALÉVY, JACQUES FRANÇOIS FRO-
　MENTAL ÉLIE, *La Tentation*, I:
　276
HALKETT, LT.-COL. JOHN CRAIGIE,
　III: 687
HALL, ABRAHAM OAKEY, III: 487,
　500
HALL, DR., II: 473
HALL, MRS., *Letter to:* IV, 330
HALL, WILLIAM, I: 459
HALLAM, ARTHUR HENRY, I: 196
HALLAM, HENRY, I: and Mrs. B.
　affair xcviii. II: 271; objects to
　T. and Mrs. B. 492; 524, 525,
　556n., 581n., 585, 617, 620;
　backs T. for Athenæum 637; 661,
　664, 706; at son's funeral 714,
　715, 717; 745, 746, 777, 814.
　III: 119n., 232. IV: 343
HALLAM, HENRY FITZMAURICE, II:
　443, 450, 468, 508n., 525, 528,
　552, 558, 569, 577, 581, 602,
　606, 617, 664, 680, 682n.; dead
　705; 706; funeral 714, 715n.,
　717; memoir of 746

HALLAM, JULIA MARIA FRANCES,
　see LENNARD, Lady
HALLÉ, SIR CHARLES [?], IV: 392,
　393
HALLÉ, LADY [?], IV: 392, 411,
　412
HALLIDAY, DR. [*G.* 56], I: 183n.
　II: 145, 189, 195, 209, 576, 582,
　587, 590, 594, 609, 726
HALLIDAY, MRS. [Augusta Thackeray
　(Elliot), *G.* 54], I: 183, 263, 447.
　II: 35, 144, 145, 174; fight with
　Mrs. C-S 189, 195; 196, 209,
　243, 494, 575; dying 576, 581,
　582; dead 586, 589
HALYBURTON, MR., IV: 400
HAMERTON, BESS, I: 359, 475. II:
　10, 23, 46, 49, 75, 86, 91, 96,
　102, 135, 139, 141, 142, 173,
　210, 250; keeping house for T.
　258; dismissed 284–86; 287, 288,
　308, 328, 334, 400, 401, 495–
　96, 587, 607. IV: 77
　Letter to: II, 284
HAMERTON, MARIA, I: 359, 475. II:
　10, 23, 135, 139, 141, 142, 173,
　587. III: 310, 325, 361, 398,
　571. IV: 77, 79
　Letter to: II, 607
HAMILTON, ALEXANDER HAMILTON
　DOUGLAS, 7th Duke of Brandon
　and 10th Duke of, III: 75
HAMILTON, ROBERT MONTGOMERIE,
　see BELHAVEN
HAMILTON, SIR WILLIAM, II: 538n.
HAMILTON, WILLIAM ALEXANDER
　ANTHONY ARCHIBALD DOUGLAS,
　8th Duke of Brandon and 11th
　Duke of, II: 593. IV: 421
HAMLEY, COL. EDWARD BRUCE, III:
　633, 687. IV: 390 [?], 398n.
　[?]
HAMMER-PURGSTALL, JOSEPH, Frei-
　herr von, *Osmanischen Reiches*, I:
　285
HAMPSTEAD COURT, *see* CROWE
　family

HAMPTON CHILDREN [Frank], III: 652, 654. IV: 80, 110, 230, 235, 279, 303

HAMPTON, FRANK, I: lxxxix. III: engaged to SSB 484; marriage 496, 516, 517, 525, 526; 555, 556–57, 558, 561, 569, 572, 586, 614, 629, 654

HAMPTON, MRS. FRANK ["SSB," Sally Baxter], I: lxxxviii. III: 142; T. in love with 149, 154; 159, 160, 164, 165, 177, 183, 184, 190, 191, 194, 204, 205, 206, 207, 210, 212, 213, 214, 216, 224, 244, 257, 260, 261, 267, 270, 271, 274, 275, 282, 307, 309, 313, 335, 356, 357, 358, 369, 370, 481; engaged 484, 496, 513, 515; married 521, 522, 523, 525, 526; 532, 542, 555, 556, 558, 559, 561, 568, 569, 572, 586, 603, 604, 609, 627, 629, 664. IV: 55, 56, 57, 81, 83, 109, 110, 213, 229, 230, 235; T.'s reaction to her death 278–79; 298, 303
Letters to: III, 150, 151, 283, 296, 314, 327, 516, 611, 652

HAMPTON, COL. WADE, III: 484n., 559, 568

HAMPTON, WADE, III: 484

HAMSTEDE, FREDERICK WILLIAM, IV: 414

HANCOCK, THOMAS, II: 805

HANDEL, GEORGE FREDERICK, I: Messiah 78n.; I.T. and 389, 440. III: 687

HANKEY, CAPTAIN, I: cxvii. II: 98, 100, 139, 140, 142, 143. III: 623, 634, 687

HANKEY, FANNY, III: 77, 634, 687

HANKEY, MRS., I: cxvii. II: 135, 634, 687. III: 634

HANKEY, THOMSON, IV: 412n.

HANKEY, MRS. THOMSON, IV: 412

HANKEY, WILLIAM, III: 77

HANKEY, MRS. WILLIAM [Cecile d'Estamper], III: 77

HANNAY, JAMES, III: T. recommends 465–66; 469. IV: 149. King Dobbs, II: 553. Satires and Satirists, III: 466
Letter to: II, 553

HARCOURT, SIR WILLIAM GEORGE GRANVILLE VENABLES VERNON, II: 508. III: 564. IV: 391

HARDING, MR., II: 145

HARDINGE, HENRY, 1st Viscount, II: 231, 546. III: 588. IV: 393n.

HARDINGE, LADY [Lady Emily Jane Stewart (James), m. 1st Viscount], IV: 393, 402

HARDWICKE, CHARLES PHILIP YORKE, 4th Earl of, II: 547n.

HARDWICKE, PHILIP YORKE, 3rd Earl of, I: 36n. II: 646n.

HARE, JULIUS CHARLES, I: 43, 68

HARE, MISSES, II: 286

HARLEVILLE, JEAN FRANÇOIS COLLIN D', Monsieur de Crac, I: 285

HARMAN, JAMES WOOLLEY, I: 493, 495

HARNESS, REV. WILLIAM, II: 337. III: 288. IV: and wife 414
Letter to: II, 490

HARPER BROTHERS, III: to publish Humourists 131, 132, 158; 280, 300. IV: 55, 58, 60, 76
Letter to: III, 130

HARPER, JAMES, III: 130n.

Harper's Weekly, IV: 92n.

HARRINGTON, LEICESTER FITZGERALD CHARLES STANHOPE, 5th Earl of, IV: 273n., 399

HARRINGTON, LADY [Elizabeth Green, m. 5th Earl], IV: 273, 399, 402, 403, 404

HARRIS FAMILY, I: 400. II: 135, 357

HARRIS, JAMES HOWARD, see MALMESBURY

HARRIS, MR. [of Baltimore], III: 543n.

HARRIS, MR. [of Cambridge], I: 496, 497
HARRISON, CAPTAIN, III: 479, 482
HARRISON, CHARLES, II: 400
HARRISON FAMILY, I: 429
HARTE, MR., I: 141, 144
HARTFORD, SUMMERS, IV: 366
HARTLEY, JAMES, II: 253, 568, 576
HASSELL, MRS., III: 689
HASTINGS, 1ST MARQUESS OF, *see* MOIRA, Earl of
HASTINGS, LADY ELIZABETH, II: 779n.
HATCH, MRS. THERESA, *Letter to:* IV, 140
HATTON, MR. AND MRS., IV: 395
HAWES, SIR BENJAMIN, IV: 331n., 391
HAWES, LADY [Sophia Brunel, m. Sir Benjamin], *Letter to:* IV, 331
HAWKES, REV. MR., III: 604
HAWKINS, MR., *Letter to:* II, 787
HAWKS, SAMUEL, I: 68
HAWTHORNE, NATHANIEL, III: on *Newcomes* 465n.–66n. *English Notebooks*, quoted III: 360n.
HAY, LORD CHARLES, IV: 188
HAY, GEN. LORD JAMES, II: 743. IV: 31, 38, 41
HAY, LADY [Elizabeth Forbes, m. Lord James], IV: 38
    Letters to: IV, 31, 41
HAY, LORD JOHN, IV: 81
HAYDN, FRANZ JOSEPH, III: 167, 268
HAYDON, BENJAMIN ROBERT, I: T. on painting of 186. II: 245
HAYNE, JULIA, III: 589, 594
HAYTER, WILLIAM GOODENOUGH, IV: 3, 387
HAYWARD, ABRAHAM, II: 202n., 265, 321; "prodigious compliments" from 449; 459, 754n. III: 127, 393. "T.'s Writings," II: 334
    Letters to: II, 312, 316, 327, 358, 635, 636, 728, 776

HAYWOOD, JAMES, II: 803. IV: 412
HAZARD, WILLIS P., III: 598n., 599n., 601
HAZLITT, WILLIAM, II: anecdote 245–46. IV: 275n. *Conversations,* II: 137
HEAD, MRS., III: 438n.
HEALTH, I: 17, 26n., 77, 79–80, 81, 126, 133, 175, 191, 290, 400, 441, 460, 468. II: 40, 43, 95, 107, 109, 112, 135, 140, 143, 145, 148, 154, 166, 211, 234–35, 346, 459–60, 554, 595–607, 677, 678–79, 694, 707, 727, 811. III: 37, 75, 82, 87, 99, 171, 246, 262, 277, 279, 280, 301, 302, 303, 322, 323, 325, 328, 332, 333, 334, 341, 342, 346, 347, 349, 350, 352, 355, 356, 358, 359, 361, 362, 375, 382, 385–86, 387, 392, 393, 396–97, 398, 401, 403, 404, 406, 407, 408, 411, 423, 426, 427, 437, 438, 449, 451, 452, 469, 481, 491, 495, 502, 503, 504, 505, 507, 509, 511, 514, 516, 518, 520, 522, 523, 534, 540, 544, 554, 558, 566, 573, 576, 584, 591, 594, 596, 598, 599, 600, 603, 604, 605, 607–08, 610, 611, 612, 613, 614, 615, 626, 627, 628, 631, 634, 644, 649, 653, 669, 670, 673, 675, 677, 686. IV: 15, 21, 25, 39, 51, 54, 56, 62, 66, 67, 68, 72, 77, 78, 80, 85, 97, 108, 109, 110, 111, 112, 127, 128, 129, 132, 136, 139, 140, 142, 148, 154, 172, 202, 203, 208, 209, 212, 214, 221, 223, 227, 231, 233, 250, 252, 255, 263, 264, 265, 266, 277, 296, 299, 307, 318, 320, 324, 327, 331, 338, 345, 350, 361, 365, 373, 390, 391, 392, 393, 394, 395, 396, 397, 398, 399, 400, 404, 408, 413, 414, 421, 425, 438, 439, 441, Appendix XXVIII

HEATH, CHARLES, I: 201, 202, 203, 205, 287. II: 139, 140n., 159
Letter to: IV, 287

HEATH, MR., IV: 121, 392, 408, 410, 413; and wife 414

HEATHCOTE, JOHN EDENSOR, I: 496

HEATLEY [or Heatly], MR., IV: 403, 409, 411

HEAVISIDE, JAMES WILLIAM LUCAS, I: 494, 495, 496

HEBELER, BERNARD, II: 843

HEBER, REGINALD [Bishop of Calcutta], *India*, IV: 262

HEDGES, SIR CHARLES, II: 541

HEGENHEIM, ORI [or Ory] D', I: 94, 95, 227, 230, 231, 232

HELPS, ARTHUR, II: 735, 739

HELVETIUS, CLAUDE ADRIEN, I: 166

HEMANS, FELICIA, IV: 330. *Homes of England*, I: T. burlesques 445–46

HENDERSON, DR., II: 822

HENLEY, IV: 392

HENNELL, SARAH, III: 437n., 438n.

HENRION, ANGELINA, II: 678, 679

HENRY, PATRICK, IV: 74

HERAUD, JOHN ABRAHAM, II: "noble madness and dullness" 24

HERBERLE, MLLE, I: 202

HERBERT, SIR CHARLES LYON, I: 367

HERBERT, HENRY ARTHUR, II: 713n.

HERBERT, MRS. HENRY ARTHUR [Grace Pollock], II: 709, 713

HERBERT, JOHN ROGERS, III: 11, 66

HERBERT, SIDNEY, 1st Baron, II: 481n.

HERBERT, LADY [Mary Elizabeth A'Court-Repington, m. 1st Baron], II: 481

HERING, DR. WILLIAM, II: 46, 52

HEROES AND HEROINES, IV: correspondence on 274–75

HERSCHEL, SIR JOHN FREDERICK, II: 581, 585

HERTFORD, FRANCIS CHARLES SEYMOUR, 3rd Marquess of, III: original of "Lord Steyne" 363n.

HERVEY, LORD, I: 36, 37

HESKITH, MR., I: 495

HESSEY, JAMES AUGUSTUS, III: 17

HEWSON, MR., IV: 366

HEYWOOD, JAMES, IV: 401, 412

HEYWORTH, JAMES I: 53, 495

HIBBERT, JOHN, III: 667, 675

HICKMAN, MR., I: creditor of T. and GP 448n. II: and *Constitutional* debts 49, 58, 95, 96, 97, 99, 100, 107–08, 112, 113

HICKS, LEONARD, I: 488. II: 112, 188, 349, 762. IV: 6, 412

HICKS, THOMAS, III: 274

HICKSON, WILLIAM EDWARD, *Letters to:* II, 48, 50

HIGGINS, MATTHEW JAMES ["Jacob Omnium"], I: biographical cxxxvii-cxxxix. II: 345, 389, 420n., 421, 450, 654, 664, 777. III: 390, 395, 426, 450, 459n., 590, 670. IV: 3; in Garrick Club Affair 121; 178, 328, 392, 396, 403, 412, 434, 438. "Paterfamilias," IV: 178

HIGGINS, MRS. MATTHEW JAMES, III: 19. IV: 396, 403, 412

HILAIRE, ÉMILE MARC ["Marco Saint Hilaire"], *L'Hôtel des Invalides*, II: 830. *Mémoires . . . d'un page*, I: 234

HILL, ALEXANDER, II: 102

HILL, ARTHUR MARCUS CECIL, see SANDYS, 3rd Baron

HILL, SIR GEORGE, II: 88

HILL, REV. JUSTLY, I: 220, 221, 418

HILL, MRS. JUSTLY [Jane-Helena Shute], I: 220

HILL, MR. AND MRS., IV: 409, 414

HILLIER [or Hillyar], MRS. AND MISS, I: 218, 219, 220

HIND, JOHN, I: 495, 497

HINE, JAMES, I: 26n., 29, 32, 39, 46, 48, 53, 55

HISLOP, SIR THOMAS, II: 516n.

HISLOP, LADY [Emma Elliot, m. Sir Thomas], II: 516n., 645

HOARES, MISSES, II: 739

HOBHOUSE, SIR JOHN CAM [Lord Broughton], II: 707n., 716, 718n., 726, 824. III: 4; "Kind dear old fellow" 5; 632, 643, 667, 672. IV: 392. Recollections, quoted II: 717n.

HODDER, GEORGE, III: 467. Memories, quoted II: 266n.–67n.
Letters to: II, 268; III, 367, 450, 467

HODGES, MR., I: 154

HODGSON, KIRKMAN DANIEL, IV: 413n.

HODGSON, MRS. KIRKMAN DANIEL, IV: 413

HOFFMAN, ERNST THEODOR AMADEUS, "The Golden Pot," I: 214. Prinzessin Brambilla, I: 225

HOGARTH, GEORGINA, II: 261, 367, 569. III: 643. IV: and Dickens separation 86, 131

HOGARTH, WILLIAM, III: 321; Sala writing on 471

HOGG, SIR JAMES WEIR, II: 364n.

HOGG, LADY [Mary Claudina Swinton, m. Sir James], II: 364

HOGG, MR., IV: 276

HOGG, MRS., III: 288

HOLE, ROBERT, I: 68

HOLE, REV. SAMUEL REYNOLDS, Memories, quoted IV: 174n.
Letter to: IV, 251

HOLL, MR., Letter to: IV, 251

HOLLAND, SIR HENRY, I: xc

HOLLAND, LADY [Saba Smith, m. Sir Henry], Sydney Smith, III: 462; IV: 440n.

HOLLAND, HENRY EDWARD FOX, 4th Baron, I: clxviii. II: 335, 647, 648. III: 68, 69, 70, 73, 667. IV: 50

Letters to: II, 575; III, 309, 349

HOLLAND, LADY [Lady Augusta-Mary Coventry, m. 4th Baron], I: clxviii. III: 68, 70, 73, 309, 667
Letters to: III, 71; IV, 50

HOLLAND, HENRY THURSTON, see KNUTSFORD

HOLLEY, MISS, III: 468n.

HOLLINGSHEAD, JOHN, II: quoted 149n.
Letter to: IV, 157

HOLLINGWORTH, SQUIRE, I: 418

HOLLOND, ROBERT, II: 663n., 843n. IV: 395, 397

HOLLOND, MRS. ROBERT [Ellen Julia Teed], II: 843, 844

HOLMES, MARY, I: biographical cxxxix-cxli. III: 16, 25, 63, 68, 71
Letters to: III, 8, 11, 12, 19, 20, 26, 28, 45, 66, 101

HOLMES, DR. OLIVER WENDELL, III: 63n.; "true poet" 152. Professor at the Breakfast-Table, IV: 231

HOME, DANIEL DUNGLAS, III: 123n. IV: 199n.

HOMER, I: 207

HOMPESCH, COUNT, I: 123

HONE, NATHANIEL, I: 161

HONEYWOOD, JAMES, III: 375

HOOD, THOMAS, III: 103. Whims and Oddities, I: 16n.

HOOD, THOMAS [the younger], IV: articles submitted CM 197; 398
Letter to: IV, 167. Letter from: IV, 183

HOOD, THOMAS, and F.F. Broderip, Memorials, IV: 196

HOOK, THEODORE EDWARD, I: 13n., 254. Peter Priggins, II: "immense vulgarity" 24–25. Sayings and Doings, I: 259

HOOKER, RICHARD, I: 428

HOOPER, MR., III: 676

HOPE, LADY MILDRED, IV: 403

HOPE, THOMAS, *Anastasius*, I: 228

HOPKINS, A. I., *Letter to:* IV, 54

HOPLEY, G. A., III: 665

HORACE [Quintus Horatius Flaccus], *Ars Poetica*, IV: 160, 167. *Epistles*, II: 766. *Odes*, I: 117, 514; II: 271; T.'s imitation of 281; 401, 463, 553n., 720, 801; III: 47, 48, 90, 201, 363; IV: 260

HORNE, SIR EVERARD, IV: 129

HORNE, REV. THOMAS HARTWELL, II: 422

HORNECK, CATHERINE AND MARY [the "Jessamy Bride"], II: 371

HORTON, PRISCILLA, I: 374

HOTTEN, JOHN CAMDEN, *Thackeray*, quoted I: 301n.

HOUGHTON, LORD, *see* MILNES, Richard Monckton

Household Words, II: 710. III: 363n., 393n., 470, 472n. IV: Dickens's separation in 86n.; 157

HOWARD, CHARLES, *see* NORFOLK

HOWARD, MISS, I: 284, 286

HOWDEN, JOHN HOBART CARADOC, 2nd Baron, II: 649. III: 309, 670. IV: 423

HOWE, ESTIS, III: 166n.

HOWE, M. A. DEWOLFE, *New Letters*, quoted III: 165n.

HUDSON, SIR GEOFFREY, I: 275

HUDSON, GEORGE, III: 651

HUGHES, MISS, III: 375

HUGHES, REV. MR., III: 604

HUGO, VICTOR MARIE, I: 224. II: "writes like a God Almighty" 44. IV: "a queer heathen" 427
    Büg Jargal, I: 133. *Dernier Jour*, I: 133. *Feuilles d'automne*, I: "poetical" 225. *Hans d'Islande*, I: 133. *Hernani*, I: 127, 133. *Marion Delorme*, I: "horrid" 362. *Notre Dame*, I: "genius" 228. *Rhine*, II: T.'s article on 42, 44, 830. *Roi s'amuse*, I: 238

HUME, DAVID, I: FG on 164, 166, 167, 169, 170. II: T. reading life of 234. *Essays*, I: 56. *History*, I: 48; II: 245, 821

HUME, JOSEPH, I: 301n., 325

HUME, MR., I: 260n., 270. II: 73; T. writes for 97, 139, 142, 147, 148, 166, 175; "India letter" 840, 841, 842

HUMMELL, JOHANN NEPOMUK, I: 127, 133, 154

HUNT, [James Henry] LEIGH, I: 446; sketch of 501. II: 14, 248, 490, 595, 723
    Autobiography, II: 711. *Legend of Florence*, I: "charming" 421. "Man of Letters," IV: 170
    Letters to: II, 307, 331, 332, 347; IV, 332

HUNT, THORNTON LEIGH, II: 595, 711
    Letters to: IV, 41, 185

HUNT, WILLIAM HOLMAN, I: 295, 329. *Pre-Raphaelitism*, quoted IV: 271n.–72n.

HUNTINGTON, LADY [Selina Shirley, m. 9th Earl], II: 473

HURLBUT, WILLIAM HENRY, III: 614n.

HURST, THOMAS, I: 264n.

HUTCHINSON, MR., III: 664

HUTTON, MISSES, II: 386

HUXLEY, LEONARD, *House of Smith, Elder*, quoted I: clxvii, clxviii, clxxii; II: 611n.–12n., 804n.; IV: 219n.–20n.

HUYSHE, ALFRED, I: 23

HUYSHE, REV. FRANCIS, I: 58, 68. II: 501

HUYSHE, MRS. FRANCIS, I: 193. II: 310. III: 9, 16

HUYSHE, HARRIET, I: 60, 62. II: 501

HUYSHE, WENTWORTH, I: 15, 42, 57, 62, 68, 91. II: 310

HYNDFORD HOUSE, *see* CARMICHAEL, Col. and Mrs.

IBRAHIM PASHA, II: 155, 237
IGNATIUS, FATHER, III: 343
Illustrated London News, III: 562, 585, 638. IV: 160; quoted 160n.–61n.; 194
Illustrated Times, IV: Yates in 119n., 131n.; 302, 417
IMPEY FAMILY, I: 230, 231. IV: 8
INGERSOLL, JOSEPH R., III: 264
INGILBY [or Ingleby], HARRIET JANE, *see* AUSTIN, Mrs. Charles
INGILBY, MARY LISCOMB, II: 286n. III: 388
INGILBY, MRS., III: 388
INGILBY, SIR HENRY, II: 286n.
INGLIS, SIR ROBERT H., II: quoted 517n.; 518. III: 667. IV: 323
INTERNATIONAL COPYRIGHT, II: Dickens and 66. III: 204, 243
INVERARITY, ELIZABETH, I: 186, 203
Inverness Courier, IV: 36n., 90n.
IRELAND, *see also* chronology, II: "who does understand?" 78; and clergy 89; T. on Irish character 130n.; P and famine 266; T. article on 352; 414. III: Irish in America 228
IRVINE, REV. ANDREW, III: 406n.
IRVINE, MRS. ANDREW, III: 406n.
IRVINE, COL. ARCHIBALD [G. 89], I: 447n. II: 609n., 617. III: 406n.
IRVINE, MRS. ARCHIBALD [Marianne Shakespear, G. 88], I: 447. II: 244, 609n., 617. III: 37n. IV: 414
    Letters to: II, 351; IV, 169, 332
IRVINE, CHARLES THOMAS, II: 643
IRVINE CHILDREN [Archibald], II: 609
IRVINE, JOHN WILLIAM, III: 406. "Newcome," quoted I: 409n. *Nineteenth Century*, quoted III: 37n., 435n.
IRVINE, MISS, II: 643
IRVING, REV. EDWARD, II: 749n.

Oracles of God, I: "finest piece of eloquence" 247–48
IRVING, JOSEPH, *Annals of Our Times*, quoted III: 627
IRVING, MRS., III: 662
IRVING, PIERRE M., *Washington Irving*, quoted III: 171n.–72n.
IRVING, WASHINGTON, III: T. meets 134; quoted 171n.; 211, 510n., 511–12, 519. IV: on T. 73–74; 191. *Crayon Miscellanies*, I: 285, 288. *Washington*, III: 512; IV: 73
ISAAC, CAPTAIN, III: 40
ISTRIE, DUCHESS D', III: 460
ISTRIE, NAPOLÉON BESSIÈRES, Duc d', III: 460
ITALY, *see also* chronology, III: 326

JACKSON, ANDREW, III: 196n.
JACKSON AND GRAHAM, IV: 397, 400, 402, 403, 404
JACKSON, REV. JOHN, II: 439
JACOB, LE BIBLIOPHILE, *pseud. see* LACROIX
JACOBS, MR., II: 405
JAFFRAY, ARTHUR, II: 39, 195
JAFFRAY FAMILY, I: 343
JAFFRAY, MRS. JOHN RICHMOND, II: 39
JAMES, EDWIN JOHN, IV: advising Yates on Garrick Club Affair 102, 106n., 116–20, 121
JAMES FRANCIS EDWARD STUART [the "Old Pretender"], III: 447
JAMES, GEORGE PAYNE RAINSFORD, II: 270; T. burlesques style 657–58. III: 131n.
JAMES, H., IV: 412
JAMES, HENRY [Jr.], *Small Boy*, quoted I: cxx; III: 142n.–43n. *Story*, quoted III: 330n.–31n., 338n., 414n., 529n.–30n.
JAMES, HENRY [Sr.], III: 142; "assaulting" T. 281
JAMES, MRS. HENRY, III: 661

JAMES, S. ["Jeames DelaPluche"], II: 647, 669, 672, 680, 725, 729, 730, 733, 747, 808, 812, 817, 820. III: 5, 22, 31, 33, 38, 44, 63, 82, 276

JAMES, MRS. S., II: 812. III: 63

JAMES, WILLIAM MILBOURNE, II: 338n., 507, 682, 756, 844. III: 377, 477, 674. IV: 287, 401 [?], 412. *Ways and Means*, I: "masterpiece" 526

JAMES, MRS. WILLIAM MILBOURNE [Maria Otter], II: 514n., 524. III: 586, 667, 675. IV: 412
    Letters to: II, 338, 507, 518, 526, 705, 756; III, 377, 477; IV, 287

JAMESON, MRS. ROBERT [Anna Brownell Murphy], II: 769; pension awarded 786. *Winter Studies*, I: attacked by T. 377
    Letter to: II, 787

JANIN, JULES GABRIEL, II: 499; T. on 500; 578; T. hoaxes 579; 580, 742. III: 309, 460, 670. IV: 409

JAY, JOHN, III: 142

JAY, MRS., III: 661

JEAFFRESON, JOHN CORDY, IV: relations with T. 410n., 416, 417. *Recollections*, quoted IV: 401n., 410n.

JEFFREY, FRANCIS, Lord, II: 538n.

JEFFRYS, NATHANIEL, IV: and George IV 12

JERDAN, WILLIAM, II: 136; promises notice of *Irish S. B.* 111; 296n.
    Letters to: I, 313; II, 131; IV, 333

JERMYN, REV. G. B., I: 106

JERROLD, DOUGLAS WILLIAM, I: and Doyle's Catholicism cxxiv; T.'s relations with cxlvi; and *Constitutional* 301n. II: 248; controversy with T. on anti-clericalism 274, 275n., 281–82; "hates" T. 308; 389, 580; "savage little Robespierre" 681; 682n., 704. III: 30; on T.'s supposed Catholicism 342; editing *Lloyd's* 363; 405; attacks T. for snobbery in Leech article 417, 418; 426, 455n. IV: 16n., 48, 139. *Black-eyed Susan*, I: 203. *Mrs. Caudle's Curtain Lectures*, II: 248n.

JERROLD, WILLIAM BLANCHARD, IV: 36

JESSE, CAPTAIN, *Beau Brummell*, III: 358n.

JEWSBURY, GERALDINE, IV: 410n.

JOAN OF ARC, II: T. likens C. Brontë to 612n.

JOCELYN, LADY ELIZABETH FRANCES, *see* LONDONDERRY, Lady [m. 4th Marquess]

JOCELYN, JOHN STRANGE, *see* RODEN, 5th Earl

JOCELYN, ROBERT, *see* RODEN, 2nd Earl

JOCELYN, ROBERT, Viscount, II: 662

JOCELYN, LADY [Lady Frances Cowper, m. Viscount Robert], II: 662

JOHN, *see* GOLDWORTHY

JOHN [a servant], II: 600n., 602n., 610

John Bull, I: 13. II: 480. III: 395

JOHNSON, JOHN, I: 323

JOHNSON, MR. AND MRS., IV: 412

JOHNSON, DR. SAMUEL, I: anecdote 444. II: 645n. III: 16n., 544; couplet quoted 565n.; 574, 619n. IV: anecdote 190n.; 390, 396. *Vanity of Human Wishes*, I: 542, 685

JOHNSTONE, MR., I: 208

JOHNSTONE, MR. AND MRS., III: 571, 572

JOINVILLE, PRINCE DE [François d'Orléan], II: 151

JONES, II: 330

JONES, C. W., *Letter to:* IV, 178

JONES, DAVID, I: 321

JONES, ERNEST, *Letter to:* IV, 189

Jones, George B., *Letters to:* III, 259, 458

Jones, Mrs. George B., III: 134 [?], 259n., 260, 458, 662

Jones, Harry Longueville, I: 228, 229, 230, 358. II: 474

Jones, Dr. Henry Bence, IV: 396, 397, 409

Jones, John, III: 426

Jones, Misses, *Letters to:* IV, 225, 248

Jones, Mr. [an actor], I: 237

Jones, Mr. [father of David], I: 321

Jonson, Ben, I: 293n.; on Bacon 345

Jope, Mr., I: 214, 218, 246

Jordan, Henry, IV: 401

Journal des Débats, II: 160, 452, 500, 578. III: 309

Joyce, Mr., IV: 58

Joyce, William, *Letter to:* II, 396

Jullien, Louis George Antoine Jules, II: 437

Jupp, Mrs., I: 358

Juvenal [Decimus Junius Juvenalis], II: "truculent brute" 553n. *Satires*, III: 207; IV: 160

Kalisch, Dr., III: 479, 482

Kane, Elisha Kent, III: 484. IV: 18, 442

Kay-Shuttleworth, James Phillips, II: 278, 279, 280

Kean, Edmund, I: 110, 141

Keane, David Deady, I: 271. "Illustrations of Discount," II: T.'s letter of protest about 103–05

Keate, George, *Pelew Islands*, II: 246

Keats, John, I: 407n. III: 298

Keeley, Mary Lucy, III: 585

Keene, Charles, IV: 162, 404, 413

Keepsake, The, I: 132. II: 420, 426, 433. III: 264n. IV: 371

Kellar, Miss, II: 373

Kelly, Sir Fitzroy, IV: 111, 117

Kelly, Lady [Ada Cunningham, m. Sir Fitzroy], IV: 111

Kelly, Robert, III: 144, 145n.

Kelvin, William Thomson, 1st Baron, III: 637n. IV: 27

Kelvin, Lady [Margaret Crum, m. 1st Baron], III: 637n. IV: 27

Kemble, Adelaide, *see* Sartoris

Kemble, Charles, I: biographical cxliii; 177, 194; "excellent fellow" 239; talk of his being knighted 433–34; drawing of 502. II: 703

Kemble, Mrs. Charles [Marie Thérèse Decamp], I: biographical cxliii; 173, 325. II: 803. III: 3, 343

Kemble family [Charles], I: biographical cxliii–cxliv; 194, 198, 205, 207, 413, 421

Kemble, Frances Ann ["Fanny," Mrs. Pierce Butler], I: cxliii; "much delighted with" 105; 170, 177, 186n., 194n. II: "dirty as a housemaid" 38–39; 702n. III: 127, 184, 230; T. "almost likes" 340; 345, 584. IV: 272n.; T. "learned to admire but not endure" 438. *Later Life*, quoted II: 778n.–79n.

Letter to: II, 778

Kemble, Gertrude, *see* Santley

Kemble, Henry, I: cxliii; "dear fellow" 172; 173, 175, 192, 239, 240, 241, 282. III: 392

Kemble, John Mitchell, I: cxliii, 172; "a forced plant" 173; 177, 192, 196, 208, 239; "noble fellow" 277; 296; and BFR 346, 374, 382, 383; 387, 398, 400; "gives himself airs" 420; 434

Letters to: I, 324, 378, 406

Kemble, Mrs. John Mitchell [Natalie Wendt], I: cxliii, 387, 398. II: 702

Kempis, Thomas à, II: 615, 616

KENEALY, EDWARD VAUGHAN HYDE, *Goethe*, II: 699. "Maginn," II: 140

KENNAWAY, REV. CHARLES EDWARD, I: 77

KENNAWAY FAMILY [Sir John], II: 763n., 764

KENNAWAY, SIR JOHN [1st Bart.], I: 60, 77n.; T. wants cornetcy from 126

KENNAWAY, SIR JOHN [2nd Bart.], I: 60. II: 763

KENNAWAY, MARIA, I: 60, 143

KENNAWAY, SUSAN, *see* NOEL

KENNEDY, JOHN PENDLETON, III: 543, 618. IV: quoted 111n.
Letter to: III, 197

KENNEDY, MRS., III: 11

KENNEDY, PATRICK, *Letter to:* IV, 114

KENNEY, CHARLES LAMB, II: attacks *Kickleburys* 728n., 751, 754
Letter to: II, 785

KENNY, MR. AND MRS., IV: 402

KENSETT, JOHN FREDERICK, III: 498, 510n.

KENT, DUCHESS OF [Princess Victoria Maria Louisa of Saxe-Coburg], I: 159, 415

KENYON, JOHN, II: 245, 247, 466, 667, 784. III: 381
Letters to: II, 483; IV, 333

KENYON, MRS. JOHN, III: 381

KER, MISS, *Letter to:* II, 317

KERRICH, JOHN, I: 160, 399. II: 5, 43–44

KERRICH, MRS. JOHN [Mary-Eleanor FitzGerald], I: 160n. II: 5, 44

KERRICH, JOHN [Jr.], IV: 408

KERRY, 4TH EARL OF, *see* LANSDOWNE, 3rd Marquess of

KEYS, MR., II: 188

KIDDLE, JOHN L., II: 95

KILLALOE, BISHOP OF, I: 430

KINDERLEY, MR., I: 185, 195, 199

KING, CHARLES, III: 250n., 497, 498, 500

KING, GEORGE, I: 44

KING, MRS. HENRY [Susan Petigru, later Mrs. C. C. Bowen], III: 569

KING, J.G., AND SONS, III: 532, 540, 544, 545, 550, 565, 570, 573, 582. IV: 66

KING, JAMES GORE, III: 497n. IV: 65n., 66

KING, JAMES KING, III: 675

KING, JUDGE MITCHELL, III: 238, 239, 665
Letter to: III, 560

KING, MRS. MITCHELL, III: 375, 560

KING, MRS., IV: 403

KING, RUFUS, III: 497n., 498

KINGLAKE, ALEXANDER WILLIAM, I: on Carlyle cviii; cxxvii; on Mrs. Procter cliv; 195, 196. II: 237, 264, 319, 505, 542, 628n., 645, 777, 825. III: 125, 126, 194; observing the Crimean War 394, 395; 403. IV: standing for Parliament 38. *Eōthen*, II: 152

KINGSLEY, CHARLES, II: 725; "little knowledge of the world" 790. III: 317. IV: 218. *Alton Locke*, II: 698, 699, 762. *Yeast*, II: 725n., 762; IV: quoted 378n.
Letter to: IV, 133

KIRWAN, A. V., II: 135, 144

KNIGHTON, SIR WILLIAM WELLESLEY, IV: 392 [?], 402, 412, 413
Letters to: IV, 267, 288, 334

KNIGHTON, LADY [Clementina Jameson, m. Sir William], IV: 122n., 267, 334, 392 [?], 402, 412, 413
Letter to: IV, 288

KNOWLES, JAMES SHERIDAN, II: 22; and Tennyson pension 225. *Hunchback*, I: 194

KNOWLES, MR., *Letter to:* III, 574

KNOX, MARIA, II: 189

KNUTSFORD, HENRY THURSTAN HOLLAND, 1st Viscount, III: 68n.

KNUTSFORD, LADY [Margaret Jean

Trevelyan, m. 1st Viscount], III: 68

KOCK, PAUL DE, II: 247
Cocu, I: 221, 222. *Laitière de Montfermeil*, I: 236. *Sœur Anne*, I: 222

KOLD, MR., III: 548

KOSSUTH, LOUIS, II: Palmerston and 816

KOTZEBUE, AUGUSTUS VON, I: T. translating 140. "Trost beim Scheiden," III: 314

KRINS, MRS., IV: 218

KUHN, MR., I: 227

KULEVCHA, Battle of, I: 88n.

LABÉDOLLIÈRE, M., I: cvii

LABOUCHERE, HENRY DuPRÉ, III: 674, 685

LACHEVARDIÈRE, I: 435. II: 841

LACLOS, CHODERLOS DE, *Les Liaisons dangereuses*, I: 213

LACROIX, PAUL, *Roi de Ribauds*, I: 225

LADD, MISS, I: 76

LAFITTE, MRS. CHARLES, II: 362

LAFOND, M., I: 277, 282

LAFONT, PIERRE, II: 142

LAMARTINE, ALPHONSE MARIE LOUIS DE, II: 493, 494; T. going to see 729; poem on d'Orsay quoted 733

LAMB, CHARLES, I: 161. II: 563. *John Woodvil*, quoted I: 161

LAMB, COLONEL, I: 4

LAMB, REV. GEORGE, *New Arabian Nights*, I: 202

LAMB, RICHARD M., I: 75

LAMBTON, JOHN GEORGE, *see* DURHAM, 1st Earl of

LAMINGTON, ALEXANDER COCHRANE-BAILLIE, 1st Baron, II: 699

LANCASTER, HENRY, and Dr. John Brown, III: quoted 43n.

LANDELLS, EBENEZER, II: 82, 98

LANDON, LETITIA ELIZABETH, *Churchill*, I: 514

LANDSEER, CHARLES, II: 192n.

LANDSEER, SIR EDWIN HENRY, I: and K. Perry cxxv; cxxxviii, 279. III: 69, 70, 451, 685. IV: illustrating for CM 183; 184, 214, 392, 397, 400, 409, 414
Letters to: IV, 176, 179, 180. *Letter from:* IV, 187

LANE, MISS, III: 463

LANE-FOX, AUGUSTUS HENRY [later Lane-Fox-Pitt-Rivers], II: 824n.

LANE-FOX, MRS. AUGUSTUS HENRY [Alice Margaret Stanley], II: 824

LANG, CAPTAIN, III: 109, 110, 170, 661, 662

LANGDALE, LADY [Lady Jane Elizabeth Harley, m. 1st Baron], IV: 402

LANGFORD, HARRIET, I: 273, 275

LANGLEY, S., IV: 86, 197, 272, 273

LANGSLOW, CAPTAIN, I: 18

LANGSLOW, ROBERT [G. 63], I: 19; and T.'s gambling debt 175; 245, 413, 506. II: suspended from judgeship 194n.–95n., 200; T. pleads Pollock's help for 207–08; "Langslow was victimized by the colonial Aristocracy" 251; 289
Letter to: I, 149

LANGSLOW, MRS. ROBERT [Sarah Jane Henrietta Thackeray, G. 62], I: 19, 68, 183n., 296. II: 194n., 211, 289

LANGSTON, DR. JAMES HAUGHTON, IV: 381

LANSDOWNE, HENRY PETTY-FITZMAURICE, 3rd Marquess of, I: cxxvii, 47. II: "jolly and kind" 662; 664, 665, 685. III: 279, 685. IV: 338, 401

LANSDOWNE, HENRY THOMAS PETTY-FITZMAURICE, 4th Marquess of, II: 685n.

LANSDOWNE, LADY [Emily Jane Mercer Elphinstone de Flahault, Baroness Nairne, m. 4th Marquess], II: 685

LARDNER, DR. DIONYSIUS, I: 438
LARKIN, WILLIAM POCHIN, I: 496
LASCELLES, MR., IV: 318
LAST, DR., III: 245
LATOUCHE, LUCIE DE, III: 138
LAUGHTON, JOHN KNOX, *Henry Reeve*, quoted I: 295n.
LAURENCE, SAMUEL, I: 348n. III: portrait of T. 99, 115, 128, 266, 269; T. writes letters of introduction for 317–19; in America 332, 498; 533, 561. IV: 270, 304
  Letters to: III, 89, 90
LAW, I: T. studying 137, 143–44, 145, 149–50, 176, 178, 181–82, 238, 243. II: T.'s comments on jury system 347–48; 625. III: 308
LAW, EDWARD, *see* ELLENBOROUGH
LAW, GEORGE HENRY [Bishop of Bath and Wells], I: 50
LAW, MR. AND MRS., III: 102
LAW, WILLIAM, I: 495
LAWRENCE, ABBOTT, III: 45, 92, 167n., 661, 664
  Letter to: III, 156
LAWRENCE, AMOS, III: 167
LAWRENCE, COLONEL, *Letter to:* III, 118
LAWRENCE, GEORGE ALFRED, *Guy Livingstone*, IV: 274n.
LAWRENCE, MRS. [of New York], III: 120, 123
LAWRENCE, MRS. BIGELOW, III: 536
LAWRENCE, SIR THOMAS, I: 515. IV: 421
LAWSON, MR., I: 434, 436n.
LAYARD, AUSTEN HENRY, III: 403, 416, 678, 683
Leader, The, II: 711, 716. III: 121, 468n., 469
LECTURES, *see also* works index
  Charity and Humour [Week Day Preachers], III: 176, 187, 189, 190; Dickens on 431, 433; 436n., 437, 440, 441, 506,

510n., 512, 519n., 577n., 598n. IV: 48n., 50, 53, 363, 391
  English Humourists, I: and Forster cxxxv. II: plans for 692, 708, 717n., 725, 736, 740, 741; reading for 754; 765; practising for 766; 770; in London 773–74, 775, 776, 777, 778; Forster reviews 779–80, 781; 783, 784n., 785; T. thinks "a failure" 795; 801, 803, 804; at Cambridge 809n.; at Oxford 810; 812; to Scotland 816, 817, success 819, 820, 821–22. III: in London 4, 5, 17; Scotland 27, 31, 33, 34; Glasgow announcement 35; 41, 42; "successful but not enormously so" 43; 44; American proposal 46–47; 48, 57, 61, 65, 66, 73; T. breaks down at Manchester 76; 80, 82, 83, 84, 87, 88; at Liverpool 89, 91; and America 92, 93; 97, 100, 101, 102; in New York 118, 119, 120, 122; to be repeated in New York 128, 129; 130, 132, 135, 136, 139, 142, 144, 145n., 148, 149; Boston 150, 154; 157, 159, 160, 161, 162, 165, 166; Providence 166n., 169, "rather a failure" 170; 171; in Philadelphia 171n., 172; papers accuse T. of Dickens jealousy 173; 176, 178, 179, 180, 181, 182, 183, 184, 185, 188, 189, 193; in Baltimore and Washington 195, 202, 204, 209, 212, 215, 218; in Richmond 220, 221, 222, 223, 225; 229, 232; in Charleston 235, 236, 238, 239; in Savannah 240, 242, 243, 245, 246; in Petersburg 248; 250, 251, 252, 254, 255, 256, 313; and Forgues' criticism 389; repeated on second American tour 594–95, 598, 599n., "failure" 600,

601; (Diary) 661, 662, 663, 664, 665, 666. IV: 428

Four Georges, III: 60; writing 63, 64, 65, 66, 67, 148, 170, 173, 176, 179, 182, 190, 218, 223, 242, 244, 245, 246, 255, 282, 357, 383, 401, 454; reading for 466; 474, 475, 477, 483; in New York 484, 485, 486, 487, 488, 489; at Williamsburg 491–92; Brooklyn 493, 494, 495; 499, 501, 503, 504, 505, 506, 507; Albany 508; 509, 511, 512, 513, 514, 515, 516; in Boston 517; 518, 519; 521, 522, 523, 524, 526; Buffalo 527, 529, 530; 532; "done wonderfully well" 533; Philadelphia 535, 536; 537; Baltimore 538; 539, 540, 541, 542, 543n.; hostile criticism 545, 546; 547, 548; Richmond 549, 550; 551, 552, 553, 554, 555, 556, 557; Charleston 558; 561; Savannah 562; Augusta 564; attacked in England 564; 565, 566, 567, 570; Macon 571, 572, 573; 574; Mobile 576; New Orleans 577, 578, 583; mistaken attack on 584; 589, 590, 592, 593; St. Louis 594, 595, 596; 598; private reading in London 612, 613; 620, 623, 627; and Mary Queen of Scots 629, 630; 632, 633; Glasgow 634; 635, 636; Edinburgh 637; 639, 640, 641; Hull 642, 644; 646, 647, 648, 650; more popular than Humourists 651, 652; 653, 654, 655, 656, 687, 688, 689, 690. IV: 3, 4, 6; Bath 7, 8; 9, 10n., 11, 12, 13, 14, 15, 16n.; "astoundingly popular" 17; 18; Halifax 19, 21; 22, 23, 24, 25; Edinburgh 26, 27; 28, 29, 30; Inverness 32; 33, 34, 35,

38, 41, 42, 43; Norwich 44; 53, 67, 68, 69, 72, 76, 84, 89, 90n., 155, 235, 249, 338, 377, 378, 379; (Diary) 390, 391; 438, 442, 443, 444, 446

LEE, GEN. CHARLES, IV: 92

LEE, RICHARD, Letters to: III, 26, 78, 450

LEE, SIR SIDNEY, George Smith quoted III: 417n.

LEECH, JOHN, I: cxxviii; biographical cxliv-cxlvi. II: 95, 105n.; "genuine humour" 263; 345n., 346, 360, 362, 367, 389, 701, 720. III: 363, 364; T.'s article on causes trouble 413, 415, 417; T.'s apology for article 418; 422, 432, 455n., 614n., 622n., 674. IV: 174n., 273, 280, 399, 404, 408, 409, 411, 412, 413. Pictures of Life and Character, III: 413
Letter to: IV, 335

LEECH, MRS. JOHN [Ann Eaton], I: cxlv. III: 73, 276. IV: 280, 408, 409, 412

LEECH, MISS, III: 276

LEEMING, MR., Letter to: IV, 132

LEEMING, MRS., IV: 132

LEFEVRE, see SHAW-LEFEVRE

LEHMANN, MRS., III: 265

LEIGH, EDWARD MORRIS, I: 495

LEIGH, FREDERICK, III: 364, 505, 506

LEIGH, PERCIVAL, I: cxlv, cxlvi. II: 247. III: 505, 625. Mr. Pips, II: 537n.; T. imitates style 700n., 767n.
Letters to: II, 103, 105; III, 349, 354, 362, 378, 418, 461

LEIGHTON, FREDERICK, 1st Baron, IV: 185

LEITCH, WILLIAM LEIGHTON, Letters to: III, 615; IV, 336

LEMAIRE, J. W., I: 318n.

LEMAÎTRE, FREDERICK, II: 737

LEMANN FAMILY, I: 235, 236, 277

LE MANN [or Lemann], MICHAEL, I: 226, 230, 231, 233, 237, 261

LEMESURIER, MR., II: 738

LEMOINNE, JOHN MARGUERITE ÉMILE, II: 452n., 502, 578. III: 309, 670

LEMON, COLONEL, I: 213

LEMON, MARK, I: 408. II: 82, 149, 267n., 328, 329, 360, 389, 712. III: 367n., 418, 432, 455n., 614n., 676. IV: 367, 404, 413
Letters to: II, 93, 281, 346, 352, 537, 757, 771

LENNARD, SIR JOHN FARNABY CATOR, II: 556n.

LENNARD, LADY [Julia Maria Frances Hallam, m. Sir John], II: 556, 560n., 664. III: 231–32

LENNARD, JULIA AND ELEANOR, III: 232

LEOPOLD I, King of the Belgians, IV: 298

LERMON, MR., I: 221

LESESNE, JUDGE JOSEPH, III: 577

LESLIE, CHARLES ROBERT, II: 371. IV: 180, 196

LESLIE FAMILY [Charles], IV: 196

LESLIE, MISSES, II: 683. IV: 397, 408

LESLIE, MR., Letter to: III, 162

LESLIE, MRS. JOHN, Letter to: IV, 296

L'ETANG, MME. DE, I: 231

LETTSOM, WILLIAM GARROW, I: 79, 124n., 410, 413, 423, 435, 436. II: visits I.T. 212; 228

LETTSOM, MRS. WILLIAM GARROW, I: 205, 465

LEVASSEUR, NICOLAS PROSPER, IV: 269

LEVER, CHARLES, I: biographical cxlvii–cxlviii. II: 66; account of dinner with T. 66n.–67n.; 89; Irish S. B. dedicated to 106; 122, 140; ends friendship with T. 164–65; 253, 270. III: 211n. IV: quoted on Garrick Club Affair

131n. Harry Lorrequer, II: 29. Roland Cashel, II: "savage" satire on T. 451n., 452; T.'s attitude toward 455; Mrs. B. on 460–61
Letters to: II, 86; IV, 143, 144

LE VERT, MME. OCTAVIA WALTON, III: 577n.
Letter to: IV, 126

LEVESON, MR., II: 814

LEVESON-GOWER, GRANVILLE GEORGE, see GRANVILLE, 2nd Earl of

LEWES, GEORGE HENRY, II: 716n. III: 437n. IV: 190n.
Letters to: II, 353, 490; III, 442

LEWES, MRS. GEORGE HENRY [Agnes Jervis], II: 716

LEWEZOW, FRÄULEIN VON, III: and Goethe 522, 523

LEWIS, SIR JOHN, I: 211, 217, 245

LEWIS, JOHN FREDERICK, I: 287, 330. II: 155

LEWIS, LADY MARIA THERESA, I: cxxvii

LEWIS, CAPT. SAMUEL, II: Cornhill to Cairo dedicated to 151

LEWIS, WILLIAM D., III: 102n., 203, 294, 535, 543, 546, 664

LEY, MR., I: 495

LEYDEN, LUCAS VAN, I: 286

LICHFIELD, BISHOP OF, see LONSDALE, John

LIDDELL, HENRY GEORGE, II: quoted on T. at Charterhouse 641n.; 642. III: 19

LIDDELL, MRS. HENRY GEORGE [Lorina Reeve], II: 641–42

LIEGEL, MISS, III: 414, 419

LIEVEN, PRINCESS, I: lxxxvi

LIGHT, CAPTAIN, III: 436n.

LIGHT, MISS, III: 436n.

LIGIER, I: 252

L'Illustration, II: pirating Mrs. Perkins 308

LINCOLN, ABRAHAM, IV: 213n.

LIND, JENNY, II: 383, 488, 510, 511, 621

LINDSAY, MRS. JOHN, II: 751n. III: 342

LINDSAY, LORD, II: 266

LINGEN, MR., II: 740

LISTER, THOMAS HENRY, *Granby*, I: 22. *Herbert Lacy*, I: 22

LISTON, JOHN, I: 233. IV: 309

Literary Gazette, I: 132. II: 111, 131, 136, 474. IV: 333

LITTLEDALE, MR., I: 196

LITTLE HOLLAND HOUSE, *see* IRVINE and PRINSEP

LLOYD, MR., I: 496

Lloyd's Weekly Newspaper, III: 363, 367n.

LOCH, HENRY BROUGHAM, IV: 215, 396

LOCKE, JOSEPH, II: 732, 743n.

LOCKE, MRS. JOSEPH [Phoebe Mc-Creery], II: 732

LOCKER-LAMPSON, FREDERICK, *My Confidences*, quoted IV: 221n. "My Neighbor Rose," IV: 222
    Letters to: IV, 221, 222

LOCKER-LAMPSON, MRS. FREDERICK [Lady Charlotte Bruce], IV: 221n.

LOCKHART, JOHN GIBSON, I: cxxviii; and Banantyne controversy 460n. III: 340, 404. *Scott*, III: 327n., 634; IV: 438

LOCOCK, DR. CHARLES, II: 560n., 739, 749, 750, 796

LONDON, BISHOP OF, *see* BLOMFIELD or TAIT

LONDON HOUSE, *see* LONDONDERRY

LONDONDERRY, CHARLES WILLIAM STEWART, 3rd Marquess of, III: 248n.

LONDONDERRY, LADY [Lady Frances Anne Emily Vane-Tempest, m. 3rd Marquess], II: 784n. III: 248, 454

LONDONDERRY, FREDERICK WILLIAM ROBERT STEWART, 4th Marquess of, II: 458, 459, 543, 544; duel over Mme. Grisi 643; 731, 736, 814. III: 248n. IV: 392, 401, 411

LONDONDERRY, LADY [Lady Elizabeth Frances Jocelyn (Powerscourt), m. 4th Marquess], II: 373n., 481, 532, 543, 731, 732, 736, 814. III: 8, 19, 54, 393. IV: 401, 411, 427
    Letters to: II, 458, 544, 627, 776; IV, 286

LONG, SIR JOHN, II: 37

LONG, MR., I: 442

LONGFELLOW, HENRY WADSWORTH, II: 821. III: 166, 172n., 514, 530
    Letter to: IV, 164

LONGMAN, MRS., IV: 413

LONGMAN, THOMAS NORTON, I: 459. II: 201, 202n.

LONSDALE, JOHN [Bishop of Lichfield], I: lxxxii

LONSDALE, ST. GEORGE HENRY LOWTHER, 4th Earl of, III: 39, 473n.

LORCHA QUESTION, IV: 447

LOTHROP, MARY, III: 173, 210n.

LOTHROP, DR. SAMUEL KIRKLAND, III: 173n.

LOTHROP, MRS. SAMUEL KIRKLAND, III: 210n.

LOTHROP, THORNTON, III: 173n.

LOTT, MR., I: 102

LOUIS NAPOLÉON [Napoléon III], II: at Lady Blessington's 362; as president 493, 495, 499, 593, 594, 729, 736, 737; and the Don Pacifico issue 758; English press's execration of 813–14, 823. III: T.'s reaction to *coup d'état* 16; 115, 132; coronation of 137, A.T.'s description of 140–41; 145n., 306; P and 432. IV: 232, 384, 421, 427

LOUIS PHILIPPE, I: 236; attempted assassination of 237; 251, 259; and Thiers 425. II: T.'s projected

article on 42, 64, 65, 66, 81, 92;
P article on 150; 151n., 163, 354,
360, 731. III: 137n., 447
LOUISE [a maid], III: 269
LOVATT, ROBERT, I: 311. III: 168
LOVEGROVE, MR., IV: 232
LOVER, SAMUEL, II: 140
LOVETT, WILLIAM, I: 421
Loving Ballad of Lord Bateman, The,
I: 380–81
LOW, ANDREW, III: 240, 241, 243,
556, 561, 562, 563, 567–68, 570,
571, 665
LOW, MRS. ANDREW [Sarah Cecil
Hunter, 1st w.], III: 240
LOW, MRS. ANDREW [2nd w.], III:
561, 563, 567, 570
LOW, AUGUSTA GEORGIANA [G. 97],
II: 609
LOW FAMILY [Andrew], III: 543,
567, 570. IV: 291, 411, 414
LOW, CHARLOTTE, *see* METCALFE
LOW, GEN. SIR JOHN [G. 82], II:
244, 609n. III: 636
LOW, MRS. JOHN [Augusta Ludlow
Shakespear, G. 81], II: 244, 609n.
LOW, MR., IV: 397
LOW, S., AND SONS, IV: 58
Letter to: IV, 60
LOWELL, JAMES RUSSELL, III: 107n.,
109n., 614. IV: 434. *Letters,*
quoted III: 464n.–65n. *New Let-
ters,* quoted III: 165n.
Letter to: III, 166. *Letter
from:* III, 161
LOWELL, MRS. JAMES RUSSELL
[Maria White], III: 107n., 167,
331. IV: 434
LOWELL, MR., II: 504n.
LOWRY-CORRY, HENRY THOMAS, *see*
CORRY
LOWTHER INHERITANCE, IV: 251n.
LOYD, SAMUEL JONES, *see* OVERSTONE
LUBBOCK, FORSTER, AND COMPANY,
I: 187, 220, 222, 230, 231, 237,
250, 379, 468. II: 73, 135, 150,
162, 177; "refuses to answer" to

T.'s respectability 225; 613, 708,
840, 841, 842. III: 12, 61, 82,
98, 274, 351, 524, 634. IV: 9,
22, 98, 178, 395, 400, 413
LUCAS, SAMUEL, IV: 321, 359, 404
Letter to: IV, 170
LUMLEY, BENJAMIN, II: 165, 269,
384
Letter to: II, 666
LUNT, GEORGE, "Recollections of
T.," quoted III: 259n.
LUSCOMBE, MICHAEL HENRY
[Bishop of Paris], I: 87, 318n.,
511
LUSHINGTON, CHARLES, II: 844
LUSHINGTON, EDMUND LAW, I: 495.
III: 423
LUSHINGTON, FRANKLIN, II: 715,
746n.
LUSHINGTON, HENRY, I: 495
LUTHER, MARTIN, I: 126
LUTTRELL, HENRY, II: 364
LYELL, SIR CHARLES, IV: 396n.
LYELL, LADY [Mary Elizabeth Hor-
ner, m. Sir Charles], III: 169n.
IV: 396, 412
LYNCY, MISS, III: 662
LYNDHURST, JOHN SINGLETON COP-
LEY, 1st Baron, II: 245. IV: 56
LYNE, BENJAMIN HART, I: 210, 213
LYNE-STEPHENS, STEPHENS, I: 262n.
LYON, SAMUEL E., III: 597n., 606
LYSLEY, WILLIAM JOHN, IV: 412n.
LYSLEY, MRS. WILLIAM JOHN, IV:
403, 412
LYTTLETON, GEORGE WILLIAM, 4th
Baron, I: xcv. II: and Langslow
207, 251; 277, 532. IV: 22n.
LYTTLETON, LADY [Mary Glynne,
m. 4th Baron], IV: 22
LYTTON, EDWARD GEORGE EARLE
LYTTON BULWER-LYTTON, 1st
Baron, *see* BULWER-LYTTON

MABERLY, WILLIAM LEADER, II:
433n.

MacAdam, George, III: 510

Macarton, Mr., I: 194

Macaulay, Kenneth, II: 390. IV: 392, 401

Macaulay, Thomas Babington, 1st Baron, I: cxxxv. II: 591; serious minded 593; 629; backs T. for Athenæum 636n.; 675n., 777, 801. III: 119n., 449. *History*, III: 38, 537, 538, 542

Macbean, Aeneas, III: 327, 332, 338, 339, 425, 671, 672

Macbean, Alexander, II: 187

MacCullagh, Miss, IV: 336

McCullagh, William Torrens, II: 392n., 820n.

McCullagh, Mrs. William Torrens, II: 820
    Letter to: IV, 336

M'Diarmid, Miss, III: 689

M'Diarmid, William Ritchie, III: 689

MacDonald, George, IV: 170

Macdonald, Lady [Anne Charlotte Ogle, m. Sir James], III: 667

Macdonald, Norman Hilton, II: 447

McDowell, Miss, III: 621

McDowell, Mr., I: 185, 190, 191, 199, 205, 206, 207
    Letter to: III, 621

Maceroni, Col. Francis, *Memoirs*, I: T. suggests revisions 344–45

MacEwen, Rev. Alexander, *Letter to:* IV, 175

MacFarlane, Charles, *Constantinople*, I: 284, 288

McGregor, Mr., IV: 414

Machabb, Mr., III: 288

Machale, John, IV: 323

McIvor, Mr., IV: 165

Mackay, Charles, I: cxix. IV: 36n.

M'Kay, Mr., III: 32

Mackay, Mr., IV: 36

Mackellop, Mr., I: 269

McKennell, J., III: 687

Mackenzie, Miss, III: 245

MacKenzie, Mrs. Colin [Adeline Pattle], I: 189n.

Mackenzie, Mrs. Stewart, II: 790

Mackintosh, Robert James, IV: 82n., 392

Mackinnon, William Alexander, *Letter to:* IV, 47

Maclaine, Maj.-Gen. Sir Archibald, III: 496

Macleod, Captain, II: 233

MacLeod, Donald, *Norman MacLeod,* quoted I: 124n., 128n.

Macleod, Lt.-Gen. Duncan, II: 291

Macleod, Lady, I: 387, 398, 429

MacLeod, Dr. Norman, I: quoted 124n.; 128n.

Maclise, Daniel, I: 280, 283, 287, 326, 329. II: 192n. III: drawing of Rogers 444; drawing of Goethe 445n.; 449, 460. IV: 304, 392. "Gallery," I: 328
    Letter to: II, 133

MacMahon, Col. Thomas Westropp, III: 633

McMichael, Morton, III: 178, 292, 293, 294, 546. IV: 135; quoted 380n.
    Letters to: III, 191, 192, 205, 410, 534

McMichael, Morton, Jr., "Thackeray's Visit," quoted III: 102n., 172n.

Macmillan's Magazine, IV: 156

Macnabb, Mr., I: 209, 245

MacOboy, Mrs., II: 65

Macon, Georgia, *see also* chronology, III: 571

Macpherson, Mr., III: 637

Macquillavray, Mrs., I: 389

Macready, Katherine, III: 127

Macready, Walter, III: 231

Macready, William, III: 127, 231. IV: 122

Macready, William Charles, I: 177n., 196, 309n., 349, 374. II: controversy with Heraud 24; T.

writing play for 38, 93; 220, 226n., 292n., 301, 302, 304, 325, 396, 701n., 702–03, 752n.; farewell dinner 755, 766. III: 127, 231, 304, 487. IV: 68; "scholar and gentleman" 72; 122, 391
  Letters to: II, 226, 237, 401; III, 500, 619; IV, 53, 68
MACREADY, MRS. WILLIAM CHARLES, II: 394. III: 127
  Letters to: II, 304; IV, 337
MACRONE, JOHN, *Letters to:* I, 327, 344
MACRONE, MRS., I: 456
MACWHIRTER, MISS, III: 385
MADDEN, RICHARD ROBERT, *Blessington*, quoted II: 390n.–91n.
MAGINN, WILLIAM, I: 191–92, 197, 199, 200, 201, 207, 208, 209, 210, 260n., 314, 350, 351, 352, 353, 354, 460n., 489, 508. II: death of 75; 140, 371; as "Shandon" 634. IV: 252
MAGINN, MRS. WILLIAM, I: 353
MAGUIRE, FATHER TOM, II: 362
MAHON, CHARLES JAMES PATRICK, II: 308
MAHON, PHILIP HENRY STANHOPE, Viscount, *see* STANHOPE, 5th Earl
MAHONY, FRANCIS SYLVESTER ["Father Prout"], I: 260n., 280; "scandal monger" 309; 326, 327, 329. II: 40, 148, 468n. III: 363. IV: 112n.–13n.
MAINE, HENRY SUMNER, II: 508, 509, 525; memoir of H. Hallam 746n.
MAINE, MRS. HENRY SUMNER [Jane Maine], II: 508, 509, 513, 543
MAINTENON, MME. DE, II: 738
MAISON DE SANTÉ, I: I.T. at cxlix. II: 3
MAJOR, JOHN, I: 209
MALAN, CÉSAR JEAN SALOMON, III: 82
MALMESBURY, JAMES HOWARD HARRIS, 3rd Earl of, IV: 330

MALTHUS, THOMAS R., *Political Economy*, I: 71
Manchester Guardian, III: 97. IV: Dickens defends self in 86n.
MANNERT, KONRAD, *Reichsgeschichte*, I: T. translating 140, 150
MANNING, HENRY EDWARD, Cardinal, II: 749. III: 343
MANSFIELD, ARTHUR, III: 476
MANSFIELD, CHARLES, III: 37
MANSFIELD, MR., IV: 393
MANSFIELD, MRS., III: 667, 685. IV: 391, 409, 414
MANSON, LADY, III: 127
MANT, REV. RICHARD, and Rev. George D'Oyly, *Holy Bible*, I: 424
MAQUET, AUGUSTE, II: 619
MARCHANGY, LOUIS ANTOINE FRANÇOIS DE, *Tristan le voyageur*, I: 237
MARGUERITE, Queen of Navarre, *Heptaméron*, II: 830
MARIE LOUISE, Queen of the Belgians, II: 731
MARKHAM, MR., I: 178
MARKS, MR., I: 459
MARLBOROUGH, JOHN CHURCHILL, 1st Duke of, II: 446. III: 37n., 254; T. reads dispatches for *Esmond* 446; 447
MAROCHETTI, CARLO, Baron, III: 387, 388, 464, 674. IV: 363, 364, 396, 438
MAROCHETTI, LADY, III: 477. IV: 396
MAROCHETTI, MAURICE, III: 464, 475, 477, 561
MARRAST, ARMAND, II: 493
MARRIAGE, I: clxiv–clxv, 267, 268, 296; account of T.'s 318n. III: 210n. IV: T. on early ones 145
MARRIOT, MR., I: 448
MARRIOT, MRS., I: 274
MARRYAT, CAPT. FREDERICK, III: 576; "vulgar dog" 591
  Joseph Rushbrook, II: 31. *King's*

Own, I: 206. *Newton Forster*, I: 206

MARS, MLLE [Anne Françoise Hippolyte Boutet], I: 88, 91, 226

MARSH, MRS. ANNE, *Mount Sorel*, II: 190n.

MARSHALL, CAPTAIN, I: 19

MARSHALL, WILLIAM, II: 548, 549n., 550, 665

MARSHALL, MRS. WILLIAM, II: 548, 549n., 550. III: 375, 675

MARSTON, MRS., II: 329

MARTCHENKO, MME., II: 792

MARTHA, *see* GOLDWORTHY

MARTHA [a servant], IV: 5, 35

MARTIN, CHANCELOR, IV: 342

MARTIN, MISS, *Letter to:* III, 64

MARTIN, MR. [of Connemara], II: 75, 76

MARTIN, ROBERT, I: 497

MARTIN, SIR THEODORE, I: quoted on T. and Dickens cxxiiin.; on T.'s gambling 506. II: 261n. IV: 284, 392, 402. *Aytoun*, quoted III: 687–88. *Helena Faucit*, quoted IV: 121n.–22n.

    Letter to: IV, 253

MARTIN, LADY [Helena Saville Faucit, m. Sir Theodore], IV: 121, 122, 402

    Letters to: IV, 253, 284, 338

MARTINEAU, ARTHUR, I: 196, 197, 207, 239

MARTINEAU, HARRIET, II: 628n. *Autobiography*, quoted I: 211n.

MARTINEAU, JAMES, III: 91. "The Church of England," II: 663

MARVILLE, ZÉLIE DE, III: 138

MARVY, LOUIS, I: biographical cxlviii-cl. II: 11, 434, 445, 454, 491, 608n., 610, 612, 613. III: 490. IV: 211, 212. *English Landscape Painters*, III: 490

MARVY, MME., II: 592. III: 490. IV: 211, 212

MARY, Queen of Scots, III: and T.'s lecture 629, 630, 653

MARZIALS, FRANK T., and Herman Merivale, *Thackeray*, quoted I: 318n., 506

MASON, EDWARD, IV: 92

MASON, JAMES MURRAY, IV: 165

MASSON, DAVID, IV: 156n. *Memories*, quoted II: 130n.–31n., 442n. "Pendennis and Copperfield," quoted II: 772n.

    Letter to: II, 771

MATHESON, MR., I: 420

MATHEWS, CHARLES, I: 14, 417n.; and T.'s play 475, 482

MATRAVEN, MR., I: 172

MATTHEW, FATHER, II: 70

MATTHEW, REV. JOHN, I: 151

MATTHEW, HENRY, I: 151, 190, 191, 198, 205, 207, 209, 494, 495, 497. II: 541–42. III: 64

MATTHEW, MISS, II: 542

MATTOCK, MATHEW, I: 48

MATURIN, CHARLES ROBERT, *Melmoth*, III: Goethe and 444. *Women*, I: 53

MAULEY, WILLIAM ASHLEY WEBB PONSONBY, 1st Baron de, II: 364

MAURICE, JOHN FREDERICK DENISON, II: 688. III: 317. IV: 392

MAURIGY, MR., IV: 136

MAYHEW, HENRY, John Binny, and others, *London Labour and the London Poor*, II: 817

MAYHEW, HORACE, III: 367, 614n. IV: 404

MAYHEW, WILLIAM, I: 497

MAYNARD, MR., III: 668

MAZZINGHI, THOMAS JOHN, I: 48, 53, 82, 187, 493, 495

    Letters to: II, 764, 765

MAZZINI, JOSEPH, II: 775

MEADOWS, KENNY, I: T. writes for 426

MEAGHER, THOMAS FRANCIS, III: 227, 228

Medical Reforms, IV: 63

MELBOURNE, WILLIAM LAMB, 2nd Viscount, I: and the Bedchamber Crisis 384n. II: 229

MELCI, M. DE, II: duel with Castlereagh 643n.–44n.

MELCI, MME. DE, *see* GRISI

MELGUND, WILLIAM HUGH ELIOT-MURRAY-KYNYNMOUND, Lord, *see* MINTO, 3rd Earl

MELOS, MME., I: 128, 141

"MEN OF THE TIME," III: 410n., 411

MENTMORE, MR., IV: 408

MEREWETHER [or Meriwether], MR., IV: 392, 393, 412

MÉRIMÉE, PROSPER, III: 460

MERIVALE, ELLA, IV: 272

MERIVALE, HERMAN, II: 662n. III: 667. IV: 133n., 172, 390, 391, 408, 409

MERIVALE, HERMAN, and Frank T. Marzials, *Thackeray*, quoted I: 318n., 506

MERIVALE, MRS. HERMAN [Caroline Penelope Robinson], II: 662. III: 4
    Letter to: III, 650

MERIVALE, J., IV: 415

MERRICK, MR., I: 449. II: 325, 381

MERRIMAN [or Merryman], DR. JAMES NATHANIEL, II: 349n.

MERRIMAN [or Merryman], JOHN JONES, II: 349, 573. III: 17
    Letter to: III, 621

MERRISON, MR., III: 543n.

MÉRY, JOSEPH, IV: 428

MERYON, CHARLES LEWIS, *Hester Stanhope*, II: 202

METCALFE, SIR THEOPHILUS JOHN [G. 96], II: 609n. IV: 408 [?]

METCALFE, LADY [Charlotte Low, G. 95, m. Sir Theophilus], II: 609
    Letter to: II, 617

MEYERBEER, GIACOMO, *Huguenots*, II: 556, 557. *Prophète*, II: 680n., 681, 682n. *Robert le Diable*, I: 208

MICHEL, F., IV: 398

MICHELET, JULES, *Histoire*, II: 16

MIDDLETON, MR., III: 623, 687

MIGNET, FRANÇOIS AUGUSTE, *Histoire*, I: 285

MIGUEL, DOM MARIA EVARISTO, I: 102

MILBURN, REV. WILLIAM HENRY, III: 532

MILDMAY, HENRY BINGHAM, I: lxxxvii. III: 150, 164, 165, 263, 265, 270, 282, 296, 307. IV: 230

MILDMAY, MRS. HENRY BINGHAM [Georgiana Frances Bulteel], IV: 230

MILDMAY, HUMPHREY FRANCIS, III: 150n., 165, 263, 307

MILDMAY, HUMPHREY ST. JOHN, III: 150n., 307

MILL, JAMES, *Political Economy*, I: 71

MILL, JOHN STUART, I: 211n. II: 662–63

MILLAIS, EVERETT, IV: 26

MILLAIS, JOHN EVERETT, III: 231, 422. IV: 26, 183, 409, 414
    Letters to: IV, 25, 26

MILLAIS, MRS . JOHN EVERETT [Euphemia Chalmers Gray (Ruskin)], IV: 25, 26

MILLER, JOE, II: 404, 408. *Jest Book*, II: 145

MILLER, MR., III: 435n.

MILLS, CLARK, III: 196n.

MILMAN, HENRY HART [Dean of St. Pauls], II: backs T. for Athenæum 635, 636n., 637; 663, 777. III: 21, 68, 667. IV: 88n., 138, 391. *Martyr of Antioch*, IV: 224
    Letter to: III, 377

MILNE, J.D., *Letter to:* IV, 34

MILNES, FLORENCE ELLEN, III: 585

MILNES, RICHARD MONCKTON [Lord Houghton], I: cxxvii; biographical cxli-cxliii; 454. II: "amazingly clever" 4; 6, 23, 163, 364, 674n.; married 807. III: 70, 119n., 125, 127, 230, 585, 667, 675, 685, 686n. IV: 170, 214, 285n.–86n.; created Baron 289; 304n., 396, 410, 411
 Letters to: I, 451; II, 27, 625, 673; III, 103; IV, 169, 339

MILNES, MRS. RICHARD MONCKTON [Annabel Hungerford Crewe], I: cxli. II: 807. IV: 285n., 411

MILNES, ROBERT OFFLEY ASHBURTON, IV: 289

MILNES, ROBERT PEMBERTON, II: 28n. IV: 21

MILNES, MRS. ROBERT PEMBERTON [Henrietta Maria Monckton], II: 28n. IV: 21

MILTON, JOHN, II: 821.
 L'Allegro, II: 25. *Lycidas*, I: 172. *Paradise Lost*, I: 104; II: 700; III: 154, 383

MINTO, GILBERT ELLIOT, 1st Earl of, II: 516n.

MINTO, WILLIAM HUGH ELLIOT-MURRAY-KYNYNMOUND, 3rd Earl of, II: 516, 819

MINTO, LADY [Emma Hislop, m. 3rd Earl], II: 516n., 819

"MISSY," *see* ELTON, Mary Agnes

"MISSY," *see* THACKERAY, Anne

"MISTLETOE, BOBBY," *see* SYNGE, Robert Follett

MITCHELL, JOHN, II: 783, 803
 Letters to: I, 299, 314

MITFORD, NANCY, ed. *Ladies of Alderley*, quoted I: clxix

MITFORD, WILLIAM, *History of Greece*, I: 47, 57

MOBILE, ALABAMA, *see also* chronology, III: 575, 577, 588

MOFFATT, GEORGE, IV: 392, 393, 397, 402, 413

MOFFATT, MRS. GEORGE [Lucy Morrison], IV: 392
 Letter to: II, 785

MOHL, JULIUS, IV: 403n.

MOHL, MRS. JULIUS [Mary Elizabeth Clarke], IV: 403

MOIRA, FRANCIS RAWDON HASTINGS, 2nd Earl of, III: sonnet quoted 473; 474

MOLÉ, COMTE LOUIS MATHIEU, I: 360. II: 731

MOLESWORTH, SIR ARSCOTT OURRY, III: 53n.

MOLESWORTH, SIR WILLIAM, I: 218, 219; supports *Constitutional* 301n. II: 397, 552. III: 53n., 317, 495, 674
 Letter to: IV, 340

MOLESWORTH, LADY [Andalusia Grant, m. Sir William], II: 397, 666. III: 277, 317, 495, 496, 508, 685. IV: 22, 183, 233, 391, 409, 423
 Letters to: II, 369; III, 302; IV, 49, 146, 340

MOLIÈRE [Jean Baptiste Poquelin], *Fourberies de Scapin*, II: 152

MOLYNEUX, EDMUND, III: 665

MONCK, CHARLES STANLEY, 4th Viscount, III: 429. IV: and Oxford election 49, 381, 382, 387, 388

MONCKTON-ARUNDELL, *see* GALWAY

Moniteur Universel, IV: 265n.

MONOD, ADOLPHE FRÉDÉRIC THÉODORE, III: 137, 138n., 141, 153, 169, 188, 198, 217, 218

MONRO, DR. ALEXANDER, I: 259n.

MONRO, MRS. ALEXANDER [Maria Carmichael-Smyth], I: 259

MONROE, MR. AND MRS., IV: 403

MONTAGUE, BASIL, I: cliii. II: 245

MONTAGUE, MRS. BASIL [Benson (Skepper)], I: cliii, 465. III: 638–39

MONTAGUE, LADY HARRIET MARY, *see* ASHBURTON

MONTAGUE, MISS, II: 6

MONTAGUE, MR., III: 232

MONTAGUE PLACE, see TURNER

MONTAIGNE, MICHEL EYQUEM, II: 245, 246

MONTALEMBERT, M., I: 278

MONTALIVET, COMTE MARTHE CAMILLE BACHASSON DE, I: 355

MONTEAGLE, THOMAS SPRING-RICE, 1st Baron, II: 509n., 577. III: 17, 317

MONTEAGLE, LADY [Mary Anne Marshall, 2nd w. of 1st Baron], II: 509

MONTEFIORE, MRS. ABRAHAM [Henrietta Rothschild], II: 644

MONTEFIORE, MRS. HORATIO JOSEPH [Charlotte Montefiore], II: 645

MONTEFIORE, JOSEPH MAYER, II: 645

MONTEFIORE, SIR MOSES HAIM, I: 467

MONTEFIORE, NATHANIEL, II: 645

MONTEFIORE, MRS. NATHANIEL [Emma Goldsmid], II: 645

MONTES, LOLA, I: cli

MONTGOMERY, ALFRED, II: 542, 617. III: 81
  Letter to: IV, 342

MONTGOMERY, MRS. ALFRED, IV: 341
  Letters to: II, 617, 626; IV, 341

MONTGOMERY, JANE, III: 586

MONTGOMERY, REV. ROBERT, II: 679
  Letters to: II, 675, 686

MONTLUC, BLAISE DE LASSERAN-MASSENCOME, Seigneur de, Commentaires, I: 201

MONTREAL, BISHOP OF, see FULFORD, Francis

MOODY, GEORGE, I: 48, 53, 55, 56

MOON, FRANCIS GRAHAM, III: 426, 674n.

MOORE, PETER, I: 506

MOORE, THOMAS, I: 112, 131, 288. II: 63
  History of Ireland, II: 245, 247. Irish Melodies, III: 335. Lord Edward FitzGerald, I: 162. Memoirs, III: 279. Sacred Songs, I: 248. Sheridan, I: 215, 216

MORALITY, see ETHICS

MORGAN, CAPTAIN, II: 683

MORGAN, CHARLES, III: 512

MORGAN, SIR CHARLES, I: 376n.

MORGAN, LADY [Sydney Owenson, m. Sir Charles], I: and "Becky Sharp" clviin.; 376, 377, 378. II: 149, 214, 476. Woman and her Master, I: 447
  Letters to: III, 373; IV, 123, 343

MORGHEN, RAFFAELLO SANZIO, I: 66

MORIER, JAMES JUSTINIAN, II: 472, 563. Hajji Baba, II: 152
  Letter to: II, 320

MORLEY, DOWAGER LADY [Frances Talbot, m. 1st Earl], II: 541, 644n., 664. III: 613

MORLEY, EDMUND PARKER, 2nd Earl of, III: 613

MORLEY, JOHN, Richard Cobden, quoted I: 386n.

MORLEY, SAMUEL, Letter to: III, 457

Morning Advertiser, The, I: 358

Morning Chronicle, The, I: E.E. Crowe and cxvii-cxviii; T. applies for Constantinople post 281, 283, 287; 376; refuses T.'s article on the Queen 384; 398. II: 164, 169, 170, 171n., 172, 216, 219, 225; resigns from 227, 229, 231, 240; 241n., 244, 245, 249, 252, 264, 353, 354, 362, 364, 365, 373, 442, 452, 459n., 482, 578; and pensions 629–35; 689, 724n., 817n. III: 267, 358n., 455n., 638n. IV: 36n., 189n., 227n., 330

Morning Herald, The, III: 393, 395. IV: 8

Morning Post, The, II: 33. IV: 361

MORPETH, GEORGE HOWARD, Viscount, *see* CARLISLE, 7th Earl of

MORRIS, LAURENCE STUART, I: 493

MORRIS, MOWBRAY, II: 390, 754, 756. III: 407, 423, 451

MORRIS, MR., II: 99, 200

MORRIS, MRS., III: 4

MORRISH, MISS, IV: 341, 342

MORRITT, MR., II: 147

MORTON, ELIZABETH, II: 227, 266

MORTON, SAVILLE, I: biographical cl-clii; 388, 453, 454. II: 38, 57, 121, 148, 227, 228, 266, 311, 366, 682, 721n., 726, 734. III: 24; murdered 114, 115

MOTHE-LANGON, BARON DE LA, *L'Empire*, II: and *Barry Lyndon* 139

MOTLEY, JOHN LOTHROP, IV: 82, 84, 231, 238, 392. *Correspondence*, quoted III: 152n.; IV: 82n., 84n., 85n.

MOTLEY, MRS. JOHN LOTHROP, IV: 82n., 84n., 85n.

MOTLEY, MISS, IV: 231

MOTTE FOUQUÉ, FRIEDRICH, Baron de la, I: T.'s translation of poem 297–99. *Undine*, I: 172

MOXON, EDWARD, III: 128, 536

MOYES, MR., I: 282

MOZART, WOLFGANG AMADEUS, I: 363. III: 268

MOZLEY, ANNE, ed. *Correspondence of . . . Newman*, quoted I: cxl-cxli

MOZLEY, THOMAS, *Reminiscences*, quoted I: 25n.

MUNRO, MR., I: 197

MURAT, JOACHIM, II: 217

MURCHISON, SIR RODERICK IMPEY, IV: 391, 402, 412

MURE, WILLIAM, III: 578

MURPHY, FRANCIS STACK, II: 370, 468. IV: 366

MURRAY, AMELIA MATILDA, III: 585

MURRAY, JOHN, III: 432

MURRAY, SIR JOHN ARCHIBALD, III: 631, 687. IV: 39

MURRAY, LADY [Mary Rigby, m. Sir John], III: 631
Letter to: IV, 39

MUSSY, HENRI GUÉNEAU DE, IV: 403, 409; and wife 412, 414

MUTTON, MRS., II: 426

MYERS, MR., IV: 70

MYLNE, MR., III: 583

NAB, MR. AND MRS., I: 204

NAIRNE, CAROLINA, Baroness, *Gude Nicht*, I: 75

NAPIER, ADM. SIR CHARLES, II: 247

NAPIER, GEN. SIR CHARLES JAMES, *Defense of England*, III: 16

NAPIER, FRANCIS, 9th Baron, IV: 384

NAPIER, LT.-GEN. SIR GEORGE THOMAS, II: 546, 593

NAPIER, MACVEY, II: 212, 482
Letters to: II, 201, 213, 214

NAPIER, MR., III: 689

NAPOLÉON I [Bonaparte], I: T. sees 3n.; 42, 45, 87, 95, 158, 182, 227, 232, 251, 252, 395, 425, 496. II: 4, 219, 734. III: 54, 95, 321. IV: 254n.

NAPOLÉON II [François Charles Joseph Bonaparte], *see* REICHSTADT

NAPOLÉON III, *see* LOUIS NAPOLÉON

NASMYTH, MRS., I: 427, 428. II: 217

Nation, The, III: 467n.

NATIONAL SHAKESPEARE COMMITTEE, IV: T. and 416–17

National Standard, The, I: T. as proprietor of 259–61, 262, 263, 264, 268, 269; T. changes name of 270–71; 508. II: 97n.

NAVARINO, Battle of, I: 17

NAYLOR, SAMUEL, I: 153

NEALD, CAPTAIN, I: clix. II: 754
NEALE, WILLIAM JOHNSON, *Cavendish*, I: 201
NEATE, CHARLES, II: 445n., 457, 458n., 622. IV: and Oxford election 381, 382, 384, 385, 386, 388. *Dialogues des Morts*, II: 463–64, 479–80
   Letters to: II, 463, 479; III, 476
NEAVES, CHARLES, Lord, IV: 40n.
NELSON, HORATIO, Viscount, II: 218
NELSON, MR., III: 219
NEWCASTLE, HENRY PELHAM CLINTON, 5th Duke of, II: 364. III: 317, 416. IV: 204, 205n., 413n.
NEWMAN, FRANCIS WILLIAM, II: in *Pendennis* 677n. III: 13. *The Soul*, II: 581
NEWMAN, JOHN HENRY, Cardinal, I: on T. cxl-cxli. II: 581n.; T. on 675, 676; 705. III: 13, 22; and Achilli 66n.; 341, 439n. *Certain Difficulties*, quoted II: 675n.–76n. *Lectures*, III: 66n.
New Monthly Magazine, The, I: cxxxviii, 196, 215. II: 24, 167, 169n., 198n., 219. III: 434. IV: 218n.
NEW ORLEANS, LOUSIANA, *see also* chronology, III: 577, 581, 588, 590
New Orleans Weekly Delta, The, III: account of attack on T. 585n.
NEWTON, SIR ISAAC, I: 35. *Principia*, IV: 196
NEWTON, JOHN, III: 93
NEW YORK, *see also* chronology, III: 123, 133, 143, 179, 193, 250, 254, 255, 514
New York Albion, The, III: 489. IV: 279
New York Herald, The, III: attacks T. 88, 120n., 121, 123, 490n., 494, 502; 505, 512, 652. IV: 435

NEW YORK MERCANTILE LIBRARY ASSOCIATION, *see also* Felt, W. L., III: 118n., 145n., 382, 383, 488n., 491, 493
New York Times, The, III: on T.'s lectures 121n.; quoted 489n., 505. IV: publishes Yates 189n., 190n.
New York Tribune, The, II: quoted 721n. III: quoted 145n.; 489, 505, 662n. IV: pirating *Virginians* 60; and Dickens-Ternan letter 86n.; 321n.
NICHOLAS I, Czar of Russia, II: 171, 362–63, 649n. III: 158, 426
NICHOLAS, CAPT. TOOP, I: 211
NICHOLSON, CAPTAIN, III: 436n.
NICKISSON, GEORGE WILLIAM, II: 130, 138, 254
   Letters to: II, 41, 103, 160, 176, 191, 254, 283; IV, 344
NIELSON, MRS., III: 536, 543
NIGER EXPEDITION, II: 43
NIXON, EDWARD, III: 148
NIXON, MRS., I: 399. III: 148n., 429
NOÉ, AMÉDÉE DE ["Cham"], II: 389, 390
NOEL, REV. GERARD THOMAS, II: 671
NOEL, MRS. GERARD THOMAS [Susan Kennaway], II: 671n.
NOKES, JOHN, I: 303. II: 49
NORCOTT, JAMES, I: 431
NORFOLK, CHARLES HOWARD, 11th Duke of, II: 363, 364
NORFOLK, DUCHESS OF [Lady Charlotte Sophia Granville, m. 13th Duke], II: 784n.
NORMAN, MR., IV: 411; and wife 414
NORMANBY, CONSTANTINE HENRY PHIPPS, 1st Marquess of, II: 495, 731. IV: 427
NORMANBY, LADY [Maria Liddell, m. 1st Marquess], II: 731, 734
NORRINGTON-EPPS CASE, I: 401
NORRIS, MR., III: 662

North American and United States Gazette, III: 178, 192, 410n., 598n.

North British Review, II: 282; quoted 538n.–39n.; 688, 771. III: 43n., 286

NORTH, CHRISTOPHER, *pseud. see* WILSON, John

NORTH, FREDERICK, Lord [2nd Earl of Guilford], II: 757. III: 321

NORTH, JAMES, I: 432

Northern Whig, The, IV: 248, 249n.

NORTHUMBERLAND, ALGERNON PERCY, 4th Duke of, III: 672

NORTON, CARLOTTA, III: 617n.

NORTON, HON. MRS. CAROLINE, I: 197. II: quoted 229n.; 316, 373n., 617. IV: 111n.
    Aunt Carry's Ballads, II: T. on 263. *Fisher's Drawing-Room Scrap-Book*, II: 264n. *Undying One*, I: 169
    Letter to: II, 263

NORTON, CHARLES ELIOT, II: 563n. Ed. *Carlyle and Emerson*, quoted I: cviii. Ed. *Letters of Lowell*, quoted III: 464n.–65n.

NORTON, FLETCHER CAVENDISH, II: 265n. IV: 111

NORTON, JOHN RICHARD BRINSLEY [5th Baron Grantley], III: 617n.

NORTON, THOMAS BRINSLEY [4th Baron Grantley], III: 617

NORTON, MRS. THOMAS BRINSLEY [Maria Chiara Elisa Federigo], III: 617n.

NOTT, DR. JOSIAH CLARK, III: 577n.

NOURRIT, I: 503

NOVELLO, JOSEPH ALFORD, III: 17

No. 60 [Regent's Quadrant], I: 186, 187, 197

No. 64 [Regent's Quadrant], I: 199

NURSEY, PERRY, I: 150, 500

OBERLIN, JOHN FREDERIC, *Memoirs*, I: 368

O'BRIEN, DR., III: 330, 425

O'BRIEN FAMILY, I: 8, 9

O'BRIEN, JAMES BRONTERRE, I: 425

O'BRIEN, WILLIAM SMITH, II: 414

Observer, The, II: 480

O'CONNELL, DANIEL, I: 483. II: 78, 98; trial of 129, 130; 165, 291, 362n., 498

O'CONNELL, J., II: 352

O'CONNELL, MORGAN JOHN, II: 333, 362, 721. III: 465n., 650. IV: 39, 232, 251, 366

O'CONNOR, FEARGUS EDWARD, I: 407. III: 681

O'DONNELL, MR., I: 355, 362, 454. II: T. on 25–26; 32; rascal 130

O'DOWD, MR., IV: 414

O'DOWD, MRS., II: 438

ODRY, JACQUES CHARLES, I: 233, 361. II: 13

OGILVY, DAVID GRAHAM DRUMMOND, *see* AIRLIE

OGILVY, SIR JOHN, IV: 29, 37, 38

OGILVY, LADY JANE [Lady Jane Howard, m. Sir John], *Letter to:* IV, 37

OGLE, MISS, II: 476, 482, 689, 814

O'GORMAN, MRS., II: 188

O'GORMAN, RICHARD, III: 228

OLIPHANT, MRS. FRANCIS [Margaret Oliphant], *William Blackwood*, quoted I: 419n.–20n.

OLIPHANT, LAURENCE, IV: 177. "Campaigning in China," IV: 177

OLLIFFE, SIR JOSEPH FRANCIS, III: 284–85, 343, 401n., 668. IV: 6, 347, 395, 400

OLLIFFE, LADY [Laura Cubitt, m. Sir Joseph], III: 285n., 668. IV: 249n., 396
    Letters to: III, 343, 401; IV, 54, 250, 252, 344, 345

OLMSTED, FREDERICK LAW, III: 614n.

"OMNIUM, JACOB," *see* HIGGINS, Matthew James

Once a Week, IV: 153n.

ONSLOW, MRS., II: 373

OPERA, *see also* under names of composers, I: 85, 91, 96, 127, 186, 199, 202, 208, 222, 230, 237, 266, 284, 363, 441. II: 109, 118, 144, 147, 157, 383, 488, 493, 556, 557, 669, 680. IV: 270

O'REILLY, MR., I: 355, 357

ORLÉANS, FERDINAND - PHILIPPE, Duc d', I: 103

ORLÉANS, FRANÇOIS D', *see* JOINVILLE, Prince de

ORLÉANS, HENRI D', *see* AUMALE

ORLEANS HOUSE, *see* AUMALE

ORMSBY, MR., IV: 403, 409

ORSAY, ALFRED GUILLAUME GABRIEL, Count d', II: 316n., 359, 360; "frank and pleasant" 362; 363, 387, 389; T.'s estimate of 390; 391n., 505n.; debts 532n.; 535; after Lady Blessington's death 593; "mad" 733–34; 750n. IV: 61

    Letter to: II, 464

ORSAY, LADY D' [Harriet Gardiner, m. Alfred], II: 316, 505n.

OSBORNE, GEORGE ALEXANDER, I: 455. II: 142. IV: 397 [?]

OSGOOD, REV. MR., III: 146, 604

OSTADE, ADRIAEN VAN, II: 118

OSY, MME., II: 744

OUR CLUB, IV: 139, 409n., 410, 414n.

OUSELEY, SIR WILLIAM GORE, III: 210n. IV: 200

OVERBECK, JOHANN FRIEDRICH, I: 278

OVERSTONE, SAMUEL JONES LOYD, 1st Baron, IV: 232

OWEN, MRS., IV: 392

OWEN, DR. RICHARD, IV: 413

OWEN, ROBERT, I: 407

OWEN, ROBERT DALE, *Footfalls*, IV: 193

    Letter to: IV, 193

OWENS, JOHN, III: 96

OXFORD, BISHOP OF, *see* WILBERFORCE, Samuel

OXFORD ELECTION, IV: T. standing for Parliament 3–4, 7–8, 28, 37, 45, 49; beaten 50, 51, 55, 56, 64, 66, 70, 71, 81; speeches 381–89

Oxford Literary Gazette, I: 39

OXFORD, ROBERT HARLEY, 1st Earl of, II: 761

Pacific, The, III: 562n.

PACKMAN, MR., II: 439

PAGE, ADÈLE, II: 590

PAGET, A. J., II: 555

PAGET, ARTHUR COYTE, I: 199, 202, 203

PAINE, THOMAS, I: 38

PAINTER, GEORGE, IV: 11

PAINTING, *see also* under names of painters, I: 91, 93–94, 100; Haydon exhibit 186; prints 235; 237, 266, 274; T. on modern French 276; 277, 278, 279; criticism 286; 288, 294, 329; at Windsor 515. II: 10; modern German 38; 76, 117, 118, 446, 503–04, 580, 730

PALESTINE, II: 154–55

PALEY, WILLIAM, *Evidences of Christianity*, I: 164, 496

Pall Mall Gazette, III: origin of 417n. IV: 302n.

PALMER, EDWARD HOWLEY, II: 345n.

PALMER, REV. MR., II: 562–63

PALMERSTON, HENRY JOHN TEMPLE, 3rd Viscount, I: cxviii, clxx. II: 625, 672n., 682n., 685; and Don Pacifico affair 757–58; 761, 811, 813; P attacks foreign policy of 816, 823. III: 3, 181, 194n., 316n., 375; "plucky" 404; 425n., 429n.; P's abuse of 432. IV: 32, 78, 170, 205n., 233n., 385, 413n., 447n.

PALMERSTON, LADY [Emily-Mary

Lamb (Cowper)], II: 622. III: 70. IV: 233

PANIZZI, ANTONIO, II: 229
    Letters to: II, 491, 650
PAPPENHEIM, DIANA VON, I: 128n.
PAPPENHEIM, JENNY VON, I: 127, 133, 142, 146, 155
PARDOE, JULIA, II: 67, 306
PARDON, GEORGE FREDERICK ["Captain Crawley"], *Billiards,* IV: 42
    Letters to: IV, 42, 46
PARIS, *see also* chronology, III: description of 269–70
PARIS, ABBÉ, I: 164
PARIS, BISHOP OF, *see* LUSCOMBE
PARKER, JOHN WILLIAM, II: 725. III: 434. IV: 15, 210
PARKER, JULIA, IV: 75
PARKER, MARY, IV: 75
PARKER, MRS., I: 427, 431, 442, 444, 449, 462, 469. II: 292. III: 364, 366
PARKER, REV. THEODORE, *Letter to:* III, 167
PARKES, JOSEPH, II: 148. III: 393
    Letters to: IV, 53, 346
PARKMAN, DR. SAMUEL, III: 662
PARKYNS, MRS. MANSFIELD, IV: 174
PARR, THOMAS CLEMENTS, II: 513, 516, 585, 594, 706, 715, 790, 794
PARR, MRS. THOMAS CLEMENTS [Julia Elton], II: 444, 513, 516, 560, 664, 715n., 790
    Letter to: II, 517
PARRY, PATRICK, I: 155
PARTHENON CLUB, III: 424
PASCAL, BLAISE, II: 279
PASHA, IBRAHIM, *see* IBRAHIM
PASSMORE FAMILY, I: 284
PATMORE, COVENTRY, II: T. helping 228, 254; 626
PATMORE, GEORGE, II: 228n.
PATMORE, PETER GEORGE, II: 228n.
PATTLE FAMILY [James], I: 189, 192, 267, 391. II: 232, 267, 436
PATTLE, JAMES, I: 189n.

PATTLE, MRS. JAMES, I: 189n., 208, 231, 237, 266, 272, 391
PATTLE, THEODOSIA, I: 267, 391
PATTLE, VIRGINIA, *see* SOMERS
PAUL I, Czar of Russia, II: 820
PAULINE [a servant], III: 301, 306, 324, 325
PAUNCEFOTE, JULIAN, 1st Baron, II: 269. III: 126
"PAUPERISM AND ALMSGIVING," I: 460
PAXTON, JOSEPH, IV: 429
PAYN, JAMES, IV: 125, 398
PAYNE, MRS., II: 394, 395, 416, 438n., 439
PAYNE-GALLWEY, SIR WILLIAM, II: 792n.
PEABODY, MR., III: 609
PEACOCK, GEORGE, I: 68, 76, 494, 495
PEACOCK, H. B., III: 661
PEACOCK, THOMAS LOVE, II: 718
PEARMAN, CHARLES, III: 276, 284, 306, 325, 329n., 334, 351, 361, 376, 477, 481, 483, 487, 490, 491, 492, 498, 505, 511, 513, 514, 518, 524, 533, 535, 554, 556, 558, 561, 562, 565, 571, 576, 578, 597, 609, 613, 624, 628, 629, 642. IV: 6, 11, 14, 25, 40, 52, 55, 57, 66, 75, 76, 80, 82, 445
    Letter from: III, 624
PEARSON, MR., I: 192, 195, 197, 206, 207
PEEL, SIR ROBERT, I: 34; and the Bedchamber Crisis 384n. II: 216, 245, 251, 465, 664, 665. III: 440, 499, 683. IV: 428
PEEL, LADY [Julia Floyd m. Sir Robert], II: 664
PEELE, GEORGE, "Man at Arms," III: 462
PEIRCE, MISS, II: 739
PELL, ALFRED, III: 662, 666
PEMBERTON, CHARLES REECE, I: 48

PENNETHORNE, JAMES, IV: 412

PENNY, REV. EDMUND HENRY, I: 26, 76

PENSHURST, see STRANGFORD

PENSIONS, II: Tennyson 225; controversy 629–35

PENWELL, HENRY C., Letter to: IV, 192

PEPE, GEN. GUGLIELMO, Memoirs, II: Fraser petitions T.'s help on 217–18; 219

PEPYS, SIR CHARLES CHRISTOPHER, see COTTENHAM

PEPYS, SAMUEL, II: style 700

PERCEVAL, SPENCER, I: 148

PERCY, ALGERNON, see NORTHUMBERLAND

PERCY, HUGH, I: 195

PERCY, DR. JOHN, IV: 409

PERKINS, JANE GRAY, Mrs. Norton, quoted II: 229n.

PERKINS, MRS., III: 516

PERLET, ADRIAN, I: 92–93

PEROWNE, J. J. STEWART, and Louis Stokes, Letters . . . of Connop Thirlwall, quoted IV: 186n.

PERRY, CHARLES, I: 15

PERRY CHILDREN [Sir Thomas], III: 81, 100, 264

PERRY, FLORA, II: 746. III: 81, 173, 263, 276

PERRY, GEORGE POTEMKIN, Letters to: II, 93, 110

PERRY, KATE, I: biographical cxxv–cxxviii. II: 374, 508, 509, 541, 569, 644, 664, 674n., 735n., 745. III: 53, 81, 124, 182, 263, 264. IV: 221, 278, 323, 423
Letters to: II, 555, 819; III, 35, 51, 132, 193, 221, 266, 458, 480, 494, 507, 547, 558, 562, 616; IV, 173, 347. Appendix XXVI

PERRY, LOU, III: 276

PERRY, MR., II: 95

PERRY, SIR THOMAS ERSKINE, II: 746n. III: 81, 173, 225, 263. IV: 404

PERTER, COLONEL AND MRS., I: 204

PERUGINI, MRS. CHARLES EDWARD [Kate Dickens (Collins)], III: 643. IV: 278n., 280, 397, 409, 410, 414

PETER, WILLIAM, III: 201, 202, 212

PETER, MRS. WILLIAM, III: 202

PETIGRU, JAMES LOUIS, III: 666

PETIT, MARIE, III: 138

PETTIGREW, WILLIAM VESALIUS, III: 75

"P. G.," "A Sketch of T.," quoted III: 124n.

PHELPS, MRS., IV: 392

PHILADELPHIA, PENNSYLVANIA, see also chronology, III: 174, 178, 179, 183, 187, 541; papers hostile to T. 545–46

Philadelphia Bulletin, The, III: hostile to T. 545n.–46n.

Philadelphia Press, The, quoted III: 192n. IV: 380n.

PHILIPPE, I: 235

PHILIPPE, ADOLPHE, and Marc Fournier, Paillasse, II: 737

PHILIPS, CHARLES, I: 451

PHILLIPS, MR. [of St. Louis], III: 594

PHILLIPS, MR. AND MRS., I: 134

PHILLIPS, SAMUEL, III: 393, 395, 407–08
Letter to: II, 751

PHILLIPS, TOM, II: 645. III: 55, 422

PHILOBIBLON CLUB, III: 686

PHINN, THOMAS, IV: 392, 399, 404, 408, 409, 413, 414

PHIPPS, CONSTANTINE HENRY, see NORMANBY

PHIZ, pseud. see BROWNE, Hablôt

PICHOT, AMÉDÉE, II: quoted 122n.–23n.; 124, 149. III: 389. IV: 403
Letters to: II, 121; III, 410

PICONNIERIE, THOMAS ROBERT BU-
GEAUD DE LA, II: 228
Pictorial Times, The, II: 188
PIERCE, FRANKLIN, III: 211, 212,
215, 218, 221, 229, 253, 549n.
PILLANS, PROFESSOR, IV: 129, 131
PINDAR, PETER, *pseud. see* WOLCOT,
John
PIPER, DR., IV: 328
PITT, WILLIAM [Lord Chatham],
II: 248
PLANCHÉ, JAMES ROBINSON, I: 23n.
Charles XII, I: 190. *Compact*,
I: 190. *Recollections*, quoted I:
416n.–17n.
Letter to: I, 416
PLUMPTRE, DR. FREDERICK
CHARLES, II: 810n.
PLUTARCH, *Lives*, I: 209
POITTEVIN, EDMOND LE, I: 266
POLE, SIR WILLIAM TEMPLAR, I: 50
POLK, SIR LAWRENCE, I: 217
POLK, LEONIDAS, III: 581n.
POLLEN, JOHN HUNGERFORD, III:
102, 337, 340, 341, 343. IV: and
wife 81, 412
PÖLLNITZ, BARON KARL LUDWIG
VON, *Mémoires*, III: 675
POLLOCK, CLARA JESSIE, III: 453
POLLOCK FAMILY [Jonathan Fred-
erick], III: 89n. IV: 62
POLLOCK, SIR [JONATHAN] FREDER-
ICK, II: and Langslow 207, 208;
241, 245, 384, 386, 440, 532, 548,
597n., 668, 701, 713, 730, 802
[?]. III: 4, 100, 454; poetry ad-
dressed to 487; 667, 686. IV:
390
Letters to: II, 596; IV, 280,
347
POLLOCK, LADY [Sarah Langslow, m.
Sir Jonathan Frederick], II: 400,
524, 548, 701. IV: 281, 413
Letters to: II, 713; III, 22, 99,
453
POLLOCK, SIR WILLIAM FREDERICK,
Remembrances, quoted II: 28n.

Letter to: II, 207
POLLOCK, LADY [Juliet Creed, m.
Sir William], II: 524. IV: 400
"POLLY," *see* CARMICHAEL, Mrs.
Charles
POMEROY, CHARLES, III: 210, 282,
296
PONSONBY, WILLIAM ASHLEY WEBB,
see MAULEY
PONSONBY, WILLIAM GLEDSTANES, I:
204, 206
POOLE, JOHN, I: sketch of 265. *Paul
Pry*, III: 395. *Pedlington*, II:
734n.
POPE, ALEXANDER, I: FG admires
166. II: 763, 821. III: 74n.
Essay on Man, I: 258; II: 801
POPE, THOMAS JOHN, IV: 409
POPHAM, ADM. WILLIAM, III: 394
POQUELIN, JEAN BAPTISTE, *see*
MOLIÈRE
PORSON, RICHARD, I: 70
PORTCH, JULIAN, IV: 302
PORTER, JANE, *Scottish Chiefs*, II:
429
PORTER, MRS. MARY B., *John Black-
wood*, quoted III: 407n.; IV: 16n.,
397n.–98n.
PORTER, DR. T. O., I: 406n.
PORTMAN, DR., II: 501
POST, JOTHAM, III: 191n.
POST OFFICE, II: T. wants position
in 427, 428, 431, 432
POWELL, CAPTAIN, III: 482
POWELL, MR., I: 428, 463, 483
POWELL, MRS., I: 443. II: 763
POWER, ELLEN, II: 362, 427, 535,
593
POWER, MARGUERITE, II: 362, 427,
433, 533, 535, 593, 734. III:
56, 60, 264n. IV: 58; T. raising
subscription for 61; 371
Letter to: II, 491
POWER, MR., I: 400; sketch of 502
POWER, ROBERT, II: 362n.
POWER, WILLIAM GRATTAN TYRONE,
I: 378

POWERSCOURT, RICHARD WING-
FIELD, 5th Viscount, III: 54n.

POWERSCOURT, LADY [Frances Theodosia Jocelyn, m. 5th Viscount],
III: 54

POWERSCOURT, LADY [m. 6th Vis-
count], see LONDONDERRY, Lady
[m. 4th Marquess]

POYNTZ, MISS, II: 800

PRAED, CHARLES TYRINGHAM, IV:
408

PRALL, RICHARD, IV: 394

PRASLIN, DUC AND DUCHESSE DE, I:
clviin.

PRATT, MRS., II: 723

PRESCOTT, WILLIAM GARDNER, III:
113

PRESCOTT, WILLIAM GEORGE, III:
674

PRESCOTT, MRS. WILLIAM GEORGE,
IV: 404, 413

PRESCOTT, WILLIAM HICKLING, III:
quoted 169n.; 170, 172n., 530,
661, 664. Philip II, II: "amusing" 537; 538, 542
    Letters to: III, 112, 113

PRESCOTT, MRS. WILLIAM HICK-
LING, III: 112n.

PRESTON, WILLIAM, III: 212

PRÉVOST, M., II: 122

PRÉVOT, CHARLES VICTOR, see AR-
LINCOURT, Vicomte d'

PRIAULX, OSMOND DE BEAUVOIR, II:
844. IV: 181, 391, 392, 408,
409, 415

PRICE, MR., I: 379

PRIDEAUX, MR., Letter to: IV, 348

PRINCE, MISS, II: 681

PRINCESS, MRS., II: 398

PRINSEP, HENRY THOBY, I: 189n.
II: 232, 487. III: 68, 279. IV:
397, 404n.

PRINSEP, MRS. HENRY THOBY [Sarah
Monckton Pattle], I: 189n. II:
232, 469, 524, 662, 694, 843,
844. III: 68, 279, 685. IV: 397,
404n.

    Letter to: IV, 348

PRINSEP, VALENTINE CAMERON, IV:
403

PRIOR, MATTHEW, II: 645n.

PRITCHARD, WILLIAM AMON GEE,
IV: 224

PROCTER, ADELAIDE ANN, I: cliv,
400. II: 14, 342, 395, 398, 435,
439, 441, 448, 492, 528; coolness
to T. 549, 550, 551; 604, 674n.,
738, 812. III: 104, 128, 343,
372, 394. IV: 122, 151, 214,
275n.
    "Fate and a Heart," IV: 194n.
    Legends and Lyrics, IV: T. on 87–
    88. "Sent to Heaven," IV: 194n.
    Letters to: II, 523, 572; IV,
    87, 182, 194, 253

PROCTER, BRYAN WALLER ["Barry
Cornwall"], I: cxxxiii; biographical cliii–cliv; 383, 398, 400. II:
7, 14, 22; lunacy commissioner
81; and Constitutional 95; 127,
245, 247, 248, 260, 298, 393,
515, 550, 559, 604, 628. III:
104, 127, 198, 228n., 232, 250,
332, 342, 343, 372, 394, 400,
441, 475, 517, 559, 572, 583,
670. IV: 393
    Essays, III: 304. Jonson, I: 377–
    78. "King Death," I: 317. "The
    Sea," III: 106–07n.
    Letters to: I, 376, 456; II,
    578; III, 303; IV, 351

PROCTER, MRS. BRYAN WALLER
[Anne Skepper], I: cxxxiii; biographical cliii–cliv; 383, 398, 457,
464, 465. II: 110, 228n.; on V.F.
312–14; 332, 334, 396, 400, 435,
451, 515, 559, 569, 572, 590,
594; accuses T. of snobbery 655;
674n., 683, 738, 751n., 843. III:
189, 277, 667, 674. IV: 182; on
heroes 274n.–75n.; 393, 437
    Letters to: I, 377, 422, 445,
    454; II, 6, 12, 14, 22, 220, 225,
    234, 235, 254, 260, 265, 269,

315, 332, 342, 384, 386, 387, 393, 394, 397, 402, 428, 448, 492, 549, 551, 573, 595, 598, 599, 603, 626, 727, 728, 763, 769, 770, 779, 781, 812; III: 104, 154, 250, 272, 305, 339, 372, 376, 381, 387, 392, 394, 430, 475, 478, 517, 583, 611, 638; IV, 150, 274, 289, 350, 351. *Letters from:* II, 312; III, 125, 230

PROCTER CHILDREN [Bryan], II: 515. III: 126, 198, 232, 387. IV: 122

PROCTER, NICHOLAS, *see* WALLER, Nicholas

PROTHEROE, MR., I: 193

PROUT, FATHER, *pseud. see* MAHONY

PROVIDENCE, RHODE ISLAND, *see also* chronology, III: 530

PRUSSIA, I: 158

PRYME, GEORGE [G. 42], I: 37, 38, 69, 71, 72
Letter to: II, 223

PRYME, MRS. GEORGE [Jane Townley Thackeray, G. 41], I: 37, 38, 46, 47, 107. II: 844
Letter to: II, 256

PRYME, RICHARD, *Letter to:* III, 10

PRYME, MRS. RICHARD, and Mrs. William Bayne, *Memorials,* quoted I: 107n.–08n.

Punch, I: and Catholicism cxxiv; Leech and cxlv; cxlvi. II: 54, 82, 97, 105n., 135, 139, 141, 142, 143, 145, 146, 148, 149, 150, 153, 156, 166, 169, 172, 180, 189; T. angry with 199; 202n., 225, 243, 247, 248n., 250, 263; "caricaturing the Irish distress" 266; 270; Parson-Snob controversy 274, 282, 283; 291, 297, 336, 360, 361, 382, 386, 448, 451n., 455, 459n., 472, 492, 494, 518, 519, 537, 538, 543, 544, 546, 569, 576, 580, 619, 628, 635, 658, 663; T. threatens resignation 618;

681, 686, 695n., 701, 702, 709, 712, 714, 719, 736, 757, 772, 810n.; abuses L. Napoléon 813; T. "in a fury" at politics of 816; resigns 823; 829, 840, 841, 842, 844. III: 121, 211, 251; and Doyle 304; 315, 342n., 363; attacks King of the Sicilies 364; 367n., 374, 386; upset over Leech article 413–14, 415, 417, T. apologizes for 418; 429, 432, 433, 614, 622n., 625, 638n., 670, 676, 686. IV: 36n., 48, 162, 199n., 217, 325, 328, 346, 367, 404n., 425, 450

Punch's Pocket Book for 1848, II: 284n.

PURCELL, MISS, I: 496n.

PURCELL, PETER, II: 63, 69, 70, 71, 80, 89
Letter to: II, 138

PUSEY, EDWARD BOUVERIE, II: 705, 712

PUTNAM, GEORGE PALMER, III: 474, 510n., 662
Letter to: III, 131

PUTNAM, MRS. GEORGE PALMER, III: 510n.

Putnam's Monthly Magazine, III: 280n., 286

PUZIN, DR., II: 41, 98, 108, 113, 121, 173, 177, 208, 216, 841, 842

PYNE, REV. DR., III: 539

QUARLES, FRANCIS, I: 163

Quarterly Review, I: Elwin and cxxviii; cxxx; against Southey 396. II: 294, 321, 334; on *Jane Eyre* 341n.; 559. III: 340n., 396, 413n., 414, 415, 417, 418, 466n., 468n. IV: Gale and 15; 16, 138, 150, 194n.

QUECKETT, REV. W., II: 709

QUEENSBERRY, DUCHESS OF [Lady

Catherine Hyde, m. 3rd Duke], II: 645n.

QUIN, DR. FREDERICK HERVEY FOSTER, I: 400. II: 150, 289, 339, 349, 359, 360
   Letter to: II, 546

QUINCY, JOSIAH P. [?], III: 166n.

RABELAIS, FRANÇOIS, I: 412. *Œuvres*, III: 494

RACHEL, MME. [Elisa Félix], II: 23

RACINE, JEAN BAPTISTE, *Iphigénie*, III: 138

RADCLIFFE, A., III: 626, 632, 644, 661
   Letter to: IV, 352

RADCLIFFE, SIR EDWARD, IV: 352

RADCLIFFE, MRS. [Ann Ward], *The Italian*, II: 55

RADCLIFFE, TEDDY, IV: 353

RADFORD, D., and H. Allingham, ed. *William Allingham*, quoted IV: 112n.–13n.

RAGLAN, FITZROY JAMES HENRY SOMERSET, 1st Baron, II: 232. III: 393n., 394n. IV: 16

RAILROAD SPECULATION, I: Major C-S and 448n. II: 215, 217; smash 233; and Major C-S 238; 258, 290; suit 333; 372, 382; Irish 459, 513, 535; 545. III: in U.S. 275, 308, 383, 385, 527, 549. IV: Irish 6; 66, 67, 68, 75, 76, 235, 290

RAMSAY, ALLAN, I: 460

RAMSAY, MAJOR, IV: 395

RAMSAY, WILLIAM, III: 689

RANDOLPH, ARTHUR D. F., "Cozzens," quoted III: 510n.

RANGEL WOOLLETT AND CO., IV: 396

RANKE, LEOPOLD VON, *History of the Popes*, I: 460–61

RANKIN, MR., III: 253

RAPHAEL [Raffaello Santi], I: 286. II: 446

RASHDALE, MR., III: 568, 668

"RATTLER," I: 154

RAWLINSON, SIR HENRY CRESWICKE, II: 699, 777. IV: 149, 426

RAY, MR., II: 352

RAYMOND, MR., II: 114

RAYMOND, MR. [of Boston], III: 600

RAYNERS, MR., I: 190

REACH, ANGUS BETHUNE, III: 638n.

REACH, MRS. ANGUS BETHUNE, III: 638, 639

READ, THOMAS BUCHANAN, *Letter to:* IV, 51

READE, CHARLES, *Masks and Faces*, III: 127

REALF, RICHARD, *Guesses at the Beautiful*, III: 10

REDDIE, CAPTAIN, IV: 64

REED CHILDREN [William Bradford], IV: 45

REED, HENRY HOPE, I: clv, clvi. III: articles on 192; 202; drowned 399–401, 536, 542
   Letter to: III, 185

REED, MRS. HENRY HOPE, III: 536, 542, 546

REED, WILLIAM BRADFORD, I: biographical cliv-clvi. III: 178n., 185, 203, 664. *Esther Reed*, III: 400; IV: 45. *Haud Immemor*, quoted I: clv-clvi, clxv; III: 599n.; IV: 137n.
   Letters to: III, 201, 292, 399, 545, 601; IV, 44, 136, 297

REED, MRS. WILLIAM BRADFORD [Mary Love Ralston], III: 546. IV: 45

REES, MARY, II: 568, 576

REEVE, HENRY, I: 184; on T. 282n.–83n.; on I. T. 295n.; 309, 310, 457. II: 12, 13, 47, 144, 278, 626; fight with Carlyle 628–29; 844. IV: 409
   Letters to: II, 279, 280

REEVE, JOHN, I: 260n.

REEVE, MRS., III: 667

REFORM BILL [1832], I: 159; T.

hears reading of 188; 190; reading in Lords 191; "Percy and Reform" prank 195n.; "gone to the devil" 199. III: 682

REFORM CLUB, I: 388, 424, 425, 428, 436, 438, 447, 460. II: 95, 115, 148, 149, 150, 165, 548, 690, 753, 800, 842. III: 74, 76n., 393, 420, 428. IV: 54, 112, 256n., 312n., 323, 394, 410, 413

REICH, DR., II: 32

REICHSTADT, DUC DE [François Charles Joseph Bonaparte, Napoléon II], I: 87, 250–51

REID, MR., III: 97

REID, MR. [a brewer], I: 191

REID, THOMAS WEMYSS, *Houghton*, quoted I: cxlii; IV: 304n.

RELIGION, I: 92; in Germany 140; 161, 248, 396, 402–03, 452–53, 464, 466–67, 493, 494. II: troubles by heterodoxy of writing 204; 205–06, 209, 253; and Brookfield 274–75, 277–78; 474, 591, 615–16, 663, 690, 711–12, 761–62. III: 20, 50–51, 66; T.'s daughters and 82, 85–87, 93–96, 141, 168–69, 188, 198, 216–18; 347–48, 350–51. IV: 128–29

REMBRANDT HARMENSZ VAN RIJN, I: 66, 150

Report of the Anniversary of the Royal Literary Fund, see ROYAL LITERARY FUND

REVEL, COUNT ADRIEN DE, II: 727. III: 61

REVEL, COUNTESS DE [Emily de Viry, m. Count Adrien], II: 727n.

REVISS, THERESA, I: biographical clvii–clx; 413. II: 382, 754

REVISS, MRS. THERESA, I: 207

Revue Britannique, I: cvii. III: 389

Revue des deux Mondes, I: 224. III: 389, 410

REYNOLDS, JOHN HAMILTON, I: 407. II: 481. III: 127

REYNOLDS, SIR JOSHUA, I: 280. II: 371

REYNOLDS, MR., I: 327. IV: 307

REYNOLDS, CAPT. RICHARD ANTHONY, I: 484

RHENANIERS CLUB, I: 114–15

RHETT, ROBERT BARNWELL, III: 556n.

RHETT, MRS. ROBERT BARNWELL, III: 556

RHODES, MRS. WILLIAM, II: 664

RHODES, WILLIAM BARNES, *Bombastes Furioso*, I: 16n.; T.'s imitation of 79n.; 132

RICE, GEORGE EDWARD, *Letter to*: III: 163

RICE, GEORGE EDWARD, and J. H. Wainwright, *Ephemera*, III: 163

RICE, STEPHEN SPRING, see SPRING-RICE

RICHARDS, MR., II: 515, 549. III: 281

RICHARDS, MRS. [Emma], II: 514–15, 544, 549, 559. III: 281

RICHARDSON, SAMUEL, II: 389. *Clarissa*, II: 500. *Charles Grandison*, I: 312; II: 815; IV: 444

RICHMOND, VIRGINIA, see also chronology, III: 220, 222, 223, 247, 515

RICHTER, JOHANN PAUL FRIEDRICH, I: 214

RIGBY, ELIZABETH, see EASTLAKE

RINTOUL, ROBERT STEPHEN, II: 403, 404, 452n.
   Letter to: II, 450

RIPON, GEORGE FREDERICK SAMUEL ROBINSON, 3rd Earl de Grey and 1st Marquess of, III: 667n. IV: 411n.

RIPON, LADY [Henrietta Vyner, m. 1st Marquess], III: 667. IV: 411

RISO, MARQUIS DEL, IV: 130

RISTORI, ADELAIDE, III: 460

RITCHIE, AUGUSTA [G. 114], III: 345, 362, 636, 646. IV: 261

RITCHIE, BLANCHE [G. 115], III: 345, 362, 636, 646. IV: 261

RITCHIE, CHARLOTTE [G. 110], I: biographical clx, clxii, clxiii; 447, 449, 461, 471. II: 35, 125, 177, 211, 287, 318, 576, 748, 750. III: 106, 144, 334, 346, 347, 348, 361, 362, 454, 616, 636. IV: 261
  Letters to: II, 173, 184, 193, 208, 575; III, 344, 645; IV, 353

RITCHIE, EMILY [G. 113], I: clx. II: 81

RITCHIE FAMILY [John], I: cxvii; biographical clx-clxiii; 192, 236, 237, 412, 415, 432. II: 142, 211, 609, 732

RITCHIE FAMILY [William], III: 454

RITCHIE, GERALD [G. 75], *Ritchies in India*, quoted I: clxii, 183n.–84n; II: 194n.–95n.

RITCHIE, JAMES, I: 189

RITCHIE, JANE [G. 111], I: biographical clx, clxii, clxiii; 296, 472. II: 35, 196, 579, 748. III: 106, 144, 334, 344, 345, 347, 348, 454, 636. IV: 261
  Letters to: III, 361, 645

RITCHIE, JOHN [G. 58], I: biographical clx, clxi, clxii; 5, 23, 30, 232, 233, 355, 415, 488. II: 499, 581. III: 645
  Letter to: I, 343

RITCHIE, MRS. JOHN [Charlotte Sarah Thackeray, G. 57], I: biographical clx, clxiii; 3, 23, 30, 231, 232, 234, 253, 266, 283, 285, 297, 317, 318n., 344, 430, 447. II: 81, 139, 287, 494, 575, 576, 579, 581, 586, 587, 590, 731, 748, 750. III: 97, 106, 144, 267, 314, 344, 345, 347, 457, 645, 672. IV: 427
  Letters to: I, 5, 6, 471; II, 34, 39, 125, 350, 499, 608

RITCHIE, JOHN [G. 112], I: clx, 415. II: 39

RITCHIE, JOHN [of Edinburgh], III: 698

RITCHIE, LADY *see* THACKERAY, Anne I.

RITCHIE, LEITCH, *France*, I: 178

RITCHIE, WILLIAM [G. 108], I: biographical clx-clxiii; 6n.; on Mrs. Halliday 183n.–84n.; 185, 199, 284, 343, 368, 381, 430. II: 39n.; 40, 72; in India 125, 184; account of Langslow troubles 194n.–95n.; married 208; 545. III: 345, 645. IV: dead 261, 276, 284; 352
  Letters to: I, 295; III, 451, 635

RITCHIE, MRS. WILLIAM [Augusta Trimmer, G. 109], I: clxi, clxiii. II: 194n., 208. III: 451, 452, 636. IV: 292n.
  Letters to: IV, 276, 284

ROBARTS, ABRAHAM JOHN, IV: 395, 396

ROBARTS, MRS. ABRAHAM JOHN, IV: 402

ROBARTS, LUBBOCK, AND COMPANY, *see* LUBBOCK

ROBBINS, GEORGE, II: 560n., 606, 715, 738

ROBBINS, MRS. GEORGE [Maria Katherine Elton], II: 560

ROBBINS, JOSEPH, IV: 59

ROBERTS, DAVID, II: 253. III: 351, 494. IV: 390, 408
  Letters to: II, 454; III, 413

ROBERTS, GEORGE, *Lady Audley's Secret*, IV: 411

ROBERTS, MISS, IV: 408

ROBERTSON, MR., II: 151

ROBERTSON, WILLIAM, I: 182

ROBESPIERRE, MAXIMILIEN FRANÇOIS MARIE ISADORE DE, III: 95

ROBINSON, BEVERLEY, IV: 66

ROBINSON, WILLIAM DUER, III: 598n., 599, 603, 609. IV: 72, 317

Letters to: III, 597, 605; IV, 65, 135, 192, 202, 223

ROBSON, THOMAS FREDERICK, III: 429

ROCHEID, MRS., I: 155

RODD, MAJ. JAMES RENNELL [*G.* 20], III: 73

RODD, MRS. JAMES RENNELL [Elizabeth Anne Thompson, *G.* 21], III: 73n.

RODD, R.-ADM. JOHN RASHLEIGH [*G.* 26], III: 72

RODD, MRS. JOHN RASHLEIGH [Wilhelmina Mary Rodd, *G.* 25], III: 72, 73

RODD, V.-ADM. SIR JOHN TREMAYNE [*G.* 17], I: 343n., 412. II: 596

RODD, LADY [Jane Rennell, *G.* 16, m. Sir John], I: 343, 412. II: 595. III: 72, 73, 674. IV: 76, 421

RODD, MR., II: 141

RODEN, JOHN STRANGE JOCELYN, 5th Earl of, II: 718n. III: 5, 672

RODEN, LADY [Sophia Hobhouse, m. 5th Earl], II: 718n. III: 5, 643. IV: 286

RODEN, ROBERT JOCELYN, 2nd Earl of, III: 53

RODEN, LADY [Juliana Anne Orde, m. 2nd Earl], III: 53

ROE, MR., I: 493, 497

ROGERS, SAMUEL, II: 245, 556, 629, 751n. III: 230, 444. IV: 343
Letter to: IV, 353, 333–34

ROLFE, FRANKLIN P., "Letters of Charles Lever," quoted I: cxlviii

ROLLES, COLONEL, I: 284

ROME, III: 326

ROMILLY, JOHN, 1st Baron, II: 514. IV: 396

ROMILLY, LADY [Caroline Charlotte Otter, m. 1st Baron], II: 514

ROMILLY, SIR SAMUEL, II: 514. *Memoirs,* III: 557

ROMILLY, LADY [Anne Garbett, m. Sir Samuel], II: 514

ROMSEY ABBEY, II: 670–71

RONALD FAMILY, II: 844

RONSARD, PIERRE DE, *Amours d'Hélène,* III: 151; quoted 152

ROOSEVELT, JUDGE JAMES J., III: 662

ROQUEPLAN, JOSEPH ETIENNE, I: 280

ROS, OLIVIA DE, *see* COWLEY

ROSE, MR., IV: 366

ROSS, MR., II: 442n.

ROSSI, COUNT DE, II: 499n., 666

ROSSI, COUNTESS DE, *see* SONTAG

ROSSI, MR., I: 360

ROSSINI, GIOACCHINO ANTONIO, *Barber of Seville,* I: 186; II: 147; III: 343; IV: 270. *Comte Ory,* I: 85, 96. *Mosè in Egitto,* I: 284. *Stabat Mater,* II: 44. *William Tell,* I: 91, 96

ROSSITER, MR., II: 767

ROTHESAY, CHARLES STUART, 1st Baron Stuart de, II: 646n. III: 54

ROTHESAY, LADY DE [Lady Elizabeth Yorke, m. 1st Baron], II: 646. III: 54

ROTHNEY, MR., II: 188

ROTHSCHILD, ALPHONSE, Baron de, IV: 30

ROTHSCHILD, LADY DE [Leonora de Rothschild, m. Baron Alphonse], IV: 30

ROTHSCHILD, SIR ANTHONY DE, II: 524n., 645, 665

ROTHSCHILD, LADY DE [Louisa Montefiore, m. Sir Anthony], II: 524, 645. IV: 411

ROTHSCHILD FAMILY, III: 69

ROTHSCHILD, JAMES, Baron de, II: 493

ROTHSCHILD, LIONEL NATHAN, Baron de, II: 524n. III: 479n., 675, 682. IV: 30n., 391, 392

ROTHSCHILD, LADY DE [Charlotte de Rothschild, m. Baron Lionel], II: 665. III: 9, 479n., 626. IV: 30n.

Letter to: IV, 29

ROTHSCHILD, MR., II: 18

ROUTLEDGE, JOHN, IV: 92

ROWE, NICHOLAS, *Fair Penitent,* III: 213. *Jane Shore,* I: 237

ROWLAND, S.N., *Letter to:* III, 446

Royal Literary Fund, Report of the Anniversary of the, II: quoted 378n.

ROYAL LITERARY FUND, Secretary of the, *Letter to:* II, 777

RUBENS, PETER PAUL, I: 286, 515. III: 123

RUBINI, GIOVANNI BATTISTA, II: 363

RUE, ÉMILE DE LA, III: 617n.

RUSH, MRS., III: 177

RUSKIN, JOHN, *Munera Pulveris,* quoted IV: 211n. *Unto this Last,* IV: 211n.

Letter from: IV, 211

RUSSEL, ALEXANDER, II: 819n. III: 698

RUSSELL, SIR CHARLES, IV: 399

RUSSELL, G., IV: 396

RUSSELL, FRANCIS, *see* BEDFORD, Duke of

RUSSELL INSTITUTION, I: 376

RUSSELL, JAMES, IV: 40n.

RUSSELL, DR. JOHN, I: 11n., 13, 15, 16, 17, 18, 22, 23; "manifest unkindness and injustice" of 24; 30

RUSSELL, JOHN, 1st Earl, I: civ, cxviii, cxix, 409n. II: and Corn Laws 216; 241n., 251; treasury statement 352; 666n.; postal regulations 686; 761, 769; and Jameson pension 770, 786, 787; 816. III: 17, 24, 279; and Crimean War cabinet 415–16; 682. IV: 233, 243, 385, 395, 403, 409; and Lorcha question 447. *Turks in Europe,* I: "silly meagre pamphlet" 284

RUSSELL LADY [Lady Frances Anna Maria Elliot, 2nd w. of 1st Earl], II: 685. III: 17, 24

RUSSELL, MISS, IV: 397

RUSSELL, LADY RACHEL, *see* BUTLER, Lady

RUSSELL, LORD WILLIAM, I: murdered 443

RUSSELL, WILLIAM HOWARD, III: at Crimea 403. IV: 54, 99n.; reporting Civil War 223, 231, 235; 400, 410, 414

Letters to: III, 455; IV: 64

RUSSELL, MRS. WILLIAM HOWARD [Mary Burrowes], III: 455n. IV: 65, 122, 398, 410

RUSSIA, I: massacring Poles 158; FG and 372–73

RYLAND, MR., II: 155

SADE, COLONEL DE, I: 86

SADLER, MICHAEL THOMAS, I: 51

ST. DAVIDS, BISHOP OF, *see* THIRLWALL

ST. GERMANS, EDWARD GRANVILLE ELIOT, 3rd Earl of, I: 214n., 246

SAINT-HILAIRE, MARCO DE, *pseud. see* HILAIRE

SAINTINE, *pseud. see* BONIFACE

ST. JOHN, II: 591

SAINT-MARS, GABRIELLE ANNE CISTERNE DE COURTIRAS, Vicomtesse de, *see* DASH

ST. MAUR, EDWARD ADOLPHUS, *see* SOMERSET, 12th Duke of

ST. PAUL, II: 591. III: 86, 141

ST. PETER's, Rome, III: 326

SALA, GEORGE AUGUSTUS, III: T.'s opinion of 470–71. IV: 36. "Key of the street," III: 470–71. *Hogarth,* III: 470n., 471

Letters to: IV, 203, 256

SALIS, PETER JOHN, Count de, III: 674n.

SALIS, COUNTESS DE [Cecilia Henrietta Bourgeois, m. Count Peter], III: 674

SALMON, MR., IV: 426

SALT, MR., I: 402, 404, 414, 420

SAMPAYO, MR., II: 257, 382

SAMS, W. RAYMOND, *Letter to:* II, 499

SAMUEL [a servant], I: 257

SAMUELSON, MR., III: 689

SAND, MRS., I: 466, 467

SANDWICH, LADY [Lady Mary Paget, m. 7th Earl], II: 731, 824. III: 316

SANDWITH, MR. AND MRS., IV: 399

SANDYS, ARTHUR MARCUS CECIL HILL, 3rd Baron, II: 645

SANKEY, DR., II: 156, 157

SANSUM, JOHN, I: 173, 174, 493, 494, 495, 496, 497

SANTI, COUNT AND COUNTESS, I: 131

SANTLEY, LADY [Gertrude Kemble, m. Sir Charles], I: 394

SAQUI, MME., IV: 254

SARTORIS, EDWARD JOHN, I: cxliv. II: 392n., 558, 740. III: 127, 230, 340, 672, 685. IV: 353, 392, 409, 413
Letters to: II, 398; III, 424

SARTORIS, MRS. EDWARD JOHN [Adelaide Kemble], I: cxliv, 207–08, 239. II: 38, 110, 391, 392, 548, 558, 559–60, 604, 740, 781, 843, 844. III: 127, 184, 230, 252, 333, 336, 337, 340, 424, 425. IV: 88, 392, 402, 403, 404, 409, 438
Letters to: II, 398, 655, 701; III, 345

Saturday Review, The, III: protests against T.'s lectures 564. IV: 190n., 215n., 227n., 409n.

SAUNDERS, DR. AUGUSTUS PAGE, I: 12n. III: 24, 435

Savannah Daily Morning News, quoted III: 553n.

SAVANNAH, GEORGIA, *see also* chronology, III: 241, 244, 247, 562, 566, 571

SAXE-COBURG, PRINCESS VICTORIA MARIA LOUISA, *see* KENT

SAXE-WEIMAR, GRAND DUKE KARL AUGUST, I: 125, 130, 136

SAXE-WEIMAR, GRAND DUKE KARL FRIEDRICH, I: 125, 130, 136

SCARGILL, WILLIAM PITT, *Rank and Talent,* I: 224

SCHEFFER, HENRY, IV: 195

SCHILLER, JOHANN CHRISTOPHE FRIEDRICH VON, I: 123, 136, 148. III: 442, 445
Marie Stuart, I: 236; II: 23; III: 460. *Piccolomini,* I: 147. *Räuber,* I: 141–42, 219

SCHLEGEL, AUGUST WILHELM VON, I: 232, 233, 253. *Litteratur und Kunst,* I: T. thinking of translating 118, 123

SCHMIDT, MR., IV: 414

SCHNEIDER, JOHN, III: 679

SCHNEIDER, MISS, I: 199

SCHÖNBERG, MR., I: 386

SCHRÖDER-DEVRIENT, WILHELMINE, I: 202. III: 443

SCHULTE FAMILY, I: 119, 120, 131

SCHULTE, FRANZ ANTON, I: 114, 116, 118, 119, 123, 131, 150, 172, 173, 191, 204, 205

SCORE, MR., I: 210

Scotsman, The, II: 819. III: 688. IV: 41, 63

SCOTT, REV. ALEXANDER JOHN, II: 282, 317n., 548. III: 96, 97, 286, 661
Letters to: II, 282, 290; III, 83, 610

SCOTT, MRS. ALEXANDER JOHN [Ann Ker], II: 290. III: 83, 84, 85, 97, 610, 656
Letter to: III, 286

SCOTT, DR., III: 574

SCOTT FAMILY [Mary], I: 429. II: 189

SCOTT, JOHN ALEXANDER, III: 97

SCOTT, LADY, IV: 433

SCOTT, MARY, I: 441. II: 135

SCOTT, SUSAN F., III: 97

SCOTT, THOMAS, III: 93

SCOTT, SIR WALTER, I: Banantyne controversy 460. II: 122n., 146,

156, 262, 378n., 737. III: 97,
634. IV: 291, 433
  Anne of Geierstein, II: 55.
Castle Dangerous, I: "poor" 178.
Guy Mannering, I: 58. *Heart of
Midlothian*, IV: 206, 411n. *Ivan-
hoe*, I: 21n. *Marmion*, I: 76.
Peveril of the Peak, I: 497. *Quen-
tin Durward*, I: 13, 206, 234.
Swift, I: 235. Waverley novels, I:
82, 84. "William and Helen," I:
169. *Woodstock*, I: 234; II: 457n.
SCOTT, GEN. WINFIELD, III: 196
SCRIBE, EUGÈNE, IV: 428
SCRIWANECK, AUGUSTINE CÉLESTE,
II: 748
SEAVER, BENJAMIN, III: 156
SEDGEWICK, MR., I: 85
SELWYN, G., III: 585
SENIOR, NASSAU WILLIAM, IV: 401n.,
403, 408
  Letter to: III, 277
SENIOR, MRS. NASSAU WILLIAM
[Mary Charlotte Mair], IV: 401,
402, 403
SEURRE, GABRIEL BERNARD, I: 294
SEYMOUR, LORD HENRY, III: 363
SEYMOUR, ROBERT, I: 311n.
SHAFTESBURY, ANTHONY ASHLEY
COOPER, 7th Earl of, III: 181n.,
273
SHAKESPEAR, ANNE, see THACKERAY,
Mrs. Francis
SHAKESPEAR, CHARLOTTE, see CRAW-
FORD, Mrs. James
SHAKESPEAR family, I: 194
SHAKESPEAR, GEORGE TRANT [G.
83], I: 6, 7, 8. II: 145, 173
SHAKESPEAR, JOHN DOWDESWELL
[G. 79], III: 334
SHAKESPEAR, MRS. JOHN DOWDES-
WELL [Marianne E. Hodgson, G.
80], III: 334
SHAKESPEAR, JOHN TALBOT [G. 51],
I: 8n.
SHAKESPEAR, MRS. JOHN TALBOT

[Emily Thackeray, G. 50], I:
183n.
SHAKESPEAR, MR., I: 8
SHAKESPEAR, SIR RICHMOND [G.
84], I: clx, 3n., 6, 7, 8. III: 447
SHAKESPEAR, SARA ELIZA DONNI-
THORNE ["Selina," G. 90], I: 204.
III: 37n. IV: 35
  Letter to: III, 406
SHAKESPEARE, WILLIAM, I: 147,
148; FG on 166; "tedious" 177;
445. II: 137, 396. III: 17, 101,
184, 203n., 293. IV: 360n.,
410n.
  As You Like It, I: 404; III:
269. *Hamlet*, II: T. on 703; IV:
169. *1 Henry IV*, II: 214. *2
Henry IV*, I: 343. *Julius Caesar*,
I: 194; III: 588. *King Lear*, II:
"bad" 392; 375; III: 502. *Mac-
beth*, I: 373; II: 603, 633, 759,
813; III: 639. *Midsummer Night's
Dream*, I: 503; II: 213; IV: 295.
Much Ado, III: 293n. *Othello*, I:
135, 145, 260n.; II: 216, 735;
III: 95; IV: 67. *Richard III*, II:
767n. *Romeo*, I: 77. *Taming*, II:
213. *Tempest*, IV: 259. *Two
Gentlemen*, I: 465
SHANNON, CAPTAIN, III: 261
SHARP, MISS, I: 89
SHAW, ANNA, see CURTIS, Mrs. G. W.
SHAW family [Francis], III: 490,
503, 551
SHAW, FRANCIS G., III: 359n., 490.
IV: 93n.
SHAW, MRS. FRANCIS G., III: 484,
490
  Letter to: III, 602
SHAWE, ARTHUR, I: clxiv; staying
with T. 424, 426, 429, 430, 431,
434; Mrs. C-S trying to evict 437;
to India 439, 441, 443, 447. II:
131; home from India 209; 210,
243, 289, 402, 405, 408, 430.
III: 397, 398, 415, 421, 637, 647.
IV: 121

Letters to: II, 305, 324, 544

SHAWE, MRS. ARTHUR, II: 306. III: 397, 415

SHAWE, COL. ARTHUR, I: 295n., 303, 305, 306n., 308, 309, 312, 321, 367, 389, 397, 398, 431, 437, 439. II: 21, 78, 89, 305

SHAWE FAMILY, I: biographical clxiv-clxv

SHAWE, HENRY, I: clxiv, 389. II: 131. III: 353; T. seeks aid for 420–21; 673

SHAWE, ISABELLA, *see* THACKERAY, Isabella

SHAWE, JANE, I: clxiv, 305, 316, 358, 359; neurotic 363–64; 368, 369, 383, 389, 413, 414, 415, 416, 429; and suitor 437, 440, 444; nursing I.T. 472, 474, 475, 476, 477, 479. II: 41; "fairly out of her mind" 305–06; 324, 381, 545. III: 325, 353, 421

Letters to: I, 429; II, 240, 430

SHAWE, MARY, I: 319. II: 78–79, 306

SHAWE, MR., IV: 396, 414

SHAWE, MRS. MATTHEW [Isabella Creagh], I: clxiv, 302, 305, 307; I.T. fears separation from 309; 310, 312; attempts to break engagement 315, 316; witnesses marriage 318n.; 319; "singular old deevil" 321; 350, 354, 356, 359, 361, 363, 364, 381, 383, 389, 413, 419; "stark mad" 424; 427, 428; "Mrs. Gam" 430n.; 433, 437, 438, 440, 443; "nightmare of a mother" 444; 450, 468, 469, 471, 473; and I.T.'s insanity 474; "really and truly demented" 476; 477; "unmotherly" conduct 479; 480, 482; advises putting I.T. in "madhouse" 486; 519, 520. II: 39; and I.T. 41–42; 73, 78, 85, 187, 210, 306, 324, 381, 430. III: 421; and "The Campaigner" 465n. IV: 145

Letters to: I, 366, 368, 414, 472, 485

SHAW-LEFEVRE, *see* EVERSLEY

SHEEHAN, JOHN, I: cxvii, 320. II: in *Pendennis* 721

SHEIL, RICHARD LALOR, II: 438

SHEIL, MRS. RICHARD LALOR [Anastasia Power], II: 438

SHELBURNE, *see* LANSDOWNE

SHELLEY, SIR JOHN, IV: 403n.

SHELLEY, LADY [Louisa Elizabeth Knight, m. Sir John], IV: 403

SHELLEY, PERCY BYSSHE, I: 49n.; debate on 70; T.'s opinion of 74; 80; T. writing on 93, 98, 99; 112, 131. *Revolt of Islam*, I: 51, 74

SHERIDAN, RICHARD BRINSLEY, II: 245. *Rivals*, II: 393; T. adapts for cartoon 758; III: "Mrs. Malaprop" 759. *Trip to Scarborough*, II: 283

SHERIDAN, RICHARD BRINSLEY [the younger], III: 675

SHERWOOD, MRS. MARY MARTHA [m. Captain Henry], *Little Henry*, III: 20

SHUTE, EMILY, I: 418

SHUTE FAMILY [Samuel], I: 41n., 64, 418

SHUTE, MATILDA, I: 418

SHUTE, MRS. SAMUEL [Anne Ricketts], I: 219, 220

SIEVRAC, MR., I: 232

SILVER, HENRY, IV: 404, 413

SIMEON, CHARLES, I: 46n., 65

SIMEON, CORNWALL, II: 647

SIMEONITES, I: 46, 65

SIMEON, SIR J., IV: and wife 400; 411

SIMONS, MISS, IV: 358

SIMPSON, DR. JAMES YOUNG, III: 686. IV: 433

SIMPSON, JOHN PALGRAVE, IV: 105n.

SIMPSON, MRS. MARY C. M. S., *Many Memories*, quoted III: 70n.

SIMS [a coachman], IV: 76

SINCLAIR, ARCHDEACON JOHN, III: 158. IV: 404, 408, 414
SINCLAIR, MISS, *Letter to:* III, 632
SKELTON, JOHN HENRY, III: 216, 217. *My Book,* I: in Yellowplush 348
Letters to: IV, 209, 253. *Letter from:* IV, 210
SKIERS, MR., II: 20
SKINNER, HELEN, III: 191
SKINNER, REV. THOMAS H., III: 191n.
SLAVERY, III: 181, 187, 198–200, 222, 223–24, 228–29, 234, 235, 236–37, 242, 248, 252, 254, 255, 559, 567, 579, 585, 588
SLEAP, THOMAS, III: 375, 376, 387
SLEAP, MRS. THOMAS, IV: 408
SLIDELL, JOHN, III: 581n.
SLOANE, MR. AND MRS. GEORGE, II: 735n.
SMETHAM, MR., IV: 401
SMITH, MR. AND MRS. ABEL, II: 644n.
SMITH, ALBERT RICHARD, II: 105n., 366. III: 63, 72, 89, 98, 221, 245, 363, 455, 585. IV: quoted 15n.–16n.; 59
Letter to: III, 22
SMITH, ALEXANDER, III: 298
SMITH, ARTHUR, IV: T.'s apology to 59n.–60n.; 86n.
SMITH AND ELDER, I: clxvi. II: 330. III: 82, 102, 243, 470n., 480. IV: contract for T.'s novels 130; 143, 144; CM arrangement 148; T. and editorship of CM 153; 157, 158, 168n., 170n., 182, 189n., 250, 261; and A. T.'s writing 272; 319, 359
SMITH, ELIZA, II: and *Pendennis* 436
SMITH, GEORGE, I: biographical clxvi–clxviii; clxxii. II: 611n., 673n., 675n., 755n., 804n., 810n. III: 15n., 89n., 99, 102, 111, 129, 135, 189; and the *Pall Mall Gazette* 417n. IV: plans for CM

130n.; 144, 148n., 168n., 189n., 190n., 197, 219n., 227, 271, 301, 391, 399, 400, 408, 414. *Memoir,* quoted I: xciv. II: 674n., 784n.– 85n.
Letters to: III, 416, 470, 618; IV, 149, 154, 156, 162, 172, 177, 180, 184, 189, 214, 215, 216, 246, 256, 257, 266, 269, 292, 295
SMITH, MRS. GEORGE [Elizabeth Blakeway], III: 471. IV: 190n.
SMITH, HORACE [Horatio], II: 320, 384n., 426, 476, 563
Gaieties and Gravities, II: 250. *Poetical Works,* II: 249. *Zillah,* I: 58, 60
Letter to: II, 249
SMITH, MRS. HORACE, II: 603
SMITH, JAMES, I: sketch of 265
SMITH, JAMES and HORACE, *Rejected Addresses,* I: 62n.
SMITH, LAURA, *Letter to:* IV, 355
SMITH, MISS, IV: 423
SMITH, MISS [d. of Horace], *Letter to:* II, 384
SMITH, MISS [of Washington], III: 205, 330
SMITH, MISSES [d. of Horace], II: 469, 601, 603. III: 392
SMITH, MR., II: 152
SMITH, O., I: 260n.
SMITH, PAUL, *La Vie d'Artiste,* II: 161
SMITH, SYDNEY, III: 462. IV: 440
SMOLLETT, TOBIAS, IV: 186. *Peregrine Pickle,* II: 144
SMOLLETT, TOBIAS, and David Hume, *History,* I: 48
SMYTH, CHARLES, I: 13, 14, 18, 19, 20, 22, 26, 30, 72, 73, 78, 80, 134
SMYTH, ROBERT, I: 381
SMYTH, WILLIAM, I: 66
SMYTHE, GEORGE AUGUSTUS FREDERICK PERCY SYDNEY, *see* PENSHURST, 2nd Baron

SMYTHE, PERCY CLINTON SYDNEY, see PENSHURST, 1st Baron

SNELLING, ANDREW S., III: 309n., 543

SNELLING, MRS. ANDREW S., III: 309, 312, 358, 370, 543, 603, 604, 609

SNELLING FAMILY [Andrew], III: 542, 570

Snob, The, I: 49n., 75, 77, 79, 93

SOMERS, CHARLES SOMERS COCKS, 3rd Earl, II: 694

SOMERS, LADY [Virginia Pattle, m. 3rd Earl], I: 391. II: 374, 381, 386, 429, 436, 437, 469, 487, 525, 527, 662; married 694, 695n., 704. IV: 323

SOMERSET, MAJ. ARTHUR WILLIAM FITZ-ROY, II: 231–32, 653n.

SOMERSET, MRS. ARTHUR WILLIAM FITZ-ROY, see WEBSTER, MRS. Henry

SOMERSET, EDWARD ADOLPHUS ST. MAUR, 12th Duke of, IV: 290

SOMERSET, LORD FITZROY, see RAGLAN

SOMERVILLE, MR., I: and J. Shawe 429, 432, 437, 440, 444

SONGS, I: 25, 36, 169–70, 432; "Nix my dolly pals" 440. II: "Bay of Biscay" 177

SONTAG, GERTRUDE [Countess de Rossi], II: 499, 655, 666. III: 112, 171n., 379

SORTAIN, REV. JOSEPH, II: 473

SOTHEBY, MR., II: 154

SOTHERN, MRS., IV: 408

SOULÉ, PIERRE, III: 581n.

SOULIÉ, FRÉDÉRIC, Mémoires du Diable, II: 143

Southern Literary Messenger, III: 411n.

SOUTHERN, MRS., IV: 149

SOUTHEY, ROBERT, I: 396. Book of the Church, II: 650, 651, 652. Thalaba, IV: 224

SOUVESTRE, ÉMILE, Mémoires d'un sans-culotte, II: 33

SOYER, ALEXIS BENOÎT, II: 149. Gastronomic Regenerator, II: 149n., 237n.

SOYRES, MRS. FRANCIS DE [Andalusia FitzGerald], I: 150n., 243, 388, 411. II: 5, 43

S. P., Letter to, III: 635

Spectator, The, I: 230, 408, 457, 465. II: 266, 403, 404, 409, 450, 452, 482, 782. III: 130, 135. IV: 286n.

SPEDDING, JAMES, I: lxxxii, cxxvii, 287n., 347, 372, 376. II: 366, 629n. III: 89n., 419, 496. IV: 285n.
    Letters to: II, 628; IV: 356

SPEECHES, II: Literary fund "smash" 540; Macready dinner 755, 766. III: Olliffe dinner 285; 426, 427; for Administrative Reform 461; Macready banquet 500–01; Shakespeare dinner 606, 674; Appendix XVI. IV: 40, 63; R. A. dinner 78; 204–05; Appendix XIX

SPENCER, CAROLINE, I: 476, 482–83

SPENCER, MRS., II: 18, 20, 31, 32, 305
    Letter to: II, 41

SPENCER, V., I: 318n.

SPIEGEL, HOF MARSCHALL VON, III: 442

SPIEGEL, MELANIE VON, I: 127, 130, 135, 142. III: 442

SPEIRS [or Spiers], MR., IV: 50, 384

SPIRITUALISM, see also Didier, III: 123, 125n., 134, 272, 338

SPINETO, MARQUIS, I: 39

SPRATT, MR., II: 57

SPRING-RICE, STEPHEN EDMOND, II: 481n., 509n., 557n., 577, 685n., 697, 711, 740
    Letter to: IV, 261

SPRING-RICE, MRS. STEPHEN [Ellen Mary Frere], II: 481

Spring-Rice, Thomas, *see* Mont-
eagle
"SSB" or "SSH," *see* Hampton,
Mrs. Frank
Staël, Mme. de, I: 118
Stanard, Capt. and Mrs. Robert
Conway, III: 540n.
Stanard, Robert Craig, III: 540n.
IV: 69, 70
Stanard, Mrs. Robert Craig [Mar-
tha Pierce], III: 540. IV: 69, 70
Standard, The, I: 197, 421, 443
Stanfield, Clarkson, I: cxxxvi. II:
253, 528n. III: 494, 643
Letter to: IV, 357
Stanhope, Leicester FitzGerald
Charles, *see* Harrington
Stanhope, Philip Henry, 5th Earl,
II: 636n., 664. III: 377, 400,
675. IV: 137. *History*, IV: 19,
21
Letter to: IV, 338
Stanhope, Lady [Emily Harriet
Kerrison, m. 5th Earl], IV: 396,
401, 412
Stanley, Algeron Charles, II:
700
Stanley, Alice Margaret, *see*
Lane-Fox
Stanley, Charles, *see* Monck
Stanley, Edward John, 2nd Baron,
I: biographical clxix-clxx. II: 571,
623n., 770, 811, 824. III: 83,
374, 425, 674. IV: 391, 392,
395, 397, 410n., 411
Letter to: II, 786. *Letter from:*
II, 786
Stanley, Lady [Henrietta Dillon-
Lee, m. 2nd Baron], I: biograph-
ical clxx-clxxi. II: 684, 755, 756.
III: 53, 64, 82, 260, 263, 632,
685. IV: 397, 410n.
Letters to: II, 570, 574, 623,
624, 699, 805, 807, 815, 822;
III, 65, 69, 87, 88, 178, 374,
403, 425, 454, 477, 649; IV, 72,
84, 110

Stanley, Edward Lyulph, 4th
Baron, II: 700
Stanley family [of Alderley], I:
biographical clxviii-clxxi. III: 97,
98
Stanley, Henrietta Blanche, *see*
Airlie, Lady
Stanley, Henry Edward John,
3rd Baron, IV: 111n., 112
Stanley, John Constantine, II:
700. III: 404. IV: 410
Stanley, Lady [Lady Maria Josepha
Holroyd, m. 1st Baron], I: quoted
on T. clxix
Stannus, Col. Sir Ephraïm G., II:
361
Starke, Mariana, *Information and
Direction*, I: 229
Staveley, Thomas, III: 622n.
Staveley, Thomas George, III:
623n.
Stead, Misses, I: 50
Stechert, Louis, I: 228
Steel, Mr., III: 689
Steele family, I: 61
Steele, Richard, I: cxxxv. II: 763.
Christian Hero, IV: 114
Stephen, Sir James Fitzjames, IV:
215, 408, 411
Letter to: IV, 227
Stephen, Lady [Mary Cunningham,
m. Sir James], IV: 411
Stephens, Henry, III: 686
Stephenson, Mr., IV: 414
Sterling, Antony Coningham, I:
430n. *Letter to:* III, 658
Sterling, Mrs. Antony Coning-
ham [Charlotte Baird], I: 430
Sterling Club, II: 629. IV: 420
Sterling, Edward, I: 295n., 306
Sterling, Edward, Jr., *Letter to:*
III, 434
Sterling family [John], I: 310,
347n., 400, 430
Sterling, John, I: ciii, 304, 310,
430n. II: 109, 629n., 829n. III:
392n.

STERLING, MRS. JOHN, II: 109
STERLING, MRS. [the elder], I: 308, 367, 430. II: 102, 109
STERNE, LAURENCE, II: 53, 312, 500, 584, 783, 799; false and wicked 800. III: 124n., 153n., 281, 284. IV: liar 281–82. *Letters*, III: 165
STEVENS, AUGUSTUS, I: 317. II: 19, 32, 116, 117, 120, 121, 124, 139, 140, 142, 143, 590, 727, 743, 840, 842. III: 267, 544, 676. IV: 353
STEVENS, MRS. AUGUSTUS [Rosa Ricketts], II: 590, 592, 743. III: 267
STEVENS, MR., I: 341
STEWART, FREDERICK WILLIAM ROBERT, *see* LONDONDERRY, 4th Marquess
STIRLING, MRS., *Fanny Hervey*, II: 562
STIRLING-MAXWELL, SIR WILLIAM [Stirling of Keir], III: 31, 33, 42, 44, 242, 451, 675. IV: 37, 40n., 396, 397, 399, 409
STOCKEN, MR., IV: 414
STODDARD, RICHARD HENRY, *T. and Dickens*, quoted III: 195n.–96n.
STODDART, WILLIAM WELLWOOD, I: 16, 18, 27, 29, 42, 53, 55. II: 810. III: 647. IV: 43
STOKES, LOUIS, and J. J. Stewart Perowne, ed. *Letters . . . of Connop Thirlwall*, quoted IV: 186n.
STONE FAMILY [of Boston], III: 484
STONE, FRANK, I: 283, 388, 398. II: 191n.–92n.
    Letters to: I, 278, 329
STONEY-BOWES, ANDREW ROBINSON, I: and *Lyndon* xcii
STORKS, SIR HENRY KNIGHT, *Letter to:* IV, 126
STORY, EDITH, III: 338n., 339n., 359, 414, 503, 523, 615
STORY, ROBERT HERBERT, *Letters to:* III, 370, 420

STORY, WALDO, III: 615. IV: 8
STORY, WILLIAM WETMORE, III: 330, 331, 341, 359, 465n., 514. IV: 229, 403
    Letters to: III, 464, 502, 506, 614
STORY, MRS. WILLIAM WETMORE [Emelyn Eldredge], III: 330–31, 341, 359; quoted 414n.; 507, 615. IV: 8, 403
STOWE, HARRIET BEECHER, III: 271; T. meets 273. *Uncle Tom*, III: 157; starts English abolitionists 181n.; 187, 199, 224, 254, 255, 273; "done harm" 293
STRACHAN, MR., I: 237, 283, 285
STRACHEY, LYTTON, and Roger Fulford, ed. Greville *Memoirs*, quoted I: cv; III: 608n.
STRANGE, MISS, I: 100
STRANGE, SIR ROBERT, I: 66, 89
STRANGFORD, GEORGE AUGUSTUS FREDERICK PERCY SYDNEY SMYTHE, 2nd Baron Penshurst and 7th Viscount, *Historic Fancies*, II: 145
STRANGFORD, PERCY CLINTON SYDNEY SMYTHE, 1st Baron Penshurst and 6th Viscount, II: 362, 363
STREATFEILD, SIDNEY RICHARD, III: 24
STREATFEILD, MAJ. SIDNEY ROBERT, III: 24n., 25
STREATFEILD, MRS. SIDNEY ROBERT, III: 24
STRICTURE, T.'s., *see* HEALTH
STRONG, BEN, III: 207, 290
STRONG, MRS. CHARLES, III: 318
STRONG, ELIZABETH ["Libby," later Mrs. Alfred Leonard Curtis], I: lxxxvii. III: quoted 147n.–48n.; 204, 207, 214, 238, 257, 260, 282, 295, 307, 308, 311, 370. IV: 57, 65, 79, 80, 109, 213, 229
    Letters to: III, 147, 289, 310, 378
STRONG, OLIVER, III: 198, 207, 232,

239, 259, 263, 274, 290, 330, 332, 370, 628, 662, 666. IV: 110
Letter to: III, 294
STRUMPF, MR., III: 207
STRUTT, EDWARD, *see* BELPER
STUART, CHARLES, *see* ROTHESAY
STUART, GILBERT, III: 180n.
STUMFF, MISS, III: 138
STURGIS, HOWARD, IV: 62
STURGIS, MR., III: 5, 6
STURGIS, RUSSELL, III: 274, 307, 496, 609, 628, 653, 675. IV: 62, 63, 357, 391
Letter to: III, 5
STURGIS, MRS. RUSSELL, III: 5, 6, 263, 299, 667, 670
Letter to: IV, 357
SUDLOW, W., III: 661
SUE, EUGÈNE, II: T. proposes article on 202
Juif errant, III: 618. *Latréaumont,* II: 202. *Mathilde,* II: 32, 202. *Mystères de Paris,* II: 92; T. translating 139, 140, 141, 159; 202, 840, 841
SUMNER, CHARLES, III: 195n.; beating of 627; 664. IV: 165
SUMNER, CHARLES RICHARD [Bishop of Winchester], II: 698
SUMNER, JOHN BIRD [Archbishop of Canterbury], II: 465
SUNDERLAND, THOMAS, I: 38
SURGÈRES, HÉLÈNE DE, III: 151
SURTEES, ROBERT SMITH, II: 622.
Sponge's Sporting Tour, III: 335
Letters to: II, 720, 769; III, 335
SUTHERLAND, GEORGE GRANVILLE LEVESON-GOWER, 2nd Duke of, II: 690n. III: 132n.
SUTHERLAND, DUCHESS OF [Lady Harriet Howard, m. 2nd Duke], II: 690. III: 132, 181n. IV: 444
SUTRO, DR. SIGISMUND, II: 422
SWAIN, JOSEPH, IV: 199, 254
Letter to: IV, 258
SWIFT, JONATHAN, I: 95, 166. II:

83, 553n.; "a bad man" 763; 776; traitor and renegade 800. III: 38; T.'s lecture on 120n.–21n. *Journal to Stella,* III: 447
SWINBURNE, ALGERNON CHARLES, IV: and T. 285n.–86n.
SWINTON, JAMES RANNIE, II: 756. IV: 393, 410, 412
SYKES, GODFREY, IV: designs CM 162
SYKES, COL. WILLIAM HENRY, *Letter to:* IV, 52
SYME, JAMES, I: ci. IV: 217
SYMINGTON, ALEXANDER, and T. J. Wise, *The Brontës,* quoted I: xciv; II: 673n.
SYNGE FAMILY [William Webb], IV: 195n.
SYNGE, ROBERT FOLLETT ["Bobby Mistletoe"], III: 302, 480, 539, 651. IV: 195n., 200, 201
SYNGE, WILLIAM MAKEPEACE THACKERAY, *Letter to:* IV, 358
SYNGE, WILLIAM WEBB FOLLETT, III: 210, 211, 220, 302, 539, 556, 599, 664. IV: 39, 53, 200; T. lends £600 to 263n.; 392, 397, 400, 404, 412
Letters to: III, 291, 335, 480, 622, 650; IV, 38, 232, 262, 358, 359
SYNGE, MRS. WILLIAM WEBB FOLLETT [Henrietta Wainwright], III: 210, 211, 263, 302, 480, 539, 599, 650, 651. IV: 201, 358
Letters to: III, 219, 291; IV, 52

Tablet, The, II: 111
TACITUS, CORNELIUS, III: 304, 668. IV: 435
TAGLIONI, MARIE, I: 85–86
TAGORE, BABOO DWARKANAUTH, II: 244
TAIT, ARCHIBALD CAMPBELL [Bishop of London], IV: 392

TALFOURD, SIR THOMAS NOON, II: 114, 144, 721n., 844

TALFOURD, LADY [Rachel Rutt, m. Sir Thomas], II: 293

TALLEYRAND - PÉRIGORD, CHARLES MAURICE DE, II: T. to write life of 172, 174, 175, 177, 185, 190; 245. *Mémoires*, II: 147

TAMBURINI, ANTONIO, II: 44

TAPRELL, WILLIAM, I: 149, 150, 176, 178, 181, 183, 185, 187, 188, 190, 197, 241

Tatler, The [1709], II: 735

TAUCHNITZ, CHRISTIAN BERNHARD, II: 444, 806. III: 280. IV: 365
    Letter to: III, 607

TAUNTON, HENRY LABOUCHERE, 1st Baron, IV: 411n.

TAUNTON, LADY [Lady Mary Howard, m. 1st Baron], IV: 411

TAYLOR, BAYARD, III: 520, 529; T. "fallen in love with" 530; 538, 614. IV: 17, 47n.–48n., 51n., 321. *Critical Essays*, quoted III: 594n. *Poems*, IV: 18
    Letters to: III, 489; IV, 46, 47

TAYLOR, SIR CHARLES, III: 674. IV: 81; and T.'s resignation from CM 256, 257; and wife 393; 396, 397, 399, 400, 410; and wife 414

TAYLOR, G., III: 689

TAYLOR, SIR HENRY, I: cxxvii. II: and T.'s apology to 697; 698, 699. III: 53. IV: 426
    Letter to: II, 694

TAYLOR, LADY [Theodosia Spring-Rice, m. Sir Henry], II: T. insults 695n.; T. apologizes 696, 697, 698; 699

TAYLOR, JEREMY, I: 428

TAYLOR, MISSES [s. of Bayard], IV: 17, 46

TAYLOR, MR., I: 81

TAYLOR, TOM, I: and T.-Forster fight cxxxiv. II: fight 296, 297, 298, 299, 300, 303; 342n., 389, 604, 614n., 625n. IV: 22, 48, 404, 409, 413. *Masks and Faces*, III: 127
    Letters to: II, 298, 303; III, 463. *Letter from:* II, 301

TAYLOR, MRS. THOMAS, II: 342. III: 73

TCHELCHAGOFF, ADMIRAL, I: 113

TEDDY, III: 144

TELBIN, MR., III: 643

TELEGRAPH SPECULATION, III: 643, 653, 654, 656. IV: 56

Temple Bar, III: 472n. IV: 203n.

TEMPLER FAMILY, I: 210, 217, 218

TEMPLER, G., I: 261

TENISON, MR., IV: 401

TENNENT, ELEANOR, II: 253

TENNENT, SIR JAMES EMERSON, II: and T.'s eastern trip 150, 177; 194, 568, 754, 843. III: 375, 667, 674
    Letter to: II, 251

TENNENT, LADY [Letitia Tennent, m. Sir James], II: 252, 683, 843

TENNIEL, SIR JOHN, III: 622. IV: 404, 413

TENNYSON, ALFRED, 1st Baron, I: and Hallam 196; 198; "clever fellow" 205; 287, 288, 346, 413, 421. II: T. on 26; "growler but a man of genius" 57; 148; pension 225; 503, 602n., 629; made laureate 710–11; "selfish" 765; 815. III: 298; read in America 497. IV: T. introduces B. Taylor to 46, 47n., 48n.; 168, 170, 171; "a great poet at 20" 372; 416
    "Grandmother's Apology," IV: 153. *Idylls of the King*, IV: T. enthusiastic 151–53. *In Memoriam*, II: 691; III: 12. "New Timon," II: 226n. "Ode on . . . Wellington," III: 128. *Princess*, II: 332. IV: 152. "Tithonus," IV: in CM 168
    Letters to: IV, 151, 360

TENNYSON, LADY [Emily Sellwood, m. 1st Baron], II: 711. III: 72

Letter to: IV, 168

TENNYSON, FREDERICK, I: 346. II: 127n., 169n., 191n., 310n., 316, 365n., 655n. III: 30n., 114, 115

TENNYSON, HALLAM, 2nd Baron, III: 73. *Tennyson,* quoted IV: 360n.

TENTERDEN, CHARLES STUART AUBREY ABBOTT, 3rd Baron, IV: 233, 395

TENTERDEN, JOHN HENRY ABBOTT, 2nd Baron, III: 426

TERNAN, ELLEN LAWLESS, I: cxxii. IV: and Dickens 83, 86, 117n., 131

TERNAN, MRS. FRANCES ELEANOR, IV: 83n., 86n.

THACKERAY, ANNE [G. 76], I: cxix

THACKERAY, ANNE ISABELLA ["Annie," later Lady Ritchie, G. 100], I: and Edward T. children cxix; born 343; and Jane T. 367, 368; "perpetual source of pleasure" 400; note from 401; eyes bad 416; "thousand charming ways" 424; "noble" 445; note from 448; and I.T.'s insanity 478, 480, 483, 518, 520. xc, cxxvi, cxxxiii, 350, 353, 355, 356, 359, 360, 362, 379, 387, 391, 392, 394–95, 396, 397–98, 404, 405, 412, 414, 419, 422, 427–28, 430, 435, 436, 440, 441, 442, 447, 449, 450, 454, 460, 461, 464, 465, 468, 469, 472, 473, 474, 476, 477, 481, 482, 484, 485, 486, 487

II: in *Second Funeral* 4; living with C-S's 46; wayward 68; preferred to H.T. 73; needs discipline 74; at school 96; "little reprobate" 123; "intelligent and affectionate" 145, 146; Yellowplushism 210; "afraid . . . she's going to be a man of genius" 240; living with T. 255–56; B. Hamerton dismissed because of 285, 286; "brains" 288; "noble heart and

genius" 292; "generous, loving and just" 379; joke of 387; and B. Hamerton 401; "awfully clever" 410; T. describes 545; "almost a young woman" 609; on European tour 788; "magnanimous and gentle" 789; "fat lump of pure gold" 796. 10, 14, 19, 20, 31, 32, 43, 47, 49, 50, 53, 55, 69, 70, 77, 78, 80, 81, 85, 88, 89–91, 95, 98, 99, 100, 101, 107, 108, 109, 110, 119, 121, 125, 131, 136, 144, 147, 155, 164, 166, 168, 170, 171, 172, 173, 175, 177, 179, 180, 181, 187, 190, 193, 194, 195, 196, 197, 200, 204, 212, 216, 218, 220, 221, 222, 231, 232, 234, 238, 239, 241, 244, 250, 255, 256, 257, 258, 262, 263, 265, 267, 269, 275, 276, 287, 289, 291, 306, 311, 317, 318, 322, 324, 325, 327, 335, 342, 347, 349, 350, 351, 352, 357, 358, 364, 365, 367, 368, 373, 380, 381, 382, 383, 393, 394, 395, 400, 403, 404, 409, 416, 417, 418, 419, 420, 427, 428, 429, 430, 431, 435, 439, 441, 457, 462, 471, 478, 480, 486, 488, 490, 503, 507, 525, 528–29, 531, 536, 541, 546, 548, 551, 558, 559, 568, 577, 581, 582, 583, 584, 585, 599, 602n., 607, 609, 622, 624, 626, 639, 640, 646, 647n., 658, 663, 664, 665, 667, 668n., 683, 685, 686, 688, 689, 699, 701, 702, 706, 715, 719, 725, 726, 732, 734, 735, 736, 737, 739, 740, 741, 745, 748, 749, 752, 754, 755, 756, 761, 762, 766, 768, 789, 791, 792, 793, 794, 797, 801, 804, 806, 810, 811, 812, 814, 816, 824, 840

III: "very popular" 24; FG leaves legacy to 29, 30 39; and religion 85–86, 141, 168–69; not

to write I.T. 187; T. worried
about religious instruction of 188,
198, 216–18; her writing 248,
251; "pleasedness and good-humour" 302; helping with *Newcomes* 313, 323, 332, 346, 375;
in Italy with T. 325, 326, 328,
329, 333, 336, 337, 338, 339,
350; scarletina 352, 353, 354,
355, 356, 362; M. Carmichael
unkind to 364, 365, 366, 427,
428; first ball 414n.; secretary to
T. 419; "drawing very good" 544;
and R. Creyke 613; nursing Mrs.
C-S 625, 628, 630, 635, 636,
640, 641, 649, 653. 3, 11, 13,
17, 19, 20, 21, 22, 34, 37, 48,
52, 60, 65, 70, 73, 76, 77, 80, 84,
91, 100, 101, 103, 104, 105, 110,
111, 115, 122, 123, 132, 135,
144, 146, 151, 152, 153, 154,
157, 160, 163, 164, 167, 170,
173, 177, 182, 186, 192, 202,
204, 214, 215, 216, 219, 220,
230, 238, 245, 246, 247, 254,
255, 256, 258, 261, 262, 263,
264, 265, 266, 267, 268, 271,
274, 279, 280, 282, 283, 285,
286, 287, 288, 289, 291, 292,
293, 297, 300, 301, 303, 306,
308, 310, 311, 312, 315, 330,
331, 342, 344, 345, 347, 348,
349, 351, 357, 358, 359, 361,
367, 368, 369, 371, 373, 376,
379, 381, 395, 397, 401, 403,
408, 409, 412, 415, 422, 423,
425, 430, 434, 439, 443, 448,
451, 452, 453, 459n., 460, 461,
464, 466, 474, 475, 477, 478,
479, 499, 521, 525, 528, 529,
531, 532, 534, 542, 543, 545,
547, 558, 561, 562, 565, 569,
570, 581, 582, 584, 585, 591,
593, 598, 599, 602, 605, 606,
608, 609, 610, 612, 616, 618,
620, 621, 622, 646, 651, 654,

656, 657, 668, 669, 673, 674,
676n.

IV: and Carmichaels 5, 6, 78;
gives "first drum" 80, 85; writing
for CM 185, 190n.; and Swinburne 285n.–86n.; on Oxford
election 381, 382. 3, 4, 9, 13,
14, 46, 48, 51, 56, 57, 61, 62,
65, 66, 74, 75, 76, 79, 81, 83,
84, 88, 109, 111, 112, 113, 115,
128, 137n., 153, 154, 155, 166,
172, 184, 186, 187, 196, 201,
202, 203, 208, 212, 213, 214,
215n., 218, 227, 229, 232, 233,
234, 235, 236, 242n., 255, 265,
269, 270, 273, 279, 287, 291,
295, 296n., 305, 308, 313, 314,
316, 318, 319, 325, 327, 331,
334, 336, 339, 348, 352, 365,
373, 378, 379, 392, 399, 412,
419, 430, 435, 436, 437, 439,
443, 444, 448

Biographical Introductions,
quoted I: clixn., 392n.–93n.,
487n.–88n.; II: 5n., 79n.–80n.,
145n.–46n., 187n., 238n.–39n.,
599n.; III: 338n., 437n.–39n.;
IV: 195n., 381. *Blackstick Papers*,
quoted I: cxxv-cxxvii; II: 436n.
Centenary, quoted IV: 177n.,
274n.–75n., 292n. *Chapters*,
quoted I: cxv-cxvi, cxliv, 127n.–
28n.; II: 647n., 673n.–74n.; III:
63n., 76n., 137n.–38n., 266n.,
327n., 328n.–29n. *Elizabeth*, III:
138n.; IV: 271–72; T.'s reaction
to bad review of 410n., 416. "Little Scholars," IV: 185, 190n.
Orphan, quoted IV: 142n.

Letters to: II, 101, 171, 210,
222, 601, 604, 605, 667, 669,
670, 691, 716, 802, 808, 817,
819; III, 4, 40, 44, 48, 55, 61,
62, 71, 81, 93, 96, 105, 106,
118, 129, 141, 189, 222, 239,
275, 322, 385, 387, 391, 480,
489, 504, 511, 513, 522, 535,

554, 566, 571, 574, 577, 586, 595, 625, 629, 630, 633, 636, 642, 644, 646; IV, 19, 20, 22, 23, 26, 28, 30, 32, 35, 40, 49, 120, 148, 261, 361. *Letters from:* III, 137, 140, 323, 526, 648; IV, 127, 229, 298, 301

THACKERAY, AUGUSTA, *see* HALLIDAY

THACKERAY, CHARLES [G. 61], II: 35, 73

THACKERAY, CHARLOTTE, *see* RITCHIE, Mrs. John

THACKERAY, EDWARD TALBOT [G. 69], I: cxix. II: 707. III: 643. IV: 304, 365, 404n.

THACKERAY, MRS. EDWARD TALBOT [Amy Marianne Crowe, G. 70], I: cxix. II: 707n., 800n. III: 325, 397, 485, 499, 506, 537, 561, 586, 613, 626, 647. IV: 9, 13, 35, 61, 62, 230, 232, 304, 404n.

THACKERAY, REV. ELIAS [G. 32], II: 79, 84, 88, 274n.

THACKERAY, ELIAS [of Hawkshurst], IV: 132

THACKERAY, EMILY, *see* SHAKESPEAR, Mrs. J. T.

THACKERAY FAMILY, *Letters to:* II, 134; III, 67, 483, 491

THACKERAY, FRANCIS [G. 59], I: 30, 31, 67, 73, 78, 150, 175, 178, 183, 185, 187, 192, 198, 204, 222, 235, 243, 245, 250, 290, 297, 413, 415, 419, 506. II: 274n. III: 308, 446, 448
    Letter to: II, 512

THACKERAY, MRS. FRANCIS [Anne Shakespear, G. 60], I: 68. II: 144, 145, 170, 173, 707

THACKERAY, FRANCIS ST. JOHN [G. 67], II: 591n., 707–08. IV: 43, 169, 396
    Letter to: IV, 139

THACKERAY, MRS. FRANCIS ST. JOHN [Louise Katherine Irvine, G. 68], IV: 139

THACKERAY, FREDERICK [G. 47], I: 58

THACKERAY, DR. FREDERICK [G. 34], I: 30, 39, 43, 46, 52, 58, 61, 62, 67, 73, 77–78, 80, 81, 82, 105, 107. II: 510, 511n.

THACKERAY, MRS. FREDERICK [Mary Elizabeth Crick, G. 36], II: 512

THACKERAY, GEN. FREDERICK RENNELL [G. 12], III: 7, 72n., 453, 478, 626, 667, 674. IV: 201, 205, 392
    Letter to: IV, 362

THACKERAY, LADY ELIZABETH [Margaret Carnegie, G. 13, m. Frederick], III: 7, 72n., 626. IV: 23, 362, 392
    Letters to: III, 7, 84, 105, 452, 478; IV, 201, 204

THACKERAY GENEALOGY, III: 446. IV: 132

THACKERAY, GEORGE [G. 46], I: 34, 41, 54, 72

THACKERAY, GEORGE [Provost of Kings, G. 14], I: 30, 50

THACKERAY, MRS. GEORGE [Mary Ann Cottin, G. 15], I: 30n.

THACKERAY, HARRIET MARIAN ["Minny," later Mrs. Leslie Stephen, G. 101], I: and Edward T. children cxix; christened 461; and I.T.'s insanity 478, 480, 481, 482, 483, 485, 487, 518, 520. xc, cxxvi, 447, 449, 450, 454, 464, 465, 473, 474, 476
    II: in *Second Funeral* 4; I.T. and 23, 43; living with C-S's 46; T. doesn't love as he "ought" 73; "amazingly advanced" 145; living with T. 255–56; and B. Hamerton 285; "sweetness" 288; joke of 387; T. describes 544–45; on European tour 788; jealousy of 789. 31, 32, 47, 50, 55, 69, 70, 74, 76, 77, 78, 80, 81, 85, 88, 89, 91, 99, 100, 101, 102, 107, 108, 109, 110, 119, 121, 125, 131,

136, 144, 146, 147, 155, 164, 166, 168, 170, 171, 172, 173, 175, 177, 179, 181, 187, 190, 193, 194, 195, 196, 197, 200, 204, 210, 212, 218, 220, 222, 223, 232, 233, 234, 238, 239, 240, 241, 242, 244, 257, 262, 263, 265, 267, 269, 272, 275, 276, 286, 287, 289, 291, 306, 311, 317, 318, 322, 324, 325, 327, 335, 347, 349, 350, 351, 352, 357, 358, 364, 365, 367, 368, 373, 379, 380, 381, 382, 393, 394, 400, 401, 404, 409, 417, 418, 419, 420, 427, 428, 429, 430, 431, 435, 439, 441, 457, 462, 471, 480, 488, 490, 503, 507, 525, 528, 531, 536, 541, 546, 548, 551, 558, 559, 568, 577, 583, 584, 592, 599, 602n., 604, 607, 609, 622, 624, 626, 639, 646, 658, 664, 667, 683, 685, 686, 688, 689, 699, 701, 702, 706, 715, 716, 717, 719, 725, 726, 732, 734, 735, 736, 739, 740, 741, 745, 748, 752, 754, 755, 761, 762, 766, 768, 789, 791, 792, 793, 794, 796, 797, 801, 804, 806, 810, 811, 812, 813, 814, 816, 824, 840

III: FG leaves legacy to 29, 39; "pertness" 40; and religion 93–96, 168, 169; not to write I.T. 187; T. worried about religious instruction of 188, 198, 217–18; "bright and pretty" 215; in Italy with T. 325, 326, 328, 329, 333, 336, 337, 338, 339, 350; scarletina 352, 353, 354, 355, 356, 362; M. Carmichael unkind to 364, 365, 366; nursing Mrs. C-S 625, 628, 635, 636, 640, 641, 649; T. worries about I.T.'s insanity and 645. 3, 5, 17, 19, 20, 21, 22, 24, 25, 37, 48, 52, 60, 65, 70, 73, 80, 84, 86, 91, 93, 100, 101, 103, 104, 105, 110, 111,

115, 122, 123, 132, 135, 139, 140, 141, 144, 146, 151, 153, 154, 157, 160, 163, 164, 167, 170, 177, 182, 186, 190, 191, 192, 202, 204, 214, 216, 219, 220, 234, 245, 246, 247, 254, 255, 256, 258, 261, 263, 264, 265, 266, 267, 268, 269, 271, 274, 275, 279, 280, 282, 283, 285, 286, 287, 288, 289, 291, 292, 299, 300, 301, 302, 303, 306, 308, 310, 311, 312, 313, 315, 323, 326, 330, 331, 344, 345, 347, 348, 349, 351, 357, 358, 359, 361, 367, 368, 369, 371, 375, 376, 379, 381, 395, 397, 401, 403, 408, 409, 412, 414, 415, 419, 422, 423, 425, 430, 434, 439, 443, 448, 451, 459n., 460, 461, 464, 466, 474, 475, 477, 478, 479, 521, 525, 528, 529, 531, 532, 534, 542, 543, 544, 545, 547, 558, 561, 562, 569, 570, 581, 582, 584, 585, 591, 593, 599, 602, 605, 606, 608, 609, 610, 613, 614, 616, 620, 621, 622, 626, 643n., 646, 651, 653, 654, 656, 657, 668, 669, 673, 676n.

IV: and Carmichaels 5; nursing A.T. 154; "absurdly young" 230. 3, 4, 9, 13, 14, 46, 48, 51, 55, 57, 61, 62, 65, 66, 74, 76, 78, 79, 80, 81, 83, 85, 109, 111, 112, 113, 115, 128, 137n., 153, 155, 166, 172, 184, 185, 186, 187, 196, 202, 203, 208, 212, 213, 214, 215n., 218, 227, 229, 231, 233, 234, 235, 255, 265, 269, 270, 271, 273, 279, 285n., 287, 291, 295, 299, 303, 305, 308, 313, 314, 315, 318, 319, 325, 327, 329, 331, 334, 339, 348, 352, 365, 373, 378, 379, 392, 399, 412, 419, 427, 430, 435, 436, 437, 439, 443, 444, 448

Letters to: II, 601, 605, 669,

670, 691, 817, 820; III, 33, 40, 44, 48, 55, 62, 71, 75, 96, 105, 106, 118, 129, 141, 171, 235, 239, 387, 391, 480, 489, 504, 511, 513, 535, 554, 566, 571, 574, 577, 586, 595, 629, 630, 633, 636, 642, 644, 646; IV, 19, 20, 22, 23, 26, 28, 32, 35, 40, 49, 120, 148, 261, 361. *Letters from:* III, 324, 526

THACKERAY, ISABELLA SHAWE [Mrs. William Makepeace, G. 99], I: biographical clxiv-clxv; T. in love with 295; married 318n.; lazy 320, 321; expecting A.T. 325, 343, 351; Jane born 366–67; H.T. expected 397, 405, 433, 436, born 446; "great deal better" 454; "languor and depression" 463; "very low" 465; "absence and depression" 467–69, 471; "absolute insanity" 474–75, 476; "profound abatement and disgust of life" 477; better 478–82; account of attempted suicide 483; worse 486, 487; appendix on her insanity 518–20. cxlix, 299, 322, 323, 324, 330, 331, 348, 374, 379, 383, 391, 392, 393, 394, 398, 400, 401, 411, 412, 413, 416, 418, 419, 420, 421, 435, 437, 438, 443, 444, 445, 447, 460, 464, 471, 472, 473, 484, 485

II: at Maison de Santé 3, 4, 5, 10, 11, 14–15; leaves Ivry 18; "mending" 21; "indifference, silence and sluggishness" 23; sudo-pathic treatment 32; to Germany for treatment 33, 34, 35, 36, 37; at Chaillot 41, 43, 46, 48; "extremely better" 92; "provokingly well" 125, 139, 141; "hopeless letter" 177; "crazy letter" 196, 204, 212; T. bringing to England 215, 216, 217; "tolerably sensible" 230, 233; "well and calm" 240; "nastiest pranks" 243;

"cholera" 324; "sinking" 334; and "Amelia" 394; T.'s reminiscing 429, 430–31, 462. 19, 20, 29, 31, 49, 57, 58, 68, 73, 81, 91, 95, 96, 98, 99, 101, 113, 121, 131, 140, 142, 143, 144 [?], 145 [?], 168, 170, 171, 172, 173, 180, 184, 185, 187, 189, 190, 193, 208, 210, 211, 222, 231, 237, 247, 248, 306, 321, 440, 545, 590, 754, 789, 804, 830, 841, 842, 844

III: 29, 39, 69, 83, 93, 99, 154, 182, 187, 247, 262, 266, 325n., 359, 360n., 365, 388, 397, 398, 415, 419, 524, 537, 577, 617, 645

IV: 62, 83, 130, 145, 214, 236, 271, 272n., 305, 366

Letters to: I, 300, 302, 305, 307, 314, 315, 317, 318, 349, 352, 354, 358, 361; II, 109, 164, 181, 209. *Letters from:* I, 368, 381, 387, 414, 426, 429, 439, 449, 461

THACKERAY, JANE [G. 102], I: born 366; 368; ill 370; dead 379–80; 447, 518, 520. II: 287. III: 239, 673. IV: 24n., 224, 278, 439

THACKERAY, JOSEPH [G. 45], I: 40, 41, 42

THACKERAY, DR. JOSEPH [G. 39], I: 109

THACKERAY, MARGARET [G. 74], I: cxix

THACKERAY, MARTIN [Vice-Provost of Kings, G. 37], I: 32, 34, 39, 44, 50, 67, 76, 78, 105, 109, 110, 285, 354; puts T. up for Reform Club 424, 428. II: 79n., 237. IV: 392, 409

THACKERAY, MRS. MARTIN [Augusta Yenn, G. 38], I: 32n., 285, 354

THACKERAY, MARY ANN [G. 19], I: 30n., 344. III: 279, 685n. IV: 392, 411, 413

THACKERAY, MARY AUGUSTA [G. 64], II: 170

THACKERAY, MARY ELIZABETH [G. 18], III: 72

THACKERAY, MISS [of Bath], Letter to: IV, 247

THACKERAY, MISSES [of Bath], IV: 8

THACKERAY, RICHMOND [G. 52], I: cxiii, cxiv, 144, 183n., 506. II: 174, 576, 609. III: 447, 448. IV: 132, 262

THACKERAY, SELINA, IV: 392

THACKERAY, ARCHDEACON THOMAS [G. 1], IV: 132

THACKERAY, MRS. THOMAS [Lydia Whish, G. 4], I: 32, 33, 67

THACKERAY, THOMAS [G. 27], I: 30, 34n., 40, 183n.

THACKERAY, THOMAS JAMES [G. 43], I: 416n.; and Lady Bulwer 434, 436n.; 447. II: 33
    Letter to: IV, 285

THACKERAY, WILLIAM MAKEPEACE [T.'s grandfather, G. 10], II: 510, 554, 608n. III: 347, 672. IV: 132

THACKERAY, MRS. WILLIAM MAKEPEACE [Amelia Richmond Webb, T.'s grandmother, G. 11], III: 446

THACKERAY, DR. WILLIAM MAKEPEACE [G. 30], II: 306

THEATRE, see also under individual playwrights and actors, I: clx, 14, 16n., 23, 29, 48, 85, 87, 88, 91, 92, 93, 96, 105, 110, 120, 127, 130, 141–42, 154, 160, 172, 177, 186, 190, 192, 194, 195, 196, 204, 206, 222, 224, 226, 231, 232, 233, 235, 236, 237, 238, 240, 250, 252, 260n., 266, 276, 278, 349, 358, 361, 362. II: 23–24, 44, 67n., 109, 124, 140, 142, 143, 147, 171, 407, 409, 429, 496, 533, 582, 588, 589, 653, 656, 663, 737n., 743. III: 61, 69, 70, 379, 387, 395, 442, 443, 460, 618, 676. IV: 411, 413, 414, 424

THELWALL, JOHN, II: 248

THIBOUST, LAMBERT, and Bernard Derosne, Aurore, IV: 413

THIÉBAULT, DIEUDONNÉ, Mes Souvenirs, III: 668

THIERS, LOUIS ADOLPHE, I: 360; and ministerial crisis 425. II: 731, 816. Histoire, I: 284, 285, 288

THIRLWALL, CONNOP [Bishop of St. Davids], II: 661
    Letter to: IV, 285

THOMAS, MR., II: 547

THOMPSON, COLONEL, I: 301n.

THOMPSON, DR. HENRY, III: 607, 611, 612, 613, 615, 626. IV: 47, 48, 67, 76, 77, 78, 85, 128, 129, 169, 217, 296, 361, 403. Pathology, IV: 129
    Letters to: IV, 177, 298

THOMPSON, HENRY L., Liddell, quoted II: 641n.

THOMPSON, JOHN, IV: 70

THOMPSON, JOHN REUBEN, III: 411n.
    Letters to: III, 171, 249; IV, 69

THOMPSON, WILLIAM HEPWORTH, I: quoted 107n.; 421, 496, 497. II: 510. III: 423

THOMSON, WILLIAM, see KELVIN

THOMSON, WILLIAM [Archbishop of York], IV: 285n., 411

THORNTON, MR., I: 108

THORNTON, WILLIAM, IV: 51

THRALE, MRS. HESTER LYNCH, I: and Dr. Johnson 444. IV: 396

THRESHER, MR. AND MRS., I: 8

THUCYDIDES, I: 43

THWAITS, MR., II: 249

THYNNE, LORD EDWARD, III: 285

THYNNE, LADY [Cecilia Gore, m. Lord Edward], II: 697, 699. III: 27, 285. IV: 425

THYNNE, JOHN ALEXANDER, see BATH

TICKNOR, ANNA ELIOT, III: 165

TICKNOR, ELIZA SULLIVAN, III: 165
TICKNOR FAMILY [George], III: 318, 613
TICKNOR AND FIELDS, III: 93, 122, 135, 493, 522
TICKNOR, GEORGE, III: 165, 170, 172n., 530, 664. *Prescott*, quoted III: 112n., 169n.
    Letter to: III, 318
TICKNOR, MRS. GEORGE [Anna Eliot], III: 540
TIECK, LUDWIG, "Trusty Eckhardt," I: 214
TILLOTSON, JOHN, I: 428
TILLY, ALEXANDRE, Comte de, *Mémoires*, III: 677
TILT, CHARLES, I: 365. II: 608n., 610n.
TIMBS, MRS., II: 753
Times, The, I: T. book reviewer for 306n.; 361, 362; T. submits bill to 375; 386n.; and Victoria 396; reconciliation with 424–25; 437; and Russell murder 443; 451, 453; and Durham's death 458; 469. II: 7, 109, 126n., 150, 170; and MC 241; 262; and Irish famine 266; 338, 390, 414, 462, 529, 646, 705, 725; "controversy with" 728, 751, 752, 754, 766; abuse of L. Napoléon 813–14. III: 112n., 175; accuses T. of slur on Washington 319–21; 393, 403, 407–08, 431, 432, 455n., 456n., 457, 461, 462, 466; and C. G. Duffy 467–68; 473n.; and war scare 495; 497, 627n. IV: quoted 13n.; 40n., 41, 54, 66, 125, 155, 170n., 177n.; quoted 205n.; 223n., 231, 233, 271, 287, 321, 409n., 412n.
TIMPSON, R. H., III: 491n.
TINLING, REV. EDWARD DOUGLAS, II: 497, 714
TINLING, MRS. EDWARD DOUGLAS [Katherine Maria Elton], II: 497n. IV: 341

Tinsley's Magazine, III: 472n.
TITIAN [Tiziano Vecelli], II: 446
TODD, MR., IV: 31
"TOMMY" [Miss], I: 302, 315
TOOKE, JOHN HORNE, II: 248
TORCY, MARQUIS DE, *Mémoires*, III: 447
TORNOW, MR., *Letter to:* IV, 362
TORRE, MR. AND MRS., I: 229, 230, 233
TORRIJOS, GENERAL, I: 173
"TOTTY," *see* FANSHAWE, Rosa
TOUCHARD-LAFOSSE, G., *l'Œil-de-Bœuf*, I: 234
TOUCHET, MRS. JAMES, II: 124
TOULIN, MRS., III: 441
TOWNSEND, MISS, III: 191
Town Talk, I: cxxi. III: 472n. IV: 89, 90, 93, 95, 100n., 101, 108, 109
TRAVERS, MR., II: 46
TRAVERS, CAPT. OTHO, I: 72. II: 69
TRELAWNEY, MRS., IV: 368
TRENCH, RICHARD CHENEVIX, I: 174n., 215. II: 698. IV: 391, 393, 402
TREVELYAN, SIR CHARLES EDWARD, III: 68n.
TREVELYAN, LADY [Hannah More Macaulay, m. Sir Charles], III: 68
TRIAL BY JURY, II: T.'s views on 347–48
TROLLOPE, ANTHONY, I: biographical clxxi-clxxiii. IV: and Yates 190n.; 262, 356n., 359, 397, 400, 411
    Framley Parsonage, IV: 158, 236. "Mrs. General Tallboys," IV: CM rejects on moral grounds 206, 207. *Thackeray*, quoted II: 433n.; IV: 263n. *Three Clerks*, IV: 159
    Letters to: IV, 158, 206, 208, 363
TROLLOPE, MRS. ANTHONY [Rose Heseltine], IV: 408, 411. *Vicar of Wrexhill*, I: 514

TROLLOPE, THOMAS ADOLPHUS, *What I Remember*, quoted I: 290n.

TROPPENEGER, MR., I: 109, 110

TROTTER, THOMAS LOWIS, I: 114

TROUBRIDGE, COL. SIR THOMAS ST. VINCENT HOPE COCHRANE, IV: 395, 411, 412, 414

TROUBRIDGE, LADY [Louisa Jane Gurney, m. Sir Thomas], IV: 395, 411, 412, 414

TROY, NEW YORK, *see also* chronology, III: 504, 508

TRULOCK, ALICE JANE, II: 668, 669, 671, 674n., 685, 689, 762, 808, 818. III: 5, 21, 25, 34, 68, 170
    Letters to: III, 100, 255

TRUMBALL, ARTHUR BLUNDELL SANDYS TRUMBULL, *see* DOWNSHIRE

TRUMBALL, JOHN, III: 195n.

TRURO, THOMAS WILDE, 1st Baron, II: 791

TRURO, LADY [Augusta Emma D'Este, m. 1st Baron], II: 791n.

TRUSLOW, MR., III: 512

TUCKER, GEORGE, III: 664

TUCKER, MRS., I: 199

TUCKERMAN, HENRY T., *Kennedy*, quoted III: 543n. IV: 111n.

TUCKETT, CAPT. HARVEY, I: 484n.

TUPPER, MARTIN FARQUHAR, IV: 120n.

TURENNE, MARSHAL DE, II: 120

TURGENEV, IVAN SERGEEVICH, IV: 82n., 392

TURNER, COLONEL AND MRS., I: 72, 73

TURNER, DR., I: clxin., 3n., 10, 175, 191, 192, 193, 195, 200, 201, 399. II: 55, 132, 136. IV: 14n.

TURNER, MRS., I: 3n., 9, 10, 17

TURNER, MISS, I: 26, 73. II: 195

TURPIN, MRS., II: 438, 527, 540, 594, IV: 420

TWIGG, MRS., I: 90, 99

TWISS, MRS. HORACE, II: 149

TWYFORD, AUGUSTA SMALL, IV: 410

TYNDALL, THOMAS ONESIPHORUS, II: 715

TYNDALL, MRS. THOMAS ONESIPHORUS [Caroline Lucy Elton], II: 715n.

TYNTE, LT.-COL. C. J. K., IV: 38n.

UHLAND, JOHANN LUDWIG, "Der König Auf dem Turme," I: T.'s translation of 297–98

UNION, THE [at Cambridge], I: 34, 38, 39, 42; T. speaks at 45–46; 52, 55, 70, 74, 80

United Service Journal, I: 76

UNITED STATES OF AMERICA, *see also* under Americans, chronology, individual cities, Lectures, Slavery, etc., II: T. plans tour in 692, 717n., 725, 736, 740, 741, 765, 797, 801, 803, 804, 810, 814. III: plans 46, 57, 61, 63, 65, 66, 67, 71, 73, 74, 76, 79n., 80, 83, 84; attacked in papers 88; 90, 93; leaving for 99–101; 104–05; opportunity in 132–33; social conditions in 174–75, 179, 181, 226–28, 245; the South 252, 254, 255; 262; project to lecture on 276; 308; upset over T.'s treatment of Washington 319–21, 327–28, 331; 370, 382, 383, 408, 420, 441, 461, 464, 466, 469, 470, 477; T.'s reactions to 496–97; the press 512; 527, 539; war scare 548–49; the South 552–53, 554, 572, 575, 579, 580–81, 584, 587, 593; 607; war scare 608; 610, 640, 651, 652, 653, 655. IV: 4, 18, 44; bank crash 55, 56; 66; Civil War 213, 223n., 231, 237; 263, 350, 434–35

VALPY, MRS., I: 429

VAN BUREN, MR., III: 330

VANDERBURCH, LOUIS ÉMILE, and
Jean François Bayard, *Gamin de
Paris*, II: 704
VAN DE WEYER, SYLVAIN, III: 686n.
IV: 396
VANDYKE, SIR ANTHONY, I: 515.
III: 317, 318
VAUDRICOURT, MME., I: 402
VAUGHAN, DR., III: 83, 343
VAVASOUR, SIR HENRY [and family],
I: 130, 131
VEDY, MRS., I: sketch of 502. II: 24
VEITCH, MR., II: 155
VELÁSQUEZ, DIEGO RODRÍGUEZ DE
SILVA Y, IV: 427
VENABLES, GEORGE STOVIN, I: cxxvii;
and T.'s nose 11n.; 206. II: 44;
"one of the finest scholars" 64;
256, 647, 777. III: 564, 613.
IV: 285n., 393, 396, 411. "Car-
lyle's Life in London," quoted I:
cix
VENEDY, JACOB, *Irland*, II: 143, 161
VENGEUR INCIDENT, I: cvii. II: 16
VERITY, DR., I: 284
VERONESE, PAOLO, I: 286
VERSAILLES GALLERY, I: "humbug"
363
VESTRIS, MME. [Lucia Elizabeth
Mathews], I: 501. II: 24
VICTORIA, QUEEN, I: and the Bed-
chamber Crisis 384; marriage dec-
laration 396; 411, 416n.; married
418; 430; anecdote on Prince
Albert and 434. II: 188, 209,
396, 397, 560n., 703; at the
Great Exhibition 768; grants
Jameson pension 786. III: 68,
228, 564, 584, 590, 592, 609n.,
649n. IV: 3, 336n., 366
Victoria Regia, The [1861], IV:
253n.
VIDOCQ, FRANÇOIS EUGÈNE, I: 223
VIEUXBOIS, M., I: 438, 441
VIGIER, M., II: 741
VIGNY, ALFRED DE, *Chatterton*, I:
278

VILLIERS, CHARLES PELHAM, II: 150,
363, 364, 365, 644n., 645, 718
VILLIERS, GEORGE WILLIAM FRED-
DERICK, *see* CLARENDON
VINCENT DE PAUL, ST., II: 279
VINING, MRS., I: 240
VIRGIL, I: 83. *Æneid*, IV: 44
VIRTUE, GEORGE, *Letter to:* IV, 252
VIRY, EMILY DE, *see* REVEL
VIVIAN, CAPTAIN, II: 145
VIZETELLY, HENRY, IV: 316, 416.
Glances Back, quoted II: 131n.–
32n., 198n.–99n., 529n.; IV: 302
Letters to: II, 188, 249, 389,
529
Voleur, I: 288
VOLTAIRE [François Marie Arouet],
I: 224, 236

WADDELL, MISS, I: 443. II: 94, 135
WADDELL, WILLIAM C. H., III:
215n.
WADDELL, MRS. WILLIAM C.H., III:
215
WADDINGTON, HORATIO, III: 670.
IV: 205, 391, 393, 397, 408
Letter to: IV, 363
WAILLY, ARMAND FRANÇOIS LÉON
DE, III: 23, 24
WAINWRIGHT, JOHN H., and G.E.
Rice, *Ephemera*, III: 163n.
WAINWRIGHT, MISS, III: 539
WAINWRIGHT, COL. ROBERT DEWAR,
III: 210n.
WAINWRIGHT, MRS. ROBERT DEWAR,
III: 539
WAKEFIELD, EDWARD GIBBON, I:
434
WALDEGRAVE, LADY [Sara Whitear
Milward, m. 8th Earl], II: 665,
731. III: 316. IV: 391
WALDSTEIN, COUNT, IV: 400
WALEWSKI, MR., IV: 44
WALKER, FRANK, IV: 270
Letters to: IV, 219, 222, 239,
244, 255, 268

WALKER, MR., I: 196
WALKER, NANCY, II: 245
WALL, CHARLES BARING, II: 359
WALLACE, MR., III: 543
WALLACK, HENRY JOHN, I: 190, 252, 253, 254
WALLACK, JAMES WILLIAM, I: 190. III: 494, 606
WALLACK, LESTER, *Memories*, quoted III: 597n.–98n., 606n.
WALLER, NICHOLAS [Procter], I: 382–83, 384
WALLER, ROBERT JOHN, *Letter to:* IV, 363
WALLS, H., III: 690
WALPOLE, HORACE, II: 645n. III: T. may edit letters 305. *Letters,* II: 90, 148
WALPOLE, MR., III: 671, 672
WALPOLE, SPENCER HORATIO, IV: 237
WALTER, JOHN, IV: 412
WALTER, MRS. JOHN, IV: 412
WARBURTON, ELIOT [Bartholomew Elliott George], II: 87, 148, 269n. III: drowned 18, 104. IV: 364, 433. "Eastern Travel," II: 145
WARBURTON, MRS. ELIOT, *Letter to:* IV, 364
WARBURTON, THOMAS ACTON, II: 269
WARD, SAMUEL, III: 484, 485
    Letter to: IV, 364
WARDE, JAMES PRESCOTT, I: 194, 241
WARENNE, WILLIAM DE, III: 152
WARNER, CAPTAIN, II: 144
WARRE-CORNISH, MRS., *Family Letters*, quoted I: clxiin., 318n. III: 459n.
WARREN, I: 20, 30
WARREN, CHARLES, I: 497
WARREN, COMTE DE, *L'Inde anglaise,* II: 161
WARREN, JUDGE, III: 152, 664
WARREN, SAMUEL, III: 393. *Ten*

Thousand a Year, I: attributed to T. 412. II: 635
    Letter to: IV, 365
WASHINGTON, D. C., *see also* chronology, III: 188, 194, 253, 539
WASHINGTON, GEORGE, II: 426. III: 134, 179, 180n., 216; T.'s supposed slur on 319–21, 327, 331; 514, 530, 677. IV: 18; and *Virginians* 66, 73, 74, 92
WASHINGTON, MARTHA, III: 179, 180n. IV: 73
WATERFORD, HENRY DE LA POER BERESFORD, 3rd Marquess of, II: 646n.
WATERFORD, LADY [Louisa Stuart, m. 3rd Marquess], II: 646
WATSON FAMILY, I: 17, 18
WATSON, SHERIFF, IV: 32
WATT, ROBERT, *Bibliotheca Britannica,* II: 651
WATTEAU, JEAN ANTOINE, I: 286
WATTS, GEORGE FREDERICK, IV: 348n., 404
WEBB, SIR HENRY, I: 424
WEBB, GEN. JOHN RICHMOND, I: 258n., 297n. III: 37n., 446, 447, 448
WEBB, COL. RICHMOND, III: 446
WEBBE, CORNELIUS, *Glances at Life,* II: 202
WEBER, BARON KARL MARIA FRIEDRICH ERNST VON, *Freischütz,* I: 199, 441
WEBSTER, HENRY BODDINGTON, II: 653
WEBSTER, MRS. HENRY BODDINGTON [Emilie de Baumbach (Mellish, Somerset)], II: 653
WEBSTER, THOMAS, I: 77
WEDDERBURN, MISS, *Letter to:* II, 345
Weekly Chronicle, II: 480
WEIMAR, *see also* chronology, I: 130. III: 442–45
WEIMAR, GRAND DUCHESS DOWAGER

Maria Paulowna of, I: 127. III: 445

Weincke, Dr., II: 32

Weissenborn, Dr. Friedrich August Wilhelm, I: 124, 132n., 154, 230, 232, 235. II: 798n. III: 189

Wellesley, Henry Richard, *see* Cowley

Wellington, Arthur Wellesley, 1st Duke of, I: 11n.; and Catholic Emancipation 34; 50, 110, 133; and Reform Bill 188n., 189; "old hero" 192; attacked 210; 430. II: 317, 580n., 768. III: 75; funeral 126; 138n., 254

Wells, Charles Rush, I: 46, 53, 60, 65, 67, 77

Wells, Edward Livingston, *Letter to:* III, 145

Wells, Mr., I: 18

West, Algernon, *Letter to:* III, 388

West, Mr. and Mrs. Temple, III: 53

Westminster Review, The, I: 386n. II: 48, 92, 663

Westmorland, Francis William Henry Fane, 12th Earl of, III: 393, 395

Westmorland, John Fane, 11th Earl of, II: 508n. III: 61

Westwood, Thomas, III: 338n.

Wetherell, Sir Charles, I: 51

Wharton, Francis, III: 203, 294, 664

Wharton, Philip, 1st Duke of, III: 358

Whately, Richard [Archbishop of Dublin], II: 84

Wheble, Mr., II: 726

Whetmore, Mrs., II: 601, 602n.

Whewell, William, I: 30, 31, 33n., 45, 49, 50, 56, 57, 70

Whitaker, Mr., II: 480

White, Frederick, I: 282n.

White, Rev. James, I: 418, 419n.,

421. II: 113, 144, 217, 274n., 322, 481, 558, 569. III: 17, 544. IV: 111, 238
"Hints to Authors," I: 346.
King of the Commons, II: 226–27.
Sir Frizzle Pumpkin, I: 346

White, Mrs. James, II: 322. III: 17, 73, 544

White, Lily, II: 322

White, Lotty, III: 17

Whitelocke, Lt.-Gen. John, I: 499; drawing of 500

Whitmore, Mr. and Mrs., IV: 404

Whitty, Edward, III: 468n.

Wickham, W. H., III: 491n.

Wieland, Christoph Martin, I: 136. *Oberon,* I: 230

Wightman, Miss, II: 450

Wightman, Sir William, II: 450n.

Wightwick, George, *Blue Friars,* I: 351

Wigram, Miss, II: 450

Wigram, Sir James, II: 450n.

Wikoff, Henry, II: 142, 144, 160; T. writes "American Letter" for 143, 158, 840, 841. III: 609
Letter to: II, 158

Wilberforce, Samuel [Bishop of Oxford], II: 672, 712, 777, 810n.

Wilberforce, William, III: 642

Wilcox, Mary, III: 264, 267

Wilde, Thomas, *see* Truro

Wilkie, Sir David, I: 279, 294

Wilkie, Miss, *Letter to:* I, 132

"Wilkins, Mr.," *see* Brookfield, William

Wilks, J., II: 130

Wilks [or Wilkes], Mr., I: 229, 231, 237

Wilks, Mrs., I. 230

William II, King of Holland, II: 117

William IV, King of England, I: 133, 157; coronation 159; 188n., 343n. II: 63, 363, 629n.

Williams, Helen Maria, I: 171

"WILLIAMS, MR.," see BROOKFIELD, William

WILLIAMS AND NORGATE, Letters to: II, 444, 806; IV, 365

WILLIAMS, WILLIAM, I: 85, 86, 87, 88, 89, 90, 93, 95, 99, 101, 103, 105, 495

WILLIAMS, WILLIAM SMITH, II: 341n.
    Letters to: II, 318, 340; IV, 197, 199

WILLIAMS-WYNN, CHARLES WATKIN, II: 751n.

WILLIAMS-WYNN, CHARLOTTE, II: 439, 751n. III: 341, 342, 353, 354

WILLINGTON, AARON SMITH, III: 665

WILLIS, DR. FRANCIS, IV: 442

WILLIS, NATHANIEL PARKER, I: T. writes on 406, 407, 451. II: burlesque of 27n.; discussion of 213–14. III: 683n. Dashes at Life, I: 407n.; II: T. writes on 202, 213–15

WILLMORE, GRAHAM, Trial by Jury, II: T.'s comments on 347–48
    Letter to: II, 347

WILLOUGHBY, L. A., Samuel Naylor, quoted I: 153

WILLS, WILLIAM HENRY, III: 393

WILLS, MRS. WILLIAM HENRY, III: 643

WILMOT, CHARLES FOLEY, II: 749n., 750

WILSON, H., IV: 411

WILSON, JAMES, III: 672. IV: and wife 393, 409n., 410. Illustrations of Scriptures, III: 422, 423
    Letter to: I, 455; IV, 83

WILSON, GEN. JAMES GRANT, T. in the U. S., quoted III: 173n., 203n., 210n., 531n.

WILSON, JOHN ["Christopher North"], I: 196n.

WILSON, MR., I: 186

WILTON CRESCENT, see HALLAM

WIMPOLE HALL, Cambridgeshire, I: 36, 37

WINCHESTER, BISHOP OF, see SUMNER, Charles R.

WINCHILSEA, GEORGE WILLIAM FINCH-HATTON, 10th Earl of, I: 50

WINGFIELD, RICHARD, see POWERSCOURT

WINSLOW, DR. FORBES BENIGNUS, IV: 397

WINSTON, MR., I: 282

WINTHROP, MR., IV: 191

WIRT, WILLIAM, III: 551

WISE, THOMAS JAMES, and Alexander Symington, The Brontës, quoted I: xciv; II: 341n., 673n.

WISEMAN, NICHOLAS PATRICK STEPHEN, Cardinal, II: "hypocrite" 83; 676, 711. III: 21; "tawdry . . . Quack" 337. Lectures, II: 83

WISTAR, DR. CASPAR, III: 202

WISTAR, DR. CASPAR [the younger], III: 203n.

WISTAR, MRS. CASPAR [Annis Lee Furness], III: 203
    Letter to: IV, 289

WITT, M. DE, II: 654n.

WITT, MME. DE [Henriette Guizot], II: 654

WOLCOT, JOHN ["Peter Pindar"], I: 158

WOLFE, MAJ.-GEN. JAMES, IV: in Virginians 137, 140

WOLOWSKI, MR., IV: 400, 402

WOOD, COLONEL, I: 30

WOOD, GEORGE, II: marital troubles 753, 755, 762. III: 429. IV: 5, 6

WOOD, MRS. GEORGE, II: 753, 755, 762

WOOD, GEORGE [of Edinburgh], II: 805, 818n. IV: 24, 35

WOOD, LADY, II: 753

WOOD, SIR MARK, I: 71

WOOD, MR., I: 178, 186, 189, 190, 192, 200, 201, 205, 208

WOOD, RICHARD, I: 27

Wood, Western, IV: 243n.
Woodford, Gen. Sir Alexander, IV: 414
Woodward, Rev. F.B., III: 334, 337
Woolgan, Miss, II: 429
Woolley, Mr., II: 157
Wordsworth, Christopher, I: 47, 50
Wordsworth, William, I: 47n., 53. II: 9, 765. "Intimations of Immortality," I: 395
World, The, III: 472n.
"World We Live In, The", I: 450
Worthington, Dr., II: 829n.
Wrackham, Mr., II: 247
Wright, Dr., I: 362
Wright, George, I: 380
    Letters to: I, 365, 367, 369, 370, 390
Wright, Thomas, ed. *Literary Remains*, quoted I: 348n.; II: 191n.–92n., 310n., 365n.; III: 30n.
Wright, Mr., II: 95
Wrightson, William Battie, III: 689
Writing, *see also* "Dignity of Literature" Controversy, II: T.'s advice on 137, 192–93; T.'s position as a writer 634. III: 78. IV: 372
Wrottesley, John, 2nd Baron, IV: 162
Wyatt, Captain, I: 237
Wyndham, Mr., IV: 408
Wyndham, Mrs., III: 403
Wynn, Mr., III: 343
Wynne, Mr., IV: 403
Wynne, Robert, II: 753
Wynne, Mrs. Robert [Eugenie Marie Crowe], I: cxvii, cxviii. II: 258, 292, 335, 374, 489, 521, 753. III: 82
Wynter, Dr. Andrew, IV: 215, 253 [?], 397

Yardley, Sir William, III: 636
    Letter to: IV, 366

Yates, Edmund, *see also* Garrick Club Affair, I: and Dickens cxx, cxxi, cxxii. IV: T. appeals to Garrick committee on 93; advised to apologize to T. 97; Russell on 99n.–100n.; 101, 102; Fladgate on 107; 108, 109; Dickens on 116–17; 118, 119; starts trial proceedings 121; 122; trial abandoned 131; 133; his later reaction to the affair 133n.–34n.; 135, 202, 203n., 245n., 255; Dickens note to 394n.; his friends and the National Shakespeare Committee 416
    "Echoes from the London Clubs," quoted IV: 189n. "Literary Talk," IV: occasions the affair 89, 90, 91, 93, 95, 97, 100n., 101, 102n., 103n., 105n., 108, 109, 117, 121, 133. *Mr. Thackeray, Mr. Yates, and the Garrick Club*, I: cxxii; IV: 131, 132. "The Theatrical Lounger," quoted IV: 119n.–20n.
    Letters to: III, 472; IV, 89, 94, 96, 99, 105. *Letters from:* IV, 91, 94, 95, 98, 103
Yates, Mrs. Edmund [Louisa Katherine Wilkinson], III: 472n. IV: 254
Yates family [Edmund], IV: 133n.–34n.
Yates, Frederick Henry, I: 497, II: T. on 45. III: 472n.
Yates, Mrs. Frederick Henry, I: 23, 260n. III: 472n. IV: 134n., 202n.
York, Frederick, Duke of, III: 682
Yorke family [Grantham], III: 438, 448
Yorke, Rev. Grantham Munton, II: 547. III: 436, 438, 439n.
    Letter to: III, 42
Yorke, Mrs. Grantham Munton

[Marian Emily Montgomery], III: 42, 77, 436, 438
　Letter to: II, 546
YORKE, JOSEPH AUGUSTUS, III: 42
　Letter to: III, 436
YOUNG, CHARLES MAYNE, I: 194
YOUNG, CORNET, II: 155
YOUNG, EDWARD, I: 158, 422
YOUNG, GEORGE, II: 253, 843
YOUNG, JAMES REYNOLDS, I: 28, 32, 53, 54, 56, 57, 61, 76, 80, 81, 84, 105, 107, 493, 494, 495, 496, 497
　Letter to: IV, 42
YOUNG, MR. [of Riverdale], III: 542

YOUNG, REV. JULIAN CHARLES, II: and wife 537; 584
YOUNG, ROBERT, III: 384
YOUNG, WILLIAM, I: 61, 62
YOUNG, WILLIAM [of New York], III: 489. IV: 18, 279

ZAMPIERI, DOMENECHINO, III: 340
ZOUCHE, ROBERT CURZON, 14th Baron, I: 177, 199; "noble little fellow" 205; 206, 208, 215, 502. IV: 397, 403, 410
ZOUCHE, LADY [Emily Julia Horton m. 14th Baron], IV: 397, 410

INDEX OF THACKERAY'S WORKS

"Academy Exhibition" [P 11 May '44], II: 169n.

Adventures of Philip, The, see *Philip*

"An Essay on Thunder and Small Beer," *see* "Thunder and Small Beer"

"Arabella; or The Moral of the 'Partie Fine' " [NMM June '44], II: 169

Ariadne in Naxos, see Projects

"Ballad of Bouillabaisse," *see* Poetry

Ballads [1855], *see also* Poetry, III: 31, 98, 298, 432. IV: 347n.

"Barber Cox and the Cutting of his Comb" [*Comic Almanack for 1840*], I: 380, 390

Barry Lyndon, Memoirs of [1844], I: and Stoney-Bowes xcii; and T.'s bill-discounting business 269n. II: 29, 38, 125; writing of 135, 139–41, 143, 144, 148, 149, 150, 151, 153, 156, 160, 176, 180; 840, 841

"Bedford-Row Conspiracy, The" [NMM January-April '40], I: 433

"Bob Robinson's First Love" [NMM August '45], II: 198n.

Book of Snobs [1846], I: quoted 27n.; 30n., 31n., 79n. II: 121n.; Lewes reviews 353; 459n. IV: T. hates 85n.

"Crump of St. Boniface," I: 30n. "On Clerical Snobs," quoted II: 274n.

"Bow Street Ballads. No. II. Jacob Omnium's Hoss" [P 9 December '48], quoted I: cxxxviii

"Box of Novels, A" [FM February '44], II: 135, 137, 139

"Brother of the Press on the History of a Literary Man, A" [FM March '46], II: 230

"Captain Warner's Discovery" [P 27 July '44], II: 144n.

"Carus' Travels in England" [MC 16 March '46], II: 227n.

Catherine [1840], I: finished 407; 408; "not generally liked" 412; Carlyle and 421; "not disgusting enough" 433; 437

"Chartist Meeting" [MC 15 March '48], II: 365

"Chest of Cigars, The" [NMM July '45], II: 198n.

Childe of Godesberg, The, see *Legend of the Rhine*

"Christmas Books — No. 2" [MC 26 December '45], I: cxxiv

"Chronicle of the Drum" [in *Second Funeral of Napoleon,* 1841], II: 7, 13, 314

"Cockney Travels," I: quoted 78n. II: quoted 51n.–52n.; 56n., 64n.

Comic Tales and Sketches [1841], I: clxviin., 397. II: 9, 610. III: 277

"The Count's" Adventures, I: cxvii, 509–12

"Curate's Walk, The" [part of "Travels in London," P November 4-December 4 '53], II: 326, 337. III: 431n. IV: 79

"Whitestock, Rev. Frank," I: cxviin.; II: 326

"De Finibus," see *Roundabout Papers*

"De Juventute," see *Roundabout Papers*

Denis Duval [1863], I: 4n. IV:

260n., 287n.; writing 291; fantasy on background of 292–94, 295

"Denis Haggerty's Wife," see Fitz-Boodle Papers

"Diary of C. Jeames de la Pluche, Esq." [P 6 December '45-7 February '46], II: and railway mania 215n.; 228n.

"Dickens in France" [FM March '42], II: 41n.; quoted 45n.

"Dionysius Diddler, History of," I: 438, 441

Doubtful Attributions, I: "More hints on etiquette . . ." 515n. II: 101n.

Dr. Birch and His Young Friends [1849], I: Charterhouse and 11n.; quoted 26n. II: Eton and 379; 444; T. doing illustrations 445; 459n.; C. Buller's death and 461n.; 466. III: 402

"Dr. Prince," I: 25n.–26n.

English Humourists of the Eighteenth Century [1853], see also Lectures in general index, III: U. S. rights 130–31; edition sold out 276; Hannay annotates 553n. IV: 192n.; errata in 204

"Epistles to the Literati," see Yellow-plush Papers

Esmond, The History of Henry, see *Henry Esmond*

"Essay on Thunder and Small Beer," see "Thunder and Small Beer"

"Exhibition Gossip, An" [AM June '42], II: 54n.

"Exhibition at Paris, The" [TL 5 April '38], I: 361

"Fielding's Works" [TL 2 September '40], I: 469. II: 462

Fitz-Boodle Papers [FM 1842-43], I: quoted 85n.; 123n.; quoted 423n.

    "Confessions," II: 54. "Doro-

thea," I: 127n. "Men's Wives. Denis Haggerty's Wife," I: clxiv, 429n.–30n. "Ottilia," I: 129n.

Flore et Zéphyr [1836], I: 86n., 299; T. requests puff for 313; 314. II: 783n.

"From the Own Correspondent of the Moniteur des Boulevards" [P 8 March '51], II: 729n.

Four Georges, The [CM July-October '60], see also Lectures in general index, I: quoted 3n. III: 276, 277, 281, 471, 537. IV: 136n., 149, 205n., 207, 443

"Gahagan, Major," see "Historical Recollections"

"Gambler's Death, A," see *Paris Sketch Book*

"George Cruikshank's Works" [LWR June '40], I: 438

"German in England, The" [FQR July '42], II: 51n., 70

"Going to see a Man Hanged" [FM August '40], I: 453

"Great Cossack Epic of Demetrius Rigmarolovicz" [FM December '39], I: 408n.

Great Hoggarty Diamond, The History of Samuel Titmarsh and the [FM September-December '41], I: cxxxviii; I.T. in clxv; Sterling on 304n.; Jane T. in 379n. II: 121n., 262n., 382, 383; "written at a time of great affliction" 440; 444, 795

"Grumble about the *Christmas Books,* A" [FM January '47], II: 263, 264n.

Henry Esmond, The History of [1852], I: lxxxvi; and C. Brontë xciv; cxx; Trollope and clxxii; and Roaldus 258n. II: and Addiscombe 361n.; Castlewood Hall and Clevedon Court 436n.; quoted

470n.; 593n.; gets idea for 708, 736; and Forster 780n.; publishing arrangements 804, 806; "cutthroat melancholy" 807; 810, 811, 815, 818. III: C. Brontë reads 15; historical data for 18; 23; "grave and sad" 24; 27, 31, 37n., 38, 41; "will be a failure" 43; finished 47; T. visits Blenheim 49, 54; "clever but also stupid" 69; 72, 74, 77, 82, 91, 92, 98, 99; "dreary and dull" 100; 102, 104, 109, 113; reviews of 121; success 125, 126; repetition in 128; S reviews 130; second edition 135; 149; Forster reviews 155; 164; TL gives bad review 175; 181, 216n.; Forster and 250; 253, 277, 286, 367, 390n., 391, 401, 410; sources for 446–48; 610, 618, 619n., 661. IV: H.T. likes best 85; and TL review 125; and morality 206; 269, 429, 432, 435, 437

"Castlewood, Lady," I: lxxxvii. "Costigan," III: 183. "Esmond, Beatrix," I: lxxxviii; III: 149, 154, 164, 183. "Esmond, Henry," II: 470n., 815; III: 49, 54, 164. IV: 274n.

"Half a Crown's Worth of Cheap Knowledge" [FM February '38], I: 407n., 515

"Historical Recollections. By Major Gahagan" [NMM March '38], I: 516

"History of the Next French Revolution" [P 24 February-20 April '44], II: 142, 162; errata for 163

History of Pendennis, The, see *Pendennis*

History of Samuel Titmarsh and the Great Hoggarty Diamond, see *Great Hoggarty Diamond*

"Hobson's Choice" [P 12 January '50], II: 628

Illustrations, I: to "Lord Bateman" 380–81; to Addison's *Journey* 513n. II: for *Irish S. B.* 90–91, 97, 98; advice on selling 114–15; *Mrs. Perkins* 249

"Important from the Seat of War!" [P 24 June-5 August '54], III: 374, 676

"Interesting Story, An" [K 1849], II: 420n., 426

Irish Sketch Book, The [1843], I: and Lever cxlvii; 459, 463, 470, 473. II: and Shelburne Hotel 61n.; Peter Purcell in 63n.; outline of travel 65n.; 69n.; Father Matthew in 70n.; 71n., 74, 75n., 77n.; and Elias T. 79n.; 81; illustrations 90–91; suggested title 93; 94; anti-Catholic bias 96; 97, 98; titled "Rambles in Ireland" 100; reviews 103, 105n., 107, 109; 110; reviews 111; reactions to 113; 126, 161, 174; selling well 229; 258, 321; QR on 334. III: 277. IV: 183

Kickleburys on the Rhine, The [1850], *see also* "Thunder and Small Beer," I: clxvii. II: 375n., 399, 421, 444, 687, 690, 691n., 692, 701, 728, 735n., 789

"Knights of Borsellen," *see* Projects

"Krasinski's Sketch of the Reformation" [TL 5 March '40], I: 375, 424n.

"Lady Kickleburys Tour," see *Kickleburys on the Rhine*

"Lady L.'s Journal of a Visit to Foreign Courts" [P 27 January '44], II: 141

"Last Fifteen Years of the Bourbons, The" [FQR July '42], II: 42, 51n., 70, 651, 829n., 830

"Last Sketch, The" [CM April '60], IV: 180n., 196

"Leaf of a Sketch-Book, A" [1861], IV: 253

"Leaves from the Lives of the Lords of Literature" [P 20 January '44], II: 139

Lectures on the Humourous Writers of the Last Century, see English Humourists

"Legend of Jawbrahim-Heraudee, The" [P 18 June '42], II: 54, 829

"Legend of the Rhine, A" [*George Cruikshank's Table-Book*, 1845], II: 141, 144, 160, 198n., 789, 840, 841

"Little Billee," or "The Three Sailors," *see* Poetry

"Little Dinner at Timmins's" [P 27 May-29 July '48], III: 161n.

"Lord William Lennox's Readings and Recitations from Joe Miller" [P 10 August '44], II: 145n.

Lovel the Widower [1859], I: clxxii; and NS 260n. IV: 136n.; and *Wolves and the Lamb* 148n.; 177n., 178, 207n., 243n.

"Meeting in Kennington Common" [MC 14 March '48], II: 364

"Memorials of Gormandising" [FM June '41], II: 281n.

Memoirs of Barry Lyndon, see Barry Lyndon

"Men and Coats" [FM August '41], II: 33

"Men's Wives," see *Fitz-Boodle Papers*

"Miss Tickletoby's Lectures on English History" [P 2 July-1 October '42], II: discontinued 82. IV: 218

"Monsieur Gobemouche's Authentic Account of the Grand Exhibition" [P 10 May '51], II: 729n., 771n.

Mr. Brown's Letters to a Young Man About Town. "Mr. Brown the Elder takes Mr. Brown the Younger to a Club" [P 12 May '49], II: 537

"Mr. Malony's Account of the Ball" [P 3 August '50], II: 686

"Mr. Punch for Repeal" [P 26 February '48], II: 352, 356n.

"Mr. Tims and a Good-natured Friend [P 2 December '48], II: 455n.

Mrs. Perkins's Ball [1847], II: designing characters for 156; 198n.; illustrations for 219, 249; Forster reviews 257; success 258; 261n., 266, 267, 290, 293n., 307; pirated 308

"New Accounts of Paris" [FQR January '44], II: 126, 135n.

Newcomes, The [1853], I: lxxxviii, cxxiv, cxxv; Charterhouse and 11n.; quoted 228n.; and bank failure 508. III: starts 67; contract for 280; 281, 283, 284, 287, 292, 293–94, 297, 298; "stupid" 299; Doyle to illustrate 300, 301, 302, 304, 305, 308; A.T. helping with 313; trouble over T.'s treatment of Washington 320, 327, 331; 322, 323, 332, 333, 334, 336, 337, 341, 342, 346–47, 349–50, 351, 352, 353, 354–55, 356, 358, 359; illustrations 362; 363, 365; instructions for illustrations 372–73; 374, 375, 377, 378, 379, 381, 382, 384, 386, 387, 394, 397, 398, 401, 403, 404, 406n., 407; doing well 408, 409, 427; Norton-Melbourne case in 428; 433; and Charterhouse 435; 437, 438n., 449; finished 459; queries on 461–62; 465–66; Elwin writes on 468, 469; 567; Tauchnitz and 607; T. on 619n.; writing of (Diary) 668, 669, 670, 672, 673, 675, 676, 677. IV: 28,

242n., 378, 379, 435, 436, 438, 439, 442
"Bayham, Frederick," III: 449.
"Campaigner," I: clxiv. "Farintosh, Marquis of," III: 102n.
"Goodenough, Dr.," IV: 275.
"Honeyman, Rev. Charles," I: c.
"Honeyman, Miss Martha," I: 4n. "Mackenzie, Rosie," I: clxv.
"Newcome, Colonel," I: cxi, cxvi, cxx, 361n.; III: 57, 334n., 341, 350, 355, 397, 435–36n., 438, 463; IV: 57, 196, 378, 379, 380.
"Newcome, Ethel," I: lxxxviii, lxxxix-xc
"Night's Pleasure, A" [P 8 January-19 February '48], II: 360
Notes of a Journey from Cornhill to Grand Cairo [1846], I: 287n. II: Diary notes for 150–57; 179; description of Lisbon 179n.; 184, 185; Crowe helping 190; 199, 201, 203; religious trouble 204, 209; chapter cancelled 212; 218n., 219, 227n.; reviews 229n.; 231, 249n.; second edition 258n.; 268, 321, 455n., 844. III: omitted chapter 96n.; 277
"Notes of a Weeks Holiday," see *Roundabout Papers*
"Notes on the North . . . Election" [FM September-October '41], II: 27n., 30, 33
Novels by Eminent Hands, see "*Punch's* Prize Novelists"

"On Alexandrines," see *Roundabout Papers*
"On an American Traveller" [P 29 June '50], I: 407n.
"On Clerical Snobs," see *Book of Snobs*
"On the French School of Painting" [FM December '39], I: 408n.
"On a Good-Looking Young Lady" [P 8 June '50], quoted II: 695n.

"On Half a Loaf," see *Roundabout Papers*
"On a Joke . . . Heard from the late Thomas Hood," see *Roundabout Papers*
"On Men and Pictures" [FM July '41], II: 19
"On a Peal of Bells," see *Roundabout Papers*
"On Ribbons," see *Roundabout Papers*
"On Screens in Dining-Rooms," see *Roundabout Papers*
"On Some Dinners at Paris" [P 3 March '49], II: 494n.
Our Street [1848], II: 323n., 333, 338n., 345n., 489n., 621

"Paris Revisited. By an Old Paris Man" [P 10 February '49], II: 494n.
Paris Sketch Book, The [1840], I: clxvii, 267n., 328; FG translations for 330n., 331–40; 397, 406n., 425, 437; finished 448, 449; reviews of 453; T. asks puffs for 455-57; 459, 461, 462, 464, 470. II: 25, 137, 555. III: 277. IV: 371
"A Caution to Travellers," I: and T.'s gambling 508. "A Gambler's Death," I: 278n., 456n. "Meditations at Versailles," I: 363n. "Napoleon and his System," I: 395. "On Some French Fashionable Novels," I: 407, 456n.
"Partie Fine, The" [NMM May '44], II: 167
"Pen and the Album, The," see Poetry
Pendennis, The History of [1848], I: T.'s boyhood and cxl, 13n., 24n.; 31n., 149n., 217n., 321n. II: 401, 411, 414, 417, 418, 420, 428, 432, 435, 436, 437, 441, 442, 444; Rintoul and 450;

452n.; making money 458; 465, 468, 469, 471, 472, 482, 498, 500, 504n., 506, 514, 519, 521, 522, 527, 530, 535, 536, 541, 542, 543, 544, 554, 555, 558, 559, 564, 565, 567, 568, 569, 575, 576; Mrs. B. on 577; and the Newmans 581; 583, 595, 602n., 604n., 614, 615, 621; and "Dignity of Literature" 629–35, 636; 644n., 648n., 652, 653; "a wicked number" 654; 657, 661, 668; Newman in 677n.; 678, 680, 683, 684, 685, 686; reviews 688–89; 693, 701, 704; finished 707, 709, 710, 713; 717n., 720, 721n., 738, 752; Masson's review 771; 806, 810n. III: verses in 13; 125, 277, 280, 308, 367, 417n.; Elwin on 469n.; 484. IV: "dreadfully stupid" 28; 104, 255, 333, 378, 419, 421, 422, 425, 442

"Amory, Blanche," I: cxi; clvii; IV: 425. "Bacon and Bungay," II: 59n. "Bell, Laura," I: cix, cxi; II: 536; III: 469n. "Costigan," III: 183n. "Fotheringay, Miss," II: 501. "Foker, Harry," II: 721n.; IV: 109. "Goodenough, Dr.," IV: 275. "Mirobolante," II: 149n. "Pendennis, Arthur," II: 437n., 500, 536, 728n. III: 297–98. "Pendennis, Helen," I: cxvi; II: 457; III: 13. "Pendennis, Major," II: 511. "Shandon, Captain," I: 192n. "Strong, Chevalier," II: 148n., 536; III: 380. "Warrington, George," I: 204n., 207n.; II: 721, 815

Philip, The Adventures of [1861], I: cxxxix; T. on clxivn.; and Constitutional 301n.; and Mrs. Shawe 315n.; and Corsair 406n.; 488n.; and Examiner 189n.; Crawford in 721n. III: quoted 68n. IV: 117n., 136, 212, 214, 216; illustrations for 219n., 220n.; 224; vying with

Trollope 236n.; instructions on illustrations 239, 244, 255, 258n., 268; 242n., 250, 256n., 257, 260, 266; titling 269; finished 270; 363, 399, 400, 403
"Baynes, Charlotte," I: clxv. "Baynes, Mrs. General," I: clxiv. "Firmin, Dr.," IV: 117n. "Goodenough, Dr.," IV: 275
"Pictorial Rhapsody, A" [FM June '40], I: 450
"Picture Gossip" [FM June '45], II: 191
"Pictures of Life and Character. By John Leech" [QR December '54], III: causes trouble 413, 415, 417

POETRY

Untitled rhymes and doggerel: I, cxxxix, 117, 145; election song 246; 501; II, 63, 114; imitation of Horace 281; 486n.–87n., 618; III, 508, 657; IV, 49, 147, 179, 265–66, 289, 312, 329, 332, 356–57
"Ballad of Bouillabaisse," I: 362; II: 140n., 494n.; III: 114–16; IV: Yates and 131n. "Battle of Limerick," I: 414n.; III: 227n. "Church Porch," III: 13. "Evening Hymn, An," I: 180–81. "End of Play," II: 466n. "Failure, A," II: 566. "Fairy Days," III: 13; quoted 14. "Field Marshall, The," I: 179–80. "Jacob Omnium's Hoss," I: quoted cxxxviii. "Jeames of Buckley Square," III: 429. "Last of May," IV: 347–48. "Legend Of Drachenfels," I: quoted 120–22. "Legend of St. Sophia of Kiev," IV: 32. "Little Billee," or "The Three Sailors," II: 483n., 484–85. "Lucy's Birthday," III: 257–58, 264. "May Day Ode," II: 766, 787. "Mrs. Katherine's Lantern," IV: 278. "Organ Boy's Appeal,"

III: 306, 670. "Peg of Lima-vaddy," II: 629. "Pen and the Album," I: cxxvii; III: 56, 60, 186n. "Sorrows of Werther," III: 411. "Stars, The," I: 154–55. "Timbuctoo," I: 74, 75n., 76. "Titmarsh's Carmen Lil-liense," II: 121n., 143. "To Genevieve," I: 77. "Weep, Albion! Weep," III: 138. "What Might Have Been," II: quoted 477n.–78n. "White Squall," III: 481n.

"Polk's First Address" [E 29 March '45], II: 190

"Problematic Invasion of British India" [FQR April '44], II: 161

"Professor, The" [*Bentley's Miscellany*, September '37], I: 328n. IV: 371

PROJECTS

Articles: I, on Shelley 49n., 93, 98; with Maginn 353; on Queen Victoria 384; on Socialist and Chartist publications 406–07; "Town of London in the Drama" 407n., 408; for BM 450–51; II, modern English comedies 48; survey of Louis Philippe's reign 42, 64, 65, 66, 81; for FQR 92, 161; "Who's Mr. Moss" 144; on Lord Ellenborough 161; on O'Connell's death 291; III, gastronomic 315

Books: I, Titmarsh in Belgium 462; on Italy 473; plots 515–16; II, Life of Talleyrand 172, 174, 175, 177, 185, 190; III, on America 108, 144, 154, 408; IV, on Henry V 85n.; Life of Queen Anne 180, 209, 210, 213, 236, 238. "Knights of Borsellen," II, 5n., 13; III, 305; IV, 260n., 272, 438

Editing of Walpole: III, 305; IV, 438

Foolscap Library: I, 438–39, 442

Lectures: III, on Men of the World 242, 358; III, on America 276

Newspaper: III, 415, 417

Opera: II, 830

Playing Cards: III, 385, 386, 387

Plays: I, William Tell 134; on loss of Amphitrite 265; II, tragedy for Macready 38, 93; *Ariadne in Naxos* 250; on Bluebeard 732, 735, 736, 739 604; errata in 613–14; 627, 789 719

Translations: Arndt I, 179–80; de la Motte Fouqué I, 297, 298–99; Goethe I, 140; Kotzebue I, 140; Mannert I, 140, 150; Schlegel I, 118, 123; Sue's *Mystères de Paris* II, 139, 140, 141, 159, 840, 841; Uhland I, 297, 298–99

"Proser, The," *see* "On a Goodlooking Young Lady"

"Punch in the East" [P January '45], II: 153n., 156

"*Punch's* Prize Novelists" [3 April-25 September '47], I: Forster and cxxiv; cxlvii. II: Dickens on 297, 336

"Barbazure," II: 270, 647n. "Codlingsby," II: 149n. "George de Barnwell," II: 270. "Lords and Liveries," II: 724n. "Phil Fogarty," I: cxlvii-cxlviii; II: 455; IV: 131n.

Rebecca and Rowena [1850], I: cxxiv. II: notes for 33n.; writing 604; errata in 613–14; 627, 789

REVIEWS

"Annuals," I: 375. "Babes in the Woods," II: 260n., 261. Blanchard's *Life and Works*, II: 230. Bulwer's *Maltravers*, I: 514. Burton's *Hume*, II: 234, 235n. Bury's *Eros*, I: 515; *Diary*, I: 515, III:

473n. Carlyle's *French Revolution*, I: 347n. Disraeli's *Coningsby*, II: 148n., 188n.; *Sybil*, II: 148n. "Fraser's Winter Journey to Persia," I: 375. Gore's *Sketches of English Character*, II: 724n. Grant's *Paris and its People*, II: 126, 139n. *Holt, Memoirs of*, I: 515. "Hugo, *The Rhine*," II: 42, 44, 830. Jameson's *Winter Studies*, I: 377–78. Jerrold's *Mrs. Caudle's Curtain Lectures*, II: 248n. Jesse's *Beau Brummell*, III: 358n. "Krasinski's Sketch of the Reformation," I: 375, 424n. Leech *Pictures of Life and Character*, III: 413, 415, 417. Landon's *Churchill*, I: 514. Marlborough's *Correspondence*, I: 515. Marsh's *Mount Sorel*, II: 191n. "Moore's History of Ireland," II: 245, 247. Norton's *Fisher's Drawing-Room Scrap-Book*, II: 264n. Prévot's *Three Kingdoms*, II: 737n. Procter's *Jonson*, I: 377–78. Ranke's *History of the Popes*, I: 461. Skelton's *My Book*, I: 348n. Smith's *Poetical Works*, II: 249. Smyth's *Historic Fancies*, II: 145. Southey's *Poetical Works*, I: 516. Soyer's *Gastronomic Regenerator*, II: 149n., 237n. Sue's *Mystères de Paris*, II: 92, 100n. Trollope's *Vicar of Wrexhill*, I: 514. Tyler's *Henry V*, I: 375. Venedy's *Irland*, II: 143, 161. Warren's *L'Inde anglaise*, II: 161. *Willis' Dashes at Life*, I: 407n.; II: 213

Rose and the Ring, The [1855], I: clxvii; and pantomines 178n. III: development of 338n.; 353, 355, 357, 367, 385, 387, 396, 405, 523, 673, 677. IV: 438

Roundabout Papers [CM], I: 3n., 22n.; quoted 496n.–97n. II:

quoted 579n.–80n., 612n. III: quoted 233n., 240n., 281n. IV: quoted 59n.–60n.; 154n., 243n., 272, 317

"De Finibus" [August '62], IV: 271. "De Juventute" [October '60], IV: 195n., 199, 200. "Nil Nisi Bonum" [February '60], II: 591n.; III: 134n.; IV: 191n. "On Alexandrines" [April '62], IV: 284. "On Half a Loaf" [February '61], III: 275n. "On a Joke . . . Heard from the Late Thomas Hood" [December '60], I: cxxxvii; IV: 196n., 238. "On a Peal of Bells" [September '62], IV: 274n. "On Ribbons" [May '60], IV: 185n. "On Screens in Dining-Rooms" [August '60], IV: 189n., 190n. "Roundabout Journey: Notes of a Week's Holiday" [November '60], IV: 282. "Thorns in the Cushion" [July '60], II: 24n.; IV: 207n., 259. "Tunbridge Toys" [September '60], I: 12n.; IV: 195

Second Funeral of Napoleon, The [1841], *see also* "Chronicle of the Drum," II: 4, 6, 7, 10, 13; "best book I ever wrote" 136

"Shabby Genteel Story, A" [FM June '40], I: 450, 469, 488. III: 146. IV: 48n., 271
    "Brandon, George," I: 151n. "Fitch, Andrea," I: 510

"Shrove Tuesday in Paris" [B 5 July '41], I: on Marvy cxlix-cxlx. II: 12n.

"Sick Child, The" [P 14 January '43], II: 82n.

"Solitude in September" [NS 14 September '33], I: quoted 265n.

"Some More Words About Ladies" [P 14 April '49], II: quoted 543n.

"Some Passages in the Life of Major Gahagan" [NMM February '38], I: 515

"Sorrows of Werther" [SLM November '53], III: 411

"Speeches of Henry, Lord Brougham" [BFR April '39], I: 378n.

"Steam Navigation in the Pacific" [TL 8 November '38], I: 375

"Stubb's Calendar; or The Fatal Boots" [*Comic Almanack for 1839*], I: 365, 369; instructions for illustrations 370–72; 377n. II: 610

"Sultan Stork" [AM February '42], II: 40, 54n.

"Tale of Wonder, A" [NS 12 October '33], I: 268

"Thieves Literature of France" [FQR April '43], II: 92, 100n.

"Thorns in the Cushion," see *Roundabout Papers*

"Three Sailors, The," or "Little Billee," *see* Poetry

"Thunder and Small Beer, An Essay on" [1850], II: and controversy 728n.; 737, 738, 751. IV: 183

"Titmarsh's Carmen Lilliense" [FM March '44], II: 121n., 143

"To the Napoleon of Peace" [P 24 August '44], II: 150

"Travelling Notes by Our Fat Contributor" [P 30 November-14 December '44], II: 145, 146, 148, 153, 180. IV: 183

"Tunbridge Toys," see *Roundabout Papers*

"Two or Three Theatres at Paris" [P 24 February '49], II: 494n., 497n.

Vanity Fair [1847-48], I: C. Brontë and xciii; xcvii, cvi; Dickens and cxxi; and title cxxvi; FG and cxxxiii; Forster and cxxiv, cliv; Chiswick in 3n.; Weimar in 123n.; 129n., 134n.; Ainsworth and 326n. II: 82n., 198n.; and Somerset family 232n.; 233, 236n., 258; Colburn refuses 262; 264, 267, 282, 286, 289, 291, 292, 294, 305, 306, 308; object of 309; 310, 311; Mrs. Procter on 312–14; 315, 316, 318, 321, 327, 337; *Jane Eyre* dedication and 340n., Lady Eastlake's gossip and 341n.; 342; illustrations 345; 346, 347, 352; Lewes on 353n.; T. on 353–54; 365, 366, 368; elaboration on end of characters 375–77; 378, 381, 382, 383, 384; finished 392, 394; 395, 396n., 400; reviews 403, 404, 409; 407, 408, 420; Bell reviews 423n.; T. on 423–25; Forster reviews 424n.; I. T. and Gaunt's madness 440n.; 450n., 458, 492, 514, 530, 531, 560n., 584, 642n., 647, 772n., 807, 810n. III: Dickens and 37n.; 98, 116, 184, 231n., 277, 367, 411, 688n. IV: 155, 242n., 419

"Briggs, Miss," II: 309. "Dobbin, Major," I: lxxxi; II: 309, 313, 376, 381, 395, 642n. "Crawley, Miss," I: cv. "Crawley, Sir Pitt," IV: 378n. "Crawley, Rawdon," II: 352n., 375. "Osborne, George," III: 363n. "Sedley, Amelia," I: clxv; II: 309, 313, 314, 335, 381, 394, 395, 407, 642n., 684. "Sedley, Old," II: 195n., 310n., 314; III: 30. "Sharp, Becky," I: clvii, clviin., clixn., II: 375–76, 377, 501. "Steyne, Lord," II: 352n., 375; III: 363n.

Virginians, The [1857], I: 238n. II: 370n. III: and Prescott 112n.; 216, 253, 471, 616, 617, 618, 620, 627, 636, 647, 655. IV: 6, 41, 44, 45, 48, 52, 55, 58; pirated 60; 62, 63, 64; doing well 65; background material for 66; 67,

68, 70, 71; background 73, 74; 76, 77, 79; "clever but stupid" 80; 81; "devilish stupid" 85n.; 89n.; provokes American abuse 92; 93; Yates in 98n.–99n., 100n., 109n.–10n.; 108; background 111n.; 112n., 115, 123, 126, 127, 135; and death of Wolfe 137–38, 140; 141, 144, 145n., 146, 147, 149; finished 150, 151n.; 155, 171, 195n., 206n., 242n., 244; original plan for 390n.; 393, 394, 448

"Esmond-Warrington, Madame," III: 216; IV: 73, 244. "Warrington, George," I: 238n.; IV: 66, 73, 111n.

"Wanderings of Our Fat Contributor" [P 3 August '44], II: 145n.
"What I Remarked at the Exhibition" [P 10 May '51], II: 771n.
"What Mr. Jones Saw at Paris" [P 8 September '49], II: 576
Wolves and the Lamb, The, see also *Lovel the Widower,* II: 515n., 648n. III: 429; rejected 430; 450. IV: 148n.
"Womanifesto, A," III: 181, 228

Yellowplush Papers [FM 1837–40], I: clxvii; T. wants more money for 351–52; 353, 357; "well received" 408; hit at Bulwer 412; original of Deuceace 506. II: new edition 9; 163. III: T. apologizes to Bulwer for 278, 395; 341, 429

"Amours of Mr. Deuceace" [February '38], I: 149n., 515. "Dimond Cut Dimond" [February '38], I: 507. "Epistles to the Literati. No. XIII" [January '40], I: 395, 412. "Epistles to the Literati. No. XIV" [March '40], I: cvii. "Fashnable Fax and Polite Annygoats" [November '37], I: 348n. "Foring Parts" [April '38], I: 350, 508. "Miss Shum's Husband" [January '38], I: 514. "Mr. Deuceace at Paris" [May '38], I: 364, 508, 516. "Mr. Yellowplush's Ajew" [August '38], I: 367, 438. "Skimmings from 'The Diary of George IV'" [March '38], I: 516
"Yesterday; a Tale of the Polish Ball" [P 10 June '48], II: 386